Goethe

Goethe

Pietro Citati

Translated by
Raymond Rosenthal

The Dial Press
New York
1974

To Elena

Originally published in Italy by Arnoldo Mondadori Editore.
Copyright © 1970 by Arnoldo Mondadori Editore

Translation Copyright © 1974 by The Dial Press

Manufactured in the United States of America

First printing

Library of Congress Cataloging in Publication Data

Citati, Pietro.
Goethe.

Bibliography: p.
1. *Goethe, Johann Wolfgang von, 1749–1832.   Wilhelm Meisters Lehrjahre.*
    2. *Goethe, Johann Wolfgang von, 1749–1832.   Faust II.*
    PT1982..C5 1974   831'.6 [B]   74–11839
    ISBN 0–8037–3006–3

Book design by Paulette Nenner

Contents

Chronology of
Goethe's Life and Works[*]

1749   August 29:   Johann Wolfgang Goethe is born in
        Frankfurt-on-Main, to Johann Kaspar Goethe and Katharine
        Elisabeth Textor.

1750   December 7:   His sister Cornelia, who will die in 1777, is
        born.

1753   Christmas: His grandmother gives the child Goethe a
        puppet theater.

1757   His first poems.

1762   Begins to study Hebrew; he had already begun to study
        French, Italian, and English.

1765   October 3:   Arrives at Leipzig University, where he takes
        courses in history, philosophy, theology, and poetics at the
        University; he also studies medicine and natural science;
        takes drawing lessons, and often attends the theater.

1768   July: Serious illness; on August 28 he leaves Leipzig and on
        September 1 is again in Frankfurt, where he is treated by
        Dr. J. F. Metz.

1769   Long convalescence. Deep friendship with Susanne von

*Compiled with the assistance of Heinz Nicolai's chronology, published in volume XIV
  of Wegner's edition.

Klettenberg, a "pietistic" lady (the "beautiful soul" of the *Lehrjahre*); reads books about alchemy.

1770   March: Departure for Strasbourg, where he studies law; meets Stilling and Herder; reads Hamann, Ossian, Shakespeare, and Sterne; falls in love with Friederike Brion.

1771   Submits Doctoral thesis *De Legislatoribus*, which is rejected; but is granted, after an oral examination, the degree of Licentiate of Law. Returns to Frankfurt in August.

1772   Friendship with J.C. Kestner and his fiancée Charlotte Buff.

1773   Publishes *Götz von Berlichingen mit der eisernen Hand*. Begins to write *Faust*; writes two acts of *Prometheus*.

1774   Autumn: Publishes *Die Leiden des jungen Werthers*. December: In Frankfurt meets Karl August von Sachsen-Weimar-Eisenach, with his tutor K.L. von Knebel.

1775   January: Engaged to Lili Schönemann; the engagement is broken off in October.
February–April: *Stella*.
March–July: Journey to Switzerland with the Stolbergs.
Summer: First scenes of *Egmont*.
September: Karl August invites Goethe to Weimar.
September–October: New scenes of *Faust*.
November 7:   Arrival at Weimar, where he meets Wieland and Charlotte von Stein.

1776   April: Karl August presents Goethe with the garden on the Rosenberg.
May–July: First visits to the Ilmenau mine, which he will be interested in for many years.
June: Appointed councillor of Weimar's secret Council, in which he is active until 1785.
October: Herder comes to Weimar.

1777   February: Begins to write *Wilhelm Meisters theatralische Sendung*, and by 1785 reaches the end of the sixth book.
November–December: Journey through the Harz.

1778   May–June: Journey with Karl August to Potsdam and Berlin.

1779   January: Karl August entrusts Goethe with the direction of the commission of war and highways.

Chronology of Goethe's Life and Works

	February: Starts writing *Iphigenie auf Tauris* (in prose). May–June: *Egmont.* September 1779–January 1780: Another trip to Switzerland.
1780	March: First idea for *Tasso.* June: Accepted as *"Lehrling"* in the Amalia Masonic Lodge of Weimar (in 1782, becomes *"Meister"*). July: Reads *Faust* to Karl August.
1781	October: Studies anatomy. November: Rents house at the *Frauenplan.*
1782	May 25: Goethe's father dies.
1783	May: Takes in Charlotte's son, Fritz von Stein, as his student.
1784	February: The mine at Ilmenau is reopened. March: Discovers the *os intermaxillare* (small jaw bone) in human cranium, and writes an essay on this subject. August: Writes the poem *Zueignung,* planned to be the beginning of the poem entitled *Die Geheimnisse.* September: Resumes study of Spinoza.
1785	March: Studies botany together with Knebel, at Jena. November: Studies Carolus Linnaeus, Swedish botanist.
1786	July–September: At Karlsbad. September 3: Departs in secret for Italy. September 14: Verona. September 28: Venice. October 29: Arrives in Rome, where he meets the painters Wilhelm Tischbein and Angelica Kaufmann, Heinrich Meyer and Karl Philipp Moritz. December: Finishes the second draft of *Iphigenie auf Tauris.*
1787	February 25: Arrives in Naples. March 29: Travels to Palermo by sea. April–May: Journey in Sicily. May 14: Again in Naples. June 6: In Rome, where he stays until April 23, 1788. September: Finishes *Egmont.*
1788	June 18: Returns to Weimar, where he relinquishes direct responsibility for his ministerial functions. July 12: Meets Christiane Vulpius. September: Becomes acquainted with Schiller.

1789   May 26: Schiller's first lecture at the University of Jena.
        June: Break with Charlotte von Stein.
        July: Finishes *Torquato Tasso*.
        November: At the *Jägerhaus*.
        November–December: *Versuch, die Metamorphose der
        Pflanzen zu erklären*.
        December 25: His son August is born.

1790   January: Completes the first reworking of *Faust*, which
        will be published with the title *Faust, Ein Fragment* in the
        first edition of the complete works.
        January: First studies of color: *camera oscura*.
        March–June: Second journey to Italy, to Venice.
        July–October: Trip to Silesia, in Karl August's entourage,
        during the maneuvers of Prussian troops.
        October: Reads Kant.

1791   January: Begins working again on *Wilhelm Meister*.
        January: Karl August entrusts him with the direction of
        the Weimar theater. Writes the *Gross-Kophta*.

1792   Several essays on the theory of colors.
        Summer: Karl August presents him with the house at the
        Frauenplan.
        August–December: Campaign in France.

1793   May–August: Siege of Mainz, which is occupied by French
        troops.

1793–1797 Reads Homer.

1794   January: Performance of Mozart's *Magic Flute* at Weimar.
        May: Finishes the first book of *Wilhelm Meisters
        Lehrjahre*; in December completes third book.
        June: Schiller invites Goethe to collaborate on his
        magazine *Die Horen*.
        July: Discussion with Schiller about the *Urpflanze*.
        October: Finishes the *Römische Elegien*.
        November: Encounter with Hölderlin.
        December: Sends the first book of *Wilhelm Meister* to
        Schiller.

1795   January: *Erster Entwurf einer allgemeinen Einleitung in
        die vergleichende Anatomie*.
        February: Sends the fourth book of *Wilhelm Meister* to
        Schiller and begins writing the fifth and sixth books.
        August: Schiller receives the sixth book of the *Meister*.

Chronology of Goethe's Life and Works

July–August: At Karlsbad.
September–August: Concludes *Unterhaltungen deutscher Ausgewanderten,* a collection of novellas.
December: Goethe and Schiller begin writing together the *Xenien,* satiric poems in rhymed couplets.

1796   February: Translation of Benvenuto Cellini's *Life.*
March–April: Schiller is Goethe's guest at Weimar.
May: Meets August Wilhelm Schlegel.
May: Writes the elegy *Alexis und Dora.*
June 26: Sends Schiller the seventh and eighth books of the *Lehrjahre;* Schiller responds with the long letter-book reviews of June 28, July 2, July 3, July 5, July 8, and July 9.
October: The publisher Unger issues the fourth and last volume (books seven and eight) of the *Lehrjahre.*
October–December: Studies fish and birds.
October–November: At Ilmenau, where there has been a collapse in the mine.
December: Writes the elegy *Hermann und Dorothea;* while he has already begun writing the epic poem with the same title.

1797   March: At Jena; studies chemistry, optics and does dissections of frogs.
March: Thinks of writing a poem about hunting, which will later be transformed into the *Novelle.*
March–May: Reads books on the epic; at the end of December writes *Über epische und dramatische Dichtung.*
April: Studies Old Testament and Aeschylus.
May–June: Writes *Die Braut von Korinth, Der Gott und die Bajadere.*
June 7: Concludes poem *Hermann und Dorothea.*
June–July: Begins again to work on *Faust,* on which he will continue to work during the coming years.
July–November: Journey to Switzerland, by way of Frankfurt and Stuttgart.

1798   January: Reads Schelling.
March: Purchases a farm near Apolda.
March–May: Begins the poem *Achilleis,* which will never be completed.
June: Essay *Über Laokoon.*
August: Studies Winckelmann, Plutarch, and Diderot's essays on painting.
August: Meets Jean Paul.

GOETHE

October: First number of the magazine *Propyläen*, to which Goethe, Schiller, W. von Humboldt, and Meyer contribute.

1799   March: Foundation of the *Weimarer Kunstfreunde*.
July: Meets Tieck.
August 11: First letter from the composer K.F. Zelter, one of Goethe's most intimate friends in his old age.
September–October: Discussions with Schelling, at Jena, on the philosophy of nature.
November: Resumes studies of colors.
December: Project for the play *Die natürliche Tochter*.

1800   April: Working on *Faust*.
September: Writes the first part of the third act of *Faust II*, which he will revise again in 1826.
November: Studies the history of Sparta.

1801   January: Serious illness.
January and the following months are taken up with the construction and decoration of Weimar's new castle.
February: Reads Cervantes' short stories. Reads several books about devils, which will be useful for *Faust I*, on which he continues to work through March and April.
June–August: Travels to Göttingen, Pyrmont, and Kassel.
October 21: Visit of Hegel.

1802   August: Studies comparative anatomy.
September–October: Reads Calderon in A.W. Schlegel's translation.

1803   January–March: Finishes his translation of Cellini's *Life*, which he publishes the same year.
March: Conclusion of *Natürliche Tochter* (first play of an uncompleted trilogy), which is staged on April 2.
July: Gives theoretical and practical lessons in the theatrical art at the Weimar theater.
October: First idea for the *novella, Der Mann von fünfzig Jahren*, later included in the *Wanderjahre*.
December: Madame de Staël and Benjamin Constant visit Weimar (until the end of March 1804).

1804   March 17: Staging of Schiller's *Wilhelm Tell*.
June: New studies on the theory of colors.
September 22: Staging of *Götz von Berlichingen*, rewritten by Goethe.
December: Essay on Winckelmann.

Chronology of Goethe's Life and Works

1805   January–February: Translates Diderot's *Neveu de Rameau* and sends manuscript to author.
January–May: Repeated illnesses.
May 9: Death of Schiller.
November: Gives a lecture on scientific subjects for the ladies of the court of Weimar.

1805–1806 Intense work on the *Farbenlehre.*

1806   January–February: Studies galvanism.
March–April: Finishes first part of *Faust* and in May sends it to the publisher Cotta, who issues it in 1808.
June: Reads the *Nibelunghi.*
June–August: At Karlsbad, where he delves into mineralogy and geology.
August–September: At Jena, where he often meets Hegel.
October: Meets Johanna Schopenhauer, Arthur's mother.
October 14: Battle of Jena: Weimar sacked by French troops.
October 19: After eighteen years of life in common, Goethe marries Christiane.

1807   January–April: Writes the polemical section of the *Farbenlehre.*
April 10: Death of the Duchess Mother Anna Amalia.
April: Meets Bettina Brentano.
May: Reads Boccaccio's *Decameron, The Thousand and One Nights,* and the tales of Margaret of Navarre.
May: Writes the first chapter of *Wilhelm Meisters Wanderjahre.*
May–September: At Karlsbad, where he meets K.F. Reinhard.
November–December: Writes *Pandora,* which he interrupts in 1808.

1808   March 2: Kleist's play *Der zerbrochene Krug* is presented at Weimar, with Goethe directing the play.
May: Plan for the *Wahlverwandschaften,* of which in June–July dictates the first eighteen chapters.
From July to December and into 1809 prepares the historical part of the *Farbenlehre,* published in 1810.
September 13: Death of Goethe's mother.
October 2 and 6: Meetings with Napoleon I.

1809   April–October: Resumes and finishes the *Wahlverwandschaften,* which he publishes the same year.

October–December: Gathers materials and makes outlines for *Dichtung und Wahrheit.*
December: Wilhelm Grimm's visits.

1810   April: Reads books on Charlemagne.
April–May: Resumes *Wilhelm Meisters Wanderjahre.*
May: Meets Sulpiz Boisserée, who gives him a closer view of medieval German art.
May–August: At Karlsbad, meets the empress of Austria, the king of Holland, and various princes, diplomats, and generals.

1811   May: New meetings with Sulpiz Boisserée.
August–October: Studies classical art together with his friend, H. Meyer.
October: The publisher Cotta publishes the first part of *Dichtung und Wahrheit.*
September–December: Reads Calderon's *Life is a Dream,* German medieval texts, and Niebuhr's *Römische Geschichte.*

1812   January: Reads Giordano Bruno.
January 23:   Stage presentation of *Egmont,* with Beethoven's music.
February–March: Reads Chateaubriand's *Atala* and *Génie du Christianisme.*
April–September: At Karlsbad and Teplitz, where he meets Beethoven.
September: The fable *Die neue Melusine,* which he later incorporates in the *Wanderjahre.*
November: Finishes the second part of *Dichtung und Wahrheit.*

1813   January: Studies Philostratus' *Eikones.*
January 20:   Death of Wieland.
March: Reads Shakespeare and several other Elizabethan dramatists.
April–August: At Dresden and Teplitz.
October: Studies China's culture and geography.
October: Meets Czar Alexander of Russia and Metternich, both of whom stop at Weimar after the battle of Leipzig against Napoleon.
December: Begins to write the *Italienische Reise.*

1814   February–May: Reads Madame de Staël's *De l'Allemagne.*

Chronology of Goethe's Life and Works

May: The publisher Cotta issues the third part of *Dichtung und Wahrheit.*

May–June: Writes *Des Epimenides Erwachen,* to celebrate the victory of the allied armies over Napoleon.

June: Reads Hafiz's *Divan* in Josef von Hammer's translation; the first poems of the *Westöstlicher Divan,* which will be published in 1819, are written.

July–October: Journey to Wiesbaden, Frankfurt, Heidelberg; meets Marianne von Willemer.

December: Studies Arab and Eastern civilization.

1815　　May: Tries to transform the first monologues of *Faust I* into arias for an opera.

June–July: Reads a collection of modern Greek poetry.

May–September: At Wiesbaden, Cologne, Mainz, Frankfurt; during August and September a guest of the Willemers: falls in love with Marianne; writes several lyrics of the *Westöstlicher Divan.*

October–November: The czarina of Russia at Weimar.

December: Studies Luke Howard's essay on the clouds.

1816　　February–November: New studies on colors.

February 18: Parts of *Faust,* with the music of Prince Radziwill, is staged at the Berlin court.

May: Conversations with Arthur Schopenhauer on the subject of colors and his theory about them. Reads Byron's complete works.

June 6: Death of Christiane.

June: The first number of a magazine, edited by Goethe, bearing the title *Über Kunst und Altertum in den Rhein- und Maingegenden* (which in 1818 will be called only *Über Kunst und Altertum*), is issued.

September–October: Second part of the *Italienische Reise* (published, together with the first part, in October 1817).

December: Plan for second part of *Faust.*

1817　　Begins publishing the review *Zur Naturwissenschaft überhaupt, besonders zur Morphologie* (ten issues up to 1824), in which he publishes many scientific essays.

April 13: Quits his post as director of Weimar's theater.

June 17: His son August marries Ottilie von Pogwisch.

September–October: Follows the studies and polemics of G. Hermann and F. Creuzer on ancient mythology.

GOETHE

October: Translates part of Byron's *Manfred*.
October 7–8: Writes *Urworte, orphisch*.

1818   February: Meteorological observations, particularly on
forms of clouds.
February–November: Studies on colors.
April 9: Goethe's grandchild, Walter Wolfgang, is born.
June: Reads Marlowe's *Doctor Faustus*.
July–September: At Karlsbad, where he meets Metternich.
October: Writes an essay on the polemics between
classicists and romanticists in Italy.

1819   January: Reads Schopenhauer's *Die Welt als Wille und
Vorstellung*.
August: Tries to continue the *Italienische Reise* (last
sojourn in Rome).
Nobember–December: New osteological studies.

1820   January–March: Gathers material and begins to write
Campagne in Frankreich and *Belagerung von Mainz*.
March–April: Reads Manzoni's *Il Conte di Carmagnola*, to
which he devotes an essay.
April–May: At Karlsbad: meteorological and geological
observations.
September 18: Wolfgang Maximilian, Goethe's second
grandchild, is born.
September–December: Begins again to write the
Wanderjahre.
November: Reads Plutarch, Appian, Dionysius of
Halicarnassus, and returns to his studies of Homer.

1821   February: Studies poetry of India.
May 8: Finishes first draft of the *Wanderjahre*, published
in 1822.
July: Reads and translates Euripides.
July–September: Travels to Marienbad, where he becomes
acquainted with Amalie von Levetzow and her daughters.

1822   January: Translates Manzoni's long poem *Il cinque maggio*.
March: Finishes *Campagne in Frankreich*.
June–August: At Marienbad, where he again meets the
Levetzow family; later at Eger.
September: The librarian Kräuter begins to gather, set in
order, and catalogue all of Goethe's published and
unpublished writings.

Chronology of Goethe's Life and Works

1823	March: Completes the lyrical trilogy *Paria*. June 10: First visit of Johann Peter Eckermann to the *Frauenplan*. June–September: At Marienbad, Karlsbad, and Eger; passion for the very young girl Ulrike von Levetzow; *Trilogie der Leidenschaft*.
1824	Edits the volume containing his correspondence with Schiller (published in 1828–1829). May: Goes back to working on the *Wanderjahre*, as he does the following year. July–August: New osteological essays.
1825	January: Begins the important essay *Versuch einer Witterungslehre*. February 25: Resumes work on *Faust II*.
1826	March: Announces a complete new edition of his works in forty volumes: *Ausgabe letzter Hand* (1827–1830). March–June: Conclusion of third act of *Faust II* (Helen's act). October: Begins the *Novelle*, which he completes in February 1827. November–December: Revision of third act of *Faust II*; plan for the two preceding acts.
1827	Publishes nineteen literary articles (on Homer, Euripides, Sterne, *Hamlet*, etc.) in the review *Kunst und Altertum*. Reads Chinese poetry, fables, and novels in English and French translations (from which is born the poetic cycle: *Chinesisch-Deutsche Jahres und Tageszeiten*); also reads *Metamorphoses* by Ovid, Victor Hugo, Béranger, and Hoffmann. January 6: Charlotte von Stein dies. April–July: Correspondence with Carlyle, which continues over the following years. May: Works again on *Faust* (first act and beginning of fourth act). August: Visit to Weimar of King of Bavaria.
1828	January–February, September–December: *Wanderjahre*. April: Begins writing the last part of *Italienische Reise*. June 14: Death of the Grand Duke Karl August. July–September: At Dornburg, where he studies books on botany and writes some lyrical poems.

GOETHE

1829   January: Finishes the first draft of the *Wanderjahre*.
January–February and December: Works on *Faust II*, of
which he reads some parts to Eckermann.
February–August: Finishes the *Italienische Reise*.

1830   January–July: *Faust II (Klassische Walpurgisnacht)*.
May: Studies Rousseau's writings on botany.
July–September: Writes *Principes de Philosophie
zoologique*, in which he studies the polemic between
Cuvier and Geoffroy de Saint-Hilaire.
October 26:   Death of his son August at Rome.
November 25–29:   Serious illness.

1831   January–October: Continuation and end of *Dichtung und
Wahrheit*.
February–July: Conclusion of *Faust II* (fourth and fifth
acts), which will be published by Riemer and Eckermann
after Goethe's death, as the first volume of his posthumous
works.
October 8–9:   Dictates *Rembrandt der Denker*.
October–December: Reads Euripides, Plutarch, Walter
Scott, Benjamin Constant, Victor Hugo, Balzac, Dumas,
Galileo, Niebuhr, A. von Humboldt, Cuvier, and Carus.

1832   January: Reads the second part of *Faust* to Ottilie.
March 22:   Death of Goethe.

Someone said: "Why in the world do you work so hard on Homer? In any case you don't understand him." Whereupon I replied: "I don't understand the sun, moon, or stars either; but they pass over my head, and when I see them I recognize myself in them and consider their regular, marvelous movement and think: 'Who can tell? Perhaps from me too something good may come.'"

Maxims and Reflections, 1037

Goethe

Wilhelm Meisters
Lehrjahre

ONE

Return
to Weimar

I

Goethe left Rome on April 23, 1788. For three consecutive nights a full moon shone brightly in a pellucid sky, canceling all the details that, during the day, distract and disturb the eye; and the great masses of light and shadow seemed to construct a simpler world, majestic and harmonious. On the last night, after having strolled down the Corso, Goethe climbed to the Capitol, which rose like an enchanted palace in a desert. Marcus Aurelius's statue reminded him of the statue of the Commendatore in Mozart's *Don Giovanni*. Lower down, the arch of Septimius Severus cast dark shadows around itself; while, in the solitude of Via Sacra, even the most familiar objects seemed strange and ghostly. Finally he approached the remains of the Colosseum and peered through the gates into the interior of the venerable ruin; but a shudder suddenly ran through him and hastened his return home.[1]

Goethe had said that in every great separation is hidden "a germ of madness," which "one must guard against cherishing and caressing with one's thought" (XI, 531: 12–14). On the stagecoaches taking him slowly toward Weimar, he did not bother to follow this advice; and with morbid, voluptuous pleasure abandoned himself to the sadness of the final separation. He closed his eyes; he tried not to look about him lest he disturb his "sweet torment." He avoided writing, so as not to dispel the delicate mist of his suffering. He fantasized; he imagined that he was Ovid, exiled to Pontus's remote solitudes, remembering the last night he had spent in Rome; he compared his own destiny to that of Tasso, dragged like himself "to an irrevocable banishment," forced to escape disguised in the pilgrim's black cape, like a savage outlander pursued by the Furies.[2]

He arrived in Florence on the first of May and stayed there for a few days, admiring the Medici *Venus* and the paintings of the *Urväter* of Italian art. But he spent most of his time in the Medici gardens; and the shade of those perennially verdant trees, the murmur of the fountains, the hothouses full of lemons and oranges called to mind the delights of the D'Estes' pleasure palace, Belriguardo, where Tasso would have liked to end his days as a gardener, each autumn covering the lemon trees with boards and interlaced rushes and tending the flowers in the flower beds. In those marvelous parks his excited senses were again struck by the world's beauty; poetry's dried-up source began to gush freely again. He had carried along the first sketch of *Tasso* and began to work on those sections that he felt closest to his present mood; by now he could attribute to his poetic double the emotions that were afflicting him, without fear of losing himself in the madness that attends all leave-takings.

In Milan he was fascinated by Leonardo da Vinci's "Last Supper"; Milan's cathedral seemed to him a barbarous "mountain of marble," which man's hands had forced to assume the "most disagreeable shapes," and he complained that those hands still continued to torture it (May 23, 1788). Climbing up onto the spire, he saw stretching out in the distance the hills around Lake Como, Grisons' high peaks, and the mountains of Switzerland, like a shore he would finally reach after a strange pilgrimage. He caught a whiff of the air of his native land. The next day, for the first time in many years, visiting a naturalist, Father Pini, he avidly examined feldspar stones and some rare crystallizations.

Just as Adam had been driven from the earthly paradise, so he was about to be driven from the realm of form and molded stone, where he had lived for almost two years. If he looked around him, his eyes no longer saw the elegant, bland, or grandiose Hellenistic statues he had admired in Rome, but only crude, savage, unformed stones, or sculptures that emulated the mountains. What could he do but adapt himself, with "the bitterness of death" in his heart, to this completely different world? And rekindle his old passion for that which is hidden *"in herbis et lapidibus"*? So, before leaving Milan, he bought a mineralogist's hammer. On the way home, as the stagecoach climbed from Chiavenna to the Splügen pass and descended through the mountains to Chur, he followed on foot, lingering among the rocks and pounding the ancient granite, feldspar, sandstone, and friable limestone with his hammer.

When he reached Weimar in the middle of June 1788 a curious relic was awaiting him. During the last months of his stay in Rome he had admired Raphael's skull, which the Accademia di San Luca preserved like something holy. Writing to his German friends, he described it as a "marvelous bone structure"; "an incredibly beautiful, well proportioned, and rounded shell without a trace of those protuberances, knobs, and bumps which, observed later on other craniums, assumed a manifold significance in Gall's phrenological theory" (XI, 256: 7; 549: 17–21). He couldn't take his eyes from that cranium in which "a beautiful" soul "could walk about comfortably" and where, perhaps, it had left some faint signs of itself. So he asked Hofrat Reiffenstein to have a plaster cast of it made, and this preceded him on another stagecoach as he tarried in Florence and Milan. When he reached Weimar he showed the cast to Duke Karl August and to all "the friends of art and nature," and kept it for the rest of his life as a kind of paperweight under which he placed his most recent poetic compositions.

No earthly hand had torn Raphael's bones and skull from their eternal sleep; in fact they lay, undisturbed, deep beneath the Pantheon. That skull, so beautiful, harmonious, and round, preserved jealously on Goethe's worktable, had been inhabited by the soul of Don Desiderio d'Adiutorio, a pious, modest priest, who in 1539 had founded the "Congregation of the Virtuous of Saint Joseph of the Holy Land of the Pantheon." Thus Goethe's "classicism" began under the symbolic protection of a spurious plaster skull.

More than twelve years had passed since that day in November 1775 when a carriage loaded with baggage brought Goethe, then twenty-six, for the first time to the obscure and muddy town of Weimar. *Die Leiden des jungen Werthers (The Sorrows of Young Werther)* had been published the year before; and an epidemic of imitations and parodies, of suicides and sermons, of exaltations and curses, of tears of bliss and scornful laughter, of gay outings to the countryside and in cemeteries had made him famous throughout Germany. The lords and ladies in the small German courts all gossiped about the new literary prodigy. "Today Hofrat Goethe dined beside me," the young prince of Sachsen-Meiningen wrote to his sister. "He talks a great deal and very well, in a unique, original and spontaneous manner, and he is extraordinarily amusing and pleasant. . . . He has his own ideas and opinions on everything. . . . I liked him very much." (B. February 4, 1775.) "Do you want me to tell you about Goethe; do you want to see him?" wrote a socially prominent doctor of Hanover to a woman patient in Weimar. "But, my dear friend, you want to see him, and yet you do not know how dangerous this lovable and fascinating man could become for you! . . . He is twenty-four; he is a jurist, a skilled lawyer; he knows and reads the

classics, especially the Greeks; he is a poet and writer: orthodox, hetero-
dox. He writes farces, he is a composer of music. He draws astonishingly
well, etches in copper, sculpts in wood—in short, he is a great genius
but a terrible man. A woman of the world, who has seen him quite
often, told me that Goethe is the handsomest, liveliest, most original,
most ardent, impetuous, tender, seductive, and dangerous man for a
female heart that she has ever encountered in her life." (B. January 19,
1775.)

As soon as he reached Weimar, Goethe proved only too anxious to
feed his own legend. In that small town of six thousand inhabitants,
where pigs and chickens roamed untended through the streets, he
strolled about in his splendid Werther-like uniform: blue dress coat,
yellow trousers, and knee-high boots. He scandalized the court with his
talented student's manners, his sudden informality of address, his curses
and unexpected cracks of the whip he carried. But, after a few months,
that "handsome master of witches," that "true monarch of the spirits,"
as Wieland called him, had charmed both friends and foes. He organized balls, masquerades, plays, country outings, bathes in the rivers,
hunts, and furious nocturnal horseback rides through the surrounding
woods.

During the long winter evenings he ordered Karl August's servants
to illuminate with torches and lanterns a frozen pond a few minutes'
ride from Weimar. He placed musicians around its banks; oboes were
played at full blast, the triangles, cymbals, and drums used in Turkish
music resounded noisily, while pinwheels and rockets traced shimmering figures of fire across the sky. Meanwhile, on the pond, Goethe taught
Karl August and the young courtiers the very new art of ice-skating. He,
too, put on the broad skates of Friesland: at first hesitant and uncertain,
he left the bank; then, almost borne along by his winged feet, with an
ever more agile movement, he glided over the ice till late in the night,
while the moon peeped in and out of the clouds as in a scene from
Ossian.

When some important guest brought news of the great world, the
dowager duchess invited the lords and ladies to her small, modest palace. The guests played faro and performed music; they discussed everything and everybody; then one of them read aloud from the most recent
issue of one of the literary reviews—*The Muses' Almanac* or *The German Mercury*—then being published in Germany. Goethe arrived
later, when the party was at its height, wearing a short green jacket,
high boots and spurs. Lost amid the elegant crowd of guests, like "a
young and graceful hunter," he sat modestly in a corner, and listened
attentively. None of the guests recognized him or took notice of him.

But finally, weary of keeping silent, he bowed politely and asked permission to read something. At first he recited an idyll by Voss or a ballad by Bürger. Then, as if the devil or the restless spirit of Mercury had taken possession of him, he read the sort of poetry that nobody had ever written. Glancing around him with his "black, shining, Italian's eyes," he would improvise in all tones and manners: hexameters, iambics, *Knittelverse;* lyrics, fables, ballads, satires, and small comedies; letting his gifts shower down on a wonder-struck audience, as if he were pouring a large basket of flowers out on the world.

He was still living in his mercurial period. As he skated over the frozen ponds or moved through rooms crowded with courtiers, his agile, sensitive nerves captured the vibrations that traversed, as Sterne says, "the great sensorium of the universe." Incredibly subtle and electric, he apprehended the movement of a falling hair or the sudden swish of a silk gown, and even what was still to be born: whims, vagrant phantoms, imperceptible emotions and impulses that had not yet reached anyone's consciousness. His soul, like Werther's, wallowed, "melted in all of his nerves" (VI, 39: 14); and none of these infinite sensations and epidermic vibrations slid over him as something indifferent and inert: each one touched some chord in him, awakened a profound echo, threw him into a kind of amorous delirium. Sometimes this continual excitation became too intense; his nerves became frayed, threatened to crack; things lost their outlines and swayed as in a single blur of anguish and neurasthenic felicity.

The entire space of a day, which we unconsciously regard as a unit, seemed to him to occupy an immense, monotonous, and unbearable expanse. So his extremely quick imagination subdivided it in "millions of parts," fragmented it in multiple and contradictory instants, each of which formed in its turn a "small eternity" (September 9, 1780). He lived minute by minute, changing in a whirlwind his face, emotion, and vital rhythm: "happy as soon as some novelty or change played a thousand different songs on the harp" of his spirit (October 21, 1779). In the course of a few hours he passed from "anguish to wild exhilaration, from wistful melancholy to furious passion" (VI, 10: 22); he oscillated between amiable fatuity and enthusiasm, between pensive frivolity and gelid ardor; contemplating ever new thoughts, which arose, intertwined, and disappeared like breathlessly compelling fireworks (June 30, 1780).

The clock of his existence ticked in accordance with two opposed time schemes. Its hands had to move much more slowly than ours, for each minute he lived embraced as many emotions, sensations, and meanings as would have filled a year in our lives. Yet, at the same time, these hands turned at an insane velocity, forced to keep pace with the

GOETHE

restless "monarch of the spirits," who broke off a conversation in the middle; dictated in an uninterrupted spate as though in a somnambulistic trance, his thoughts rushing ahead of the pen; and who went through the world with his mind crammed with very rapid images, which gushed forth all at once and then got clogged and confused, generating multiheaded phantoms.

Like Euphorion, he let himself be swept away by his passion for frivolity. Whatever task he accepted, he did not seem to notice its weight; and even in the midst of governmental affairs, while dealing with taxes and roads, he retained his enchanter's charm. If he suffered, he would obligingly wear the elegant garb of sorrow and despair; if happiness took him by storm, it seemed that he reveled in it only because of the unexpected lightness which then animated his body and spirit. He glided over the surface as though nothing of what seethed in his depths could move or preoccupy him. "My life," he wrote, "is like a sleigh ride, gleaming and resonant, but there is little for the heart, a great deal for the eyes and ears" (October 14, 1770). And five years later: "Like a sleigh ride my life goes, quickly away, bells jingling and parading back and forth" (November 22, 1775). Pushed along in a kind of vertigo of frivolity, without the slightest ballast, he was afraid of being mistaken for one of those *Luftphantomen*, one of those insubstantial, airy figures his imagination produced; afraid that ghosts were playing with him, sucking him into their demonic celestial sphere.

He lived always at the margin of his being, going out to meet others in a great transport of self-abnegation. He made an effort to identify with all of his friends and correspondents. Depending on the person he addressed, he would change his ideas, his tone, even the style of his letters: Mephistophelian and sentimental, natural and complicated, naïve and ephemeral. Then, suddenly, he would study them with a cold eye, from a distance, uninvolved and aloof, as if he wanted to use them as a subject for a treatise on physiognomy. Sometimes his friends and all the people he loved seemed only fragments, trifles, atoms of his heart which—long before, perhaps in another life—he had flung into the world with the gesture of a sovereign creator. Now all these creatures stood outside of him—the severed limbs and scattered fibers of a still unknown being. He tried once again to gather them around him, to fuse them in a single emotion of sympathy, a shadow of the great vagabond love that travels inexplicably over the earth.

Soon after he arrived in Weimar he met Charlotte von Stein, whose silhouette cut out of paper in the fashion of the period had been shown him the year before by a friend of Lavater. During those days, in 1776, his manservant began knocking at the door of her house, delivering airy notes from Goethe written at the end of a ball; or a few lines dashed off in haste during his administrative duties; or long, minutely detailed pages from his diary; or poetic masterpieces flung down on a sheet of paper and forgotten. Along with the letters, the manservant brought Goethe's whimsical gifts: the first rose to bloom in his garden; three violets and some hyacinths; six lemons, when grapes were still unripe; large panniers of asparagus and strawberries; a roasted kid or thirty larks for dinner.

When he was traveling or composing *Iphigenie* and *Tasso*, a thousand associations would lead his thoughts back to her. "I live with you, whether present or absent, asleep or awake" (December 1, 1782). "Only this evening I wrote to my Lotte, with whom I have conversed silently for all this time. I would prefer that throughout the day you were invisible around me, and then in the evening, when I am alone, you would step clear of the wall . . ." (September 9, 1783), as if she could traverse space and envelop him, even from afar, with the power of her look and voice. For a number of years he tried to live wholly in Charlotte von Stein's light and shadow, not even attempting to keep anything for himself. Like a child he continually thanked her for her love; he asked her for protection and advice, and would have liked all his actions to be pleasing to her.

When he tried to delineate her figure, his imagination always suggested the same image. Charlotte was like a star of morning and evening, which sets after the sun and rises before the sun; or the North Star which never sets and weaves above our heads an eternally living crown; or like an eternal star which, faithful and friendly, shines athwart the mobile rays of the aurora borealis. Beneath this astral light, so steady, cold, distant, mitigatory, and soothing, "the noisy movement of rapid life," which in the past had fascinated him with its colors, turned into a shadow, a pale veil of mist quickly lost in the night (*An Lida*, verse 4 ff.).

After so many years of wandering, living like a pilgrim or wayfarer "in tents and huts," he felt he now inhabited a house with deep-laid foundations, "where one could live and die and conserve all of one's possessions" (February 11, 1782). His iridescent fantasies, his flights as an ice skater, his demonic improvisations, his nervous deliriums, his continual changes of mood, that excessive frivolity, those sudden moments of élan, and that cold detachment—all of the incredible strength which he had at one time scattered over the world's surface now gathered around a motionless center formed in his spirit like a soft and compact amorous mass.

When they were together, they did not lose themselves in the "happi-

GOETHE

ness of dream," in "dream's dangers," in the illusions and intoxications of young love. They were unlike other people, who do not know their own hearts and who love without understanding, grow excited and rush here and there, victims of unforeseen sorrows and hasty joys (*Warum gabst du*, verse 1 ff.). Goethe's intelligence, rendered sharper and more penetrating by love, understood the most delicate secrets of her intelligence and was understood in turn. He embraced her soul with a single glance and was embraced; without illusions he accepted their real relationship; so that, united with her, he could clearly grasp men's destinies, the movement of history, the signs of the future, the proportions of the universe. During their walks along the Ilm River, while reading and drawing together, or amid his administrative tasks and duties, always an ecstatic monotony enfolded his life, expunging all boredom and dispersion. A full, rich, tranquil happiness dripped into Goethe's heart; it almost overwhelmed him, and finally overflowed and rushed out of him, like a richly abundant spring.

These common treasures, gathered and defended with so much care, could not remain hidden in the house and garden on the Ilm. Just as Wilhelm Meister dreamed of appearing on the stage together with Mariane, saying to men's hearts what for so long they had yearned to hear, so Goethe imagined appearing on the stage of the world, bestowing his wealth on the great and humble of the earth. "Of what use," he wrote, "are all love's tribulations and blessings, if it does not become active?" (December 10, 1781.)

Far from the events of the great states, in which disharmony, unhappiness, and stupidity triumphed, the small, poor duchy of Weimar could become the first nucleus of the future kingdom of God—"Mount Ararat," as Wieland said, "where good men set foot, while the universal deluge covers the rest of the world" (B. October 7, 1776). So, at Weimar, perhaps for the last time in Europe's history, poetry tried to take over the governing of the state: Goethe donned the uniform of a privy councillor and for many years tried not to distinguish his political activity from his moral and artistic life. With the same spirit in which he had written *Iphigenie* or *Grenzen der Menschheit*, he shouldered every sort of practical task. He presided over long administrative meetings, drafted bureaucratic documents, dealt with matters concerning roads, bridges, canals, the mines of Ilmenau and the University of Jena; he trained the firemen, endeavored to reduce the costs of running the court and the small army. Only thus could the kingdom of God be born, patiently, from the sum of many humble sacrifices offered in a pure spirit.

During these years Goethe continually felt at his side the presence of superior beings observing his life. Hidden in the clouds a spirit bore a torch, lighting up the mountain trail; "sacred destiny" stood behind him, and he could hear its breath, at times he even glimpsed its ambiguous countenance. An emissary of the gods took him by the hand, leading him benignly toward his goal. A thousand mysterious signs were revealed in the flight of birds, the sudden presentiments of his heart, the beckonings of chance. But what did these celestial forces want from him, what did they ask of him? What did their beckonings mean? Sometimes he feared that they wanted to make him lose his way. When he found himself at a junction, facing a choice of several roads, he would have liked somebody to decide for him; but, at that moment of extreme uncertainty and distress, the gods would proffer contradictory advice. With a gesture they would point to this road; and with a smile, a wink, they would invite him to travel down the opposite one; or a third, a fourth. Every road seemed to be the right one, and yet only one road was his. The others would have led him to that perdition which, though completely guiltless, he would nevertheless deserve.

In a world teeming with gods and signs, Goethe soon learned the complicated art of the soothsayer. Like his ancient predecessors, he understood that the first secret of honest divination was to venerate all the signs that came from the heavens, whatever they might be. "My life proceeds," he wrote, "in accordance with the decisions of the gods, whom I honor in my profoundest presentiments" (March 10, 1777). "Only the gods know what they want and what they want to do with us. Their will is done" (December 4, 1777). He tried to keep his vision clear so that the slightest warning should not escape him; he did not let his desires befog his sight, nor permit ideas, rules, or examples to limit the scope of his horizon.

Since the gods change pace continually, he tried to be changeable as they were. Sometimes he received some barely whispered invitations, which nobody else would have comprehended, and, like Egmont, he mounted with a leap on the chariot of his destiny. At other times he seemed to miss quite obvious signs; he delayed for eleven years his journey to Italy, for fifty-three years the conclusion of the *Meister;* for fifty-seven years the completion of *Faust.* When he acted, no effort, no tension or anxiety agitated his spirit. Each action detached itself from him with the calm, objective necessity of a natural event, like a ripe fruit falling from the tree. "He reached his goal as though he were carried [by the gods]" (*Die natürliche Tochter,* 2708). Thus he managed to assimilate completely what he did, felt, and thought, enriching the substance of his organism. Nothing was wasted; even renunciations and things that failed to come off obeyed some sort of logic. All the real and

GOETHE

imaginary threads of his life intermingled in a compact fabric which rose before him like a collective work on which innumerable hands had collaborated.

Some of his friends, many of his adversaries, and all the unfortunate persons who tried to repeat his example were astonished by this mode of life. Some of them said he had an iron will, a grim spirit of self-restriction. Others, however, thought they could see an ecstatic, almost monstrous, passivity in his frame of mind. Both groups were right. Long training taught Goethe to carry out the will of God as if it were his own, or to live in so impersonal a fashion as to make his own acts coincide with the desires of the Almighty. Like a shuttle, he moved in obedience to the propulsions of an unknown hand; but like a skilled weaver, he would put the finishing touches to a cloth whose design he had known from the very start.

But who can deny that his "sacred destiny" seemed at times that of a clown, a lovable juggler, a young girl who mocks at grown men? As if he sought to imitate destiny, on some days Goethe amused himself by playing with his skills, carrying out some small mystification. He performed willful, almost gratuitous acts; then he would attribute them to his destiny, pretending to be actuated by his sacred inspiration—certain that the gods and demons who watched over him would never disavow him. And so in fact it went: the gods or demons blessed these all-too-human acts with a smile and sent them out into the world, consecrating them with their capricious seal.

This happy period also came to an end. "By transplanting me here," he wrote to Charlotte in November 1777, "destiny has done just what one does with lime trees; one prunes the topmost branches and all the beautiful lateral boughs so that they receive new strength, otherwise they would die from top to toe. . . ." And four years later, writing to his mother and friends in Frankfurt, he repeated: "People see only what I sacrifice, and not what I gain, and cannot understand that I become richer each day, although each day I sacrifice something" (August 11, 1781). But, as the years went by and God's kingdom was not realized even in the small duchy of Weimar, Goethe began to ask himself whether, in his effort at purification, he had not lopped off too many boughs, too many leaves, too many bushes of his undergrowth. The uniform of the privy councillor had almost hidden the free garb of the poet; and *Iphigenie*, the *Meister*, and *Tasso*, the works he had begun during those years, still lay unfinished on his worktable or in his traveling bags. His love for Charlotte von Stein had enclosed him in too exclusive a circle; a thousand wrinkles dug their furrows in his soul; his spirit had become rigid, while resignation hid joys and sorrows under the grayness of habit.

Wilhelm Meisters Lehrjahre

On September 3, 1786, a few days after his thirty-seventh birthday, Goethe left Karlsbad at three in the morning without telling anyone. He traveled in a mail coach, taking along a small valise and a portman- teau. On the night of September 9 he left the hotel on the Brenner pass, the horses plunging at a gallop down the road to Italy. As he descended toward the south, Goethe again took interest in the things of the world. He observed the great granite backbone of the Alps, cloud formations, lights, shadows, and colors, the light bluish mists produced by the at- mosphere; churches, palaces, statues, ruins; Palladio's Rotonda, Venice, that "republic of beavers," with San Marco's "enormous crustacean," the temple of Segesta surrounded by wild fennel; Vesuvius's lava, the mythical *Urpflanze* in the botanical gardens at Palermo, the carnival at Rome.

At the court of Weimar he had spent his time "thinking, wishing, reflecting, commanding, and dictating" (XI, 25: 22–23). Now, exposed to the fresh air and the journey's impressions, he felt he was swimming in a sea of youthfulness. The wrinkles in his soul were smoothed away; once again his spirit became lively, mobile, and resilient, as in the past. With an ever more overflowing enthusiasm, he kept writing his friends in Germany that he had become another person, that he had changed to the marrow of his bones, that each day he sloughed off another layer of dead skin, another crust, and that his eyes were fresh, washed clean, purified.

As was his habit, he interpreted this new state of mind in the Biblical language of the New Testament. His biological rebirth became the outward sign of a profound spiritual transformation and regeneration, such as every sinner experiences by being born again through Christ. "I count a second birth, a true rebirth, from the day I entered Rome" (December 2, 1786). But he added, repeating the words Christ said to Joseph and Mary in the temple: "I live happily, because *I am in that which is of my Father.*"[3] Now he no longer had to look forward, as at Weimar, to the time when his love and its works would prepare the future kingdom of God. All the desires and dreams of youth had been fulfilled; felicity was finally there before him, immediate, uncondi- tional, instinct with plenitude; and he felt that he could see and touch it. He had reached the very acme of his existence. He lived "in that which was of his Father."

Having returned to Weimar in June 1788, he sat in his garden, behind a trellis covered with roses, trying little by little to return within him- self. But the cloudy sky swallowed and extinguished the colors; the barometer sank; and in a little while the rains would conceal the hori- zon, forcing him to shut himself up in the house and sit before the burning fire. Winter soon came. The year before he had strolled among the orange trees, enjoying the full pleasure of living; now he had to remain in ambush behind the window panes, spying on the transparent crystallizations—like trunks, roots, stems, leaves, branches, and vine tendrils—with which the frost tried to imitate the forms of vegetation on the panes. Enclosed in his rooms like an onion beneath the snow, he was not visited by inspiration. It seemed to him that Italy was the only country made for him, and every "breath" coming to him from the south grieved him profoundly.

At Weimar, with the trusted friends whom he had lived and grown with, for eleven years, he had hoped to reelaborate the profound impressions he had brought back from Italy. But as he described the temples in Rome and Paestum or the original city plan still visible at Palermo, his friends' lack of attentiveness became less and less polite. His enthusiasm for Italy, "his sorrow and laments" for what he had lost, seemed to offend them (XIII, 102: 7). Nobody understood his new language or enfolded him with sympathy. Karl August dreamed of wars and armies; Knebel was living a hypochondriacal existence at Jena. And Herder, writing from Rome to his wife, protested that he didn't want to have anything more to do "with that great artist, with that single All who reflects the All of Nature, who regards even his friends, and everything that happens to him, merely as a sheet of paper on which to write, or as a color on the palette with which he paints" (B. May 7, 1789). The delightful monarch of the spirits seemed to have lost his old powers.

Even the long relationship with Charlotte von Stein was disintegrating. Deeply wounded by his flight to Italy, she had become nervous and excitable; she drank too much coffee and spent her time interpreting her dreams, losing her way among the night's vain phantasmagorias. She could not bear seeing him so changed. If he wanted to speak, she would silence him. If he told stories about his travels, she accused him of indifference; she subjected all his gestures and movements to scrutiny, criticized his character, distrusted him. On June 8, 1789, Goethe wrote to her: "I have never known a greater happiness than in my intimacy with you, which has always been boundless; and since it has been taken away from me, I have become another man and will change even more in the future. . . . Give me back your confidence . . . and I can then hope that everything between us will be recomposed in a purer, better way."

The letter was never answered and Goethe actually did become another man. But how could he forget that pure, monotonous, enclosed life, without the "happiness of dream" or "dream's dangers"? Or those eyes which knew every aspect of his being, which spied out the most delicate vibrations of each of his nerves, poured "moderation in his hot blood" and directed his "savage and errant course" (*Warum gabst du*, verse 29 ff.)? After that, Charlotte's image, always different yet always recognizable, continued to live in Goethe's poetic creations. The heroines of *Iphigenie auf Tauris* and *Torquato Tasso* preserve something of Charlotte's spirit. Natalia, the heroine of the *Lehrjahre (Wilhelm Meister's Apprenticeship)*, is, like her, the eternal star that shines through the moving rays of the aurora borealis; Makarie, in the *Wanderjahre (Wilhelm Meister's Travels)*, is Charlotte sanctified. And in the Utopia of "true love," heavenly and unrealizable, Goethe expresses the consoling emotions and fantasies of his long friendship with Charlotte von Stein.

In July 1788, a month after returning from Italy, Goethe met Christiane Vulpius in the park at Weimar. She was twenty-three and great clusters of black curls wreathed her face. A few days later he hid her in his country house; and soon he settled her in his city house, *Jägerhaus*. The tone and atmosphere of his life changed completely. Charlotte von Stein dressed always in white; she would perform the rarest dances with "the lightness of a zephyr," with "infallible dexterity"; she read, drew with elegance, acted, wrote plays and poems, and, as her doctor and friend, Johann Zimmermann, assures us, "the light of the moon and the silence of midnight filled her heart with a divine calm." Christiane Vulpius had worked in a factory, making artificial flowers. She preferred dresses with loud, strident colors; she barely knew how to read and write; she loved to dance at peasant festivals and to shoot with bow and arrow. With her robust arms she kept the house spick and span, and when night came she would slip, like a royal servant, into the master's bedroom. Now Goethe's *commissionnaires* no longer as in the past brought roses, lemons, hyacinths, and strawberries—the poetic gifts of a fanciful magician. From Frankfurt and Dresden, from Zurich and Jena, the diligences delivered to his house only domestic gifts: skirts, scarves, shawls, and from Sankt Gallen Swiss eyelets and muslins; swan's feathers and true or false garnets; half a pound of pins, two hundred sewing needles, twelve tin spoons; almond cakes, sausages, and cheeses.

He no longer traveled willingly. When Karl August obliged him to leave Weimar for a few months and stay among Silesia's "rags and bedbugs," or in Venice, "this maze of stone and water" (April 15, 1790) where the spring was without greenery, he sighed with nostalgia and desire. "Call me home! Why in the world must a gardener travel!" (April 4, 1790). "I will no longer have a happy hour," he wrote to the Herders, imitating the images of Horace and the Latin elegists, "until I shall have dined with you and slept next to my girl. If you continue to cherish me, if some good people remain my friends, if my girl is faithful, if my child lives, if my large stove heats us—then I desire nothing else" (September 11, 1790).

He had drawn a "very tight magic circle" around the walls of his house. All the world's tumults must remain outside, while within the silent rooms reign order, calm, regular repetition. If at one time he had changed his propensities with almost anguishing speed, now he obeyed the rhythm of the large pendulums measuring out the time in his rooms. If in the past he had traveled through the world like a vagabond or a guest, now he had become a prudent householder, a shrewd treasurer, an epicurean cupbearer, an architect who delighted in elegance and luxury. When he directed the restoration of the *Frauenplan* house, he demonstrated the same meticulous pedantry that he had execrated in his father. His workers built a large neoclassical stairway, like those he had admired in Italy. He ordered gilt cornices, from Nothnagel, a merchant in Frankfurt; draperies and rose-encrusted braids from Brussels and Brabant; and he was concerned about the wallpaper, which he wanted in iridescent hues, from blue to russet. From England he obtained Chester cheeses and smoked fish, along with old wines for his rich cellar.

While he lived hidden in this way, he was no longer visited by hopes for the world's future, hopes which had pursued him during his first years at Weimar. And he no longer thought, as he had during the months spent in Rome, that happiness could appear each morning before his very eyes. Disillusioned but tranquil, mature in a melancholy way, he realized that the gods had not granted even him the chance to live a life illuminated by joy, immersed in love, touched by the presentiment of eternity. Nor could he inhabit "that which was of his Father." Just like any other mortal he accepted long moments of boredom, pleasures and limitations, anxieties and care, shutting himself up behind the ever higher walls of his house, as if behind the bronze walls of necessity.

He lived nearly isolated, writing and speaking to a very few friends. Indeed, could he still call them his friends? Both the old trusted companions and the new people he met during those years were no longer a part of him. He had learned that "others" obey laws we do not know. He scrutinized them with curious eyes, tried to discover their secrets, dealt with them with skill and tenacity; but he no longer hoped to receive sympathy and comprehension. He began to dictate his letters to a secretary—interposing between himself and the others, between himself and his own soul this mute witness who obliged him to employ ever more impersonal formulas. Thus nobody could now observe his hand's nervous movements, the sudden abbreviations of his handwriting, the caprices and effusions of his spirit. With his usual rapidity, in the course of a few months, he covered himself with defenses, masks, simulations. The temperature of his life, once so ardent, sank suddenly to an arctic level, as though he were living beneath a sheet of ice.

His old friends no longer recognized him. The swift ice skater, the young, graceful hunter in the green jacket, the handsome master of witches, the gay artist of Rome was turning into a plaster statue with a fat frowning face and a chest covered with decorations. Young visitors, who wished to talk to the author of *Werther* and *Tasso*, met at the head of the Italian-style staircase amid a pantheon of statues, plaster casts, and paintings, a "cold, monosyllabic, mute divinity," eyes gleaming with a disagreeable light, who spread about him a distressing frost.

What had happened? Many years later Goethe, then an old man, replied in the *Wanderjahre* with a complicated parable to the question his friends had so often silently addressed to him. When charcoal burners prepare charcoal—Jarno explains to Wilhelm Meister—they pile the thick pieces of wood one on top of the other; a close-set, regular lattice in which the air can circulate freely. Then they light the wood; and as soon as the fire bursts through each crack they stifle the flames with a cover of grass and soil, so that each piece of wood burns in a uniform manner, pervaded and compenetrated by the fire. At the end they shut all the air vents, stifle the last sparks, and the whole burning mass is gradually doused, turns into charcoal, and grows cold. Then the charcoal burners sell their goods "to the blacksmith and coppersmith, the baker and cook, and when it has served and benefited so many good Christians, it can still be used as ashes by laundresses and soapmakers" (VIII, 39–40).

With the passing of time Goethe, too, like Jarno, had become "a basket of good beechwood charcoal." During these years he no longer burned in great impetuous flames with the love and yearning that filled his soul, scattering them like useless ashes on the world; rather he hid them, made them cold beneath gestures, clichés, conventions. Of what use to men were his amorous raptures? Rather than flames and scattered ashes, he wanted to offer them only good beechwood charcoal with its precise capacities and limited abilities, like the technical skill of a botanist or mineralogist, the culture of a scholar of ancient art, the prudence of a diplomat, the wisdom of an artisan of words. If the charcoal burner's charcoal could be used by blacksmith and coppersmith, baker and cook, his modest charcoal could be useful to both the great and humble of the earth, to scientists and artists, philosophers and

GOETHE

literary men, to all those minds and spirits that desired precision.

But just as the wood, when covered by soil and grass, burns in silence, so love continued to burn unseen within him, completely imbuing and compenetrating him. The soft, shapeless mass of emotions and anxieties he had repressed, the hopes he had given up, the happiness to which he had bidden farewell—everything which in the past had glittered brightly on the surface—he had slowly concentrated into a symbolic substance, hard as a diamond, which did not cease giving off its very sweet, incomprehensible irradiations.

The French Campaign

II

A few minutes by carriage from Weimar, on the slopes of the Rosenberg, Goethe owned a garden, which Karl August had given him as a gift in April 1776. At that time the place was deserted and uncultivated. On the hill, covered with wild roses, the duke's woodcutters had chopped down trees or thinned them out with their axes; deer, fox, and wild goats could be seen in the scrub; in the winter, hunting horns rang out over the snow-covered valley. Right below the hill, winding in tranquil curves, ran the Ilm River, which sometimes flooded the lower part of Goethe's garden. Weimar was not far away. But the branches of the alders, ashes, poplars, and birches of the large English-style park, which the duke had planted in 1778, concealed the town's towers and buildings. "There one felt immersed in the peace and the deepest solitude of nature," Eckermann wrote, "for the great silence is only broken by the lonely chatter of the blackbird, the shimmering, intermittent song of a thrush. From these dreams of a solitary life we are awakened from time to time by the tolling of the tower clock, the cry of peacocks wafted down to us from the top of the park, or the roll of drums and blare of trumpets in the barracks" (E. March 22, 1824).

When Goethe visited his garden for the first time, the ground was covered with rocks and dry scrub; poisonous snakes had their nests among the bushes; a bed of asparagus promised a scanty harvest; and only a very large, extremely old juniper tree, so rare in that region, attracted his attention. But a growing number of laborers—twenty-six by the end of June—began to divide the slope into a series of terraces.

GOETHE

They dug out paths along the summit of the hill and descending to the river; enriched the unfertile terrain with soil and loam from nearby fields. Then came bricklayers, carpenters, and painters, who restored the small, very modest two-story house. Furniture designed by Mieding, "the court's master cabinetmaker," included two sofas, a few armchairs, a Viennese desk, chairs with red cushions, and large mirrors with black frames.

On the evening of May 18, 1776, Goethe began to live in his new house. In the summer he slept, stretched out on a straw pallet and wrapped in his blue cloak, on the house's high balcony. During the winter, the snow and rain would wake him several times a night and force him to retire to a more sheltered corner, barricading doors and windows, as a seaman caulks his ship against the assault of the waves. He took long walks in the Ilm valley, hunting for wild ducks and fishing with the gamekeepers; he learned to swim in the river; wrote the first draft of *Iphigenie;* or sat beneath the juniper tree, drawing a rose, Wieland's face, a tree, a bush, the moon over the river, a winter view of the park in Weimar.

The hill often echoed with the shouts of children, who were searching for colored eggs and oranges hidden in the corners of the garden. The duke, the dowager duchess, the young duchess, Lavater, Lenz, Knebel, Wieland, Herder, later on Schiller and Humboldt, would discuss the major problems of science and literature with him as they walked. But if his friends or some of the Weimar aristocrats threatened his quiet too often, Goethe would lock the gate to the three bridges which, after crossing the Ilm, led to the foot of the Rosenberg. "Every time I tried to visit him," Wieland wrote, "I found the gates shut; and since one could not reach his house unless one had brought along an artillery piece or at least a couple of servants who could open up a path with axe blows, an ordinary man like myself was forced to renounce the adventure" (B. April 12, 1778).

In the spring of 1777, the duke's gardeners planted lime trees, oaks, elms, firs, beech and birch trees. On the top of the hill a few apple and pear trees, even some grapevines, which had come from distant Frankfurt, gave the promise of cheering Goethe's table. Hedges of honeysuckle protected the garden from the road; bushes of jasmine, laburnum, and colutea, lilies and gladioli grew along the slope; strawberries gleamed among the bushes; while mallows, tall as a man, their large flowers of bright burning yellow, soft pink, and festive violet, stood like sentinels along its paths. A magnificent, very dense espalier of roses—Frankfurt roses, cinnamonea roses, damask roses, eglantine roses—climbed on the house's walls and roof, their first green leaves sprouting in April, the buds in May, and the flowers' full luxuriance in June.[1]

When he was a child, he had watched admiringly as his grandfather, dressed in his ankle-length dressing gown, a black velvet cap on his head and wearing a pair of old leather gloves, looking like an Alcinous or Laertes in eighteenth-century clothes, grafted roses, sorted out the bulbs of the tulips and tied the espaliers to the branches of the peach trees. Now, followed by the court gardener, Gentsch, he imitated the gestures of that family figure; he got to know the habits of the plants and acquired the calm eye, silent application, and patience of old gardeners. He, too, trimmed the rose bushes, planted oak, beech, and fir trees, tended the flower beds and grapevines, setting grafts on the young trunks; and conversed with his beloved trees, which swiftly rose to the sky, "burying many joys and sorrows beneath their roots" (December 16, 1780).

On the slopes of the Rosenberg Goethe began to leaf through the book of nature: the only book that "offers us great substance on all of its pages" (XI, 196: 22). But what efforts he made at the beginning to decipher those gigantic and invisible characters, scattered among rocks and flower seeds! As Heraclitus had said, "Nature loves to hide"; it does not want us to know the life that it eternally bestows on us. "Now it contracts in abbreviations what, if clearly developed, would have been so easy to comprehend; now it dallies in intolerably long pauses, lining up sentences written in a broad, flowing calligraphy: it reveals what it had hidden and hides what it had revealed" (W. VIII, 137: 11). Many pages of the great book are scattered among the most impregnable mountains or on the surfaces of Jupiter, Mars, and other planets, where men have never reached.

With his apprentice's enthusiastic fervor, Goethe sought advice from the scholars and scientists at the University of Jena, pharmacists, court gardeners, the duke's mining inspectors: from that whole manifold fauna of dilettantes and artisans who were then studying the life of nature. He appointed a nineteen-year-old boy, Friedrich Gottlieb Dietrich, as his "botanical herald," and received help from Knebel and Frau von Stein. He studied Linnaeus's *Botanical Philosophy* every day; on his walks and excursions he took along, condensed in a small notebook, Linnaeus's *Fundamenta*, and Gessner's *Dissertationes*, so as to memorize the names of the trees and flowers. When traveling, instead of abandoning himself to his thoughts, he would stop the coach each time his attention was caught by a clump of grass or bushes he had never seen before. As a result, his apprenticeship did not last long. He soon learned how to spell out those immense pages, those illegible words, those abbreviated messages; he began to have faith in his own powers; and he told his friends that he knew how to read nature's "large, beautiful characters" (August 23, 1784).

When he reached Italy he felt lost among the trees, fruits, vines, and flower beds in the eternal bloom and luxuriance of Alcinous's garden, as it had offered itself to Ulysses's gaze. All the plants he had seen in hothouses bloomed here in the open air; in the cities' gardens lattices of lemons and oranges curved to form arbors, walls of red oleanders lured the eye, unknown trees from the tropics spread out their strange ramifications. Bordering the roads in Sicily, between Monreale and Castelvetrano, the wild bushes and shrubs gleamed in a mad profusion of flowers; the lentisc, so covered with yellow flowers like butterflies that one could not see a single green leaf; the hawthorn producing cluster after cluster of blossoms; the aloe standing stiffly on its stalk, announcing the flowering soon to come; and hibiscus, insect-orchid, rhododendron, hyacinths with closed bells, amarathine clover, borage, alliums, and asphodels formed illimitable carpets of flowers that spread for miles.

In the midst of this unhoped-for wealth of vegetation, Goethe's lucid and inebriated eye thought it had discovered "the most surprising creature in the world," the *Urpflanze* or Primal Plant, which included all existing plants and all those that ever could exist; and he thought that nature itself should envy him (XI, 324: 3–4).

When he returned to Weimar, he resumed his botanical studies. Soon after, in the winter of 1789, he wrote the most famous of his scientific essays, *Versuch die Metamorphose der Pflanzen zu erklären*, which was published in 1790, on Easter Day. In this small book, which he later summed up in an elegy, he told how each plant grows from the seed and entrusts to the grace of light the very fragile structure of aborning leaves; how the leaf expands, becomes indented, divides into parts and points, grows ribbed and notched on the swollen surface; how it contracts, delicately and rapidly lifting the stalk and opening the calyx, to lavish colorful, sumptuous rosettes; how the flower sways on the agile armature of shimmering leaves and finally contracts once again, forming the countless seeds enclosed in the fruit's maternal womb.

During those same years he had a *camera oscura* built for him; set up optical instruments in the open air and in a darkened theater, reproducing the phenomenon of the rainbow under all possible circumstances; and he wrote the two *Beiträge zur Optik* (1791–1792), the essay *Von den farbigen Schatten* (1792), and many other minor studies that anticipated the grandiose *Farbenlehre* published in 1810. Like a "true son of the light," he took on the task of defending the eternal clarity of solar light, which had been divided and besmirched by the "calumny" of Newton, whom he described as master and prince of the wicked, and whom he detested as much as Campanella had execrated Aristotle. So he tried with all of his powers to destroy Newton's doctrine, which he compared to an uninhabitable fortress, full of weird tunnels, bizarre arcades and passageways, a nest for owls and mice, defended by a handful of old, ineffective soldiers, who were still convinced that they were well armed.

While recounting light's "deeds and passions," he was gripped by his youthful propensities and began drawing again "the ancient, mysterious hexagon" of colors, dear to the alchemists (XIII, 521: 9). On one side of the hexagon he set out the active colors: yellow, the color closest to light, merry and tenderly stimulating, which expands the heart and soothes the spirit; reddish yellow (orange), which gives the eye a sensation of warmth, recalling the sun's rays at sunset; and extremely violent reddish yellow (red lead), energetic, crude, primitive, which seems to transfix the gaze, enrages animals, and generates an incredible excitation in us. On the opposite side he set the passive colors: blue, which contains something dark, draws us into the distance and immerses objects in a cold, sad light; bluish red, which makes one tender and disquieted; while reddish blue, if it looks out at us from a tapestry, constitutes an almost unbearable presence. At the point of lowest encounter between yellow and blue, Goethe placed green, where eye and heart find true rest. But at the point of highest encounter between the two lines, sublime purplish red ostentatiously exhibits itself—the color that contains in fact and potentiality all other colors and which cloaks the grace of youth and the dignity of old age, the sumptuous color of sovereigns and popes, the terrible color that will light up heaven and earth on the day of the Last Judgment.

He continued to study the metamorphosis of insects, the structure of rocks, the history of the earth, the anatomy of men and animals. While composing the *Lehrjahre,* he wrote the *Versuch über die Gestalt der Tiere* (1790), the *Erster Entwurf einer allgemeinen Einleitung in die vergleichende Anatomie* (1796), and the *Beobachtung über die Entwicklung des Schmetterlings Phalaena grossularia* (1796). Friends in Italy, friends, acquaintances, and admirers whom he counted in Germany and every part of Europe sent him rocks of lava, basalt, feldspar, agate, jasper, and pieces of granite; giraffes' skeletons, walruses' jaws, the skulls of monkeys, elephants, and mandrils, paws of polar bears, and antelope horns; precious treasures or insignificant oddities, which he held in his hand, observed, and classified for his collections, adding another page, another word, another letter to the by now unveiled book of nature.

Thus he spent the years of his maturity scrutinizing flowers and plants, mountain rocks and animals' bones, the spectacles of light and color; and, wherever he might be, he knew he had before him "all of nature," in the full complexity of its laws (XIII, 315: 22). Like an ancient Greek naturalist, he searched in the wealth of phenomena for the "single model" on which the universe had been constructed. Among all existing plants he identified the primal plant, the archetype hidden in each of them, at once the unattainable idea and the real object we can see with our eyes and draw with our hand. The manifestations of every plant—stem, calyx, flower, fruit, and seed—were characterized by the aspects of a single fundamental organ, the leaf; one could trace in the bodies of monkeys, giraffes, fishes, and men an "anatomical type," a "universal form," containing the forms of all possible existing animals (XIII, 172: 14–15); the same antithetical and conciliatory forces can be found again among colors and clouds. As he proceeded by successive analogies, by ever more general formulas, "all became one, all was born from one and returned to one" (July 19, 1810).

But nature does not like rigidity and immobility. As soon as it has shaped an essential form, nature "plays with it and, by playing, produces manifold life" (July 10, 1786). Under the touch of its fingers, the *Urpflanze* and the *Urbild* (primal anatomical structure) were manifested and hidden in an uninterrupted series of metamorphoses: they contract and expand, change appearance and function, spurt out and slip away right before us, more changeable than Proteus, swifter than the creatures of the sea—as swift as God, who flees past Job before he can see him. At first, our eyes are disconcerted by this extraordinary versatility. Then we learn to discover in the most inferior formations the traces of a law. Finally, we appreciate how the order of nature dissolves in the cadences of a rhythm, how repetition and variety are intertwined, and gravity is able to assume the appearances of a free game.[2]

When it amuses itself so amiably, nature seems to possess the prodigious, sumptuous fantasy of an Oriental writer of fairy tales—of Scheherazade, who was never without resources and each night, faced with whatever difficulty, hit upon an imaginative, elegant solution. And yet, beneath its magnificent appearances, nature is infinitely prudent and balanced and never wastes or dissipates its strength, as cautious as an experienced businessman or a shrewd householder. When it intends to spend more than is permitted under one heading of its ledger, it makes sure to save under another heading. If, for example, it varies the structure of the "anatomical type" by lengthening the giraffe's neck, immediately it economizes by constricting its body; if it swells a fish's flesh and body, it curtails its extremities and accessory organs. In this way, as Goethe remarked, the imaginative and prudent nature guiding our lives "never falls into debt and never goes bankrupt" (XIII, 176: 20–21).

While Goethe at Weimar was studying the metamorphoses of plants, everything on earth was in agitation and dividing—"as if the world, the formed world, wanted to dissolve and return to chaos and night, and form itself again" *(Hermann und Dorothea,* IX, 273–274). The States General were meeting in Paris, the mob had destroyed the Bastille, Louis XVI was imprisoned and deposed, opposing factions were in a bloody contest for power; and soon revolutionary armies would cross the Rhine and the Alps. The temperature of the world was rising, igniting hopes and fears, fervent friendships and ferocious hostilities. "Everyone is going about with bellows," Goethe observed, "whereas it seems to me that this would be more the time to grab the water buckets" (July 24, 1794).

Enclosed in the "very tight magic circle" of his house, he would have preferred that not even the newspapers, his "most dangerous enemies" (August 18, 1792), could disturb his quiet occupations; he hoped to disappear in a dense cloud like that which surrounds the gods of Epicurus, and so be spared having to hear "the uproar made by that noisome ghost which is called the spirit of the age" (July 17, 1794). "The whole does not worry about us," he wrote to his friend Meyer, "and so why in the world should we worry about the whole more than is just?" (June 13, 1796). "As far as I am concerned, it becomes more and more clear that each person must seriously do his own job and take the rest as it comes. A few verses interest me much more than important things, over which I have no influence . . ." (August 10, 1797). At that moment he had only to prepare the form of the *Meister,* study the laws of nature, praising God with a "pure breast," together "with Raphael and other good spirits . . ." (July 17, 1794).

In August 1792 Goethe had to leave Christiane and his son, his books, his *camera oscura,* and the quiet hills of Thuringia. The emperor of Austria and the king of Prussia were attempting to restore the monarchy in France; and Karl August, who commanded a Prussian regiment, wanted Goethe to accompany him.

For two whole months the horizon of Champagne was covered by the dark veil of an obstinate downpour; cloudbursts and sudden showers drenched men and animals to the core. Their encampments were set up in seas of muck; water-rotted tent ropes broke one after the other; the ditches around the camp swarmed with nauseating garbage, which the rain at night washed up around the tents. The terrain of Champagne had become a vast, red, sticky morass of mud. Military vehicles, columns of soldiers, and the light open carriage in which Goethe traveled pushed forward with great difficulty amid broken wheels, cannon and transport wagons abandoned along the road, in fields and swollen streams.

On the morning of September 20, 1792, the Allied and French artillery began bombarding each other from the hills around Valmy, and continued until sunset. That night the French troops still occupied the same hills. The road to Paris was blocked and nine days later the duke of Braunschweig, commander-in-chief of the Austro-Prussian troops, gave the order to retreat. On the way back, beneath the incessant rain —hourly fearing the attacks of French volunteers—soldiers in uniform, strays, refugees, elegant emigrants, women and children streamed in a disorderly mob among the wagons, ambulances, carriages, and vehicles of every description. There was no food or water; the wells were polluted by the carcasses of dead horses. To slake their thirst, some dipped up the muddy water puddled in the horses' tracks. So an epidemic of dysentery and typhus began to rage in the army. The sick died by the thousands in hastily set-up fever hospitals, attended by careless, unscrupulous doctors and nurses; and the bushes along the roads hid human bodies, savagely stripped and plundered.

During those two months Goethe lived as in a bad dream, "amid mud and misery, worry and discomfort, danger and torment, amid ruins, cadavers, carcasses, and piles of excrement" (October 16, 1792). But he never shared the passions that darkened the hearts of his companions. "As for me," he repeated, "I care not at all about the death of either aristocratic or democratic sinners" (August 18, 1792). He had come so far, wrested unwillingly from his garden, and he gazed at the excogitations of universal history as an indifferent and curious spectator might watch a clumsy military parade. He tried to survive and to perform each day the actions and duties his new existence set before him. Calm in the midst of disheartenment and despair, he tried to soothe the spirits of his companions; he protected the persecuted and defended French peasants from looting and requisitionings.

With his firm-willed tenacity, he shut his eyes to the sights of war. Amid miseries and horrors he was still capable of discovering some untouched fragment of his natural world. As soon as a ray of sun fleetingly broke through the clouds, he saw the soldiers' rifles and bayonets gleam as if they formed a vivacious waterfall or a tranquil river. As the army fled toward the Rhine, he noted the moonlight on sleeping soldiers, the white horses restless because of hunger, the white covers on the wagons, the opulent white sheaves of hay. . . . In the houses of

French peasants he came across scenes of "an idyllic, Homeric" flavor: the hearth set level with the earthen floor, the box of salt, the *pot-au-feu* filled with beef and cabbages, the kitchen utensils disposed in impeccable order, the clay soup tureen filled with white bread and hot broth; a pig which had just been slaughtered and now hung alongside an immense master bed.

On the last day of August, while Allied mortars bombarded Verdun and incendiary rockets furrowed the air like long-tailed meteors of fire, Goethe examined a ditch filled with limpid springwater, in which fish of the most varied colors flashed about. But suddenly he discovered that those fish, when removed from the water, lost their variegated hues. A piece of majolica had fallen to the bottom of the ditch; brighter than the bottom, it sent to the surface prismatic colors, like flickers of blue and violet, pink and yellow flames. That night, his mind still overwrought by this phenomenon of refraction, he met an old acquaintance, Prince Reuss, the Austrian ambassador to Berlin, and immediately began to explain to him his new theory of light and Newton's "crimes." Throughout the night, pacing up and down on the wet grass, protected by the vineyards' stone walls, he talked about the graceful and immutable life of nature, while all around him universal history continued its noisy displays.

During these months of disorder and misery, Goethe got to know the mechanisms of universal history at first hand. Sitting in his unhooded carriage, with his valise containing his notes on the chromatic scale, he looked about him like a curious spectator. But who were the people he observed? Were they the kings, the generals, the ministers, the leaders of the peoples, the great creators and interpreters of history? Were they the ones who acted without obstacles or impediments and "moved here and there with a strange power, meting out life and death without counsel or judgment" (*Natürliche Tochter*, 2013–2014)? No, for they too were only spectators of a drama of which they knew nothing. Like playwrights or presumptuous stage directors, they had written a play or selected this or that script from their repertory; then they went bustling about, distributing parts to the actors and hoping that their intelligent labors would actually produce a spectacle to which posterity would attach their names. But, as soon as the actors and supernumeraries stepped on the stage, an unknown character hid himself in the prompter's box and forced them to speak lines that no king, minister, or general had ever imagined.

When Goethe thought back over these years of European history, he found not even a vestige of what "philosophers so willingly call human

GOETHE

freedom." It seemed to him he saw "brooks and torrents which, obeying a natural necessity, plunge down into each other from innumerable mountains and valleys; and finally provoke the growth of a great river and flood, in which he who foresaw it and he who didn't even suspect it are both destroyed. In this monstrous necessity there is nothing but nature . . ." (March 9, 1802). But in this strange nature he failed to discover any of the laws that rule in the realm of plants and colors. Where in history could he have found something as universal as the *Urbild?* Or the regular, progressive metamorphosis of the leaf? Laws and principles did not exist in the world of history: there was nothing unitary and harmoniously mobile; only a senseless saraband of instances, arbitrary acts, and machinations constructing around us an even more ironclad trap than that of ancient fate.

True enough, history sometimes seemed to sketch a development, draw the track of a spiral, or venture up that road which Goethe's contemporaries loved to call "progress." But how do the movements of history come about? Whereas the leaf's material is infinitely soft and plastic, capable of becoming stem, calyx, flower, blossom, fruit, and seed, while always remaining the same, the material of which history is made is rigid, fixed, tending to harden into forms that resist any regular and continuous change. Thus he who wants to change history must destroy these old forms and throw them into that picturesque old flea market, that desolate refuse heap which is our past (*Faust,* 582). Then he can draw a new form, which soon becomes rigid in its turn and which another hand, equally pitiless, will dump in the sad wastes of time.

The history of men knows neither prudence nor equilibrium: in a few months it wears out, wastes in frightful dissipations a quantity of power which nature would employ to form the most beautiful and delicate of its creatures. Then it becomes sluggish from exhaustion, dragging out a spectral existence for decades. It produces monsters: giraffes with both neck and body overgrown, fish with swollen bodies and huge extremities; and it always seems on the verge of going into bankruptcy. In the end, after so much blood and destruction, it should at least give us the consolation of seeing new countries! But its "spiral movement" continually twirls around on itself, carrying us to places humanity has seen many times before, places where one repeats the same truths, the same mistakes, the same events, the same struggles between slaves and tyrants; where the same pompous and ridiculous puppets, dangling from Satan's hand, meet and clash (XIV, 7: 26–32).[3]

As the years went by, the remembrance of the months spent in France and beneath the walls of Mainz, the memory of those enthusiasms, those hopes and fears, never left Goethe's mind. Whether defeated or victorious, the French Revolution had indelibly marked the world. History, after that, would never again travel the old roads. But what had the Revolution been? What was its real significance? Why had it awakened so many men's hopes? Why had it caused so much destruction and would it continue to cause more and more? When he wrote *Hermann und Dorothea* (1796–1797), Goethe tried to interpret it, using the great images from the Bible which since the years of his youth he carried in his imagination as the richest of treasures.

When Moses grazed Jethro's flocks, Jehovah appeared to him on Mount Sinai as "flame of fire" in the midst of a bush that burned but was not consumed; and Jehovah said to him: "I am the God of thy father, the God of Abraham, the God of Isaac, and the God of Jacob. . . . I have surely seen the affliction of my people which are in Egypt . . . and have heard their cry. . . . And I am come down to deliver them out of the hand of the Egyptians, and to bring them up out of that land unto a good land and a large, unto a land flowing with milk and honey; unto the place of the Canaanites, and the Hittites, and the Amorites, and the Perizzites, and the Hivites, and Jebusites. . . ." (Exodus 3: 1–8). Some time later, in the third month of the going forth of Israel from Egypt, Jehovah descended again upon the top of Mount Sinai: like a devouring flame, enveloped in smoke and hidden by thick, dark clouds, and while the sky flung down thunder and lightning, the exceeding loud voice of the trumpet was heard, and the mountains quaked greatly. Hidden in this impenetrable cloud, Jehovah made a perpetual pact with his people, giving Moses the tablets of stone, the Law and the Commandments (Exodus 19–24).

After the death and ascension of Christ, on the day of the Pentecost, when the Apostles were gathered in the same place, the Holy Ghost came down out of heaven like a mighty rushing wind; and "there appeared unto them cloven tongues like as of fire, and it sat upon each of them." And as the prophecy of Joel had announced, they began to praise the greatness of God in all tongues: in the languages of the Parthians, Medes, Elamites, Phrygians, Libyans, Cretes, Arabians, Egyptians, and the dwellers in Mesopotamia and Cappadocia (Acts 2). But the Son of man, whom they announced, would only be fully revealed at the end of time. Then, as Jesus said to his disciples, many shall come in the name of Christ; nation shall rise against nation, kingdom against kingdom; there will be famine, pestilence, earthquake, frightening prodigies in the heavens. Then Christ's followers will be hated, persecuted, tortured, and killed, while false prophets will deceive even the elect with their miracles; brother will kill brother, and the son will condemn his father to death; the men of Judea will flee to the mountains, Jerusalem will be trampled underfoot and not a stone will be left standing of its temple. Then the sun will grow dark, the moon will no longer shed any light, "the stars of heaven shall fall, and the powers that are in heaven shall be shaken"; "and then shall appear the sign of the Son of man in heaven: and then shall all the tribes of the earth mourn, and they shall see the Son of man coming in the clouds of heaven with power and great glory" (Matthew 24; Mark 13; Luke 21).

All these revelations of God in history had been repeated during the sublime and terrible years of the French Revolution. "Truly, our time," one of the characters in *Hermann und Dorothea* says, fusing together the two passages from Exodus, "resembles the most extraordinary times that history records, sacred as well as profane. . . . Oh, yes, indeed, we could be compared to those to whom at a grave hour the Lord God appeared in the burning bush: for us too he has appeared in clouds and fire" (*Hermann und Dorothea*, V, 229–237). During those years, men had believed that God wished to free them from the chains and afflictions of ancient oppression, as he had freed the children of Israel from the power of the Egyptians; and that he had tried to lead them to another land of Canaan, rich in milk and honey, where they would live obeying new laws cut on the purest tablets of stone.

Weren't the leaders of the Revolution, the "first heralds of the message," similar to the Lord's Apostles? Also among them lived God's "inflamed" spirit, which infused everyone's spirit with "high intelligence and feeling," lifted the heart to the "new Sun," and filled "a freer breast with purer heart beats," and released the once mute, stiff tongues of the old, mature, and young men. At that time, "the loftiest things *(das Höchste)* a man can think proved to be near at hand and attainable." Hope, which everyone had futilely nourished for so many long centuries, again attracted people's eyes to barely opened roads, dangling before them a near-at-hand, radiant future. The kingdom of God seemed just about to be incarnated on this earth (*Hermann und Dorothea*, VI, 6–8, 17–19, 28–29, 32–33, 36–39).

At the end of *Hermann und Dorothea*, a young German revolutionary, about to reach Paris where he will meet prison and death like Christ in Jerusalem, pronounces an eschatological discourse, similar to that of the Son of man: "Everything now suddenly moves on earth, and everything seems to be falling asunder. The fundamental laws in the most solidly based states are dissolving, property leaves the hands of the ancient master and in the same way friend leaves friend; love takes leave of love. . . . Only a stranger, as one rightly says, is the man here on earth; and now more than ever everyone has become a stranger. The soil is no longer ours; treasures emigrate; gold and silver fuse, giving up their ancient sacred forms. All is in motion, as though the world, the formed world, wanted to dissolve and return to Chaos and Night, and form itself again" (*Hermann und Dorothea*, IX, 262–266, 269–274, 276–277). What does it matter if the old world plunge into the Chaos from which it had come? As at the end of time, there already moved above the ruins of the world the first new creatures, "transformed and free and independent of destiny"—agile and extremely light, like pilgrims who set their "mobile feet" on all the places of the earth without belonging to any of them; similar to those whom Jesus Christ had forever freed from the servitude of the Law.

Nobody could therefore deny that the French Revolution, in which the three fundamental moments of Biblical revelation had been incarnated, represented a decisive turn in that "spiral movement" which leads humanity toward some shadowy goal. But sometimes supreme evil, capable of all the adaptations, tries to imitate the features and language of supreme good. The French Revolution might resemble the kingdom of God, but as its inverted image, its grim, infernal counterfeit.

On the new Sinai God had not handed down to his people the tablets of the Law, nor had he pointed into the distance to a land of Canaan. He simply revealed his terrible, fiery countenance. The apostles of the Revolution had proven to be a "corrupt race," incapable of anything good; and they had killed each other in turn, plundering both great and small and ferociously crushing their new brothers. The tongues of young and old, finally released from restraint, had pronounced lying words; once again Hope had been deceived and disappointed. As for the new creatures who, liberated from fate, should have been able to act freely on the ruins of the old world, liberty had revealed in them all the evil which the harsh powers of the Law had hidden in the most remote corners of their hearts (*Hermann und Dorothea*, VI, 51, 79–80).

Thus, because of the Revolution, not only the old world but also the entire world "formed" by the patience of centuries was plunged into Chaos and Night. Bonds were torn apart, loyalty was wounded (VIII, 317: 15–16); friends parted from friends, lovers abandoned lovers; the old sacred forms, the statues of gold and silver adorning the temples, were melted down by impious hands. As in *Natürliche Tochter* a dreadful nocturnal nightmare had devastated the world's marvelous face: the splendor of houses, towering masses like rocks, the circle of the squares, the churches' noble edifices, the expanse of the harbor crowded with masts; everything which, in the past, when lit by the sun's rays, had seemed "founded and ordered for eternity." Now a stormy shudder raged in the dark and gloomy air. The steady earth vacillated, the

GOETHE

towers of the churches swayed, the joined stones split asunder, the sea's currents filled the harbors with sand and mud; and the few survivors clambered sadly up the just created hills, where each ruin marked a grave (*Natürliche Tochter*, 2786–2808).

So the French Revolution had revealed to Goethe the dangers hidden in every attempt to create the city of God here and now, in the history surrounding us. "What does the city of God mean?" Goethe asked. "God does not have a city but an empire, not an empire but a world, not a world but many worlds" (M. March 28, 1830). He refused from then on to confuse the spheres of religion and politics. As the years went by, he became more and more convinced that men must not try to realize the hope, nor incarnate the radiance of myth within the confines of this earth. Mediocre and cautious bureaucrats, such as those in the small duchy of Weimar and the German courts, were quite adequate to rule the destinies of our states.

But at the very moment he renounced giving Utopia a face, Goethe defended its profound essence. His eschatological aspiration remained pure, uncontaminated, without earthly shadow, as perhaps in no other modern writer. The fragile hope, which frees itself with a flap of its wings from the bronze walls of necessity; impossible love, as distant as the farthest star; the full felicity, which cannot be possessed; symbol and myth, which we must not incarnate; ineffable poetry, which throws off the bonds of form; the eternally future vision of a free people—around this delicate woof of analogies was later unfolded Goethe's poetry in *Natürliche Tochter, Pandora,* and the late figurations of *Faust II.*

The
Son of Kish

III

Having gone through the *Lehrjahre* with Wilhelm Meister and shared his thoughts and emotions for so long, we realize that we cannot remember the face of our amiable companion; nor his figure, nor the way he speaks, gestures, and walks. We know that he is young, but we dare not assign him an exact age. Only once does Goethe let slip a precious clue. As Wilhelm is explaining Hamlet's character, a role he is preparing to act on the stage, he attempts to draw for Serlo and Aurelia, a picture of the Dane's physiognomy. In his opinion, the prince of Denmark was blond and had blue eyes like all men of the North; and "his wavering melancholy, his soft gloom, his active indecision" were the traits of a pudgy, corpulent man (306: 34–36). With a sort of sad resignation, Wilhelm adds that he will certainly make a very poor Hamlet, since not a single one of his features recalled those of Shakespeare's character.

So we know the hair, eyes, and figure Wilhelm Meister did not possess, and it seems right to us that he should conserve only the reverse —the negative of a face. For in the gallery of portraits in the *Lehrjahre* this passive, indeterminate character, uncertain in both personality and temperament, is more the victim than the protagonist of his deeds, and is guided like a puppet by the potentates of the tower. But we too, like Goethe, can let ourselves be helped by the imagination: by staring for a long time at this misty, negative portrait until we perceive, behind Hamlet's lineaments, those of the actor who will play him. Then may we amuse ourselves by drawing him in the full light, as if we were painters. We need only another small clue, and this Philine pretends to let fall by chance (VII, 101: 22). The good-natured hero of the *Lehrjahre*, the naïve bourgeois Hamlet, the German emulator of the prince of Denmark is a young man with brilliant black eyes and brown hair; thin, slim, and agile, as befits someone accustomed to walking through the world on foot, acting on stages, and fighting courageously with the sword.

Like Goethe, Wilhelm Meister descends from a rich, upright bourgeois family. During the first decades of the eighteenth century, grandfather Meister had amassed a precious collection of classic marble and bronze statues, Italian paintings and drawings, coins and semiprecious stones. When grandfather Meister died, Wilhelm's father sold the collection and invested the money in the company owned by Werner, a well-known and very competent merchant, thus greatly increasing his capital. Although he venerated money as a diety, he had inherited something of his own father's artistic disposition; he loved luxury. He had built for himself a house in the latest style, where everything was solid, massive, sumptuous: furniture, tableware, drapes. Growing up in this large, wealthy bourgeois house, Wilhelm breathed in the dense, voluptuous atmosphere that order, cleanliness, and luxury weaves about things. In his room, which he transformed into a small kingdom, the curtains and bedcovers seemed like those around a throne; rugs covered the tiled floor and the worktable; and all the books and objects were arranged in meticulous order, as in a still life by a Dutch painter.

But Wilhelm did not prepare himself to become a good merchant and to transform his life into an orderly balance sheet of profits and losses, for the demon of imagination bound him in firmer, more enchanting chains. In the evening, when he had no fear of being disturbed, he wrapped a white turban around his head, put on a kind of Oriental robe, tied a silk sash around his waist, and stuck in his belt a dagger found in some old armory. Thus disguised, he abandoned himself to the flights of his tragic imagination, or, kneeling on the carpet, recited his prayers. When he was a child he had lived in the puppets' enchanted world. Hidden behind the flies of the wooden stage, he would manipulate King Saul, Jonathan, David and Goliath, Darius and Cato, Moors and blacks, shepherds and shepherdesses, dwarfs and gnomes, completely sharing the passions of his heroes. When he grew up, love struck him like a theatrical spell and reawakened the treasure of his romantic desires. The first female creature to move him is a character in one of the most pathetic of poems: Clorinda, from Tasso's *Jerusalem Delivered*. He loves Mariane because he sees her behind the footlights; the countess's attraction is the scintillation of her jewels and necklaces, the grace of her gowns, and her aristocratic mien; and in Natalia he thinks he can see Clorinda's image, which fascinated his adolescence.

How many times did his father, mother, friends, unknown messengers, even books, try to wrest him out of his soft, youthful cocoon! Yet no sooner does he read Shakespeare's plays than Wilhelm thinks he sees flung open before him "the dreadful Books of Fate, through which whistles the tempestuous wind of the most agitated life, tossing them to and fro at great speed" (192: 5–8); and he would like to plunge into the heart of reality, immerse himself in the currents of existence. But reading Shakespeare also has the effect of rekindling the caprices of his imagination. Traveling with a third-rate troupe of actors, he imagines that he is Prince Hal in *King Henry IV* and that, like him, he enjoys living and conversing with crude, vulgar companions. He flings a short cape over his loose jacket, puts on long knitted wool trousers and short jackboots, twists a silk sash around his waist, wears a round hat with a big feather and a lovely, particolored ribbon, and shoves a brace of pistols into his belt. Then, like a vagabond prince, a romantic gypsy, he guides his band of tatterdemalions through a Germany bloodied by war.

Wilhelm Meister goes through life the prisoner of his gilded imagination, of his froth of dreams. He does not look at the things of the world: he cannot judge the persons with whom he lives. In his dealings with people he seems the first child of creation, who with moving benevolence contemplates the lions and monkeys, the sheep and elephants that surround him. He does not know himself, since an invincible predisposition leads him to delude himself as to his true state. The childhood and youth that he leaves behind him, the maturity whose first hardships he is beginning to experience are a graveyard of unrealized projects: unfinished readings, tragedies of which he has written only the first act, works left dangling halfway through. Thus, when he reaches thirty, nourished and consumed by the force of fantasy, he realizes that he has not yet learned a trade, and fears that he has compromised his destiny forever.

One night we see him in the square of his city, his hands raised to the sky. He feels that all is beneath him; he soars aloft in an atmosphere of abounding hopes, strains toward the infinite, thinks that he is embracing something great: "and only the cry of the night watchman reminded him that he was still walking on this earth" (43: 9–11). But soon his spirit's arms lie broken on the ground; nothing great allows itself to be grasped, disappointments pile up. Yet Wilhelm continues to search and to develop his tendencies to the good and beautiful. He will not let the luminous spark, placed in his breast by the gods, be covered up by the ashes of everyday necessities and indifference. He stirs that fire, continues to feed it with new fuel, nurses it with a conscientious and naïve scruple. As he passes through the world, animated by a beneficent mission, he continually spreads around him the beautiful blossom of understanding and trust: he comes to the aid of a strange little girl whom he meets in a group of tumblers, chooses a mad harpist as the companion of his destiny, offers the gift of his time and money to mediocre and envious theater folk, goes out of his way to console the anguish of the unhappy.

Pure and ingenuous as he is, Wilhelm tries to instill his dreams of moral perfectibility in other human beings and the enigmatic reality of things. He tries to educate princes, actors, and bourgeois—even loose women, who admire the beauty of his big black eyes and would simply like to share his too jealously guarded bed for a few nights. When this pedagogical mania attacks him, Wilhelm becomes clumsy, scholastic, pedantic—half idealist and half philistine; while Goethe, concealed in the wings, enjoys making mock of him. For example, one day Wilhelm decides to use the weapons of moral condemnation to attack an aristocratic libertine, who has deserted a desperate woman with a very young child to support. Diligent as always, he composes a fine pathetic speech and learns it by heart, so as to recite it before the guilty man. But destiny does not look kindly on professional pedagogues; a few days later Wilhelm will learn that the child is his own son by Mariane, whom he allowed to die in pain and despair.

These educational manias do not restrict Wilhelm to that prison of laws, preconceptions, principles, and obsessions in which so many persons voluntarily immure themselves. He bears within him a fresh and youthful sensibility, which bends, adapts itself, changes in accordance with the occasion and succeeds in making its own the most diverse spiritual experiences. Like the young Goethe, Wilhelm can become, involuntarily and even unwittingly, soft, ductile wax, the vibrant, faithful echo of the persons he encounters. In the *Lehrjahre* no one—not even the Abbé—possesses so rich a sensibility. Wilhelm is capable of understanding the opposed qualities of both Mignon and Theresa. His indiscriminate receptivity allows him to love Jarno's coldness, Lothario's virile elegance, Aurelia's inspired neurasthenia, the "beautiful soul's" pietistic religion, and his uncle's humanistic religion, the plays of Racine and those of Shakespeare. Someone might say that Wilhelm is even too ready to understand others and share in their experiences. As Jarno remarks at the beginning of the *Wanderjahre*, Wilhelm is like "the pilgrim's staff, which has a marvelous ability to grow green in whatever corner it is planted, but does not strike root anywhere" (VIII, 40: 4–26). Thus he runs the danger of not existing as a person, of not finding a center around which he can live, of not discovering his true homeland in any place in the world.

The experiences through which Wilhelm lives, the persons who influence him, the books which predisposition or chance places in his hands lead him to reflect continually. Alone or in the company of friends, Wilhelm examines the emotions of his soul, the events that occur around him, and those he senses and anticipates. His attentive and scrupulous mind follows scarcely apprehended impressions—the irrational nuances of every phenomenon. Reason's precise concepts do not suffice for him and, in order to pursue the truth which eludes him, he orchestrates the most fantastic images and now and then loses himself in a kind of lyrical tempest. Yet, despite appearances, Wilhelm has not much in common with Werther. His intellectual passion is deeper and more authentic, for he always endeavors by every means "to translate each particular thing into a more universal formula" (Schiller, July 5, 1796): He tries to make the perfect and immobile light of the Idea shine on the changing and contradictory surface of appearances.

Among the vocations he wonders whether or not he possesses, among the professions he mistakenly undertakes, Wilhelm overlooks his true vocation. He is a great essayist and one of the most acute literary critics of his time, although no magazine publishes his inspired illuminations. The very fine essays that he dedicates to poetry (Book II), *Hamlet* (Books IV–V), and the traits of aristocracy and bourgeoisie (Book V) certainly owe something to Goethe, reflecting some ideas of his youth and maturity. But Wilhelm is a more systematic essayist than his creator, who so readily indulged in uncertainties and contradictions. As he theorizes, enthusiastic and extremely lucid, as he discusses with Werner or Serlo, we often have the impression of listening to the voice of Schiller, who during those very years was about to write or had just written the great studies *Über Anmut und Würde* and *Über naive und sentimmentalische Dichtung*.

As soon as Wilhelm Meister left his paternal home to plunge into the world, female hearts began to beat faster because of him. As with Tasso, "women's favor" (*Tasso*, 2020, 2057) seemed to be his natural right. His candor, his scrupulous gravity, the romantic fantasies in which he loses himself, the ardent force of love living in his breast, his anxieties, and even the noble awkwardness with which he ventures out into the waters of life—all aspects of Wilhelm's character arouse every woman's tenderness. Mariane, a frivolous actress who sets fire to provincial audiences, knows for the first time, with him, the joys of amorous passion. Philine's naughty blue eyes try to find their reflection in Wilhelm's deep black ones. Clumsy Frau Melina does not hide her fond feelings for him, and the beautiful countess, surmounting the abyss of birth and social condition, clasps him tenderly to her bosom. For him, Theresa seems disposed to forget her love for Lothario, and even in Natalia's heart, seemingly so cold and distant, a secret passion is born for the young man she has saved.

The male characters in the *Lehrjahre* do not always seem to share these sympathies: Werner thinks of Wilhelm as a capricious idler, and Lothario and Jarno view him with good-natured hauteur. While Schiller felt that Wilhelm resembled him, many modern readers regard Wilhelm as a kind of social climber who has undeservedly pushed his way into the company of such authentic heroes of the novel as Tom Jones, Fabrizio del Dongo, Stavrogin, and Prince Andrei. Even Goethe seemed to hold the same opinion when, talking with Chancellor von Müller, he remarked that Wilhelm was only "a poor dog" (M. January 22, 1821).

Who is right? Natalia or Werner, Schiller or the Goethe who converses with his friends? If we consider the problem from the standpoint of psychological characterization, all of them are right. Wilhelm can be considered as much a feckless dreamer as a noble idealist, a philistine, a very sensitive soul, or a man without character. But in this case, the simple psychological consideration does not suffice. In a deeper region of his being, Wilhelm possesses a strength that escapes consciousness as well as the instruments of intellectual analysis. What "he is," the innermost core of his being, the significance of his destiny, are not revealed to him either by the emotions he experiences or the deeds he performs; but all these are untranslatable archetypes that nature has left in his memory.

During his youthful years, when amorous impulses began to assail him, Wilhelm read Tasso's poem, *Jerusalem Delivered.* "Hundreds upon hundreds of times, when walking in the evening on the balcony set between the house's chimneys and looking over the town, when on the horizon still flickered the tremulous gleam of the sun that had already set, the stars began to appear, night advanced from every corner and depth, and the crickets' reverberant song shrilled in the solemn hush—then I would tell myself again the story of the dolorous duel between Tancredi and Clorinda . . . I could never pronounce the words:

> But now the fateful hour has struck,
> Clorinda's life has reached its end.

without tears rushing into my eyes, which flowed like rivers when the unhappy lover sinks his sword into her breast, opens her helmet as she falls, recognizes her and runs, shuddering, to get the water to baptize her" (27: 4–25). The woman he dreamed of was like Clorinda; she did not possess any of Armida's violent and artificial erotic attraction (27:2); but rather a sort of vague androgynous aura (*Mannweiblichkeit*, 26: 36) veiled her feminine lineaments.

During those same years Wilhelm would stand for a long time before a painting in his grandfather's collection, in which some seventeenth-century Italian painter had depicted a story told by Plutarch in his *Life of Demetrius*. The young prince Antiochus, the son of Seleucus, king of Syria, fell in love with Stratonice, "his father's bride" (70:4). Tormented by his guilty passion, full of remorse for the dreadful desire he harbored, he let himself waste away, no longer took care of his body and stopped eating. When the young stepmother entered the sick man's room, Plutarch says, he unfailingly manifested all the admonitory signs that Sappho describes: "His voice faltered, his face was covered with blazing red flushes, his sight blurred, he suddenly began to sweat, his pulse beat became irregular and confused and, finally, when his soul was taken by assault, he felt completely lost and bewildered, and lay there dismayed and deathly pale." "This painting," Wilhelm remarks ten years later, "made an indelible impression on me. . . . How sorry I felt, how sorry I still feel for that young man forced to shut his tender instincts inside himself, the most beautiful heritage which nature gives us, and conceal in his breast the fire which should have warmed both himself and others . . ." (70: 18–27).

These two youthful images—that of the androgynous warrior and of "his father's bride"—for a long time led a secret, separate existence in his soul, indelible despite life's experiences. When Wilhelm met Natalia dressed like an Amazon and saw her bend down over him as he lay gravely wounded, it seemed to him that the two images of his youth had merged in a single face. "All of the dreams of his youth were tied together in this figure. He believed that he had at last seen the noble, heroic Clorinda with his own eyes; and the king's sick son came to his mind, whose bed the beautiful, compassionate princess had approached with silent modesty" (235: 24–29).

At that moment Wilhelm had grasped Natalia's essence. Like Clorinda, the noble Amazon was wrapped in a vague androgynous atmosphere, and the erotic fascination of Armida or Philine did not perturb her mild figure. Like Stratonice, Natalia was "his father's bride"—the mother so long dreamed of and desired. But how many other names we must give her! Wilhelm could have well repeated the words that Goethe had written to Charlotte von Stein: "Ah, in times gone by you were my sister or my mother!" (*Warum gabst-du uns*, 27–28). He could have called Natalia, as Goethe had called Countess di Stolberg, "friend, sister,

GOETHE

lover, fiancée, bride"; and yet none of these names by itself would have sufficed.

Every absolute love, every passion directed at the perfect female image therefore pursues all of a woman's possible aspects: mother, sister, friend, fiancée, and wife. Then, mixed up with other emotions there creeps into the tormented heart, the prostrate limbs, a terrible incestuous force: the desire for mother and sister, and, immediately after, the horror of sin and of the divine prohibition is born. Struck by dismay and fear, some flee and get as far away from this celestial image as possible; others violate the sacred interdiction, falling victim to the furies; and only very few men—the happy few—are able to purify their passion and obtain "the father's bride" as a gift from heaven.[1]

How should we interpret Wilhelm's double propensity? Nothing prevents us from adopting the most obvious analytical interpretation, and affirming that Wilhelm Meister, terrorized by the violence of Eros, incapable of overcoming the Oedipal phase of sexuality, prefers pale, cold, unfeminine women. But the psychological explanation is far from exhaustive. How is it—we ask ourselves—that incest and the androgynous are so closely linked, both in Wilhelm's and Augustin's parallel stories? The only way to understand this passage in Goethe is to search for its sources.

The combination of the androgynous and incest, which triumphs in the *Lehrjahre*, has precedents in the classic religious tradition. King Mausolus, married to his sister Artemisia, honored Hermes and Aphrodite by a joint cult; and Caligula, who willingly wore feminine clothes, had incestuous relations with one of his sisters.[2] But Goethe's direct source is less remote. In the alchemist's art, the highest sign of perfection—the snow-white, elegant, luminous philosopher's stone—presented this double aspect. In his youth Goethe fervidly absorbed the books about alchemy, and they later formed for him a great repertory of symbols and metaphors. Inasmuch as it reconciled all the contrary elements of the universe, the philosopher's stone was considered hermaphroditic. But at the same time it embodied man's female aspect and descended into the soul as virgin, bride, sister, and mother. In the allegorical representation of the *pietra* that Starkey gives us, the Golden King, seeing the Mercurial Queen in danger, "knew her to be his Sister, his Mother and his Wife, and compassionating her estate, ran unto her, and took her in his Arms." "The king," Starkey added, "is Brother to his Wife,/ and she to him is Mother."[3]

Many years later, when he wrote the *Wanderjahre*, Goethe wanted to emphasize more openly Wilhelm Meister's exceptional qualities. This time, he gave him the intuitive knowledge of "true original nature" (*die eigentliche Originalnatur,* VIII, 273: 36–274: 1), compared with which everything we learn afterward is but a pallid copy. In the course of a few hours, on the day of Pentecost, the boy Wilhelm experiences for the first time the immense freedom of the world: the green of the fields and meadows, the bright buds already sprouting on the bushes, the blinding white of the trees; the flower beds full of tulips, narcissi, jonquils, ranunculi, and many-blossomed lilies. He knows the ambiguous fascination of water lit up by the sun; the microscopic, Dionysian agitation of animal life along the banks of a river; the ants swarming on all sides, the dancing grasshoppers, the varicolored beetles hanging from the branches. He has awareness of the fluffy opened seeds or "the sun's little virgins" which floated and swayed at his feet like the very spirits of nature. He knew the resplendent beauty of the human body beneath the rays of the sun. He was attracted and almost swept away by the ardor of friendship; he glimpsed the presage of love; he suffered that last, desperate form of love which is death. Thus, on that day, all the sensations, impulses, and emotions, which in life are distinquished into separate forces, were still fused together in Wilhelm Meister's spirit as an indistinct, amorous fire capable of infinite warmth, like a humid pool of light that irradiates every object and every shadow, like an abundant spring that continues to well up, flowing through and bathing the entire world.

Now we can understand why that youthful dreamer, that virtuous pedant, who has excited the antipathy of so many readers of the *Lehrjahre,* was called "nature's favorite" by Goethe (77: 30), as he was in the habit of calling mankind's geniuses. Wilhelm was not a genius. But, while his *entelechia* was wandering along the orbits of other stars, the "gods," "grace," "the higher government of the world," had seen in him "a vessel worthy of receiving the divine influence" (E. March 11, 1828); and they had adopted him as one of their favorites. Even before he set foot on the earth, they had incised in his mind a sublime mark of perfection, like the alchemists' brightly white and luminous *lapis philosophorum.* They had hidden in his soul the intuition of "original nature" in which were contained all the symbols of life, similar to that "original fount" enriching Faust's spirit with its inexhaustible gifts (*Faust,* 334).

With the silent assistance of the archetypes he bore in his heart, Wilhelm Meister could travel all the roads of somnolent, provincial, eighteenth-century Germany without fear of getting lost. No attack of bandits would ever succeed in mortally wounding him in the meadow among the beech trees. Nor would love affairs, bad companions, clashes, and foolhardy experiences have been able to draw him far from his predestined goal. The purpose of his life, the loftiest and most unhoped-for happiness he will receive from fate—Natalia's love—was already contained in his childhood. If he wished to grow and mature, if he wished to end his years of apprenticeship, he had to look back to the presentiments of his childhood, where the images of the noble Clorinda and the mild, compassionate "father's bride" awaited him. As Pindar said, he had only to "become who he was."

The road Wilhelm must travel is long, tortuous, and difficult. Like a stranger, he leaves his paternal home; he loves Mariane and Philine, Theresa and Natalia, meets Mignon and Jarno, the harpist and Lothario; he works in his father's business, plays the part of Hamlet, and has a son. He knows the depths of sorrow and the sudden, vaulting impulses of joy, tranquility and disarray, plenitude and dissipation, violence and frivolity. As a sort of modern Gil Blas, he undergoes all the experiences a young bourgeois can face in Germany at the end of the eighteenth century. He shares aristocrats' castles and the picturesque taverns inhabited by actors; he experiences the calm of small towns and the violence of war; and becomes involved, without knowing it, in the plots of a very powerful secret society, capable of changing the world.

When they consider Wilhelm's life as a whole, many readers of the *Lehrjahre* perceive in it a regular, continuous metamorphosis, which at last leads him to his marriage with Natalia. In this view, he grows like an oak tree, striking root in propitious soil and lifting its trunk to the sky; or he traverses step by step the spacious stairway of his existence. No sooner does he encounter a new environment or a new person than he understands and suffers this experience to the very bottom; he appropriates the nature of Hamlet and Theresa, of Jarno and Lothario, of bourgeois and aristocrat. Thus he is formed and learns to know reality each time he adds a new branch to the trunk, a new step to the stairway of his life. At the end of his peregrinations, he conquers perfection; or, to use Schiller's words, he leaves behind "the empty and indeterminate ideal" of his youth in order to enter "an active and determined life, without losing his idealizing strength" (July 8, 1796).

If all this were true, Novalis would have been right when he judged the *Lehrjahre* a "silly and boring" book. But Wilhelm is not this *exemplum* from a bourgeois textbook; he is not the ideal protagonist of a *Bildungsroman;* he does not grow with the unbearable regularity of an oak or a flower; he does not climb step by step up the stairway of his life in the same way that, beneath the tepid spring sun, a well-mannered tourist mounts the steep stairs that lead to the *Erechteion* or the *Ara coeli*. The *Lehrjahre* bears in its title the image of a series of experiences in time. Its paradox is that its protagonist does not change at all—neither in character nor propensity. It is as if only for him—the immobile motor force of his own book—time does not strike the hour on the world's clocks.

Wilhelm Meister could well repeat Goethe's words: "It is strange how I resemble myself, and how little my inmost being has suffered because of the years and events" (XI, 525: 24–26). Instead of maturing and letting himself be educated by so-called reality, he remains unconsciously, obstinately faithful to the deeply rooted youthful germ bestowed on him by the gods. In any case, what need has he to "have experiences"? Wilhelm Meister possesses the same quality as great artists who carry hidden in themselves, almost by anticipation, all the elements of the visible world, so that by presentiment they have already known and lived the real things that will be offered to their sight. Like a true poet, Wilhelm imagines the objects of nature without having seen them; he comprehends the heart's most obscure emotions without having experienced them; he understands the significance of Shakespeare, the character of Hamlet, of the aristocracy and bourgeoisie as soon as his glance skims these different worlds.[4]

If he had possessed Faust's extraordinary psychological power, he could have lived enclosed in himself and reduced his relations with reality and other human beings to a kind of fanciful theatrical game. But Wilhelm is weak, uncertain, desirous of orientation; he needs others, and tries to reflect their natures and experiences in his mobile spirit. He reads Shakespeare's plays in order to know reality; he travels for years on end with a company of actors, lives in aristocratic castles, lets himself be accompanied by the messengers of destiny. When we must add up the sum of each of these experiences, the conclusion is always the same: Wilhelm fails to learn anything, or almost anything, from what life offers him. It is as though a sort of pathological weakness stood in the way of his appropriating and putting into practice the things that his intelligence understands perfectly. At the end of these long years, he learns only to disguise himself as Prince Hal did. He does not see everyday reality, he does not repeat even one of the light, spontaneous exploits performed by Lothario and the other aristocrats. He does not know how to interpret the signs destiny benevolently drops on his path.

At the end of the *Lehrjahre*, Wilhelm contemplates the spectacle of his life, and his eyes dwell with fright on a bleak forest of mistakes and aberrations, similar to those of a child incapable of growing up. All of his experiences seem to him to be a futile tangle of steps, gestures, words, and actions. Indeed, the sum of his existence seems to him one unforgivable blunder: something to be denied and flung away with a gesture (446: 22–24; 459: 25–27). When he utters these bitter words, who can say he is wrong? What are these unfulfilled experiences, which have led to nothing, if not mistakes, perhaps even sins? And yet Wilhelm is wrong. As the Abbé says, it is not he who must try to ascertain the final sum of his life. This task belongs to an infinitely wiser being. It belongs to destiny, which has all of our account books in its care, sets a value on each of our deeds, transcribes it in figures, adds, subtracts, divides, and multiplies; and, at the end, calculates the total sum of our lives.

When we read the book of destiny, when we perceive the signs and abbreviations of that mysterious calligraphy and know all the relations and connections of which Wilhelm is unaware, how different his life seems to us! Studied in that book, his mistakes, his strayings, his futile or poorly assimilated experiences acquire significance. Contemplated in the book of destiny, Wilhelm's gait is no longer that of someone who gets lost in the forests, or clambers up mountain trails, halts when he comes to a cliff and is about to fall into some frightful gorge. Rather it is the sure and tranquil step of the wayfarer who travels down the main highway and knows every stage of his journey.

Even though Wilhelm is unaware of it, all of his experiences, even those that seem most insignificant and dispersed, come together around that fundamental one—to lead him little by little to Natalia's arms. The youthful elated passion for Mariane leaves him Felix, at whose bedside Natalia's hands join forever with his. If he had not traveled about with the actors, the bandits would not have wounded him and the Amazon could not have succored him. His love for the countess anticipates his love for Natalia; and Mignon guides him right to her feet. Thus to all Wilhelm's adventures destiny adds that incalculable, unknown quantity, transforming chance into law, mistake into salvation, the senseless wanderings of a fugitive into the journey of a providential pilgrim.

As we shall see, Wilhelm Meister maintains that *Hamlet* is a drama that unfolds on two levels: the hero's and destiny's. The same could be said of the great, pellucid, and incomprehensible book of which he is the protagonist. While he continually makes mistakes, destiny impels him not to take a single false step; while he wanders about without plan or goal, destiny draws the clear plan of his life. While he stumbles without prescience, destiny juggles with events like an author writing a novel in installments; while he fantasizes and dreams, destiny is precise as a bookkeeper; while he moralizes, destiny plays jokes on him and everyone . . . If, in the end, Wilhelm succeeds neither in learning anything nor in transforming himself, destiny nevertheless flings in his path a great many adventures and experiences, which cluster around him and slowly alter him.

Wilhelm Meisters Lehrjahre

Thus, as always happens in the *Lehrjahre*, we must return to the point of departure and affirm that which we have denied. Like oaks, flowers and, perhaps, human beings, Wilhelm Meister grows and matures, although he is not aware of changing and his readers find him always the same. Like the tourists who climb up the *Erechteion* or the *Ara coeli*, he climbs at a steady pace up the spacious stairs of his life, although nobody perceives these stairs. They appear, as if by a miracle, only at the end of the book. And, finally, he is truly the hero of a *Bildungsroman:* even though he does not know how to educate or train himself, and the pedagogue who, unbeknown to him, educates him resembles a coarse clown and a theatrical mystifier.

If we were asked to establish this change with the instruments of psychology, describing what he has learned at each stage, what new branches he thrusts in the air, what new steps he ascends—what would we reply? We could say nothing; for we do not know what happens in Wilhelm's heart, neither at the beginning nor at the end of each of his experiences. Only at the close of the book can we observe, repeating Werner's words, that Wilhelm's external appearance has changed: he has become taller, his forehead is broader, his eyes deeper, his nose finer, his mouth more loving than in the past. But as to the changes in his inmost being, how he has "become" who he already was, what distinguishes the spirit of the young Wilhelm who loved Mariane from that of the almost thirty-year-old Wilhelm who is about to marry Natalia —all this we shall never know, either from Goethe or from destiny.

Wilhelm
Meister's
Experiences

IV

When he was ten years old, Wilhelm Meister for the first time encountered the puppet's magical world. On the evening of Christmas Day, after the usual distribution of gifts, he was seated with his friends before a door to another room. When the door opened he saw a "mystic curtain," a "mystic veil" (12: 32; 17: 26), behind which something glittering could be seen. Finally the half-transparent veil rose, revealing to his eyes a "sanctuary" (19: 15) in which were celebrated "mysteries" that had never been witnessed before (21: 30; 22: 21).

Inside a temple painted bright red, "the High Priest Samuel appeared with Jonathan, and their strange alternating voices seemed to me infinitely venerable. Soon after, Saul came on stage, terribly embarrassed by the impertinence of that huge, clumsy warrior, who had defied him and his people. But you can imagine my joy when Jesse's son, who had the stature of a dwarf, came bouncing out, with his shepherd's crook, pouch, and sling, and said: 'Almighty king and sovereign lord! Let no one be cast down because of this; if your majesty will grant me leave, I will go out to battle with the powerful giant.' The first act ended and the spectators burned with curiosity to see what would happen next —each hoped that the musical interlude would soon be over. At last the curtain rose again. David dedicated the monster's flesh to the birds of the air and the beasts of the fields; the Philistine spoke mockingly, violently stamped his feet on the ground, and fell down like a tree trunk, providing the play with a splendid conclusion. And then the virgins sang: 'Saul hath slain his thousands, but David his ten thousands,' and the giant's head was borne before the diminutive victor, who was given the hand of the king's beautiful daughter in marriage; and yet, despite all my joy, it grieved me that the prince of felicity was portrayed as a dwarf" (12: 39–13: 24)

That evening Wilhelm went staggering to bed, drunk with happiness; but he couldn't sleep and continued to wonder about the fascinating world he had seen. The next morning, as soon as he awoke, he returned to the room. But the magical apparatus of the day before was gone. Someone had taken away the "mystic veil," had dismantled the wooden "sanctuary" and hidden the royal puppets, and in the place where so many prodigies had occurred only the bare, cold jambs of a doorway remained.

After that day, with a heart full of curiosity, fear, and reverence, Wilhelm tried to look upon the mysteries celebrated and hidden behind the half-transparent veil. One day one of the doors of the storeroom was left open. There together with prunes, dried apples, and candied oranges, Wilhelm discovered the heroes of his theatrical dreams: King Saul with his golden crown and black velvet robe, Jonathan with his yellow and red cloak, David, Goliath, and the High Priest Samuel. But his childhood powers were insufficient to know the mysteries more intimately. As happens in all religious cults, a master "initiated" him (21: 30; 22: 21), led him behind the veil and revealed to him the secrets of his art; taught him how to work the strings and to speak with the voices of Goliath and David. The enchanted child is tranformed into a magical enchanter, the layman into a priest who at his pleasure manipulated heroes and heroines, unleashed stormy seas and thunder and lightning on the stage of a small wooden theater.

This episode anticipates the course of Wilhelm's life. Starting with his passion for puppets, all his experiences—whether amorous, theatrical, or aristocratic, concerned with his destiny or astral influences—propose again and again the same religious itinerary. Hidden behind a door or a "veil," he senses something secret and alluring in the shadows stretched out before him. With the assistance of a human or divine messenger, he penetrates into the "sanctuary," where he is initiated. He descends to its profoundest depths, experiences the mysteries which are taught there; or he discovers that the temple is deserted and that the magic veil conceals a terrible emptiness.

A young actress, Mariane, was the amiable divinity who introduced Wilhelm into the as yet unknown "sanctuary" of love (74: 2). Passion seized him at his first sight of her, just as it happens in the elegantly stylized loves of Italian tales, in which Romeo and Juliet, as soon as they set eyes on each other, stare for a long time "with unaccustomed joy," pouring forth "the fiery rays of sight," filling the air with ardent sighs, each drinking in from the other "the sweet, amorous poison." Seated at the back of the hall, Wilhelm saw Mariane on the stage of his city's theater; she was wearing an officer's red uniform, white satin cloak, and large plumed hat—her figure, her voice, her gestures immediately enthralled him, and soon he attended only the plays in which she acted.

One day he dared slip onto the stage; timidly he approached her, spoke to her, brought her a glass of lemonade. From that day on, he spent a great deal of time in the wings! For hours on end he would stand by the light frame, inhaling the dense smoke of tallow candles, trying to catch a glimpse of his beloved; and if she gazed at him tenderly, he felt transported into a paradisial world. Amid that framework of laths and beams, the most ordinary theatrical props could make him happy. The stuffed lambs, cloth waterfalls, paper roses, and one-sided huts awoke in him poetic visions of ancient Arcadia.

At night, when everyone in his house was asleep, he would wrap himself in a cloak like a thief or a lover in a play, and would slip down to the garden and run all the way to Mariane's house. She would meet him on the stairs in her white negligee, a red ribbon tied around her head. She would embrace him passionately, lavish on him the caresses which nature and art had taught her; and then welcome him behind the curtains of her bed. The next morning, through a haze of happiness, how surprised Wilhelm was as he looked about him at the tables, chair, and floor! Accustomed to the orderliness of a bourgeois house, he saw the "remains of an ephemeral, false and frivolous elegance, lying about in the wildest disorder, like the glittering skin of a scaly fish. The articles of personal cleanliness—combs, soaps, towels—with still visible traces of their use, were not concealed. Musical scores and shoes, linen and artificial flowers, pincushions, hairpins, rouge pots and ribbons, books and straw hats—none of them disdained the proximity of the other, and all were united by a common element—face powder and dust. But Wilhelm, since . . . everything that belonged to Mariane and had touched her became dear to him, came at last to see in this disorder a charm which he had never felt in his own large, sumptuous home" (59: 9–24).

For some months, living alongside this young, naïve, impassioned, and frivolous actress, Wilhelm was immersed in the very element of love, which enveloped him as water envelops and supports a swimming man. With its many hands, its touch that makes one shiver, love skimmed lightly over the strings of his soul; it filled and possessed him, transmuting every other thought and emotion into the same enchanting music. Beneath that hand's disquieting touch, the most romantic illusions were aroused in him, his heart was exhausted from tenderness, his senses assailed by intolerable desires. A kind of religious ecstasy tore the very weight from his body, and an insatiable *Taumel* and *Wonne*, a beatific intoxication led him to lose himself beyond the confines of this earth (67: 1–4). As though magnetized, all images precipitated around him: Biblical, classical, alchemical images, drawn from the life of nature, from pietistic treatises and scientific books, launched by love into the sky like fireworks or worn by love as the most magnificent of gowns.

Two hearts that love each other—Wilhelm thought—are like two magnetic clocks always pointing at the same signs: "Whatever moves in one must move the other, for a single element works in both, the same form penetrates them" (72: 33–36). As he hugged Mariane in his arms, Wilhelm told her the story of his childhood and youth: he revealed his emotions, thoughts, ultimate aims, pouring out the superabundant richness of his soul. When Mariane was far away, scarcely had he touched a dress, a book, some memory of her than he felt swathed in her presence. He thought that he had finally abolished the divisions between bodies and the distances between souls, the inevitable condemnation of all creation.

He dreamed of entering the country of the future, holding Mariane by the hand, like a bridegroom who, during the sacred marriage ceremony, stands on the solemn carpets before the "mysterious curtains from which love's grace whispers out to him," full of happy omens of the new world which, soon, would flower within him. As his imagination mounted to the highest regions, he pronounced the noblest words and abandoned himself to the most flattering hopes. Soon he would leave his father's house and the stagnant bourgeois existence in which he lived as in a jail, spying on freedom. Soon, with Mariane, he would appear on the stages of the German theater.

From the height of a pulpit, like that of a temple, he would shower on the world the love that filled his soul. Like a good spirit, he would offer men the words they had for so long yearned to hear. He would nurse the spark that lives in them beneath the ashes, impressing a free and pure movement on their benumbed spirits, spreading noble sentiments, worthy of God and nature (66: 20 ff.; 10: 8 ff.). Thus Wilhelm's love for Mariane, like Goethe's for Charlotte von Stein, became the germ of a project for the complete redemption of the world.

Robinson Crusoe's laborious existence is continually accompanied by signs, warnings, and the extremely visible messages of Providence. When, propelled by rash desires, he runs away from his father's house,

GOETHE

the divine hand flings violent winds and waves as high as mountains at his ship; when, loaded with merchandise, his ship sails toward the Guineas, the same hand makes him a prisoner of the Moors, and later blesses his modest existence as a cultivator of tobacco and sugar. But Crusoe does not want to see the signs by which God tries to guide him. Like a man who is blind and deaf, he refuses to admit that his life has a single providential design.

Only when, seated on the grass of the unknown island, he contemplates the sea which has swallowed his companions, only when God appears to him through the power of an earthquake and in the nightmares of a fever—only then does Crusoe understand that Providence wishes to transform his silent life into a marvelous example. From that day on, "locked up with the eternal bars and bolts of the ocean," he performs simply, as do the elect, the tasks which are proposed to him from on high. He measures out the passage of the weeks, months, and years on a square cross; he builds two houses, makes shovels and hoes, bakes crude pots in the fire, gathers grapes, citrons, and lemons, grows barley and rice. Like a biblical patriarch, together with his old dog, his gentle cats, his domesticated goats, he lives an orderly and tender idyll, protected by the invisible hand, visited by the light breath of God.

From the day on which the son of a Cripplegate butcher, the trader in woolen goods and groceries, brickmaker, pamphleteer, and spy who bore the name of Daniel DeFoe wrote *Robinson Crusoe* to the day that Goethe finished the *Lehrjahre*, almost eighty years had passed. In this period of time, the world's Providence had hidden itself; and no longer revealed itself in events and hearts with the manifest clarity which had persuaded Robinson Crusoe's hardened heart. Now it sent down on the earth a thousand ambiguous, uncertain, and confused signs; and often some mystifier assumed the task of impersonating it. So Crusoe's simple Puritan faith would no longer have saved him from shipwreck. During the last years of the century, while Wilhelm Meister wandered about Germany like a vagabond, only a refined intelligence such as Goethe's could choose, from among that multitude of signs, the few, authentic celestial messages and spontaneously obey them.

But Wilhelm Meister did not know this art. While he loved Mariane, he thought he was moving in a world crowded with very obvious signs. Just as the Oriental poets (II, 189–190) and faithful pietists interrogated Providence, slipping their thumbs at random in the Book and accepting as an oracle the passage thus designated, so he continually sensed providential omens and welcomed them in a faithful and devout spirit. "Do not worry," he wrote to Mariane. "It is Fate that worries about love" (65: 12). These signs, incised with inexpungeable calligraphy on the surface of things, told him that he was being protected by a beneficent force which offered him Mariane's lovely hand to pull him out of the bourgeois world and start him on his way to the theater (35: 2; 42: 32; 71: 13).

During his youth, Robinson Crusoe had sinned through a lack of faith, but Wilhelm sinned through an excess of faith. Who can claim to be able to meet Providence at every street corner? Who can be sure of feeling continually at one's side the breath of a benignant divine force? As the "tower's" first messenger gave him to understand, he was like Eduard, the protagonist of *Die Wahlverwandschaften79 e (Elective Affinities)*. With the help of fantasizing and imagination, Wilhelm had also unwittingly fashioned a multitude of imaginary celestial signs and venerated them devoutly. While he thought he was honoring the will of superior beings, he was following only the promptings of chaos or the fluctuating allurements of his passions (71: 25 ff).

Destiny had never blessed his love for Mariane and his generous theatrical projects. The pretty actress, with her plumed hat and red officer's uniform, was not the lovable goddess, the priestess of the "sanctuary," of whom he had dreamed. When he was with her, Wilhelm was alone: no magnetic clock beat time with his; and the dulcet voice he thought he was hearing was really that of an invisible interlocutor, the voice of an echo repeating his words' last syllables.

One night, as Wilhelm was walking in the square in front of Mariane's house, it seemed to him that the door opened and a dark figure came silently out. Then he thought he saw this figure walk past a white house farther ahead; when he halted and strained his eyes, the phantom was gone. "Like a traveler at night, when he had seen part of the country he is traversing lit up for an instant by a flash of lightning, will, immediately after, with dazzled eyes, seek in vain in the darkness for the suddenly glimpsed forms and the continuation of his path—so it was with Wilhelm's eyes and heart" (74: 16–20). Having returned home at the first cockcrow, he hoped daylight would chase that unexpected apparition out of his mind. Finally, to soothe his heart, he picks up one of Mariane's scarves and brings it to his lips; at that moment a note from Norberg, the young actress's other lover, falls with a rustling sound to the floor.

"As when by chance, in the preparation of some firework, one element is ignited before its time, and the skillfully bored and loaded barrels which, set up and lit according to a preestablished plan, would have traced in the air a magnificently varied series of flaming images, now hiss in disorder and dangerously, exploding all at once—so now, in his breast, happiness and hope, pleasure and joy, realities and dreams become all confused as they sank together . . ." (76: 24–32). All his desires were shattered. His spirit's arms, with which he had hoped to embrace something immense, were broken, and he lay on the ground like a daring acrobat who has vainly tried to fly through space. He suffered desperately and wanted to suffer; he tried to hold on to the happiness escaping him; overwhelmed, destroyed, so great a part of himself killed—until nature, so as not to let its favorite die, contrived to make him fall sick.

When he began to recover, Wilhelm "looked with fright into the tormenting abyss of his arid misery, as one looks down into the hollow crater of an extinct volcano. . . . He despised his own heart, and longed for the balm of tears and despair. To reawaken these within him, he would parade before his memory all the scenes of his past happiness. He would paint them in the liveliest colors, try to immerse himself in them, and when having attained, exhausted, the greatest height, when the sunshine of past times seemed again to animate his limbs and alleviate his breast—then he would look back into the fearful chasm, would feast his eyes on that dismembering depth, plunge down into its horrors, and thus wrest the bitterest pains from nature" (78: 1–18).

Many months, perhaps years, passed before he could completely accept his misfortune. But at last he succeeded in destroying in himself all hope of love, all faith in his own capacities, convincing himself that his verses were only student exercises and that not a trace of acting talent inhabited his limbs. One winter evening, having lit the fire in the hearth, he threw into the flames the gifts Mariane had given him and which, until then, he had preserved like relics. In a few instants, a bouquet of withered flowers that had blossomed in her hair, her notes in which she had told him the time of happy appointments, ribbons that had rested on her breast disintegrated in the smoke and flames. Lastly, his youthful attempts at poetry revived the languishing fire.

For some time Wilhelm completely renounces his dreams; and the images of Clorinda and of the princess, the hopes of love and poetry no longer tempt his benumbed heart. Joylessly, with the silent, obstinate diligence of someone doing his duty, he works in his father's business. He spends his days at the office and stock exchange, the store and warehouses. He talks with customers, keeps the accounts, takes care of the correspondence with foreign firms, dispatches with care everything that is entrusted to him.

A few years later we find him on horseback, his saddlebags behind him, exhilarated by the motion and the free air, traveling through the valleys and hills of a mountainous region. For the first time he sees around him those sheer cliffs, murmuring brooks, grassy slopes, and deep chasms among which had lived the characters of *Aminta, Jerusalem Liberated,* and *Pastor Fido,* whom he had pursued in his youthful dreams. He feels rejuvenated by this sight; all the sorrows he has suffered are washed from his spirit. In a cheerful mood he recites passages from *Pastor Fido* which, in those solitary places, come swarming into his memory (87: 5–19).

Wilhelm has merely to pass through the walls of a town for the theater to send its messengers, its humble and imaginative seductions out to meet him. Even in a village lost among these mountains and impenetrable forests, some factory workers are performing a crude comedy of intrigue; and later a group of miners act out an allegorical pantomime before a rustic tavern. When Wilhelm reaches a town on the banks of a river, a small troupe of rope dancers and jugglers are exhibiting their talents in the market square. A clown dashes about playing pranks in the crowd; acrobats execute somersaults in the air, leap on swords and through a hogshead; and a clump of men, women, and children, standing on each other's shoulders, form a living pyramid. Then, amid the audience's cries and enthusiasm, Monsieur Narciss and Demoiselle Landrinette walk across a rope stretched between trestles.

It seems that all of Germany's unengaged actors arrange to meet in this town at the foot of the mountains. At the window of an inn a young actress, Philine, leans out, her hair falling over her shoulders. A young actor is fencing in the large parlor of Wilhelm's hostelry. From a stage-coach alight Herr Melina and his wife who want to rejoin a company of players; a poor devil, stammering and ridiculous, in a worn topcoat and threadbare wig, who usually plays the parts of the pedant and pedagogue; and a rubicund and jovial old man who plays himself on the stage, together with his young daughters who have just begun to act. Finally they add to the group a harpist with a long white beard, and a small, melancholy acrobat, who says that her name is Mignon. Thus, in the course of a few days, a company of strolling players is formed, and Wilhelm becomes, almost without realizing it, its financier, director, and poet.

After so much time Wilhelm again steps behind a theater's wings and inhales the smoke from tallow candles. The rustic houses built on the stage still resemble those that the peasants inhabit in the surrounding countryside; the waterfalls are made of cloth, the rose gardens of cardboard, the lambs are stuffed with rags. As before, the actors wear the old costumes of Turkish and pagan warriors, the cloaks of Jews and Magi, and the caricatural garments of farce, or the armor of medieval knights and the tatters of Gypsies, which for some years now excited the

audiences' enthusiasm. Now at last Wilhelm knows the real existence
of actors to whom in the past he had ascribed the noblest emotions. He
knows the misery, the insults, poor joys, envies, disappointed hopes, sad
frivolities, petty ambitions, and vain pride of theatrical life; the great
drinking bouts of punch; the frenzied banquets after opening night,
which leave one's head dazed by wine fumes. None of this frees him
from the theater's enchantment. The scenery, props, and costumes, the
picturesque confusion, the smell of makeup and dust, of adventure and
rags still retain for him some of their old romantic fascination.

This fascination has an unmistakable aspect of *déjà vu*. As Wilhelm
is about to begin his new theatrical existence, Philine appears before
him at a window, her blond hair streaming over her shoulders, a black
mantilla thrown over her white negligee; and she capriciously asks him
for flowers. Soon Philine's voice, songs, laughter, and physical presence
fill Wilhelm's life. Her high-heeled, graceful slippers tap up the stairs
of the inn, like the motif of an eighteenth-century rondeau. Slithering
with a rustle before his door, they step into his bedroom and drop on
the floor, and their sound expresses the most spontaneous joy of life.
Who is happier than she? Like a cricket she lives in the present, minute
by minute; she obeys all the fickle notions that flash through her head,
and goes through the world borne on a rosy cloud of unconsciousness.
Generous and prodigal to the point of wild abandon she flings all that
she has out of her window: money, shawls, and hats; and her peals of
laughter pursue the pedants and tightfisted everywhere.

We ask ourselves at times whether this simple creature does not hide
some secret. Her naïve eyes suddenly become cold, perspicacious, and
astute, they look around intently, discover other people's frailties. The
generous cricket turns into a crafty flatterer, who avidly clutches the
keys to her treasures. With fierce feminine penetration, Philine calls
attention to her dark eyebrows which contrast strangely with the blond
hair, and the scar that marks her forehead like some horrible sign of
infamy. We begin to feel that something shady and repulsive surrounds
her life. And yet who would dare to be angry with her? Hardly does she
sing a song or sip the froth of a glass of champagne as if it were a
delicate, airy creature than everyone around her smiles and feels at
peace. Despite her promiscuity, Philine preserves a kind of childish
innocence, reappearing on her face when we see her asleep, smiling,
with her hair cascading over her breast.

We are not told with what success she treads the boards; but certainly
she acts without passion or study, driven by her spontaneous talent for
mimicry. She knows only one trade, one pastime, one diversion, one joy.
With ever renewed enthusiasm, in all places and on all possible occa-

sions, she makes love to aristocrats, actors, merchants, young servants, even the chief of a band of highwaymen. She courts Wilhelm as soon as she sees him, curls his hair, teaches him to dance, caresses him, and brazenly kisses him before everyone. Yet it seems at times that Wilhelm's black eyes wound her deeply. But, immediately, she begins to play again, as if it were merely a game.

Wilhelm, too, is attracted by these charms, and as soon as Philine comes close to him he feels enveloped by the "sweet cloud" of her youth. Protected by his armature of virtuous scruples, didactic and moralistic, he would like to keep her at a distance; several times he rejects her, pushes her away. But how can he resist so obstinate a sinner? So his virtue yields without too many twinges of conscience when Philine slips between his bed curtains, smothers him with kisses, and hugs him in her arms.

Together with his troupe of actors, Wilhelm traveled through Germany, performing in small provincial theaters and in the halls of noble castles magnificently festooned with lights and tapestries. On some nights they slept at inns, on others in the cold, smoky rooms of an old, uninhabited building. They sail up a river in a boat; on foot or in a carriage, beneath the sun or rain, they travel over muddy, unsafe roads, frequented by Gypsies, jugglers, and menacing bands of highwaymen. But what do they care about dangers and privations? Wilhelm and his friends roam about as heedlessly as birds, giving themselves up to fantasy's varicolored illusions, imagining that they formed a nomad republic, a free vagabond state, like charcoal burners and woodcutters.

At their head strode Wilhelm with a rapid and cheerful gait, wearing his short cloak, a silk sash around his waist and a round, plumed hat on his head. The others followed behind him, armed with rifles and hunting knives. The weather was fine, the landscape enchanting; and at noon the strange adventurers stopped in a clearing in the woods. Here they drank water from a spring and warmed their food. But suddenly from the nearest bush a pistol shot rang out: a horde of bandits plundered the coaches, ripped open the actors' trunks, slashed the luggage, leaving Wilhelm on the ground, seriously wounded, in the arms of Mignon and Philine.

As night threatened to fall, the first help arrived: a surgeon dressed Wilhelm's wounds, a young lady spread a greatcoat over him. Then a group of peasants loaded him on a litter made of cut boughs and twigs and carried him down the mountain, reaching a village late at night. There Wilhelm was lodged in the house of the parish priest, and Philine, Mignon, and the harpist surrounded him with their care. His wounds slowly healed: inertia, anxiety, known and unknown desires tormented him. Without waiting until he was completely cured he and his companions left the village.

A few days later Wilhelm reached a mercantile city in the north where performances were being given by one of the most famous theatrical companies. The group was directed by Serlo, whom he had known at the time of his first passion for the theater. From the poor, ignorant players with whom he had lived, he had not learned anything. But now he found himself in his natural element, conversing with acute connoisseurs, with artists who have a felicitous talent and a limpid knowledge of their art. While he sat in the audience, watching Serlo and his sister Aurelia perform, he had before his eyes the highest models symbolizing theatrical art.

Whoever knew Serlo found in him the very type of the actor, as Diderot has described him in *Paradoxe sur le comédien.* "In society, unless they are buffoons," Diderot said, "I find them polished, caustic, and cold; ostentatious, wasteful, spendthrifts, and selfish, struck more by our absurdities than moved by our misfortunes; quite composed at the spectacle of a troubling incident or the recital of a pathetic story; isolated; wayward, at the beck and call of the great; little morals, no friends, and almost none of those holy and tender ties which associate us to the pains and pleasures of another, who in turn shares our own. I have often seen an actor laugh off stage; I do not recall ever seeing one weep."[1]

Offstage, Serlo also did not cry. His cold heart loved no one; his sister's pain and death awakened in him no emotion of sympathy; and only music, certain beautiful paintings, certain good poems, and the pleasure of fame, wealth, and libertinage attracted his spirit. He never confided in anyone, nor did he ever reveal his real thoughts. He liked to speak ironically, like a sophist, masked behind simulations, theatrical tricks, elegant witticisms.

When Serlo performed, the audience followed him moved and persuaded. Perhaps some of them thought he shared the passions he interpreted; that those tears, those cries, those outbursts of laughter, seemingly so natural, were actually his; and that his inner life coincided with that of the characters he portrayed. But this was not so. With the greatest circumspection, cold and subtle, a sheet of paper on his knee and a pencil in his hand, Serlo had studied the outward spectacles of human nature. He would stand in front of a mirror and rehearse a cry of pain, a gesture of despair, a hypocritical smile, a suspended word, a slurred sound.

Just as a collector gathers paintings or porcelain figurines, so he had hoarded in his memory a vast mimetic collection (272: 37–38): gestures, expressions, significant attitudes. Each time he had to interpret a new character, he would select from his collection some of these strokes, combine and fuse them together. But as soon as he walked onto the stage, what an extraordinary metamorphosis took place! This whole long, laborious exercise, this cold simulation was transformed into spontaneous, fluent behavior. Each evening, for everyone's pleasure, he gave birth again to the miracle of theatrical art. The spectators were caught up in the illusion and persuaded; before them stood an ever different character, reconstructed in its most subtle nuances. Each evening the stage's boards became a temple, and cardboard flats painted green were turned into Shakespeare's forests (309: 30 ff.).

Aurelia's life had not been happy. During her childhood and adolescence she had lived with an aunt who gave in to all her instincts, slave to the most shameful fetters. Living with her, Aurelia had learned to have contempt for men—obtuse and clumsy before they possessed you, sated and overbearing after they had gratified their desires. As soon as she began to act on the stage, admirers tried to circumvent her. She knew all ages, all conditions, all types: The sentimental shop assistant, the conceited merchant's son, the bizarre student, the crude country baron, the astute man of the world, the impetuous prince—all seemed to her ridiculous and disgusting. She could not bear them—as if an atavistic, hysterical female instinct drove her to avenge the insults her sex had suffered through the centuries.

She ended by making a loveless marriage to a mediocre, ordinary man who helped her brother administer the theater. A few years later, having lost her husband, she met a young nobleman who had fought for the freedom of the American colonies. She fell in love with him with the same violent passion with which she had detested the male sex in the past. She lived only for him; she began to act with a talent she had never before possessed and it seemed to her that all the words she spoke on stage were said only in his honor and praise. But this relationship did not last. Before long the young nobleman abandoned Aurelia and she fell into boundless melancholy, overcome by headaches and gripped by a continual feverish agitation.

Her excessive and violent character did not allow her to forget. Her memory kept delving tirelessly into the past, and memories became the sole reason for her life. As though a vengeful demon had taken possession of her, she suffered and wanted to suffer, despaired and wanted to despair. She twisted the knife in the wound; she punished every drop of her blood, every fiber of her organism. By the sheer strength of her will she made her attacks of fever more acute, day by day destroying

58

GOETHE

her beauty and talent. So, when Wilhelm met her, her existence had
become a perennial performance, grave, tenebrous, and dazzling. It
included a touch of the ferocious and artificial—daggers savagely bran-
dished, mad acts, strange pronouncements and tears, sudden moods of
tenderness, luminous outbursts of intelligence. While her brother knew
how to dominate his fictions, Aurelia became more and more entangled
in the net of her hysterical inventions.

She was a born actress: the backdrops, the lights, the smoke from the
orchestra, the sound of applause, the prestige of the theater moved her
deeply. No sooner did she walk onto the stage, wearing the costume of
Ophelia or Orsina, than she continued her daily declamation. She
opened the last floodgates of her sorrow; she tore away every veil
between her soul and the character she was playing. Beneath each
theatrical disguise she repeated the unbearable story of her existence.
Although neither Diderot nor Serlo would approve of this mode of
acting, Aurelia was a great actress. When the dark and ardent notes of
her voice imitated the voice of Ophelia, abandoned, rejected, scorned
by Hamlet, forced to drink the bitter cup of heartbreak—the audience
was enthralled by this extraordinary communion of two destinies in a
single person.

Holed up in the most remote chamber of an old castle, Wilhelm
began to read Shakespeare's plays, completely losing himself in them,
as in an illimitable sea. When he opened *Hamlet, Macbeth,* or *King
Henry IV* he felt that he was not looking at a book written by an earthly
hand. His young and eager eyes saw flung open before them "the Books
of Fate, through which whistles the tempestuous wind of the most
agitated life, tossing the pages to and fro at great speed" (192: 5–8). The
characters moved around him, filling every corner and crevice of his
room, like the spirits that crowd a necromancer's cell. . . . They seemed
human creatures with bodies like ours; but they belonged to an unex-
ampled breed. "Extremely mysterious and complicated," they act
before us, Wilhelm says, "as if they were clocks with crystal cases and
faces; they indicate, as is their purpose, the course of the hours, while,
at the same time, permitting us to discern the mechanism of wheels and
springs that turns them" (192: 23–30).

Scarcely had he gazed into these shining crystal spheres than it
seemed to him he knew all the enigmas of the world and man he had
barely intuited until then. The universe was illuminated by a blinding
light; sensations and abilities he had not even suspected were awakened
in him. But had he tried to extract from Shakespeare's plays this or that
"reply," what could he have heard? Like all great poetry, Shakespeare's
poetry reveals the mysteries of earth and heaven without confiding or

explaining them; the light that traverses it is infinitely enigmatic; it does not offer the key to a single solution.

Having looked for the first time at Shakespeare's plays, Wilhelm immediately felt impelled toward an active life. Precisely he, so immured in his dreaming inner world, was stimulated by these books "to take more rapid steps into the real world" and "mingle in the stream of destinies, decreed on that world" (192: 31–34). This—Goethe seems to add—is the natural fate of great poetry, for it is not born from reality but tends to lose itself in that reality. But even this time Wilhelm fails, as we know, to immerse himself in the waves of life. He cannot penetrate the crystal sphere where the symbols of the universe can be read. From Shakespeare's plays, which he understood with so inspired an intelligence, he learned only to disguise himself in Prince Hal's boots and round hat.

Fat, blond, blue-eyed, soft, and melancholy, Hamlet occupied Wilhelm's thoughts for a long time, and at first he did not understand the contradictions of the Dane's nature—until, gathering the most hidden clues, he managed to reconstruct the story of his life. With Hamlet, he believed, the heroes of history and of the ancient tragedies relinquish the field, perhaps forever, to a new kind of man. The ancient heroes had "a character" (307: 27), their inclinations united around a center to form a delimited organism. With an exclusive vocation, they cultivated their heart's emotions. They allowed themselves to be swept away by the passion of love and revenge, burned with hatred, fell victim to ambition and the desire for power. When they conceived a plan, they carried it through with iron determination. If any human or divine obstacles rose in their path they pushed these aside or succumbed to forces greater than their own.

Like the ancient heroes, Hamlet was destined to become a king. "Gently and nobly cultivated, this noble flower had sprung up under the immediate influences of majesty: the idea of justice and princely dignity, the feeling for the good and decorous together with the consciousness of high birth, had all been developed in him simultaneously. He was a prince, a prince by birth; he wished to reign, but only so that good men might be good without impediment. Pleasing in appearance, well-mannered by nature, gentle of heart, he was meant to be the model of youth and the joy of the world" (217: 32–218: 2) But, unlike classical heroes, Hamlet did not have a character. The mass of his inclinations formed a fluctuant, limitless ensemble. No passion had marked him with its exclusive seal; hatred and warlike ardor struck no roots in his soul; ambition and the desire for domination provided no aims for his existence.

When his father suddenly died and his mother remarried, Hamlet's inner world came crashing down in ruins. He felt oppressed and humiliated. Though neither sad nor reflective by nature, sadness and reflection had become the heaviest burden of his life. Finally, on the bastions of Elsinore Castle, his father's venerable ghost stalked toward him, signed to him, spoke out, and made its terrible accusation. "When the ghost has vanished," Wilhelm says, "who do we see before us? A young hero who thirsts for revenge? A prince by birth who rejoices at being called to challenge the man who has usurped his crown? No, amazement and melancholy crush the lonely man; he grows bitter at smiling villains, swears never to forget the dead man, and concludes with a significant sigh: 'The time is out of joint: O cursed spite,/ That ever I was born to set it right!'

"In these words, I believe, will be found the key to Hamlet's entire behavior; and it is clear what Shakespeare meant to represent: a great action imposed on a spirit who was not born to act. . . . An oak tree is planted in a precious jar, which should have received only pleasant flowers in its bosom; the roots expand, the jar is destroyed. A beautiful being, pure, noble and highly moral but without the hero's sensual force, succumbs beneath a burden which he can neither bear nor cast away" (245: 28–246: 8). Thus, throughout the play, Hamlet never gives himself a goal. He tries to punish the guilty according to an idea of rigidly actuated revenge. He advances, retreats, delays, and continually confuses himself. But the active force rests, not in Hamlet, but in the very firm hands of destiny. "Neither the inhabitants of the earth nor those of the nether world can succeed in doing what is reserved to destiny alone. The hour of judgment comes. The wicked fall together with the good. One generation is mowed down, another begins to sprout (254: 38–255: 3).

Swayed by Wilhelm's enthusiasm, Serlo decides to present Shakespeare's play for the first time in Germany; Wilhelm will play the part of Hamlet, Serlo Polonius, while Aurelia will invest Ophelia with her sorrow. But who will play the part of the Ghost? While Wilhelm and Serlo are still undecided, they find a note in the theater. In it, written in bizarre characters, a mysterious correspondent promised that the Ghost would appear on the stage at the right moment and play its part. And this is just what happened on the evening of the first performance. When Horatio cried out: "Look, my lord, it comes!" Wilhelm whirled around, "and the tall, noble figure, the low inaudible tread, the light movements under the heavy-looking armor, made such an impression on him that he stood as if turned to stone, and could exclaim only in a half-voice, 'Angels and ministers of grace defend us!' He stared at the form; several times drew a deep breath and pronounced his invocation to the Ghost in so confused, so broken and distressed a manner that the greatest artist could not have said it with more effectiveness. . . .

"Then the scene changed; and when the two reached a farther point, the Ghost suddenly stopped and turned; so Hamlet was too close to him. With longing curiosity he immediately looked through the lowered visor, but could only see two sunken eyes and a well-formed nose. Timidly trying to spy, he stood before the Ghost; but when the first sounds issued from the helmet, and a somewhat hoarse yet deeply resonant voice pronounced the words, 'I am thy father's spirit,' Wilhelm, shuddering, started back some paces, and the audience shuddered with him. Each imagined that he knew the voice, and Wilhelm thought he noticed some semblance to his father's. These strange sensations and memories, the curiosity he felt at discovering his mysterious friend and the fear of offending him . . . all this drove Wilhelm from one side of the stage to the other . . ."(321: 24–32; 322: 6–24).

So, along with the audience of the large mercantile city, we are present at a symbolic miracle, no less great than the miracle of the loaves and fishes; a magical transmutation of physical presences. On the stage of Serlo's theater, the "gentle royal flower," the blond and melancholy prince of Denmark lives again in the body of an intelligent, naïve German bourgeois. Wilhelm shares fully in his character's fate: An unknown actor frightens and petrifies him, just as so many centuries before the ghost of Denmark's king had terrified his son. The hoarse voice of Hamlet's father seems to him the voice of his own father who only a short while ago had gone to the house of shadows.

It has been suggested that Goethe, when he imagined Wilhelm's figure, wished to draw the Hamlet of modern times: the Hamlet of the Germany that was about to be converted to Romanticism. Wilhelm has many psychological traits in common with the prince of Denmark. Like him, Wilhelm does not have a character; no exclusive and violent passion dominates him; he does not know his own desires and, when he acts, he makes mistakes, becomes confused, and defers the fate prepared for him. But this identity is not complete: it takes place for only an instant, on the stage of a theater, like a miraculous illumination. What's more, the fat, blond, melancholy prince of Denmark casts only a shadow, a vague and continuous resemblance, on the thin, brown-haired German bourgeois who plays him on the stage.

With the performance of *Hamlet,* the second experience, Wilhelm Meister's true and proper "theatrical mission," comes to an end. At the start, when he agreed to act with Serlo, he had dreamed of the favor of the great and the sympathy of women. He had hoped to perfect his persona and his tendencies to the good and beautiful, whose development his bourgeois birth had hampered. But soon these hopes abandoned him, and he realized that the theater did not deserve the best part of his strength and intelligence. The audience did not understand; his fellow actors were egotists, unaware and ungrateful; he himself probably did not have a true theatrical talent, like that which enabled Serlo to transmute himself, like Proteus, into all possible forms.

When he thought over the time he had devoted to the theater, he felt he was looking into an "infinite void" (422: 1–4). Of all his labors, nothing remained; and full of regret he remembered his youth, when an immense inspiration had still swelled his breast. So Wilhelm decides to leave Serlo's company; the best part of his spirit was already looking forward to a new homeland.

On hills and mountain slopes, in the middle of a cultivated countryside, the traveler who journeys through Goethe's novels encounters the castles and manor houses in which the German aristocracy lived out its tranquil existence. Sometimes a high wall wards off the glance of the visitor or a deep ditch prevents him from entering. But if the custodians welcome him in, his eyes can admire dense, English-style parks, full of plane trees, oaks, poplars, bushes, ponds, windmills, and brooks; or dwell on trim, orderly walks shaded by noble lime trees, surrounded by flower beds and hothouses where gardeners prepare the spring's luxuriant flowering. Many castles, with their towers, pinnacles, and courtyards, still recall the German Middle Ages. Some of them are crumbling into ruin, and only the tattered tapestries and inlaid pavements preserve signs of their old magnificence. Meanwhile the new eighteenth-century palaces gather within their walls broad neoclassical staircases, the most recent elegancies imported from England, and with lanterns and thousands of candles light up fields already wrapped in the shadows of night.

The son of rich burghers, Wilhelm had never stepped across any of these thresholds. But how often did his naïve snobbery carry him in his imagination into these castles! There, he thought, live those who are "triply happy, those whom birth has raised above the inferior grades of humanity." Whereas, during the difficult voyage of life, other men derive "little profit from propitious winds and soon, their strength exhausted, sink in the storm," noblemen from the moment of birth are placed on a magnificent ship, enjoy favorable winds, and avoid all contrary ones. From the height of their observatory, they observe life with "a just and universal look"; they know the vanity or value of earthly things and turn their spirits to what is "necessary, useful, and true" (154: 18–31; 35–155: 2).

The day came when Wilhelm, too, could approach this happy world. He was invited, together with a troupe of actors, to perform in a count's castle before a prince who is a diplomat and soldier. The audience is a group of aristocrats. But reality amused itself—as usual—by disappointing him. At the castle Wilhelm and his companions were welcomed like criminals off the street; insulted and mocked by the servants; lodged in an old building that lacked beds, tables, or enough fireplaces to keep them warm. When Wilhelm was taken into the countess's chamber to read his writings, he was mistaken for a hairdresser or haberdasher. The "just and universal" vision, the cold, disillusioned judgment that he had attributed to aristocrats seemed to exist only in his imagination.

But the countess's beautiful eyes and lovely demeanor left their mark on Wilhelm's heart. When she appeared before him, covered with ribbons, laces, curls, and glittering jewels, she seemed to him a goddess issuing from the corolla of a flower. Petrified, he stared for a long time at her, suspended over the abyss of birth and social condition that separated them. He loved her grace and sweetness; he adored in her the splendor of luxury, the unfamiliar scintillation of jewels and necklaces. Meanwhile two cunning go-betweens, the Baroness and Philine, weave around them an equivocal network of small intrigues and sensual blandishments. A few days before leaving the castle, Wilhelm dropped on his knees before the Countess, pressing her beautiful hand to his lips. "He wanted to stand up; but as in a dream the strangest things are born from something stranger, and take us by surprise; so, without knowing how it happened, he found himself embracing the Countess, her lips were resting upon his, and these ardent kisses made him experience the bliss which we mortals enjoy only from the first sparkling foam that brims over the freshly filled cup of love" (201: 25–32).

At the castle, in the petty, gossiping aristocratic crowd, Wilhelm met an officer with large, bright blue eyes that glittered frigidly beneath a high forehead. Immediately, he was impressed, although such haughty ways repelled him. He understood that Jarno was the only person in the castle's society to look at reality with the penetrating vision which he had attributed to all aristocrats, and to possess qualities unknown to him. Wilhelm was not mistaken. Since his youth Jarno had loved "clarity"; and at the center of his world he had set the clear, untainted light of reason, the cruel precision of a mind that sees things as they are. He had become a soldier; diplomatic missions had taken him to France, England, and Italy, initiating him into the most secret political affairs. He was among the first in Germany to read Shakespeare's plays and looked at reality through his extraordinary "magic lantern." But these experiences did not make him gentler. The more he came to know the world, the more he became hard, cynical, sarcastic, cold as a stone; and men's lives seemed to him a muddle of mistakes, idiocies, and illusions.

Certain things, however, escaped the comprehension of his keen blue eyes. One day, with a voice reeking with disgust, Jarno lashed out against Mignon and the harpist, deploring the fact that Wilhelm had given his affection to "a wandering balladmonger and a silly, ambiguous mongrel" (193: 29). These words which deeply offended Wilhelm make us wonder. How can this experienced man of the world, himself protected from the winds of chance, rage with such spiteful and vulgar cruelty against the victims of destiny? With these words, Jarno simply revealed that divine grace had never touched his soul. His intelligence had remained sharp and dry, like Mephistopheles's; it did not understand passion's tenebrous richness, nor destiny's habit of instilling in its victims values superior to those it cultivates in its favorites.

Some years later Jarno took refuge in the mountains, among the very ancient masses of granite which had lifted their peaks through the clouds when the primeval waters still covered the earth. There he carried on long, silent, and impenetrable colloquies with the mountains, his "silent masters." He scrutinized the folds in the rocks, beat the stones with his mineralogist's hammer, delved into the rich veins of gold and silver. Living continually among the rocks, Jarno tried to rid himself of every last vestige of love and emotion. He grew to scorn even more bitterly the "spirit" of men, the heart's enchantments and illusions, the useless treasures in whose pursuit Wilhelm vainly consumed his time. Finally he became an *Einseitige*, a limited man, with only a single face, a specialized master in his profession (VIII, 57: 15).

Some reader might suppose that, up there in the mountains, Jarno would end by losing himself in a desert of spiritual aridity and technical precision, like some grim Mephistopheles of geology. But, precisely up there, Jarno saved his soul. The *Einseitige*, the man with a single face, the circumspect and scrupulous technician became a mystic, who devoutly perused Nature's secret characters and prophetic mysteries. At this great height, of what use to him were the heart's imaginative and imprecise passions—everything that is exclusively "human"? His frigidity, which he had succeeded in creating within himself, his sarcastic destruction of all emotions, permitted him to contemplate without error the immensely distant, ethereal, beatific orbits which the stars trace in the sky and in the pure spirits of some of us.[2]

After departing from the castle, Wilhelm tried to sum up his experiences in a long letter to Werner, his brother-in-law, who administered the commerical enterprise owned by their fathers. According to Werner, it is not the princes of this world but the daring men of business who know how to seize the significance and relations of all things. Their spirit is broad and enormously alert; because of their system of double-entry bookkeeping their minds are accustomed to order and clarity. "I am convinced," Werner said, ". . . that if you once could take a proper zest in our affairs, you would be persuaded that certain faculties of the mind can also find their free play here. Believe me, all that you lack is the view of some great activity to make you ours forever; and when you return, you will gladly associate with those who, by means of every kind of shipment and speculation, are able to draw toward themselves a portion of that money and that prosperity which circulate by necessity through the world. Cast a glance at the natural and artificial productions of all parts of the universe and consider how they have become, one after the other, indispensible! And what a pleasant and intellectual task it is to know, at any moment, all the things which are most sought and yet are lacking or hard to find; to supply easily and rapidly to everyone what he desires; to lay in your stock prudently and to enjoy at every moment the advantage of this great circulation!" (38: 4–8, 11–25.)

Wilhelm, who aspired only to the formation of his personality, his "I," replied that a bourgeois can never ask himself: "What are you?" but only "What do you have? What intelligence, what knowledge, what talents, what wealth?"(291: 16–18). A bourgeois is not a unitary and harmonious person but an aggregate of isolated attitudes, which exclude and contradict each other. If he wants to break out of his limitations, if he tries to "become visible" and to possess a public persona like a king, an aristocrat, or even an actor, he becomes ludicrous and tasteless. Werner had only to look at himself in the mirror. In a few years he had accumulated a large amount of capital; but while his coffers were being filled, he had become a "laborious hypochondriac," very thin, bald, with too long a nose, faded cheeks, bent shoulders, and a shrill voice.

Yet, Wilhelm adds, if we might imagine taking from an aristocrat his wealth, his capacities, and his talents, there still would remain a very rich residue. We would know his persona: that ensemble of perfectly balanced qualities that transpire in the daily exercise of forms. When an aristocrat appears on the quotidian stage of life, we, sitting in the audience, admire his beautiful, resonant voice, his noble, natural movements, his reserved demeanor, his ability to be continually equal to himself. We esteem the extraordinary art with which he manages to introduce a kind of "solemn grace" in common things and an "elegant lightness" in those that are serious and important. We respect the atmosphere of equilibrium, measure, and harmony that accompanies his entire existence, like a sprightly musical cortege.

Thus, despite humiliations and disappointments, Wilhelm's first experiences with the aristocracy concluded much more positively than his experience with the theater. It seemed to him that he had not learned anything on the stage. In the castle's halls and gardens he had found the signs of a spiritual and formal harmony, which he dreamed of appropriating for himself. But, as always, while composing his letter to Werner, Wilhelm's imagination had succeeded in anticipating what his eyes had not seen or had glimpsed confusedly. The castle's world was a small-scale mediocre incarnation of aristocratic civilization. Only later, in another castle, would Wilhelm know the true propriety of forms, the "just and universal" look which descends from on high like a divine gift, illuminating the true and false, the necessary and useless.

After leaving Serlo's theatrical company, Wilhelm traveled again through one of those mountainous landscapes to which Goethe entrusted the task of healing his characters' wounds. It was spring; a storm lashed violently over mountain and plain, the sun returned, and a rainbow appeared against the sky's gray backdrop, blessing the new stage of Wilhelm's life. A few hours later, he knocked at the portal of Lothario's ancient castle, where he met an abbé and a doctor whom he had already encountered in the course of his travels. Jarno, too, was at the castle.

A few days before she died Aurelia had asked him to give her last letter to Lothario, the lover who had abandoned her. Wilhelm had formed an unusual idea of this charge; he wrote a pathetic speech to reproach the faithless man. As he rode through the mountains he repeated it to himself and learned it by heart, imagining the gestures and inflections of voice with which he would pronounce it. But as soon as he arrived in the castle's main hall and was surrounded by the portraits of noblewomen and knights, ruffs and coats of mail, as soon as Lothario stood before him dressed with the elegant simplicity of a country squire, all these intentions vanished. He accepted Lothario's invitation to join the company of his friends; and he began to praise, with almost feminine devotion, his new friend's excellence—the most "estimable" man he has ever met.

At first we think that Wilhelm's snobbery has been seduced by the young nobleman's charm. But Wilhelm is not alone in this. All who know Lothario are in love with him: tranquil and hysterical, terrestrial and celestial women; contemplative men and men of action; and even Jarno, when he speaks of Lothario, lays aside his habitual coldness and irony. All are inclined to forgive Lothario for almost any deed, as if he possessed certain secret and incommunicable perfections. As for us, we are less enthusiastic; and we fail to understand what these exceptional qualities of his consist of. He seems to us only a fatuous, idle young man, who never grows tired of having his little adventures, his modest amorous intrigues with young actresses, mature promiscuous ladies, and capricious colonels' wives.

Yet Goethe loves Lothario as much as Wilhelm, Jarno, and his thousands of female adorers. Obviously, he considers him the most perfect and elegant flower of the great aristocratic civilization that Wilhelm had drawn in his imagination. If we wish to understand him—Goethe seems to tell us—we must not examine his deeds, speeches, and thoughts one by one; none of these is able to express completely what he "is," as is the case with all exceptional beings. The central fire of Lothario's personality is an ineffable strength, a hidden yet continually visible quality, of which we are apprised by the grace of his bearing and the adoration which he quite naturally arouses at every step.[3]

All the qualities that remain incomplete in other human beings achieve their full maturation in Lothario's figure; all the propensities which, in his friends, contradict and harm each other in turn, find in him their balanced and felicitous expression. He is calm, measured, tranquil, but he does not know Jarno's pitiless frigidity. He reasons lucidly, but he is not subject to the dangers of the rational intelligence; he acts like a force of nature, but he does not destroy or overturn the world. The delicate, almost morbid sensitivity which at moments we sense in him, does not lead him to lose himself, like Wilhelm, in the vertiginous depths of the past and the heart's emotions. While he thinks, talks, acts, guides himself and others, how can one help but admire the fluent harmony, the grave lightness, the sober charm enveloping his entire existence?

Lothario is devoid of the inspiration, the extraordinary spiritual intensity which at times illumines the life of an incomplete person. The world of Mignon and the harpist—the anguish of destiny and misfortune, the chasms of heaven and earth—is alien to him. Unlike Wilhelm he does not know the ecstasies of passion. More balanced than Jarno, he lacks his extraordinary intellectual acumen. But he possesses an even more extraordinary form of intuition; the objective kind; reality stands before him open, evident, luminous. He seems born to act; he reflects, decides, gets rid of the obstacles he encounters in his path. More, he kindles the enthusiasm of others, interprets their desires, and drags them impetuously along with him (553: 19–23; 608: 6–12).

When he was quite young the spirit of adventure had led him to fight under the flag of the American colonies. On returning to Germany, he realized that in the world of high politics, man pursues a spurious dream of dominion: "He governs nothing while he thinks he governs everything"; he dissimulates when he wishes to be frank, he is false and wishes to be honest; and "in order to attain a goal that he will never reach, he sacrifices at every moment the supreme goal—harmony with himself" (452: 24–33). So, although he is a man of action, he renounces insinuating himself into the places where the destinies of the universe are plotted, where states are administered and revolutions prepared.

His mind pursues a political ideal, which he likes to symbolize in the image of the wise, calm, foresighted housewife, who moves about her house, plants and harvests, spends and conserves, repeats the regular cycle of her existence, like a star that regularly travels its orbit and presides over night and day. Like a housewife, Lothario wants to exclude violence, chance, and disorder from history; he tries to achieve complete mastery of the means and ends of his activity (452–453). Having taken refuge on his estate as revolutions are about to rock Europe, he starts to carry out reforms and studies a very ambitious plan: the creation of a great Utopian society. This is to be spread in Germany, Russia, and America, and will attempt to assure progress in the world in accordance with nature, the harmonious female, and stellar rhythm.

In Lothario's castle, where old and new, utility and elegance are all so marvelously wedded, Wilhelm begins living in a freer, richer atmosphere. No longer does he inhale the thick, acrid smoke of tallow candles; he no longer slept in the hazardous rooms of inns, among jugglers, actors, and noblemen's grooms. He had rediscovered comfort, orderliness, tranquillity, habit—all of which he had renounced during his years of vagabondage. But he discovered so many other things in Lothario's castle! A group of intelligent, experienced men, members of that mysterious "Society of the Tower," converse with him, and their words reveal to him unsuspected possibilities, which cast a flattering light on his future existence.

Now that a joyful period was about to begin, Wilhelm felt impelled to bid farewell to his past, that time of illusions, aspirations, and confused conflicts, during which he had almost been lost. So he returned to the places of his theatrical activity; he again met Laertes, Horatio, Herr and Frau Melina, Serlo and Elmira. Frau Melina's last words removed all bitterness from his definitive separation. But a deeper nostalgia tortured him. During all those years Mariane's loving shadow had never left him. Though he had lost all trace of her, he hoped to find her again, dressed in her red officer's uniform, on the stage of some town in Germany.

The first night that Wilhelm had spent in Lothario's castle, Mariane had appeared to him in a dream. Like all revelatory dreams, it took place toward morning, as the sun's rays burst into his room. He felt that he was in a garden, amid alleys, hedges, and blossoming flower beds, when Mariane approached him and spoke to him sweetly, as if no discord had ever divided them. Soon after, his father, dressed as for the house, and with a rare, affable expression, came to them. When he grasped Mariane by the hand and left with her, strolling down a tree-lined walk, Wilhelm wanted to join them and ran after them; but his father and Mariane seemed to flee him, almost flying down the garden path. What were these silent familiar spirits trying to tell him? They ran away from him because they both belonged to the shadows' populous realm, yet they forgave him for the sorrows he had inflicted on them. His father, too, whom he had never understood or known how to understand, in those early morning hours took leave of him in a mild and peaceful manner.

Wilhelm, unlike Lothario, did not possess the art of being consoled by nature and of leaving his own experiences behind him: nor did elves hover about his head as around Faust's, bathing him in the waters of Lethe. That morning dream did not suffice to free him from Mariane's memory. Like all brothers of Epimetheus, Wilhelm must resurrect his past once again, desperately exacerbate its sufferings, and drain the bitter cup of memory.

Some days later he rediscovered Barbara, Mariane's maid and confidante, behind the lights of a stage. Then at midnight, the hour of the spirits, the old witch knocked at the door of his room. As in the past, at the time of his happy love, Barbara set out three glasses on the small table and filled them to the brim with champagne. "Drink," she cried, after quickly swigging down her frothing glass, "drink before the spirit evaporates! The third glass must lose its froth without anyone drinking it, in memory of my unhappy friend. How red her lips were when she replied to your toasts! Ah, and now they are pale and stiff for eternity!" (476: 3–8.) Like a "Sibyl," like a "Fury" (476: 9), like a classic witch, whose tripod and holy vestments were all she lacked, Barbara savagely called up the past, evoked again her mistress's love and suffering. Then Mariane's ghost seemed to return from the nether world and her pale, cold lips seemed to drink the glass of champagne that had been poured for her.

Seated opposite Barbara, in the dim light cast by the candle, Wilhelm let himself be overwhelmed by this tragic, furious evocation of the past. "Give me back my Mariane!" he cried. "She lives, she is near at hand. Not by chance did you choose this late and lonely hour to visit me. . . . Where are you keeping her? Where have you hidden her? I believe all, I will promise to believe all, if you but show her to me, if you restore her to my arms. The shadow of her I have seen already: let me clasp her once more to my bosom. I will kneel before her. I will beg her to forgive me. . . . Come! Where have you hidden her? Don't leave her, don't leave me any longer in this uncertainty! Your object is attained. Where have you hidden her? Come, let me light you with this candle, let me once more see her sweet face!" (481: 10–26.) But Mariane was hidden where neither the light of the sun nor the candle's familiar company could reach—in the dark abode, from which she would never again run to meet a lover.

During the course of this night Wilhelm built a solemn funeral monument to Mariane, cruel and grotesque, like all the monuments that the men in Goethe's books erect with stones and words over the bodies of the dead, to honor them, keep them at a distance, and continue living. After that, his nostalgia for Mariane no longer troubled him; and he abandoned her, as she wished, in the fields where the shadows of the dead flit about silent and sad.

When leaving him forever Mariane had entrusted him with her most precious legacy: Felix, the son she had had from him; a lovely boy with gay eyes, blond hair, and thin, dark, gently arched eyebrows drawn upon a very white brow. Wilhelm did not want to believe that Felix was his son; and he took him before a mirror, anxiously examining the resemblances between the child and himself. He then realized that, since nature had given him the child, he must truly make him his son a second time, observing his gifts and gradually recognizing himself in the boy.

Surrounded by the new wonders of the world, Felix ran about in Lothario's garden, asking his father the names and uses of the plants, the origin and end of all things, where the flame goes and whence the wind comes. Wilhelm was unable to answer these questions. Until then he had been like a bird, his house a pile of quickly gathered leaves that wither before he deserts them. He lacked the sense of duration; he did not know the names of all things that exist on the earth's surface. Living close to his son's inexhaustible curiosity, Wilhelm realized he must learn to know the world as gardeners, artisans, and technicians know it. The time had come for his life to have a foundation; the time had come for him to own a house and garden where he could plant trees that would grow together with Felix. While educating his son, he would also be educating himself.

One morning, before dawn, Jarno conducted Wilhelm into a hall. It looked like a deconsecrated chapel: A large table covered with a green cloth had taken the place of the altar; a curtain seemed to conceal a painting; and built into the walls were shelves holding rolls of parchment behind fine wire netting. Suddenly a vaguely familiar voice seemed to issue from the altar, ordering him in a shout to sit down. While Wilhelm sat in an armchair, the first rays of the morning sun, passing through the window's colored panes, struck his eyes and dazzled him. Standing like this, with one hand shielding his eyes, Wilhelm watched in astonishment a strange ceremony, reminiscent of both a Masonic initiation and the show of an illusionist.

With a light rustle, the curtain over the altar opened to reveal a dark and empty aperture, into which stepped, one after the other, three men whom Wilhelm had known in the past, and who greeted him by pronouncing pedagogic aphorisms. Finally the curtain parted for the last time; and in the aperture, wearing the ghostly garb of the king of Denmark, stepped forth the mysterious figure who had so moved and frightened him during the performance of *Hamlet.* Just as then, it seemed to him he was hearing his own father's voice saying: "I am thy father's spirit, and I depart consoled since my wishes for you are accomplished beyond all my hopes. Farewell, and think of me when you will enjoy what I have provided for you" (495: 31–37). With this theatrical solution, Goethe lets us know that the obscure wound left in Wilhelm's heart by the difficult relationship with his father was now healed. His "father's spirit" had blessed him, accepted his past life, and directed him trustingly toward the future.

When the spectacle ended, the Abbé came into the hall, sat down behind the green table and handed Wilhelm a small roll of parchment containing a "Letter of Instruction": "Art is long, life short, judgment difficult, the occasion fleeting. . . . Every beginning is cheerful; the threshold is the place of expectation" (496: 11–14). He showed him the rolls of parchment containing the *Lehrjahres* of Lothario, Jarno, and himself, along with those of many unknown youths. And finally, in an exultant and solemn voice, like Sarastro's or the two armed men who meet Tamino and Pamina at the end of their peregrinations, he announced that Wilhelm's *Lehrjahre*—his long, confused, anxious years of apprenticeship—have been completed. "Ask not," said the Abbé. "Hail to thee, young man. Nature has emancipated you" (497: 36–37).

Soon after, we find Wilhelm again in Lothario's garden. Only a few hours have passed. But we have the impression that in the blank space, the imaginary interval of time which divides the seventh and eighth books of the *Lehrjahre,* Wilhelm has changed. He no longer seems the young man who sat in the ancient chapel, his soul in turmoil and his eyes dazzled, waiting to be emancipated by nature. Now he is a mature man. Like all those who have left youth behind, he has bidden farewell to the shadow of his father and to his old, deceptive love; he lives with his son;

72

GOETHE

and he is about to take his first sure steps into the immensity of the
world. That very evening we learn that he has even changed physically.
As Werner assures us, his physique is taller and stronger, his forehead
broader, his eyes deeper, his nose finer, his mouth more loving than it
was in the past.

This serene satisfaction, this ease—communicated to us in the first
pages of the eighth book—leads us to imagine that, in a short while, with
one of his rapid, light strokes, Goethe will bring the *Lehrjahre* to an
end. A final scene, perhaps an unexpected recognition scene—and Wilhelm will attain the goal of his existence. But the end of the *Lehrjahre*
is still far away. The novel is like a grandiose and bizarre castle whose
top floors, towers, and subterranean tunnels which should connect the
outlying buildings with the principal one have not been built; other
characters, other tumultuous adventures are about to erupt into this
edifice.

Whoever attentively reads the scene of the initiation ceremony will
understand that it is not at all the definitive consecration of Wilhelm's
maturity that Goethe may have wanted to lead us to think. At the first
light of day, the Abbé and the tower's "messengers" solemnly introduce
the young pupil into the society of the elect, revealing to him the
fundamental principles of their extremely lucid and mysterious philosophy. On the one hand, by means of these rapid apparitions, they teach
him that his life is formed around a providential design, which will lead
him happily to the goal prepared for him by destiny. On the other, they
also teach him the secret of pedagogy: "To guard men against error is
not the educator's duty, but rather to guide the erring pupil, indeed to
let him quaff his error from overflowing cups—this is the educator's
wisdom. He who merely tastes his error, will lodge it for a long time in
himself and will take delight in it as in a singular felicity. But he who
drains it to the dregs must, if he isn't crazy, learn to know it" (494:
38–495: 6).

But Wilhelm does not understand: the initiate does not accept a
single one of the teachings offered him. Whereas, when he was a young
man lost in the ecstasy of his love for Mariane, Wilhelm saw everywhere
benign signs and warnings—now, after so many years of roaming, he
has lost his youthful trust in destiny. In the past he sinned out of an
excess of faith, now he sins from a lack of faith; and he can see in his
past only a series of mistakes and aberrations. Like all those who do not
believe in the harmony of the world, he has become a moralist. The
"pedagogy of error" repels him. "If so many men were concerned about
you," he exclaims, "if they knew your life and knew what you should
make of it, why didn't they guide you in a severer and more serious

fashion? Why did they favor your silly games, instead of drawing you away from them?" (495: 21–25.) He prefers the opposite kind of pedagogy: a pedagogy of laws and rules capable of inculcating the path that must be followed (527: 19–21, 25–28).

During this period Wilhelm meets Theresa, who had been on the point of marrying Lothario. Theresa lives in a small country house painted white and red, where all is clean and orderly. The house still smells of paint; bowls and pots gleam brightly in the kitchen; in the courtyard the firewood is stacked in neat piles; and in the garden vegetables and fruit trees take the place of useless ornamental plants. Just as a young duckling immediately searches for water, so in her early youth Theresa sensed that the kitchen, pantry, granary, and attic were her natural element; the house's order and cleanliness seemed her sole instinct and preoccupation. Even now she keeps the accounts, directs the servants, administers her property, and travels the ever identical circle of a housewife's life, obeying the same rhythm as the constellations in the sky.

The greatest stars of Goethe's female constellation revolve in so remote a point of the sky that their light seems to us pale or enveloped by very dark shadows. Yet when Wilhelm looks at Theresa's blue eyes, transparent and clear as crystal, it seems to him that he is moving beneath the sharp, precise, and constant light of a delightful minor star, limning the real outlines of things and showing us the road's dangers and obstacles. But how many things Theresa refuses to illuminate! Everything that reveals the least shadow or shines out too glaringly proves to be incomprehensible and strange to her. For her, Mignon's shadows and Aurelia's inspired hysteria belong to an unknown world; every theatrical fiction seems ridiculous to her; she does not like to read. She reduces God and religion to a kind of exquisite moral diet; and love has never revealed its joys to her.

This clear and precise light fascinates Wilhelm who, after having been the prisoner of the illimitable and indistinct, hopes to inhabit the sure world of reality. So, a few days after the initiation ceremony—and concealing the fact from his teachers and guardians—he writes a long letter to Theresa, offering her his hand. With the eyes of imagination he already sees Mignon and Felix, till now left to themselves, running through the fields and woods and flourishing in the open air under Theresa's guidance. "The decision to offer my hand to Theresa," he later observes, "is perhaps the first that came wholly from myself. I had made my plan after much reflection, and my reason was completely in agreement" (534: 22–25). This marriage should initiate a new period in his life: he would become the master of his destiny.

GOETHE

Wilhelm, victim of the worst illusions, neglects to interrogate his archetype—the loving images of Clorinda and the princess—which a superior hand had placed within him. Like Prometheus in *Pandora*, like Pylades in *Iphigenie*, and Montecatino in *Tasso*, like all irreligious men, he is idolizing the actions determined by reason alone and carried through by the force of will. Yet correct actions derive from both the deepest desires of our nature and the will of the gods. They well up from us as if we had not determined them, necessary and natural as the figures in dreams.

But the "Society of the Tower" watches over Wilhelm. It cannot permit him to fail his destiny when he is so close to realizing it, and so it removes Theresa from his path. Not understanding that the men of the tower are preparing his happiness, seeing mysterious designs and machinations everywhere, Wilhelm wrathfully protests. He cannot stand being guided by those omnipotent hands, like a pawn in an incomprehensible game. But, in the end, he becomes resigned: "I put myself completely at my friends' disposal and their guidance: in this world it is futile to try to act according to one's individual will" (594: 37–39). As he sadly utters these words, he does not know that all of his desires are about to be fulfilled.

Wilhelm's first meeting with Natalia took place in a mythical landscape, like those he had dreamed of while reading *Aminta* and *Pastor Fido*. A clump of beautiful beech trees encircled and shaded a large clearing in the mountains; bubbling up through the grass a brook ran down the slope. Windmills, villages, and towns appeared in the distance between the ravines and wooded peaks, and another range of mountains rose at the line of the horizon. Wilhelm lay on the ground, his wounds barely bandaged and his head in Philine's lap, while Mignon, with her hair askew and bloodied, knelt at his feet and embraced them in tears. By now night was falling and no one had come to help the wretched man.

Suddenly the hooves of a troop of horses resounded over the mountain; and, from behind the bushes, riding a white horse, appeared a young Amazon accompanied by an elderly gentleman and a retinue of servants and Hussars. The strange woman turned her horse toward him, halted and dismounted, her shape hidden, for she wore a man's greatcoat, to protect her from the dampness of the night. Scarcely had Wilhelm seen her than his eyes could not leave that sweet, calm face bent over him: he felt that he had never seen anything so noble and lovable; and the beneficent look in those compassionate eyes made him forget his wounds. Finally the young Amazon took off her greatcoat and stretched it delicately over Wilhelm's body. "At this moment, as he wanted to open his mouth, and stammer out some words of gratitude, the vivid impression of her presence worked so strangely on his already disturbed senses that all at once it seemed to him as if her head were encircled with rays; and a resplendent shining light seemed gradually to spread itself over her entire figure. Just then the surgeon, preparing to extract the ball from his wound, gave him a sharp twinge. The angel faded away from the eyes of the fainting patient; Wilhelm lost consciousness, and when he came to his senses again, the horsemen and coaches, the beautiful woman and her attendants, had vanished like a dream" (228: 18–32).

During the following days, lying in his sickbed, a thousand times he felt that he heard again the sweet sound of that voice: he saw her as she let the greatcoat slip from her shoulders, and as her face and figure faded away in the light. He thought he had contemplated the amorous archetype of his youth, at last incarnated on this earth. Clorinda's noble, virile femininity had appeared before his eyes; the beautiful princess had bent maternally over his wounds, just as when the stepson lay sick with love.

When Wilhelm tried to see the Amazon again, all signs of her had disappeared as if she had returned to the forests of *Jerusalem Liberated* or had stepped back into the painting whence she had come. No book, no map mentioned the place where she had fled the dangers of war; no manual of genealogy recorded her family's name; and Wilhelm feared that he would have to renounce the hope of finding her again. But one day, rummaging in the pocket of the greatcoat, he found a note in her handwriting. Enormously moved and astonished, he realized that the handwriting resembled the countess's: it seemed to him that their faces were those of twin sisters, and in his memory one apparition was transformed into the other. Thus the Amazon's image began gathering about itself the different threads of Wilhelm's past.

Months, perhaps years, went by. While he was acting in *Hamlet* and Lessing's *Emilia Galotti*, or pursuing Mariane's ghost, Wilhelm never forgot the "figure of all figures" (445: 35). Even in the world of the theater, some sign, which he could not interpret, led him to her. As he will discover later, Lothario, of whom he had heard Aurelia speak, is the Amazon's brother. Reading the confessions of the "beautiful soul" with Aurelia he had unwittingly penetrated into her house, meeting her "noble figure," her "tranquil temperament," her "even, unchanging pursuits."

When he was taken into Lothario's castle, the Amazon's traces multiplied. In a woman's face portrayed in an English etching he thought he recognized her features; in a doctor's hands he thought he saw the bag of the elderly surgeon who had treated him in the woods. During his first night in the castle, in the prophetic moments that precede dawn, the Amazon appeared to him in a dream. Twice she saved Felix from the mortal dangers of water and fire; then she grasped Wilhelm by the hand and led him along a garden's alleys and flower beds where he had played in his childhood. Thus, by means of the dream's vague shadows, the Amazon indicated her double maternal function—Felix's adoptive mother and Wilhelm's guide, guardian angel and female image.

A few days later Wilhelm and Felix left Lothario's castle. They departed at dawn, the weather serene and cold; and night had already fallen when the coach halted with a clatter in the courtyard of a large, unknown palace. Two servants holding torches come to meet them. Wilhelm picked up the sleeping Felix in his arms, entered the house, and found himself in the most severe, majestic, and harmonious place he had ever seen. A dazzling lantern illuminated a large neoclassical staircase divided into two ramps; statues and busts stood on pedestals and filled niches. As he mounted the stairs, Wilhelm recognized some works of art from his grandfather's collection. With even greater amazement, he saw in the antechamber the painting that had fascinated his childhood. Right before his eyes, just as twenty years ago, the king's son was being consumed by his love for the princess. . . . Now he had arrived: the road that led to the culmination of existence had brought him back to his youthful treasures; and Clorinda, "his father's bride," awaited him in a room close by.

"There, behind a lamp shade, which cast a shadow on her, sat a young lady reading. 'Oh that it were she!' said Wilhelm to himself at this decisive moment. He set down the boy, who seemed to be awakening, and was about to approach her, when the child, drunk with sleep, sank to the floor. Then the young woman rose and came to him. It was the Amazon! He could not restrain himself, fell to his knees, and cried, 'It is she!' He seized her hand, and kissed it with unbounded rapture. The child was stretched out on the carpet between them, sleeping softly" (513: 13–31).

In the harmonious neoclassical palace, Wilhelm again encounters Mignon, dressed in a long white gown, like an angelic spirit about to leave the earth. And when the terrible palpitations of her heart cease and she falls with a cry at Natalia's feet, Wilhelm is left silent and deeply perturbed. Theresa vainly speaks to him, embraces him, clasps him to her breast—"only the images of Mignon and Natalia flitted like shadows before his imagination" (545: 5–7).

Days go by and Wilhelm must admit to himself that he loves Natalia with all the strength of his being. If he closed his eyes, behind the tightly closed lids he found her figure, which had already filled his romantic imagination. If he opened them, he saw her shine refulgently before all things, like the reflection which a dazzling image leaves on the retina. How could he still live without her, how could he look with joy at the sun, the thousand spectacles of nature, other human beings, any good thing of the earth, if she did not accompany him? But he dared not approach Natalia. She seemed more unattainable than the character in a poem or the heroine of a painting; and he thought his love would not be reciprocated.

He could not find peace. While the others slept he roamed restlessly through the large house, attracted and repelled by the works of art. At times he felt his life was that of a disembodied, vagrant spirit. All the threads of his existence had led here, to confront his grandfather's statues and paintings, to confront Clorinda and "his father's bride." Destiny, the blacksmith, had hammered out the ring of his life, and now the ring refused to close. "It is painful," he thought, "to be always searching, but it is far more painful to have found and to be obliged to leave it. What can I now ask of the world? And where can I continue to search? What region, what city possesses such a treasure as this? And must I travel on, only to find things that are more and more tenuous! So life, then, is like a racetrack, where we must turn back immediately and swiftly as soon as we have touched the finish line? And are the good and excellent like a fixed, motionless goal, from which we must flee on swift horses the instant we think we have attained it?" (569: 2–13.)

But no longer would Wilhelm wander through the countries of the world, shunning the barely glimpsed goal. A few days later, after a dizzying succession of *coups de théâtre* Wilhelm and Natalia are convinced that Felix has drunk a mortal dose of poison. "The night passed sleepless and full of anguish for all. Felix would not leave Natalia. Wilhelm sat before her on a stool; he had the boy's feet on his lap, while his head and breast were resting on hers. Thus did they divide the sweet burden and painful anxiety, remaining till day broke in this sad, uncomfortable position. Natalia had given her hand to Wilhelm; they did not say a word; they looked at the child, and then at one another" (602: 31–39; 603: 4–6). The next morning, Felix was safe. During the night, Natalia had adopted him as her child.

A few days later, Friedrich, madcap younger brother of Lothario and Natalia, revealed that something equally decisive had taken place in Wilhelm's heart that night. With all the palace guests gathered in the main hall, he began mocking Wilhelm and Natalia; then he opened the doors and pointed into the antechamber at the painting that depicted the story of Antiochus and Stratonice. "What call you that king?" he cried. "What call you that goat-beard there with the crown on, seated at the foot of the bed and so distraught over his sick son? How call you the beauty who enters, and in her modest, roguish eyes, brings at once poison and antidote?" (606: 1–8.)

Friedrich's words reveal that in the painting, where we thought only the figures of Antiochus and Stratonice were represented, there was another figure: the old king, Seleucus, seated at his son's feet. But at the same time his words put in a wholly different light the relationship between Wilhelm and the characters of the painting, symbol of his destiny. In the *Lehrjahre's* first book, Wilhelm identified his childhood aspirations with those of the prince made ill by incestuous love, and forced to hide in his heart the fire of his instincts (70: 4–6, 23–25). In the fourth book, when he lay wounded, he also shared the thoughts of the prince, while Stratonice's face was confused with that of Natalia (235: 27–28). In the eighth book, if we wish to believe Friedrich's clownish interpretation, Wilhelm was no longer like Antiochus: after a night of sleeplessness and terror he had become like the old king with the white beard, who exhausts himself with worry beside his son's bed.

Lothario and Natalia's young brother had understood what had happened in the depths of Wilhelm's heart. During the anxious hours of that night, while Wilhelm held the sleeping Felix on his lap and clasped Natalia's hand, the incestuous emotion tying him to her, the incarnation of his female archetype, had been purified; and pain had consecrated him as the father. So his spirit was now wholly free from all taint. No inner or celestial prohibition could prevent him from marrying "the noble, tranquil" Clorinda, "the lovely, compassionate princess," who had come down into the world out of love of him.

As we are about to reach the last pages of the *Lehrjahre*, we may imagine that the mysterious, ironic destiny—which has pulled the strings of the long series of events—will appear solemnly before us to explain the remote and immediate causes, the true and apparent significance of everything that has happened in the book. But destiny does not like to show men its true lineaments, its noble or dwarfed figure, its regal or scurrilous gestures. Instead, it entrusts Friedrich with the task of concluding Wilhelm's story, confirming once again its predilection for "gnomes" (558: 7), gay, wild, mercurial sprits and coarse clowns. Naturally, Friedrich hastens to obey. He comprehends the symbolical significance of the painting and furnishes its final interpretation. He eavesdrops at doors, reveals secret oaths; like a "wizard," he discovers the most precious of all the treasures (608: 31–32); through his "own strength and will," but also "by the grace of God," he grants Natalia's hand in marriage to Wilhelm. Finally, assisted by his recent Biblical scholarship and historical erudition, he sums up Wilhelm Meister's experiences in a few words: "I can not help but laugh when I look at you: to my mind you resemble Saul, the son of Kish, who went out to seek his father's asses and found a kingdom" (610: 6–9).

Saul had not "found" a kingdom. Without doing anything to deserve it, God had chosen him from among his servants, had filled him with the strength of his spirit; and had anointed him prince of Israel (I Samuel 9–10). In the same way, Wilhelm had not obtained Natalia as a prize for his deeds, for even to the last instant these remain—like those of every man—blundering, inappropriate, and confused. "Natalia," he rightly says, "is a happiness that I do not merit" (610: 12). What many of us think we conquer is therefore a grace, a "celestial fruit of gold," a gift that comes to us "long and sagaciously prepared" by the prudent and loving hands of the gods (*Iphigenie*, 1103–1104, 1111).

If we ask why the gods who rule the *Lehrjahre* have decided to reward Wilhelm rather than another, nothing remains for us but to recall a maxim from the Gospel of St. Matthew: "To he who has will be given in superabundance; to he who has not, from him will be taken even that which he has" (Matthew 13: 12). When he was born Wilhelm had received by chance an archetype, a luminous and divine germ; and now it was "given" to him in superabundance. But the Gospel of Luke adds: "To he who has been given much, of him will much be asked; and to him whom much has been entrusted, even more will be asked" (Luke 12: 48). If the pure desire of good, if honest disquietude, if tormenting scruples, if noble searching and not finding had not been the moving cause of Wilhelm's spirit—certainly the clownish messenger of grace would not have granted him Natalia, the gift long and sagaciously prepared by the hands of heaven.

The
Guardians
of the Tower

❧ 〜❖〜 ◦

V

When the visitor caught sight of Lothario's castle from the top of the mountain, he received a curious impression. There, amid the fruit trees and vegetables, stretched an extravagant labyrinth of rock. Around an irregular castle, bristling with towers and pinnacles, someone had constructed more modern buildings, some close by and others at a certain distance, linking them together with a network of arcades and covered passageways. Within the castle's walls, this impression of a bizarre atmosphere and mystery became even more intense. Certain rooms were always locked; certain strange arcades led off to God knows where; while an ancient, heavy iron door prevented one from reaching the tallest tower.

In this medieval tower and these hermetically sealed rooms gathered the members of a Masonic lodge, the "Society of the Tower." Several years before, it had been founded by a group of young noblemen, among whom were Jarno and Lothario. At that time, with the natural passion of youth for all that is secret, the young initiates would solemnly hold their ceremonies in a deconsecrated chapel. As if they were members of a mystical guild of artisans, they took the titles of "apprentice," "aide," and "master," and gathered the flower of their wisdom in enigmatic sentences. Some years later, the members of the tower came to know a mysterious abbé, probably Catholic and of French origin (419: 15; 421: 33), who belonged to a very powerful secret association. Under his guidance, the society was transformed and spread throughout Europe and into Russia and America, as a great society of reform. By now the youthful inclinations—those solemn ceremonies, those enigmatic sentences, that eccentric atmosphere—have become almost ludicrous relics; but the Abbé and his friends preserve them, ironically concealing their new activities behind this theatrical veil.

The masters and guardians of the tower, like a group of dilettante biographers, enjoy writing the lives, indeed the *Lehrjahre* of each of their disciples; and they collect a real archive of biographies on the wire-netted shelves of the desanctified chapel. When Wilhelm was admitted to consult the parchment containing his *Lehrjahre*, "he found the minutely detailed story of his life, delineated in large, sure strokes; neither isolated incidents nor narrow sensations disturbed his view; the most loving general observations admonished him without shaming him; and for the first time, he saw his own image from the outside; not, indeed, a second self, as in a mirror, but another self, as in a portrait. We do not, it is true, recognize ourselves in every feature; but we are delighted that a thoughtful spirit has so understood us, that such great gifts have been employed in representing us, and that an image of what we once were exists and may endure, when we ourselves are gone" (505: 10–12).

As for us, having read Wilhelm's *Lehrjahre* in Goethe's version, we ask ourselves whether the tower's guardians and messengers are really scrupulous biographers. Are they satisfied, like Plutarch, like Suetonius, to gather together the episodes of Wilhelm's life, to interpret and recount them honestly in their rolls of parchment? Something prompts us to be suspicious. The guardians of the tower do not confine themselves to watching over Wilhelm's journey. They also intervene in his life, disguised like the ancient gods when they visited men. They offer him advice, prevent him from marrying Theresa, and even go so far with their collaboration as to perform with him on the stage.

As if nothing could escape their knowledge, they know all their disciple's intentions, thoughts, and emotions; even those he dare not reveal to himself. Jarno, for example, knows that Wilhelm has written a long speech to shame Lothario (433: 6–9). During the initiation ceremony, the voice of the "king of Denmark" responds to the tormented doubts Wilhelm is silently addressing to himself (495: 26). Many members of the tower intuitively guess that their pupil's deepest aspirations center around the painting of the "king's son" (70: 3; 495: 20; 601: 1 ff.). But that is not all. If we follow the plot of the *Lehrjahre* closely, we often suspect that they have provoked events we had ascribed to chance. We do not know precisely which ones, since they operate so completely in the dark. Although the Abbé and Jarno are sometimes singularly without scruples, I do not wish to maintain that they push their cynicism so far as to pay the bandits who wound Wilhelm in the clearing so that he will be succored by Natalia. But it is probable that they were the ones who invited Wilhelm's actors to the castle. It is also they who induced old Barbara to conceal Felix's existence from him until the moment when they consider him worthy of calling himself a father.

Shut up in the tower and in their fantastic labyrinths, the Abbé and his friends are therefore not satisfied to write minutely detailed, honest pedagogic biographies. If they possess such a talent as psychological omniscience, if they know how to invent incidents and transform them into dramatic events—what then distinguishes them from the world's great novelists? Both dispose of a power that can be compared only with that of God the Creator. Of the two, the guardians of the tower are much closer to the creative force of God, for the protagonist of the novel they are writing lives, has a body, a voice, moves about before them. No novelist has ever succeeded in looking at the face of Madame Marneffe or Andrei Bolkonski. Thus, we can imagine we know, incarnated in a group of characters, the wise and ironic narrative power that constructs the *Lehrjahre.* The Abbé is nobody else but the novelist Goethe; and the roll of parchment he keeps in the chapel's covered shelves simply recounts Wilhelm Meister's *Lehrjahre.*

Why has Goethe entrusted his power as a narrator to precisely these meddling and witty Masons? While they talk, travel, draw up plans, the Abbé, his brother, Lothario, Jarno, and all the other acolytes of the tower are, so to speak, "double" characters. Behind each of their deeds, there vaguely transpires the deeds of a great invisible character: destiny, the omnipotent lord of the world, the sovereign of gods and novelists, who has entrusted them with the task of representing him on the stage of the *Lehrjahre.* But destiny cannot entrust all the indefinite expressions of his countenance, all the actions that he likes to perform, all the facets of his multiform figure to a small group of men. In the *Lehrjahre,* he does not delegate all of his powers: he keeps for himself the terrifying flashes and the tenebrous, tragic, and incomprehensible acts that reveal his omnipotence. He asks the guardians of the tower to portray only his most amiable aspect, which men know less well. These include the strange sympathy and benevolence with which he contemplates our efforts from the summit of his sky; the theatrical, ironic, and mystificatory atmosphere behind which he prepares his portentous machinations.

With the scrupulousness and precision of consummate executants, the tower's messengers carry out their task. Just as destiny prefers traveling incognito and is unwilling to confide in the incompetent eyes of the groundlings, the messengers are also hidden behind a cloud of discretion. Some of them, such as the "unknown" or the stranger of the first book (68: 21; 68: 26; 494: 21), conceals his existence right up to the end of the *Lehrjahre.* The Abbé's life is shrouded in the most profound secrecy; we never succeed in discovering his name. His twin brother, a trifle taller than he, wears or wore the clothes of a Lutheran minister (119: 5; 421: 32; 494: 34; 551: 30–32); although nobody can exclude the possibility that the Abbé impersonates two different roles at the same time.[1] The plots which they prepare are infinitely complicated: their extremely mysterious combinations, and a network of informers and spies more powerful than that of a modern secret service, permit them to be present, active, and hidden everywhere on earth (533: 4, 22; 547: 14–21).

As they appear on the stage of the *Lehrjahre* they are accompanied by a kind of formula. "On the boat stepped a handsome man, who by his dress and venerable expression *one could have taken* for an ecclesiastic." "Beside the count stood a gentleman, who *had the air of being* an officer, although he did not wear a uniform." "A strange man, who *was regarded as* a French ecclesiastic, although one did not know his origin exactly. . . . " "I do not know what change has taken place in him: in the past *I had taken him for* a Lutheran country pastor, today *he seems to me* rather a Catholic priest" (421: 30–33). (Italics added.) Thus none of the messengers of destiny possesses a definite character or profession: none of them "is" something certain. In exchange, they "seem," "are regarded as," "have the air of being," "leave the impression," "could be taken for" this person or another.

Unseizable and unattainable as destiny, the guardians of the tower are performing before our eyes a theatrical role. This is the sole certainty in their existence. Without having to read the manuals of playacting, without studying Diderot's *Paradoxe sur le comédien* or Stanislavsky's theories, they naturally possess all the qualities of great actors. They love mystification and deceit; they adore the surprising *mise-en-scène* and the shocking gesture which provoke cries of amazement from the audience; they alternate the coldest lines with the most emotional ones; they come swiftly from behind the wings or prompter's box and disappear with the same incomprehensible velocity: they descend from the height of the heavens or step from behind a bush, a boat, a hill, a wall, a palace, like the *deus ex machina* in Euripides's tragedies. So, at times—and we do not know whether it is to amuse us or to offer us some examples of perfect dramatic art—they step on stage, side by side with third-rate players like Melina or the finest craftsmen like Serlo. The Abbé's brother (or the Abbé himself) finds it amusing to improvise, together with Philine, Wilhelm, Laertes, and Melina. It is he who plays

GOETHE

the part of the king of Denmark, modulating his voice to resemble the voice of Wilhelm's father. At the end of the seventh book, all the members of the tower stage an illusionistic spectacle in the deconsecrated chapel; and early in the morning, with the assistance of the sun's blinding rays, they appear and disappear like phantoms, interweaving voices and pronouncements, as if they sought only to enchant their pupil's soul.

What gravity, what seriousness could we expect from a troupe of actors? Indeed, in the old tower, the sealed rooms and labyrinths where destiny resides, his messengers let themselves be guided by the spirit of playfulness. They pretend to imitate the attitudes of the supreme powers; but their truest passion is that of arranging or preventing marriages. At times it seems that they want to compete with the most fertile and improbable popular novelists of the eighteenth century. They whet our attention, excogitating ever more extraordinary events, positing insoluble enigmas, or suddenly interrupting their plots. From their conjurers' sleeves they pull miraculous coincidences, unsuspected recognition scenes, providential deaths. So, at the end, we wonder whether the Abbé is not a great imposter, a kind of new Cagliostro, capable of devising the most astounding deceptions, illusions, and hoaxes.[2]

The Abbé, like Cagliostro, never reveals his real intentions to his favorite pupil, as though he considered him a child to be deceived for his own good, or a puppet to be dangled from a string over a wooden stage. He follows Wilhelm's life; at its gravest moments he admonishes him and gives him the benefit of his wisdom, as enigmatic as the Sibyls. But it could be said that everything he does is designed to prevent Wilhelm from understanding his teachings. How could Wilhelm grasp these obscure revelations? He would have to study them with the same attention with which we study them today in Goethe's novel; and he would still not understand anything, for destiny's allusions must be intuited instantly, with a kind of miraculous sympathy.

As soon as they meet Wilhelm, before a glass of punch or strolling along the banks of a river, the tower's messengers start a discussion about destiny's qualities. Naturally, we imagine that they sing the praises of their master, and that they never tire of reminding Wilhelm of the misery of men, fragile as the leaves of the forest. But, in the *Lehrjahre*, destiny enjoys confusing us continually. Thus, in the first two books, he seems to entrust his defense to a young incompetent like Wilhelm Meister. Indeed, Wilhelm venerates the sublime force that "guides all things for our benefit" (71: 14). He exalts the pedagogic wisdom of destiny which adopts some men as his children, endows them

with a happy nature, and educates them in accordance with his principles (120: 25, 36–37; 121: 20–21).[3]

The sole preoccupation of the tower's messengers seems to be to
discredit their master, as if he were a ridiculous god from some oper-
etta. With a kind of hypocritical condescension, they admit that up
there above the clouds, destiny exists and they affirm that they have the
greatest veneration for his wisdom. But destiny—they add—does not
possess any power of his own; and he is forced to entrust his decisions
to such a clumsy and inept assistant as chance, who "rarely executes
exactly and precisely" what destiny has preordained (121: 26–28).

For example, destiny wishes one of his favorites to become a good
actor, and another a great painter. But this is where chance intervenes.
It leads the first man to a puppet theater where he waxes enthusiastic
over some performances in bad taste, which leave an indelible mark on
him. It has the second man grow up among filthy huts, stables, and
granaries, in a vulgar and impure world which stamps his temperament
forever. And so, two geniuses are stifled in their very cradles. As a result,
what terrible confusion reigns on this earth! Sovereign decisions that
nobody respects; impotent intelligence and clumsy, inept activity;
events that begin by revealing great significance and then produce only
foolishness (121: 33–34): a fabric in which a very swift shuttle knots,
entangles, or destroys a delicate warp that had seemed precise and
elegant.

As for men, since nowhere on earth does a providential and harmonious celestial force operate, they can trust only in their lucid reason and
their unconquerable will (71: 22). Like astute and knowing politicians,
they must accept the laws of necessity; limit their desires and dreams;
and so, according to the tower's messengers, succeed in utilizing and
directing the forces of chance. When they need help, instead of select-
ing a costly and useless teacher like destiny—as Wilhelm would have
preferred—it is much better that they trust in the precepts of a human
teacher. If men act thus, shaping their lives only with their hands—then
they will become gods of the earth, as God wanted them to be. They
will be kin to sculptors, who impose their intentions on soulless masses
of stone (71: 25; 72: 10).

Listening to the first messages from destiny, we expect to hear concepts so lofty and rare that man's intelligence is incapable of elaborating
them. What is offered us, however, is nothing but the modest wisdom
that men elaborate every day. Precisely the representatives of that
unfathomable force, which not even the gods can understand, proffer
the maxims of the most irreligious Enlightenment. Their speeches remind one of those of Pylades in *Iphigenie*, of Montecatino in *Tasso*, and

GOETHE

of Prometheus in *Pandora*. They recall all those who see in the universe only "the iron hand of necessity" (*Iphigenie*, 1680–1681), who value what men can obtain by "work, effort, gold, the sword, shrewdness, and perseverence" (*Tasso*, 2324–2328). They do not admit—at least, not willingly—that the gods enrich our lives with gifts "long and sagaciously prepared." Thus, for an instant, we fear that destiny, having now reached the threshold of the modern age, is about to declare its definitive bankruptcy.

But these sentences do not contain the tower's entire philosophy and pedagogy. Destiny is not a simplistic and dogmatic instructor, like human teachers who know only one educational system and propose it to all men and on all possible occasions. Versatile, eclectic, and colorful, his pedagogy tries to adapt itself to every psychological situation. At this moment, for example, the tower's messengers are trying to educate the young Wilhelm. When he praises the harmony of the universe and the providential significance of his life, how can they who know the archetypes of his spirit contradict him? But Wilhelm's excessive confidence in portents runs the risk of ruining him. Thus, on one hand, destiny reveals his ambiguous countenance to Wilhelm, showing him that no sign blesses his love for Mariane. But, at the same time, the messengers also furnish Wilhelm, as a provisory antidote, with precepts that can be of use to him during the first phase of his life.

On the second level of this pedagogic edifice, the anonymous messengers yield the floor to the Abbé, prince and inspirer of the tower's guardians, who dictates the sibylline sentences of the Letter of Instruction. Among all human deeds and works, how can one recognize—the Abbé asks himself—the excellent ones, so as to propose them to men as models? Virtuous actions, beautiful books and paintings, harmonious buildings all have this in common: They are encircled by darkness and do not like the rational light of theory around them. "No one knows what he is doing when he acts aright; but of what is wrong we are always conscious." "He who knows art by half is always mistaken and speaks much; he who possesses it fully, only loves to act and speaks rarely or tardily" (496: 30–32, 20–23). But even these virtuous acts, even the book or the painting touched by beauty, are merely the faulty and uncertain reflection of an ineffable perfection. The supreme value, *das Höchste, das Beste*, is the spirit we bear within ourselves; it cannot be expressed completely either with words or with works (496: 28–29). The principle underlying every incarnation—it is never completely incarnated; father of all forms—it refuses to assume a form.

Thus, while he pretends to be drawing the chart of a specific pedagogy, the Abbé pokes fun at any pedagogic attempt. He ridicules every ethical and esthetic system, every rule, every precept which tries like a futile net to imprison the force of our spirit. As for reason and human will so greatly exalted by the tower's first messengers, it would be absurd to imagine that he had much faith in their power. Like a true son of the Enlightenment, the Abbé believes only in the benign and loving wisdom of nature (or of destiny, Wilhelm would have said). For nature implants in us certain inclinations, certain faculties, certain innate instincts, which find in themselves the strength to fulfill themselves. Just so does Wilhelm's profound instinct for the images of Clorinda and of the princess fulfill itself (520: 19 ff.; 552: 36–38).

Like pilgrims sure of their goal, men must go down the same road Wilhelm has traveled, and which nature has silently pointed out to them. Some, like Natalia, find it immediately and follow it without difficulty; others, like Wilhelm, delay, turn their back, sometimes even get lost. But, though "he makes a mistake about his proper road" (520: 34–35), though he sips and empties to its last drop the bitter cup of his mistakes, he will end by recognizing and conquering them completely. At the close of his peregrinations, instead of finding a happiness that does not touch or concern him, like that so often proposed to us by human teachers, he will encounter the sole happiness that is truly his and will reach the place which in the depths of his soul he has always wanted to reach.

The true educator remains in the darkness, enclosed in his towers and labyrinths, tolerant and enigmatic as destiny. He lets his young pupil commit ever more serious mistakes, wander lost in a wilderness of fantasies and illusions, waste time playing like a child. Having faith in the beneficent signs of nature, he is satisfied to study the disposition and ineradicable instincts of the man he is protecting. When he wants to guide him he issues for a moment from his hiding place and points to the distant goal by indirect, almost incomprehensible hints—like those which, during Wilhelm's journey, remind him of his life's archetypes.

How different are the concepts of the tower's messengers from those of the Abbé! The first see in the universe a continual discord between the decisions of destiny and the activity of chance. For the Abbé, however, chance acts as destiny's most diligent pupil and assistant. While one secretly decides the fate of men, the other lifts the mask that covers destiny, looks it straight in the face, examines its expression, understands all the intentions of its lord and master. Then, faithfully applying these intentions, chance stages this or that event, exploiting the resources of its own inexhaustible imagination. Thus joined, great destiny and small chance, the wise lord and the bustling servant transform the earth into a perfect sphere, where order and the plentitude of significances reign.

Therefore the philosophy of destiny denies what it had at first affirmed, and affirms what it had at first denied. The panorama which we contemplate from the higher level of the tower contradicts completely the panorama we had glimpsed from the lower one. Below, the mistrust of the order of the universe; on high, faith in the gifts of the gods and the harmony of the universe. Up there, the image of man the artificer, who builds his life with his own hands; down here, the image of the man who is satisfied to collaborate humbly with his own destiny. Having attained the highest point of the tower, we hear from the Abbé's lips the same eulogy of destiny we had heard so long before from Wilhelm's. Youth, love, the enthusiastic uprush of the spirit contain, though confusedly, the light of truth; or, at least, one of its multiple refractions.

As Jarno observes, the majority of men are limited and unilateral. There is the man who knows only the instinct for the useful and the man who experiences the pleasures of art. One man travels to the ends of the world, another shuts himself up in his house. There is the man who studies the sacred books and another man has eyes for the vivacious immensity of nature. Not satisfied that he possesses a single faculty among many, each man esteems only his, and wants this faculty to be the only one to develop and spread among all the others (552: 6–8). If the profoundest desires of each of us were realized, mankind would be exclusively composed of businessmen or pious souls, carpenters or vagabonds, violinists or mineralogists.

But, suddenly, men are gripped by the desire to overcome these individual limitations. They would like at each instant to exercise the richness of their propensities, and to seize in everything the plentitude of the All (573: 18–20). Thus, for example, if they read Virgil's poetry, if they look at a painting by Titian, if they contemplate a Greek statue or attend a performance in the theater, they are not satisfied to admire the beauty of the images, the splendor of the colors, the harmony of the proportions, and the words coming from the stage. They savor a book —that is, a work of art—with the tongue and palate as if it were food, a work of nature. They want the painting to instruct them like a philosophical text, the play to improve customs, and the marble statue to imitate the softness of wax or the transparency of a veil. If things gave heed to their desires, the world would lose all its forms, which distinguish and hold it together. The sphere on which we live, which embraces the elements of fire and water, light air and heavy earth, which sees the harshest of mountains rise alongside green plains, burning deserts and lakes covered with mist—all would dissolve into an identical, "formless" material, a soft, tedious muck (573: 34 ff.).

Wilhelm Meisters Lehrjahre

From the height of the tower, the Abbé, almost unique among human beings, contemplates things with the benign, patient, impersonal gaze that the All lets fall on the details: the whole of mankind looking at the millions of individuals that compose it; and Goethe looking at the different parts of his own novel. His intelligence knows no limits; all human faculties and inclinations fill him with joy (552: 3–5). It comprehends the simple instinct of the craftsman and the feats of the most refined artist; the enterprises of merchant and warrior; fleeting, frivolous loves as well as ardent, durable passions. It encompasses the knowledge of material objects and the hopes and presentiments of a paradisial future. Helped by this capacity to understand, he can penetrate into each person's heart, seizing predispositions that still elude consciousness.

The specter of that false universality, though it misleads the human spirit, does not confuse his intelligence. Like a true representative of the All, he defends the distinctions of the universe: the forms created by nature, the forms men sculpt in marble or instill with the life of colors, words, and sounds; the institutions, rituals, and laws they model seriously or out of playfulness. In the course of his educational work he advises his disciples always to separate clearly their own faculties, and to form in themselves a host of organs independent from each other. So each of them will be able to enjoy food with his own palate; will be able to appreciate books and paintings with the most refined senses; and will, depending upon the occasion, obey either the laws that govern the states, or the laws of knowledge, or the principles that inhere in works of art (573: 6, 17–18).

When, in the last pages of the *Lehrjahre*, we live under the Abbé's influence, we have the feeling that we inhabit the edifice which the All, humanity's nature and spirit has prepared for us. A quiet light illuminates each room, each hallway, each corner, setting off sharply both persons and things. The book's various characters all try to attain the individual perfection of their innate form: Lothario pursues the ideals of action, Theresa governs house and garden, Natalia helps the poor, Jarno is cold and sarcastic, Wilhelm marries Natalia, and Friedrich marries Philine. But none of them is shut up in himself: all gather, come to agreement, find a point of understanding around the Abbé, as though around their own centers. If it is true, as the Letter of Instruction affirms, that "only all men form mankind, only all forces together compose the world" (552: 11–13), at the end of the *Lehrjahre*, beneath the Abbé's protection, we receive a clear presentiment of this.

Many may wonder whether the *Lehrjahre* might have reached its culmination with the figure of the Abbé. At first it seems difficult to doubt it. Yet the Abbé's pedagogy is not addressed to all human beings.

GOETHE

When he advises us to give in to our natural inclinations, he presupposes that Nature has watched over our birth and lovingly protects our course through life. As we have seen, this is the case with Wilhelm. But who can exclude the fact that Nature might lift its vexed gaze from our cradle, and that no succor might descend to sweeten the burden of misfortune? In this case, the Abbé's pedagogy is not only useless, it is downright harmful. What sense would there be in advising the harpist, who has sinned against the Law, or Mignon, victim of a sin which she has not committed, to drain the bitter cup of their mistakes to the last drop?

The edifice of which the Abbé is the master gathers within its walls only Nature's favorites, and an immense territory eludes its jurisdiction, which at first seemed illimitable. Beyond the tower's protection, in the inhospitable deserts of the world, where one labors in vain, live the innocent and guilty victims of destiny. There, weeping bitter tears and dying unjustly, live all those in whom the Abbé is not interested. Now and then he thinks of them with strange cruelty, as if they belonged to a mistaken part of the universe. Thus he excludes Mignon from his educational experiments and, with the emptiest of attentions, is preoccupied with the problem of embalming her body. As for the harpist, is not the Abbé the one who brings about, even though involuntarily, his ruination? But this cruelty should not surprise us. The tower's pedagogy is the pedagogy of destiny, which protects and educates its favorites while it abandons to their own resources all those whom it has condemned.

Thus the fate of Mignon, of the harpist, and of all the victims that are presented in the *Lehrjahre*, casts a troubling light on the wisdom of the tower and of those who rule the universe. Isolated in their labyrinths, the Abbé, Lothario, and Jarno do not ask questions, but continue to write and consult the elegant parchments of fortune's favorites. Meanwhile the readers of the *Lehrjahre* anxiously ask themselves whether some form of salvation does not shine on the luminous and cruel edifice of the All.

The Grandsons of Tantalus

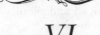

VI

When Zeus drove Tantalus, once his favorite, from Olympus and imprisoned him in the ancient shame of Tartarus, the Fates intoned a "savage hymn":

> Let the race of men stand
> In fear of the gods!
> Power they hold
> In eternal hands
> And they can use it
> As they see fit.
>
> He whom they lift up
> Should doubly fear them!
> On rocky peaks and clouds
> Chairs are made ready
> Around tables of gold.
>
> If a dispute breaks forth,
> The guests, abused and dishonored,
> Are hurled into the nocturnal depths
> And there await in vain,
> Fettered and in darkness,
> A just judgment.
>
> But they, the gods, remain
> Eternally feasting
> Around tables of gold.

And they stride from peak to peak:
While from the jaws of abysses
Wafts up to them the breath
Of stifled Titans,
Like the perfume of sacrifices,
A light mist.

These lords avert
Their blessing eyes
From entire lineages,
And refuse to see in the grandson
The once beloved and silently eloquent
Features of an ancestor.

Sometimes the gods, distracted or faithless, consider the race of men as they do their own. Then they let grace fall upon one of them and raise him to the banquets of Olympus. But if this person, overwhelmed by this sudden celestial favor, commits a sin whose guilt they too would bear (*Iphigenie auf Tauris,* 315 ff.), they cast him into the depths of the abyss.[1] Then, around the forehead of his sons and grandsons, they nail a strip of bronze, hiding from their eyes the moderation, wisdom, and patience which could have saved them. Thus is formed, in the sequence of the generations, the atrocious destiny of Tantalus: Pelops conquers Hippodamia by treachery and murder; Thyestes and Atreus kill their older brother, Thyestes dishonors Atreus, Atreus drives him out of the city, both murder their sons in turn; Clytemnestra and Aegisthus fling a net over Agamemnon's head, who falls in his own blood. Finally, renewing the ancient curse, the last, tender heir of Tantalus, Orestes, sacrifices Clytemnestra at the place where a pale mark recalls his father's murder.

In the solitude of the Tauris, when she is about to succumb to the curse on her lineage, Iphigenia sacrifices herself. She offers her life and that of Orestes in a holocaust, so that the benign face of the gods may triumph over their malign shadow. From the summit of the heavens, the new gods of light bless the prayer that rises from her pure heart like the flame of a sacrifice. They release men's anxious expectation in joy, scatter over the earth the wise superabundance of their gifts, mirroring on leaves wet with rain Iris's many-hued face. And yet this rainbow does not promise complete reconciliation; Iphigenia's victory is not definitive. Her sacrifice has not freed the world forever from the shadow of the divine face; a faltering voice intones, for each new generation, the terrible song of the Fates.

Wilhelm Meisters Lehrjahre

Just as in *Iphigenie auf Tauris*, so also in the *Lehrjahre* the "celestial powers" reveal an infinitely ambiguous figure. The destiny presiding over Wilhelm's life does not charge him with the sins he has committed, but rewards him for actions he has not performed. But in the world of the harpist and Mignon, the faces of the "celestial powers" undergo a change. As the harpist sings, they fling their victims on this earth, where heaviness and guilt reigns; they lead them into temptation and induce them to sin. When these wretched people moan with horror at what they have done, eating their bread amid tears and spending their anxious nights in lamentation, the celestial powers withhold the grace of forgiveness. Stricter than human judges, they demand revenge; they impute to the victims the crimes they have unknowingly committed, the crimes for which their fathers are responsible, and the crimes caused by heaven's deceptions. If the sufferer flees, they pursue him; if he begs for pity, they strew his path with malign signs and obstacles that nobody could overcome. Finally, when the wretch thinks he has reached safety, they propel him insidiously toward death (136: 25–32).

Old Marquis Cipriani was the new Tantalus of this dynasty of destiny's victims. Like his prototype, he sinned out of "disproportion." With a noble character, a proud and stately comportment, grandiose in both ideas and imagination, he insisted that his life obey the most severe and tyrannical principles. Inflexible toward himself, he expected others, too—the state, his neighbors, his children, his servants—to observe the laws he had established. He was never happy, for nothing happened as he had hoped. The houses he had built never equalled his fantasies, the fine lands he had acquired seemed to promise disappointments and sacrifices, his children did not follow the plans he had made for them.

Shut up in his manor house near Lake Maggiore, he spent the last years of his life in grim and bitter solitude. When it appeared that he was now traveling on the road to death, he was subjected once again to the passions of the senses and his wife had a child. Devoured by his maniacal susceptibility, he could not bear the possibility that someone might comment jokingly on his ardor as a belated lover. So he forced his wife to give birth in secret; the girl child, to whom he had given the name of Sperata, was taken into the country and a friend of the house adopted her as his daughter. A number of years passed; when the marquis, Marchioness Cipriani, and the adoptive father died, only the family's confessor remained aware of the secret.

Marquis Cipriani's third son, Augustin, lived in a monastery, where he gave himself up to the turbid pleasures of a "holy phantasmagoria" (581: 16). At times he enjoyed the loftiest, sweetest plenitude when it seemed to him he was being exalted to the third heaven. At other times he sank into the "desert of emptiness, annulment, and despair" (583: 18–19), and his soul, poisoned to its depths, doubted everything. A few years after his father's death, this mystical crisis seemed to be placated. With the excuse of teaching singing and the harp, Augustin gained admission into Sperata's house; he fell in love with her and generated a child in his sister's womb. He believed that "benign Nature" had healed his wounds, saving him from perdition and leading him to the arms of that "heavenly girl," with whom for the first time he had experienced the "vivid, true, indestructible pleasures of pure love" (583: 31–32).

No one had healed Augustin's old wounds. As often happens with neurotics, the illness had only changed its outward aspect. A new, more powerful, perhaps more insidious poison was finding its way into him and corroding the fibers of his spirit. With the same fury, the same ecstasy, the same savage restlessness that had propelled him into the deserts of exaltation and mystical despair, he now adored Nature, its charms and its teachings. While, in the past, he had cursed life, now he blessed it frantically—like a Dionysian and lonely *Stürmer*, one of those unfortunate and obstinate young men whom Goethe had known at the time of *Werther*.

When the confessor revealed to him that Sperata was his sister, Augustin tried to deny what he considered "an incredible fable," a "frightful specter" (582: 24, 27). Then, persuaded of its truth, he kept staring insistently at the sin he had involuntarily committed. With all his hysterical pathos, he attacked the moldering parchment rolls, in which men enclose their absurd ordinances, and also the fires of hell and purgatory, which seek to consume the joy of pure love. The only true law of the universe is written—he proclaimed—in the pages of Nature, which protects the cypress trees, the myrtle's tender flowers, the espaliers of lemons and oranges, and the infinite passion of love. "When Nature abhors, she speaks it aloud; the creature that shall not be, is not produced; the creature that lives with a false life, is soon destroyed. Sterility, painful existence, premature destruction, these are the fruits, these are the signs of her severity." But when has Nature ever condemned incest? "Look at the lilies: do not husband and wife shoot forth on the same stalk? Does not the flower which bore them hold them both? And is not the lily the very image of innocence, and its fraternal union fruitful?" (584: 10–18.)

We cannot decide whether Augustin uses this image unconsciously, swept away by the tempest of his lyricism; or whether he adopts it with allusive intent. But Goethe certainly leaves it here, partly hidden and partly obvious, so that we may observe it attentively, analyze it in its separate parts, and compare it with the images of all the other flowers, of all the other symbolic stones in his novel. This "lily of innocence" was not born in the fields of the earth; but rather in the books of alchemy, in which Paracelsus and Starkey call the lily "the most precious treasure," "the noblest thing," the "greatest pearl" of the universe—the *lapis philosophorum,* the philosopher's stone. Like the *lapis,* the lily is white, exquisitely elegant and luminous; like the *lapis,* it unites the qualities of the two sexes and around it hovers the memory of incest between brother and sister.[2]

Thus the motif of the *lapis,* which accompanies Wilhelm's life as a sign of election and perfection, surfaces in this distant territory of the *Lehrjahre.*[3] This reappearance is not by chance; for Augustin, son of the Lombard marquis, reminds us of Wilhelm, the son of the German burgher, like an older brother. The love that pushes him into Sperata's innocent arms is as ardent as that which inhabited Wilhelm's twenty-year-old heart. The words he prefers, the images that fall most easily from his lips—"the noblest instincts," "the loftiest, sweetest plenitude of phantasmagoria," "These horrid dregs of the cup, so alluring at the brim," "the breast of a heavenly girl," the "vivid, true, indestructible pleasures of true love" (583: 12, 17, 21–22, 26, 31–32)—remind us of the style of young Wilhelm's long letters and fluvial speeches, so drenched in romantic lyricism.

But everything is turned upside down, everything is distorted and contaminated; for, leaving the serene plains where Nature's favorites live, we have entered the steep, rocky, wild regions where the sons and grandsons of Tantalus gather. Augustin is a dark shadow, a rhetorical caricature of his German brother, and the style of his speeches is alien to the soft, abundant, dulcet grace of Wilhelm's prose. Absolute love, which guides one youth to the sublime felicity of life, hurls the other into misfortune and horror. Whereas Natalia is a "saint" enhaloed by light (228: 29), Sperata, the "heavenly girl" adored by Augustin, is the dark saint venerated by superstition (592).

With strange ubiquity, the symbolic theme of the *lapis* is hidden in opposed places of the *Lehrjahre.* It is found where light reigns and where darkness triumphs, among lives that arouse the favor of the gods and lives that excite their anger. This ubiquity of images may surprise many readers of the *Lehrjahre,* who begin to experience that dizziness, that confusion of horizons and points of view which Goethe's books are so adept at suggesting. But, this time, all is simple—or almost simple. Also in the verses of *Hermann und Dorothea* a single image expresses two opposed aspects of the world. The burning briar and the cloud of fire, both of which hide the face of the Lord; the gift of tongues, which

GOETHE

the Holy Ghost confers on the Apostles; the end of time, which announces the advent of the Son of man—these confide to us at one and the same time the supreme revelations of God and the infernal revelations of the French Revolution.

The identical symbolic event is repeated in the pages of the *Lehrjahre* and on the streets of Paris. While Wilhelm's love for Natalia casts off its incestuous aura, Augustin, blinded by the gods, generates a child in his sister's womb. While God does not possess "a city but an empire, not an empire but a world, not a world but worlds," the leaders of the Revolution embody the kingdom of God, so long dreamed of by men, in the mediocre places of this earth. Both Augustin and the French revolutionists do not know how to preserve the signs of perfection in their memories. They cannot transmute them as hopes, Utopian images, distant perspective lines capable of guiding them—not by human merit but by the grace of God—all the way to the fulfillment of their dreams. Overwhelmed by an identical derangement, they try to possess and realize them; and so God shows his fiery face, the world plunges into Night and Chaos, and love generates monsters.[4]

By committing incest, Augustin violated both human and divine laws. But he did not know that Sperata is his sister; he approached her not knowing the prohibition; and earthly judges would have blamed the muddles produced by chance and his father's insane manias. Much less compassionate than human judges, destiny condemns him irredeemably. What does it matter to destiny that he was ignorant of his blood relationship? All sons of Tantalus, all victims of heaven are guilty of sins committed unawares; they are guilty even of thoughts which have visited them for an instant, and of confused dreams which have filled their minds during "nights full of anxiety."

If destiny were summoned as a witness before a supreme court of appeal, he could testify: "Just as once I tempted Oedipus by inducing him to kill his father and share his mother's bed, so now I have pushed Augustin into his sister's innocent arms. When the abominable, immense, irresistible cloud of darkness was stretched over Oedipus's head, he did not invoke a human justification: with his eye sockets streaming with blood, he cried that he was the most criminal of men, the scourge of the universe. But Augustin did not want to admit his sin; he has justified it by attacking, like the lowest of outcasts, the divine and human laws of the universe. . . ."

After killing his mother, Orestes, another grandson of Tantalus, left Mycenae. The spirits of revenge pursued him, like a pack of wild dogs sniffing his blood-drenched tracks, through all of Greece. Vertigo enveloped his brow, an inextinguishable fire accompanied him; for the memory of the crime, "the eternal consideration of the perpetrated deed" (*Iphigenie auf Tauris*, 1064) never left his mind. Finally he reached the banks of the Tauris, where he met Iphigenia. When his mind seemed to be overcome by the final despair, he was visited by the grace of sleep, which descended on him "like pure felicity, not besought, not supplicated" (IV, 452: 32–33); he drank the cool waters of Lethe, lying down in abandon at the spring of oblivion. At that moment the curse is ended; and the Eumenides flee into the Tartarus, closing behind them the great bronze doors with a crash of fading thunder.

Like Orestes, Augustin could not bear the burden of sin; remorse tortured him and the old, never extinguished religious impressions of his youth, his "Furies," once again master his soul. Forcibly imprisoned in a monastery, he spent a few years of apparent calm, singing and playing the harp. Then he fled, and reached the chapel where Sperata's corpse was laid out—white, diaphanous, miraculously intact. He looked at her furtively and grasped her hand not realizing she was dead. At last he left the banks of Lake Maggiore forever and reached Germany by traversing the Grisons, as if he sought to cancel every vestige of his past.

But Augustin never knew the pure felicity of sleep and the cool joys of forgetfulness. Although he had canceled the story of his life from his consciousness and his love for Sperata reemerged only confusedly in his memory, the past, "the eternal consideration of the perpetrated deed," continued to imprison him in his sick mind. His flights, his long wanderings over mountains and valleys had not driven the savage laughter of the Furies from his path. Scarcely did he try to rest than the spirits of revenge gathered around his bed. Among his nightmares there appeared a child, threatening him with a naked knife. It seemed to him that his very presence frightened happiness—even the light of the sun, when it rose above his head, tinged the pure horizon with flames.

Like all victims of the Furies, wherever he might go he remained a "stranger." The variety of the seasons had been expunged forever from the world; no terrestrial sight attracted his spirit. Completely thrown back on himself, he stared only at his empty ego, which seemed to him a bottomless, immeasurable abyss. He could see "nothing else before him, nothing else behind him but an infinite night, where one found oneself immersed in the most frightful solitude" (436: 24–26). There, neither persons nor words appeared, nor the comforting signs of time and space, high and low, before and after; nor the radiance of some known divinity. He felt no emotion, save that of his guilt—a distant, shapeless ghost.

Sometimes, overwhelmed by this dreadful indifference, he cried des-

GOETHE

perately: "Eternally! eternally!" But "this strange and incomprehensible word was clear and luminous compared to the darkness of his condition" (436: 31–34). What existence could be more painful? What horrors could vie with those experienced by his soul? And yet, if something seemed to convince him that reality existed, that friendship and love lived on the surface of the earth, that time and things changed—then, instead of running with open arms toward the world, he was overwhelmed by anguish; and he chased away the tempting sights, retreating into his void as into a precious refuge.

His face marked by pain and the imaginary weight of time, Augustin journeyed like a beggar through Germany's cities and towns. His appearance changed within a few years. When Wilhelm saw him for the first time, "his bald crown was encircled by a few gray hairs; and a pair of large blue eyes looked out softly from beneath his long white eyebrows. Beneath a nose of beautiful proportions hung a long white beard, which did not hide his loving lips; and a long, dark brown garment wrapped his slim body from neck to feet" (128: 3–9). He carried the harp that so many times had consoled his sorrow; and his voice, accompanying the now gay, now heartrending chords of the music, exalted the happiness of minstrels, the joys of friendship and of souls who meet again, the pomp of great lords, the audacity of knights, the comfort of wine.

When he picked up his harp, Augustin forgot the frightful night of his soul and the mystical and Dionysian ecstasies of his youth. As though he inhabited a spirit of other times, he became akin to a Homeric singer or a wandering *Minnesänger*. He seemed one of the ancient poets, "masters, prophets, friends of gods and men" (83: 18–19), who bear in their hearts the flower of wisdom and look with clear eyes at the confused dream of life; who know the past and foretell the future. In those days poets flew above the world like birds, building their nests on the mountain tops. They lived at the courts of kings, at the tables of the rich, before the doors of lovers. They lived where everyone listened to them, shutting ears and souls to any other voice. "The hero listened to their songs, the conqueror of the world paid homage to the poet, for he felt that without him his prodigious existence would pass away like a tempestuous wind; the man in love wanted to hear of his longing, his multiple and harmonious pleasure, as only inspired lips can describe them; and even the rich man, if he looked with his own eyes at his wealth—his idols—found them less precious than when they appeared to him illuminated by the splendor of the spirit, which feels and exalts all the values of the world" (84: 2–19).

But who could resurrect those happy times? What bards, what *Min-*

nesänger could live in modern Germany? The harpist's voice resounded now in poor German taverns, before a few third-rate actors and a young, naïve bourgeois who thought he resembled the singer. That majestic white beard, that long, dark brown garment, that harp, the minstrel's entire symbolic arsenal, were the remembrance of something solemn and ancient, gone from the earth forever. In the evening, when the harpist returned to his miserable lodgings, the voice that had celebrated the happiness of minstrels and the joys of wine remembered "the bread bathed in tears," "the troubled nights spent weeping on his bed." It faltered, broke, mingled with his harp's plaintive sounds, revealing at what a high price a singer or *Minnesänger* had been reborn in eighteenth-century, bourgeois Germany.

Toward the end of the *Lehrjahre,* Augustin came under the tower's pedagogic influence. Lothario's doctor and a country minister became concerned about him; and they induced him to give harp lessons, work in the kitchen garden, read the newspapers, and distribute these activities according to a precise schedule. They tried in this way to prove to him that reality exists, and that his fate, his happiness, his talent as a poet were not, as he thought, exceptional but rather slight deviations from the natural course of things (346: 37–39). Under the guidance of these skilled educators, the harpist began to look for the first time outside his own ego and to accustom himself to live among human beings. He taught music to the boys with the patience of a true *maestro;* he ate the cabbages he had planted; and with great curiosity read the newspapers to learn what was happening in the world. But he would not cut his white beard or give up the dark brown cassock which had accompanied him in his wanderings. It was as if he wanted to preserve the funereal marks of his destiny and of his sacerdotal and poetic dignity.

Sometimes the terror of death would seize him again. One day he decided to put an end to his anguish—he would go to meet the one whom he feared. But at the very moment he stole a flask of liquid opium from the minister's pharmacy Augustin was cured. The possibility of ending his sorrows forever by drinking a few drops of poison gave him the strength to bear them; the everyday nearness of death brought him closer to life. Even if he had not forgotten his sin, now he possessed symbolically in that opium-filled flask—which he carried about with him like a talisman—the salutary immersion in sleep, the victory over the obsession of memory, the beatific death of the "I"—everything that had saved Orestes from the persecution of the Furies.

He believed he understood that his destiny was similar to that of all other human beings who work in the fields, buy and sell, raise a family, and conscientiously read the newspapers. Why should he still conserve

GOETHE

the fateful insignia of the poetic vocation? So he relinquished the white beard and the long garments and had his hair curled. Even the deep lines disappeared from his face, as though Nature herself wanted to bless the harpist's metamorphosis. When he reached Natalia's palace, he no longer seemed a Homeric singer or *Minnesänger,* or an inhabitant of Nullity and Darkness; but rather an elegant eighteenth-century gentleman traveling about the world bent on his own education. Wilhelm, seated near him in the main hall, looked at him for a long time without recognizing him.

This sensational *coup de théâtre* fails to convince us. How is it possible —we ask—that symbolic fetishes can take the place of lived experiences? That a few drops of opium kept in a glass flask can render useless the consolatory grace of sleep and forgetfulness? All the veneration and terror we felt before the "heavenly powers," the obscure destiny that persecutes the sons of Tantalus, are on the point of vanishing when we discover that all one needs is a mere talisman to fend off or delude the wrath of the gods.

But destiny had only prepared one of those small, terrible pranks it stages so willingly behind the backs of its victims. The tower's guardians and messengers had carried out—perhaps involuntarily—their master's instruction. The doctor had spoken of a "cure." But had the emissaries of destiny really cured the harpist? Or had they killed a sublime lyrical poet—something neither the precepts of destiny nor those of the tower could ever have fabricated—forcing him to plant cabbages, give music lessons, and read those newspapers which Goethe considered his own "most dangerous enemies"?

At the end, so that what had been written by the hand of heaven might be fully consummated, the most astute of destiny's servants intervenes: chance. When Augustin had arrived in Natalia's palace, he was given the room used by the Abbé, who had left in it somewhere, in a chest or on a table, the manuscript which recounted Augustin's life. Tantalus's last son read it, and shuddered as he recalled all that had floated confusedly in his memory: the life in the monastery, the act of incest, Sperata's death, the flight across the mountains. Seized by terror, he took out the flask of opium, poured it into a glass and brought it to his lips, but a feeling of revulsion swept over him and he set it down again. Soon after, Felix comes into possession of it. Convinced that he has caused the death of Wilhelm's son, Augustin cuts his throat with a razor, and when the doctor treats and bandages his wound, he tears off the bandage and dies in a pool of blood.

As Augustin abandoned our earth, no one pronounced over his grave those words of mournful regret that the guardians of the tower wrote so willingly on walls and parchment rolls. In Natalia's palace nobody remembered his name—as if he had never lived, had never sung of the happiness of poetry, the joys of love, the tears of the unhappy, the anguish of solitude. A few days of disquietude and disorder pass; then the Abbé and his friends resume their task of arranging marriages among those whom destiny has favored.

During the course of a children's party in Natalia's palace, Mignon puts on a long, light, white dress, a pair of large golden wings, and a golden sash. A diadem adorns her jet black locks and a lily flowers in her hand, as it does in Gabriel's when he appears before Mary. A strange grace accompanies her gestures, her words seem charged with an enigmatic significance; and Natalia believes for an instant that an angel from heaven has made its appearance before her. Who, then, is Mignon? A human creature like all others, merely accoutered as an angel? Or does some superior spark live in her weary limbs? Natalia's amazement is not unreasonable. During the party, Mignon frees herself from the shadows, burdens, and sorrows which during her life had stifled her, and her profound nature completely shines forth. That white dress, those wings, the lily are the "veil," the "outer envelope," the symbolical "appearance" of her heavenly nature (515: 31, 37).

Mignon's true country is not the earth but the luminous, pellucid ether. Up there, as she sings to the sound of her cittern, "heavenly creatures do not ask whether one is a man or a woman, and no garment, no drape covers the transfigured body" (516: 1–4). Is heaven therefore populated by the same androgynous figures that, according to the Talmud and Böhme, inhabit the earthly paradise? It is enough for us to know that, in the angels' eternally youthful chorus, no one remembers the fateful division between the sexes, with which the decadence of creation and the history of the world began.

An unknown hand tears Mignon from this blessed state of innocence and flings her down to earth, in the impure body of the daughter of Augustin and Sperata. Perhaps as a belated kindness of the gods, the place where she falls is a sort of earthly paradise. Around her, on the banks of Lake Maggiore, lemon trees blossom, "golden oranges flare in the dark leafage," pomegranates redden on the branches; while a gentle wind, descending from an eternally blue sky, breathes over the myrtle and laurel. Immense cloisters, country manor houses, smiling villages, the scattered houses of fishermen cluster around a neoclassical villa, which rests its roof on tall columns and scintillates with grand halls in which motionless marble images stare at her with petrified eyes. At her back rise the Alps—misty, cloud-covered peaks from which rocks

GOETHE

and torrents plunge down, and caves, filled with gigantic crystals, in which the ancient, fabulous "race of dragons" lives. But not even in this earthly paradise can Mignon live freely. Even among "golden oranges" and ancient statues, the sin of Adam and the error of Babel impose the division of the sexes and the multiplication of tongues.

Forced to assume a female body and to speak the language of humans, Mignon tries to preserve the signs of her heavenly origin. When the strolling players want to force her to wear women's clothes, she obstinately refuses to don them (207: 31; 237: 1); as if the masculine jacket and long boots were meant to recall her mythical sexual completeness. A vague atmosphere of the androgynous continues to accompany her on earth, too. Whoever sees her questions at first whether these picturesque clothes conceal the body of a boy or a girl (91: 22–23). Jarno, who likes to distinguish with the precise and limited acumen of reason, deprecates her precisely because she is an ambiguous, hybrid, hermaphroditic creature (zwitterhaftes Geschöpf, 193: 30). So the prophecy that issued from Augustin's lips did not lie: "The fraternal union," the amorous encounter of two flowers on the same stalk, generates the white hermaphroditic flower, the lily, "the image of innocence." A new relationship draws closer together the opposed spheres in which Wilhelm and the grandsons of Tantalus live. Just as the harpist is Wilhelm's shadow, so the sign of the precious, androgynous lapis accompanies both the figure of Natalia, toward whom the incestuous ardor of Wilhelm's passion leaps out, and the figure of Mignon, the innocent fruit of fraternal incest.[5]

Of her heavenly origins Mignon preserves another, more significant memory, which nobody will ever succeed in taking from her and to which she entrusts the dolorous voice of her soul. One morning Wilhelm listens to her sing before the door of his room, accompanied by the enchanting sound of the cittern. The grace of the melody, the expression of Mignon's voice, now solemn and grandiose, now mysterious and gloomy, now full of nostalgia, now supplicating, now imperious, fascinates and troubles him deeply; but for him many words of the song remain obscure. So he calls her into his room, persuades her to repeat and explain the stanzas. He transcribes them into German, translating her stammered, broken words and bringing harmony into her disconnected phrases. But, as he writes, Wilhelm realizes that he is killing the powerful "originality" of Mignon's locutions. The firm logic of syntax, the precision of meanings, and the rigor of connections is destroying the "childlike innocence" of her expression. Thus *Kennst du das Land, wo die Zitronen blühen*—one of the most famous lyrics of universal literature—is only the pale, mediocre reflection of a sublime song no man has ever heard (145: 36–146: 7).

So in what language did Mignon sing that morning before the door of the inn? With what words did she try to express the nostalgia consuming her? Since Goethe informs us that when Mignon speaks she mixes up Italian, French, and German forms (110: 12), we can suppose that *"Kennst du das Land"* was originally a disconnected *impasto* of verbal fragments: a strange linguistic detritus. But the material sources of Mignon's "style" do not have great importance. As soon as the worn-out and degraded words of our languages reach her lips and mix with the touching sounds of the cittern, they overturn that network of relationships and combinations which forms every language's "system." Broken, jagged, disconnected, yet immensely expressive, these words reveal to us the profound voice of the soul before the intelligence interprets it and translates it into the language of men. They are a somber and effulgent glimmer of that "language of the spirits" in which, Goethe said, poets should express their great intuitions (E. June 20, 1851).

Some years later Mignon is also torn from her lemons, oranges, and noble, classic palaces, for which she continues to feel an irresistible nostalgia. A troupe of Gypsies and tumblers kidnap her, carrying her toward the frozen lands of the north. When Wilhelm meets her for the first time Mignon seems to be one of them. Her makeup barely permits one to see the brown color of her face; her long black hair is knotted in braids around her head; and a silk vest with Spanish-style sleeves and narrow, long pants cover her clumsy, childish body. While Pagliaccio entertains the spectators with his pranks and the tumblers perform gay somersaults, Mignon executes the strangest, most difficult, and laborious contortions; or dances with her eyes blindfolded, accompanied by the music of a violin, stepping among eggs laid out on a carpet.

Mignon hates the world of tumblers, tightrope walkers, and actors with whom she is forced to travel. Nor does she like the stages of theaters and the public squares where the others force her to display herself. When Wilhelm frees her from her slavery, she refuses, even for fun, to go on the stage, the triumphant milieu of the qualities she lacks —lightness of soul, gay sensuality, empty appearances, mimetic coldness, the formal decorum of gestures. Those leaps, contortions, and dances among the eggs, for others simply a trade, are for her the memory of a very ancient esoteric art. She can practice this only before Wilhelm, her soul's new companion, the "beloved," "father," and "master" whom she has miraculously encountered on her path.

Like other Goethean demons, like the Homunculus, the "boy charioteer," and Euphorion, Mignon is possessed by the desperate vertigo of lightness; and she would like to leave the rigid soil of the earth with a single push of her feet, a single beat of her wings. So she climbs up on

GOETHE

wardrobes, jumps from tree to tree, walks on the roofs of the houses, slides agilely between the rocks, as if she were trying to prepare herself for the definitive leap. But her demon brothers are more fortunate than Mignon. Homunculus has no body, a winged chariot transports the "boy charioteer" toward the brightness of the sky, Euphorion scarcely grazes the earth with his foot than he leaps like Antaeus toward the steps of space. Mignon remains miserably among us. No wingéd chariot saves her from this world's confused and savage phantoms; the earth weighs on her in an irremediable fashion. A kind of fatal torpor binds her limbs, and they cannot throw off their chains.[6]

On the surface of the earth, where time is measured by clocks, where men have names, reason or think they are reasoning, count their money, perform each day actions they believe to be useful—everything repels and offends the white, hermaphroditic lily. What can these human conventions mean to Mignon? In the place where she lives and continues ideally to live, intelligence dissolves into the indistinct life of the soul; time does not obey the beat of the clock. The person who falls from heaven like Mignon has no name or has only the name—ignominious perhaps—others impose on her. She has no concept of numbers, cannot subtract, multiply, and divide; she is incapable of counting the money spent and saved by men. If she tries to work, to sweep a room or make a bed, if she tries to learn the simplest notions, in short, if "she acts" as we act every day, everything becomes unbearably burdensome and difficult for her (98: 25–26; 106: 33; 107: 6; 262: 9; 489: 23–24).

She lives in the very deep shadows of the soul, enveloped in the silence of her own inwardness. She does not know herself, or suspect what desires consume her heart. That gay light of the spirit which permits her brother demons to sojourn among the world's creatures is not part of her. She does not know how to express herself. Only the stammering words of angelic language and the sounds of the cittern can manifest a part of her emotions. But when she tries to employ the signs to which we resort every day, what a useless, painful labor it is for her! No matter how much she forces herself, the words of our languages— the Italian of childhood, the French and German of her peregrinations —come distorted from her lips. The letters of our alphabets, which she painfully inscribes on paper, are twisted, uncertain and irregular (98: 30; 110: 11–13; 135: 22; 262: 9–10; 587: 1–2).

When Philine descends the stairs singing or sips a glass of champagne we are conquered by the ease of her movements and understand that naturalness is the grace of one who harbors no secrets and lives at peace with himself. But an angel or demon relegated to the earth—bound again to the earth—a creature who does not understand, who does not know how to act or express himself—cannot be "natural." So Mignon constructs for herself a strange ritual of poses and uniform signs: a private code of artificial or privileged gestures. To greet someone whom she knows but slightly, she puts her right hand on her heart, her left hand on her forehead, and executes a perfect bow; and she salutes Wilhelm by holding her hands crossed over her breast (98: 20; 110: 6). In the same way, Ottilie, the protagonist of the *Wahlverwandschaften*, joins her hands, lifts them high and carries them to her breast, when she must repel something that revolts her; when an emotion upsets her, her left cheek turns red and her right cheek grows pale (VI, 279–280; 473).

How should we interpret these rituals, which to some might seem grotesque? The demon incarnate, the imprisoned *lapis*, cannot reveal the dense tangle of emotions he bears in his soul. He allows only the tiniest part of his upheavals and feelings of tenderness to appear on the surface of his being. Even if his heart is deeply troubled, he speaks in dry, cold, impersonal tones; he does not laugh, does not sigh, does not lament or cry, and gesticulates in an almost automatic manner. But each of Mignon's staring looks, incomprehensible words, and always uniform gestures spread over her days a sublime gravity and fantastic solemnity, which permit the inhabitants of our world to catch a glimpse of a denizen of other worlds who has come down among them (98: 31; 116: 14–15; 146: 8; 283: 14; *Theatralische Sendung*, A. VIII, 682).

One day, in order to console Wilhelm's afflicted soul, Mignon performs one of the most difficult exercises of her repertory. She spreads a carpet on the floor and distributes some eggs on top of it. Then she binds her eyes and begins moving about, guided by the music of a violin, which in turn is accompanied by the striking of castanets. Light and precise, with strong, sure steps, now close together, now wide apart, making swift turns and at times even leaps, she glides among the eggs, without trampling on them or even grazing them. As he presents this scene, Goethe compares Mignon to a "mechanism, which someone has wound up" (*wie ein aufgezogenes Räderwerk*, 115: 34–35), and which advances as irresistibly as a clock (*unaufhaltsam wie ein Uhrwerk*, 116: 7). A few pages farther on, he compares a gesture of Mignon, who flings her arms around Wilhelm's neck, to a "spring" that retracts violently (143: 23–24).

In Goethe's books these expressions are not surprising. Shakespeare's characters resemble clocks, with dials and crystal cases that let us see the mechanism of wheels and springs that moves them (192: 26–30). At the end of the *Wanderjahre*, Makarie too, who like Mignon bears within the light of other worlds, is called "a living armillary sphere," a

GOETHE

"spiritual cogwheel," a cosmic "clock" that measures the course of the stars (VIII, 451: 11–16). When we compare them to human beings, so imprecise and inexact, heavenly creatures in contrast seem artificial constructions: clocks, mechanical dolls, holy automatons, wound up by an unknown hand and measuring the course of the stars, the pulse of time, the music of human and divine instruments.

If we look through the crystal case into the heart of Shakespeare's characters, if we contemplate Makarie's luminous, astral spirit, those wheels, those springs, those mechanisms, which move with such exquisite elegance, give us a presentiment of the mechanism of the spheres and the harmonies of universal music. Although she glides swiftly among the eggs, Mignon is only a poor, spoiled automaton, a sick clock. As she descended to earth, the machinery that moves her was severely damaged; and with the passage of time the damage became more and more serious. Indeed, toward the end of the *Lehrjahre* we constantly fear that it will stop with a sudden jerk or an infinitely painful crash.

Obscure emotions and desires consume the oil of her life like a flame. At the beginning she silently conceals them, but, since her nostalgia for something or someone remains unappeased, an hysterical anxiety compels her to twist threads in her hands, to fold and unfold handkerchiefs, to chew nervously on pieces of wood. If a violent emotion wounds her, a spasm shoots through her heart; it grows and spreads through her entire body in the form of convulsions. Her heart suddenly stops and her breast is burdened with a leaden weight; she can no longer breathe and her limbs lie broken on the ground, like those of a dead person. No sooner does life return to animate her than her heart's very rapid pulsations make her suffer; but finally the tremor is calmed and her rigid body revives, becomes soft again, and melts in a flood of tears.

When Natalia witnesses one of these heart attacks, she cannot repress a sharp movement of revulsion, as if a "worm" were twisting on the ground before her feet (524: 31). Natalia is not mistaken; there is something monstrous and repugnant in Mignon, as in all those whom the gods have afflicted with a sacred disease. She is a creature who refuses to choose a sex and who does not know how to speak our languages— the only ones that have been given us. She seems impeded and incomplete in her physical and intellectual development. In her body she confuses the mechanical perfection of automatons and the obscure nervous illnesses of men—how could she help but arouse our pity and our horror? Thus the *lapis*, born from the amorous encounter of a brother and sister, reveals to us its two antithetic faces. If we remember the heaven she once inhabited, Mignon appears to us as an angelic spirit, akin to those who do not wrap dresses or flowing garments around their purified bodies, a white and innocent lily, a soul who has caught a glimpse of the perfection of heavenly language and the harmony of the spheres. But if we remember the incest consummated on earth, the crime committed where oranges flare in the dark leafage, Mignon seems to us only a dark, monstrous creature, from whom gods and men turn their heads with a shudder of disgust and horror.[7]

Wearing Wilhelm's colors, gray and blue, Mignon accompanies him on his peregrinations. She lives with him in inns and the castle's deserted chambers; she cleans his room, combs his hair, brings him his breakfast, heals his wounds. If Wilhelm pursues "his sister, mother, fiancée, and bride" in the image of the Amazon, Mignon's devotion to Wilhelm is no less absolute. She waits on him like the most devoted of servants; she bathes his feet with her tears, just as the sinner sprinkled ointments on Christ's feet (225: 3–4; Luke 7: 37–38). She venerates him as the "father" and "protector" who will lead her back to the earthly paradise from which she has been driven; and she dedicates to him, as to the "beloved," the wealth of her unconscious amorous desires.

Living in Wilhelm's shadow, Mignon dreams of gathering in all the feelings of affection and the passions that once had made his heart beat wildly. Inspired by an infallible intuition, she induces Wilhelm to give her the only souvenirs he had preserved of Mariane; the few things that the fireplace's flames had not consumed—a pearl necklace and a scarf. It is as if she were indeed trying to guard and symbolically possess his past (80: 35; 222: 16–17; 356: 16–18). When Felix is in danger of dying in a fire, a mysterious voice beating in her heart and head reveals to her that the child is Wilhelm's son. From that moment on, she never leaves him alone; she plays with him, teaches him her songs, laboriously reads books to him, hugs him to her breast with the tender love of a mother.

As the intimacy of their common life grows, this silent love of servant and child no longer satisfies her barely budding heart. In the evening, when she says good night to Wilhelm, and in the morning when she brings breakfast to his room, Mignon squeezes his hand, clasps him in her arms, and kisses his cheek, mouth, arm, and shoulder with such ardor as to leave him upset and dismayed. After the first performance of *Hamlet*, excited by the wine she has drunk and by a kind of frantic hysteria, she decides to slip into Wilhelm's room and spend an innocent night in the arms of her "beloved," "protector," and "father." But she has barely mounted the stairs when she hears a rustling sound and sees Philine's white dress slip into Wilhelm's room. An unbearable pain assails her sick heart; violent jealousy is confused with the upsurge of an unknown desire, and terrible convulsions fling her—"like a worm"

GOETHE

—at Augustin's feet. The next morning, when she enters Wilhelm's room, "she seems to have grown taller overnight: she stands before him with so noble and solemn an air, and gazes so seriously into his eyes, that he cannot bear her look" (328: 26–33). After that night, Mignon no longer clasps Wilhelm in her arms, and if she shakes his hand or kisses him, she does it without any tenderness and with grave solemnity. Instead of calling him "master" or "father," she now calls him Meister, giving him a surname, like all reasonable and mediocre human beings.

As if that shock had transformed her, Mignon seems to emerge from the indistinctness in which she had lived. She acquires a melancholy serenity; she abandons her boy's attire; and she employs the language of men with more perspicacity, and on her lips flower sentences and opinions we were not used to hearing from her (488: 32–33, 36–37; 489: 23–24; 525: 30–33). The androgynous creature is about to enter the world of knowledge, language, and distinction—the world where we live. But this seals her fate. How can she live in a world so different from her own? She begins to fade away, turns pale and thin; and a short walk is enough to tire her—she who in the past climbed agilely among trees and walked over mountains. Wrapped in her long white dress, her black hair falling over her shoulders, she holds Felix in her lap and clasps him to her heart, like a celestial spirit who bids farewell to life forever.

Mignon's light is similar to that of the stones of the carbuncle, dear to alchemists, which "glitters in dark caves and with their soft, precious light sweetly vivify the mysterious shudders of the desolate night" (*Die natürliche Tochter*, 65–68). Who can see it, so hidden, enclosed in its cave full of horrors and darkness? Who can recognize its gleam behind the shadows that seem to envelop it? But if someone, like Wilhelm, knows how to turn his eyes from the world's splendors; if he frees his eyes of the murky clouds that close off men's horizons; if he lives together with the precious stone of the carbuncle,[8] protects it from offenses, guards it like a talisman, then the hidden light in the caves will light up his road as much as the star of day or stars of night.

Like a "tutelary spirit" (282: 31; 490: 7) Mignon watches over Wilhelm's life. She knows the road he must travel, the goal that awaits him at the end of his peregrinations—the obstacles, dangers, errors, and diversions that threaten him. Similar, at least in this, to the potentates of the tower, she bestows on him prophetic signs and warnings. When, for example, Wilhelm is about to sign the contract with Serlo, Mignon clutches his arm and tries to restrain his hand from the document that would have bound him to that theatrical world of fictions and games, gestures and appearances which she so profoundly fears and hates (293: 18; 172: 36).

When she dies, her last earthly gesture is even more eloquent. Just as Wilhelm and Natalia are leaving the "Hall of the Past," where the corpses of the dead and the symbols of life are gathered, Theresa arrives, flings herself into Wilhelm's arms and kisses him, swearing her eternal love. Mignon watches the scene. Overcome by jealousy, she suddenly puts her left hand on her heart, violently stretches out her right hand, and with a cry falls dead at Natalia's feet. If he had married Theresa, Wilhelm would have belonged to the world of reason and order, in which Mignon had never known how to live. While Natalia is his symbolic sister, the immaculate, perfect, and happy face of the *lapis*, Mignon is its imperfect and unhappy face, at once white and darkling. With her last gesture—falling dead at Natalia's feet—Mignon therefore tries to send Wilhelm to the arms of the heavenly sister who would protect him as another "tutelary spirit" (471: 23), illuminating his path with more radiance than the nocturnal light cast by the carbuncle stone.

Immediately after Mignon's death, Theresa comforts Wilhelm, who is seated in a corner, silent, lacking the courage to look at her. Theresa embraces him and promises to share his sorrows forever; but when Wilhelm feels her heart beat against his chest, he realizes that he does not love her: "In his spirit, all was deserted and empty; only the images of Mignon and Natalia flitted like shadows before his imagination" (545: 5–7). So Mignon's last act is not without an echo. A few days later, Augustin's suicide brings forever closer, before the sweet, dolorous weight of the sleeping Felix, Wilhelm's hand and Natalia's. Thus Mignon and the harpist, the two victims of destiny, have concluded their mission. As in an unconscious propitiatory sacrifice, they have immolated themselves so that at their expense Wilhelm's amorous dream can be fulfilled and the world's harmony safeguarded in the fate of him who helped and loved them.

Augustin and Mignon both abandon the earth for which they were not born. One lies we do not know where; the other, dressed in her angelic clothes, embalmed and with an appearance of life on her face, is buried in the Hall of the Past, among granite sphinxes, precious marbles, classical sarcophagi, and the voices of an invisible choir. But if from the profundity of their graves, we look once more at the tower and its labyrinths, how changed the majestic edifice of the All appears! None would cast doubt on the wisdom destiny inspires in the Abbé, the ironic universality of his look, his ability to intuit still confused traits, the elegance with which he grasps the world's diverse forms and brings them into accord. And yet, among the tower's messengers and guardians, no one possesses those pristine and inspired faculties that the gods

GOETHE

bestow on men. No one knows the language of the spirits and the gestures of transfigured bodies; no one plays the songs of the ancient singers on the harp; or immolates himself to safeguard the world's harmony.

In the *Lehrjahre* the supreme values are not in the line of destiny and its representatives. They move far above it, among the stars where Natalia lives, or they hide beneath the line of destiny, in the shadows of the world, among the unhappy, the victims and persecuted whom the Abbé's pedagogy will never succeed in curing. The values are in the lives of those who have experienced, like Christ, "abasement and poverty, mockery and scorn, shame and misery, pain and death" (VIII, 157: 11–12).

The Stars

VII

Close to the surface of the earth, where clouds, winds, and rains gather, the air is humid, heavy, and misty. But, if we ascend higher, it becomes progressively hotter and dry, until, suddenly, we reach a completely different region. Above the restless gusts of the air, though without mixing with them, runs very light ether, similar perhaps to purified air or transparent and subtle fire. This engendered and indestructible *quinta essentia,* on which the minds of classical philosophy pondered, flows with a uniform and tranquil momentum, like the Pontus's calm waves. It clasps all things in an avid embrace and forms the farthest confines of the earth.

On earth, we live in darkness. Night, tempests, storms, clouds, smoke, shadows hide the light from us, and a few sparks travel with difficulty down the cramped roads of our eyes. Up there, however, where the mobile ether triumphs, night never alternates with day; the clouds, smoke, and shadows dare not obfuscate the purity of the heavens. A thousand constellations draw their fixed orbits, five planets embroider their errant orbits in the ether's eternally serene and even splendor.

High up, around the Pole, revolve the two Bears. Between them is insinuated, like an impetuous river, the grim Dragon or Draco; its temples are marked by a double gleam, two beams issue from its eyes and a star glitters on its chin. Alongside Draco, Serpentarius clutches between his palms the Serpent twining around his body; and his feet press against the Scorpion's eyes and chest. Beneath the diaphragm of the Boötes shines Arcturus; Virgo holds a luminous ear of corn; Leo, or

GOETHE

the Great Lion, gives off a tremulous flame. Shaking its mane, the famous Centaur touches Andromeda's head with its belly, while a star tries to tie an eternal knot between the two constellations. The icy breath of the Eagle flays Perseus; Capricorn releases a gelidity from its powerful half-bestial body; the Raven flutters its lucent feathers. Near the tail of the Dog glides the ship Argo, which touches the banks of a river beneath Ariës and scaly Pisces.

Below the constellations, the five planets carry out their evolutions. The most distant from the earth, Saturn, cold, white, and windy, protects the regions of ice and snow, thunder, lightning and thunderbolts. Jupiter emanates a mild and salutary glow, and Mars glitters with a sinister redness. Beneath the sun revolves Venus, which rises before dawn—like another sun it hastens the coming of the day; and it shines after sunset, the moon's emulator. While Venus spreads over the earth its fecundating dews, protects births, fertilizations, germinations, the pleasures and pains of love, Mercury, like the wingéd god whose name it bears, travels across the sky, dominating the waves in our seas and oceans.

The stars of the sky are living creatures and have a soul, a mind, and senses like human beings. But what a great difference separates us from them! Our bodies, composed of water and earth, air and fire, nourished by heavy foods, dissolve within a few years and prevent us from knowing the truth and practicing the supreme virtues. The stars, on the contrary, belong to the blessed race of the gods; their bodies, immortal and immutable, pure and beautiful, are formed of the most subtle part of the ether and are fed by marine and terrestrial vapors. Their senses are extraordinarily acute; and their intelligence, devoid of passion, knows all the secrets of the universe, practices the virtues, and is alien to any sort of vice.

None of those casual events, those vain confusions, those capricious, headlong disorders, which disfigure the spaces under the moon, occur in the spaces of the ether. Beneath a very pure light, all is truth, Providence, order, necessity, constancy, and harmonious rhythm. The stars, fixed as well as wandering ones, continue to execute the circular orbit that the Demiurge established for them at the beginning of creation. The first stars move from east to west, never changing their routes; the second stars appear and disappear, advance and retreat, accelerate their course or slow it down, and now and then halt for a while. But all of the constellations and planets go back eternally over their own tracks, as in a cadenced dance, occupying at every hour of the day, every season of the year, the same point among the sky's embroideries.

As they revolve, the stars produce a sound. The highest and fastest orbit leaves behind it an acute, vibrant note; the lowest, a very deep echo; and all these tones together form an incredibly sweet music. Just as blacksmiths in their forges no longer hear the crash of their hammers; just as the inhabitants of Catadupa, where the Nile plunges down from very high mountains, are deprived of hearing by the enormous roar, so we on earth cannot hear this astral music. But if by chance we could hear it, what irresistible love, what impassioned desires would be born in us! Forgetting to nourish ourselves, we would no longer swallow the food and drink of mortal creatures. We would receive through our ears a nutriment of celestial chords, as if we were marked out for immortality.

When we leave this earth, those of us who have led a virtuous life will ascend to the scintillating whiteness of the Milky Way or will travel across the sky, dragging behind us a headdress of flames. Then we shall freely contemplate the stars and the order of the universe. From that vantage point the Earth will seem to us a cramped sphere—for even now a few days suffice, when a good wind swells the sails, to take us from the ports of Spain to the most distant shores of India. It will seem to us puny, desolate, covered by the sea and vast deserted spaces; burned by the sun and immobilized by ice; and so who could look without smiling at the precious mosaics of the rich, their arcades, ceilings in which ivory gleams, and water streams through their houses?

Even during the course of this life we can contemplate the stars. What does it matter where we live? Whether it be in Rome or Corsica, among the savage Scythians, where the Achaeans built their cities, or in Persia? Wherever we set our restless feet, our gaze travels the same distance to reach the sky and sees with the selfsame joy the uninterrupted spectacles, the admirable festivals and choruses offered us by the architect of the cosmos. At the start our minds are disturbed and our thoughts are confused. But gradually we slough off the errors, stains, and disturbances of becoming. With the mind's eye we follow the pure periodical movements, the exact circular revolutions of the celestial intelligence, trying to reproduce them in the movements of our thought. Thus, while still alive, hidden in a body made of water and earth, pilgrims or exiles, we transform ourselves into stars. Beatifically and serenely we converse with the gods.[1]

Like Plato, Aristotle and Seneca, Lucretius and Aratus, Goethe gladly raised his eyes to the realm of the ether, where the stars, always equal to themselves, mark the hour and day (VIII, 119: 30–33), and "the sun, according to ancient custom, emulates the song of its brother-spheres" (*Faust*, 243–244). Like Cicero, he imagined that the "spirit of the world" summoned to itself, after death, the entelechies of the most excellent men, to whom it entrusted ever new activities (March 19, 1827). Some of them, such as Wieland, participated in the pleasures of the gods, and crossed the sky in the form of a star of the first magnitude, spreading around itself the serene restorative power of its light; while Euphorion rose in the sky like a brilliant comet.

Also on earth, Goethe discovered some rays of the ethereal stellar substance. But he sought it in vain among men, for they shed blood, triumph by the use of force and cunning, conquer wealth, and administer states. Men fling themselves frantically on all present and particular things, act or think they act, command or think they command; and they lose sight of the loftiest aim of life: harmony with themselves (*Iphigenie*, 1829 ff., 2064 ff., 2142–2145; *Tasso*, 1024 ff.; VII, 452: 31–33; VI, 245: 32–34). If he wanted to find an astral sign, a trace of the imprint of the rhythm of the universe, Goethe had to look in that calm female world, which he had represented for the first time in *Iphigenie auf Tauris*.

Some of these women watch over the sanctuaries of the gods in distant lands; others live in aristocratic castles; or run the kitchen, wine cellar, and small family garden in bourgeois houses, planting and harvesting, saving and spending. Some of them cluster around the knees of the Mater Gloriosa; some, finally, live in Weimar, akin to the Pole Star that weaves above our heads an eternally living crown. All these women, wherever they might live, maintain the order and decorum of the universe; they protect the delicate network of relationships that keeps the world united. In addition, they calm overexcited spirits, conciliate separate spirits in a single music; and they quietly travel the orbit of their existence, like stars that regularly traverse the sky and preside over day and night (*Tasso*, 773–776; VII, 453: 6–13; VI, 245: 35–38).

The major star of the female constellation of the *Lehrjahre* is the "noble, heroic Clorinda," dreamed of by the child Wilhelm—the "beautiful, compassionate princess" depicted in his grandfather's painting; Natalia, the bride promised by destiny to Wilhelm's love. But what do we know about the light of the great stars? How can we describe the figures of Andromeda, Boötes, Virgo, the North Star, fixed in the enormous distances of the sky? Even if we look at them through a telescope only an infinitesimal portion of that light, only a very vague outline of those figures reach our eyes. Thus, whenever Natalia appears in the *Lehrjahre*, a kind of pale veil extenuates Goethe's prose. Behind this veil we can catch a glimpse not so much of a character as of an emblem or symbol of a character: a face with "soft, noble, tranquil features" (227: 3), a "heavenly, modest, and serene smile" (529: 20); while the sole precise detail Goethe furnishes about her, "the thinly tapered arms," is canceled or forgotten in the definitive version of the *Wanderjahre*.[2]

When Natalia makes her first appearance, she is surrounded by the landscape of pastoral epic poetry, and until the second chapter of the eighth book, Wilhelm remembers her only as the "beautiful one," the "noble Amazon." This expression has a striking effect on us. Seduced by Wilhelm's adventurous and romantic fantasy, we imagine that Natalia, hidden in the wings of the *Lehrjahre*, runs swiftly through rocks and woods, like a spirit of nature. We picture her pursuing deer and breaking furious colts, like Eugenie, the Amazon of *Natürliche Tochter*. Perhaps she wields bow and arrow or sword, like the warrior heroines whom Ariosto and Tasso described in their poems. But Wilhelm's fantasy has led us astray. After that first encounter, Natalia never appears again in the open air, among woods and mountain glades, riding a colt. She lives shut up in her palace full of books, paintings, and scientific collections, surrounded by her poor people and orphans, like a priestess in her temple. Although there are few indications to comfort us, we suspect that for her nature is a kind of Italian-style garden, where an architect has designed alleys, pavilions, and waterfalls, and a group of gardeners stand guard each day around the capricious branches of the trees, and at every season plant and gather flowers (526: 27).

Why, then, did Goethe insist on calling Natalia an Amazon? What associations did this mythical image awaken in his mind? In September 1786, when he was traveling to Rome, Goethe saw in Verona a painting depicting St. Ursula and the eleven thousand virgins. A month later he admired at Bologna a painting, which he thought was by Raphael (but in fact was by Guercino), with the figure of St. Agatha in prison (XI, 46: 2–3; 107: 18; W. III, I: 306). The faces of the two saints seemed to him very much alike; each had a noble and virginal expression, without feminine charm *(ohne Reiz)*, but also with no touch of coldness or crudity; and they appeared to be Amazons. Also in *Iphigenie auf Tauris*, in the first version as well as the definitive one, Goethe associated Iphigenia's gentleness of spirit with the fact that, according to a tradition, the daughter of Agamemnon and Clytemnestra descended from the race of Amazons.[3] In all these instances, the Amazon was not for Goethe an adventurous warrior or a daring huntress; but rather a noble, mild, well-bred woman, without the intense or artificial erotic charm such as the boy Wilhelm disliked (or feared) in Armida (27: 1–2).

Like Iphigenia, St. Ursula, and St. Agatha, like Eleonora d'Este, Natalia belongs to this group of Amazons. Her face with its "soft, noble, and tranquil" features and her "heavenly, modest, and serene smile" reveal not even a trace of the sensual female qualities of Mariane and

Philine, those two small, delightful, theatrical Armidas. One would never dream of covering Natalia's arms with Mariane's white negligee, or of putting on her feet Philine's bedroom slippers. None could mistake her for one of those "light little clouds," for that soft-hearted populace of female sinners who so gladly let themselves be seduced by a "glance, a greeting, a caressing breath," and at the end of *Faust* gather around the knees of the Mater Gloriosa.

At once fascinated and disappointed by the androgynous atmosphere that envelops the figure of Natalia, the readers of the *Lehrjahre* wonder what is enclosed in the heart of the woman whom Wilhelm has so long pursued. At first sight, Natalia seems alien to the passions that agitate the characters of the *Lehrjahre*. She has neither the élan of the emotions which produces Wilhelm's joy and anguish, nor the nostalgia for birthplace and heaven which consumes Mignon's life. She knows neither Philine's profane love nor Aurelia's hysterical fury, nor even the vague phantasmagorias that propel the "beautiful soul" toward visible and invisible beings. Many readers wind up imagining that the heart of this pale secular nun is either empty or indifferent. If some emotion does throb in her, it must resemble Eleonora d'Este's passions as an envious woman friend describes them: "They illumine like the moon's calm light parsimoniously illumines the nocturnal path for travelers: they do not warm or pour out either pleasure or joy of life" (*Torquato Tasso*, 1956–1959).

But Natalia's calm, clear stellar light seems cold only to one who is a prisoner of the emotions' illusions. The fire of the affections has retreated to the most intimate corner of her being; not in the heart, if the heart is the divinity of Wilhelm and Augustin, but rather in that which, in the past, moralists called the "profound center of the soul" or the "summit, the highest point" of our spirit. There all human faculties, which usually appear to us divided, fuse and harmonize with a tender strength. Thus no one can say what separate inclination moves Natalia's acts; in her, reason coincides with a boundless aspiration; coldness with warmth, maternal and fraternal affection with passion.

To this indistinct and compact force, living in her and continually welling up out of her, what name can one give but—love? As St. Paul said, "Love is farsighted and kind; love does not burn with passion, does not boast with words or puff itself up with pride. Love does nothing that is indecorous, does not look for its advantage, or let itself be moved by fire, it does not reckon with evil. . . . Love bears all things, believes all things, hopes all things, endures all things" (I Corinthians 13: 4–7).[4] This profound, patient, and steady love, this love rich in hope and faith, this love which coincides with the formal instinct of the universe, constitutes, as Schiller said, Natalia's "permanent nature and character."[5] She loves at every instant and on every occasion of her life, and even when she appears in dreams she cannot renounce this unique instinct of hers. With the same mild sympathy she cares for the poor and wretched, educates Felix, shares in Lothario's existence, alleviates the pain of the last months of Mignon's life, and throws her "tapered arms" around Wilhelm's neck.

Like Theresa, Natalia never remains inactive. When she is still an adolescent, an invincible instinct drives her to respond to other human beings' needs and desires. If she sees a poor man covered with rags, she remembers the superfluous clothes that fill her family's closets; and she cuts and resews them, adapting them to the people she takes under her wing. If she sees children saddened by lack of care and attention, she remembers some rich lady who is dying of boredom amid her wealth. If she sees many unfortunate people forced to live in a single room, she thinks of the large, half-empty chambers in her aristocratic palace. With the passing of the years, this pedagogic vocation attracts her spirit ever more intimately; and when Wilhelm comes to know her, Natalia is taking in poor girls, helping them, instructing and educating them in accordance with simple moral laws.

There is something unique about Natalia's incessant activity. While almost all men end by letting themselves be overwhelmed by their activity, as if the world existed only for this, Natalia maintains a kind of intellectual distance from her actions. It is easy to imagine that tomorrow, on a new occasion or in a new milieu, she might dedicate herself with the same elegance to a completely different task—such as establishing the laws of the ideal city or doing the work of a carpenter. Although she is never inactive, Natalia does not need to act. Unlike weak and uncertain spirits, no impulse compels her to fling herself into the world's agitated sea. If no worthy task offers itself to her attention, she remains in her corner, immobile and silent, tranquil and patient; but whoever contemplates her repose, already senses in it the future occupations which, in a short while, will call her back among men (417: 33; 418: 1).

Plato asserted that man's loftiest task is that of reproducing in his mind the pure periodic movements, the exact circular revolutions of the celestial intelligence (*Timaeus*, 47 b–c, 90 c–d). There is no character in the *Lehrjahre* who comes closer than Natalia to this ideal. Just as the stars traverse the sky in an "eternally cadenced dance," so Natalia inhabits the Earth to bear witness to the measure of a rhythm. Her life is alien to the abrupt jerks, the sharp differences in intensity of our existence. Alien, too, to our gray moods and gaieties, feverish agitations and boredom, her life conserves the same temperature and repeats the same tone. When we see her move, there comes to mind the words that describe Ottilie's life: "Her tranquil attention remained always uniform with itself, like her calm activity. Ottilie sat, stood up, went and came, fetched, carried and sat down again without the slightest shadow of anxiety: it was a perpetual change, an eternal, pleasant movement" (VI, 284: 2–7). He who knows Natalia profoundly sees the fusion of continuous movement and perfect repose; the insatiable course of the stars and the absolute quiet of the universe.

Even during his years of maturity and old age Goethe did not forget the physiognomical passion of his youth, when he studied portraits, silhouettes, and known and unknown handwritings. He made the characters in his novels write love notes or business letters, subjecting their handwriting to an implacable examination. The distorted, uncertain, jagged lines traced by Mignon reveal the darkness of her spirit; Ottilie's slow and rigid handwriting points to her psychological weakness (VI, 265: 15); and the countess's handwriting expresses an excess of grace and study (240: 27–28). Only one handwriting seems perfect to Goethe's physiognomical mania: Natalia's. The hand of this astral woman writes in a very free fashion, without awkwardness, uncertainty, or interruption, revealing that "ineffably easy-flowing harmony" (240: 30) which constitutes the true secret of her nature.

As soon as Natalia appears in the novel, a cortege of evangelical allusions and religious images accompanies her steps. The first time she meets Wilhelm, he is lying wounded on the ground. Crying, Mignon embraces his feet and dries the blood from his wounds with her black tresses (225: 3–5, 19–20), just as the woman sinner in the Gospel of St. Luke (7: 38) bathes Christ's feet with her tears and dries them with her hair; while Philine, in whose lap Wilhelm rests his head, is called the "frivolous Samaritan" (226: 36). This grouping of the two sinners—the victim of the darkness of sin and the gay flower of everyday sin— prepare, by contrast, the coming of Natalia, who appears as a "saint" (228: 29).

The second time Natalia appears before Wilhelm is in a dream; Felix is about to drown in a pool, and she "stretches her right hand toward the child," who miraculously goes through the water in the direction of her finger (426: 13–14). Natalia's gesture recalls that of Christ, who stretches out his hand to save Peter from the water of Lake Gennesaret (Matthew 14: 31) or to cleanse the leper (Matthew 8: 3); while the right hand of Jehovah is that which saves, supports, and performs miracles (Exodus 15: 6; Psalms 17: 7; 20: 6; 60: 5; 118: 16). And finally the house in which Wilhelm rediscovers the Amazon is a temple (519: 18), "the most sacred and severe place" Wilhelm has ever seen (512: 31–32); and Natalia is its "worthy priestess" (519: 18–19).

With the figure of Natalia, the book of the *Lehrjahre* achieves its culmination. Goethe has gathered all the superlatives of his prose to describe her celestial face. Natalia is a "saint" who in her dreams performs miracles like Christ: she is "the figure of all figures" (445: 35), the loftiest woman whom Wilhelm's eyes and, perhaps, those of almost any other man, could ever contemplate. In her double aspect of Amazon and father's bride, she recalls the "greatest pearl" of the universe, the pure white philosopher's stone. Why be amazed, then, if all the people in the *Lehrjahre* "delight in this apparition" and kneel devoutly before her (608: 24–25)? If her aunt gazes at her with "wonder" and "veneration," and Theresa considers her worthy of the "adoration" of the entire world (417: 30; 459: 10)?

This chorus of attributes and superlatives does not exhaust Natalia's ultimate essence, which obstinately escapes our eyes, like the essence of all supreme beings. Even Wilhelm succeeds in glimpsing it only once, and then aided by the weakness of the senses when he lies wounded in the mountain clearing and sees "some rays surround her head and a splendid light spread little by little over her entire figure" (228: 25–27). Like the ethereal stars in the sky, like truth, like beauty, Natalia is a splendid irradiation of light that fills the soul with felicity and dazzles men's eyes.[6] The marvelous epiphany vanishes immediately from Wilhelm's sight; and those rays become part of his memory of her, a memory that pursues her through the rocks and woods (229: 26; 235: 24; 293: 14–15).

When Wilhelm rediscovers Natalia in her uncle's palace, among the paintings and statues of his childhood, a "lampshade" casts a shadow on her figure and its lineaments (513: 14, 29–30). From that day on, Wilhelm will never see again the radiant splendor of their first encounter.[7] He has rediscovered the Amazon and thinks she will illuminate him, but a veil conceals her from him. And so it must be. No mortal can long bear the blinding sight of the absolute, unless—Goethe thought—it appears to us mildly screened; no man can stare straight at the pure white philosopher's stone.

Meanwhile, as if to seal her definitive transformation, Natalia gives up the Amazon's attire and man's greatcoat which protected her during her first meeting with Wilhelm. While Mignon tries desperately to protect the symbolic insignia of her androgynous condition, Natalia renounces them and steps down from the mythical pedestal Wilhelm's fantasy had created for her; she accepts going hidden through Goethe's

GOETHE

book.[8] Thenceforth she sews the clothes of the poor, discusses this or that with her friends, inhabits a house, and lives in clock time—like all the human characters of our novels.

But even this veiled light must vanish from the world's stage. In the opening pages of the first draft of the *Wanderjahre*, the marriage of Wilhelm and Natalia—joyously announced by Friedrich at the end of the *Lehrjahre*—has not yet taken place. After thinking he was close to heaven, after an instant of supreme happiness, Wilhelm leaves Natalia's house, Germany, the waters pouring down from the Alps and flowing toward her garden. Like the wandering Jew, he travels through the world alone, repressing his laments, his involuntary tears, hiding in his heart the sadness of infinite separation. But one day, having climbed to the peak of a mountain, he catches sight of a group of people, almost all women, standing on a large rock. One of them, who seems to stretch out over the abyss, catches his attention. When he picks up his spyglass, the lens as in a magical spectacle brings before his eyes Natalia's "pure, sweet figure" and "tapered arms," "appeared to him so compassionate, and finally, after unhappy sorrows and confusions, embraced him affectionately, if only for a few moments."[9]

In the definitive version of the *Wanderjahre*, even this consolation is denied him and Wilhelm's travels multiply, the years pile up, while Natalia's face disappears in the distance. At the end of the book, when all the other narrative threads are tied together and the destinies of Lothario and Theresa, Flavio and Hilarie, Jarno and Lydia, Lenardo and Susanna are fulfilled, no sign announces their approaching or even distant reunion.

Why in the world has Wilhelm lost this rare happiness, this incomparable treasure? Someone might imagine that an error had closed the doors of heaven to him forever; that a sin has kept him from the unattainable goal he thought he had attained. But Wilhelm has committed neither errors nor sins; just as he had not deserved Natalia, so now he loses her through no fault of his. He loses her because he cannot help but lose her. While he loves Natalia, Wilhelm knows absolute love; he is on the point of possessing, though veiled and screened, a heavenly star. But on this earth, full of rocks and stones, where the heaviest of the elements holds sway, who can live with a great star? Absolute love is the Utopia of all Utopias, the heart of all hopes and all dreams; it cannot tolerate closeness, possession, the quotidian warmth of happiness. Like the city of God, its reign is not "here" and "now," but in the illimitable distances of space. If he wishes to preserve Natalia's love, if he wishes that the thread woven between them not be broken for eternity, Wilhelm must renounce the idea of living with her. He must not speak to her, see her, or write to her, and their amorous relations are similar to those which, in the vault of the sky, silently draw two stars together.[10]

In the course of his wanderings, Wilhelm reaches a wall encircling a large garden. He rings the bell; a portal opens by itself; in the garden a group of boys are joyously working. At the back, among oaks and beech trees, he sees an old castle, all of whose decorations are strikingly new, as if a gang of masons and stonecutters had just left it. When he is ushered into the vestibule, a woman is embroidering at a frame and a steward leads him into a hall. It is completely paneled in wood, furnished with massive oak benches, its walls hung with historical paintings. In the next room, in the library's bookcases, someone has classified by subject the most significant maxims that the world's wisdom has enclosed in books and disseminated in conversation. At night, on a circular tower, an astronomer contemplates the wonders of the starry sky.

This singular milieu smacks somewhat of a prim girls' boarding school, a monastery, and a center of scholarship, but does not ignore the simple worldly traditions of the German aristocracy. Here Wilhelm meets Makarie, the star which in the *Wanderjahre* takes the place of Natalia's light.[11] A green curtain parts and two girls push forward an armchair in which an old woman is seated, a venerable lady who pronounces the simple and divine words of an "ancient Sibyl" (VIII, 65: 30–31). All those afflicted and confused, souls who are lost, those who want to find themselves again and do not know how, turn to her for help and advice. Makarie, immobile in her armchair, protected by the mysterious green curtain, offers them no moral precept. Her glance pierces the heavy individual mask covering every person, removes the decayed and sinful crust, contemplates the profound being, the still healthy core of his soul. As in a magical mirror, she shows each person the inner beauty he felt he had stained. She caresses his brow, and the afflicted heart is relieved of all burdens, the confused soul rediscovers itself, thoughts become limpid, emotions are pacified.

On his first night in the castle, after studying the sky with the astronomer, Wilhelm flings himself down to sleep on a cot. A dream reveals to him Makarie's nature and the source of her therapeutic qualities. He thinks he is in an oak-paneled hall. The green curtain parts; Makarie's armchair gleams with gold, moving by itself as though it were alive; a soft light enfolds the "ancient Sibyl" covered with sacerdotal vestments. A cortege of clouds suddenly forms at her feet and rises toward the sky, lifting the venerable figure on its wings; then the cirrus clouds divide; Makarie loses all human features and ascends ever higher, like the loving and radiant morning star, until she reaches the other stars of the firmament.

As Wilhelm's truthful dream reveals, Makarie is a star of the zodiac. When she looks within herself, she seems to see gathered there all the light of the sky. While the eyes of the body contemplate the sun and moon, the inner eyes see another sun, another moon, more resplendent than the real ones; and all the stars, all the constellations of the zodiac repeat their elegant and happy orbits in the spirit. When the mists of the mind hide from her the sight of her celestial companions, Makarie lives and acts in the world, succors and counsels. But no sooner does her inner zodiac shine again than she leaves all activity and gives herself up to calm and quiet, like a contemplative saint.

Though the old sick body still lives among us, its spirit has already left the earth a long time ago. Like a planet it revolves around the sun; following the movements of a spiral, it penetrates deeper into the spaces of the sky. Soon it travels past the orbit of Mars, approaches Jupiter, gazes astounded at its splendor and its moons; catches sight of planets unknown to man. Then it also leaves behind the orbit of Jupiter and advances through the infinite heavens, toward Saturn. "No imagination could follow her that far," Goethe concludes; "but we hope that an entelechy such as Makarie's will not completely leave our solar system. When it will have reached its borders, we hope that it will be seized by the desire to turn back, to act again in terrestrial life and bestow its benefits on our distant grandsons " (VIII, 452: 2–7).

The Architecture of the Lehrjahre

VIII

"Except for the hero's passion," Stendhal said, "the novel should be a mirror."[1] But a mirror of what? The naïve reader who in 1796 knew only *Moll Flanders* and *Tom Jones*, Marivaux's *Paysan parvenu* or *Pamela* would have given the same reply as the reader of the future who gave himself up to the pleasures of *Lost Illusions*, *War and Peace*, *The Old Curiosity Shop*, and *Remembrance of Things Past*. "The novel," they would have replied with one voice, "is the mirror of reality."

In this great mirror all the events of universal history leave marks, as though the novel were the only eternity they could possibly merit. On the morning of the battle of Austerlitz, Napoleon, mounted on a small gray Arab horse, sits motionless before his marshals. In good spirits, refreshed and joyous as a young man in love, in that happy mood when everything seems possible to us and everything succeeds, he contemplates the mountain tops rising out of the mist, the slowly moving Russian troops. No sooner does the sun appear than he takes his glove off his small, shapely hand and gives the order to begin the action. Some time later, the colors of youth have left Napoleon's face. With a sallow, swollen face, his eyes blurred and his voice hoarse, he crosses the damp and smoky field of the battle of Borodino. Tens of thousands of men lie dead on the meadows where for hundreds of years the peasants of the villages of Borodino, Gorki, and Shevardino had reaped the harvest and grazed their livestock. When Napoleon enters Moscow, the city is deserted; the stores and portals are shut; only the singing of drunks, the screams of a group of lunatics, the shrill caws of a flock of crows on the wall of the Kremlin break the silence; and soon the first tongues of fire rise from the roofs of the wooden houses, the walls crumble and collapse, the streets are obscured by wavering clouds of smoke, then illuminated by the sparkle of flames.

Detailed and meticulous—whether placed in a country lane, at the corner of a city street, or in the secrecy of luxurious apartments—the mirror of the novel takes in the swift and contradictory spectacles of everyday life. In it we find reflected London in the first years of the eighteenth century—this enormous city, this sudden and monstrous excrescence full of unscrupulous aristocrats and greedy merchants, of drunkards, sluts, thieves, and adventurers from every country. Then the mirror grows dark; and London shows us, a century later, the damp and rotting houses of its slums, scarcely built and already falling to pieces; miserable hovels constructed from the flotsam of sunken ships. Tall, dark chimneys are densely packed together, pouring out a scourge of smoke and covering with ashes the tangled litter of nettles, withered leaves, faded flowers, and coarse grass in old gardens.

If we shift our mirror over Paris and the France of Louis Philippe, what a tumultuous and exorbitant spectacle is offered to our eyes! Napoleon's paymasters pursue their obscene and senile passions. The imagination of usurers distills gold, and the fantasy of great criminals prepares devilish machinations capable of overthrowing an empire. Young provincials vainly seek wealth and glory, while workers pile up stones, omnibuses, and gas pipes on the avenues of Paris, bursting into the palace like a swirling river. In the countryside, peasants creep into the mysterious and dense sixteenth-century parks, clear them for tillage and divide them into thousands of plots, like tailor's swatches. We cannot overlook anything of what then existed, neither the shirts with golden buttons, nor the trousers with rich pleats and the small frockcoat that tightly clasps the dandies' waists in Paris. We see the advertisements for *double pâte des sultanes* and *eau carminative* which César Birotteau pasted on the walls along the boulevards; or the sticky buffets, the huge tables covered with wax, Argand's dusty lanterns. We take in the cracked, decaying, shaky, and worm-eaten furniture that depressed the guests of Vauquer's boardinghouse.

Whoever tries to flee from the real world—the place where space divides, where things crush with their weight, where chance and disorder trace their sinister and pathetic embroideries—will be hard put to find some consolation in most of these novels. If he passes through the mirror like Alice and the light wall of glass dissolves like gauze before his steps, he will encounter in the novel's world the same brutal, unassailable divinity who makes our existence both happy and unhappy. Space will acquaint him with its measures; time, weight, volume, chance, and disorder will prove to him that nothing has changed. His only consolation is that everything in existence that seemed to him faded and mediocre will become marvelously intensified and immensely magnified.

When he reads a novel he discovers the same space that the cartographer draws on his maps. As in reality, he recognizes the altitude of mountains, the curve of hills; plains extend into infinity, measured by the march of armies. He becomes familiar with the torrents and rivers that flow precipitously down into a valley or proceed with a slower tempo toward the sea. He rediscovers the same distances—two days by carriage or three hours by train—that divide two cities. Even if he is shipwrecked on Robinson Crusoe's island, he learns its latitude and longitude, its flat or rocky coastline, the distance between two caves and the rule of the rainy season. Over his head slide minutes and hours, weeks and months, seasons and years. What does it matter if time seems to him incredibly faster and more high-spirited than real time; or, instead, so slow and minute that neither sentences nor pages nor books suffice to exhaust even a single hour of it? In both cases, he sinks into the element of time as into a liquid: inside time, which transforms society, which bends and masks bodies, scores faces with wrinkles, hardens our arteries, tinges our hair and beards white, makes our legs heavy as though each of us wore shoes of lead.

As he is reading, his small room is suddenly filled by a character who leaps from the open pages. The reader knows everything about him: the color of his mustaches, the dark or ashen hue of his face, the makeup that thickens his skin; his ancestors right back to the thirtieth generation. He knows the character's nervous, dramatic, insolent, theatrically virile gestures; his regal benevolence, fierce fits of anger, irresistible *bons mots*, deplorable sexual inclinations. He understands when the protagonist's looks are dilated by attention, now daring, now prudent, now arrogant as those of a royal prince, now insinuating as those of a spy, now devout, timid, ecstatic, and bashful. The reader hears and responds to the strident voice, deafening as a storm, tender as a choir of young girls and sweet sisters; he is familiar with the little laugh, so delicate and light, like that of his Bavarian or Lorrainese ancestors and the sound of certain ancient musical instruments, which today have become very rare.

At the end, having lived with Monsieur de Charlus for some months, how can one be surprised if the roles are inverted? Just as gigantic spirits fill the old Gothic chamber, driving out the wizard who evoked them, so the marvelous paper figure seems to possess all the strength

GOETHE

and blood, all the volume and weight of reality, while we, with our feigned body of flesh and bone, become so small and unreal—silly shadows clinging to the edge of a small night table.

If we continue to live amid the figures and events of our novel, we end by realizing that our author has at least one attribute in common with the unknown master of history. The writer, too, does not distinguish between the inventions of destiny and those of chance, universal things and insignificant ones, symbolic matters and apparent ones, and he does not try to discover even the shadow of a law in all that is illegal and catastrophic. He has no plans, he obeys no patterns, he does not know where he wants to arrive. He does not know what he is writing. He walks in the midst of his inventions as if he were going at night through a dense forest; he does not see the characters and the constantly different stories to which he gives birth. He gets lost, strays off, follows the most absurd bypaths, finds himself in unexpected clearings. He is unable to reject any of the invitations with which the road lures him on, and at the end he seems more amazed than we by the wealth he has managed to collect.

Thus the novel is not an organism but rather an accumulation of living organisms: an aggregate of persons, animals, and things living one on top of the other, like algae and marine excrescences—a very large bag in which is collected everything that, in the course of a couple of months or years, occurred to a writer's imagination. We can find everything in it: the history of printing in France, or the crisis of the majorat in southern Italy, or a treatise of political economy. It contains a whole concert for string instruments, an essay on the philosophy of clothing; travels in India or beneath the earth. No sooner does a character conceive ideas on God or death than he immediately wants to tell them to us, even though it has no connection with the overall design of the book. The principal sections are barely sketched; secondary details are finished with excessive care, as if they must reveal some secret to us. Many threads mentioned in passing, many themes proposed at the start are suddenly abandoned in some odd corner; while a distracted hand fills a large empty space with a black splotch.

When we have reached the last sentences of the novel and the word "End" forces us sadly to stop reading, we no longer know in what world we are now living. Sometimes, in the pages that have flown before us, we have sensed certain intentions, significances, and symbols. But how often they seem to us to continue our own existence! We will never be rid of this perplexity. As Jacques Rivière has said, the novel is like a monstrous tree: It feeds on living and dead things, real and imaginary things; it absorbs almost any ailment, and immeasurably enlarges its branches and shoots, its innumerable tentacles and vines. We do not know what force propels it or what law it obeys. But with an always new pleasure, we enter this marvelous conglomerate, this picturesque mix-up of men and animals, trees and cities, paper and earth, blood and ink.

"The play lasted for a long time. Old Barbara went more than once to look out the window, hoping to hear the noise of carriages. She was waiting for Mariane, her pretty mistress, who, in the afterpiece, dressed up as a young officer, was delighting audiences. She was waiting for her with more impatience than on other evenings, when she could offer her only a modest supper. This time, however, she would be able to surprise her by giving her a package which Norberg, a young and wealthy merchant, had sent by the mail, to show his beloved that even when far away he still thought of her" (9: 3–12). Can one think of anything more tranquil and reassuring than the opening paragraph of the *Lehrjahre?* As in a clean Flemish mirror, we see an old maid, a frivolous actress, and the rich merchant who keeps her; and, in a short while, we shall meet the naïve young man to whom Mariane has given her heart. So the reader thinks that he has started a splendid costume novel, full of highly colored, realistic details, cities and towns, picturesque adventures and, perhaps, extraordinary historical events.

If we proceed with our reading, the first impression vanishes, and the Flemish mirror reflects ever more incomprehensible lights and shadows. Goethe did not seek out eccentric subjects, as Novalis has claimed; he continues to represent a reality everyone can recognize. But many small hints arouse the suspicion that he has tried to transform completely the thousand-branched tree, the monster of a thousand tentacles, which continued to grow luxuriously around him.

The action of the *Lehrjahre* takes place in Germany; Goethe does not name the region. Nor does he name the city in which Wilhelm spends his youth, nor the farming town where he meets Mignon and Philine (90: 12). Serlo's company performs "in a large mercantile city" (266: 21).[2] The only geographical name recorded in the entire novel is the very common one of Hochdorf, the mountain village where Wilhelm watches the factory workers act in a play (87: 26). One cannot imagine what distance separates Wilhelm Meister's city and Hochdorf; or how many days of travel divide the count's castle from the mercantile city where Serlo performs, or that city from Lothario's castle. All this is certainly not by chance. With these systematic reticences, Goethe tries to shade out or erase the objective space in which Wilhelm Meister and his friends must move about. The only space he lets us see is the purely mental space drawn by the book before the eyes of its readers.

GOETHE

Just as geographical indications are lacking, so temporal ones are also absent. A pedant or a person who loves precision will never know in what year or month Wilhelm Meister met Mariane or Natalia. In the background, the echoes of only two historical events are heard. Lothario meets Aurelia just after he returns from America where he fought in the army of the United States (263: 8–10); and a war runs through the fields of Germany, a warrior prince inhabits the count's castle together with his staff. No one doubts that it was the war of American independence in which Lothario has fought, but the other war remains mysterious. Some people might believe it is really a theatrical spectacle, staged by order of the guardians of the tower.

History seems to have dozed off, as if some skillful enchanter had managed to free it from revolutions and catastrophes. Germany is immobile, shut up in its modest patriarchal existence. The nobility still possesses its privileges and castles, and incarnates, in the eyes of young intellectuals, the supreme values of civilization. Merchants trade with neighboring or distant countries, accumulating wealth, but they do not try to go beyond the confines of their own class. The peasants, shopkeepers, and workers in the city do not even dare to appear in the novel's mirror. What does it matter whether the Germany of the last decades of the eighteenth century actually resembles Goethe's description of it? This tranquil and backward provincial country is also the ideal land where, as one reads in *Natürliche Tochter*, everything seems "founded and ordered for eternity." Here the fundamental laws are stable, possessions do not leave their masters, gold and silver remain in their sacred forms, and the towering houses, the circle of the squares, and the noble edifices of the churches shine immobile beneath the rays of the sun.[3]

At one point, Jarno observes "that great changes threaten us and in almost any place property is no longer secure." But this is only in one of the last chapters of the book, and only in passing (563: 21–22). The shadow of the French Revolution seems therefore to graze for a moment Natalia's and Lothario's palaces. These social and political changes do not succeed in making their way into the novel, where everything remains calm and tranquil, perhaps for the last time in the history of men. The "ties have not yet been broken," "faith is not yet wounded." This will occur thirty years later, when the bizarre construction of the *Wanderjahre* will reproduce the lacerations and upheavals of the modern world. Nobody could imagine, while Goethe was writing, that history was savagely reawakening, Robespierre had mounted the scaffold, the French armies had crossed the frontier of the Rhine, and soon Napoleon would be going down the same roads traveled by Wilhelm Meister and his friends.

To try to establish the measure of time embraced in the *Lehrjahre,* one must recall that Wilhelm is ten years old at the time of his grandfather's death (68: 27), and that at fourteen he writes a poem against commerce (32: 36). At the beginning of the first book, when he loves Mariane, he is twenty-two (69: 18). Although he dedicates "some years" (76: 15) to commercial activity, it is probable that he is twenty-five or twenty-six when, in the third chapter of the second book, he leaves his paternal home and rides on horseback over the valleys and mountains. The events recounted in the second, third, and fourth books should take only a few months. As for the succeeding events, described in the fifth, seventh, and eighth books, Goethe furnishes two contradictory indications, and we do not know whether about nine months or a few years elapse between the first performance of *Hamlet* and Mignon's death.[4]

We could suppose Goethe is amusing himself, as in the *Wanderjahre,* making fun of clock time, convinced that "in the novel and universal history" our temporal calculations are all mistaken and that "we cannot ever know what happens before or after."[5] But, in the *Lehrjahre,* Goethe does not make fun of time; he ignores it. As soon as we enter the great novel, the clocks stop ticking, and the years, months, weeks, and days of which Goethe speaks are conventional terms to which he has recourse so as not to offend the mind of his readers. Just as the space of the book does not reproduce geographical space, so the only time in the *Lehrjahre* is that measured by the construction of the book.

Within this ideal space and this ideal time wander creatures without name or surname. Goethe remembers the surnames of Norberg, Melina, and Marquis Cipriani, but Meister's is a symbolic surname, and the family name of Natalia and Lothario is not registered in any dictionary of genealogy (239: 3). The "beautiful soul," the "uncle," the "baron and baroness," the "abbé," the "count," and "countess" do not even have names. The names of Narziss, Philo, and Philine are obvious moral allegories; those of Serlo and Jarno (of whom it is said: "they called him Jarno, but they did not know what to think of this name" [162: 36]) seem extravagant monograms. Goethe found it amusing to deny his characters the most certain and humble mark of personal identity, the label by which we are made to exist in the registers of civil status and which welcomes us, as protagonists or supernumeraries, into the ranks of society and history.

If we wish to know the stature, the slow or rapid step, the nervous or dramatic gestures, the laugh's strident or soft timbre and the different *toilettes* of each of these characters; if, in a word, we seek to find on paper that massive physical relief which Balzac and Proust reproduce so willingly, we should not turn to Goethe. Like those portraitists who suggest only an "idea" of their subject, he lets his attention fall

GOETHE

on very few elements, to each of which he attributes a symbolic value. He tells us that Philine has blue eyes, long blond hair, and small Parisian bedroom slippers; that Mignon has black eyes and a black, piercing look; that Jarno's eyes are large and pale blue, and Theresa's eyes clear as crystals. So he lets the reader compare these facts, complete them with his imagination and draw in his mind the portrait in oils of Wilhelm Meister and the miniatures of Philine and Theresa.

No character employs those recurring words and expressions, those dialectal modes or syntactical twists and turns which in everyday life distinguish every individual. Nobody speaks by slurring his words, with a lisping voice, or so incredibly fast as to make it hard for us to follow. Every character knows only one style: Goethe's. The great pedagogue and the poor strolling player, the ardent lover and the frigid man of the world, the cultivated writer and the hardworking merchant, the celestial star and the old procuress use the same metaphors and with the same ability gather the arduous flowers of rhetoric. While Plato, Cervantes, and Proust seek to give movement to the levels of dialogue and oppose them to those of narration, Goethe tries to merge them in a single verbal surface.[6]

A novelist in the analytical tradition possesses (or thinks he possesses) intellectual instruments with which he can illuminate almost any situation. If he had to tell Wilhelm's sentimental story, he would be capable of explaining in detail the origins of his Oedipus complex, and its transformation and sublimation in his love for Natalia. Goethe, however, ignores (or pretends to ignore) any sort of psychological instrument. With the lightness of the great classical writers, he tells us only that Wilhelm as a boy loved an episode of *Jerusalem Delivered* and spent hours gazing at a painting. Then Goethe brings these memories together around the image of Natalia. Finally, he transforms the description of the painting in an almost imperceptible fashion. Thus he concentrates the whole, rich, tumultuous story of a soul—to which another writer would have devoted hundreds of pages—in an elegant interweaving of silent symbols that possess an irrefutable objective clarity. He never explains anything. He does not reveal to us what secrets are hidden in Wilhelm's soul, but he hints at a possibility which remains wrapped in a cloud of suggestions. And he lets us translate his very clear and mysterious symbolic language into our labored and dry intellectual speech.[7]

While the nucleus of the *Lehrjahre* is explored by means of this symbolic psychology, Goethe, in the more external parts of the book, simply tells what happens. But, also in these parts, what marvelous rapidity and lightness of touch! The most spectacular events, which should provoke tempests of sorrow and joy in the characters' souls, are recounted in a few sentences, and only a hundred pages later, from a gesture or a gaze staring into the distance, do we find out what Natalia or Wilhelm have felt.

An analytical novelist is not a single figure but rather a compromise or combination between a storyteller and a psychologist or moralist who, by insinuating himself in the story's flow, interprets the events and the characters' emotions. Goethe, on the contrary, fuses the narrator's different functions in the story's smooth uniformity. If it is necessary for him to interpret what happens, he combines the objective story and the intellectual interpretation in a single *impasto* in which one cannot distinguish the voice of events, of the character, and of the writer. He more willingly entrusts the role of interpreter to a metaphor or a group of metaphors. Wilhelm's amorous despair becomes a plague, a malign fever, a firework exploding violently. All these images embody emotions, concentrate them in figures that never exhaust them and through a thousand figures connect them to other images which shoot across the book like sumptuous and fantastic comets.[8]

Hidden behind the wings of the *Lehrjahre*, like the Abbé in the tower's labyrinths, Goethe, lucid, detached, and ironic, camouflages with intelligence the impetuous inventions of his free-ranging imagination. He woos the mystery without putting faith in it. He proposes to himself and his readers the most marvelous adventures, "the strangest and most diverting secrets." It is as if he wished to imitate the popular novels of the eighteenth century or to anticipate the *feuilletons* which were about to invade Europe's newspapers. For, without batting an eyelash, he trots out stories of Gypsies and bandits, acts of incest and superstitions, coincidences, disguises and unsuspected blood ties, sudden recognition scenes and providential deaths. Our interest never slackens. We keep asking ourselves right to the end: What has happened to Mariane? Who will the mysterious Amazon be? Will Wilhelm succeed in finding her again? We hang on his lips with bated breath as on those of the most brazen charlatan and enchanter of the rabble. In these incredible adventures there is nothing unreal and truly fantastic as in the tales of the *Thousand and One Nights* or the *Three Musketeers*, for instance. Goethe wants to show us that the plots of novels are inevitably artificial, and that a book is a chessboard on which destiny performs its elegant and unpredictable moves—moves to which no human chess player will ever succeed in replying.

These indications, which I have quickly mentioned, permit us to see that Goethe wanted to untie all the bonds that could have connected the *Lehrjahre* with everyday reality. In his book nothing reminds us of the spaces of the world; clocks do not tick, the events of history do not dare introduce their crash and rumble. The characters do not have names, surnames, or an individual language, they display symbolic faces and conceal their emotions from the eyes of psychiatrists; and their adventures are more artificial than those dreamed of by the wildest imagination.

So what is left of reality? The loves of Wilhelm and Mariane, the scenes of the puppets and the German theater, the inns and castles, actors and aristocrats, a whole picturesque and multiple life, which Goethe has perceived in the world, has been completely transformed by his firm but light hand. The Flemish mirror, set up along country roads and in rich castles, has caught the most enchanting reflections of reality. It has held the images for a long time, distilling their significant essences; then it has directed these reflections and their shadows into that concave mirror, that empty, polished, and uniform sphere that is a book.

In the spring of 1794, when he took from his bookcases the six books of the *Theatralische Sendung*, Goethe must have been disconcerted. This very fine work, which lay open on his desk, seemed a mine of inspired poetic fantasies from which he could have drawn novels, essays, and lyrical poems; or it seemed a palace, crumbling to the ground beneath the weight of the treasures adorning its rooms, the balconies in its façades, the towers growing above its roof like tropical vegetation. Love stories, colorful brawls, scenes in costume, picaresque adventures, fragments of dramas, ardent bouquets of metaphors and lyrical inventions, reflections on life and literature confusedly filled its pages without following the slightest design. One motif would find, not very far off, its double; a note of color stood out with unwarranted gaudiness; certain very fine realistic scenes (such as the story of Bengel and De Retti) lacked structural justification; while a scintillating lyrical mist seemed to enfold the entire book.

So, in the first phase of his work of revision, Goethe ends by knocking down that marvelous ruin. He breaks the *Theatralische Sendung* into its smallest constituent parts. With the skill of an anatomist, he reduces the material stretched over his desk to fragments: slivers of characters, atoms of scenes, crumbs of reality. Among these fragments he sacrifices with no feeling of regret the useless fine details, the capricious notes of color, the splendid realistic scenes, the wanderings in the depths of the forest—all of which constitute the charm and weakness of the *Theatralische Sendung*. At the end of this first phase of revision, the book that Goethe is writing seems an immense mosaic, subdivided into its prime elements. All the tiny bright and dark stones, all the precious gems glitter brightly and wait to be composed in a new design.

In the second phase, like Howard when he studied the forms of the clouds, Goethe "reunited" what he had first "separated" and "distinguished" (*Trilogie zu Howards Wolkenlehre*, I, 6). He hits upon continual analogies among the thousands of stones scattered over his desk and transforms the simple linear structure of the *Theatralische Sendung* into the complete and all-encompassing symphonic structure of the *Lehrjahre*. In the first, each theme is executed with a certain abundance, producing a complete portrait of a character or a broad realistic scene; yet it remained distinct from other themes with which it could enter into relationship. In the second, however, each motif develops slowly, by means of small, almost imperceptible touches. Sometimes these minute steps follow each other at a distance of a hundred pages: appearing, disappearing, and returning, now loud, now muted, now obvious, now masked, and sometimes ending by including a great number of minor motifs.

The first time that it is presented in the *Lehrjahre*, the Natalia motif is still disguised; we do not know that the memory of Clorinda and the painting of the "father's bride" are an anticipation of its fundamental notes; and that the figure of the beautiful countess constitutes a minor variation. When the Amazon suddenly appears from behind the bush, the subterranean motif emerges strikingly. Then she disappears again, and the note found in the greatcoat, the morning dream, the revelations of the "beautiful soul" and of Theresa present new variations— until, after so many delays and postponements, Wilhelm rediscovers Natalia beneath the veil of the lampshade. In the same fashion, the motif of destiny runs, hidden or on the surface, all through the *Lehrjahre*. Like a triumphant prelude, Wilhelm's ingenuous words exalt its benign force; the guests of the tower come forward with their denigratory falsetto; the songs of the harpist and the reading of *Hamlet* permit one to catch sight of destiny's dark and terrible countenance. Then the roles are reversed; Wilhelm loses all faith; from the top of the tower, the Abbé again gives voice to the luminous and optimistic sounds which we had almost forgotten. All the while, around and above them, destiny brings to fruition what it had long ago decided, condemning to death the "sons of Tantalus" and crowning Wilhelm Meister through Friedrich's words.[9]

Whereas in *Theatralische Sendung* he left the various motifs isolated, Goethe now weaves them tightly together. Sometimes he brings them close to each other, so that they can reveal the symbolic antitheses that make them clash and the resemblances that dissolve them into a superior unity. He inserts a minor motif into a major one, thus forming curious Chinese boxes or elegant telescopic structures. In other instances, although they might be extremely distant, he sets two motifs out in parallel or corresponding positions, repeats or turns a verbal formula (or a symbol like that of the *lapis*) on its head, so as to illuminate them both. Any musical note or motif of the *Lehrjahre* is reechoed at every point of the symphonic tessitura, and the entire surface of the book is traversed by thousands of hidden vibrations that multiply meanings and suggestions *ad infinitum*.

Just two examples will suffice. In the first book of the *Theatralische Sendung*, obeying a simple linear technique, Goethe recounts the story of Wilhelm's childhood and his passion as a puppeteer (Book I, chapters 1–10); then his love of Mariane (Book I, chapters 15–23). Only much later, when Wilhelm has already suffered Mariane's betrayal, Goethe reports the discussions with Werner and Melina about poetry, commerce, and the theater (Book II, chapters 3, 7, 8). In the *Lehrjahre* this material is completely refashioned, Wilhelm recalling for Mariane his childhood and his fantasies as a puppeteer, while Goethe slips into the love story his ideas about commerce, the theater, and literature. So the dreams of Wilhelm's childhood, the hopes of his youth, the expectation of a mystical revelation, the religious vocation for the theater, the ardent force of love, the image of the poet as the prophetic master of men—all the motifs of the first book are merged in a single musical figure.

When Wilhelm, in the third book of the *Theatralische Sendung*, reaches the town at the foot of the mountains, he meets only the noisy company of the tightrope walkers and acrobats (*Theatralische Sendung*, III, 2); several days later, in another city, he sees Mignon coming swiftly down the stairs; while Philine appears in the tenth chapter of the fourth book. In the *Lehrjahre*, these different and opposed motifs appear at the distance of a few sentences. As soon as Wilhelm enters the inn on the market square, the rope dancers have a noisy brawl, Philine makes her smiling appearance at the window of a nearby inn, and Mignon descends the stairs as swift as a flash. In this way, Goethe can counterpose Philine's blue eyes and blond hair against Mignon's dark eyes and hair; the noisiness and frivolity of the theatrical world against the mysterious silence and embarrassment of the unhappy celestial creature.

In the last book of the *Lehrjahre* all the characters—whom Schiller liked to compare to the planets, satellites, and comets of an unknown "solar system" (July 2, 1796)—are gathered in Natalia's palace. We discover that they are or are about to become relations. Who would ever have believed that Philine—with her free sexual attitudes, her white, not too clean, dressing gown and that touch of the equivocal accompanying her—could become the sister-in-law of Lothario and the noble Amazon? That Mignon was the harpist's daughter, and that Mignon and the harpist were tied to Lothario's family? That the son of the merchant would marry the descendant of a great aristocratic family? All these marriages and romantic recognition scenes render triumphantly visible the unity between motifs and characters, who until now had traveled through the *Lehrjahre* without ever meeting.

When the last marriage is about to take place, the symphonic score achieves its definitive note: the mosaic scintillates with the harmonious light of all its gems; and the over-decorated and generous ruins of the *Theatralische Sendung* are transformed into the closed architecture of the *Lehrjahre*. The architect of this edifice has designed foundations so deep as to elude our eyes. He has devised retaining walls that are almost invisible although they support the pressure of an exorbitant quantity of materials—and very broad and commodious stairs, like those that lead Wilhelm into Natalia's palace. Nothing that can possibly attract the visitor is missing: Mountains and hills, rivers and the world's highways are reproduced in miniature; a few foreshortened views of the sky; books in the libraries, frescoes on the walls; defiladed rooms, like huts in a garden, where the visitor forgets what surrounds him; and tombs sheathed in marble, among which to meditate on the life and death of men and things. Looking around one finds not a single useless or decorative detail. Even the balconies, the embellishments on the façades, the color of the bricks and the veins of the stones, the frescoes on the walls or the treasures hidden in the strongboxes—all the elements of the edifice possess a necessary and constructive function.

Perhaps for the first time in the history of literature, Goethe freed the novel from its long, fascinating subjugation to the colorful whims of chance. Like Flaubert, he compels this so intimately illegal creature, this tree with a thousand branches, this mix-up of earth, blood, and ink to bow its head before the inflexible force of law and form. If in the past the novel resembled a *suite* of thoughts in the mind of a drunk, Goethe transformed it into a work of philosophy, connected and continuous as a theorem. If in the past necessary and possible places alternated in it with utter fickleness, Goethe fashioned its surface so attentively, introducing in it correspondences and relations, cutting, distinguishing, and reuniting to such a point that all its motifs and words become as significant as the verbal space of a poem.

I believe that the most faithful readers of novels—those who turn to books to pass the time, to swim in the consoling sea of fantasy, and to know, even if only through another person, what reality is—will not be enthusiastic about these metamorphoses. When they read a "real

GOETHE

novel," they give it a sentimental, distracted attention; they doze over a page, skip a maxim or a chapter of reflections, skim their eyes over the description of a landscape or an interior. They are sure they have not missed anything, for in a succeeding chapter they will find a page repeating the one they have skipped. If, however, they overlook a single paragraph of the *Lehrjahre,* it is quite possible that they will misunderstand the book's meaning. If they remove a brick from its façade or a small stone from a corner of the mosaic, the entire edifice runs the risk of collapsing with a crash. But Goethe had no desire to neglect even this very large audience, which approaches works of art with its mind full of good-natured confusion. The person who does not grasp the pattern of symbols, who is blind to the *lapis* gleaming everywhere, who fails to comprehend why the guardians of the tower behave in such an extravagant fashion can still run swiftly over the surface of the book and identify his destiny with Wilhelm Meister's, fall in love with Mariane, be wounded in the forest, and weep over Mignon's fate. It is not certain that his pleasure (and his comprehension) is less than ours.

When Goethe visited the fabulous public gardens in Palermo, everything there reminded him of the Phaeacians' blessed island. If he looked to the north, dark blue waves were struggling to enter the bay's inlet. Around him, espaliers of oranges and lemons curved to form graceful walks, tropical trees spread out their ramifications, walls of oleanders fascinated the eye with thousands of red flowers; in large ponds, gold and silver fishes hid among moss and rushes. But what struck him above all was the intense, light blue haze over everything, like the glaze a painter applies to a canvas. This atmospheric apparition permitted one to distinguish the distant profiles of mountains, the masts of ships in the harbor, the oleanders' red blossoms, the orange and lemon trees and the reciprocal distances between things. At the same time, it seemed "to dissolve the mountains, sky, and sea in a single element" (XI, 298: 35–36; 240–241).

That is what happens to us as we read Wilhelm Meister's adventures. The extraordinary light, bathing every part of the book, outlines precisely the contours and shadows of things and persons, constructs sharp ensemble scenes, distinguishes from each other yellow bricks, reds of walls, and small objects—a comb, ribbon, or scarf—abandoned in a corner. It measures distances and proportions, as if it were illuminating a painting by Vermeer; and, sometimes, it passes through things and beyond them it searches out very bright shadows. But this strange light diffuses over all points of the book a soft haze, a light shadow, a delicate veiling, dissolving them in a uniform substance. No place, no character, no adventure retains a memory of having been removed from the world of reality, where it lived together with us. The cracks and roughnesses of walls, the splotches of color and dampness, the knots in wood have disappeared; differences in style and language, dissonances and sudden changes in tone, the abysses between story and dialogue, narration and interpretation are nuanced and amalgamated. Goethe's hand has spread over the book that ineffable essence that, as Proust said, constitutes the ultimate secret of art: *"le Vernis des Maîtres."*[10]

He who travels with Goethe through the realm of nature meets certain phenomena of a privileged rank. Granite, which lies in the bowels of the earth and raises its shoulders above the earth's surface, is "the oldest, firmest, deepest, and most unshakable child of nature," "a very old, eternal altar, built immediately on the depths of creation," which imitates the divine Trinity in the structure of its parts. In the same way, the hexagon of colors achieves its "zenith" (XIII, 445: 8) in the color purple, which contains in itself all other colors, mediates between opposed poles, unites extremes and, translated into numbers, represents the Trinity. Lower down, at the base of the granite and the color purple, lie the most inconstant and feeble parts of the creation: ruins, the detritus of recent rocks, colors that excite or disturb our eye. To represent the creation in a drawing, we would have to imagine a pyramidal construction which from step to step leads toward a supreme point where nature reveals its entire meaning.[11]

In other places in Goethe's scientific writings, one can find an opposite image of the universe. Nature has no favorite sons; and the prickly thistle of the fields is as dear to him as wheat, the monkey as dear as man, the jackel as dear as the elephant, the tiny pilot fish as dear as the great blue shark. All phenomena, even the lowest, most extravagant, and bizarre, reveal to us the formal laws of "all of nature." If one of us is blind, it will be enough to open and sharpen his ears: "From the lightest breath to the most savage crash, from the simplest sound to the most complicated chord, from the most violent cry of the heart to the most caressing word of reason, it is nature which speaks and manifests its being, its force, its life and its relations" (XIII, 315: 22–31). In these pages the creation somewhat resembles a flat surface, where all points are equally important and significant.

The *Lehrjahre* also resembles a pyramid of perfection. At the summit, almost beyond the reach of mortal sight, stands Natalia; below her, the Abbé, Lothario, the "beautiful soul," and Jarno; Mignon and the harpist bring together darkness and the celestial spaces. Despite his mistakes, Wilhelm also stands on a very high level, since he is the only

GOETHE

one to glimpse the white light of the philosopher's stone. Below them, although Goethe is full of compassion, doubtlessly stands an arid and pedantic man like Wernèr, this "laborious hypochondriac" with his strident voice, pale cheeks and drooping shoulders; and the clumsy, sentimental, and rhetorical Frau Melina. But an unusual event occurs. As Wilhelm moves toward the summit of the pyramid, sometimes the characters who stand on the lowest levels of the pyramid offer him images of perfection. So, for example, when Werner praises the broad-minded spirit of the merchant who contemplates the All, distinguishes things with order and clarity, and relates them to one another, he already in some sense anticipates the Utopia of the tower and the later Utopia of the *Wanderjahre*. And when Wilhelm leaves the theater and it seems to him that nothing has remained of all of his work there, it is neither the Abbé nor Jarno but actually Frau Melina who speaks noble and intelligent words, which free him from his past and direct him toward a loftier life (491: 4–7, 14–22).

Confronted by these metamorphoses, some readers imagine that Goethe is amusing himself by freely shifting the characters around, making them occupy first a very low place, than a mediocre or sublime one, thus transforming the *Lehrjahre* into an edifice shaken by an ironic and vertiginous movement. But these hypotheses are unfounded. Werner remains a petty merchant and Frau Melina a boring speech-ifier. Like the colored stone in a corner of the mosaic, like the note of a symphony, each of the book's characters and motifs occupies a precise place, and we cannot remove them from it.

Yet nature has been built according to a unique model: the wheat and the prickly thistle, man and monkey, sight and hearing reveal to us the same laws. Who then can deny that the apparently lowest places in the book conceal sublime revelations? That the truth might have chosen the lips of a Werner or a Frau Melina to mani-fest itself to Wilhelm and to all of us? At every point of the *Lehr-jahre*, in the most mediocre character, the least defined image, the idea seemingly least rich in meaning, the ancient granite can con-ceal its divine structure; and purple can leave a reflection of its re-gal and terrible light.

So, in the *Lehrjahre*, two images of the universe that seem and are contradictory dissolve into a paradoxical unity: The pyramid of perfec-tion, built according to a very evident hierarchy of values, is continually transformed into a broad, flat surface where all points stand at the same distance from the center. We do not know whether a God lives there. If he does, he manifests himself only on the tallest peaks, where Natalia's light and the profoundest archetypes of the human soul shine forth. But, at the same time, this God likes to reside in odd corners of the book, even on the miserable stage of a company of strolling players, in the most equivocal of inns, along roads traveled by bandits, in the soul of a modest housewife, or on the lips of an actress without talent.

Faust II

TWO

Goethe's Last Years

I

Having walked the dusty, sun-beaten roads that lead from Hanover into Thuringia, Johann Peter Eckermann arrived in Weimar in June of 1823. A few days later he was invited to the *Frauenplan*. He mounted the broad, neoclassical staircase, wandered through the brightly lit rooms filled with paintings and prints, admiring the huge heads of Juno and Antinous and the copy of the *Aldobrandini Wedding.* For the first time in his life the modest, extremely poor, young man of letters sat beside the princes of this earth: famous writers and scientists, elegant ladies and fashionable pianists who, like him, gathered in their notebooks the sublime and insignificant words the diety of Weimar let fall from his lips.

But Eckermann disliked the splendor of the official receptions; he preferred going to the small study near the garden, where he could talk alone with his "infallible Pole Star." He sat beside Goethe in "tranquil, loving conversation." With his knees grazing Goethe's knees, his eyes never were satiated with looking at that "robust, brown face, full of wrinkles"; his ears listened to the slow, measured words, like those of a monarch burdened by the years. Seated thus, he felt unspeakably happy, "like one who, after much toil and long expectations, finally sees his dearest wishes gratified." Thus passed almost nine years, during which Eckermann renounced living his own life. Straightforward, sensitive, infinitely receptive, endowed with a calm, meditative intelligence, he let himself be possessed by that immense force boiling there beside him. He welcomed it into his spirit with devout and loving faithfulness.

GOETHE

He absorbed its last, incomprehensible complexities—even *Faust II* revealed to him secrets that remained hidden to interpreters so much more acute and presumptuous than he.

When Goethe died, Eckermann stayed on in Weimar. He continued his usual life. He catalogued Goethe's collections; together with Riemer he put in order and prepared books and still unpublished writings for the press. He gave English lessons to Prince Karl Alexander; sometimes he was invited to the court by Karl August's son. But after Goethe was gone, he felt in exile at Weimar. All force, joy, love, and desire had abandoned his spirit; existence weighed on him like a nightmare. Almost completely alone, sadly shut up in himself, he indulged in the passions of his childhood. He walked through the countryside and the woods with young friends. There he practiced archery, studied the molting of the blackcap, the yellow-headed blackbirds, and golden orioles, the cuckoo's strange customs, the soft, melancholy song, like the sound of a flute, of certain solitary larks. He transformed his room into a small zoo, in which young falcons, hoopoes, sparrow hawks, a hunting dog and marten moved about freely.

Long, unbearable months went by, during which no memory had the strength to germinate and blossom within him. Then, after days of emptiness and desolation, Goethe appeared to him in a dream. He wore a dark overcoat and had the fresh, ruddy face of someone who lives in the open air. "People think," Eckermann said to him, with a smile, "that you are dead. But I have always said that it's not true; and now with great joy I see that I was right. Isn't it true, that you are not dead?" "What fools," Goethe replied, looking at him ironically. "Dead? Why in the world should I be dead? I've been traveling; I have seen many men and many countries. Last year I was in Sweden" (E. November 14, 1836).

Consoled by these dreams, Eckermann, during the day, managed to penetrate undisturbed into the depths of his memory. The past surfaced in brighter colors; he saw Goethe again as if he were alive; and he listened to the beloved sound of his voice. "When the weather was fine, he was with me in the carriage in his brown surtout and blue cloth cap, with his light gray cloak laid over his knees. The color of his face was brown and healthy as the fresh air; and his genial words flowed forth in the free world, sounding above the jolting noise of the carriage. Or I saw myself in the evening by the quiet candlelight, transported again into his study. He sat opposite me at his table, in his white flannel dressing gown, and was as sweet as a day well spent. We talked about things great and good: he opened before me the noblest part of his nature, and his mind kindled my own—the most perfect harmony existed between us. He extended his hand to me across the table, and I pressed it; I then took a full glass which stood by me and, without uttering a word, drank to his health, while my glances, passing over the glass, rested on his eyes" (E. part III, Preface).

During those years how many other persons tried to summon up a picture of the living Goethe! Great conservative statesmen and obscure nationalistic students; geologists, classical philologists, historians, actors, violinists, archaeologists, astronomers, tenors, and Hegelian jurists; affected lady painters and gossipy matrons; Russian and English noblemen; French journalists, Jews from Bohemia; Heine and Grillparzer, Mendelssohn and the Grimm brothers, Schopenhauer, Alessandro Poerio and Mickiewicz. Envoys from all parts of the world had come to Weimar; they had talked with Goethe for a few hours, and now they were leafing through their notebooks, reelaborating old impressions. Many had understood nothing. Some of them took Goethe's words and fancifully embroidered them; others, who had approached him "with bated breath and a head swathed in mist," recalled only a few unimportant gestures. But all these reports are equally important. Perhaps this is how the aged Goethe must be known, through a thousand echoes and almost anonymous reflections, as if his power preferred to manifest and irradiate itself over all human beings.

Indeed, we barely open our album of oil portraits, drawings, and silhouettes than once again we see Goethe in his "yellow room," surrounded by a group of his friends. At times he resembles his own legend: calm, grave, tranquil, talking in a low deep voice about philosophy and literature, art and science; and he passes fluently from one idea to another, suffusing each of them with a broad light, which clarifies and fascinates. Though the circle of his friends becomes narrower, the tumultuous energies still working in him wake him from sleep and discharge "the excess of his vigor by means of spiritual lightning bolts and thunderclaps" (M. March 6, 1828). His dark look scintillates and shines as in the years of his youth; the fiery and rapid gesticulation of his hands accompanies the fury of his speech, which pours out frothing like a mountain torrent in a spring freshet.

Suddenly a mask of boredom makes his feature heavy. He sees around him always the same persons: his son, his mother-in-law, his grandchildren, Chancellor von Müller, Eckermann, and Meyer; and he cannot bear their loving devotion. Nobody contradicts him; nobody amuses him. But he can't live without distractions and excitations; he needs to pass from one interest to another with the rapidity with which one changes a suit. He should move in a gay, vivacious society, but there, at Weimar, a long, insupportable winter awaits him—so he imagines opening his house every day at teatime: "Everyone could come and stay

GOETHE

as long as he liked, and could bring along some guests, whomever he prefers. The rooms would always be open and lit up after seven o'clock, and there would be tea and everything one wishes in abundance. We could play some music, play games, read aloud, gossip, according to one's inclination and the occasion. As for me, I would appear and disappear, as my mood suggests. And if sometimes I did not appear at all, this should not upset anyone. . . . So we would organize an eternal tea party, like the eternal lamp that burns in certain chapels" (M. October 2, 1823).

But when the doors of Goethe's house open and his friends cheerfully gather to play games, read, and sip tea, other moods reign in the royal seat of the *Frauenplan.* A side door of the yellow room silently opens; and before the guests appears an old, powdered gentleman dressed in black, who wears all of his decorations on his chest and moves about stiffly, as if he had to conceal a feeling of embarrassment or pretend a majesty he does not possess. The old gentleman grumbles, mutters to himself something incomprehensible; regales his subjects with advice on manners, and it seems to his friends that "a freezing, searing wind were blowing over the snowfields" (E. part III, Preface).

This gelid, cutting wind seems to be guided by a malign will, which wants to strike out, offend, restore the breath of Nothingness in the world. The old, bepowdered man abandons the mien of a courtier and assumes Mephisto's grandiose and trivial manner. His eyes darken, his voice becomes bitter, his words mock at men, "this absurd breed, basely and methodically absurd." They contradict, deride, and vituperate the most sacred things, so much so that his terrified auditors feel they are among the witches of Blocksberg. Since Mephistopheles is the prince of all conservatives, Goethe also plays the part of the angry conservative. While young liberal students are agitating in the German universities, he criticizes freedom of the press, attacks the law that authorizes marriages between Jews and Christians, and takes the side of the Turks against the Greeks, of the constituted order against whoever, in Germany, Spain, or Italy, wants to overthrow it.

When a young man from Geneva permits himself to affirm that "His Excellency," if he had been born in England, also would have denounced the mistakes of society and government, Goethe is unable to restrain his indignation. "But whom do you take me for?" he says in the tones of Mephistopheles. "I should have gone hunting for these abuses and uncovered and denounced them into the bargain—I who in England would have lived on abuses? If I had been born in England I would have been a rich duke, or a bishop with an income of thirty thousand pounds a year . . . I would have been a hypocrite and I would have lied in poetry and prose . . . I would have done everything to make the night of ignorance, if possible, even darker. Oh, how I would have caressed the good, silly crowd; and how I would have guided the darling youths in the schools, so that no one should realize, or even have the courage to observe, that my splendors were founded on the most scandalous abuses" (E. March 17, 1830; Soret, March 19, 1830).

In the morning, as soon as he awoke, Goethe consulted his diary in which during the last years he registered all of the day's events and thoughts. He had divided it under different headings, each with a Latin title. There were the headings of *Publica*, *Politica*, and *Oeconomica*, *Religiosa* next to *Privata*, *Domestica* and *Vinariensia*, *Botanica* and *Ottica*, *Chromatica* and *Osteologica*. *Grammatica*, *Poetica*, and *Rhetorica* guided the long procession of *Graeca et Latina*, of *Orientalia*, *Sinica*, and *Theatralia*. Local affairs were handled under *Coloniensia* and *Francofurtensia*; *Psichcia* was the rubric for passions of the heart, and *Novissima* and *Varia* were ready to welcome the surprises that every morning the world might reserve for him.

He inscribed on a leaf of the diary the things that he planned to do —as he put it, in his "agenda"—and, in the course of the day, as he gradually did them, he canceled them with a stroke of his pen. As soon as they were registered on the leaves of his diary or in the capacious archives of his mind, all events seemed to assume the same importance: the arrival of a fossil, an old coin, or the letter of a mediocre royal highness became something "significant" and "incalculable," like the *Klassische Walpurgisnacht* or Faust's descent to the Mothers. All things were loaded with recondite meanings and symbolic resonances; and they became, at the same time, majestically deprived of significance.

Late in the morning he would take care of his very heavy correspondence. As he paced up and down his study with his hands behind his back, his secretary, Herr Kräuter, sat at the small table. Herr Kräuter would take a sheet of paper, leaving a broad, elegant margin on all sides; and he would begin to write, delicately dipping his pen in the inkwell, which was never too full. How many precautions he had to observe! Each face of the letter had to contain the same number of lines; no drop of ink could stain or darken the whiteness of the paper. When the letter was completed, Goethe would take Herr Kräuter's place, as though he considered him incapable of bringing it to its final perfection. He never sprinkled it with powder; he preferred letting it dry for a few minutes in front of the stove. Then he would pick up a small box, in which he kept tiny squares of paper, each about an inch in diameter; and he would take out a square and place it where he was to stamp his wax seal. So the wax, when it melted, could not blemish a single word of his small epistolary masterpiece.

In his mind everything was distinct, ordered, and precise. But what

GOETHE

was happening outside his small study, among the "basely and methodically absurd" men who dared to crowd into his rooms? Sometimes he must have regarded the world as an immense, extremely dusty archive, full of documents in disorder; as a library, in which someone had piled up at random masses of worn and illegible books. Every so often he would come out of his retreat. Convinced that his mental hygiene, his mania for precision were indispensable to the world, he insisted that the clerks in the libraries of Weimar and Jena should keep a diary. They were to note in it variations in the weather, visits they had received, new books, work accomplished—everything that had happened in the course of the day. Or he would shut his novels' characters in a castle and set them the task of drawing topographical charts, preparing schedules, listing documents, copying papers and contracts, as if they too were diligent archivists and scrupulous notaries.[1]

During those years he was writing the *Wanderjahre* in which, as in Plato's *Politics* and *Laws*, he sought to establish the world's ideal laws. Families, associations of artisans and artists, pedagogical communities, colonies of emigrants—all groups of society in the *Wanderjahre* received their institutional charters; this would safeguard them from dangers of the future. They were strange laws. At the beginning of the book we learn that the members of the "Society of Renunciants" accept only "external and mechanical duties," such as never sleeping for more than three nights in the same house (VIII, 12). All the boys educated in the "pedagogic province" cross their arms over their chests and raise their eyes joyously to the sky, or they put their arms behind their backs while looking at the ground—without knowing the meaning of their gestures. As for the American colony of the *Wanderers*, where we might imagine that the spirit of Utopia would triumph, there too legislators are concerned only with multiplying the clocks in houses and offices and preventing their subjects from ringing bells and beating drums (VIII, 405: 20–21; 406: 14–15).

How much time had passed since the days when the "young, charming hunter" had tried to realize the kingdom of heaven! Now Goethe no longer prescribed religious commandments or moral imperatives. He did not say: "Love your neighbor as yourself," or "Do not bear false witness." Like an old Chinese mandarin teaching the ceremonious rituals of courtesy, like a very wise Pharisee studying in the Torah the signs that regulate ablutions and tithes, he recommended the abstract order and preestablished forms of existence—the elegant letter of the Law. Whereas Romantic Germany claimed to listen only to the immediate voice of the heart, Goethe advised his young friends to keep their diaries in good order, to carefully seal their letters, to set their books and documents on the shelves with great care, to listen to the clock's rhythmic beat.

Protected by this crust of formal conventions, Goethe finally felt free and light as never before in his life. Nobody could believe that the bizarre commandments of his decalogue were as serious and binding as Sinai's ten commandments, or the voice of the categorical imperative. Like the members of the Society of Renunciants, Goethe pedantically observed the small laws and rites that he prescribed for himself and others. Then, suddenly, they eluded him, casting an impalpable irony on the code he had elaborated with so much patience. The Pharisee poked fun at the Torah, the mandarin revealed the grace of a humorist. Thus circumvented by irony, these commandments did not become empty forms to be flung into the dead sea of conventions. Irony set them in quotation marks, underlined the elegance and senselessness of the letter and, at the same time, hinted that behind it extended unknown expanses, even more enigmatic meanings, forests of symbols, which can reveal a different face to each person. So there are many, many advantages to that formal life, which the young romantics refused to comprehend! When a person repeated to himself, "keep your diary in order," "seal your letters carefully," "listen to the clock's sound," "bend your eye to the earth," he brings precision into his life. And, too, he advances cautiously into the symbolic place where the gods administer the metaphysical order of the universe and marvelously regulate the flow of time.

"To live for a long time means to survive many people"; and one after the other those whom Goethe had known and loved dissolved into the air, consumed by the fires of life, like a roll of the Sibyl's leaves (March 19, 1827). In far-off 1805 Schiller had died—"half of my existence"—ten years younger than he; Wieland in January 1813; his wife Christiane in June 1816 and in atrocious pain. Ten years later Charlotte von Stein begged that her coffin should not pass beneath Goethe's windows. Grank Duke Karl August died in June 1828. And in November 1830 his son August, the cause of so much anxiety, was also buried in the Protestant cemetery in Rome, close to Shelley and Keats.

What thoughts saved him from the anguish of death? When he was consumed by the fires of life, no noble, strong, and vivacious human monad dissolved into the eternal void. The spirit of the world entrusted it with ever different activities in the spaces of the ether, or in other earthly existences.[2] And, on the other hand, what did it matter if the individual turned into dust and wind? If that father, that mother, that young bridegroom lost name and memory? While individuals were

GOETHE

wiped out, the archetypes of life survived victoriously in the generations. Thus, for centuries, the mother would hug her child to her heart;
for centuries the father would play with his son; the bride would wait
blushing for the bridegroom; the wise man would continue his tranquil
meditations; while kings and peoples would be allied before the solemn
altars of the gods.[3] When some of his dear ones left Weimar forever,
Goethe would repeat to himself these old thoughts, which instilled him
with new hope in the uninterrupted metamorphoses of the universe.

But, suddenly, all these hopes in the immortality of monads and forms
seemed vain. If he looked back, if he considered that picturesque and
confused abyss we call "history," he would repeat Mephistopheles's
words: "The past! A stupid word. Why the past? *Past and pure nullity,
absolutely the same. . . .* 'It has passed!' What does it mean? It is as if
it had never been, yet it runs wildly in a circle as if it existed" (*Faust,*
11595–11602; italics added). The history of men seemed to him a vast,
frightful desert, an abyss as deep as had reigned over the universe
before the creation—where one lost all memory of those who had
known the warmth of existence.

Oppressed by this nullity, Goethe tried to convince himself that Mephistopheles was wrong, that something had truly existed in the history of
men; and he set about collecting relics and testimonies of the past. But
he was not interested in conserving great events and immortal works
of art, which our piety is anxious to preserve in museums and history
books. He tried to collect that ephemeral part of men's life that fails to
transform itself into an historical event or a work of art, that returns to
dust and is miserably dispersed by the winds. The face of a man who
had touched so many hearts—putrified in a grave; the voice that had
revealed the inventions of a colorful fantasy—fell into the confused
graveyard of sounds; and even the marks of calligraphy, in which the
ineffable essence of a person was perhaps expressed, lay forgotten in
drawers and would soon disappear forever.

Thus Goethe began to acquire family portraits and compositions in
which the dead would continue to show him their earthly faces. He
searched for manuscripts, letters, and even the simple signatures of
illustrious men; drawings, plaster casts, stones, coins, relics, any object
that harbored the shadow or aura of the past. He had his letters copied
and bound; he narrated his own existence in a number of autobiograph-
ical writings, as if he were attempting to preserve something of the
persona condemned to death. His large house became a large, gloomy
museum. Hundreds of portraits hung on the walls, thousands of letters,
autographs, and drawings turned yellow and musty in the cupboards,
dust-covered books and sealed newspapers filled the rooms. The house

could no longer contain this unceasing lava flow of dead objects.

In the meantime a throng of antiquarians, mild and maniacal, gathered in he castles of the *Wahlverwandschaften* and the *Wanderjahre*. Some of them collected medals, coins, seals, vases, weapons, and tools found in the tumuli of ancient peoples; incisions in wood or copper, reproductions of medieval paintings. Some lived among clocks that had struck the hour of birth and death for many; poured tea from a teapot, the witness of a thousand family gatherings; stirred the fire with a poker used by many generations. Others built solemn funerary monuments or chapels, illuminated by an eternal light, there to preserve, miraculously embalmed, the bodies of Mignon, Eugenie, and Ottilie. Who could exclude the possibility that in those bodies a shadow of the immortal soul might still live? Or that the dead, laid beneath funerary stones or crystals, might have a "a second life" (VI, 370: 15); a quiet, twilight continuation of the existence they had known on earth?[4]

Goethe, like a prince of antiquarians, roamed through his collections. He contemplated the portraits, leafed through the manuscripts, autographs, and yellowed drawings in his drawers and cases; read the letters he had written to the friends of his youth. But was he only a simple antiquarian, warmed by the comfortable tepidity of ancient things? Or rather was he a maniacal embalmer, a fetishistic custodian of the shadows of the past? Probably, in the depths of his soul—although he would not have dared admit it to himself—he imagined that he had imprisoned a populace of ghosts within the walls of his house, in its chests, and on its walls. Just as Mignon and Ottilie lived their "second life" beneath slabs of marble or crystal, so around him other noble individual essences experienced their silent, tranquil second life. His house had little in common with other museums. It was akin to Hades, where, among asphodels and unfertile willows, heroes and elect spirits continued to live a pale reflection of their former existence.

When Goethe's senses were weaker and his imagination more acute he was sure to discern, on the walls of his rooms, the infinitely light shadow of those by now familiar persons; and to listen to "silent conversations," small silent ripples of laughter, the whisperings and batlike squeaks of the company of ghosts he had shut up in his house. Perhaps, at even more dizzying moments, desperate dreams tempted his mind. The witches of Thessaly called souls back into their bodies; Faust obtained permission from Persephone to carry Helen's ghost back into life; and perhaps, by dint of wandering among the shadows of the past, he too, would finally acquire the same power.

When he was young he had thought that the past was a "book closed with seven seals" (*Faust*, 575–576); and now all the world's history could

GOETHE

not satisfy his longing for knowledge. With a rich imagination, nourished by precision, he summoned up the peoples of gods and monsters who reigned over the origins of Greece; the rough, mighty walls of Mycenaean fortresses; Moses, this "taciturn and solitary shepherd," as he crossed the desert with his people. He called into his world Zoroaster, Mohammed, the Barmecide caliphs in Baghdad, the audacious tropes of Oriental poetry and the fables of the *Thousand and One Nights,* all strung on a very mobile thread. He evoked the builders of cathedrals and the painters of Madonnas from the German Middle Ages; the castles as smooth as steel, packed with halls and escutchens, built in Greece by crusading knights; the imperial alchemists, who distilled the philosopher's stone and prepared the birth of *homunculus* in their Gothic laboratories. He restored the German cities he had known in his childhood—Cologne, Frankfurt, Leipzig—with their old wooden houses and new outlying districts traversed by a mob of carriages and industrious ants.

As soon as Goethe contemplated them, these historical figures and images left the soil in which they were born. Covered with ruins and dust, steeped in the color of time, with still lively remains of their language and customs, they flitted like ghosts across tens of unknown centuries, to reach the small Weimar of 1817, 1826, or 1831 and invade the present in which Goethe lived. Like a gallery of statues, busts, and plaster casts, the images were set out before his eyes; faithful to their own time and completely free from the succession of times. He stared at them one by one, studied their most hidden details, copied in words a Doric column, the style of Aeschylus's choruses, the images of Hafiz, or the language of the alchemists. Finally he mixed them all together, as if in a paradoxical phantasmagoria—and the Mycenaean fortresses were transformed into the castles of crusading knights, Helen trilled and warbled like a singer in an opera, the image of the Holy Family lived again, after eighteen centuries, in the family of a modest German carpenter.

Meanwhile Goethe felt that he was no longer that particular individual born in Frankfurt eighty years before whom destiny had decreed could live only once. He had become a suprapersonal being, a mythical figure similar to Alexander the Great, who had felt the hopes and deeds of Achilles and Cyrus reborn in his person. While he listened to his foolish visitors or the tedious noise of the carriages on the streets of Weimar, a part of himself inhabited all points of time and space. He existed in the fortress of Mycenaean Sparta, amid the stones of the desert of Palestine, in the Baghdad of the caliphs, and the Frankfurt of his childhood. A thousand other existences, perhaps but grazed in his dreams, were reborn in his: the words of Homer and Hafiz, the myths of Plato, the fantasies of Ovid, and the hoaxes of Cagliostro. Sometimes it seemed to him that his life was "double, triple, quadruple"; infinitely multiple, like Helen's resurrected from the kingdom of the dead (*Faust*, 9254–9255). Thus all the instants he still had to live—the last instants fate granted him—became rich and vast, profound and full, like those of no other living person.

These continuous epiphanies of the past also bore their bitter fruits. Called up from the void, the past introduced into the present a frightful, spectral shadow (X, 32: 28–29). Guests who visited his house moved as in a dream, and daily events lost their delightful vivacity. He was living a mythical existence—in Sparta and Baghdad, imperial Rome and old Cologne. But was he really alive? Did he still exist? Or, rather, had he lived so long among the shades that he too had glided along the paths of death, "in bitter, gray Hades, full of elusive images, regurgitant, eternally empty"?[5]

There were days when Goethe seemed to have changed. The old gentleman garbed in black, his chest covered with decorations, the pedantic archivist, the gloomy custodian of the Museum of the Past, left the house in Weimar. Like a pilgrim who travels about the earth murmuring the chants of eternal separation, Goethe left his possessions, collections, the honors and dignity of a notable bureaucrat. He renounced the mania for order, the complicated rituals, the almost unbearable weight of the past; the faithful friendships. He turned his back on the books he had written and was still writing; the fame he had, as few others, enjoyed and of which he knew the senselessness.

At such moments some of his older friends recognized the airy master of the spirits, the elegant skater who so many years before had charmed the court of Weimar. But now his life was even lighter. In those far-off years, his spirit had been oppressed by a turbid and disquieting intoxication. Those passions were now gone. He had neither regrets nor a feeling of nostalgia for the past, nor any desires for the future; no anxiety, no nervous tension, no feelings of tenderness toward himself. His faculties were purified; thoughts crossed his mind reduced to their linear essence; emotions burned in him without warmth or softness. Consumed and lightened, almost without human shadows, there shone in him only that deep crystal, that very bright, immaterial fire he called the entelechy. The long, laborious, very painful metamorphoses were completed; and soon the chrysalis would leave the cocoon that had held it for so long.

Seated in the garden behind his house, wearing a very white dressing

GOETHE

gown—which made him look like "a large white ram"—he contemplated the eternal beauty of the world. Like an old mandarin, "sated with giving orders, weary of serving" (I, 386: 25–26), he looked at the narcissus, its calyx rimmed with red, as it bloomed prematurely in his garden. He saw the boldly winking tail of the peacock spreading in glory in the sun's rays at sunset; a belated rose bud; the ardor of the moon in the regions of the East. Amid the greenery and waters, he cheerfully drank and wrote—"cup after cup, sign after sign"—as though he knew only the moment he was living. His existence had become an uninterrupted contemplative present; a series of equally beatific instants, each of which reflected the immobile light of the eternal.

He gazed at the clouds: the large cumulus clouds, dense, magnificently rounded masses, looking like the ridges of mountains. Soon the clouds broke apart and began drifting to the heights, dissolving in fresh and luminous ribbons, in very light and tender cirrus formations, disappearing into infinite space. Up there, in the pure region of the ether, were gathered his world's loftiest symbols; and noble souls like Wieland's crossed the spaces in the form of stars of the first magnitude, or guiding the nebulous essence of some comet. Soon he, too, consumed by the flames of life, would live among the stars. So he chose a star, as one day he said jokingly to Chancellor von Müller, where "he hoped to continue his little games in peace."

Meanwhile destiny, forgetting that he too was made of nerves, veins, and arteries, put him to some terrible tests (November 21, 1830). Death pursued him right into his house; the pain he tried to control overwhelmed him and violent discharges of blood made them fear for his life. But Goethe had by now accepted, once and for all, the unfathomable will of God: he bowed his head before the necessary movements of life, which repeats itself and returns before our eyes, like a circle or spiral. So the grimmest clouds soon cleared from his horizon; the strength of the pain was mitigated; his despair became absolute, almost serene. A strange gaiety slowly descended in his soul, warm with gratitude for the beauty of the world and, at the same time, cold and inhuman as the light of the stars where the spirit of the world would soon call him.

He left his small study at the back of his house quite reluctantly. The windows, lit by the sun, opened on the garden; a vase of flowers adorned the sill; an oaken desk was filled with minerals, ledgers, and silhouettes. A large desk contained his grandchildren's savings and the glass given him as a gift by Ulrike von Levetzow. He lived shut up in there, as in a monk's cell, going for months without speaking to anyone, "especially if to speak means to say to someone else what one thinks" (September 20, 1820). He was too old to understand the ideas of others, nor had he any desire to make himself understood. If there came to see him some old friend with whom he thought he might have a long conversation, he soon realized that the things one could discuss were quickly exhausted. "Only stupidity is infinite," Jarno says (W. I, 25; II, 12). Seated like this in silence, for hours, facing Meyer, every so often he would let fall a sentence, a few words, a grunt of assent or bad humor. He entrusted his secrets to sheets of paper.

He had no time to lose. As a young man, he had imagined he could rule a state; he had drawn trees, landscapes, and figures and had lost himself in the realm of plants, colors, and stones (E. April 20, 1826). If he had not wasted so much time, he too perhaps would have become an old, very wise artisan like Aeschylus or Lope de Vega, capable of shaping the German language as he wished. Now his powers had abandoned him; but *Faust* was still a superb, incomplete construction, the first draft of the *Wanderjahre* did not satisfy him, and many sketches and studies remained among his papers.

He tried to use wisely whatever energy he still had. During the sleepless hours of the night, he pondered what he could do the next day. And during the first morning hours, restored by sleep, he recounted the astral experiences of Makarie, the flight of the wild beasts and the sounds of the flute in the *Novelle*, the spectral swarming of mythical figures in the *Klassische Walpurgisnacht*. He exploited the tiniest fragments of time, unexpected, very rapid tremors of inspiration, even moments of weariness. Like a superb Oriental tyrant who surrounds himself with slaves and lives in them and from them, he had transformed the court of his friends into a prolongation of himself. He entrusted them with his papers, so that they might put them in order and publish them and make known to the world the last, most inspired illuminations of that "collective being that bears the name of Goethe."

The
Sleep
of Poetry

II

After Pandora's desertion, Epimetheus returns every day to the place where he had seen her disappear into the sky. Lingering there for a long time, he sees her again in that sudden gesture of farewell. He hopes to meet her again on the earth; he dreams that "the most immobile star of the night" (*Pandora*, 772) will yield to the force of his yearning. But Pandora does not return to his arms, and he remains alone in "an eternally orphaned time" (*Pandora*, 741).

So Epimetheus begins to shun the daylight. He fears the crow of the cock, the too precocious brightness of the morning star, the rays of sunlight that distinguish forms and illumine men's paths. He would like to see an eternal night engulf the world. While the race of Prometheus grazes sheep, shapes iron, and stretches nets in the waters, Epimetheus fantasizes and drowses, lost amid the mists of his twlight world. When darkness maternally covers men and beasts, no sleep comes to restore his lost strength or to cancel the memory of his sufferings and felicities. Anxious, insomniac, burdened with cares and grave thoughts, he roams the fields sunk in nocturnal shadows.

Overcome by a morbid lunacy, Epimetheus cannot bear to see the past disappear in the abysses of time. With the violence of a passion tortured by intelligence his anguished spirit sinks into the shadows of the past. He lingers on events that happened quickly and immediately vanished, torturing them, calling them back into the present. Everything that has existed must come to rest, like an inexpungeable shadow, in his sleepless eyes, in his memory, unable and unwilling to forget. All dimensions become confused in his mind; past and present events, things that actually occurred and those imagined in dreams, real things and illusory things become as changing as smoke and dissolve "in the murky realm of possibility which confuses the figures" (*Pandora,* 12).

Again and again Epimetheus tries to summon Pandora's image. It advances trembling, approaches him; it sways and flutters in his mind, similar to itself and to a thousand different figures; then it disappears once again. Finally his eye possesses her as if a painter had painted her effigy inside his pupil. He sees again the brown hair, rich and exuberant, falling about Pandora's temples; the crown of flowers casting its shadows on her forehead, dousing the ardor of her gaze; the delicate pearl of her ear—— But the beautiful apparition lasts for only an instant. Scarcely does his eye shut than Pandora goes off into the air and fades away, and the flowers of her necklace are scattered through the universe. No labor is emptier and vainer than that which he has carried out; the past cannot be possessed; memories flee and unfaithful images vanish in swarms and leave us all alone.

Many poets like Epimetheus lived in Goethe's time! They, too, shunned the clear light of day and sought the shadows of night. "Nocturnal wayfarers, full of care, weighed down by grave thoughts" (*Pandora,* 314), they roamed about sleeplessly in an eternal twilight. The force that impelled them to write was born from what they had lost: a dangerous Pandora, an ambiguous gift of the gods, a creature of air and bronze, whom they would never see again. They contemplated the tragic experience of their life; they tortured their minds, forcing themselves to wander in the "murky realm of possibility which confuses the figures"; and they let themselves be imprisoned by the face of Medusa who so often possesses memory.

If Apollo did not visit them, if the divine delirium never descended on them, they tried to provoke it with the violence of artifice. Like Epimetheus, like Goethe's Tasso, like Wilhelm Meister in *Theatralische Sendung,* they sought help in alcohol, coffee, drugs—in a procured insomnia. They searched their savage dreams, the turbid, extremely mobile shadows that fill the agitated imagination. What extraordinary poems came from their hands! There was, in these poems, something convulsed, neurasthenic, enervated, infinitely soft. There was, too, something strident and forced, as in all creations compelled to mature before their proper time. Their images still fill us with wonder, they are so new and inspired; and yet they dissolve and fray before our eyes like the flowers of Pandora's necklace.

At various periods of his life Goethe also ran the risk of resembling Epimetheus; but each time he overcame this danger by transforming his own emotions into those of a dramatic or lyrical character. He disliked the spectacles of tragedy. If the wings of death or suffering grazed him, he would force his frightened and intimidated eyes to look away. While Epitmetheus's children morbidly cultivated their feelings of anguish, he would let the suffering discharge itself silently within him and he did not permit his words to dwell on the still open wound. He waited for sleep to come—"like pure felicity, not besought, not supplicated"—and close his eyes and refresh his sick temples: he waited for sleep "to untie the knots of adamant throughts," cleansing him of the horror he had lived through (*Faust,* 4623 ff.).

So memories abandoned him, plunging him into the deep waters of forgetfulness (June 6, 12, 1820). There he sojourned for a long time; while on the surface of the earth he experienced a new existence, his memories lost their anguishing rigidity and began to move about freely, living a richer, more agile life. They encountered affinities, analogies, and significances the intelligence would never have been able to find, and were transformed into a yielding mass, organized like a poetic motif. At this point, everything seemed ready: the material of his existence waited only to be gathered into a book.

But Goethe was in no hurry to start writing. If the sudden shock or joyous tumult of inspiration did not excite his mind, he spent the unproductive hours, days, and months in utter idleness—without trying to awaken his poetic faculties with alcohol and drugs, like Epimetheus's sons. "Forced" works, born from delirious violence or from audacious intellectual premeditation, had never convinced him. The only excitants he recommended to his young friends were those that nature offers to every man: quiet and sleep, during which the poetry is formed within our spirit; movement, which frees impeded and benumbed thoughts; the water of the sea, into which Byron dove and on which he sailed so daringly; and above all the fresh air of the open country, where God's spirit breathes immediately on man (E. March 11, 1828).

When he considered his own poetic gift he understood that he was inhabited by the selfsame biological force which each season makes the trees grow and ripens fruits on the light-suffused crust of the earth. Who can compel peach trees to blossom in cold December, or cauliflowers to decorate the dinner table during the summer? His books were also plants; and neither arbitrary wishes nor whims could force them to be born unnaturally. *Tasso* grew slowly, like a fragrant orange tree (December 16, 1789); *Faust* "was born from the soil like a great family of mushrooms," which are born and then disappear with the changing of the season (July 1, 1797). Usually, the full flowering of his poetic garden occurred during the months of spring and summer, when trees are covered with leaves, flowers, and fruits. During the winter months the readied paper remained blank; and Goethe hid himself from the snow, like an onion beneath the earth, waiting for warmth and south winds to revive his chilled, cramped inspiration.

Sometimes, as in the case of the *Lehrjahre* and *Faust II*, he prepared a complicated intellectual construction, elaborating a quantity of levels and schemes. But he always distrusted his own programs, since he knew that too obvious an architecture would frighten away his "airy phantoms" (July 1, 1797). He left his levels in a drawer; and meanwhile the books grew without his even realizing it. Like plants, they were soon pushing their roots and branches far in all directions, forming a forest so dense and so tightly interlaced that it seemed incredible to him that he had planted it with his own hands (November 14, 1827).

Like all plants, his books needed loving and continuous care: They feared sudden frosts, badly executed prunings, hasty grafts. They feared above all to be wounded by the violent light of intellectual analysis. So he tried to protect them by the deepest silence, by a boundless secrecy. If someone asked him about them, he would avoid replying: like that character in the fairy tale who, while a thousand voices lured and threatened him, walked silently and without looking about him to the place where the talisman was buried and for which he had searched for years (X, 459: 5–20). Only at the time of the *Lehrjahre* did he listen with fascination to Schiller's explanations and proposals, a "true prophet" and interpreter of his poetic dreams (June 22, 1797). But after a few months, assailed by superstitious fright, he had suddenly broken off all discussions with him.

The ripening of his books took place in the slowest, most cautious and hesitant fashion. The *Lehrjahre* had to wait for twenty years before finding definitive form; and *Faust*, capricious as a family of mushrooms, required almost sixty seasons to push into the light. When all was ready within his spirit, the execution came to him with incredible speed. His imagination ran on so swiftly that his hand could not keep up with it; he would stumble on the paper, mixing up letters and words (November 24, 1812). His friends could never stop being amazed by this. "While we," Schiller wrote, "must gather and painstakingly sift, so as to slowly produce something mediocre, for him it suffices to give a slight shake of his tree to bring down the finest fruits, ripe and heavy" (July 21, 1797, to Heinrich Meyer).

Sometimes the verses burst into being with the joyous and capricious rapidity of a flash of lightning. It was night; he was fast asleep; suddenly a poem would form in his dreams, would wake him and, when he had opened his eyes, was already completed. But nocturnal creation ran the risk of being lost; like Petrarch, he would have liked to own a hairy

GOETHE

leather vest on which he could fix with his fingers the words born unexpectedly in his dreams. With his eyes bleared and his mind still drowsing, he would get up from his bed and run to his writing stand like a somnambulist, writing down the poem from beginning to end. He did not like to use a pen, which grated and dug into the paper, threatening to wake him from his poetic sleep. He preferred instead to entrust the quick nocturnal words to the docile marks of a pencil.

When inspiration attacked him with such extraordinary violence, he thought that "most precious gifts" are not born from the σωφροσύνη, "wisdom," of men; but, as Plato says, "from a delirium, which is certainly bestowed as a divine gift" (*Phaedrus,* 244 a). At those privileged moments he had the impression that the gods had sent him one of their unhoped-for and unforeseeable gifts (E. March 11, 1828). He was only the conduit, witness to a higher force—the somnambulistic hand dashing down the nocturnal words, the inspired mouth pronouncing them during wakefulness or in sleep.

"Live well, my dear, my venerated friend!" Schiller had written to Goethe immediately after reading the *Lehrjahre.* "How moved I am when I think that what we must otherwise search for and find with difficulty in the remote distance of a happy antiquity, I have so close to me, in you. You should not be surprised if there are so few people able and worthy of understanding you. . . . It is one of the most beautiful happinesses of my life to have witnessed the fulfillment of this production, at a period when my energies are always in movement, so that I can still draw from this pure source; and the fine relation that we have imposes on me the religious duty of making your book mine, of educating all that in me is simple reality to become the limpid mirror of the spirit alive in this guise; so as to deserve, in the highest sense of the word, the name of your friend. How vividly I have felt, on this occasion . . . that confronted by the supreme things there does not exist any freedom but love" (July 2, 1796).

During these very intense days of the summer of 1796, Schiller encountered one of those masterpieces that so completely upset mental attitudes and received ideas that men can but dimly perceive them. For the first time he met greatness incarnated in the simple figure of a friend; and this greatness towered over him, almost made him doubt his own existence, endangering his own poetic and intellectual activity. Many people would have protected themselves, keeping that threatening and destructive force at a distance. But for a noble and gentle soul like Schiller's, loving admiration was able to overcome all conscious and unconscious resistances. It forced him to abandon his ideas and attitudes and to transform himself into the "limpid mirror" of Goethe's work. Almost at first glance he understood the *Lehrjahre* and described in an incomparable manner its architecture, tone, characters, and most hidden nuances.

Yet, despite his dedication and intelligence, even Schiller did not succeed in completely overcoming the limitations of his own nature. Certain aspects of the *Lehrjahre* continued to elude him. For example, he would have liked Goethe to render his themes more evident, and to formulate their intellectual significance with greater precision. "It seems to me" he wrote, "that you have pushed the free grace of the movement farther than poetic gravity can support; and that, due to your repugnance for all that is heavy, methodical, and rigid, you have approached the opposite extreme. . . . It would be necessary to render a bit more meaningful to the reader everything that up till now he has regarded in too light a manner, and to legitimatize also in respect to reason those theatrical inventions in which he could perhaps see only a game of the imagination, connecting them in a more emphatic fashion to the high seriousness of the book, as has happened, till now, implicitly but not explicitly" (July 8, 1796).

The next day Goethe replied to Schiller. "I beg you not to stop pushing me, if I can put it that way, beyond my limits. The fault, which you rightly remark on, comes from my most profound nature, from a certain realistic 'tic' that makes it seem pleasant to me to hide my existence, my actions, my writings from men's eyes. So I always enjoy traveling incognito, I choose a modest attire rather than a better one and, when speaking with a stranger or someone I don't know very well, I prefer an insignificant subject or a less significant expression. I seem more frivolous than I really am; and, I should like to say, I interpose myself between my real self and my appearance. . . . Undoubtedly the apparent results, as expressed by my book, are much more limited than its content; and it seems to me that I am the sort of person who, after having drawn up a long column of large sums, in the end purposely makes mistakes in addition so as to diminish, God knows because of what caprice, the total sum." And he added: "If it must happen . . . that the final significant words do not want to come from my breast, I beg you to add yourself, with a few bold strokes of your brush, what I— bound by the strangest necessity of nature—cannot succeed in pronouncing. . . ."

The "final significant words" never came out of Goethe's breast. Nor, to our good fortune, did Schiller's daring brush add them in the margin of his manuscripts. Like a vegetable gardener who grows all kinds of delicate, early produce for the rich spring markets, Goethe did not

GOETHE

bring his works to complete ripeness. He arrested them just a moment before; he plucked them from the stems while they were still green. Instead of rendering all the motifs explicit and intelligible, as Schiller would have preferred, he left them in the shadow. With a "hint," a "fleeting allusion" (September 8, 1831), he touched lightly on the greatest problems. Half consciously and half unconsciouly, he committed his small, obstinate mistakes in addition. Behind a frivolous note or a theatrical game he concealed tragic depths; he indicated the just path and then departed from it. Only the return of a comparison, after hundreds of pages, illuminated a profound meaning.

But behind the almost cruel formal calm, how many forces remained hidden and unspoken! All the richness, which, in other works, shines and sparkles on the surface, we must glimpse indistinctly here. On one page an idea has not been developed fully; on another page, a whole swarm of metaphors has not been explicitly expressed, but rather is radiated into all the veins of the work and continues to communicate its imaginative excitement to us.

The Veil
and the Clouds

III

Reading Goethe's youthful letters and certain parts of the *Theatralische Sendung* one feels he can see the young hunter in the green jacket as he improvises before the Weimar audience, stunning himself and us with the elegant ardor of his images. Like the *Knabe Lenker* in *Faust II*, he squanders in a moment an imaginative wealth sufficient to supply an entire guild of poets; he snaps his fingers and his images—pearl necklaces, gold brooches, precious stones, mysterious flames, brightly colored butterflies—take flight and go fluttering through the air. Some of them wither sadly, incomplete and uncomprehended. Others are lost in the sky like restless fireworks that have escaped from the hands of the person who prepared them. Many of them come from the books of the Old and New Testaments; or from the language of the alchemists, pietists, and scientists of the period; or they have just been culled from the lips of the inhabitants of the German courts. Whatever their origin, these metaphors share every tone of Goethe's emotions; they gather in the sudden changes of mood, the bizarre inventions of his poetic frenzy, and carry all the way to us the echo of an always changing, very rapid conversation.

When Goethe wrote *Faust II*, he had certainly lost many of his youthful gifts. He no longer converses with his audience; he writes on sheets of paper, closeted in his study, addressing everyone and no one. The vivacious imaginative tumult, which once ran like a shiver through all the images, rarely reappears. Goethe's imagination seems stiff and crystallized; like his life, it hides behind a grill-like layer of cold, spent coals.

GOETHE

If in the past he tried to give his style the freedom and movement of verbs, now he prefers nouns, transforming even the adjectives and verbs into substantives. He has recourse to formulas, stereotypes, set forms, strange clichés; more and more he cultivates his own sclerosis. Certain images recur, barely changed, in the most diverse occasions—as if Goethe could conceive the world only through the variations of a few basic formulas.

This process of stylistic fixation should make it easier to read *Faust II* and allow us to know more fully the significance of certain privileged expressions. But if we isolate an element of Goethe's "late style" and ask ourselves what the adjective *bedeutend* (significant or relevant) means or why Goethe resorts so frequently to images of the "veil," everything blurs before our eyes. The semantic confines of the images and words stretch out farther and farther, until they are lost in utter indistinctness. Each element of the style seems to contain the entire wealth of the dictionary. At the end we are convinced that *Faust II* was written in an absolutely private language, freighted with meanings and equivalences to which no one has given us the key.

So the task of every reader of *Faust II* becomes similar to the linguist's search for the key to an unknown language, collecting on his desk all the testimony he possesses concerning linear *B* or Etruscan. We, too, when we read *Faust II*, are forced to gather all of Goethe's similar or related metaphors—all the places, for example, where he has drawn the images of the veil and the cloud—and then ask ourselves what affinity links the morning mists and the veil of *Zueignung* (Dedication), the pestilential clouds of the *Natürliche Tochter*, the airy figures of Pandora, and the soft cirrus clouds of the penitents clustered around the Virgin.

We must go back to the *Zueignung*, a lyrical poem written in 1784 and published as the prologue in the edition of Goethe's complete works. At dawn, as he leaves the hut in which he has spent the night, the poet walks along the mountain paths, contemplating the marvels of the new day. From the damp meadows rise wisps of mist, which condense and grow around his head like a "turbid blossoming" (*Zueignung*, 14), blotting out his sight. But the mists soon dissolve; the sun's first light spreads over peaks and valleys, drives away the darkness and illuminates the world, blinding the poet with the fiery violence of its splendor.

When an impulse leads him to open his eyes again, he sees above the clouds in the sky a "divine woman" (*Zueignung*, 30). She speaks to him in words full of love. Only at the end of the *Zueignung* do we learn her name. The "divine woman" is the truth (*Zueignung*, 96) who acquaints men with her "soft light" (*Zueignung,* 56). But the truth's rays are different from those of the sun. Infinite source of all light, the sun blinds us and forces us to look down at the ground. Like a suave celestial mediatrix, the truth interrupts and filters the solar rays. It robs them of all their violence so as to transform what was a terrible gift into a benediction. At other times, the "divine woman" had appeared before us in Goethe's books under the name of Charlotte von Stein and Iphigenia. Like Frau von Stein, who "dripped moderation into his hot blood" and controlled Goethe's wild and errant course (*Warum gabst du,* 29–35), the truth infuses one with calm when the passions rage without rest (*Zueignung,* 43–44) and pours "a very pure balsam" on the wounds inflicted by life (*Zueignung,* 36). Like Iphigenia, who refreshed perturbed hearts with the "pure breath of love,"[1] the truth refreshes the brow with a touch like that of celestial wings (*Zueignung,* 45–46).

Not even the mitigated light of truth can descend with impunity on the earth. Its rays wound many people's eyes (*Zueignung,* 52): if someone possesses it or thinks he possesses it, he encloses it within himself and tries to conceal it from other men (*Zueignung,* 56). So even the "divine woman" is compelled to choose a symbol of mediation. Smiling at the poet kneeling at her feet, she stretches out her hand. Seizing the morning mist and the lightest ribbons of cloud, she weaves them into the brightness of the sun and forms the "very pure veil" of poetry, which moves and swells in the sky in a "thousand folds" (*Zueignung,* 81–96).

As Goethe had written in a youthful letter, "Beauty is not light and it is not night. Twilight: the birth of true and false. A thing in between" (February 13, 1769). In the same fashion, one encounters in the veil of poetry the extreme poles of the world: light and darkness, true and false. But, as they meet and dissolve in the same texture, they are transformed completely. Darkness leaves its obscurest and heaviest part at the bottom of the valley—the "turbid blossoming." It purifies itself, becomes thinner; and the shadow remaining in the hands of the "divine woman" is imbued with light. The sun's rays lose their ardor, welcome the damp freshness of celestial creatures; the truth reflects a face always the same in the veil's thousand shimmering folds, where we know it only as if in shadow.

If the limpid veil of poetry accompanies us along the paths of life, nothing can fail us or wound us. We possess all the light we have need of on earth—we live in a protective penumbra; we see the eternal, while the spirit plays with appearances and terrestrial illusions. When the misty, sultry heat of midday prostrates us, we wave the veil in the air and immediately the fresh winds of afternoon, the perfume of flowers and roots envelops our existence. If the night terrifies us, poetry will make it luminous for us. If the waves of life and passion torment us, everything, at that touch, will become calm and soft; and even the grave will seem to us "a bed of clouds" (*Zueignung*, 102). So, around the veil of poetry, Goethe gathered his "friends," the small germ of that Utopian society he dreamed of during those years. And with them, he went to meet the "new day" (*Zueignung*, 109).

When Goethe wrote *Torquato Tasso* (1780–1789), the antithesis between the sun and the clouds again attracted his imagination. The real world, in which the astute calculators of politics act, seems to Tasso similar to "the day's splendor" (*Tasso*, 2261). As for him, he compares himself "to the calm light that gives you joy at night, and with its light irresistibly lures your eye and heart"; but the day roams about like "a feeble, pale little cloud" (*Torquato Tasso*, 2257–2261). If he listens to the words of knowing politicians, it seems to him that he disappears from himself; he fears "vanishing like Echo before the rocks," of getting lost like a reflection, a nothingness (*Tasso*, 797–800). Even the verses he offers to the world are figures of air, with "sounds and light images" fluttering before our spirits (*Tasso*, 2025–2027). Thus the images of *Zueignung* return in the verses of *Tasso* with another significance. The lightness of poetry does not protect poets from the torments of life: it leaves them helpless, like very pale clouds, a barely audible echo, when confronted by the triumphant splendor of the real world.

No sooner does the Princess d'Este set a crown of laurel on Tasso's head than he cries: "Oh, take it off my head, take it away! It scorches my curls! And like a ray of sunlight that might strike too hot upon my head, it burns the power of thought and tears it out of my brow. A feverish heat agitates my blood! Forgive me! It is too much!" (*Tasso*, 488–493). Farther on, he insists: "My poem . . . I will change it, I will never complete it. I feel, I feel indeed that great art that nourishes us all, that strengthens and restores the healthy spirit, will ruin me, will drive me away" (*Tasso*, 3132–3136). In the verses of *Zueignung*, poetry is regarded as a tranquil possession, an everyday blessing that refreshes and perfumes. Here everything is turned upside down. The demon of poetry that lives inside Tasso, the fulfilled and perfect art that at times visits him, burns with the same strength as the sun's rays—they strike at the temples, confuse and wipe out thoughts, agitate the blood, plunge their victims into the final ruin. If Tasso wants to survive, he must drive poetry away from himself: lift it up into the ether and pursue it endlessly, like an apparition floating "high, always higher and out of reach" among the clouds of the sky (*Tasso*, 499–502).

After Eleonora d'Este's entreaties, Tasso accepts the crown of laurel;

but he wants to run away and wander in the woods, where trees and rocks are mirrored in a fountain. Possessed by imagination, which as always incarnates all of his desires, he believes that he is already there, in the thick of the woods, and that he is contemplating his own shadow reflected in the water. His troubled mind becomes lost in vertiginous fantasies, everything before him becomes confused. The shadow he thinks he is staring at does not seem to be his but rather that of a young, unknown poet of other times whom someone had "marvelously crowned."[2] The trees, rocks, and sky mirrored in the waters seem to him those of the Elysium, and soon the heroes and poets of ancient times, Homer, Achilles, Alexander, perhaps Virgil, gather around his shadow. So Tasso's delirium is placated. The sun of poetry transforms him into a specter, a distinct reflection of himself; it takes him far from life and sets him traveling toward the silent realms of Hades. But at the same time, it cures and saves him, welcoming him into the great tradition of heroic poetry.

In a later play, *Die natürliche Tochter* (1799–1803), the images of the clouds, the veil and light are intertwined even more richly. A duke has two children. The "turbid mind" of the male son generates "clouds" that darken the father's horizon (*Natürliche Tochter*, 61–62). On the contrary, his natural daughter, Eugenie is akin to the "carbuncle stone" that inhabits the dark caves and gladdens with its light "the night's mysterious horrors" (*Natürliche Tochter*, 64–67). Yet Eugenie is not satisfied to illumine the night; she would like "to become visible" (*Natürliche Tochter*, 1067) and shine at court, dressed in the "splendor" of the regal sun (*Natürliche Tochter*, 265–269; 376–377; 1080–1086).

One day her father presents her with a casket full of gowns and jewels, which she must wear before the king, but he forbids her to open it. Overcome with impatience, Eugenie disobeys; and her gaze is riveted to the gold of the cloths, the mild gleam of the pearls, the glittering rays of the jewels (*Natürliche Tochter*, 1025; 1033–1036; 1060–1063). With this rash deed, uncovering what must remain hidden, Eugenie sins against the law of her own nature and brings about her condemnation. The light of the world "blinds her." Powerful enemies confront her with this alternative: either leave her country and live on an American island, where "the sun's fiery darts" (*Natürliche Tochter*, 1983), the swamp's poisonous "vapors" (*Natürliche Tochter*, 1768), "clouds" of pestilential insects (*Natürliche Tochter*, 1997) will wear away her strength; or renounce forever the splendor to which she had aspired, "veiling" her face in the mediocrity of bourgeois life (stage direction, Act IV, Scene 1).

After begging and weeping, after seeking in vain for help, Eugenie

GOETHE

bows her head and shuts herself up in the secrecy of a house in the country (*Natürliche Tochter*, 2901). Buried once again in darkness, "veiled" like an "invisible divinity" (*Natürliche Tochter*, 2943–2947), she again reveals her true essence, which life in the world was on the point of disfiguring. Like the mythical carbuncle stone, like a "pure talisman" (*Natürliche Tochter*, 2853), Eugenie illuminates the shadows, preparing the future resurrection of the world (*Natürliche Tochter*, 2913–2914; 2854–2855). Her veiled figure is the image of hope.

When Pandora travels across the earth she seems a gigantic classical statue. A net of gold woven by Hephaestus tries vainly to hold her brown, swollen headdress; Amphitrite flings the pearls of the sea around her neck; a diadem adorns her head, flowers bedeck her breast, bracelets encircle her arms, rings her fingers, winged sandals encase her feet; and enormous flowers, lions and roe bucks are born miraculously on her path. Like all divine figures, Pandora concentrates in herself the light of the sun. Her glances, with their "infallible strength of arrows," dazzle man's eyes (*Pandora*, 135; 617–618); and they hopelessly bind the soul, which finally knows "the fullness of beatitude" (*Pandora*, 655) and becomes the slave of their splendor.

We might expect that the universe, almost in competition with her, fills up with statues of marble, bronze, and gold—closed and perfect plastic forms gleaming brightly "in accordance with sacred measurements" (*Pandora*, 675–676). But the cortege that accompanies and remembers Pandora does not resemble her. When it descends from Olympus it bears with it a vase. A "light vapor" (*Dampf*) comes from under the lid, as if "incense wished to thank the gods"; "airy illusions," "gay daughters of the air" (*Pandora*, 119, 122) flutter about, playing while suspended, and merge with one another, according to the swaying of the smoke (*Pandora*, 113–114). When Pandora leaves the earth, her memory "still hovers" in Epimetheus's mind. "It oscillates," "vacillates," "waves," "fades away," "dissolves," "thins out," and "vanishes like a figure of mist" (*Pandora*, 793 ff.).

Elpore, too, the daughter whom Pandora had carried with her into the sky, has a gown made of air. In the morning, when men give vent to their desires by dreaming, she visits them fleetingly. He who wants her must neglect wealth, strength, honor, and power. If, in the silence of early morning, he listens to a "whispering sigh," she will appear in his dream and promise him everything he desires (*Pandora*, 386–402). She tricks men with illusory promises and false hopes; she changes shape, becomes veiled, and vanishes like the echo (*Pandora*, 331, 340, 401, 747–750). But Elpore's deceptions are not perverse, her illusions console, her breath "refreshes" the suffering forehead (*Pandora*, 327), her hand casts a loving veil of mist over the harshness of existence.[3]

With her capricious charms Elpore shows us one of the two faces of Hope. The other image of Hope—Goethe called it Elpis or *Hoffnung* —is an aerial being and as unattainable as she. But Elpore is content to sweeten our present life, encircling us with a mist of pleasant illusions. Superior to Daimon, Tyche, Eros, and Ananke, Elpis does not enclose us in the prison of time. With a flap of her wings, she shatters the bronze walls of necessity, conquers death and leads us above "blankets of clouds, mist, rainy whirlwinds" into the boundless realm of the eternal future (*Urworte*, 33–40: *Des Epimenides Erwachen*, 620–623).

Until now we have encountered only images of perfumed veils, of clouds, mists, and light figures of air. After the publication of the *Farbenlehre*, the metaphorical nucleus born with *Zueignung* is amplified, attracting metaphors of colors that allude to the same symbol. As we have seen, the "veil of poetry" was a sign of mediation between light and darkness, between true and false. Similarly, in the two famous poems of *Westöstlicher Divan* the colors of the dawn and those of the rainbow mediate between light and darkness, between the sun's rays and clouds of rain.

At the beginning of time, at the origin of the universe, as sung in the strophes of *Wiederfinden* (September 1815), all things lie on God's eternal breast, immersed and commingled in a happy unity. When with a single word God created the world, a painful "Ah!" reverberated through space. The All broke into infinite realities, that fled each other in turn; the darkness separated from the light. The elements were concentrated in themselves, became more rigid (*starr*) and heavy, and opposed one another, each pursuing "wild, desolate dreams" of dominion (*Wiederfinden*, 21). The harmony of sounds no longer echoed over the deserted spaces; the strength of love had departed from the universe, which was about to consume itself and plunge into nothingness (IX, 352: 6–9). God was alone, abandoned by his creation.

At that moment God extended over the desolate abyss the dawn's many colors; and the first sign of mediation pacified the world. Light and darkness, which had separated like enemies, embraced again in the spectrum of colors. Hostile elements joined together and expanded amorously, while the harmony of sounds again echoed above the reconciled cosmos. Since that day, the amorous force of the universe has captured our hearts: Every man searches fervently for "the sweet echo of his joys" (*Wiederfinden*, 5–6); and both eyes and emotions turn "toward an infinite life" (*Wiederfinden*, 35). If the night of absence divides

GOETHE

us, if pain tortures us and makes us shudder, we shall soon be consoled. From the moment God gave colors to the world, every separation contains the certainty of a coming encounter.

In *Hochbild,* another famous poem from the *Divan,* the sun travels the roads of the sky, contemplating the spectacle of the universe. As if happy spaces did not exist, it looks only at Iris, the young goddess of rain who lets dolorous tears fall on earth. The sun sinks into her suffering, kisses all her tears, lets rays of joy fall into each drop, each pearl. Finally, recovering her serenity, the daughter of the clouds turns her rainbow-crowned face aloft where the sun and rain both reflect their own images. But love begins and ends in this delightful mirror. If the sun approaches Iris, if it tries to know her and identify itself with her, it yet fails to reach her; the rainbow dissolves under the strength of the sun's rays, and the "adamant law of fate" (*Hochbild,* 21) forces them to separate forever.

Thus the symbol of mediation reveals to us both a benign and a terrible face. Shining on a hostile world, the colors of the dawn and the rainbow bring together divided elements, resurrecting the harmony of sounds and eternal love among men. But the same colors proclaim the fatal law of renunciation. When our arms try to clasp the beloved images, reflected in the many gradations of a shimmering mirror, they grasp only fugitive shadows. Love, which has created and guides the universe, protects and saves us on the condition that we renounce, as individuals, the consolations of love.

In the years that followed the writing of the *Divan,* atmospheric phenomena, which until now had freely appeared and disappeared from Goethe's verse, were subjected to an analysis based on the principles set forth in the *Farbenlehre.* According to the *Versuch einer Witterungslehre* (1825), two opposed tensions regulate everyday life on earth—the force of "warmth" (or "expansion"), considered by Goethe analogous to light, and the force of "attraction," similar to darkness. Just as colors are born when an opaque or transparent body is interposed between light and darkness, so clouds are formed when the forces of expansion and attraction meet in the atmosphere (XIII, 311: 16–26).

The varied forms of clouds owe their origins to the relations between these two rival energies. If the force of attraction defeats that of expansion, veils of mist cover the swamps, heavier layers swath the mountains' slopes (stratus); or the clouds sink toward the earth (nimbus), provoking rains and hurricanes. If the battle remains undecided, large cumuli, masses of dense, magnificently shaped clouds looking like the ridges of mountains, travel through the atmosphere continually changing pattern. If, finally, the force of expansion conquers its adversary, the cumuli begin to dissolve; numerous flakes (cirri) detach themselves and rise toward the upper regions of the atmosphere, fresh, light wisps wander about bizarrely and disappear into the pure light of the ether (*Wolkengestalt nach Howard; Trilogie zu Howards Wolkenlehre*).

So, for Goethe, the sky becomes a symbolic alphabet, which merges with the symbols of colors and the "veil." In the figures of the cumuli, where the opposing forces of the universe are kept in equilibrium, he sees nature's mediatory and plastic qualities.[4] In the cirri, he finds the memory of Elpis rising above the "blankets of clouds, mist, rainy whirlwinds" (*Urworte*, 37). In them, too, he traces the sign of lightness that frees itself of material weight and ascends into the sky; and also the image of Christ, who leaves this earth and returns "*in sinu Patris*," where he lives eternally.[5]

In the "pleasant region" in the Alps, where Faust has slept so deeply, lulled by the songs of the spirit of nature, it is already dawn (*Faust*, 4679 ff.). The earth breathes, restored by the night's repose; the forest resounds with a thousand-voiced life, the trees' branches awake from sleep and colors stand out vividly against the misty background. Finally, the sun's rays descend through the valleys and attack the world with the violence of their light and a tempest of sounds our ears cannot perceive. An "immeasurable flame" bursts from the sun's eternal chasms; a "sea of fire" dazzles Faust's sight; while the light's roar deafens nature's spirits.

Also in the verses of *Zueignung* the sun dazzled the wayfarer's eyes, and the voice of the celestial woman helped us to remember that our minds are too weak to take in the full refulgence of "the truth, identical with the divine" (XIII, 305: 26–27). But now the sun, image of all that is loftiest, seems to contain something of darkness, something we cannot grasp. What are these immeasurable flames coming from its chasms, that "sea of fire" where love is confused with hatred (4710)? Is the "divine" an ambiguous force like the gods who, in the *Lehrjahre*, illuminate and blind Mignon and the harpist? Goethe does not reply; he barely grazes the supreme mysteries of creation.

Without sorrow or regret, Faust turns his back on the sun and directs his gaze toward earth "to hide himself in the youngest of veils" (4714). As in the verses of *Zueignung*, this veil is the morning mist that creeps up from the mountain valleys. But it is also the moist veil of the rainbow. Roaring through rocks, a waterfall plunges from ledge to ledge; the sun's first rays strike the water, and the rainbow's "many-hued reflection," now sharp, now vague and evanescent, is drawn in the air, spreading "cool vaporous shivers."

The verses of *Zueignung, Pandora, Wiederfinden, Hochbild,* and

GOETHE

Urworte gather their meanings around this passage from *Faust II*. If we cannot stare at the light of eternity—Goethe reminds us—we still know it every day in its enchanting reflections. We catch sight of it in the multiform aspects of life, in symbols, examples (XIII, 305: 26–31) mutable as the folds of the "veil," as clouds, and the creatures of air and smoke that accompany Pandora. We contemplate it in the iridescences in which water, air, and light come together in peace, in memory of that time when God reconciled the elements and made his arc scintillate amid clouds of glory (Genesis 9: 13; Ecclesiasticus 50: 8).

Protected by this celestial mediation, Faust can proceed trustingly on the earth's roads. As the rainbow recalls, he lives in the element of love, although the sun can never clasp the waters of the waterfall and the "sweet echo of our joys" eternally flee us (*Wiederfinden, Hochbild*). Those humid colors reflect his existence and remember his past just as the figures of mist preserve something of Pandora. Those vaporous shivers refresh his brow like the well of poetry (*Zueignung*), and the spume, futile as Elpore's charms, eternal as Elpis's power, propels him toward "an even higher existence" (4685) beyond "all human limits."[6]

At the death of Euphorion, his mother Helen, the mythical beauty, she who dazzles the eye like the sun's rays (924), hides again in the realm of darkness. But on earth something recalls her new existence. Helen's dress and veil remain for an instant in Faust's arms; then they are changed into a large cloud, which lifts him up and carries him away across Europe's mountains and seas right into the heart of Germany. There the cloud stops and lets him descend on the jagged, solitary ledge of a mountain. Then it slowly drifts away without dissolving. It condenses before Faust's marveling eyes; divides while moving in the sky, changes, undulates, seeking a form, until it seems the gigantic figure of a woman, Juno, Leda, or Helen, stretched out on pillows lit up by the sun. Again it changes aspect, broad, shapeless, towering, like a "distant mountain of ice," it returns to the Greece where it was born (10039–10054).

The structure of the image is what we are familiar with. On one hand, the splendor of the sun; on the other, the veil, dress, and cloud merged in a single metaphoric *impasto*. Just as the veil of *Zueignung* and the rainbow of *Anmutige Gegend* reflect the sun's light, so the dress, veil, and towering cumulus reflect Helen's vanished light. If it were legitimate to interiorize so spendidly objective an image, we might add that these celestial visions are Faust's remembrance of Helen, just as the wavering figure of mist was the memory that Epimetheus possessed of Pandora. But unlike Epimetheus, Faust is neither prey nor victim of

memory. No figure of mist disappoints him. All that he keeps of her—
the veil and the cloud lit by the sun—is an inestimable gift that reflects
"the vast meaning of fleeting days" (10054) and continues to guide him,
above "everything that is vulgar," toward the highest ether (9952–
9953).[7]

While the cumulus drifts off to the east, a "soft, luminous wisp of mist"
(10055) envelops Faust's brow. It cheers him, "cool and caressing"; it
condenses, taking the form of a cirrus cloud, and it ascends to the height
of the ether. In this image Faust thinks he sees Gretchen's reflection.
When the cirrus cloud rises, the distant treasures of his youth, "that first
quickly felt and scarce comprehended look," which could have conquered all other precious things, are awakened and carry his best part
on high. Here, too, the simplicity of the image conceals a great many
allusions: the recent scientific studies of clouds, the "coolness" of the
veil and rainbow, the spirit freed of its mortal remains, Hope which will
soon celebrate its triumphs in the sky.

Other cirrus clouds traverse *Faust's* last scene. A "small morning
cloud" (11890) rises among the trees bearing in itself the souls of newborn infants. On high, in the tent of the sky, some "light cloudlets," a
"tender populace" (12014–12015) of sinners gathers about the knees of
the Mater Gloriosa. Thus childish innocence, the sweetness of amorous
sin, the lightness of hope at last fulfilled, gather once more in the image
of those cirrus clouds Goethe had contemplated among Karlsbad's gardens and waters.[8]

We have finished describing the veils, all the light and heavy clouds,
the mists, the figures of air and of rainbows one encounters in Goethe's
poetry. The result is surprising. These images which belong to completely different books, written over a period of almost fifty years, all
come together, form a pattern, merge in an immense "metaphoric
complex," coherent and unitary.

This metaphoric complex embraces three groups of fundamental images. On the one hand is the sun which blinds and consumes (*Zueignung, Torquato Tasso, Natürliche Tochter, Pandora, Hochbild, Anmutige Gegend, Helen*). At the very opposite pole are the heavy, dark
clouds of *Zueignung*, the mortal vapors (*Dünste*) of *Natürliche Tochter*,
the shadows of *Wiederfinden*, the force of attraction in the *Versuch
einer Witterungslehre*. Halfway between these two extremes, Goethe
sets out a very rich group of equivalent images: the veil, the light clouds
(cirrus), the vapors or morning (*Duft*), the mist, echo, smoke, figures of
air, colors, rainbow, and garments. If the series "sun" and "darkness"
are naturally antithetic, a relation of mediation can exist between the

series "veil" and "sun" (*Zueignung, Pandora, Wiederfinden, Hochbild, Versuch einer Witterungslehre, Anmutige Gegend,* "Helen's Death"), or of antithesis *(Tasso, Natürliche Tochter),* or of simple succession (the memory of Pandora). Finally, one might add that the image of the cirrus clouds tends to occupy an autonomous position as a pure symbol of lightness *(Trilogie zu Howards Wolkenlehre,* Gretchen, the end of *Faust).*

During the last years of his life Goethe preferred to call himself, rather than a poet, "an ethical-esthetic mathematician" (November 3, 1826); and all of his images are rapid formulas in which he summed up his most profound intellectual convictions. In the veil and rainbow were reflected his studies of color, his ideas on the theory of knowledge, on language and symbol, and the image of God and society which had formed in his mind. But the reader cannot translate "veil," "rainbow," and "clouds" into exclusively intellectual terms. At the beginning of *Faust II* and the opening of the fourth act, he contemplates the sun as it is mirrored in the spray of a waterfall, and the clouds clustered around a high mountain peak. "Ideas," to use Goethe's words, are hidden behind these stupendous landscapes: "unreachable" and "unpronounceable," infinitely alive and active and infinitely mysterious (XII, Maxim 749).

With a vague and approximate description, we can point to only a few of the meanings and associations that gather around each image. For example, the light of the sun alludes to God, to the truth *(Zueignung, Anmutige Gegend),* to poetry *(Tasso),* to the political world *(Tasso, Natürliche Tochter),* and to feminine beauty *(Pandora,* Helen). The clouds, vapors, veils, and colors express the mediating force *(Zueignung)* and the elusiveness of poetry *(Tasso),* the marvelous and terrible levity of poets *(Tasso),* the changing nature and force of memories *(Pandora,* Helen's disappearance), the vanity and reality of hope (Elpore and Elpis), the possibility and impossibility of love *(Wiederfinden, Hochbild),* childish innocence *(Faust's* last scene), the love of youth (Gretchen), our vaulting impulse toward the heights, Christ's ascension to heaven *(Trilogie zu Howards Wolkenlehre).*

So the same image bestows its outer guise on contradictory ideas. The spectrum of colors affirms the possibility and impossibility of love; the cloud reveals to us the mutability and strength of memory; a figure of air expresses both what is illusory and supremely real in hope. Also, a single idea embodies opposed images—poetry burns like the sun and cools like morning vapors and evening winds. Goethe's great characters and major intuitions also reveal similar contradictions. Mephistopheles is the lord of rock and fire, a conservative and nihilist. That force which

Goethe liked to call "daimonic" is as much a gift of heaven as a diabolical energy; it contains something both human and inhuman, spiritual and physical, providential and casual.

If we wish to use once again an image dear to Schiller, every one of Goethe's fundamental metaphors, every one of his great intellectual intuitions, every eminent character in his books is like a small solar system. Quite often the center of this system eludes our penetration. Our eyes discern but a cortege of planets and satellites, each of which possesses an autonomous existence and follows its own orbit, which seems to lead it very far from all the others. Goethe could not proceed in any other way; separate considerations, single observations, distinct ideas, images without a system did not attract his mind. Like the Greeks, who included the most radical contradictions and antitheses under the sign of the same god, he tries to discover a compact nucleus in a thousand apparently disconnected and opposed aspects of the universe. He then gathers them together in a system of metaphors, a great character, or a single intellectual intuition.

If we ask ourselves what element holds together all the planets and satellites of this solar system, making them revolve around the same center, we would not know what answer to give. Who could define intellectually the mysterious cohesive element the Greeks called Hermes? We are only granted the privilege of admiring an indescribable divine figure: A youthful face, an elegant gesture, teaches us the cunning of nighttime thieves and the skills of inventors, the shrewdness of merchants and the grace of celestial messengers, the intelligence of great mysteries and the interpretation of words. So, in Goethe's case, with an intuitive flash, every reader perceives the mysterious Mephistophelian element that inspires an apparently disparate metaphysic, cosmology, and ethic. He understands that the metaphor of the veil expresses a force of opposition and mediation active at every point of the universe, in poetry and colors, in love and clouds, in memory and hope.

During his last years the poetic delirium visited the "ethical-esthetic mathematician" less and less frequently. Cold, "in complete awareness," he thought that poetry might "command," as he wrote jokingly to Wilhelm von Humboldt (December 1, 1831). Like an old, very skillful weaver, he sat before the loom of images, where the threads of the warp were all prepared, an enchanting design announced the strangest of tapestries and the shuttle awaited only the movement of his hand.

As soon as the shuttle began to move, Goethe realized that it was drawing lines, figures, colors, and shadows he had never foreseen; and perhaps, behind that first design, other lines and other figures were hidden. He was struck ever more sharply by the impression that *Faust*

GOETHE

II was slipping through his hands, like a creature of which he was not the master. He could reason and calculate coldly, "command" his poetry as he wished. But the metaphoric system had become so broad and multiple that he could not control all the combinations and relations in what he was writing. All he could do was to entrust *Faust II* to his present and future readers and hope that they would collaborate with him, uncovering what he had hidden unknowingly. "Since a poetic work is written for many," he said, "many must receive it; since it has many aspects, it must be seen from many sides" (November 14, 1827).[9]

In an effort to meet with Goethe's last wishes, a thousand pairs of eyes have since then scrutinized the multiform tapestry of *Faust II;* a thousand hands have composed and recomposed it, thread by thread. There are those who have interpreted every "hint," every "slight allusion," while others have tracked down the "large sums" and placed them one after the other, trying to correct the addition that Goethe wanted to have incorrect. There are those who have reconstructed the value of each symbol and the analogies tying the symbols to each other. So we have discovered many secrets Goethe did not know. But perhaps we do not understand *Faust II* better than the old weaver who, some one hundred and forty years ago, devoted to it his last days of work, his last sleepless nights.

God, Faust, and Mephistopheles

IV

When the theater of heaven opens, three archangels step onstage
before God and the angelic hosts, singing in praise of the wisdom of him
who embraces all, upholds all, and governs all. The God they praise is
the Creator to whom Greek, Christian, Renaissance, and alchemical
knowledge has consecrated the edifice of the world. At the beginning
of time he fashioned the cosmos; in the center of the heavens he set the
sun which from then on, with the noise of thunder, continues to fulfill
its prescribed course. The stars revolve around it, intoning the ineffable
Pythagorean music while days and nights alternate on the Earth's magnificence, above wild mountain ranges, hills descending gently to the
valley, and bays warmed by the sea. In God's world there reigns an
unblemished harmony and order; the spirit of natural law mildly shapes
all figures, large and small phenomena correspond, the macrocosm is
reflected in the microcosm, and "each thing is woven into the All"
(447–448).

To the person who knows how to listen to it and contemplate it, the
world reveals everywhere the sign of God. He or his messengers (but
who can distinguish them from each other?) are present in everything
that "eternally works and lives" (446), in everything that becomes,
transforms, expands, dies, rises up again, and continually surpasses its
own limits. Thus we are aware of its sign again in "new fresh blood"
(1372) circulating through the veins of creation, in the thousand germs
of air, water, and earth, "in the sweet, reviving look" of spring that frees
the rivers and streams from crude winter's ice and fills the world with

GOETHE

new colors (904 ff.). The sign is visible in the blessed amorous force that agitates, "invisibly visible" beside us, and fills our heart as it fills the ardor of the sky (3446 ff.).

But the song of the archangels brings to mind less cheerful spectacles. From the summit of the heavens their eyes discern a paradisial radiance alternating with "deep, dreadful night"; the sea's foam assails rocks, storms rage in rivalry over earth and water, lightning bolts flash in the air, bringing fire and ruin. As the reader proceeds in *Faust II,* the consoling image of the *harmonia mundi* is more and more often contradicted and offended. If we contemplate the sun, benign heart of the universe, boundless flames, hostile seas of fire try to envelop us and destroy us (4708 ff.). If on a luminous night we look aloft, meteors cross the sky, whistling fearfully (7910 ff.). If we look around us, a savage fury flings the elements against each other: Waves of the sea try to drag the land into the depths (10198 ff.), fire seizes and consumes all that can burn, volcanoes continually disrupt the beautiful surfaces created by the hands of God (7503 ff.).

Between these two opposed images of the universe, conciliation seems impossible. We are unable to believe that the same celestial hands have made the light and darkness, formed harmonious growths and disasters, constructed a peaceful world and an illegal, violent chaos. Thus some might imagine that two hostile principles are at war in the universe; they might think they see an ambiguous shadow on God's luminous countenance; and might believe that he entrusts part of his powers to a daimonic spirit, such as the spirit of the earth which, seated at the "rumbling loom of time," weaves "the living garment of the deity" (508–509). Others affirm that the harmony of creation is a flattering and illusory dream produced by our imagination; or they repeat that the phenomena of the universe seem irregular only to our enfeebled and uncertain eyes.

The long, interminable debate concerning theodicy and the mysteries of the creation which runs all through *Faust II* begins in the "Prologue in Heaven" in which the three archangels offer us the solution of purest faith. They know that evil—the dreadful night, the moan of tempests, the crash of lightning—"works and lives" in the universe side by side with good; but they do not try to explain it. Like devoted and obscure servants, they bow their heads before the incomprehensible vision that God conceals in his works (248–268), and they continue to exalt the paradoxical miracles of the *harmonia mundi.*

The new character, who bears the strange name of Mephistopheles and who strides forward through the convocation of angels, does not share their awe at God's wisdom. The archangels' cosmic "pathos" seems to him ridiculous. The Pythagorean orchestra of the spheres, the velocitous course of the stars, the beauty of the world, the perfect correspondence between macrocosm and microcosm—all the *topoi* of Greco-Christian knowledge leave him skeptical and indifferent (275–279). For his part, he knows only the world of men, and here he sees not even the slightest trace of that order, harmony, and felicity that should reign in the universe. "This little god of the world," he says, addressing God, "is still the same breed and is as bizarre as on the first day he was made. He might live a trifle better if Thou had not bestowed on him the appearance of heavenly light; he calls it reason, and makes use of it only to be more bestial than all the beasts. He seems to me— with Your Grace's leave—one of those long-legged grasshoppers that always flies and, while flying, jumps, and sings the same old ditty in the grass" (*Faust*, 281–292). This bizarre grasshopper likes to poke his nose into every sort of filth. He grubs in garbage, and, immediately after, he desires unearthly food and drink, the fairest stars in the sky, and the highest joys on earth. Nothing satisfies him, neither base things nor sublime, neither nearby things nor distant can soothe his "deeply agitated breast" (307).

Summoned to the front of the stage by Mephistopheles, God also makes his appearance in the theater of heaven. Despite his effort to exhibit the indulgence and urbanity of an Enlightenment *grand seigneur,* he seems rather annoyed. He does not like the idea of Mephistopheles ceaselessly criticizing the beautiful work which, thousands of years before, had issued so splendid and incomprehensible from the light play of his hands. Why does he insist on these quarrelsome accusations, this eternal opposition, this deliberately adopted position of dissatisfaction? So God directs a singular reproach at his ancient adversary; he accuses him of never having been satisfied with anything. Perhaps God has forgotten that it was actually he who, some thousands of years ago, entrusted Mephistopheles with the task of negating and destroying all that exists.

Soon God drops his reserve and agrees to explain, though quite hastily, the supreme mysteries of the theodicy. He does not reject the description of the human race that Mephistopheles has presented. He even admits that men, moved by the most obscure desires, serve him "confusedly" (308), and that their lives are a vast wilderness of "mistakes" (317). But this concession is incapable of denting his optimism. At the origin of every man, at that point where he begins to detach himself from matter, lies a very pure "source," which no one will succeed in muddying (324). It does not matter that man makes mistakes and is confused; that he travels the road of Satan instead of the road of God.

GOETHE

In the depths of his soul he unconsciously knows the right way; and, at the end of his long journey, he will reach the goal that God so long ago prepared for him.

When God concludes his brief philosophic dissertation, it is likely that many readers of *Faust* are disappointed. From the Lord of the universe, from him who should know the mysterious motive and secret operation of all things, the reader could have expected something more original. Is that all there is to theodicy? This muddle of a few sentences lifted from Rousseau and Leibniz? One is led to think that God, busy running the ever more complicated machinery of the universe, has in recent times forgotten to delve deeply into the major problems of philosophy, that he is satisfied to listen to the most fashionable thinkers in Germany and France. What's more, even experience does not support the Lord's optimism. As the *Lehrjahre* and *Faust* remind us, only a few among us can call on a "primal source" as do Wilhelm Meister and Faust; very few men are guided all the way to the predestined goal. Why, then, are some people chosen and others, like Mignon and the harpist, abandoned to a bitter bed of tears?

God's philosophy is akin to the one that Abbé professes in the *Lehrjahre* and Thales in the *Klassische Walpurgisnacht*. It is the philosophy of those in Goethe's books who accept the marvelous and senseless task of defending the reasons for *harmonia mundi*. The symbols they represent—the music of the spheres, the architectonic beauty of the world, the benignity of the law, the providential activity of nature—are the most splendid things that man's creative imagination has produced. But, at the inception of time, a division of roles had taken place. Analytical intelligence, intellectual precision, psychological acumen, all that makes up the endowment of an honest philosopher and a good moralist, had not been given to the representatives of the All. It had been given rather to the adversary, to the negator, to Mephistopheles, "the part of the part" (1349), who will always find it easy to demonstrate the inadequacy of God's constructions and of his exegetes.[1]

Though he is but a middling philosopher, God possesses other talents, perhaps more useful to him in ruling the world. Just as a skilled parliamentary leader terrifies and flatters his opposition, so he, too, governs his celestial and infernal entourages with a firm hand, at times alluring, at other times plunging the party of his adversaries into the basest ignominy. He knows Mephistopheles's profoundest weakness: his old gentleman's snobbery, a gentleman who has gone to seed, become rather vulgar, and is sunk in debt and vices. He also knows that, despite his obstinately repeated "No," the devil wants above all to converse urbanely with him in that comfortable celestial theater where he had once lived. He realizes that at the bottom of his heart the devil would like to win the approval of the God he is always trying to offend.

So, with the exquisite graciousness of an old-fashioned host, God tries to reassure Mephistopheles—"I have never hated the likes of you," he tells him. Then he woos him, setting him apart from the innumerable breed of the wicked: "Among all the spirits who deny, you are the one who gives me the least trouble" (*Faust,* 336–339). These courtesies are not at all disinterested. Like a parliamentary leader, God wants to renew his pact of collaboration with the devil. He does not ask him to leave the infernal hosts and join the angelic choir to sing wholeheart-edly of the paradoxical glory of his works. What use could he have for another angel? Mephistopheles must keep his smell of sulphur and his horse's hoofs; he must repeat his sarcastic remarks against the order of the universe; he must critically define, arrest, and limit the course of the world. Precisely in this way, he will always be giving a new impul-sion to men's activity (340 ff.; 7134 ff.).

With Mephistopheles's tacit consent, the pact of collaboration be-tween light and darkness is renewed. "The force that always wants evil and always accomplishes good" (1335–1336) remains in the world of God. Does that, then, assure universal harmony? Does the alliance between God and the head of his opposition permit that order which the philosophy of the heavenly schools has not been able to demon-strate? It is impossible to say. The true enemy against whom God must fight is not Mephistopheles, but God himself. It is his hostile face that shines out amid the sun's flames, his messengers, his emanations, fright-ening as the spirit of the earth, which trouble the universe.

As suddenly as it had opened, the theater of heaven closes. In a corner, before the spectators, Mephistopheles is eager to ponder over the words—so "human"—that the Lord has addressed to him. God must also be satisfied with this encounter. He finds Mephistopheles—indeed, *der Schalk* as he prefers to call him—quite pleasant. He feels for him the same friendly feeling Zeus experienced at first sight for another *Schalk,* Hermes (9652); the small gnome, the humorous and clownish god, master of tricks, thefts, and disguises. All the cunning shifts, the scurrilous inventions and traps, all the energy Mephistopheles employs in a cause defeated from the start, never cease to amuse him (7137). How could he spend his time up there on high, surrounded by the monotonous sound of the spheres and the eternally unvaried strum-ming of his angels, without his incomparable infernal buffoon?[2]

On the sixth day God fashioned man in his "image" and "likeness" (Genesis 1: 26; *Faust,* 516, 614). He infused him with a gleam of the

GOETHE

celestial light, a naturally good "primal source" (284–324); and he wanted man's soul, emotions, and body to correspond with universal nature as "microcosm" to "macrocosm" (1802, 430). What has become of his creatures thousands of years after the world's creation? The youthful "splendid emotions," which gave us life, have stiffened and died, killed by earthly life (638–639). Our imagination, which should turn trustingly to the eternal, has shut itself up in a small space. There it is transformed into incessant anxiety secretly gnawing at our hearts and forcing us to worry about our house, our family, the fire that could attack us, the imaginary poison that undermines our existence. So we live amid necessities, conditions, very heavy iron chains we ourselves have forged. We are no longer worthy of the ancient, proud name of "microcosms"; we are barely individuals, wretched and limited "persons," who perhaps have lost all resemblance to God.

Unlike other men, Faust continues to insist on his affinity with the Creator of the universe. With what inexhaustible yearning does he try to slake his thirst at the distant "founts" of his life! Like Wilhelm Meister, he calls back to memory the days of his childhood, when the "kiss of heavenly love" descended on him in a solemn Sabbath hush, the song of the bells resounding full of presentiments, and "every prayer was impassioned bliss." He remembers the days of adolescence, when "an incomprehensible, sweet desire" impelled him to run through the meadows and woods and, "amid countless burning tears," he felt a world come into being within him (769 ff.). Even now, holed up in the old Gothic chamber, the same youthful force of love burns within him. Like a single wave, like an indistinguishable and indivisible passion, this force fills his being, it impels him to embrace all things. He wishes to be eternal, and he tries vainly to express himself with the most solemn, the loftiest words, for neither God nor love can be named with the words of this Earth (3060 ff.; 3192 ff.; 3455 ff.).

If other men have become persons, Faust is still a "microcosm" (1780–1781, 1802)—or dreams of being that. He wants to share the fate of all mankind: its blessings and misfortunes, its loves and hates, its joys and sufferings. He wants to gather in his breast all of men's qualities—the fiery blood of Italians and the constancy of Nordics, the vital joy of the boy and the solemn gravity of the patriarch, the courage of the lion and the swiftness of the deer. Each of his passions should embrace all extremes, such as "painful pleasure," "enamoured hatred," "the annoyance that comforts" (1765 ff.). But Faust's greatest dream is to rediscover in himself a harmonious correspondence with universal nature, which surrounds him with "its active force and its seeds." No sooner does he contemplate the symbol of the microcosm in Nostradamus's mysterious book, no sooner does he see how everything is woven into the whole and one element works and lives in another, than his heart's tumult is placated and a youthful felicity runs through all his veins and nerves (433–434).

With these presentiments in his heart, Faust leaves the narrow, high-vaulted Gothic chamber where the sunlight must penetrate the darkened, small panes of glass. He leaves his prison, the "world of moths," where worm-eaten books are piled among sooty parchments, old ampuls, and empty skulls. When the "sweet reviving look of spring" melts the ice, frees the greenery, and makes the hope of felicity surge up in everyone, he goes into the countryside; and if a storm rages over the woods, the safe depths of the caves welcome him. He does not wander about like a distracted guest in the regions God has prepared for him. Nor does he try to grasp the mysteries nature does not wish revealed to the human spirit by means of the cold instruments of science—levers, cogwheels, and cylinders. He looks into her breast as into the breast of a friend; and the bushes, water, and air, the moonlight, the thousands of spirits hovering between earth and sky are his true brothers.

Close to nature's vital forces, Faust realizes how profound is the affinity that ties him to her. Just as everything in the universe becomes, expands, and is transformed, his life also obeys the rhythm of metamorphosis. He is not content with the "accursed *here*" (11233), which wants to enclose him in the day's cares and anxieties. What he knows is not enough for him—the books he has read or the words he has written on paper. Nor are the pleasures, the instants of his experiences—his very *I*—capable of claiming and possessing him forever. An incessant drive forces him to shatter every situation and every limit, to slough off his old skin and transform himself, passing through life like an impetuous torrent. Just as Christ in the chants of the faithful each year dies and is resurrected, just as universal nature dies and rises again each instant, so the extremely mobile soul knows the continual joy of becoming.

Although Faust affirms that all his joys rise from this earth, a tender, yearning impulse guides him toward his celestial homeland. When the sun sets and hastens elsewhere, there to arouse new life, he envies the bird its wings. He covets the lightness of the lark that trills its pealing song, the strength of the eagle that flies above the crags and fir trees, the speed of the crane that returns to its native shores. If a wing could lift him from the earth, he would see the world at his feet in the rays of an eternal sunset—all the mountain peaks lit, the tranquil valleys, gilded streams, the sea with its warm bays. Then would he hasten even farther away, the day before him and the night behind (1070 ff.). But, as long as he lives in the prison of the body, no wing can lift him to the

GOETHE

sky. So, oppressed by anguish, he wants to kill himself, turning his back forever on the "sweet sun of this earth"; and "crossing the ether on new roads, toward new spheres of pure activity" (704–705). Only there, perhaps alone in infinite space, the unsatisfied force of his nature will be able to express itself completely.

All this restless activity, these Platonic surges toward the sky, these impossible desires are distasteful to a cold, ironic, and limited spirit like Mephistopheles. Faust's passions seem to him a wild and senseless intoxication, a ridiculous "fermentation" (302). But in the illustrious theater of heaven, among the hosts of archangels and angels, God looks at Faust, "my" servant (299), with completely different eyes. He can still see in him, though stained and confused, the celestial lineaments he had given man at the time of the creation. His madness, his amorous desire for totality, his very lively *Streben* assure him that Faust is made in "his image and likeness."

Like God, Goethe contemplates himself in Faust's image. In his youth he has entrusted him with his feelings of disgust and his profoundest hopes; he admires with him the sign of the macrocosm, scoffs with him at Wagner's bookish knowledge, struggles against and is defeated by the "spirit of the earth." In his old age, as well, when he has become wiser and more serene, he likes to confess through Faust's mouth. At the beginning of the second part he awakens with Faust on the meadows of the "pleasant region" in the Alps. He lifts his eyes to the burning light of the sun and then looks down at the ground, willing to know the splendor of the eternal in the evanescent, colored froth of the rainbow, "the reflection, the example, the symbol, in single and similar phenomena" (XIII, 305: 26–34).

This affinity between the two old men, between Goethe who is preparing himself for death and Faust who enjoys an impossible youthfulness does not last long. Despite a lively capacity for metamorphosis, Faust has changed less than his creator. He did not take the journey to Italy, he has not understood the laws that govern the realm of colors, he has not shut himself like a statue in the house of the *Frauenplan,* and he could never write cold, unfathomable books like the *Wanderjahre* and *Faust II.* So, having proclaimed with Goethe the metaphysics and ethics of the symbols, he immediately forgets them; or he leaves them in a corner of his mind, neglecting to make use of them. In contrast to Goethe, he does not know how to live under the mediatory sign of the rainbow. The enchanting reflections, the creatures of air and smoke, life's multiform apparitions do not reveal to him the meanings that are confided to the eye of his poet.[3]

As in the first part of the play, the most impossible desires, dreams, and hopes continue to throng tumultuously in Faust's breast. When he lived in the dark Gothic chamber, he would have liked to drink at the sacred founts of life and lose himself in the veins of nature, enjoying a felicity akin to that of a god (455, 619–620). Among the masked balls and processions of *Faust II*, when his soul should be wearier and wiser, he imagines that he could conquer something that will remain eternally beyond human strength. As Plato's most enthusiastic pupil, he tries to establish "the double, great realm" (6555) in which the absolute forms of being and the figures of reality live side by side. Like an ancient wizard and alchemist, he attempts to call up again the spirits of Hades and make peace among the warring elements, divesting nature of its violence.[4]

None of the world's fresh appearances reveal to him the shadow of eternal beauty (11293–11297). No joy makes him lighthearted, no conquest satisfies him, neither near nor distant things "bring contentment to his deeply agitated breast" (306–307). So he is forced to run ceaselessly from one goal to another, from what he has to a new possession, which immediately in its turn loses its attraction. Propelled as he is by anxiety, restlessness, and ever more anguished and insatiable impatience, he goes through the world like a "fugitive," like "a homeless man," like "a monster without goal or peace," like "a cataract which, avidly furious, leaping from rock to rock, crashes down toward the abyss" (3348–3351).

What does he leave behind him? Curses against the wretched counterfeits of immortality that deceive us on this earth; Gretchen in prison; destruction, ruin, fragments of Mephistophelian spectacles, a false paradise on Earth, the blood-covered bodies of Baucis and Philemon in the burned hut. . . . So man, fashioned in God's "image and likeness," the proud "microcosm," runs the risk of becoming the great guilty one, cursed by the laws of nature.

As Mephistopheles appears on the stage of *Faust* dressed as a wandering student or a noble knight we wonder what his hierarchical rank is in the complicated infernal world. In the theater of heaven, where he remains modestly among the hosts of angelic "servants" (274), God regards him merely as one among the many "spirits who negate" (338). On this earth he does not enjoy greater prestige, and it seems that rats and mice, frogs and flies, bedbugs and lice, ringworms and beetles are the true subjects, the sole citizens of his miserable kingdom. So we become accustomed to consider him as one of the lowest emissaries of a large anonymous infernal association which has dispatched its most important representatives to other books or other worlds.[5]

GOETHE

If Mephistopheles is a servant, where are the great demonic spirits? What is the face, what are the gestures and mien of the lord of evil, the prince of the inferno, the undisputed sovereign of darkness and fire? During Walpurgis Night, Faust hopes and believes that he knows him. Together with Mephistopheles, he climbs the Harz Mountains, converses with will-o'-the-wisps, sees crags that bow and hiss and howl, roots that twist and stretch like snakes, the turbid light of Mammon that slithers and slides through the deepest gorges. Wild winds rage over chasms, terrified owls fly away, huge trees crash down grimly. Witches ride sows, singing strident choruses and rushing in a swarm toward the summit of the Brocken, where, amid "flames and whirlwinds of smoke" (4038), great Satan is enjoying his triumph. All seems ready for the revelation of absolute evil. But Faust sees nothing. Despite Faust's anxious insistence, Mephistopheles, with a series of strange excuses, prevents him from climbing to the top of the Brocken; and so he continues not to know what distinguishes the prince of hell from his very modest servant.

At the end of the play we will understand that Goethe and Mephistopheles, bound together by an invisible alliance, have been playing with us. If he had gone up among the Brocken's rocks and flames, Faust would have met only a dusty ghost, an old infernal puppet, governed by Mephistopheles's arts. Faust has no need to know Satan. He has lived with him for a long time. He has talked with Satan about good and evil, creation and chaos; he has made a pact with him, signing it with his blood; and he could not wish for a more experienced and knowledgeable traveling companion. The prince of the inferno, the lord of evil is none other than Mephistopheles; the small wayward and scurrilous devil, hidden with so much modesty among the melodious ranks of God's children.[6]

During the glorious centuries of the Middle Ages, Satan flaunted his own name and the marks of his infernal nature: the horns, tail, claws, and smell of sulphur. In this strange modern epoch God, by ignoring "traditional customs amd ancient rights" (11621), is conquering many territories which in the past belonged to the devil. He establishes himself as master among the countless lively germs of water and air, builds his realm on the flight of becoming, and even entrusts the abysses of the "demonic" to a spirit who is faithful to him, the earth spirit. So old Satan, dispossessed of his powers, must choose a new name of very uncertain etymology from an obscure folk book. He gives up his ravens, renounces the horns, claws, and tail, at one time his pride, and hides his horse's hoofs beneath a pair of fake calves. After so many centuries of uncultivated crudeness, he, too, has learned to dress like a respectable person. Now he appears before us as a "wandering student"; now as a frivolous German baron, with a red suit, short silk cloak, and long, pointed sword; and now as a curious and splenetic English gentleman traveling incognito through classical ruins.

To anyone meeting him on the world's highways he certainly does not recall his past tragic battles with the Creator of the universe. Even Mephistopheles has forgotten them, and he willingly relinquishes to men's puerile innocence the Promethean poses, the shadowy and grandiose attitudes of a noble, defeated Titan, which the bad taste of human artists had attributed to him. Modest, jovial, without pretensions, full of discretion and *understatement,* * with the greatest good grace he renounces the ancient royal prerogatives. *"Ich bin keiner von den Grossen,"* "I am not one of the great," he says with a smile to Faust (1641). If we sought to awaken in him some regret or nostalgia for his past grandeur, Mephistopheles, with a touch of furtive smugness, would reply that he has never been as happy as he is now, made fun of by God and abandoned by his followers.[7]

He no longer possesses a place where he can reign with the insignia of an absolute sovereign; even death and hell—where in the past nobody dared to oppose him—scarcely recognize his rule. Like an old aristocrat, having transformed himself into a soldier of fortune, he has become a part of God's immense and contradictory world, where he grows increasingly conscious of his special function. He knows that evil is as necessary as good to the providential organization of the universe. He understands that, if he stopped concocting crimes, conflagrations, and sacrilegious acts, he would embarrass the Lord of the heavens. And so here he is, carrying out his diabolical duty every morning with the scrupulousness of the most diligent bureaucrat.

Seated at his desk Mephistopheles composes his tragedies, comedies, and infernal farces. He writes them himself and with men's help. He designs the scenes, prepares tricks and illusions, arranges the positions of extras, choruses, and actors, hides in the prompter's box, and sometimes he himself performs under the stage's smoky lights. The success of these "pieces" depends on many different factors. Mephistopheles's state of grace, chance's assistance or annoying defiance, the adeptness or awkwardness of the human actors whom he is forced to use in his performances. Quite often the youthful audience, seated in a corner of the orchestra, does not applaud; and other older spectators, dazed by the vicissitudes of existence, can barely grasp the most pointed cracks. But what does it matter as long as his compositions manage to wrest a smile, or even imperceptible applause, from the bored Lord of heaven?

*English in original.

GOETHE

Suddenly, as we listen to him as to a character in a play, Mephistopheles rips apart the thick veil of modesty and irony behind which he has hidden; and he towers onstage in all of his ancient and grandiose infernal stature. He is no longer Mephistopheles, but Satan; he is no longer God's humble and grotesque servant, but the haughty and pitiless adversary. As if to set the seal on his own new pretensions, in Faust's study he draws in broad strokes his proud genealogical tree, his extremely aristocratic coat-of-arms. Before him, no Christian devil had ever made such great claims; no demon had tried to take from God the leading role in the history of the universe. Although he has esteem for the Old Testament, Mephistopheles forgets that, according to Genesis, "in the beginning" God's spirit hovered over the deserted expanses of the primordial ocean. Leaving his Christian upbringing behind him, he accepts the version the Greek Genesis gave of the origin of things: Hesiod's *Theogony*. He tells us that "in the beginning" there was "Mother Night," "Darkness" with her womb full of prodigies (1350–1351, 8665); and, together with her, very ancient "Chaos" (1384, 8027). From their atrocious and clumsy coupling, which occurred at some unascertainable time but certainly before Night gave birth to Light, Mephistopheles was born, the strange, "dearly beloved son of Chaos."[8]

What Mephistopheles did in the empty universe; what language he spoke before the invention of languages; how he spent his time before the birth of time—every reader can provide his own answers to these unknowns. But one thing is certain—Mephistopheles is the oldest among *Faust*'s characters; only the Phorkyads, his aunts or sisters on his father or mother's side, know the world of Night as he does. The Sphinxes who squat before the pyramids, the ghosts of ancient Greek mythology who swarm in dense ranks through the *Klassische Walpurgisnacht* are infinitely younger than he. God has experienced his *Lehrjahre* a few centuries before, studying the texts of Paracelsus, Spinoza, and Leibniz; and Faust is a Baccalaureus who has just grown up, a son of Hamann, Herder, and Swedenborg, a presumptuous offshoot of *Sturm und Drang*.

An atrocious disaster shattered the beatific, frightful nothingness of the origins. Night, unwilling to remain alone in the deserted universe, rose from her own depths and generated Light (1350). And Light, like an ungrateful and proud daughter, extended quickly over the universe, disputing both the space and ancient rank of her mother.[9] Then were born the new gods of creativity who covered the earth with sprouts, green grass and trees, animals and reptiles; then filled the waters with fish and sea serpents, the air with birds. They formed man from mud. From that day on very fresh blood circulated ceaselessly in nature's veins (1371–1375). Thus the child of Chaos and Night found himself confined in nature, where he paces back and forth like a prisoner in his cell. When Faust takes refuge among the fraternal creatures of the air, water, and forest, Mephistopheles cannot follow him, since he would feel as though he were living "like an owl in caves and rocky clefts," or like a toad that slithers "in the soggy moss and between trickling stones" (3273–3275). He feels a very intense disgust for everything that grows and flowers, vegetates and is transformed, for seedlings, plants, men, animals, and simple embryos which are born and pullulate continually from God's creative play. Even the gentle force of spring does not stir his old bones, which would prefer to encounter ice and snow on their path.

Mephistopheles cannot bear the absurd spectacle surrounding him on earth. What does this eternal "something," so favored by God, really mean? This creation of always new figures, which after a few years—a crumb in the immensity of time—sink again into nothingness? With the cynical passion of a nihilist, he tries to cancel with a gesture all signs of life—the sky, earth, and sea; the "accursed brood of beasts and men" (1369), and that bad imitation of nothingness which is the past, where memories are lost without an echo, like words in the void (11600 ff.). Like Momus, also the son of "black Night" (*Theogony*, 214), Mephistopheles comes down among men and with his infernal breath scorns, mocks, insults, and destroys all the enthusiasms, illusions, and hopes that warm their breasts.

Some of these gestures and words let us feel what the icy breath of Chaos must be like; the caliginous voice of Night; the desolation of the "eternal void" without sun or moon, stars or seas, without space or time, reason or language. But Mephistopheles's great nihilistic plot fails irremediably. God's "clumsy world" continues to reproduce itself before his eyes, like a forest full of lymph. Very few human beings let themselves be tempted by the traps of boundless negation. Almost all live, speak and do foolish things, die, are buried and forgotten together with their undertakings, without ever understanding the devil's dreadful and exquisite mockery.

Defeated as a nihilist, Mephistopheles makes an alliance with two of the four elements in God's world. Like all devils he likes to live among intensely hot flames. But his fire is not the fire of Prometheus; it is not the fire that announces the light of the sun and daily activity, shapes bronze and iron, and burns inconsumable before the altars of the gods. Mephistopheles's flames are infertile, savage, and violent; they creep under the ground and suddenly appear above it, bringing everywhere destruction, catastrophes, and explosions.

GOETHE

Meanwhile Mephistopheles's emissaries, tyrants thirsting for blood or frenetic revolutionaries, also leave the sign of fire in human history: they cause upheavals with their "tumults," their "violences," and their "absurd actions" (10127); they provoke senseless revolutions, stir up bloody, grotesque wars, like the war which, during the course of the *Klassische Walpurgisnacht*, sets the ants, pygmies, and cranes at each other's throats.[10]

When he leaves the flames of hell, Mephistopheles is happy to live among the rocks, among dead layers of sandstone, where grass cannot grow; among innumerable, horrible, gaping rock masses, which Moloch's hammer has strewn over the summits (10070, 10109–10111); along the mountain slopes, where veins of minerals are hidden and the wood of the fir tree and beech is transformed into dry charcoal. For him and his pupils, rocks represent the symbolic place where "matter" and "the force of concentration" triumph. Their impenetrable, dark surfaces do not permit the fecundating rays of light to enter. With their weight, they vanquish the wings of lightness, and with their rigid, immobile forms they try to halt the universe's continual impulse of "expansion" and transformation.[11] So Mephistopheles's eyes relinquish their savage tiger's look, and the wrinkles on his brow and in his heart imitate the folds in the rocks. Seeing this immobile face and fixed look, who could think that he also brings with him the fire's violence? The mythical figures Mephistopheles prefers at these moments are the ancient stone Sphinxes, who sat for thousands of years before the pyramids without changing expression or moving from their place.

Everyone around him is trying to destroy the past. God dislikes stable institutions; Faust regards the past as an ignoble pile of trash (575–582); Baccalaureus scorns experience, white hair, and uselessly dusty books. The French Revolution, which Mephistopheles had favored, throws Europe into confusion; industry's machines and "paper money," which he discovered in the course of a single night, transform the relations of production. But Mephistopheles looks with deepest skepticism on this revolutionary madness, these excesses of imagination and presumption; and if respect for the Creator of the world did not restrain him, he would reproach him for his culpable levity. Like old conservatives, he knows that the world does not change and history repeats itself. So *it was*, so *it is*, and so *it will be* eternally (6956 ff.); and no one, not even Satan, can think "something foolish or something judicious," not already thought by our ancestors (6809–6810).

When nihilism or the spirit of fire do not tempt him, Mephistopheles tries to arrest life by turning the world into a landscape of stones and fossils, jagged and steep as impervious mountain peaks. He defends, like

Metternich, the established order and institutions, the small absolute monarchies of the eighteenth century. He would retain unaltered the adorable Gothic cities of old Germany, with their narrow, dark, and twisting alleyways, their houses with pointed roofs, their market stalls covered with turnips and cabbages. He feels for the past—which with another part of his soul he continually destroys—a kind of affectionate friendship and perhaps, as often happens with cynics, a sentimental regret. If we were familiar with all of his peregrinations, we might often find him in the shops of antique dealers: old, wrinkled, softhearted, surrounded by clocks that have struck for many the hour of birth and of death, and old tea sets, the witnesses to a thousand family gatherings.[12]

If he reviews the very distant years of his youth, when he lived in the boundless spaces of Chaos, the All created by God—the cosmos with its stars, the earth with its mountains and seas must seem to him a pebble flung by a childish hand into the ocean's immensity. But when he lives on earth, constricted by the twisting alleyways of medieval cities, pride leads him to select the road of limitation. With a kind of scorn, he abandons the All to God, who lives up there, beatific in his eternal splendor; or to man, "Mr. Microcosm," who hopes to be able to take into his breast the meanings of all things (1780–1782, 1802). As for him, he says that he is only "a part"—indeed, "a part of the part" (1349). He proclaims that he is a fragment of darkness within nothingness; a spark of fire facing a sea of flames, a sharpened stone as compared with a range of mountains, a piece of sarcasm or mockery without the slightest general notion; he is something incomplete, limited, and "unilateral," like the technicians who are inaugurating the modern age.[13]

His mind lacks that inspired architectonic imagination that forces men to create great philosophical systems—or the most mediocre "house of cards" (6641). With his lucid, precise, and pitiless eyes, Mephistopheles sees things as they are; he measures ideas and words with the yardstick of reality. He knows the art of reasoning, and an infallible instinct leads him to discover all the contradictions, distortions, and stridencies that render the life of man absurd. While God is negligent about the exactness of his philosophical demonstrations, while the angels are optimistic by profession, and Faust lets himself be intoxicated by words, Mephistopheles never has any illusions. No sooner does a deception swell up under his eyes like a varicolored soap bubble than he pricks it with the pin of irony and shows us what is behind it: "flies' mugs and mosquitos' noses."

Men's everyday life, so hemmed in and mediocre, full of mean anxieties and joys, pleases him greatly. He loves "small roles" (4045), mea-

GOETHE

sure, moderation (1760), the art of remaining within the limits that fate has fixed for us. The pleasures he desires are those of a modest epicure. He wishes to enjoy in peace, sordidly, "some tasty little morsel" (1691), some senile lust, some equivocal pleasure accompanied by filthy gestures and obscene *bons mots;* and half-ironic and half-puerile dreams of Sardanapalesque grandeur and voluptuousness (10170 ff.). Perhaps, at certain moments of tedium, he would willingly leave the spaces Mother Night has assigned to him, so as to live on earth. "When from time to time I come among you," he will say a few years later to Ivan Karamazov, "my life goes by with an appearance of reality, which pleases me more than all else. The fantastic actually makes me suffer, and so I love your earthly reality. Here with you, everything is determined, everything is formula and geometry; whereas among us there are only indeterminate equations! . . . My dream is to become incarnate myself, but definitively, irrevocably, in some fat merchant's wife who weighs seven *pudy,* and to believe all that she believes."

Seated in his old armchair beneath the friendly light of the lamp, Faust translates the first verse of the Gospel of St. John using Luther's translation, *Im Anfang war das Wort,* "In the beginning was the word." But this does not satisfy him. "I cannot," he says, "esteem the word so exaggeratedly" (1226). The word—sound and smoke misting over the fires of heaven. So, supported by Herder's advice, he writes: "In the beginning was the thought"; then, "In the beginning was force"; and, finally: "In the beginning was the act."

If he were concerned with New Testament exegesis, Mephistopheles would certainly translate as Luther did: *"Im Anfang war das Wort."* The written word, the word drawn on parchment, printed on paper, incised on marble, or fused in bronze enjoys his highest consideration. While God and Faust can scorn words, since they put their trust in the power of love and the activity of the universe, Mephistopheles builds on words the foundation of his earthly kingdom. He knows that something obscurely Mephistophelian is hidden in all the words of human tongues. Each word tends to forget or deny the spirit that has given it life; it wrests itself from the lively course of time; it separates every phenomenon from the others to which it is bound, defines it, limits it, makes it rigid, helps it to die. At some moment of ironic fantasizing it must dream of its ideal world as a mass of file cards: as a single, immense, universal dictionary.[14]

Like many cultivators of words, Mephistopheles is a legalist, and he finds himself at his ease in the temples of justice and the offices of notaries, surrounded by dusty, yellowed parchments and old inks left to dry in the inkwells. Nobody could induce him to offend the laws of the infernal world, to violate the customs tying him to God and the rules of His honest commerce. If he must stipulate an agreement, he claims to respect all the preestablished forms: the pen dipped in blood, the signature that commits one for eternity. But he has the misfortune to deal with adversaries who are much less honest than he, such as God and Faust, who are accustomed to putting the spirit of things before the letter and are always ready to make fun of his intolerable pedantry (1716).

We do not know how Mephistopheles spends his leisure hours; but it is pleasant to imagine that he spends them like Wagner, who loves and cultivates words, *auctoritates*, and well-organized discourses. During the long nights of winter, while the north winds swoop down with sharpened teeth and tongues as pointed as arrows, perhaps Mephistopheles also opens his most cherished books, leafs through them page by page, unrolls old parchments, while a beatific life warms his limbs. In his leisure hours or his long pilgrimages he has had the time to obtain an excellent culture. His profession has forced him to learn the Old and New Testaments by heart: Genesis and Kings, Job, the Gospels and St. Paul's Epistles. But he has also read Homer and Aeschylus; he knows Mycenaean architecture, Doric temples, Gothic churches and castles, and on occasion is even able to counterfeit them quite well. He is not unfamiliar with ancient and modern music. As for the most recent literature, he prefers his country's old and new poets, from Hans Sachs to Wieland. But he does not disdain foreign literatures; Voltaire and the fables of the *Thousand and One Nights* equally enchant his spirit and imagination.[15]

All the witty remarks he gets off, all the inventions of his imagination, all the verses he shapes with so subtle a skill reveal the taste of a great creator of style. I do not know whether he proposes to train guilds of Mephistophelian poets to put to rout forever the artists devoted to the Lord of the heavens. But he has certainly created a poetic tradition, much more fertile than the one inspired by a Faust or Wagner. As a consequence, Dostoevsky tried to transplant his figure among the Russian gentlemen of his time; Heine and Brecht learned from him how to write verses; Baudelaire owes to him some poems in *Les Fleurs du Mal* and many prose pieces in *Spleen de Paris;* Eliot did not know that he was one of his pupils; Freud memorized his witticisms; and Mann and Musil discovered among his words the starting point for some of their finest inventions.

Mephistopheles dares not compete in the realm of lyrical poetry, for which he possesses not the slightest inclination. He lets the archangels loudly chant their neo-Pythagorean hymns, and permits Faust to find the source of a grandiose lyricism in the heart's sweet repining and the soul's nostalgia for heaven. He rates Horace over Pindar, Pope over Virgil, Wieland over Goethe and Hölderlin. His cold, dry imagination prefers intellectual precision and calculation to the religious Platonic "delirium." He is partial to concrete, pointed, piercing words in brilliant contradiction to those words wrapped in secrecy and shadows. The "average" or "plain" tone, the *"sermo humilis"* recommended by St. Augustine for revealing the mysteries of Christian revelation appeals to him, rather than the "sublime" tone of the classic poets.

From the summits of the heavens, God does not laugh (278); the Word incarnate does not laugh on earth. In the earthly paradise, the twisted creases of irony do not deform the still ingenuous lips of Adam and Eve. Even Virginia, barely reaching Paris after issuing from the hands of nature, still gilded by the sun of the tropics, her eyes full of the great primitive images of seas, mountains, and forests—even she does not know the scandal and vice of laughter. Faust, the man created in God's "image and likeness' does not laugh. To whom, then, belongs the realm of laughter? Who can claim suzerainty if not Mephistopheles, Momus's brother? While he lives in the abysses or on earth, among infernal flames or mountain's rocks, he shows us that he knows all the tones of irony, ridicule, comedy, farce, satire, and epigram.

Looking down on the world from the heights of his cynicism, he mocks at everything that exists. Now dark as nothingness, now flaming with rage, now cold as a stone, now limited as reason—he leaves behind him a taste of poison, a stench of sulphur, atrocious *pointes*. But the spirit of evil cannot grant itself the naïve pleasure of always being wicked. So Mephistopheles likes to crack jokes like a jovial old man who knows past and future things; like an amiable conversationalist, full of worldly elegance and exotic spleen; or like a vulgar, plebeian ham actor who makes fun of himself before the complicitous audience of the universe. Whatever cord of irony he touches with his adept hands, his witticisms reveal an inimitable lightness, an enchanting precision and sharpness of style, as if only infernal laughter could confer on words the dry sharp light they need.

As a realistic writer, Mephistopheles has neither the time nor the patience to compose a big novel, rich in social frescoes, well-rounded characters, love stories, mishaps, tears, and furious avarice—like those of Balzac and Dickens. For him "realism" is still a literary genre, as for Horace, Pope, or Hogarth. It is a way of isolating some "small worlds" within the "large world," and of describing them with neat, acrid elegance. When Goethe depicts the foolish gaiety of the students of Leipzig, the house and conversation of Marthe Schwertlein who has been abandoned by a drunken husband, the blond and brunette ladies who request remedies for freckles and the sufferings of love, the gabble of the courtiers when confronted with Helen's appearance—each time he yields the brush to Mephistopheles's knowing hand.

The infernal territory over which Mephistopheles rules is a jumble of bric-a-brac in the worst possible taste: fourth-rate witches, monkeys who play checkers or with a ball, smoking cauldrons, and senseless refrains, scenes of wood, and canvas of the city of Dis with its clumsy swarm of devils. Instead of infusing a new, imaginative life in this worn-out mythology, Mephistopheles takes pleasure in emphasizing the grotesque degradation of his kingdom. Like a very adept vaudeville juggler, he travesties, parodies, and brings abreast of fashion the old informal world, strewing it with literary allusions and political *bons mots*. So he himself is forever destroying the reality of hell. After his appearance on the stage of literature, the realm of evil will no longer be a theological place, but rather the place where the satanic spirit of pastiche triumphs.

In *Faust II* Mephistopheles's literary tastes become more complicated and refined, and the satiric epigram, the realistic print, the grotesque fantasy no longer meet his imagination's needs. With constantly renewed inspiration he leaps into territories he had barely glimpsed until then. He investigates the world of being and the wings of theaters, the boundless solitude of oceans and the gloomy caverns of the Phorkyads, the illusory colors of the Fata Morgana and the phantoms of myth. When he leaves us forever, hiding in his inferno, it seems to us that a great part of "modern poetry" has come from under Mephistopheles's short silken cloak. Perhaps without him one could never imagine that the poet could combine analytical precision and metaphysical élan in the same verse, the mind's aridity and the wildest fantasy, irony and nothingness, the heat of fire and the mute, impenetrable coldness of rock.

Faust's dramatic action has its origin in two different wagers. The first, which takes place in the theater of heaven, finds God and Mephistopheles confronting each other. God trusts in Faust's original good nature (324) and in the strength of his *Streben*, which is still uncertain, confused, and obscure but will end by purifying itself and finding the right road (308, 311, 317, 326–329). Mephistopheles seems equally certain that this strange scholar, who desires the most beautiful stars in the heavens and the highest pleasures on earth, will soon succumb to his flattery. Then Faust will have to eat dust, like Mephisto's cousin, "the celebrated serpent" of the earthly paradise (335).

During the second wager, Mephistopheles offers Faust two pieces of

GOETHE

advice. "Believe me," he says to him, "this All was made for God alone" (1780–1781). Man is not a "microcosm"; he cannot reconcile the lion's courage and the deer's speed, the Italian's fiery blood and the Northerner's steadfastness, the warmth of youth and the mature strength that calculates and foresees. "You are in the end . . . what you are. Put on wigs with millions of curls, put buskins a yard high on your feet, you will still remain what you are"[16]—an individual. Like every human being, Faust must learn to walk through life in the enclosed, limited, and commonplace world where real men live; and to know the joys of the senses, savoring in peace some honest pleasure, some "tasty morsel."

Scorned by the "spirit of the earth," nauseated by all human science, Faust lets himself be tempted by Mephistopheles. He decides to placate his "ancient passions in the abysses of sensuality" and to plunge "into the noisy tumult of time, the whirl of events" (1750–1755). In any case, while he welcomes Mephistopheles's proposals, he transforms them completely. In the real world into which he is about to venture, his profound *I* retains the ambition of achieving the All because he wants to know, enjoy, and suffer everything that fate has granted to all mankind (1768 ff.). Before the door of limited existence, he recalls again his eternally dissatisfied nature which will never rest on the bed of sloth, will never be deceived by pleasure, or be induced to contemplate the moments of beauty (1692 ff., 1700 ff., 1759). So Faust renounces not even a molecule of his own nature, and the signature he leaves at the bottom of the old parchment is a mark without importance destined to gather dust in the inferno's archives. The sole agreement to which he subscribes, the true obligation to which he obstinately wishes to remain faithful is what he undertook toward himself when he was born. Now, too, in the company of his obsequious Virgil, amid the pleasures of sensuality and the noisy tumult of time, he obeys only his *Streben*, that restless entelechy God has placed in his care (1676, 1742).

So the wager seems to be decided from the very start. When in the world will Faust be able to savor in peace some "tasty morsel"? What can a "poor devil" offer to so restless a soul? (1675.) But Mephistopheles is not at all that poor devil whom, out of cunning or politeness, he sometimes pretends to be with us mortals. Mephistopheles is old, and Faust is too young to know him well. Mephisto does not expect to see his new servant and master sprawled out on the bed of sloth surrounded by the allurements of vulgar pleasures. Like God, he trusts in the rash, headlong insatiability of Faust's *Streben*. If that soul will always be driven by the same fury, no food will calm his hunger, no drink will slake his thirst, and every refreshment will flee from his lips. Without peace, without a goal, without pause, Faust will be forced to continue down the terrible road until he plunges into ruin (1856–1867).

So the wager between God and Mephistopheles and the wager between Mephistopheles and Faust reveal their true meanings. Seated at the table of fate, the three contenders do not choose different cards but stake all their assets on the selfsame card: Faust's *Streben*. God stakes his reputation as a creator, Mephistopheles his debatable dignity as a modern devil, and Faust his *daimon*. Half troubled and half amused, we witness the double wager. The conditions are so subtle, the yes and no, the negative and positive are so confused that at the end of the play we must turn to a legal adviser for help. The stakes are immense. The fate of the modern world, our very fate hangs by a thread. We do not know whether Faust's *Streben* will leave behind only blood and anxiety, or whether it will reveal the same impulse that guides Makarie past the confines of our solar system.

We know the three main characters of the play and the commitments binding them, all that remains for us now is to follow them through the five acts of *Faust II*. Just as Lamb told Shakespeare's plays to children, just as in the past students used to turn the *Iliad* and *Odyssey* "into prose," so we, too, will tell everything that happens (or seems to happen) on stage or behind the wings to the characters and ghosts of *Faust II*. We shall try not to forget anything; and above all not to mix any of our childish inventions with Goethe's great inventions.

The
Magic
of the Wise

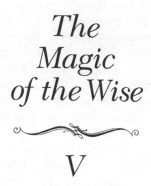

V

Mephistopheles and Faust at the Imperial Court

The piercing, joyous sound of trumpets announces, as in an Elizabethan play, the Emperor's entrance into the throne room, between two ranks of magnificently dressed courtiers. Soon the Chancellor, the Commander of the army, the Treasurer, and Majordomo will stalk onto the stage to pronounce their stylized speeches. Everything in the great hall seems to express triumphant regality, unlimited power, the ostentatious splendor of forms, self-satisfied opulence. What is more, the cheerfulness of the Emperor, the coming masked balls of the carnival season, the witticisms of the court jester, and the predictions of the astrologer all seem to promise boundless felicity and joy.

This splendor is an empty façade. The feckless sovereign seated on the throne between his astrologer and jester possesses neither power, nor authority, nor money. The coffers of his treasury are empty; for months his mercenaries have not received their pay, the usurers own the wheat before it is harvested and seize the pigs before they have been fattened. The ancient prestige of the Holy Roman Empire of Charlemagne and Frederick I of Swabia has come to naught. Almost as though competing with one another, the kings of Europe have hastened to forget their feelings of awe. The Church's domains are constantly enriched with new donations and privileges, mountains and forests, rich pastures on the uplands, lakes swarming with fish, fertile valleys and hills, tithes and payments in kind. The nobles, holed up in their nests of rock, reign like sovereigns over their estates; and the burghers, protected by the cities' walls, carry on their commerce undisturbed.

Faust II

Anyone looking down from on high on the empire's regions can see only confusion, anarchy, and feverish ruin. He may think he is having a nightmare teeming with frightful monsters who continually generate even more frightful monsters. Small and great do battle; knights attack knights, cities destroy cities, guilds war against aristocrats, bishops war against communes, brothers exile and kill each other. While choirs and naves, towers and portals are raised to the greater glory of God, murderers immolate their victims on the barely consecrated stones, thieves tear precious crosses, chalices, and candelabra from the altars, and rob pilgrims on the highways. And if the innocent turn to the courts, what a mockery! The judges sit pompously on their high benches while the robbers of flocks and holy trappings, the criminals with bloodstained hands, plot together to the detriment of innocence.

Mephistopheles and Faust appear in this sumptuous and deceptive setting. We do not know where they come from. We left Faust in the "pleasant Alpine region," facing the sun's first rays; and we had seen Mephistopheles for the last time in Gretchen's prison. We do not know how much time has passed since then; nor what adventures, pranks, or crimes they may have shared. But, at least in appearance, their relationship has changed. Mephistopheles no longer seems the vulgar, arrogant, infernal tempter; nor Faust the noble soul, the proud and romantic *grand seigneur* who, with an annoyed gesture, rejects all tasteless pleasures. At the imperial court, amid the marshals, treasurers, pages, and heralds surrounding the Emperor, Faust and Mephistopheles behave like two bizarre adventurers trying to make their fortunes in the most illicit fashion, or at least wanting to amuse themselves at the world's expense.

Mephistopheles, with a stratagem, succeeds in getting the fat court jester drunk and takes his place at the left of the Emperor. While the dignitaries are making their solemn speeches, he amuses himself by imitating an Elizabethan fool,* weaving together riddles and brazen flatteries, vulgar jests and pungent, acrid truths. A short time passes and Mephistopheles, without apparently changing his mask, changes his manner and style. Those listening to him think they are hearing one of those talented impostors, one of those astute mystagogues, who crammed the courts of Europe during the superstitious century of the Enlightenment, charlatans such as Cagliostro, who claimed to have lived among Egyptian Sphinxes and the ancient Brahmins of India and insisted that he knew miraculous jewels, the language of the spirits, and Solomon's secret alphabet.[1] Mephistopheles is more modest. But he too

*English in original.

GOETHE

surrounds himself with mysteries, speaks in the obscure and deceptive language of the mystagogues, and declares that he possesses the profound secrets of "eternal dominant Nature" (4985).

Like one of those very adroit charlatans, Mephistopheles has an astonishing "project" all prepared (4888). During the barbarian invasions and the wars that have plagued the empire, thousands of fugitives hid their wealth in mountain caves, cellars, and the most secret subterranean tunnels. Nobody has ever dug up these treasures. Mephistopheles takes delight in describing the pots full of gold, the packets of gold, the golden beakers, bowls, and salvers, the goblets studded with rubies, the jewels, gems, and essences of very old wines still buried in the darkness. Since the treasures in the ground belong, by law and custom, to the Emperor, all that has to be done is bring them to light and so fill the coffers of the exhausted imperial treasury.[2] In this project, the crowd packing the rear of the palace hall sees only *Chymisterei* and *Kalenderei* (4974)—the deceptions of alchemists and astrologers. Even the naïve Emperor suspects that such a flaunting of mysteries conceals a colossal hoax. "What's the point of obscurity?" he says. "If a thing has value, it must reach the light of day. Who can recognize the rascal in the dark of night? All cows are black then, and all cats gray . . ." (5033–5036). Wise, at least this once, the Emperor is repeating unawares the words which, so many years ago, Goethe had written to Lavater, who had been deluded and blinded by Cagliostro's skills: "Believe me, he who does not know how to evoke spirits by day and under the open sky, will not exorcise them even at midnight, in a crypt . . ." (June 22, 1781).

The new Mephistopheles has many other surprises in store for us. As he is speaking with the Emperor, he gradually draws the same picture of the world that Faust had proposed at the beginning of the play. As though he were a follower of Paracelsus, he maintains that the universe is a unitary and harmonious construction in which each element acts in a hidden way on all the others. Each of the stars in the sky reflects its power in a metal, the sun in gold, the moon in silver, Saturn in lead (4955 ff.). The macrocosm is reflected in the microcosm; all the treasures of heaven and earth have their correspondence in ourselves, in our "spiritual and natural" strength (4896 ff.). At the close of the scene, Mephistopheles reverently names the *lapis philosophorum* (5064) and the "lofty art" that produces it, "the magic of the wise" (6316). So we cannot be astonished if he recommends, through the mouth of the astrologer, all the qualities necessary to those who wish to perform the alchemical *opus:* moderation (5048), inner concentration (5050), goodness (5053), patience (5055), and, actually, "faith" (5056).[3] All seems clear. The prince of hell has converted, becoming a devout Christian alchemist trying to reconcile God with nature's secret forces.

What does this incredible conversion mean? How is it possible that the mortal enemy of nature, he who shudders with horror when he stays for a while amid grass and moss, the creatures of air and water, now extols "eternal dominant Nature" (4985)? We could more easily imagine him shut behind the walls of a monastery draped with hair-shirts and Agnus Dei, and performing the most ascetic mortifications. It is not easy to understand Mephistopheles's intentions, or determine how much seriousnes and how much playfulness are mingled in his words. But it is quite probable that his intentions are manifold, hidden one within the other like the gifts inside the fairy tale's miraculous nut. In the first place, he delights in mocking the chancellor-archbishop, who believes that "nature is sin" and "the spirit is a devil" (4900). "Oh," says Mephisto, "there I recognize the learned man! What you do not touch lies leagues away from you, what you cannot grasp does not exist at all for you. What you cannot calculate you regard as untrue, what you cannot weigh has no weight for you . . ." (4917–4922). Thus he makes fun of philosophy and alchemical images, both of which he is actually using lavishly (4955–4970, 4985–4992). Finally, he proposes to his listeners, in the guise of cosmology, piety, and Christian faith, the fundamental principles of hell's alchemy.

According to Mephistopheles, the principles of vision are enclosed in the subterranean world—in caverns, gorges, labyrinths, beneath the walls of houses, in the "deepest, most profound abyss" (4892–4894, 5014–5017, 6284). They lie buried in darkness, wrapped "in night and horror" (5029). Therefore, the true wise man does not explore on the crust of the earth and in the light of day, where things are obvious even to a superficial glance. Like the patient miner, like Jarno in the *Wanderjahre*, the wise man hides in the subterranean shadows; and down there without fear, rest, or anxiety he examines the profound mysteries of knowledge (5051–5052). If Mephistopheles had become a Christian alchemist after having delved in the abysses and darkness, he would have brought his discoveries back to the summit of heaven, to the light of the stars where God, the beginning of all knowledge, triumphs. But Mephistopheles has only disguised himself in the ideas of Paracelsus and Böhme. So his wise man does not turn his eyes to heaven: he continues to live in the caves and night, studying what is dark, heavy, rigid, impenetrable to the divine lightness of the light. If this sort of knowledge had spread, the Christian universe would have been overturned, and the force of "concentration," matter, and darkness would again rule the world.[4]

Faust appears on the stage only much later. In the imperial throne room, where Mephistopheles simultaneously plays all these parts, there is not the slightest sign of him. During the long carnival masquerade, in which he participates dressed as Plutus, we do not hear his name; and only the morning after, when the conjuring tricks have dissolved in the air like figures of mist, does Faust bow before the emperor. If he could have heard Mephistopheles's speech, Faust, for the first and only time in the entire play, would have agreed with many of his companion's affirmations. His father had been an old alchemist who locked himself up in his laboratory, mixing antagonistic elements in his alembic—the red lion and the whitest lily—in order to distill the miraculous remedy, the "young queen" (1034 ff.). As for himself, though he had scoffed at his father's science, he owes all of his persuasions to the "loftiest art," which explores the mysteries of knowledge. The books that continue to nourish his mind are those of Paracelsus, Böhme, Basil Valentine, and *Aurea catena Homeri* and Georg von Welling's *Opus mago-cabbalisticum*. If he thinks of nature, his inner eye sees a chain of magical correspondences, a compact net of relationships traversing the universe from stars to minerals, from sky to earth, from the germs of air and water to the blood of creatures, from the "sweet gaze of spring" to the force of love that burns in every man's heart.

Faust, like Mephistopheles, believes that in the symbolic depths of the earth there lies—frozen and unused—a "superabundance of treasures" (6111), an "unlimited wealth" exceeding the most far-reaching thoughts and surpassing imagination's most ambitious flights. But the portrait of the wise man, indeed of the spirit "worthy of looking deeply" (6117), which he proposes to men, is the opposite of that presented by Mephistopheles. Like the great Renaissance alchemists, the true wise man beloved by Faust is animated by an enthusiastic religious emotion, an impetuous abundance of imagination, an "unlimited faith in the illimitable" (6118).[5] He lives down there, in the darkness, digs up the gems, the symbolic golden jewels, the noble essences shrouded in the night, and boldly brings them to light; he crawls through the labyrinths of the underground, and there discovers the supreme forms and values of existence.

After describing Mephistopheles's and Faust's "alchemy," we know the pattern around which Goethe composes the verses of the first act of *Faust II*. In the halls of the imperial palace, during the course of a tumultuous carnival masquerade, Faust and Mephistopheles use images and words, illusionistic feats and prodigies to present the opposed forms of gold, the great symbol of alchemy. Each chooses the aspect most congenial to him. Full of "unlimited faith in the illimitable," Faust shows us the sublime gold of the soul; while, with a thousand conjuring tricks, Mephistopheles distills on the stage the base gold prepared in the cavities of hell. The descent to the Mothers is also a metaphor, though distant and veiled, of the *opus magnum*. Alchemists called the "mother" that "prime material," that original substance they would ennoble by actually extracting from it the philosopher's stone. Similarly, Faust, with the help of the magic of the wise, descends to the Mothers to receive in exchange from them the "treasure," Helen.[6] The relationship between the two characters remains unchanged. While Mephistopheles teaches us to see in the abyss only the eternal void, nothingness, Faust tries to wrest the ineffable, full forms of Being from the Mothers.

Mephistopheles the Illusionist

At the Emperor's court the carnival continues on its mad way. But there are no macabre dances, devils, and clowns to remind us that we are on German soil. The masked processions winding through the sumptuously decorated hall resemble those which a few decades before had brightened the court of Lorenzo the Magnificent and which Anton Francesco Grazzini had illustrated and collected in a book. Here is a group of flower girls with bright artificial flowers twined in their black curls, silken floss and bows, green stems, golden bellflowers, and other multicolored blossoms, never seen in nature, are mixed in their baskets with peaceful olive branches, roses, and ears of wheat.

Accompanied by mandolins, some of the flower girls praise the strange fantasies of fashion while others proclaim the triumphs of the reign of Flora, setting out their wares beneath the festoons of a pergola. As the mandolins and theorbos continue to play, the flower girls carry baskets full of cherries, peaches, plums, and apples. Crude woodcutters, fishermen, and bird catchers armed with nets, fishing lines, and snares step out on the flower-bedecked stage. Cunning, clumsy Punches in light jackets slither away like eels on their slippered feet. A mother tries to marry off her daughter, parasites catch a whiff of a free meal; and a drunkard stretched out on the pavement drinks and sings boisterously.

Then the herald announces a more solemn procession. Figures from Greek mythology appear, wearing modern masks. The Three Graces, Aglaia, Hegemone, Euphrosyne, bestow graciousness on life; the Three Fates have sheathed the scissors that cut short so many young lives; and

GOETHE

the Furies, who embitter the joys of lovers and married couples, seem three young girls full of smirks and affectations. The last group is more openly allegorical. On an enormous elephant, covered with brightly colored rugs, sits a delicate woman, Prudence, who guides the animal with a thin wand. On either side of her walk Fear and Hope, two of men's worst enemies, tightly wrapped in chains. On high, with her wings outstretched, clothed in dazzling splendor, the goddess Victory, mistress of all human activities, sits on her throne.[7]

As he describes these modest allegories, Goethe's imagination is lazy, slack, and bored, as when Karl August insisted that he prepare scenarios, plays, and choruses for Weimar's festivals. But suddenly everything changes. Unnoticed, Mephistopheles has taken the place of the Emperor's choreographer. He begins to animate a disquieting carnival feast, dragging onto the stage the courtiers dressed like fauns, satyrs, gnomes, giants, and nymphs, and even the Emperor himself, disguised as Pan. The lord of the inferno is not satisfied with simple human arts; he is much more than a choreographer. Mephistopheles is the most ancient of wizards, the greatest among all the equivocal and imaginative illusionists that populate heaven, earth, and the abyss. Everything that deceives the senses, that does not have a body and yet seems to have it, that does not have a voice and speaks like men falls within his sovereignty. Everything that is empty and seems full—air bubbles covered with colors, smoke that gleams, formless mists, musical compositions which no orchestra is playing, resplendent Fata Morganas—all are products of his art. Everything that is born in the delicious and dreadful no-man's-land where the dreams, specters, deceits, tricks, and mystifications of poets and jugglers flourish—all this belongs to his immense kingdom.

In the first part of *Faust*, Mephistopheles had extracted Rhine wine, champagne, and Tokay from a poor tavern table. At the imperial court such tricks must seem to him worthy of a mediocre provincial charlatan and so he tries to surpass himself (5487, 5501). As imaginative and fecund as Scheherazade, he flaunts before the aristocratic audience the conjuring tricks and deceptions of his old repertory, which till now he had revealed only to the vulgar crowds in hell. Like the great illusionists, he finds a point of departure in everything his avid eyes have read and seen. He finds inspiration in Homer's and Ovid's verses, in the *Thousand and One Nights* and medieval chronicle, in the figures of Greek mythology and the Barmecidal caliphs, the *Farbenlehre* and the *Westöstlicher Divan*.

He snaps his fingers and specters, "airy phantoms" (5487, 5501), come streaming through the palace windows and whistle about the heads of the spectators, entangling them in their coils, four winged horses arrive vomiting flames. The magic wand flashes; it traces invisible circles, empty columns of fire, imaginary clouds; and vying with the wand, words draw palaces and marine monsters.[8] When we penetrate into Mephistopheles's world, who can distinguish the choreographic spectacle from the phantasmagorias—the theater of men from that of the ghosts? Sometimes we cannot tell whether a figure in the masquerade is a disguised courtier or a ghost who has come among us from the spaces of the sky or the cavities of hell.

In this illusionistic world, everything wavers and is transformed. Mephistopheles presents himself on the stage in the garb of the dwarf Toilo-Thersites. No sooner does the herald touch him with his baton than he bends, writhes, twists, curls up like a ball into a loathsome shape; he becomes an egg which swells up and divides in two, a viper wriggling in the dust, and a black bat which flies toward the ceiling. Thus Mephistopheles reveals that he has at his command the same force of metamorphosis that dominates nature, that transforms the seed into the fruit and generates new life. Mephistopheles's metamorphoses are even more prodigious, and do not respect that prudent economy and wise caution of nature's activities. But Mephistopheles does not create even the shadow of life; everything that issues from his enchanter's hands is audacious and sterile; nothingness is transformed into nothingness, the void generates another void, the ambiguous and unseizable irony provokes infinite, ever more ambiguous and laughter-provoking games. . . .[9]

At the back of the spacious imperial hall, lost amid the masked crowd, or seated before a desk with an open copy of *Faust II*, the spectators let themselves be enchanted by this carnival masquerade. Few of them understand that, behind the choreographic spectacle, is hidden the symbol of alchemy in the double version presented by Faust and Mephistopheles. But what does it matter if these delightful appearances, these exquisite games succeed in beguiling—for a few hours, perhaps a few days—the unbearable boredom, the ever denser tedium of their existence?

GOETHE

Poetry and Wealth

Scarcely have the viper and bat disappeared than a glittering shower of colors, whimsical gleams of stars, reflections as from a magic lantern announce the arrival of a chariot drawn by four winged horses, furious as a tempest. As the herald observes them, the noble steeds turn into dragons vomiting flames from their scaly jaws (5521, 5680–5681). But of what material are they made? Perhaps of wood and cardboard, as the crowd suspects (5673). Perhaps they are as light and incorporeal as our dreams, since they pass through the crowd without even touching it; perhaps they are as robust as draught horses, since they drag such heavy loads (5685–5689). Do they make their appearance here only for a few hours, invented by Mephistopheles's magic? Or does this furious horse-drawn chariot eternally travel the heavenly spaces, beating audacious wings and conquering more new trophies? (5612–5621).

If Goethe had not helped us, we would not recognize Faust in the mythological god-king seated on a magnificent throne in the chariot. We do not know whether he has donned a mask of cardboard or silk; whether before coming onstage, a skillful makeup artist has not smoothed away his wrinkles and transformed his face with cosmetics and the artful tricks of his craft. In any event, behind the shadow of fiction there does not transpire even the memory of the anxious and impatient, yearning and violent expression that usually accompanies his figure. At least this time—at least during the course of a fast-moving night of carnival—Faust seems completely serene. Like almost all the maskers who obey the Emperor's classical tastes, Faust impersonates a god of Greek mythology. Not Prometheus, Hercules, Cronus or some other Titan, none of the great rebels, heroes, or defeated gods, whom he resembles, has attracted his theatrical interest. Leafing through Hesiod's *Theogony*, he has tracked down, in a probably spurious passage, the figure of Plutus, the god of wealth, who was born in the field "of a flat country town in Crete" from the lovemaking of Demeter and young Iasion, and who courses over the earth and the vast ridges of the sea, bestowing his opulence on all men (*Theogony,* 969 ff.).

Faust is not concerned with respecting the colorful historian of the god he represents; he is acting in *Faust II,* where history is only a phantasmagoria, and he obeys the orders of Mephistopheles who mocks at such things as the unity of place and time. So, instead of studying Greek statues and cameos, he has looked at a Persian miniature. The turban adorning his head, the long, pleated tunic flowing around his limbs; the face round as the full moon, the well-padded cheeks, the tumid mouth, the dignified and solemn gestures—everything in his costume recalls one of those wealthy, powerful, and extremely cultivated Barmecidal caliphs whom Goethe had exalted in his note to the *Westöstlicher Divan.* This Greek god, this peaceful Oriental sovereign does not know the devouring force of desires (5556); his strongboxes are crammed with gold, his domains measureless, his soul majestically tranquil. Seated on his throne he looks at the world as from a distance. His is the mild, calm, and benign eye of one who for a long time has contemplated the vicissitudes of this world without acting (5703). If he interrupts his repose, it is only when "the pure delight of giving" invites him to spread his treasures among men (5558). All of his majestic, measured gestures and words leave the impression of perfect plenitude and spiritual harmony.

The handsome, very young ephebe who drives the winged horses, recalls the figure on a cameo, in a bas-relief, or in a classic hymn. His ardent black eyes are fiery; a ribbon of jewels brightens his night-black curls, a perfumed cloak glittering with spangles and a purple hem enfolds his soft, feminine limbs from his shoulders down to his ankles. Whoever knows him thinks he is seeing Apollo's ephebic image as he watches the games of the inhabitants of Delos or the dances of the goddesses of Olympus. But the boy charioteer has also known the splendors of the Orient. Luxury has nourished him, superabundance has educated him in some celestial palace, even more sumptuous than the Hellenistic palaces—in Alexandria or Antioch—where ephebes lend an atmosphere of gaiety to the dances and banquets.

As he talks with the herald, the boy charioteer, with the adolescent's naïve and brazen narcissism, makes a boastful display of his talents and exploits. All goals seem attainable to his boundless daring: today flights in space, tomorrow women's charms and love. But will this enchanting Cherubino really have a tomorrow? Will his limbs acquire virile strength, will his beauty take on substance, will his emotions achieve the composure of maturity? Everything leads one to think that the young charioteer—perhaps miraculously untouched by time, perhaps swept away by the wild rush of the winged horses—will forever be a prisoner of the unlimited, imaginative world of adolescence.

Like Euphorion and Mignon, his demon kin, the boy charioteer has received from heaven the incommensurable wealth of poetry, no less great than the wealth Plutus guards in his strongboxes. Numerous palms of glory and crowns of laurel have already rewarded his labors.[10] If he were older he would know how to conserve this bounty. Surrounded by the books in his study, he would compose and polish long and short verses, lyrical poems and comedies, tragedies and novels for himself and a few trusted friends. But the young charioteer cannot and does not

GOETHE

want to hide himself—every breath betrays him, every gesture reveals him (5704–5706), and a fatuous, dolorous desire forces him to bestow himself, to lavish all that he possesses, to burn up his poetic inventions once and for all (5573–5576). When he appears to us at the end of the third act in the guise of Euphorion his dissipations lead him, after having traversed in a few hours the vertiginous steps of space, right into the arms of death. Here, at the carnival celebration, his follies still belong to the sphere of the theater. Encircled by the crowd, the charioteer suddenly snaps his fingers, and immediately something gleams and shines forth. As if by enchantment, pearl necklaces, gold brooches and earrings, diadems, faultless combs, and rings encrusted with gems take flight; while small flames, which should communicate the genial force of poetry, burn over now one head, now another.

The crowd hemming in the chariot does not understand the treasure that poetry gives away through the hand of the *Knabe Lenker*. As they try to seize them, the pearl necklaces become beetles which crawl over their hands and fly off with a buzzing sound; the gems, diadems, and brooches soar over their heads like many-hued butterflies (5584 ff.); and the small flames burn for an instant and then are sadly doused. So it occurs in fables, too: When someone is unworthy of a conquered or inherited treasure, he sees it turn into a stone that weighs down his knapsack, or a frog that hops away from him down a muddy road.

Disappointed and humiliated, the young charioteer laments the sad fate of his talents and blames the crowd's blindness. But, as the herald suspects, this explanation is not complete. Isn't poetry perhaps a "veil" with a thousand folds, in which light and darkness, immutable truth and shimmering illusion are confused? Isn't it perhaps a fresh, deceptive rainbow? So, with the same fatuous and sorrowful gesture the charioteer bestows on us pearl necklaces and buzzing beetles, the purest gems and butterflies, perennial flames and fleeting will-o'-the-wisps. His generous spirit is quite different from Mephistopheles's acrid and limited one. Nevertheless, when the charioteer spreads abroad these real and empty treasures, he, too, is a mystifier like the prince of hell; he, too, uses the glitter of the fictitious to attract and mock at men.

The earthly mission of the *Knabe Lenker* has been completed. Nothing obliges him to linger any longer on this earth where heaviness imprisons the wings of his spirit and he is surrounded by men's confused and savage gesticulations. Heeding Plutus's call, he leaves the masquerade and his horses carry him to the heavens, to that solitary place where poetry constructs another world (5694–5695). Up there in pure space, or in a palace similar to the sun's, made of gold, ivory, pyrope, and silver, his clear eyes contemplate the light's "gentle brightness" (5693); up there he delights only in that which is "beautiful and good"

(5695). If he strews around him the flame of inspiration, he will find those who nourish it with jealous and devoted care; if he flings rings and diadems among the heavenly host, no enchantment will change their forms.

Before the charioteer leaves the procession, Plutus paraphrases the words that God the Father had pronounced at Christ's baptism (Matthew 3:17): "If it is necessary that I be a witness for you, I gladly say unto you: you are the soul of my soul. . . . I announce this word of truth to all: This is my beloved Son, with whom I am well pleased" (5622–5629). The young charioteer responds with the same affection, declaring himself Plutus's "worthy envoy" and his "closest kinsman," and weaving wreaths of laurel around his brow (5697–5698, 5617–5621). These mutual declarations of love, these close ties of kinship will surprise many readers of *Faust II*. What relation can exist between the god of wealth and the god of poetry—between the fat, tranquil caliph and the anxious ephebe decked out in frills? The ancient readers of Homer, Pindar, and Callimachus, or modern alchemists would have understood Goethe's intentions. They knew that gold "scintillating like the flame that shines in the night" (Pindar, I *Olympian Hymns* 1 ff.) is a multiple element, a universal symbol. They knew that when Apollo was born, the island of Delos was completely covered with gold; that Apollo's bow, lyre, sword, fasces, sandals, and hair were made of gold; and that his celestial palace, built on tall columns, gleamed with gold like the palaces of the kings, potentates, and lords of the earth. So they would have accepted the idea that the god of wealth was the father and protector of the god of poetry.

During the course of the carnival masquerade, gold shares its symbolic abundance between Plutus and the *Knabe Lenker*. It confers its irresistible flame of inspiration, the active spirit of poetic creation on the continually mobile and active ephebe (5624–5625, 5703–5704).[11] To Plutus, possessor of strongboxes crammed with precious metal, it consigns less obvious gifts. The god himself says that he is less "rich" than his son (5579, 5625). But spiritual plenitude and the gaze of serenity, symbolically revealed by gold, permit him to propose certain goals to the audacious flights of the young charioteer (5614–5615, 5624). When Plutus and the boy charioteer are united by the loving bonds that link father and son, they offer to men an ideal image of existence: the noble gold of the soul. The dignified and majestic deeds of maturity join with the restless grace of youth; wisdom sustains irrepressible inspiration and is in turn illuminated by it; the contemplative stance is in accord with the active life; and spiritual fullness pours out lavishly and—so deep are its roots—inexhaustibly.

Hidden behind Faust's or Mephistopheles's shoulders, or perhaps

even farther away, at the rear of the hall among the carnival supernumeraries and the prodigies of water and fire, Goethe does not reveal
his own inclinations. But if Eckermann had questioned him further, if
he had asked him at what point in that great scene he had painted his
self-portrait, perhaps he would have confessed that the beturbaned
Oriental caliph was one of the most faithful images he had ever given
of himself. Like Plutus, he had become one of the great ones of the
earth; the powerful came to his house, bringing him tokens of homage
and veneration, knightly orders to hang about his neck, decorations,
fossils and ancient coins. But as soon as they left his house, he called up
from within himself the ghost of the ephebe with flashing black eyes,
who scattered unreal prodigies over the earth and then drove a winged
chariot far into the solitary regions of the sky.

Fire, Water, and Paper Money

In a rejected scene of *Faust II*, Satan appears on a peak of the Harz
Mountains, with his grotesque retinue of fetid he-goats and stinking
she-goats, like Christ in heaven on the day of the Last Judgment. The
infernal choirs honor the potent lord. Satan's children prostrate themselves before him; and pilgrims from every part of the world come to
hear his "precious words," his incomparable teachings, which illuminate the sign of "eternal life" and "profound nature." Thus after centuries of silence, Satan finally reveals his wisdom—those *logoi*, which until
then his disciples had confided in whispers and had transcribed in
esoteric books. Turning to the he-goats, seated to his right, he proclaims:
"For you there are two great and magnificent things: shining gold and
the female womb. The first buys, the second swallows, so happy is he
who obtains both." Turning to the she-goats, who are at his left, he adds:
"For you there are two things of precious splendor: blazing gold and a
resplendent phallus. Therefore, my dear ladies, may you learn how to
enjoy money, and even more than money, to value the phallus."*

More discreet than his alter ego, more skeptical than he concerning
the profundity of his knowledge, and less inclined to general ideas,
Mephistopheles is content to hide these traits behind carnival fictions.
While Plutus and the boy charioteer exchange their "couplets," Meph-

*See *Faust* in the Artemis-Ausgabe, *Paralepomena*, Page 553.

istopheles remains seated, on a chest crammed with metal coins, high in his allegorical chariot. He is wearing the miser's old folk mask—extremely thin, consumed by the fascination for gold as though he were being devoured by hunger and thirst. He moralizes, as stock characters in masques often do; he regrets the good old days when women kept the hearth fires burning, saved, and filled chests and cupboards with thalers. Today, he says, they dissipate their husbands' wealth on dresses and frills; they eat, drink, and support the ill-omened throng of their lovers. When a bevy of beautiful women approaches the chest full of gold, yearning to see and snatch, Mephistopheles is assailed by lust and seeks to court them with the most brazen words and gestures. But how can he clearly express his lubricious intentions? Mephistopheles plunges his hands in the chest and seizes a handful of gold. Kneading it between his fingers as if it were dough or wet clay, he squeezes it, shapes it, and models from it a huge, glittering, resplendent phallus, that phallus—Satan assures us—which women prize even more highly than money.

So Mephistopheles shows us the satanic aspect of the very ancient metal confined in the caves of the earth, in the bowels of infernal caves. He certainly does not lavish it with the inspired abundance of Apollo, Plutus, and the *Knabe Lenker*. He accumulates it in his strongboxes; that generous, joyous river of gifts, which leaves a presage of felicity along its banks, he transforms into a pile of cold metal conserved by the miser's sterile passion. This gold contains the symbol of erotic force, as he conceives of it—a filthy, all-powerful activity, composed of sordid couplings, gestures, displays, flauntings, obscene words and *bons mots* typical of an old *voyeur*, with not even a trace of the love that continually creates life.

When Mephistopheles has completed his private show, the carnival procession is animated by new crowd scenes. Now there rises the song and tumult of a "savage army" as it swoops down from mountain peaks and wooded valleys. Hosts of fauns with pointed ears, snub noses, and oak leaves in their curly hair dance joyfully, and satyrs leap about on goat hoofs and thin legs, reminding the inhabitants of the valleys and plains of the free and pure atmosphere of the lofty mountains, where they lead their happy lives. Then trot out groups of little gnomes, wearing suits made of moss, each carrying a small bright lantern. They bustle about helter-skelter on every side and work away, teeming like luminous ants. They live in the mountains, hidden in the darkest grottoes, like a populace of troglodytes; they swarm through the labyrinths discovering veins of gold with a divinatory wand. Like surgeons they bleed the turgid veins in the rocks, gathering into great piles the

GOETHE

precious metal for which men will rob, corrupt, and spill the blood of their brothers. From the top of the Harz Mountains descends a mob of wild giants, naked as nature made them, wearing the crudest aprons of leaves and twigs, each holding the trunk of a fir tree in his hands. A group of nymphs surrounds the Emperor who, dressed as the "great Pan," is covered with resinous boughs, a crown on his head and a false beard on his chin. The nymphs form a circle around him, twirling lightly and rapidly, extolling the peace of midday, when no leaf stirs on the boughs, balmy perfumes pervade the still air, and creatures abandon themselves to nature's terrible sleep.

All the groups of the carnival masquerade have now reached the imperial hall, where Mephistopheles can finally bring his illusionist spectacles to a close. Gold crowns, chains, and rings, gold vases, gold coins fill to the brim the bronze chest, which was transported by the winged chariot. Plutus merely touches the locks with his rod and they open: a wave of gilded blood suddenly gushes forth, swollen and seething, threatening to fuse and engulf the treasures. He but dips the rod into the burning liquid and it begins to flash, crackle, and shoot out spellbinding sparks. Then the bronze chest becomes a "fountain," a "well of fire" (5716, 5907, 5912), a volcano that communicates with the bowels of the earth; and from its black gaping mouth flames, vapors, and a strange froth of pearls pour out in boiling confusion. So, even in the course of a theatrical game, gold reveals its essence to us. The noble metal dreamed of by alchemists, the metal of caliphs and poets, of misers, of lewd and violent men, dissolves in the element of fire. So we should not be amazed that Mephistopheles was so willing to direct the representation of one of the elements that he prefers.

The Emperor approaches the volcanic fountainhead, surrounded by his courtiers wearing the costumes of fauns and gnomes, giants and nymphs. As he looks into the fire, it seems to him that he is living in an abyss as black as night. Thousands of flames rise from the pits and unite, twisting up into a very high vault, like the contorted columns of a cathedral continually being formed and decomposed. Thousands of salamanders—his entourage of courtiers—move along the columns of fire and pay homage to him. When the Emperor recounts these marvels, his voice is almost touched with emotion; and at the beginning of the fourth act, he will confess that at that moment he reached a turning point in his life, dreaming confusedly of "victory and glory" (10416 ff.). Perhaps the Mephistophelian game of illusions is about to be shattered, and the Emperor is about to penetrate into the true realm of the elements. Like Tamino and Pamina who, hand in hand, protected by the sound of the flute, are transformed and go through the heat of the flames and the crash of the waters, he, too, perhaps will issue regenerated from the supreme trial of fire.

But it is only a fleeting impression; Mcphistopheles does not abandon his direction of the masquerade. New prodigies are announced. The Emperor's false beard catches fire, burning his crown, head, and chest. The flames summoned by the fiction flare up and spread. They envelop the groups of courtiers, the hall's decorations, the grove of trees and resinous boughs left by the last group of maskers, and lick at the ceiling's beams, threatening to reduce the imperial palace to ashes. With another conjuring trick, Plutus dissolves the imaginary danger. At a wave of his magic rod the air fills with cool vapors; very moist clouds and mists rush in from all sides, flowing, hissing, curling, slipping in and transforming the flames' vain spectacle into flickers and flashes.

The next morning Mephistopheles, dressed decorously but not ostentatiously, meets the Emperor and his court in the garden. Kneeling before the Emperor, Mephistopheles is congratulated by him for the night's prodigious pranks. In the first light of the sun, Mephisto does not resort to the wizard's imperious, nocturnal gestures. Words can also deceive like Plutus's magic rod. So Mephistopheles vies with profane poets who possessed the lightest, most opulent imagination, who, like Ovid and Scheherazade, loved metamorphoses, fables, miracles, and baseless tricks.[12]

How enchanting the bottom of the wild ocean is! Like the pearl fisherman diving with his bell, the Emperor flings himself boldly into the water where a thousand oysters decorate the underwater rocks. As he touches bottom a magnificent circle forms flowingly around him; he is heart and center of whatever he encounters. Green, luminous, agile, purple-fringed waves swell up, tracing stupendous aquatic palaces that move in time with his steps. Along their walls, which also delight in the multitudinous teeming of marine life and the movement swift as the darting of fish, monsters surge from the depths, varicolored, golden-scaled dragons, repelled by the constantly changing outlines of the regal edifice. Attracted by the new, mellow light, the shark vainly gapes its jaws. Young Nereids, shy and lascivious as fish, swim close by, full of curiosity; and even Thetis offers a second Peleus her hand, mouth, and rulership of the ocean.

While the Emperor is conversing with Mephistopheles, the Marshal and Treasurer rush in to announce the good tidings. The empire, which a few hours before seemed on the verge of bankruptcy, has been saved by Mephistopheles's arts. Last night, during the course of the masquerade, the Chancellor and Treasurer had the Emperor sign a sheet of paper money, the first that men's eyes have ever seen. On it was written: "To whom it may concern: This note is worth a thousand crowns. As a certain pledge it guarantees him an infinity of wealth buried in the Emperor's land. Now it provides, until the rich treasure, as soon as it is dug up, will be used to redeem it" (6057–6062). That very night skilled artisans had printed thousands of banknotes of ten, thirty, fifty, one hundred, and one thousand crowns. Swift and festive as springtime lightning, these very light sheets of paper scattered over the empire and spread everywhere an outpouring of life and joy. The commander of the army pays danger money to his brawling Lansquenets who rush off to taverns and girls; the marshal of the court is freed from the usurer's claws. All the cities of the empire awaken from their mortal sleep. The citizens go back to guzzling and swilling in the wine shops, amid the aroma of roasts and the clatter of plates. They strut about in clothes just sewed by the tailors' hands, buy rings and necklaces for their women, purchase fields, houses, and livestock, woods for the hunt and fish-filled streams . . . The priest devoutly hides the miraculous sheets between the pages of his breviary; the hardened gambler loses his new fortune at dice; with a wave of these banknotes the libertine conquers the beautiful woman who strolls alone on the terrace promenade and ogles him from behind a superb peacock fan.

Neither the Emperor, nor his Chancellor, nor the Treasurer understand that at this instant, before their astounded eyes, something is taking place that will change the history of men forever. From this morning on, gold—splendid as the sun, red as blood, ardent as fire, the emblem of Apollo, princes, and poets, of misers and alchemists—is no longer the universal sign of wealth, the scale that measures our needs and desires. A miserable sheet of paper, with the signature of an emperor, a king, a minister, or banker, has taken its place. So wealth's symbols and figures take on a different aspect. Those who spread it about are no longer mountain gnomes, but instead artisans, capable of multiplying thousands of banknotes in a single night. And the person who prepares the forms is no longer the wise craftsman, who studied the die and the weight of talents, escudos, and florins. Instead it is the printer who with the most delicate inks draws on paper Gothic and Latin characters, numbers, allegorical images, and the faces of sovereigns and potentates of the moment.

When they offered or received a metal coin, the treasurer, merchant, lord, or peasant could not deceive or be deceived. The "value" of each coin was the coin itself: the more or less precious, more or less heavy, metal compared to the supreme metal, gold. If they bought bread, they gave a piece of lead or copper in exchange; if they bought a stove, they gave a piece of silver; if they wanted to cover their women with jewels, they took many gleaming yellow coins out of the strongbox. What a perfect scale, what a marvelous universal key was gold! He who possessed it entered into relationship with that complex play of affinities, the macrocosm, for it reflected the light of the sun in the caves of the earth, just as silver reflects the light of the moon and lead the cold, distant rays of Saturn. On this basis the traditional economic life was founded, and from the perfection of money it derived its solidity, its concreteness, its affinity with the operations of nature.

But what is the value of banknotes of a thousand, fifty, or thirty crowns scattered like lightning flashes over the earth's surface? As their inventor says, these banknotes are only "paper ghosts" (6198, 10245), printed and signed phantoms, to which corresponds a value fraudulent as the treasures Mephistopheles imagines buried under the empire's soil. Thus, under the sign of paper money, economic life becomes the place of illusion and of appearance, something profoundly akin to the false winged chargers, the empty spectacles of fire and the legendary underwater palaces summoned up by Mephistopheles's magical and verbal arts. Nobody can be surprised if the tricksters and mystifiers, the Laws and Cagliostros, the stock market speculators and financiers who build and destroy fortunes with the rapidity with which Mephistopheles plays with flames, from this moment begin to guide the world's destinies.[13]

Thus during the final hours of a night of carnival, modern economy is born from the imagination of a devil who tries to distract the tedium of a thoughtless Emperor. That Mephistopheles loves his new invention; that he takes joy and pride in the rustle of banknotes traversing the world with such great speed; that he regards with pleasure the possibilities it offers of corruption—all this cannot be doubted. But it would be absurd to think that a many-sided devil like Mephistopheles would advise the adoption of only one program of political economy. As the lord of illusions, he invents paper money; as the lord of stones, the prince of conservatives, the king of misers, he continues to advise us to hoard gold in our cupboards—the ancient talents, ducats, escudos, florins, Louis d'ors, and zecchinos that promise us the surest hopes of felicity.

So, in the early hours of the morning, when the mind is still weary from the night's passions, the carnival show—the great alchemical representation, from which some expected who knows what revelations—ends in the most grotesque manner. Those profound symbols leave us holding in our hands only a few sheets of worthless paper; some banknotes more discredited than John Law's or the *assignats* of the French Revolution. Everything—Mephistopheles seems to add—was simply a hoax. Just as the flames were an empty game and the water an enchantment cast by words, just as gold has given us pieces of paper, so Plutus and the boy charioteer also counterfeited the serene richness of the spirit and the infinite prodigality of poetry.

But it is not certain that Mephistopheles is right. The pranks and mystifications we have contemplated resemble Elpore's promises. They are vague veils of mist, futile colored flashes, elusive airy figures, fleeting echoes behind which the splendor of truth can be hidden. Neither Plutus nor the boy charioteer has deceived us. As a sort of ironic prelude, the double spectacle of fire and water already announces the hymn to the reconciled elements, which will resound triumphantly at the end of the *Klassische Walpurgisnacht.*

The Mothers

Beyond the confines of our world, far above the vault of the sky, Plato imagines that there stretches the Plain of Truth. Up there exist the Ideas, motionless on their sacred pedestals. They have neither hands, faces, bodies, colors, nor forms; they are unaware of generation and death, growth and decay, change and movement. Always the same and always equal to themselves, emanating a pure and radiant light, they live out their eternal, felicitous lives.

The procession of gods and men moves toward the Plain of Truth. The great warrior Zeus is at its head, whipping on his winged chariot; behind him advances impetuously the army of the gods and the troop of demons, each of whom occupies the place and performs the task assigned to it for eternity. With their very docile horses, they perform wondrous and beatific circular orbits; they easily mount the harsh slopes leading beyond the celestial vault. When they have reached the summit, they are raised above the ridge of the sky and contemplate the Ideas: Justice and Temperance, Beauty and Thought. Then they sink again into their own sky and return home, where they lead the horses to the feeding trough and offer them the ambrosia and nectar gathered on the Plain of Truth.

Following the procession of the gods, our souls would like to reach the supracelestial place. But how different are the chariots of the gods and those of men! One of the two winged horses harnessed to our chariot is beautiful, good, and docilely obeys the reins; the other horse kicks, resists, and pulls the hand of the unskilled charioteer toward the earth. As the chariots rise, they are devoured by desire and envy and try to pass each other, clash, collide, and are engulfed by the crush and tumult. Thus many souls are crippled and limp about painfully, the wounded wings of others are torn and broken forever, and they return to earth to lie benumbed inside this tomb that is our body, prisoners of the empty dreams of opinion. Only very few souls rise, like the gods, above the ridge of the sky and attain the Plain of Truth, where their horses find pastureland suited to the lightness of their wings. There they are initiated into the world's supreme mystery; they contemplate the immutable splendor of Ideas, unite with them in the happy integrity of their nature. They know true knowledge and perfect beatitude.

When Goethe composed the episode of the Mothers, *Phaedrus's* great myth must have occupied his imagination as a conscious or unconscious symbolic model. Like Plato, he tried to visualize in the myth of the Mothers the conflict between the sphere of Reality and the sphere of Being. He contemplated daily life where the forms of time and space dominate, where ever new images strike our eyes, ever diverse sounds reach our ears, and the solidity of things surrounds us and protects us at every step. He juxtaposed this against the other world, which none of us has ever known, where time and space no longer exist (6215), where we cannot see images of any kind (6246), or listen to sounds (6247), or meet and touch any real object (6248). But the version he gives of the supracelestial place is not at all one of those brilliant, elegant variations, so dear to the Neoplatonic centuries. Instead, the episode of the Mothers seems a programmatic confutation of the *Phaedrus* myth, since it contradicts all of its most significant points.[14]

Plato had placed the Plain of Truth on high, above the vault of the sky, where the movement of our world is arrested. The Mothers could not live up there, for, in Goethe's books, the summit of the sky is agitated by incessant movement, by the eternal becoming of God. The Mothers live beneath those caves, those gorges and subterranean labyrinths where the gold of alchemy is hidden amid "night and horror" and Mephistopheles invites us to know the great mysteries (5032). Even lower down, in the ultimate bowels of the earth, at the deepest point (6220), in an abyss so profound (*im tiefsten, allertiefsten Grund*, 6284) as to terrify even Mephistopheles, live these mysterious and solemn goddesses.[15]

Scarcely do the winged chariots set off impetuously for the homeland of Ideas than an immaculate joy and beatitude invades the souls of the gods, demons, and noble men. In *Faust*, there is not a trace of these ecstatic emotions. If one of us tries to reach the place of Being, traveling a road never traveled, never sought by men, he will experience the most absolute solitude; a desolate desert (6213, 6226–6227, 6551–6552) similar to that which reigned over the universe before God's spirit hovered over the waters. Wherever he turns his eyes, searching anxiously, he sees "eternally empty distance" (6246). He sees nothing; not even the forever equal piling up of waves in the most remote part of the ocean, nor dolphins racing through green and tranquil seas, nor the passage of the clouds, nor the orbits which sun and moon draw in the sky's immensity. He does not even hear the echo of his own footsteps; he can find nothing solid on which to rest. What anguish and what horror surrounds his soul on every side—what vertigo faced by the illimitable! As he travels this frightful route, the only ecstasy he can feel is a negative one—the atrocious experience of nothingness.

When he arrives he does not contemplate the pure light that shines on the Plain of Truth. The only gleam illuminating the bottom of the abyss is from a burning tripod. Close to that feeble flame cluster the Mothers: Some sit, others stand or move about continually, sad, funereal, and blind as ghosts; and around their heads, like a cortege of clouds, flit the "images of all creatures" (6279, 6289, 6430). In Goethe's verses, the splendor of the light belongs to our world, in which, according to Plato, we live imprisoned as in the darkness of a cave.

At the end of the frightening journey, the earthly traveler hopes to know the great Ideas—eternal, immutable, and incorruptible—which existed before the earth's multiple creatures. He hopes to see and preserve in the depths of his eyes Beauty, Justice and Thought, as Goethe imagined them; or perhaps some of those *Urphänomene*, such as the *Urpflanze* or the *Urtier*, that play so important a part in his natural science. But this last hope is also disappointed. The images thronging around the heads of the Mothers are not archetypes that existed before earth's persons and phenomena. Like pallid copies they reflect "that which once was" (6431), something that existed at one time (6278); they are dead and yet they still continue to be feebly agitated (*regsam, ohne Leben* (6430).[16] Immured in this gloomy jail, spectral as the Mothers, the felicity of Plato's Ideas is unknown to them. This misty immortality, this life without life, this movement without joy cannot attract them; and they want only to return to the earth, where they once had lived (6432).

So the traveler imagines that Goethe and Mephistopheles have deceived him; or he thinks that, terrorized by solitude and blinded by the void, he has taken the wrong turn at some crossroads. If he contemplates "that which once was," "something which has not existed for a long time," how can he be in the world of being, so alien to the dimension of time? Has he perhaps penetrated, without knowing it or wishing it, into the realm of the past, where the dead are gathered and time accumulates, into the sad cemeterial museum of Hades "eternally empty, full of elusive images" (9120–9121)? But Hades does not have burning tripods or goddesses like the Mothers. If the assistance of some divinity might permit him to set foot in the meadows of asphodels, the traveler could see Helen, Paris, Achilles—all those who bear a glorious name and have lived nobly, gathered around the throne of Persephone. There they continue to enjoy the reflection of their own earthly existence. They possess the shadow of their "figure" (*Gestalt,* 7439), they conserve the outlines of their persona (9984) and, among themselves, as when they lived beneath the walls of Troy, engage in melancholy and interminable colloquies. Although they are dead, they still belong to the sphere of Reality.

As soon as they penetrate silently into the world of the Mothers, the former earth creatures break down the light walls, pass through the invisible doors that lead outside of reality; they become "patterns" (6290), "absolute images" (*in der Gebilde losgebundne Reiche,* 6277)— "ideas" of themselves, if we may use Platonic language so improperly. What does it matter that these images are not archetypes, like Plato's Ideas? If once they belonged to time, now they do not know it; if they inhabited a place, now they have forgotten the existence of places; if they possessed a persona and a form, they have lost them; if their eyes saw, their lips spoke, their ears listened to words, their hands palped things, now blindness, silence, deafness, and the void hide them with their wings. So the earthly traveler has not taken the wrong road. The habitation of the Mothers is truly the Museum of Being: anguished and dark, as Goethe imagined it.

But who are the Mothers? Who are these large, venerable, subterranean goddesses, whose "strange" name strikes Faust like a bolt of lightning (6217, 6266)? When Eckermann, shaken by the same shudder as Faust, asked Goethe to tell him who the mysterious goddesses were, the old thaumaturge cloaked himself in enigmas, gazed at him with his great staring eyes and repeated the verse: "Mothers! Mothers!—so strange a sound!" (6217). Then, as if to help both his confidant and his future readers, he told him that he had discovered their name in the *Life of Marcellus,* where Plutarch says that in Sicily there existed the small city of Engyon, "very ancient and famous for the apparition of goddesses who were called Mothers." It should be added that in the fourth book of the second oration *Against Verres* Cicero reports that the Magna Mater was venerated in the sanctuary of Engyon.

So we think of her whom Goethe called the "great Mother of gods

GOETHE

and men" (VIII, 79: 22–23); of the ancient female divinities who populated the shores of the Mediterranean under different names. We recall
the inexhaustibly fertile goddesses who generated from their ample
loins the starry sky and the tall mountains, and Oceanus, the Titans, the
Cyclops, the giants with fifty heads and the gods of Olympus, while
innumerable demons or gnomes rose out of the earth at a touch of their
hands. But our perplexity increases instead of diminishing. What have
the empty, gray, sterile, Goethean Mothers in common with these extremely fertile divinities? And when before has Goethe surrounded the
womb and name of Sacred Nature with so much precaution and circumspection?

Although Goethe owes the name of the Mothers to Plutarch, I believe
that another Platonic myth had influenced his imagination. In a much
debated passage of *Timaeus* (48e–52e) Plato, after having invoked the
help of God, remembers having distinguished between two kinds of
beings: on one hand, intelligible and immutable Ideas; on the other, the
visible copies, which are born and die before our eyes, and which move
and are transformed in space and time. Alongside these two kinds of
beings, there exists a third kind, obscure and hard to conceive of. It
cannot be considered an intelligible form, although it can be as invisible
and immutable as Ideas; and it does not possess a real figure, since it is
not air, earth, water, or fire and resembles none of these existent things.
This third kind receives in itself the images of eternal beings, as a
"mother" receives the father's seed (*Timaeus*, 50d). It welcomes all
possible impressions, like a soft, smooth, formless substance, and it furnishes a "place," a "receptacle" for all bodies that are born and die.[18]

So what are the Goethean Mothers? These solemn, solitary goddesses
belong to the realm of Being. Since they live outside of space and time,
they cannot see human faces and the phenomena of this world, and
they do not hear the earth's sounds (6290). There in the depths, near
the burning tripod, they fulfill a double function. Just as in Hades Persephone conserves the persons and figures that have lived, so they
conserve their absolute images in the abyss. In a word, the Mothers are
the custodians of the Museum of Being, just as Persephone is the custodian of the Museum of the Past; and they guard it jealously so that of
all that which has been created nothing is lost and the world preserves
all the possibilities established by God.

Side by side with this conserving function, the Mothers carry out
another, even more essential, one. Just as the "third species," the
"mothers" of *Timaeus*, mediated between Ideas and the things that are
born and die, so the Mothers constitute the sole possible relation between the two extremes of Being and Reality. They oversee "formation

and transformation" (that is, *Gestaltung, Umgestaltung);* "the eternal play of the eternal mind" (6287–6288). As God's sublime handmaidens, they gather the misty images fluttering unhappily around their heads and with their omnipotent strength change their nature. They transform the empty pattern into a limited and individual person whom until now no man has ever contemplated: the absolute image into a figure *(Gestalt)* that until now has never appeared on earth. They give them new eyes with which to see, new ears with which to hear, new lips with which to speak, new hands with which to touch. And finally, they force the images to go over the same road they have already traveled infinite times. They reincarnate them in the "sweet course of life," "beneath the tent of day and the vault of night," beneath the light of sun and moon (6434–6435), distributing them in ever new places and new times.

Although the Mothers are not as fertile as Gaea or Demeter, although they do not generate mountains or oceans, demons, gnomes, or even human beings, their function, in the equilibrium of the cosmos, is no less fundamental. Everything leads us to suppose that God, or whatever one wants to call the creator of the universe, had shaped an unlimited number of beings; and that, from a certain moment on, his creation of images and types halted. Thus to the Mothers falls the task of nourishing and regenerating the ongoing life of nature: of transforming a single model, such as that of Helen, into a multitude of persons who follow each other in time, all different from each other, yet united by the mysterious resemblance which is conferred by the same immortal pattern.

The way in which this process of formation and transformation occurs is among the greatest mysteries of both the universe and *Faust II.* Our minds can conceive of pure forms, which are never born and which will never die; our eyes see every day thousands of beautiful, changing terrestrial figures. But how is it possible that these two worlds can communicate; that something which "is" falls into "becoming"; that a pure thought can take on substance and occur in a given time and place? As we shall see, Faust will come to know the tragic significance of this paradox.[19]

GOETHE

The Magic Spectacle

Among the many singular things in this episode, we have not mentioned the most singular—the Virgil who helps Faust go down the road
"never traveled," "never sought out"; the poet who describes for us the
habitation of the mysterious divinities is Mephistopheles, the lord of
nullity and fire. And with what profound veneration does he speak of
the sublime goddesses enthroned in solitude! He has never felt such an
emotion for God, whom he addresses, in the theatrical and worldly
celestial court, with the servile respect and vaguely top-lofty irony
which he might use with a "great lord" of this earth (352). One might
say that for him the Mothers represent what we call the sacred. He is
reluctant to name them (6219); speaks of them with religious embarrassment (6215); surrounds his statements with caution, shadows, circumlo-
cutions. Even his style changes. No cynical and vulgar tone renders his
words jagged and sharp; a strange pathos seizes precisely him who has
proclaimed himself incapable of any sort of pathos. A master of syntac-
tic precision, he now constructs ambiguous, almost incomprehensible
sentences (6287–6289), as though feigning a Pindaric obscurity. He
transforms verbs into abstract nouns (6222–6223), willingly has recourse
to such typical pathetic-rhetorical instruments as the exclamation (6216,
6222, 6275, 6277, 6280, 6293). So the poet of the plain style and basso
register, the realist and extremely elegant satirist becomes a sublime
metaphysical poet—a solemn chanter of hymns to Being.

What has happened? Has Mephistopheles suddenly been converted?
Or, as many people maintain, has Goethe exchanged the moving tim-
ber of his own voice for the adversary's arid and cold one? Not at all.
Mephistopheles experiences no revulsion for the eternal immobility of
Ideas; he hates only the divine impulse which compels things to become, to be transformed, to die and be reborn at every instant. When
he thinks of the Mothers, who live silently in the "illimitable" (6240), in
the "eternally empty distances" *(ewig leerer Ferne,* 6246)—the realm of
Being reveals to him his own affinity with the "eternal void" *(das Ewig-
Leere,* 11603), the "pure nothingness" (11597), the confined darkness of
which he is the child.

When he speaks of the Mothers, Mephistopheles's voice takes fire at
the thought of abysses deeper than those the demons have ever inhabited; of mysteries which his lucid intelligence almost cannot penetrate.
That void, that solitude terrify and attract even one like himself who
has known the deserts of Chaos. There is only one part of the Mothers'
activity he does not love: the fact that they oversee "formation and
transformation" (6287) and therefore collaborate in the process of

becoming. So he leaves to Faust the task of explaining how the Mothers distribute images in the gentle course of life (6428–6438); and, during the magic spectacle, he tries to discredit the miraculous apparition of absolute forms. This is the significance of Mephistopheles's new alchemy—the "stone" he extracts from the abyss, the "treasure" (6315) he keeps ready for us is the suggestion that the science of Being is nothing but the dark science of nullity (6256).

While Faust is descending to the Mothers, Mephistopheles grants us a small interlude, as if to relax our too tense attentions. In a hall of the palace, the ladies of the court crowd around him. Every summer a hundred brownish freckles cover the very white skin of a young blond lady; a frostbitten foot prevents a brunette from dancing and curtseying; while another lady, neglected by her lover, suffers the scathing pangs of jealousy. Like a cunning smalltown charlatan selling his potions and remedies in the market square, Mephistopheles advises the first lady to smear her face, on a day of the waning moon, with a lotion of frog sperm and toad tongues, distilled under a full moon. As for the second lady, he treads on her sick foot with his horse's hoof; and he orders the third to swallow a piece of infernal coal.

But the Emperor grows impatient, and the Chamberlain orders Mephistopheles to stage the new spectacle immediately. Like a procession of ghosts coming down long corridors and tunnels, the courtiers gather in the hall of knights; old armor ornates the niches; tapestries on the walls recall the battles of the Emperor's glorious period; while a weak light spreads about, as if to announce grim prodigies. The Emperor and his courtiers occupy seats in the first rows; at the rear of the hall, where the crowd is packed and jammed on benches, lovers also await the strange hour of the spirits. Before this very attentive audience, Mephistopheles's new magic show begins. That he now proves himself to be the most daring of magicians; that he knows how to summon up unprecedented prodigies, fantasies impossible and therefore worthy of belief; that he can vie with the architects of the Parthenon and Romantic composers—all this will astonish no one. But the new show does not come entirely from the repertory of the prince of hell. This time he confines himself to supplying a framework and suggesting a scene. The forms of Helen and Paris, perhaps hidden suggestions of the Mothers, will add to the spectacle a beauty and awe he has never been able to insinuate into the inventions of his highly colored, insidious mind.

The tapestries vanish as if a fire had shriveled them up, the walls open and, turning on themselves, form a deep stage illuminated by a mysterious glow. On the stage appears a massive Greek temple supported by Doric columns, capable, like Atlas, of bearing the world's great bulk.

GOETHE

Having stepped onstage, the astrologer invokes the stars' protection for the inventions of his imagination; Mephistopheles just peeks out from the prompter's box. In the audience, a fashionable architect comments contemptuously on the devil's archaeological masterpiece, and praises the Gothic churches with their slim columns and their pointed-arch vaults, which lift the soul toward the infinite.

When Faust ascends from the abyss, wearing a crown on his head and priestly garb, the burning tripod tags after him like a servant, giving off an odor of incense. He touches it with a shimmering key Mephisto has entrusted to him, and instantly a dense mist engulfs the stage. It slithers, waves, distends, agglomerates, entwines, and divides, imitating clouds —strati, cumuli, and cirri. Immersed in vapor, the spirits of Helen and Paris take shape. An ineffable melody accompanies them; the music frozen in the temple's walls, the notes hidden in triglyph and columns begin to resound again. Finally the veil of mist settles on the stage, and, in time to the music, Paris appears, a "radiance of flourishing youthful strength" (6453). We see him lie down gently, crook an arm behind his head and sleep, while all about him there spreads a soft perfume of ambrosia, the perfume of his adolescence. Soon, Helen approaches him, as the Moon approached Endymion, bends down and kisses him, drinking in his breath.

So we witness the formation of two of those patterns that fluttered around the Mothers' heads. What was illimitable becomes limited; what was indeterminate is determined; what was dark is illuminated; the subterranean mists and the vapors of incense imitate the definite forms of the clouds and become two human figures. An analogous process takes place when the creatures' images leave the Mothers and are incarnated in the "sweet course of life." But, whereas in this case they renounce their nature as "patterns," now a very light wall continues to divide the two images of Helen and Paris from our world. They still remain there, outside of space and time, not persons but absolute forms knowing only the incomprehensible words of the world of Being.

What an extraordinary transformation! Close to the Mothers, absolute images had appeared to us as lifeless figures which stir feebly, like gray, spectral clouds. But during the course of the magic spectacle they show us for a few instants their sublime countenances. Like Plato's immobile and beatific Ideas, they too offer the ambrosia desired by the winged horses of our souls. They cast an immortal light on our existence, making the world—in which they roam lost and uncertain—as steadfast and indomitable as the supracelestial place. Thus they will justify the words that Faust, before descending to the Mothers, had said to Mephisto: "In your nullity I hope to find the All" (6256).

Save for Faust, nobody understands this marvelous event. Seated in the hall of knights, the Emperor and his courtiers think they are watching only a program of light entertainment, which could be entitled "The Rape of Helen" (6548). A lady wants to sink her lips in the fresh and succulent peach which is Paris; another lady goes into an ecstasy over the perfume his adolescence emanates; a few of them consider him rather unrefined and graceless; while to the men he seems a crude shepherd lad, ignorant of the manners of the court. Helen is even more unfortunate: One of the ladies thinks her head is too small, a second lady says that her feet are thick and ungainly; and other ladies put her down as a brazen, vulgar trollop, a jewel without value, who has passed through too many hands . . . As always, men never realize when something unearthly fleetingly visits them.

Love, Veneration, Delirium

Sometimes when we travel about the earth, prisoners of our bodies as the oyster is of its shell, it may happen—so Plato recounts—that we see a face with a divine look. The apparition flashes before us; and once again we see in our memory the supracelestial Beauty as we have contemplated it once, resplendent on its pedestal. We are stunned and deeply touched, we are no longer in control of ourselves, a shudder of sacred horror assails us, some of the fears of that past time creep into our spirit. We look at the beautiful terrestrial image and we venerate it deeply; and if we were not afraid of being thought insane, we would offer it sacrifices, as to the image of a god.

Meanwhile an unusual sweat, an unfamiliar heat dissolves and melts the rigid crust that covered our soul and prevented it from budding and developing. Because of the heat's generating and nourishing power, the quills of our wings swell and begin to grow, starting from the roots. The entire soul bubbles, tingles, ferments, throbs like an infant whose teeth are about to break through the gums; and one's eyes look aloft, as a bird whose wings have just sprouted, impatient to begin flying. So man possessed by amorous passion attains the loftiest state granted by the gods to their favorites—*mania*, religious delirium. It is the same emotion that invested the prophetess of Delphi, the priestesses of the temple of Zeus at Dodona, the Sibyl possessed by the divination of the god; and also the delicate, immaculate souls of true poets.

GOETHE

In the episode of the Mothers, Faust's initiation passes through the same phases. As soon as Mephistopheles pronounces their name, Faust jumps with fear (6212). That word seems to him very strange (6217); a shudder of horror and revulsion seizes him (6216, 6265), like the character in *Phaedrus*. That name he does not want to hear strikes him like a lightning bolt (6265), and he understands that it conceals a mysterious, terrible reality. But this fear does not induce him to seek protection behind a carapace of coldness and indifference (6271). The violence of his revulsion is equal to the fascination the forbidden name exerts on him; and the shudder of anguish that seized him becomes, as in *Phaedrus*, the religious amazement, profound excitement (6274), and enthusiasm (6281) we feel when faced by the highest things.[20]

So, as the most faithful among the "neophytes" (6250), he decides to confront the trial that the worship of the Mothers demands of him. But how can he descend all the way down there? How can he find his way into the bowels of the earth? Like a cunning mystagogue, Mephistopheles helps his pupil, giving him a small key with extraordinary properties. As Faust squeezes it, the key suddenly grows in his hand, grows and flashes while an unsuspected force suffuses his heart and fills his spirit. Without further delay, Faust stamps the earth with his foot and leaps out of time and space.

We can scarcely imagine Faust's experiences during his journey. The anguish of solitude: nothing to see, nothing to hear, nothing to touch; the vertigo of the illimitable, the fear of the absolute . . . But the journey is very rapid; the miraculous key sniffs out the residence of the Mothers just as the wand of a water diviner scents water, guiding him to the burning tripod. At last Faust sees the Mothers enthroned in the solitude, surrounded by the images of the creatures. He does not even graze them; obeying Mephistopheles's advice, he keeps them far from his body. He goes to the tripod, touches it with the key, and the tripod follows him to the surface of the earth.

When Faust rises again into the light, his initiation has been completed. The overwrought and enthusiastic neophyte, who did not dare listen to the name of the Mothers, has become the noble priest, the solemn sorcerer of being; and someone has consecrated him, covering his limbs with priestly robes and encircling his head with a crown. So he has reached the highest point of his existence. He knows the absolute forms, which other men neither know nor wish to see; he sees the rich spring of beauty gush up before his eyes (6488). The world, in which he once roamed as in an insensate, inhospitable desert, for the first time seems to him "desirable, firmly based, enduring" (6492). All the wild impulses of passion and enthusiasm, all the love, veneration, and madness which in the past led his mind astray, are reborn in him and reecho a hundredfold. Faust seems beside himself, swept away by "delirium"[21], and Mephistopheles mocks him. But his delirium is not the madness of one who succumbs to the soul's dark passions, to the nerves, violence, and fantasies of the darkened spirit. Like the Pythia and the Sibyl, like the delicate souls of true poets, like those philosophers who love Plato, Faust receives in his delirium the most unhoped-for gifts of divine wisdom.[22]

What would Faust's life have been if he had halted at the height of this moment? Like Plato's pupils, he would have devoted himself completely to the contemplation of beauty and to pure intellectual activity. But Faust was too tortured by violent passions to be able to devote himself to the contemplative life. As he is delivering his monologue, Paris, onstage, awakens from his sleep. Astonished, he looks around him, goes to Helen, picks her up, and, like a mythical hero, is about to abduct her. Furious with jealousy, Faust wants to interrupt that embrace, forgetting that an impassable wall shuts these two images within their sphere.

A great dream suddenly fills his delirious mind. Until that moment no god and no man had been able to fuse the realms of Being and of Reality; and the Mothers, too, when they distribute the creatures' images in life, cancel their qualities as forms. As the most talented demiurge of the silent goddesses, Faust would like to prepare an infinitely richer world than the one we live in. On the earth's firm soil he would build "the double, great realm" where, side by side, absolute forms and men's living bodies can lead the same existence. He would render eternal that moment when delirium had illuminated him and the world had seemed as marvelous and enduring as Ideas.

With his vulgar, smug, common sense, Mephistopheles urges him to surrender to the limitations of existence; three times he tells him that he is only watching a comedy of spirits, a *Fratzengeisterspiel,* which he has helped to stage, and he should be satisfied with his part as an actor (6501, 6514–6515, 6546). But when the absolute forms stand close to us so visible and bright, what noble soul could accept the barrier dividing us from them? Faust ignores Mephistopheles's warnings: He clutches Helen and touches Paris with the luminous key. Her beautiful figure becomes murky; an explosion is heard; Faust faints and falls to the ground, while the spirits dissolve and vanish in the same vapor from which they had come.

During Faust's descent to the Mothers and during the magic show we have shared, in turn, Faust's, Mephistopheles's, and the courtiers' view of things. As for Goethe, we know nothing. We do not know whether

GOETHE

he accompanied Faust down into the abyss, wearing priestly vestments, or whether he chose a privileged position—due an old Weimar minister —alongside the Emperor. Perhaps, on the contrary, he hid himself beside Mephistopheles in the prompter's box; and of course we wonder what he thinks of this strange spectacle.

I believe that in the two figures of Faust and Mephistopheles, in their viewpoints which contradict and complete each other, are expressed all the emotions the realm of the Mothers aroused in Goethe's spirit. The world of Being seemed to him that limitless and frightful nullity the prince of hell had described. He, too, is amused at representing the most sacred things on the frivolous stage of a court theater, as if he wanted to mock and insult them. He knows there is no passage that permits us to travel across the frontier between the two realms. But when the mysterious envoys reached this earth; when certain illuminations, certain unexpected ideas, certain startling moments touched him for an instant—then he would experience the same shudders, the same terror, the same veneration that had assailed Faust's soul. Although he may have ended like all men by resigning himself, perhaps during these moments Goethe, too, dreamed of founding "the double, great realm" where man would live happily in the midst of immortal forms.[23]

The
Classical
Walpurgis Night

VI

Professor Wagner

At the beginning of the second act, the imperial palace with its ceremonies and illusions has disappeared from the scene together with the ghosts who had risen from the depths of the abyss. Once again we are in the Gothic room where so many years before Faust had vainly invoked the spirit of the earth and Mephistopheles had appeared before him dressed as a wandering scholar and noble knight. Everything seems carefully preserved, as in the shop of the most jealous antiquarian. The colored window panes, even darker than before, hide the sunlight; spiders continue to weave their webs between the pointed arches; thousands of books, gnawed by worms and dust covered, are piled up to the ceiling; shards of pottery, blackened sheets of parchment, skulls with huge, empty sockets, ampuls, vases, and cogwheels fill the shelves along the walls with mold and decay. On the lectern, where Faust had kept his futile vigil for so many nights, the ink has dried in the inkwell. The paper has turned yellow, and deep in the quill of the pen with which he signed the pact with the devil there is still a small drop of blood.

All the characters of the play's first part are here, as though nothing had ever happened. Mephistopheles again dons the long, hairy fur cloak, Faust's "coarse pelt," which hangs from a nail; and a strident chorus of moths, beetles, bedbugs, and cockchafers fly out buzzing and joyously salute their old master, the "lord of flies and mice," who has returned to his own people. Having become a bachelor of the arts, the scholar, with his hair cut short and his head packed with fashionable nonsense, runs up the stairs. Another famulus, Nicodemus, has taken Wagner's place. Faust has also returned to his room. But he lies unconscious on the patriarchal bed, bound by the ties of love, paralyzed by his mad passion for Helen.

As for Wagner, he has mounted the rostrum of his old professor who disappeared so mysteriously. From there he teaches every day, he shines and glitters with fame and glory as crowds of listeners gather around him, as if around the chair of St. Peter. But he, too, has not changed. As in the past, the spring greenery does not charm his soul, the birds' free wings do not remind him of his celestial homeland. He lives on the earth, holed up in his house, among his beloved books, lovingly unrolling the ancient parchments, "a beatific life warms his limbs . . . and the whole sky descends on him" (1104–1109). He believes that men have discovered the truth in the far-off past and have enclosed it in books, the "sources" of all knowledge, capable of slaking forever our thirst for knowledge. So he venerates them as holy objects. He consults them, studies them, trying to wrest their secrets from them; and humbly, patiently, he again ascends the path of tradition.

In the first act, Wagner seemed an honest sixteenth- or seventeenth-century humanist. He had read a few Greek tragedies, became exalted while declaiming Cicero's orations, Livy's histories, and Plutarch's *Parallel Lives,* studied antiquity's most famous treatises on rhetoric. Perhaps he collected the codices of Origen and Valerius Maximus; and, among the most modern texts, he particularly loved Erasmus's dialogues and Martin Opitz's *Poeterey.* After so many years his culture has been enriched, as if to emulate the encyclopedic mania of his vanished master. He, too, has "given himself up to magic" (377); that is, to alchemy. If we could slip into his laboratory, we would find open on his desk, among the retorts and alembics, the books of Nostradamus and Paracelsus, J. Valentin Andreae's *Die Chymische Hochzeit,* and *Aurea catena Homeri.* When he speaks from the rostrum or with Mephistopheles, the symbols and endings dear to the adepts of the *opus magnum* come thronging to his lips, as in a grotesque dance.[1]

Faust would not have liked Professor Wagner's alchemy. When Faust consulted the book of Nostradamus, he sought the authentic face of universal nature: to live and immerse himself in the daimonic creative activity coursing in its veins; and he imitated and emulated it in his own existence. Wagner, on the contrary, was content to regret for an instant the "sweet, generative force" of nature (6841); but immediately after that he declares that nature "is no longer fashionable" (6838). The extremely new goddess, to whom he consecrates all of his talent, is audacious, proud, analytical reason, which distinguishes, divides, and lucidly counterfeits nature's mysterious organic processes in the laboratory. So the medieval color surrounding Wagner's enterprize and the alchemical terms flocking to his lips arc just a bizarre veil that in fact conceals a new substance. Behind the alchemist's cloak, Wagner is a modern experimental scientist, a precursor or student of Newton, "the sink of every iniquity," "Baal Isaac," as Goethe, at moments of bad temper, liked to call him.

When Mephistopheles returns to Faust's house, Wagner has not set foot in his room for several months. Like a mole he has burrowed into the profound silence of his laboratory among the fantastic scientific instruments the Middle Ages bequeathed to him. Filthy and black as coal, his eyes red and bleary, he blows with his bellows at the fire in the small furnace, stirs up the embers with tongs, and anxiously awaits the extraordinary event. The *opus magnum* (6675, 6834), vainly dreamed of by generations of lonely scholars, is to be fulfilled before him. The small gleaming phial held in his modest, skillful hands is the womb, the cradle in which modern science is trying chemically to produce a new human being.

Until that moment, all the men, all the animals of the earth, water, and air had been generated by Mother Nature who for hundreds of centuries had used for her purposes the amorous encounters between two creatures. Then life had leaped forth from a "tender point" (6840), from the "sweet force" of the seed, which was released from within a human being, joined with another seed, taking and giving, appropriating for itself similar and alien substances, and developing in accordance with its inner law. So there developed and grew that mysterious entity, that unitary creature, complex and indivisible in all its parts, which is a living organism. Wagner declares that this way of being born is now antiquated; worthy only of gladdening the animals of earth and air. From now on, producing human beings will no longer be the casual whim of a dazed pair of lovers but rather the proud task of experimental science. Hidden in his laboratory he analyzes the hundreds of elements which go to form man's vital substance; then he encloses them in a retort, mixes, combines, and distills them many times (6849–6854). The new man, whom he tries to create chemically, does not possess the "sweet [inner] force" of the old unitary organisms. Instead he is the mechanical aggregation and combination of different elements, a "crystallization" (6860), similar to the patterns formed on winter days by thousands of drops of water aggregating on the panes of our windows because of the frost's external power.[2]

Although Wagner had exchanged the robes of the humanist for the smock of the modern scientist, his attempt was similar to that of the past. When he read Cicero and Martin Opitz he believed that if one wanted to write immortal books it was enough to string together the words and images of the ancients, distributing them according to the precepts of rhetoric. Therefore, he turned out dead books, pieces of interwoven paper, ragoûts made of staples consumed by other mouths, piles of ashes left behind by more generous conflagrations. Now, in his alchemical-scientific laboratory, Wagner gathers, blends, and distills the "elements of life" (6990), hoping to generate new human beings. As in the past, he understands neither what an authentic organism is nor that the children of analytical science, the monsters it distills with so much care, have nothing in common with the life that "Sacred Nature" mysteriously produces every spring, every day, every minute.

The Birth of Homunculus

It is a summer night, perhaps the night of June 6 or August 8,[3] and a favorable conjunction of stars protects the most extraordinary discoveries and adventures. In Faust's study, Mephistopheles pulls the cord of an old bell. At that strident and frightening sound the sooty walls tremble and shake, the shelves sway, the floor buckles, chunks of plaster rain down from the ceiling, the doors are flung open by a powerful force. Meanwhile, through the panes, one can see the lightning flashes of a distant storm. Is the force of the inferno intervening to help Wagner and his *opus magnum?* Shut up in his fantastic laboratory, Wagner also hears these prodigies and he understands that, after months of expectation and anguish, the task of his life is finally about to be accomplished.

At this moment in the small phial, the process described in the alchemists' books is renewed. Just as during the preparation of the philosopher's stone, the *nigredo* of the raw material is transformed into the *rubedo* and then into the *albedo.*[4] Soon in the depths of the phial, the darkness "brightens" (6825). Something akin to a living coal, or a gleaming red carbuncle *(rubedo)* flares, radiating flashes in the darkness; the light becomes clear, white, then whiter and whiter *(albedo).* The mass at the bottom of the glass seethes, rises up, flashes, and agglomerates. The phial tinkles, shaken by a gentle violence. Inside the glass, the flame assumes the form of a graceful little man. He gesticulates, and immediately we hear the high-pitched cheerful sound of Homunculus's voice:

Well, my little daddy, how goes it? This was no joke.
Come, clasp me tenderly to your heart!
But not too roughly, so the glass won't break.*

Around the luminous, resonant phial stand Homunculus's two parents: Wagner, his father "according to the flesh," delicately holds in his hands his "dearly beloved son" (6902); and with maternal tenderness he contemplates the perfect artificial creature he had for so long dreamed of. But he does not realize that during the last moments, as the *nigredo* was being transformed into *rubedo* and *albedo,* a very potent infernal force had cooperated with him, successfully producing the chemical combination among the different substances in the retort (6684, 6885–6886, 7003–7004). So Homunculus's other parent, his father "according to the spirit," is Mephistopheles. At a moment like this, when it is a matter of helping the triumph of artifice, how can the mortal enemy of nature fail to be at hand, he who hates the "sweet force" from which life gushes?

Thinking of the two fathers who have generated him, one might suppose that Homunculus is a bookish Mephisto, a very erudite demon who knows all the books of this earth and all the flaming infernal archives. Or he might be a great nihilist who venerates only words and forms; a crystallized and mechanical brain, an experimental scientist allied with the savage forces of darkness. But as soon as we see him move in the phial, these hypotheses collapse. From his two fathers, Homunculus has inherited almost none of his intellectual qualities. Thus we imagine that at that solemn hour protected by a favorable juncture of the stars, another unknown, beneficent force presided over his birth.

Who, then, is Homunculus? In order to understand him one must go back to the sources, the clear or confused suggestions Goethe preserved intact since the years of his youth. At that time, in his beloved Neoplatonic and Hermetic texts he had read that our νοῦς, our divine "intellect," does not live only in this prison which is the body of earth and the human soul. Before descending into the world or after having abandoned its outer covering, it lives for itself, marvelously alone. Then the νοῦς garbs itself in the only body that corresponds to its very penetrating nature: a pure tunic of fire, like that worn by the demons; and it

*Nun Väterchen! Wie steht's? es war kein Scherz.
Komm, drücke mich recht zärtlich an dein Herz!
Doch nicht zu fest, damit das Glas nicht springe.
(6879–6881)

enjoys an uncontaminated life in the immensity of space.[5]

When he imagined the figure of Homunculus, Goethe recreated and reinterpreted this Neoplatonic and Hermetic myth. The child of Wagner and Mephistopheles, the flame which stirs, scintillates, and tinkles inside the "tunic," the glass phial, is the agile and pure demon of fire in our minds. Within those artificial walls, Homunculus has no body; he knows no weight, no darkness, no limitation such as matter communicates to the movements of intelligence. From birth, he has no need for the accumulation of sensations and novelties we call experience: Faust's restlessness and unrealized aspirations, Euphorion's rage, the cynicism that makes Mephistopheles's laughter so acrid and vulgar, the too many parchments perused during the long winter nights which constrict Wagner's understanding (8248–8250; E. December 12, 1829).

Since none of us has ever met an intelligence separated from the body, it is hard for us to believe that the small demon of fire belongs to the genus of humanity. Is not intelligence, as Mephistopheles has just remarked (6809–6810), composed of much reading, of transformed sensations, of intellectual labors—in a word, of accumulated experience? But Goethe has also imagined Homunculus so as to make fun of our pride as educated and knowing men. Without a body, having read no books, lacking experiences, the small demon possesses at birth certain qualities that no man will ever succeed in emulating. While we reflect laboriously with our brains, Homunculus's flame "sees" all the things of the world, and for him they become as transparent as his walls of glass. We study history in books—he knows by intuition or by a kind of "magical sympathy" everything that has happened in the past, that is happening, and is about to happen in the visible and invisible world. We are accustomed to misunderstand each other—he, cleverer than any psychologist, understands men's hearts at a glance. With the same facility with which he could describe a painting hung on the wall, he reads and interprets the dreams locked in our minds. And he knows how to heal troubled and weary souls. There is only one thing that has no interest at all for him—the history of philosophy. The great metaphysical and philosophical "problems" which have tortured men's minds for centuries—such as the relations between the soul and the body—seem to him a ridiculous mass of absurdities and clichés (6891 ff.; E. December 16, 1829).

No other mind in *Faust* is as limpid and luminous as the mind of this visionary demon. As soon as Homunculus utters one of his quick, sparkling witticisms, the most difficult things become clear, the mists of uncertainty are driven away, doubts and mysteries are suddenly resolved; and the world is immersed in the same triumphant *albedo* that accompanied his birth. To understand fills him with joy; to agitate the resonant flame like a character in *The Magic Flute* amuses him. To speak in a clear-cut, pointed style, with the elegance of an eighteenth-century writer and a celestial spirit, gives him a feeling of boundless intellectual gaiety; and the pungent, airy irony winding its subtle way through his speeches, seems the natural language of our minds.

When he flits through the air inside the gleaming, tinkling glass phial Homunculus resembles one of those lively childish elves encountered in folk tales. He was newly born and already had all the vices of boys who are too talented. Cruel and irreverent, he does not respect the two fathers fate has bestowed on him. He mocks the tender affection Wagner feels for him, scoffs at his manias of a scholar lost among the rolls of parchment. The Middle Ages, so dear to Mephistopheles, seems to him a revolting hodgepodge of priests, knights, moldiness, and Gothic arches. At times he is as unbearable as an *enfant prodige*, who continually flaunts his knowledge. But he also has the candor and charm of all such brilliant youngsters; the irrepressible curiosity that compels him to chase after all "new, marvelous things" (7069). He possesses, too, the almost painful yearning for love, which will lead him to incarnate and immolate himself in the waves of the Aegean Sea.[6]

If he possesses so many charms, why should we be astonished at the fascination he exerts on the characters in *Faust?* Wagner watches him with the anxious devotion of a mother; Mephistopheles grows tender at the thought of his secret son; Anaxagoras and Thales fight for his collaboration. But perhaps only Proteus, agile and swift as he, can understand what a joy it is to live beside a creature who unites the charm of youth and the understanding of maturity; who combines the clear precision of intelligence and the élan of love; the splendor of fire and the freshness of water.

Life and Death, History and Myth

In the first six, hardworking months of 1830, during which he composed the 1483 verses of the *Klassische Walpurgisnacht*, Goethe always kept open on his worktable a lexicon of mythology, the Hederich-Schwabe, just as today a poet could not write about the gods of Greece without the Pauly-Wissowa. With his inexhaustible encyclopedic curiosity, he rummaged through all the books searching for *mirabilia*, odd facts,

GOETHE

mythological examples and insights in the *Odyssey* and the Homeric *Hymns,* in Hesiod's *Theogony,* the tragedies of Aeschylus and Euripides, the poems of Virgil, Ovid, and Lucan. He delved into the histories of Herodotus, the lives of Plutarch and Diogenes Laertius, the *Eikones* of Philostratus; the geographic and scientific writings of Pausanias and Strabo, Seneca and Pliny.

If he needed to look directly at the creations of the ancients, he would leave his study to examine again the coins, bas-reliefs, Hellenistic vases, and plaster casts in his collection. Or he forced his memory to summon up again Raphael's and Carracci's mythological frescoes he had admired in Italy almost half a century before. Then, like Friedrich and Philine in their castle, he would leaf through the historico-mythological complications of the baroque writers. He would travel through modern Greece with the most recent tourists, the "young Anacharsis," Chateaubriand and Dodwell. Torn between hostility and an equally profound agreement, he studied Creuzer's inquiries into the symbolism of Greek mythology and Schelling's on the "gods of Samothrace."

Surrounded by the multitude of Greek gods, the immense "Legions of Hellenic saga" (7028), Goethe carried out a singular selection. From the inferno of the *Klassische Walpurgisnacht* he excluded all the great gods of Olympus: Zeus and Apollo, Neptune and Aphrodite, Hermes and Artemis, as well as the heroes who defeated the monsters and fought beneath the walls of Troy. He let the first group lead a beatific life on the peaks of Olympus (8146, 8197) and abandoned the others in the chasms of Hades at the foot of Persephone's throne. He permitted only a few minor figures, such as Galatea, to inherit their qualities; and only Chiron and a few primitive peoples could remember and celebrate, during the brief moonlit night, the absent gods and vanished heroes.

Goethe preferred to represent the infinitely more picturesque and extravagant gods who had lived before, alongside, and after the gods of Olympus. Thus he resurrected the Phorkyads, who seem to be lost in the darkness of Night and the silence of Chaos. They are the very ancient gods, without precise shape, who are transformed and multiply, as if to express the still fluid world of our origins. Together with these, he described the divine and bestial monsters, the magnificent and ferocious beasts of legend, who ruled over earth and sea before the exploits of Hercules and the Argonauts. He re-created the horrible nightmares of the night, the same demonic forces that triumph on the Blocksberg. Until that day no modern poet had ever dared to show Greek mythology in so archaic, witchlike, and monstrous a light.

In his travels among the "fabulous figures of ancient days" (7030), Goethe was not only guided by his mythological imagination. He was also inspired by caprice—the love of unexpected names and encounters —a taste for the bizarre that violated all verisimilitude and flung up in a corner, or at the very center of the scene, the most unexpected images. So, among these archaic gods, these hairy monsters and revolting witches, there appear some of the most conventional figures of Greek mythology, such as the water Nymphs, Nereids, and Tritons, by now smoothed and polished by classicism's literary and plastic representations. And with them there are also primitive populations, half real and half legendary, such as the Telchines, who are metal workers, the witches Psylli and Marsi, Herodotus's obscure Arimaspians; and even two philosophers, Thales and Anaxagoras, with whom we penetrate to the heart of Greek civilization in Periclean Athens. These gods lived at one time in the light of the sun, near Thebes, on the shores of Cyprus, in a cave on Mount Pelion, near the lake of Stymphalus, or the lake of Lerna. Then they died; or someone killed them. Today they lead the degraded and mysterious existence of "phantoms" (6946, 7043, 7046, 7843), of "spirits" (7200, 7447, 8337) in remote subterranean caves; and some of them harm and insult living things with their very breath (7036–7037). Once a year they again assume their own bodies, and repeat the gestures of what was their true existence. Like northern witches they gather once a year on the summit of the Brocken; on the night of June 6 or August 8 these ghosts hold a meeting on the fields of Pharsalus, the banks of the Peneus, and in the bays of the Aegean Sea, to celebrate their "feast of horrors" (7005), their "free night of jubilee" (7109).

So we can expect to travel through the kingdom of the dead, to be fascinated by ghosts or terrified by the funereal effluvium rising from open graves. But just at this point, Goethe introduces us to the youthful prodigies of nature. A mountain is born from the bowels of the earth; the ground opens and swells up continually. The pygmies and Dactyls burst into the light like miraculous creatures; a meteor falls from the sky. And on the shore of the Aegean Sea, where life is born, air and earth, water and fire embrace. How can we think that the creatures of the Aegean Sea are only ghosts? How can we admit that the Nereids and Tritons, who swim faster than fish, do not possess the gift of life? What about the Dorides, lovingly united with the sea's foam, and beautiful Galatea and Proteus who are transformed like the very force of nature?

Some of the figures in the *Klassische Walpurgisnacht* reveal the same naïve mythical consciousness as the creatures of the classical poets. We know that at Cyprus, as in all the places of the world, history raged savagely. The temples of Aphrodite and Galatea no longer stand; Romans and Crusaders, Venetians and Turks fought there incessantly, covering the earth with blood and destroying cities and harvests (8370 ff.). We know that Phoebus's great statues, the work of the Telchines which adorned Rhodes, were razed to the ground by an earthquake. Thousands of years have now passed and ingenious craftsmen have fused them together in new and different forms (8305 ff.). But if we listen to Galatea and the Telchines, nothing seems to have happened. Today, on Cyprus, Galatea still has the temples of Paphos, where she is venerated and honored by the piety of the crowds, and around which gather doves with wings as white as the light (8146 ff.; 8339 ff.). At Rhodes, the mountains, cities, and shores still enjoy the protection of Apollo, and an eternal springtime enfolds the statues of the god, which no earthquake tremor has ever dared overturn (8289 ff.). So Galatea and the Telchines are unaware of the events that so rapidly transform the surface of our Earth. They are enclosed in the impassable circle of myth where all is immobile or repeats itself eternally, and in which they live out their fresh and vivacious existence, unaware and innocent.

The majority of the figures in the *Klassische Walpurgisnacht* do not share this naïve intimacy with myth. Like the children of the modern age, they are sure of belonging to the unrepeatable time of history—in which one is born, lives, dies, and plunges forever into Hades. Moreover, they know the age in which they lived and disappeared with the precision of a scholar of classical mythology. The Sphinxes know that they ruled over Egypt and Greece at a very remote and monstrous epoch, destroyed by the deeds of the heroes. Chiron knows that he lived in the first true historical age—when Hercules shone like a god, the Argonauts set out for the conquest of the golden fleece, and Helen, while still but a child, played havoc with the world's amorous imagination.

The culture of these divinities, which should belong to a single historical epoch, envelops and covers their future, touches all civilizations and all possible times. The Sphinxes of Egypt and Thebes are not unfamiliar with the art of fencing and asceticism (7135); Erichtho has read the sixth book of *Pharsalia*, just as Don Quixote read the novel Cide Hamete Benengeli had devoted to his exploits (7007–7008). Chiron has just consulted Hederich-Schwabe's manual of mythology and an account of the battle of Pidna (7427, 7465 ff.); Nereus knows to perfection the Enlightenment interpretations of mythology (8347). Agile, ironic, and disrespectful as gnomes, these gods glide through all the periods of human history, live contemporaneously in Cheop's Egypt and archaic Greece, in the Athens of Pericles and Alexander; in a Cyprus dominated by Crusaders or Turks; and in the libraries filled with the Enlightenment and Romantic historians of classical antiquity.

Finally, the divinities born from time, on whom time has let fall its debris, abandon the region that has nourished them and, like Galatea and the Telchines, reach the tranquil world of myth. Although they died with the advent of the heroic age, killed by Heracles's civilizing ferocity, the Sphinxes still sit today in front of the pyramids, their expressions unchanged, regulating the days of moon and sun (7245–7248). The Psylli and Marsi abandon the surface of Cyprus where men are going berserk; and they hide in the deep caves where they preserve —unchanged and unchangeable, like the very spirit of myth—the chariot made of seashells that belonged to Aphrodite (7429–7433).

All the distinctions we are accustomed to establish dissolve into the multiple and paradoxical life of the Sphinxes and Chiron, of the Psylli and Marsi, of Nereus and Proteus. If we could delve into their consciousness, we would understand that they dwell at once in the immobile world of myth and the disastrous world of history. If we could know their minds, we would discover that their thoughts are limited and conditioned like those of a person who knows only a single epoch; ironic and phantasmagoric as the thoughts of him who flies swiftly over the expanse of the centuries; firm, immense, and profound like the intuitions of him who trusts only in eternal repetition.

Our first journey in the *Klassische Walpurgisnacht*, among creatures of night and of books, has ended. For a few hours we have visited an inferno, where bestial and anthropomorphic gods, ancients and moderns, fabulous animals, witches, sibyls, men of legend and reality converse in different languages. We have inhabited a vortex in which the "pallid hosts" of the dead (8337), the ghosts who offend the living, the nightmares which crowd the labyrinths of night insinuated themselves among the most humid, most perfervid images of life. We have known the only world where time and myth exist side by side, one within the other, one over the other, like the shell and the nut, like the madreporic incrustations that conceal and reveal the great ocean reefs. Many readers—those more tied to the principle of noncontradiction, those who do not love the realm of "possibility which confuses the figures," the realm of smoke and subjunctives—have experienced the same feeling of malaise as a person who walks on volcanic terrain. What meaning has all this, they ask; this defiance of the dimensions and categories of our existence? What does this unfettered tone of parody intend to demonstrate? But other readers—the simpler and more subtle, the readers of fables and the readers of mathematical allegories—find a source of new joy in their malaise; and they walk forward on the moving ground, the vertiginous space, with the curiosity, exaltation, and calm of him who experiences the extremes of the world, finally reunited.

GOETHE

The Style of the Klassische Walpurgisnacht

During the first months of 1830, Goethe stopped reading books and newspapers; he even ceased to read *Le Temps* and *Le Globe* (E. February 21, 1830), although a revolution was being prepared at Paris. To the guests who thronged his house he seemed distracted and lost in thought. As at all difficult moments, he retired to his study and its windows looking out on the garden. At night, during the long hours of insomnia, he thought of the Sphinxes, the Lamiae, the Phorkyads, and sudden revelations would fill his mind with light. In the morning, refreshed by sleep, helped by the "mood and strength of the moment" (E. January 15, 1827), by the same favor of the stars that had watched over the birth of Homunculus, he composed entire scenes of the *Klassische Walpurgisnacht.*

During his life he had read so many books and on that desk had written many poems, plays, and novels. All of these now stood at his right hand, contained in the volumes of the *Ausgabe letzter Hand;* and by now little of what he had read and written seemed marvelous or surprising to him. But this time he was unusually pleased. He had the impression that something or someone had taken him beyond his usual limits and propelled him to a place he had not thought he could attain. While talking about a thousand different things with Eckermann—a letter from the king of Bavaria, the death of the grand duchess, Ninon de Lenclos, Gozzi and the theater—he confessed that he was actually producing some "marvelous things" which astounded him and went far beyond all his expectations (February 10, 14, 1830).

What were the sources from which these "marvelous things" gushed forth? What force pushed him, as adventurous and undaunted as Ulysses, beyond the limits nature had assigned him? During his last years, as Gottfried Benn has said, he seemed a magnificent baroque God, with miracles, prodigies, and mysteries dangling from his coattails; an unreal, motionless god on a balcony. He conjured up ever new clay pipes and straws from which he blew gleaming iridescent soap bubbles —ephemeral nocturnal volcanoes, wild round dances and battles of ghosts, spectacles composed of air and fire, duets and choruses of theatrical marine divinities. Then in the midst of the prodigies that popped out from under his coattails, there arose wise wizard Merlin who sought the philosopher's stone among the grasses; a magnificent poet-scientist or poet-theologian, like those who flourished at the beginning of the Greek world. Like the ancients he enunciated by hints and to a very few readers his theory of the elements, of time, of myth and symbol, of redemption and salvation.

Just as Proteus changed himself into a dolphin or a sea turtle, a bull with immense horns and a tree with dense foliage, a trickle of water and a very bright flame, so he too, old, almost decrepit, burdened with pains and worries, his hands stiffened by fatigue, had learned to modulate in his verses all the notes of the universe. He could be as ardent as Faust and as cold as Mephistopheles; as airy as Homunculus and as pedantic as Wagner. He was as immutable as the Sphinxes and as changeable as the clouds, wise and infinitely audacious. At once grave and ironic, extremely tender and frivolous, melancholy and profoundly gay, he was sensitive to all the nuances of colors. Attracted only by the spectacle of pure darkness and pure light, he was like those mystics whom, as he liked to repeat, all of us become as we grow old.

With the passing of time, he had acquired an amazing abundance of literary talents. He knew how to write in every style, in every combination of styles. He had become the prince of poet-librarians, the Ovid Nonnus* of modern poetry; and in that library crammed with bookshelves, storerooms, and secret niches which was his book, he gathered all the literary fantasies that man had ever imagined. He knew the exact weight of each word: the curves, clashes, and mortise joints they form on the page; their sounds and their colors; rhyming couplets and free verses, small pungent strophes and verses immense as bedsheets; his own language and the languages of others. Like an old carpenter he knew the different kinds of wood, the glues, varnishes, stuccoes, and enamels of his trade. Sometimes he would parade his knowledge. But more often he seemed to forget the cunning tricks of art and write in the language of the spirits he had dreamed of in the years of his youth.

Before beginning the *Klassische Walpurgisnacht* he hesitated for quite a while, and many doubts and difficulties assailed his mind. He drew up very detailed outlines containing many figures he would later pass over; then he put them aside and thought he would never be able to fill the gap between the first and third acts of *Faust II*. He did not know how to make his spirits speak, the spirits that roamed in the vortices of "the night of ill-fame," the divine figures that appear at the "gay festival of the sea." What language, what style, should he give to creatures who live at once in myth and history; who move with the same fluent grace in Greek antiquity and our times; who are dead yet so alive as to protect the birth of life?

He could not have recourse to the absolute, uniform, and polished language of Racine's heroines and of *Iphigenie auf Tauris*. Instinct

---

*Born in Panopolis, Egypt, fifth century A.D., epic poet, author of *Dionysiaca* and *Paraphrase of St. John's Gospel*, both valuable for mythological learning.

forced him to create a grandiose pastiche, similar to that in the third act, where each figure would speak in his own historical style. Thus, before the Homeric formulas pronounced by Helen and the Aeschylesan choruses sung by her maidservants, we would have listened to the archaic, enigmatic voice of the Sphinxes, the bestial language of the Griffins, the liquid messages of the old men of the sea, the still formless stammerings of the Phorkyads. But this solution also ran up against insurmountable difficulties. So much precise antiquarianism would have stifled these vivacious demons. What language would the gods who came out of the womb of Chaos and the loins of the Earth have spoken, when human languages did not as yet exist?

During those sleepless nights, those patient and tenacious days, Goethe hit upon the solution almost by chance, giving himself up to the richness of his talent. He started with a kind of homage to his own exploits as a *pasticheur:* by representing Erichtho, he began again to shape the heavy iambic trimeters of tragedy, the grave formulas borrowed from Homer, gathered up again in his German the echos and resonances of Greek as he had attempted in the act dealing with Helen. Immediately after he dared to use all the forms of the modern grotesque, granted himself the most scurrilous amusements, accumulated buffooneries, parodies, and strident, off-key notes. In this fashion, he succeeded in depicting crude and extremely powerful, "horrible and marvelous" gods (7157) akin to the archaic statues in the Museum of the Acropolis. When he described Faust's dreams, he imitated the pictorial softness, the quivering lightness of the idyls of Correggio and Tasso. He made Chiron speak like a didactic eighteenth-century poet. The war between the pygmies and the cranes was orchestrated in the abstract rhythms, the shrill phonic games he had attempted in *Pandora.* He forced Anaxagoras to pray to the moon like a romantic poet inebriated by the inspiration of the demons.

But Goethe reserved the most extraordinary stylistic effects for the end of the act, where he gathered all the forms and genres of existing art. Amid the "rocky bays of the Aegean Sea" he built an illusory and fluctuant stage. And on this stage he directed the dances and gyrations of marine divinities, making them act out small comic scenes and strange, riddling games, as in a farce or comic opera. He brought before the spectators groups of ancient flute players; he vied with Hellenistic and Renaissance painting; he induced his characters to intone mythological and sacred hymns. Meanwhile he transformed the scene into a lyric opera: recitatives dissolve into duets; two masses of chorists oppose and respond to each other; a soloist, swept away by enthusiasm, sings an aria, supported by the sounds of an entire orchestra; and, finally, all the divinities of the sea, the Sirens and Nereids, Dorides and Tritons, Telchines and Psylli and Marsi, burst into a triumphant hymn of glory.[7]

Without effort, without undue labor, aided only by the happy abundance of his talent, during those first months of 1830 Goethe solved the problems and difficulties that had distressed him. He had forged a fluent, multiform style to produce the impression of a vortex of ghosts and a lively festival, of an historical inferno and a mythic phantasmagoria. With a few indirect touches, with no antiquarian encumbrances, he suggested the historic epoch when the Sphinxes, Griffins, and Phorkyads had lived. At the same time he put on their lips the words of all epochs and all countries: the words of monsters and heroes, of late Latin poets and baroque playwrights, of the tenors and sopranos who, while Goethe was just finishing his work as a writer, continued to warble and trill in the theater at Weimar.

Erichtho

In the Gothic chamber, Faust is still sleeping on his old cot surrounded by darkened window panes, blackened stones, skulls, and worm-eaten books. His soul dreams of bubbling springs in the woods, Zeus's splendid swans, the splashings of the nymphs, Leda's beautiful body refreshed by the waves. How can he be cured of the paralysis with which he is stricken? Homunculus has a remedy to hand. The night approaching in the sky is the same that, so many times before, preceded the battle of Pharsalus. It is that night of the year during which "the legions of Hellenic saga" come together; nothing remains but to take the sick man to the soil that bore Helen's body. The long journey begins. Mephistopheles mounts his magic mantle, it is swollen by combustible air and envelops the still-unconscious Faust; Homunculus guides him like a luminous coachman. Wagner remains in Germany among his parchments to conquer gold, honor, glory, and perhaps knowledge and virtue.

As swift as meteors, the three travelers cross Europe and reach the soil of Thessaly, sacred to gods, witches, and the bloody trials of Mars. In the background the travelers can see the snows of Mount Olympus where the gods live; at the foot of the mountain a dark tunnel leads to Persephone's kingdom. Eastward tower the rocks of Ossa and Pelion, with which the Titans and Seismos tried in the past to scale the sky;

while to the west Mount Pindus extends its farthest ranges, covered with ancient oaks. Down below stretches the plain of Pharsalus, where Pompey dreamed of reenacting the triumphs of his youth and where Caesar defeated him, lacerating forever the crown of Roman freedom. Here, too, is the sandy plain of Pidna, where the defeated king of Macedonia lost his kingdom to the Roman legions. But the landscape bears no sign of these sad triumphs. As in the time of the gods and nymphs, the Peneus River runs through the plains; a hundred springs feed it from every side. Rushes, reeds, canebrakes, willow bushes, and the branches of poplars shade its banks and protect the waters descending freely to the shores of the Aegean.

A thousand fires burn on the fields of Pharsalus, throwing up glittering red lights. As on the night preceding the battle between Pompey and Caesar, the moon rises in the sky—not yet full but already bright and luminous. Its splendor spreads, illuminating the entire soil of Thessaly; and the fires, which give off a bloody color in the darkness, "burn blue" (7033). The hour so long awaited has now come; attracted by the brightness of a summer night, the "fabulous images of ancient days" are arriving from all over to attend their annual festival—the *Classical Night of Walpurgis*.

On this same nocturnal landscape, on the same fields swarming with the legions of Pompey and Caesar, Lucan had imagined Erichtho, the greatest witch of Thessaly. She was dreadfully thin, pale as the waters of the Styx; wreaths of serpents were twined about her tousled locks; and the night's most lugubrious mist hung around her head. There issued from her throat the howlings of dogs, the baying of a wolf, the quavering hoot of one kind of owl, the screech of another, the shrieks and groans of wild beasts, the hissing of serpents. The thudding crash of waves upon the rocks, the murmur of forests, thunder tearing through a cloud—all were mixed together on her lips as in the most horrible and most discordant of orchestras.

She lived in dark subterranean caves, close to the chasms of Dis; in deserted graveyards and profaned tombs from which she had driven away the shades. She dwelt among corpses as though in the most trusted company. From the heart of funeral pyres she would steal the still smoking ashes and burning bones. She dug beneath gravestones, flinging herself avidly on the pale, withered limbs, sinking her fingers into the sockets to tear out frozen eyeballs. With her teeth she would rend the mortal bonds of hanged men, pull down corpses dangling from crosses, bearing away guts and marrow bones beaten by the wind and cooked by the sun, gathering up the black decay that dripped from their limbs. When she needed a jet of warm blood for her rites, she would tear fetuses from the bellies of mothers or blooming cheeks from still adolescent bodies.

Erichtho's power had an influence on every aspect of the universe. It modified the course of events established by Fate and summoned up the ghosts of Erebus, announcing the future with veracious prophecies rather than the ambiguous and confused words of the prophets and divine Sibyls. If she gestured, the night was prolonged, the world arrested in its course, the stars descended from the celestial vault. The moon, pursued by the poison of her enchantments, paled, burned with black flames, and sank toward the earth, casting foam on the grass. Rain clouds, thunderclaps filled the serene sky; the sea was swollen, though not a breath of wind stirred; mountains lowered their peaks, waterfalls hung motionless from precipices, rivers ran backward along their beds, and the Nile ceased to fertilize the plains of Egypt.

Adorned by these trophies of horror and by the reputation of her irresistible power, Erichtho became the only divinity in a universe completely infested with evil. Standing above her shone an unknown god who lived in the invisible parts of Tartarus. But all the other gods, celestial or infernal, dared not resist her threats. When her sinister songs penetrated the recesses of the ether, the celestial gods, seized by mysterious terror, hastened to grant her any sort of abomination. When her imprecations descended into the abyss, Chaos, always eager to confuse innumerable worlds, obeyed them, as did the Furies who were afraid of being called by their true names. Hecate, too, obeyed so that Erichtho would not show the gods her infernal, pale, and putrefied face; and Persephone, so that Erichtho would not reveal what banquets kept her underground and what a scandalous pact of love bound her to the lugubrious king of the night. She was even obeyed by Pluto, the worst among the masters of the universe, who feared the threat of being blinded by the sudden glare of the sun.

The long spectral shadow, which at the beginning of the *Klassische Walpurgisnacht* roams about the fields of Pharsalus, is like Lucan's witch Erichtho. But she does not rage among the corpses, does not predict the future, does not overturn the laws of nature, does not offend the will of the gods, does not glorify the evil of the universe. Immobile at the beginning of the *Klassische Walpurgisnacht* as a sepulchral pillar, in the verses of *Faust II* Lucan's witch becomes the melancholy custodian of that sad grave, the pitying conserver of that mournful museum which is the world's past.

She lives on the same fields that, so many centuries before, witnessed Caesar's victory over Pompey. At that time the entire valley was "whitened by the wave of gray tents" (7009–7010), the armies of Caesar and

GOETHE

Pompey gathered around the bivouacs. Caesar remained awake, observing the swaying pointer on the scales of his destiny; and Pompey dreamed of the triumphs of his youth. Even now Erichtho remembers the "night full of anguish and horrors" (7011) which preceded the battle of Pharsalus. It seems to her that she can see again those gray tents and bivouac fires; she thinks she can still breathe in the smell of blood uselessly shed.

The spectacle Erichtho sees in the night is only a figment of her hallucinated memory: a trick of the imagination, which is time's prisoner. When the moon rises in the sky, those nonexistent tents vanish and around the fires gather the ancient gods of Greece. So the figures of myth punctually return each year to the rendezvous we have with them. On the contrary, the exertions of the memory to hold what has happened in history are wearisome and futile. No sooner does the light strike us than the fragments we have painstakingly collected—the drawings and autographs, the relics of an ill-omened battle—rapidly disappear like the shades of the dead.

Meanwhile Erichtho continues to think slow and laborious thoughts about the world's history, over which she is forced to keep watch. She looks back, recalls the events she has experienced, muses on the prides, envies, revolts, and battles she has witnessed. This spectacle does not console her. The history of men is merely a continuous repetition, an incessant, boring, unbearable retracing of their steps in time. At Pharsalus, as Mephistopheles has said, slaves fought against slaves; and behind it all, manipulating the strings of this absurd comedy, stood Satan (6956–6963). At Pharsalus, Erichtho more mercifully corrects him, one man tried to wrest the empire from another man who had conquered it by force and dominated it with force. The sweet, multiple crown of Roman freedom was torn apart and a rigid laurel wreath encircled the victor's head. But after that, how many times has the battle of Pharsalus "been repeated! and will repeat itself into eternity!" (7012–7013). How many times in the course of history have Caesar and Pompey, while bearing different names, faced each other in battle! How many similar events, similar to each other as the body and its shadow, as a thing and its mirrored reflection, clasp hands across the expanses of history! Man does not change. "He who cannot govern his inner being will all the more readily govern the will of his neighbor, in accordance with his proud mind" (7015–7017).

Repetition also triumphs in nature. The leaf expands in the fruit and concentrates itself in the seed, according to an always identical metamorphosis. The rose and lily blossom obeying the same laws, each year the same seasons follow each other; and water and fire, air and earth, as we shall see at the end of the *Klassische Walpurgisnacht,* embrace and repeat the same "rare adventure." All these leaves, these roses and lilies, these dolphins cleaving the waves of the sea, each time seem fresher and more vivacious, as if their return in the very same mold increased their powers. The contrary occurs in the realm of history. The new battles of Pharsalus, the new wars of tyrants and slaves are like a squalid echo of the first battle of Pharsalus, which is preserved in Erichtho's mind. All the new events, which step forth presumptuously on the stage of history, are worn out, empty, and spectral copies of an ancient model.

Thus, in the places sacred to the past, in the tombs where the departed continue their existences, in the museums where our piety collects the signs left by time, in books where our intelligence tries to recount them—the breath of the dead is exhaled. Around Erichtho, who pitifully guards what happened, reigns the same sad atmosphere; and the words she pronounces—Helen's iambic trimeters—are wrapped in the dust of the museum. If some living creature approaches her, Erichtho offends him, we do not know how, perhaps by diminishing or stifling his vital energy (7037). But Erichtho does not like the mortal spell that emanates from her person. When she sees the magic mantle of the three travelers in the sky and "gets a whiff" of the life about to descend on the soil, she runs off with long strides and is lost among the fields of Pharsalus. From then on, we no longer see her among the figures of myth. Her realm is not here, among the Sphinxes and Griffins, the Nereids and Tritons, but among the men who, sleeping and dreaming, continue to plan their futile exploits.

Greece's Ancient Monsters

Whenever the ancient wayfarer traveled, propelled by his desire for adventure or the longing for wealth, the will of the gods or the élan of love, the bloodiest monsters waited along his route and attacked him with their deadly claws. And the traveler who, after years of peregrinations, returned home, alone or with chance companions, would describe to an ever vaster multitude the Griffins and ants, the Sphinxes and Sirens, the prodigious flora and fantastic fauna that decorated the façades of the temples and the large Ionic vases. The legend was enriched in the verses of Homer and Hesiod, the histories of Herodotus,

GOETHE

the tragedies of Aeschylus, Sophocles, and Euripides—until, after centuries, these monsters, which some still saw in nightmares, inspired Ovid's marvelous fantasy and Aelian's decorative grace.

To the north of Scythia, where Hercules had coupled in a cave with a woman serpent, the traveler encountered immense, desolate, and deserted lands. The earth was all covered with feathers; the air was thick with feathers; the sea was frozen, the waters of the rivers and lakes were turned to ice, a harsh frost tortured men and animals. Up there, at the base of the high mountains, the Argippaei slept beneath trees wrapped in white felt, nourishing themselves on the fruits, and did not bear arms. Farther on lived men with the feet of goats: the people of Issedones, among whom ventured Aristeas of Proconesus, inspired by Apollo. There, too, lived the daring one-eyed people of Arimaspi, their tawny locks bound by a strip of gold.

Even farther to the north, where the cold was more atrocious and feathers continually whirled in the air in eddies, the ancient wayfarer saw the Griffins, whom Nature had created in order to bizarrely confuse the species. "The sharp-beaked dogs of Zeus, who do not bark," as Aeschylus liked to call them, they had the lion's body and claws and the eagle's head, beak, and wings. Their eyes jetted fire; the feathers on their backs were black, those on their breasts red, and on their wings extremely white, while deep blue feathers drew friezes and embroideries around their necks. No animal could elude the clutch of their claws and the speed of their wings. Except for tigers, as Philostratus says, these animals are faster than the wind. Zeus had given them the task of guarding the treasures from the cold; and their robust limbs rested avidly on piles of rocks speckled with spangled lights and golden gleams and drops. But cunning succeeded in defeating strength. Coming up from the southern regions on horseback, the tawny Arimaspians carried off the gold guarded by the terrible winged beasts.

In India's hot deserts, the adventurous merchant came across ants of an unprecedented nature and dimensions. These ants were "larger than a fox and smaller than a dog"; they did not yield in speed and ferocity to the tiger. They dug their burrows in the sand, unearthing the precious, hidden gold. So in these deserts, too, cupidity flourished, and the events which in the ice of the North had counterposed the Griffins to the Arimaspians were repeated. Early in the morning, when the sun was high and the ants were holed up in their burrows, the Indians would venture into the desert. Each Indian was mounted on a female camel, torn from its tender young, and led two male camels, tied to a rope. As soon as they reached the region of the ants, the hunters quickly filled their bags with sand and tiny particles of gold, and then started for home in great haste. But, just at that moment, alerted by man's unusual smell, the swift, cruel ants would begin to chase them. If cunning had not helped them, none of the seekers for gold ever would have seen home again. When the colossal ants were right behind them, they would untie the rope and, one after the other, abandon the two male camels, already exhausted by the race. The ants would stop to devour the prey, while the female camels loaded with gold continued the long journey across the desert, guided by the thought of their distant young.

The wayfarer who sought monsters did not have to go to Scythia or India, where the imagination begins to dream and rave. Monsters lived along the roads at home, on the mountains, in caves, in rock crevices, lakes, and hills where the shepherd tends his quiet flock. In one of these caves Echidna was born: an irresistible monster who in the upper part of her body seemed a young woman with lovely cheeks and shining eyes and in the lower part an enormous, horrible snake lost in the bowels of the earth. In that same cave Echidna coupled with Typhon and generated the most tremendous maledictions of nature: Orthos, Geryon's two-headed hound; Cerberus with fifty heads and a voice of bronze; Lernaean Hydra; the Nemean lion; the fiery Chimera with three leonine heads; and the Sphinx of Thebes.

Like her mother, the Sphinx had the face of a virgin, the breast, paws, claws, and tail of a lion, and the wings of a bird. Sent by Hera, Dionysius, or the gods of Hades to devastate Thebes, she lay in wait on the outskirts of the city, crouching on the slopes of a mountain. Then, flying over the walls, she swooped down on the market square, where the Thebans were gathered in council. The Muses had taught her an ambiguous, intricate, indecipherable riddle which she sang in her "mountain monster's" harsh, coarse voice. It was a crude, discordant, graceless song which the chords of the lyre did not sweeten. No Theban, not even if he had consulted the oracles, was able to answer her. So the "infamy of Thebes," the "rhapsodic bitch," the "monster of the mountains" bore off in her claws a young man, dragged him into the spaces of the ether, slit his throat and devoured him. And the laments of mothers and sisters resounded in the houses; and songs and cries of sorrow, sobs and clamors burst out in the streets of the city with the violence of thunder.

The Sirens, who were the daughters of Achelous, a fluvial god, and one of the nine Muses, had something in common with the "coarse singer" of Thebes: the same virgin faces, the same bird's wings, the same predator's claws, sometimes resembling the claws of a lion. They had been seen everywhere in the world. Some people had seen eight of them, each seated in one of the eight rotating circles of the sky—the eighth more rapid, the seventh more brilliant, the fourth reddish, the

GOETHE

third very white . . . The Sirens sang and their voices, their different tones rose in accord and composed a single harmony. Some people had watched them in the nocturnal palace of Persephone and Pluto, where the great enchanters were enraptured and spellbound by the beautiful *logoi* of that consummate sophist who was the lord of Hades. Some people had met them in the dark, dense forests of Sicily, where the humid earth continually generated flowers like Tyre's purple violets and lilies. But Homer forever tied their home to an island, not far from Circe's, covered by a "blossoming meadow." No sooner did the ships come near than the fury of the wind and wave was arrested as if to announce that other more insidious quiet which would shackle the listeners to the Sirens forever.

Like the "coarse singer of Thebes," the Sirens cultivated the pleasures of poetry; and the Muses, who did not inspire the Sphinxes' discordant song, liked to protect the words of their elegant and cruel wingéd daughters. Seated on the island's meadow, they sang in "divine" and "harmonious" voices, with a "sound of honey," accompanied by the chords of lyre, flute, and syringe, "about everything that the Argives and Trojans suffered by the gods' will in the wide land of Troy" *(Odyssey*, XII, 189–190). Their songs were the most illustrious themes of epic poetry, the same subjects as the *Iliad*, Achilles's wrath, Hector's exploits and death, and the death of Patroclus . . . He who listened to them— in the ships halted by calm or in the depths of Hades—knew the same joys that in Ithaca's and Alcinous's palaces were felt by the listeners to Phemius and Ulysses. They enjoyed the "delight" which lightens the spirit (XII, 52, 188), and the enchantment which charms, persuades, deceives, and heals it (XII, 40, 44).

The Sirens' poetry brought to an extreme point those enchanting, healing qualities that, according to the ancients, distinguished great poetry. It was at once very sweet and demonic. In Alcinous's palace, Ulysses's audience wanted only to spend the sleepless night listening to tales of journeys in the world of Circe and Polyphemus. He who heard the voice of the Sirens would land on the island and be lost there. He forgot his own existence and was healed, bewitched, deceived, and inebriated by those honeylike melodies. He lost his memory and never returned home again to be near his wife and children. Perhaps, like the young men of Thebes, he was strangled and killed by those ferocious and amiable witches; perhaps he stayed there, listening to the great deeds of the Greeks and Trojans until the end of his days. Death overtook him on the island; and his body remained there to putrefy and be consumed on the "flowering meadow," a useless warning to the future victims of poetry.

Faust II

The traveler who descended from Corinth toward Arcadia ran into the small swamp of Stymphalus, reeking with miasmas and exhalations, and the swamp-born river that flowed for a short distance and disappeared into a gorge. A very dense wood, where deer lost their way, surrounded the unhealthy banks. If he halted on those banks, overcome by weariness, or if he ventured among the trees of the wood, seized by a passion for the hunt, a dark flock of very swift birds would obscure the light of the sky. Overwhelmed by fear, he would see strange birds as large as cranes and resembling the ibis, but with bronze beaks, wings, and claws. Like a mortal cloud, these birds spread terror and grief, damaging the harvests with poisonous droppings, killing the flocks with their bronze feathers, pouncing on human creatures and mortally wounding them with their beaks, for these could pierce the strongest bronze armor.

Farther south, in Agamemnon's kingdom, between Argos and the shores of the sea, stretched another swamp, the swamp of Lernae. On its banks covered with reeds, grass, and plane trees, on the calm, quiet, almost motionless water, reigned a silence that no flight, no song, no bird's screech dared break; and nearby a tunnel led into the Tartarus. But this silence concealed a new danger. If the wayfarer dived incautiously into the water, a mysterious force sucked him down into those dark, unattainable depths, which perhaps communicated with the infernal abyss. Through the grass slithered "a horrible hissing beast" (*Aeneid*, VI, 288), the Hydra of Lernae, which murdered men and flocks with its breath and the stench of its tracks. On a monstrous dog's body waved eight or nine serpents' heads, perhaps fifty, a hundred, and even ten thousand—he who tried to cut them off with a sword or to break them with a club, described how they would be reborn from the blood, like thousands of branches of an eternally living tree.

There was no place in the world, no hour of the day and night which the monsters did not infest with their grim, gloomy presence. The retinue of ghosts that accompanied Hecate lived in cavities of the earth, woods, mountain caves, or old abandoned towers. But, when the solitude of the night was illuminated by the moon or when the sun was at its highest point in the sky, the Lamiae and Empusa appeared to wayfarers, continually changing form, as the apparitions of our dreams change and fluctuate—now looking like young, rich, refined women, now like bitches, cows, and repugnant donkeys with one leg made of bronze and the other of excrement. And they brought misfortune, nightmares, frightful nocturnal visions, madness, and epilepsy. Some of them, devoted to the pleasures of Aphrodite, preferred to entrap young, handsome men; they lured them by singing exquisitely and by offering them very sweet wine. They lay with their victims during the night or afternoon siesta, behaving with the lascivious abandon of prostitutes and sucking their blood like vampires.[8]

<hr />

The Monsters of Faust

All these legendary monsters and fabulous beasts can be found in *Faust II*'s extravagant library. As the moon continues to climb in the sky, the monsters warm themselves around the fires burning on the fields of Pharsalus and along the upper banks of the Peneus River. Some of them rapidly appear and disappear before the wonder-struck eyes of the three travelers. The birds of the swamp of Stymphalus cross the sky, honking loudly, moving their powerful wings, their vultures' beaks and ducks' feet, swifter than the fury of the infernal wind. For an instant they darken the light of the lunar night, then they vanish at the horizon, while the hundred heads of the Hydra of Lernae, still separated from the body, creep in among them, hissing and whistling.

The winged Griffins, the populace of tawny Arimaspians and gigantic ants do not live in such distant places as the frozen surfaces of Scythia and the hot deserts of India. Instead, they remain clustered together near the fires, bizarre allegories of the voracious longing for wealth that rages among monsters and men. The ants seek out the layers and crumbs of gold glittering in the rock clefts, and they collect them secretly in the mountain caves. The old winged Griffins, with their screeching, nasal voices, avidly guard these treasures with their claws, stronger than any lock; while the astute hosts of Arimaspians rob the fabulous piles of gold and consume them wildly in the "free night of jubilee."[9]

The Lamiae and Empusa in their old hiding places have forgotten their faculties as dangerous vampires, spirits of midday and midnight, capable of making human beings lose their wits. Meeting them in *Klassische Walpurgisnacht*, with their shameless eyes, laughing mouths, faces covered with rouge and powder, their bodies clasped tightly in a fashionable bodice, one might think them vulgar prostitutes like those in Paris or Weimar. If the Empusa, who has the head and feet of a donkey, revolts even the "lord of flies and mice," the Lamiae, with their lewd gestures and amorous promises, drive men, devils, and monsters mad with desire; and then, as in ancient Greece, they reveal their abilities as quick-change artists. When the laughing mouths, the painted faces, and wriggling bodies dissolve, all that is left of the "charming chorus" is a grotesque round-dance of brooms, lizards, snakes, thyrsi, pine cones, rotten, dust-filled mushrooms, and bats flitting insidiously through the night.

The Sphinxes who warm themselves at the fires along the banks of the upper Peneus have the face and breasts of young girls and the body and claws of lionesses (7083, 7146–7147, 7149), like the monster of Thebes. Before Hercules's great deeds, they ruled over Greece; and a bastard with pierced feet, the son of Laius and Jocasta, stopped one day before them, solving the enigma which weighed on the life of Thebes. But at the same time they are the enormous granite Sphinxes towering before the Egyptian pyramids, regulating the course of the days, months, and seasons (VII, 539: 36). If for Goethe granite was "the most ancient, most solid, most profound, most unshakable child of nature," the "eternal altar, erected immediately on the depths of creation," the keystone of the earth, the solid foundation on which the immense variety of other rock formations rested (XIII, 255: 11–12; 256: 6–8 ff.), the Sphinxes of granite and flesh which appear in the *Klassische Walpurgisnacht* are equally ancient, rigid and unshakable: solemn symbols of conservation. Whatever may happen in the universe, they "do not change aspect" (7248); whatever event erupts, "they do not change position" (7528), do not let themselves be torn from the "sacred seats" (7581) they have occupied since the beginning of the world. No one could make them bend, or convince them to become less tenacious in their own defense. Nobody could ever prove to them that, in the history which they too must undergo, some perennial value does not persist.

Around the Sphinxes, in the vortex of the *Klassische Walpurgisnacht*, everything trembles, undulates, and is transformed. The shock of earthquakes and meteors creates landscapes that last only a single night; mythical figures alter in appearance; pygmies and herons uselessly spill their blood. But each time, the Sphinxes, constant and patient, intervene to reestablish the threatened order of the universe. With their robust lioness's claws, their powerful granite paws, they halt the odious tempest of the earthquake. When history goes berserk and men start their wars, regular and disastrous as floods, they bring them quietly before "the high tribunal of the peoples" (7246), which, unknown to all, stands near the millenial pyramids.[10]. Nothing in the comportment of these great conservative divinities recalls the dark and brutal ferocity of the "infamy of Thebes." Seated between the fires, they help the wayfarers just as our world's most scrupulous guides do. They speak as if they were in a drawing room; and their conversation is full of social

GOETHE

graces, elegant morality, and a scorn so deeply rooted and profound that it cannot help but express itself in an incomparable courtesy. Thus Goethe must have spoken during the last years of his life; but no sooner does some more acrid remark come to their lips than we seem to be hearing the voice of Mephistopheles, the lord of rocks and fire, who is conversing with them near the banks of the Peneus.[11]

Hidden among the branches of the poplars, a group of Sirens begins to warble, accompanying themselves with the sounds of the lyre and flute (7173, 8034). We do not know whether their voices are still as harmonious and enchanting as at the time of Ulysses; or whether death, the long silence, the changes in poetic modes may have dimmed their grace. Certainly nobody here lets himself be seduced by their honeyed voices. The Sphinxes mock them, the Griffins think only of gold and German etymologies; and Faust flees, driven by the thought of Helen. As for Mephistopheles, who reveals a musical ability we would never have attributed to him, the Sirens' trills do not succeed in touching his old, wrinkled, unfeeling, and leathery heart. Why this ineffectiveness, more astounding than the failure the Sirens suffered when Ulysses heard their singing but did not stop his ship? On the high banks of the Peneus, among the solid mountains and venerable oaks where the stone Sphinxes reign, the Sirens find an alien and hostile milieu. The element to which they belong is the "green water"; the life they exalt is the free, mobile life that gods, fishes, and men know in the waves of the sea (7208, 7495 ff., 8060). Only on the banks of the Aegean could we admire all their power as witches, priestesses, singers, musicians, and heralds of the kingdom of the sea.

The Sirens in *Faust* are also multiple and ambiguous: insidious and benign as the waves of the Aegean, which have known both the birth of Venus and the shipwreck of the Greek fleet on its return from Troy. While they announce the most luminous joys, the claws of the sparrow hawk hidden among the branches of the poplars threaten to grasp, wound, perhaps kill those who listen to their flattery. They love the lie, as when they tell how Ulysses stopped on their island, and everything leads one to think that in a near or distant time their songs have wrecked many ships and made many crews perish (8055, 8182). But at the end of *Klassische Walpurgisnacht*, during the Aegean festival, the voices of the Sirens, by throwing off these demonic vestiges, change in accent. Becoming more moving and benign they exalt the two great celestial twins, Apollo and Artemis, venerate the ancient Cabiri, encourage piety and devotion to the gods, and celebrate the amorous force that embraces the entire universe.

The monstrous divinities and legendary animals sculpted by the

Greeks on the façades of their temples and painted on their vases are completely transformed in Goethe's hands. Everything which in the verses of Homer, Hesiod, and Euripides was so obscure and solemn, everything which in the books of Aelian and Philostratus was sumptuously decorative, seems in the verses of *Faust II* only gay, strident, and jovially grotesque. Who could any longer recognize Aeschylus's Griffins in Goethe's? Forgetting their heraldic fascination, the Griffins have become dirty old misers, moody and splenetic, who talk through their noses in a shrill voice and have a strange competence in the field of etymology:

> Not gray! Griffins!—No one likes
> To be called gray. In every word resounds
> The origin from which it derives and which conditions it:
> Gray, gruesome, grumbling, grim, graveyards, and griping
> Which etymologically have a similar sound,
> Sadden us.*

The Sphinxes find it amusing to discuss astrology and to solve charades together with Mephistopheles, they are familiar with asceticism and the art of fencing, and insult the Sirens in the tones of old women gossips. The Sirens seem like inept Italian sopranos; Mephistopheles, who likes to call himself Old Iniquity as if he were performing in the theaters of London, carries off some of his finest buffooneries; and the hundred heads, which Hercules cut off the Hydra of Lernae, pursue and pay court to the Lamiae like old roués in the street.

With these grotesque fantasies, Goethe did not intend to parody the gods of Greece and consign them to the ridicule of farce. The world of monstrous divinities and legendary animals he had decided to represent, the world of Sphinxes and Sirens, Griffins and Phorkyads, must have seemed to him still lost in the abysses of Chaos and the hostile womb of the earth. But the ancient works of art, which he knew, had not helped him to render these accents. Hellenistic statues and vases made the monsters' lineaments precious and softened them, while Homer's style was already an "historical" style in which a heroine like

---

> *Nicht Greisen! Greifen!—Niemand hört es gern,
> Dass man ihn Greis nennt. Jedem Worte klingt
> Der Ursprung nach, wo es sich her bedingt:
> Grau, grämlich, griesgram, greulich, Gräber, grimmig
> Etymologisch gleicherweise stimmig,
> Verstimmen uns.

(7093–7098)

Helen could express herself, but not such immensely more archaic figures as the Sphinxes and Phorkyads.

So he turned for help to Mephistopheles's grotesque imagination, tested the most acute tones and mixed together the broadest modern desecrations, as in an infernal cabaret. The grotesque acts as a kind of chemical reagent, scraping off the patinas and varnishes that time had accumulated on the mythical figures. So Greece's ancient monsters once again reveal the "horrible and marvelous" faces, magnificently, robustly repugnant, which they showed to Heracles and the first heroes of Greece (7157, 7182). We are no longer reading *Faust II;* we are no longer with Mephistopheles. Rather we are in the hall in which stood the statues that decorated Athens's archaic temples. We are where the Sphinx proudly extends her wings and the famished lioness sinks her fangs into the bull's neck, where serpents gape their enormous jaws and Heracles strikes down the Hydra of Lernae with the blows of his club; while the Triton smiles with his three faces, thrashing his sea serpent's colored tail.

Anaxagoras and Thales

Strange commotions threaten the tranquillity of the moonlit night. A hidden shudder, a frightful tremor agitates the waters of the Peneus, rousing the sleeping nymphs. The earth vacillates; the pebble-covered bank of the river begins to smoke and then cracks, the water froths and foams, rushes backward and overflows its bed. From the subterranean caves one hears the grumbling and uproar of an old giant. With his back arched, his shoulders raised strenuously and his arms tensed, he pushes, presses, labors—he raises the pebbles, gravel, and sand of the river and breaks the surface of the valley. At last he comes up out of the ground to his waist, carrying on his back a mountain covered with woods and bushes—like an Atlas bearing the earth, a colossal caryatid supporting a baroque palace.

When the gods of Olympus lived in our world, Zeus's brother Poseidon agitated the earth; he shook it with the force of an earthquake, struck the mountains with his trident, flung huge rocks into the currents or set them at the bottom of the abyss. In the Aegean he brought volcanic islands into existence, accompanied by flames and violent winds. And so he made whole continents and regions disappear.[12] In the

Faust II

Klassische Walpurgisnacht, Poseidon has become Seismos, one of the Titans, a descendant of Night and Chaos. With pride in his lineage, he boasts of enhancing the world by pushing mountains into the blue of the sky; he proclaims that at the time of his youthful follies he played ball with Pelion and Ossa, and lifted up Jove's throne. Together with his name, Seismos has lost the dignity of the Olympian gods. When he raises the stones with his back and arms, he seems an athlete from a street fair; and the Sphinxes' look falls ironically on him, as on all the things of our world.

All of a sudden, a great swarming of life animates the mountain of Seismos! A thousand leaves and droplets of gold tremble in the fissures of the rocks, the large ants move about quickly, search, delve in all the niches, separating gold from the rock, the winged Griffins stretch out their claws to seize these new treasures. Then from cracks in the ground, behold! a host of potbellied pygmies with bandy legs, sons of Mother Earth, stream out, and also a multitude of tiny Dactyls, the invisible servants and witches who pay attendance on the Great Mother. But the savage violence of human history erupts even during the nocturnal festival of the ghosts with the rapidity of dreams. As soon as they were born, the pygmies made the Dactyls and ants into slaves, forced them to extract metals, prepare charcoal, and fabricate weapons for their army. They wear helmets and breastplates over their potbellied bodies and are armed with swords, bows and arrows. Just as the strength of Seismos, emerging from the depths of the earth, has rebelled against celestial beings, so the small telluric monsters attack the free, noble, and peaceful herons, the splendid children of the sky, who build their nests near the banks of a pond. "Cries of slaughter and laments of death," "anguished flapping and beating of wings" (7660–7661), groans and sighs rise to the sky. The pond is red with blood; and the herons' white feathers decorate the pygmies' grotesque helmets.

When he lived in Athens, Anaxagoras, the friend and teacher of Pericles and Euripides, glorified the force of the νοῦς that sets in order everything which in the past "existed together" (Diogenes Laertius, *Life of the Philosophers,* II, 6). He revealed to his disciples the real cause of the annual floodings of the Nile (Seneca, *Naturales Quaestiones,* IV, a); and he explained how all things can be decomposed and divided into infinitely smaller parts, the bone into very tiny bones; flesh into equally minute fragments; blood into a multitude of drops joined to each other; earth, water, and fire into infinitely divisible particles (Lucretius, *The Nature of Things*). The new, strange Anaxagoras, who appears in the *Klassische Walpurgisnacht* immediately after the victory of the pygmies, repeats none of his most proverbial theories. This savage, hysterical phantom has not a single trait in common with the "powerful hero," whom Goethe had gotten to know from the *Lives of the Philosophers.* He bears no resemblance to the man "eminent for his noble birth and wealth, but also for his magnanimity," who in his old age devoted himself to the contemplation of nature.

From what sources did Goethe derive this singular portrait of the teacher of Pericles? Perhaps he remembered Plato's *Phaedo* in which with furious sarcasm Socrates recounts how he read Anaxagoras's Συγγραφή, "writings." One day Socrates learned that for Anaxagoras the νοῦς was the ordering cause of all things. This idea filled him with enthusiasm; he thought that he had finally found the man capable of explaining to him what was the best and worst solution for anything: why the earth was flat or round, why the sun shone, why the stars revolved at a specific speed. And he flung himself on Anaxagoras's book, devoured by feverish impatience. His disappointment was enormous. The presumed universal cause seemed completely inert and ineffective, and earth, ether, fire, or some other mechanical cause provoked the actions and reactions of the universe. It was as though a man, after maintaining that Socrates was guided in all his acts by intelligence, might then explain them, instance by instance, by the structure of his body, the shape of his bones, by his muscles which contract and relax, his ears, or his vocal cords (*Phaedo,* 97c–99a).

But Goethe's principal source was a passage in the *Naturales Quaestiones,* in which Seneca recalls Anaxagoras's theory of seismic phenomena. Within the bowels of the earth, Anaxagoras said, oscillated thick, dense clouds, similar to those in the sky; and a very violent wind breaks and shatters them using the same force with which it sweeps away the clouds from our world. When this wind is fastest and the clouds collide, suddenly a furious fire explodes, expands, searches for an outlet, and destroys all obstacles. In the end, bursting through the cracks in the ground or forcibly opening an exit, the subterranean fire reaches the crust of the earth where its violence disrupts everything (*Naturales Quaestiones,* VI, 9). As Seismos shatters the surface of Thessaly, Anaxagoras repeats to the letter the theory of *Naturales Quaestiones.* The cause of the seismic phenomena is the conjoined action of subterranean winds, "the explosive force of the Aeolian vapors" (7865), and the "wrathful Plutonic fire" (7866); what he calls with a single word *Feuerdunst,* "fire-vapor" (7855).

But this explanation is not for him, as it was for the real Anaxagoras, a simple scientific theory. Under the inspiration of his furious and dogmatic mind, fire-vapor becomes the beginning of a systematic ideology, which explains every phenomenon in nature and history. As a philosopher of nature, Anaxagoras considers only sudden forces (*einer Nacht,* 7859) and catastrophic forces (*Gewalt,* 7864–7865) such as the revolution of Seismos, while at the same time he claims that he does not see forms that change slowly in obedience to the laws of order and harmony. His political ideal is expressed in the contorted, potbellied hordes of pygmies—these plebs without a past, born suddenly from the "nethermost depths" (10090), who murder the elegant herons and spread the violence of fire everywhere. Thus the "very powerful hero of the mind," the noble friend of Pericles and Euripides is transformed in the *Klassische Walpurgisnacht* into one of Mephistopheles's followers. Like his master, he can live in all times and all places, in the Athens of Pericles and medieval Germany, in Berlin, London, or Weimar at the beginning of the nineteenth century. But Anaxagoras especially resembles the most modern student of the lord of fire, such as the political and literary theoreticians of the French Revolution. His natural theories all remind one of those of the "vulcanists" who dominated the science of nature while Goethe was writing *Faust II.* His imaginative and hysterical violence is the same as that flaunted by the *Stürmer* and the Romantic poets.

At the start, everything that happens in the *Klassische Walpurgisnacht* seems to justify Anaxagoras; despite the Sphinxes' resistance, a mountain is born in a few minutes; and with the same criminal speed obscene, potbellied pygmies murder the celestial herons. But Anaxagoras's joy does not last for long. Coming from the sea, flocks of cranes threateningly approach to avenge the murdered herons; they alight on the ground, and with their sharp beaks and clawed feet attack the deformed and rebellious race of pygmies. Neither the shield, nor the sword, nor the helmet with its shining plumes can avail against the cranes' implacable strength; and so new blood reddens the ponds.

Impotent and stunned, Anaxagoras watches the slaughter of "his people" (7904); and he no longer asks for help from the subterranean powers, who until then seemed to have assisted him. After a moment of uncertainty, he turns to the celestial powers for help. In the solemn tones of a priest he invokes the potent divinity with three names and three forms. He supplicates the divinity who, like the Moon, "shines calmly in the sky" and "enlarges men's breasts" (7905–7906), who reigns on Earth in the guise of Diana, and who, like Hecate, has dominion over the nether regions and possesses the supreme secrets of magic (7908–7909). But in reality, he prays only to the ultimate form of the three-named divinity. What could he have asked of the mild queen of the sky, who soon will protect the spectacles of the "Aegean festival," or of the huntress Diana? The ardently invoked moon is the demon of the night, the star of wizards and witches who perform their atrocious feats beneath its disquieting rays.

Before being born again on Anaxagoras's lips, Hecate's prayer had resounded in classical times whenever a miracle, an enchantment, a philter, evocation, or curse was about to offend nature's order and laws. Thus in the *Aeneid* the invocation to "triple Hecate," "powerful in the heavens and in Erebus" sounds out three times. Once when the witch of Massilia, who can halt the water of rivers and force the stars to change their courses, concocts a philter out of poisonous herbs gathered in the moonlight; again when Dido calls down the divine curse on Aeneas and his lineage. And finally it is invoked when the Cumaean Sibyl sacrifices the young bulls beside the great rocky cavern, the lake, and pitch-black wood, before leading Aeneas into the empty houses, Dis's hollow kingdom (IV, 511 ff., 609 ff.; VI, 247 ff.). In the *Metamorphoses,* the magical background is extraordinarily embellished, as if Ovid wanted to gather together everything that had inspired Hecate's name and fame. We see Medea come out of the house in the mute, mortal silence of midnight, while the full moon pours the wealth of its daimonic rays on earth; she crosses the fields like a somnambulist, with bare feet and hair hanging loosely over her shoulders. She raises her arms to the sky, turns herself around three times, sprinkles her hair with the river water three times, and three times flings out a strident howl, invoking "triple-headed Hecate." Then she mounts a cart pulled by winged dragons and gathers the magic herbs growing on the slopes of Ossa, Pelion, Pindus, and Olympus, the roots and flowers sprouting along the margins of the Po and Peneus, and the dew that fell from the moon. These, together with the wings of an owl, the entrails of a wolf, and the fillet of a water tortoise, must form King Aeson's new blood. But the same long, strident howl, the same atrocious invocation resounds through the forests and brushwood of the Italic countryside after the king of Ausonia has been transformed into a bird with feathers of gold and purple. As soon as Circe prays to the gods of night and to Hecate, the forests leave their places, the earth groans, the trees turn pale, the grass is soaked with drops of blood, the rocks emit raucous moans, the dogs bark, the ground is covered with obscene snakes. She prays and the sad and tenuous souls of the dead twist and turn in the air, and the bodies of the living become the limbs of savage beasts (VII, 179 ff.; XIV, 345 ff.).

While he declaims his prayer, Anaxagoras certainly remembers these typical passages from classical literature. As though to defend his prestige as a rational philosopher, he protests that he does not use any magic formula and that he has nothing in common with the witches of Thessaly and Massilia, with Medea, Circe, and the Cumaean Sibyl (7909). But in reality little or nothing distinguishes him from them. At this moment the impious worshipper of fire and violence, the "vulcanist" and Jacobin, is only an infernal witch, a ridiculous apprentice sorcerer. This is what happens, Goethe seems to imply, to the Anaxagorases of all times; especially to those who plagued his epoch, when so many rationalistic scientists and so many defeated Jacobins, disappointed by the "subterranean powers," had suddenly flaunted the witchlike deeds of the philosophy of "fiery vapors."

What does Anaxagoras ask of the grim divinity of night? His request seems enigmatic. "Open," he says to Hecate, "the horrible abyss of your shadows" (7908). This time, too, the hidden correspondence with the passage of a classical author reveals Goethe's intentions to us. In one of the *Moralia*—namely, *De facie quae in orbe lunae apparet*—Plutarch explains that on the moon there are vast, very deep cavities, like the Caspian Sea, the Indian Ocean and the channel between the columns of Hercules. The largest of these is called Hecate's abyss, and there are two long passages, one connecting it to the face of the moon turned to the sky, the other to the face turned to our world. In Hecate's abyss live a host of souls, who are being punished for sins committed after having left earth and body and having assumed the attributes of demons. These spirits await purification until a "second death," when they will leave the soul, too, and their very pure νους will reach the sun. Not far away hover the souls of those who in their first existence were ambitious, irascible, active, and enamoured of the body; they seem to sleep and memories of terrestrial life are their dreams. But the violence of old passions sometimes returns to possess them and push them toward our world, where they will don new limbs and commit crimes as terrible as the crimes of Python and Typhon. Every six months the tranquillity of this limbolike life is disrupted. The earth's shadow covers the moon for a few hours. Torn from the light of the sky and plunged into darkness where they can no longer hear the music of the spheres, the souls cry out in terror and anguish until the moon, accelerating its movements, again reaches the spaces illuminated by the sun.

So Anaxagoras's invocation becomes comprehensible. In this moment of great misfortune for his people, he prays to Hecate to open the doors of her abyss; and to all the demons gathered up there—perhaps, above all, those who resemble her, the souls of the ambitious, irascible and violent—to come down to the Earth to help the overwhelmed pygmies. Just as the witches of Thessaly summon up the souls of the dead on nights when the moon is full, so Anaxagoras, who also belongs to the "pale ranks of the spirits," tries to summon up an army of ghosts who could throw new fuel on the guttering fires of war. But the miracle does not take place. Indifferent, impassive, or defunct like the other gods of Greece, Hecate does not open the gate which would lead the demons to our globe. Yet something perturbs the night's serenity. As he looks up at the sky, Anaxagoras believes that the rotund throne of the goddess is descending rapidly, becoming larger, more immense and terrifying, threatening to destroy men, earth, and sea. Despite a new invocation, it seems to him that the moon's luminous disk grows red, then dims and darkens, and that it shatters with a crashing noise on the ground, amid sparks, flashes, thunderclaps, and the fury of the winds.

Because his mind is nourished by every possible tradition of witchcraft, Anaxagoras cannot have doubts or hesitations. That first bloody and then blackish color spread over the surface of the celestial globe, the thunder and the winds' fury announce that an eclipse is about to take place; and that he has repeated the most famous exploit of the Thessalian witches, wresting the moon out of its starry orbit. Deeply troubled by the conviction of having dared to do something so sacrilegious, Anaxagoras throws himself face down on the ground and asks for forgiveness from the triple divinity whom he fears he has offended. But this time too, he has let himself be seduced by an imagination all too ready to abandon itself to the readings of his youth. As Thales and Homunculus immediately observe, the moon has remained tranquil and resplendent in the pure summits of the summer sky. From its surface has been detached an enormous rock, like the meteor of Egospotami whose fall Anaxagoras had predicted in real life (*Diogenes Laertius*, III: 3, 10). The selenic rock has traversed space, flashing, hissing, and whistling, and has fallen on the mountain created by the labors of Seismos, impartially killing both pygmies and the cranes. Thus nature derides him who tries to arouse its daimonic force. It kills him who disturbs its tranquillity with ridiculous brawls; and it displays its admirable qualities as creator and prestidigitator, capable of continually transforming the earth's spectacle.

During the vicissitudes of the *Klassische Walpurgisnacht*, Anaxagoras met another Greek philosopher—Thales, the oldest and most venerable of the seven wise men, the one whom the oracle had called "the man who knows and unveils present, future, and past" (*Diogenes Laertius* I: 33). As happens to philosophers of different schools, Thales and Anaxagoras immediately begin a dispute, right before the eyes of Homunculus, who could not have known two more opposed temperaments. While Anaxagoras raves like a magus, poet, or demagogue, Thales possesses the qualities tradition attributes to the "wise man"; that mixture of candor and tenacity, of sweetness and obstinacy, of abstraction and grace, which alone seems to permit men to construct great philosophical "systems."

Nature, in which he believes and which he venerates as the image of all that is "true and beautiful," does not recognize its symbol in fire but rather in the eternal generative force of water. Peaceful and mild, obeying the "eternal norms" (8324) God has taught it, it has no recourse to violence even in its greatest creations (7864). While we calculate time according to days, hours, and minutes, it moves according to time that is slower, more gradual, never sudden and precipitous. It is similar to the time the waters of rivers and oceans obey. And many of its effects can be measured only by the clock of the centuries (7861–7862).[13]

In the course of the *Klassische Walpurgisnacht*, this philosophy seems vulnerable to the most sarcastic confutations. That which happened and continues to happen—the sudden appearance of the mountain, the swift fall of a comet—isn't this born from nature's violence *(Gewalt)* and from nature's anxious creative haste *(einer Nacht)?* Thales is quite unruffled by so clamorous a refutation of his thesis. He barely admits that Seismos might have raised a mountain with the Plutonic strength of his arms, but he insists that, unlike authentic natural creations, this illusory creature of night and fire will not have a future (7869). As the nymphs of the mountains believe, it will perhaps disappear at the first crow of the cock (7817–7818). In the case of the meteor, his attitude is even more unusual. As the moonstone hisses, flashes, and falls with a crash at his feet, he affirms, calm and imperturbable, that he neither sees nor hears anything (7930–7932). Everything has occurred, he declares to the astounded Homunculus, only in Anaxagoras's diseased imagination (7946).

We do not know whether Thales is really lying; whether he sees the moonstone and claims not to see it; or whether his unconscious faith in *harmonia mundi* is so deep it prevents him from seeing and hearing what is actually happening in the *Klassische Walpurgisnacht*. His old philosopher's dogmatic optimism remains so pure and lovable as to keep even to the end Homunculus's sympathy and that of the readers of *Faust II*. But a subtle persiflage, a slight comic aura accompanies his words, as it does all those words in Goethe's books that pronounce theories too persuaded of *harmonia mundi*.

We have neglected until now the third great philosopher of nature, the man who in his youth had lived on Rosenberg hill, and in the years of his maturity was lost in Alcinous's garden. We have not discussed the naturalist who studied the phenomena of light and colors; and at seventy, like the old magician Merlin, strode with a grave and solemn step across the Dornburg valley, now dallying near an isolated tree, now beating the stones with his mineralogist's hammer, while the shadows of night and death stooped down to envelop him (M. April 29, 1818). When Thales and Anaxagoras were debating about fire and water,

GOETHE

where was Goethe—the old magician Merlin—hidden? To which of them, or to what verses in *Faust II*, had he entrusted his philosophy of nature?

For many years Goethe no longer believed, like Thales, that nature revealed only harmony and order to the eyes of its admirers. Anaxagoras was not mistaken. Just as in the tumultuous world of history, so also in nature there functioned a catastrophic, arbitrary, insensate force which on its passage destroyed all possible laws. The waves of the sea swelled with arrogance, moved to the assault of the beaches and tried to drag the earth into the abyss. The air turned against the earth, flaying it with tempests, lightnings, and meteors; insatiable fire seized everything that could burn and overturned the world with the force of seismic phenomena; the earth tried to become the master of the water and turn it into ice or stone.[14]

But Goethe could not bear the fact that someone—like Anaxagoras and his modern pupils—saw only these events, and that they drew from it an hysterical ideology which exalted fire and disorder. Anyone who looks with a pure spirit, with eyes not obfuscated by intellectual passion, could see in a part of nature the "eternal norms" (8324) joyously extolled by Thales. To such a one was evident the "law according to which the rose and lily blossom" (E. November 7, 1829), the animal "type," the leaf, the slow transitions of metamorphosis, the providential memory of Biblical creation (VIII, 262: 11–17). These were the sublimest images that had ever populated the earth. Man must continue to shape, develop, and enrich them within himself, draw them in picture and books, even if, around him, the elements unleashed their fury.

What would be the fate of the world? Would water still defeat the earth; would fire upset all order, would air be eternally traversed by lightning bolts? In a corner, oblivious to what was happening, would some Thales continue to exalt the "eternal norms"? The philosophy of the old Goethe did not accept the conditions of the universe; it tried to change them radically. The task it prescribed for man was to overcome the violence and arbitrariness, sterility and absurdity that accompanied nature, making shine out everywhere the law of the rose and the lily, the perfection of metamorphosis, the harmonious sound of the spheres.

This miracle would not be performed by the scientists who studied the origin of the world and the causes of seismic phenomena; nor even by the engineers, although they built dikes capable of holding back oceans and dug canals to dry up the swamps. Nature could be saved only in the sphere of myth. The redeemer of the elements must again perform the deed of the Golgotha—sacrifice and immolate himself like

Homunculus, so that water and air, earth and fire could peacefully embrace. This deed must be repeated incessantly, "renew itself continually through all the time of becoming and being" (IX, 353: 5–7). Only in this way, perhaps, even on the real earth, the one where Mephistopheles's artisans and engineers labor, would all shadows abandon nature's beautiful countenance.[15]

Faust's Double Dream

We have reached the halfway mark of the *Klassische Walpurgisnacht*, and soon we shall set foot on the shores of the Aegean Sea But what has happened to Faust? And what fate has befallen Mephistopheles? The protagonist of *Faust* had in fact begun his journey to Greece a few hours before the others, as he lay in a faint, paralyzed by his violent love for Helen. As at the beginning of the first act, Faust's strength, fatigued by his vigil, gave up the light of consciousness and the tension of speech to seek refuge in the consoling darkness of sleep.

As he slept on his narrow cot, Faust dreamed of a well of limpid, pure water, protected by dense bushes, in which a hundred springs—not murmuring, but barely dripping—gathered from all sides. Young, charming women undressed. They went into the water, their lovely limbs reflected by that dank mirror to the eyes of the happy spectator. They swam timidly or boldly and, shrieking, they splashed each other. Among this group of women, one figure shines like a goddess: Leda, Tindar's bride, the queen of Sparta. Now she hides in the green density of the bushes as in a "sacred spot" (7306); now she advances toward the light, plunges her foot in the water's transparent clarity, and "the noble body's sweet flame of life is refreshed in the pliant crystal of the waves" (6909–6910). But, suddenly, a loud splatter, a swish of rapidly beating wings breaks the quiet. A flock of swans comes down the river's curves. Majestic and tranquil, they move their heads and beaks, agitate their shining feathers. One swan among them glides swiftly like a wave above the waves. Proudly it ruffles its feathers, sailing along like a ship; then it ventures behind a bush where Leda is hidden and presses tenderly and brazenly against her knees. . . . At this point a veil of mist descends into Faust's sleeping mind: a thick veil envelops "the loveliest of all scenes" (6920), and prevents us from witnessing the embrace of Zeus and Leda, from which Helen, "the peerless form" (7439), is born.

GOETHE

This dream, melodious and elegant as a painting by Correggio, which we know through Homunculus's eyes, dissolves the paralysis that shackled Faust's mind. It retempers his forces, and a new spirit burns freshly within him. To be completely cured, he had but one last step to take. When his foot finally touched the soil of Greece, when he knew the ground that bore Helen's body, saw the wave that ran toward her, and breathed the air her tongue had moved, Faust felt himself reborn to a new life, just like Antaeus each time his foot touched Mother Earth.

Among the fires of the *Klassische Walpurgisnacht*, he sees the ferine divinities: the Sphinxes, before whom Oedipus had halted; the Sirens, who attracted Ulysses with their songs; the Griffins who faithfully guarded the treasure. But "his" Greece, the land of which he had dreamed for so long, is Olympic and heroic Greece. It is the Greece of Zeus and Hermes, of Apollo and Ares, the Greece of semidivine heroes who won the golden fleece, vanquished monsters, and fought before Troy. His was the Greece of the sculptors who tortured stones to represent gods and men; and of the bards who sang of their "glory," invoking the Muses.

Although they may have belonged to history, for Faust the figures of Olympian Greece have an absolute, paradigmatic value on which no historical vicissitude could ever cast a shadow. They awaken in his spirit the same emotions awakened by the images torn from the Mothers, a noble and grave enthusiasm that carries him to love, religious veneration, adoration, and delirium (6500). How could he be content to contemplate those images for just a few hours, images which at the first cockcrow will vanish into the void? The nostalgia and ardent desire swelling his breast compel him to try at least to summon up a figure of that marvelous world; they force him to face every challenge, provided he can see Helen next to him, the absolute beauty, "the eternal creature, equal to the gods, great and tender, august and loving" (7440–7441).[16]

While Faust pronounces these fiery words, Goethe must be seeing himself again during the years when he lived in Italy, animated by the same enthusiastic veneration of beauty. Perhaps he sees his friend Schiller and even Hölderlin, who sang about cranes and the Archipelago's "islands in flower," thrones, temples, vases, nectar-filled song, and the silent oracles of Delphi. But his classical season now seemed to him immensely far away. Having reached eighty he had rediscovered, alongside Olympian Greece, the Greece of the *Theogony*; and many other emotions besides veneration inspired him. Irony, playfulness, a parodistic spirit; an acute historical sense that transformed even Greece's gods and heroes into historical figures, a profound mythical sense; a devotion to nature that derides all human and divine forms . . .

After having seen the archaic monsters and resisted the Sirens' temptations, Faust reaches the lower banks of the Peneus. Here he finds a soft, idyllic landscape, which Tasso would have loved. Along the river's banks the waves chatter and the wind plays, the reeds rustle, the canebrakes give off a light odor, the clumps of willow trees barely murmur, the quivering branches of the poplars accompany one's dreams. But to whom do these melodic and caressing voices belong? This *hauchen* (soughing), *säuseln* (rustling), *lispeln* (lisping), *rieseln* (rippling), *flüstern* (whispering) of all things? Perhaps only to the waves and branches, grazed by soft nocturnal winds; or among these branches, these bushes, these fragile canebrakes is hidden the ancient Peneus River, barely awakened by Seismos's jarring shocks. There, too, are the river nymphs, who invite Faust to restore his weary, restless limbs in the water's coolness.

In the landscape so similar to the one he had just dreamed of, the image of Helen's conception once again seizes Faust's mind. He is not sure it is a dream or, on the contrary, whether a memory might have accompanied him from a previous life (7275). Something in the past has found its way inside him; it has filled him, made him happy; and this vision rises to his eyes and fills his pupils. Faust cannot hide this joy in himself, just as Erichtho projected on the fields of Thessaly the memory of the battle of Pharsalus, his eyes extract the "incomparable figures" (7272) who inhabit it and project them magically on the Peneus's water and bushes.

So the empty banks are again inhabited by Sparta's noble queen, her swimming maidservants, the triumphant "prince of the swans" and his court. Faust's happy dream vision now stands before his eyes, spread over the aquatic landscape where he can contemplate it clearly. More real than a real spectacle, it seems to happen now for the first time, as if the myth had never told the story of the lovemaking of Zeus and Leda. Everything is transformed. The midday sun which, though never named, lit up Faust's mind during his dream, also shines brightly on the banks of the Peneus, for some moments blotting from the sky the moon of the eighth of August.

His description of Faust's dream had revealed in Homunculus the elegance of a painter and poet of Hellenistic training. Faust's hand is lighter and more emotional. Though almost vying with Homunculus, he retouches some of the dream's details; and he recalls more lovingly the pure depths of the water, the play of its currents, the grace of the wet, youthful limbs, the swan's triumphant movement. But we are struck above all by an omission. Whereas Homunculus had remembered the embrace of Zeus and Leda, Faust conceals Helen's mother behind a bush as if some obscure fear prevented him from extracting her from his mind and contemplating her in the river's water.

What do these dreams, which fill Faust's heart with happiness, mean? When he thinks back over Helen's conception, it seems to us that he is trying to rediscover in his own ego the "tender point" (6840) from which the incomparable figure had leaped into life. For an instant we believe that in the course of his illness he has acquired magical powers; that he might know how to give birth to Helen with the sole assistance of imagination and desire. We imagine that we shall soon see appear among the Peneus's willows and poplars "the figure of all figures" (8907), miraculously alive and real. But Faust's journey to Helen still has a long way to go and will lead him, like a second Orpheus, down into the regions of Hades. His double dream—the dream contemplated by Homunculus and the dream he has strewn on the waters—is only a slow preparation of his soul, which must dwell on Helen's birth, imbue itself with the colors of her world and anticipate her in himself, before being able to meet her on the shores of Peloponnesus, inebriated "by the waves' restless rocking" (8490).

The pounding of rapid hoofs suddenly reverberates and echoes in the night, rousing Faust from his dream. The centaur Chiron, who once ruled over Pelion's peaks, offers him his white and shining back and carries him into the vortex of the "infamous night" (7482). He never stops, he never slackens his swift pace; galloping across the Peneus, he skirts past Olympus, reaches the plain of Pidna, runs tirelessly in a circle, like the very genius of time (7332, 7479–7481).

In Pindar's verses, the very ancient mountain and rustic god possesses the sublime gift of prophecy. He knows the termination of all things and the routes they take; the number of leaves the earth puts forth in the spring and the grains of sand rolled by the waves of seas and rivers; and even Apollo, the god of divination, asked him for his prophecies. Whoever had been wounded by stone or bronze, whoever bore painful ulcers in his flesh, or was tormented by the heat of summer or the cold of winter had recourse to his mild enchantments, his bland medicines that healed diseased limbs. But Chiron possessed still rarer qualities. As the first and greatest pedagogue, endowed with unlimited goodness, wisdom, and sweetness, he trained the children of men and gods. He also sacrificed for others, as when he took on Prometheus's sufferings and descended in his stead "into lightless Hades, into Tartarus's dark pit."[17]

When he appears in *Klassische Walpurgisnacht*, Chiron simply reminds us of an amiable gentleman, a wise, skeptical educator of the period of the Enlightenment whom we could have met in Paris or London, together with Voltaire or Gibbon. Like them, he harbors certain doubts about the existence of the gods (7383–7384). He possesses no qualities of divine origin, he scorns prophetic gifts, and his ancient medical witchcraft has become a modern science (7352, 7455). The qualities he esteems are human and terrestrial: strength, decisiveness, charm, and astuteness. As for men, he has for them the same feelings of benevolence, goodwill, and irony we attribute to the most attractive figures of the eighteenth century. He protects them, helps them, educates them; he even speaks of some of them with enthusiasm. But he has no faith in humanity; he does not like the mistakes, enthusiasms, and impossible ideals that perturb our diseased minds; and a slight contempt colors his kindness.

Chiron feels ill at ease among the specters of *Klassische Walpurgisnacht*. His Enlightenment spirit is revolted by the monstrous divinities of the origins: the strident-voiced Griffins, the bestial Sphinxes, the Sirens with the feet of sparrow hawks, the Lamiae who transform themselves. If at one time he shared the gifts of the Sibyls, now he scorns their "guild" (7455–7456) and their savage dens dug in the depths of the mountains, the hundred apertures and the hundred doors. He rejects the divine delirium, the rage, fury, and anguish which swell the breast. The frightening gestures, the tangled mane, the frothing mouth, the inhuman voice pronouncing dreadful enigmas—the whole sublime and horrible ritual of the Sibyls seems to him only a grotesque theatrical machination (7456).

The world that Chiron loves is the same heroic world venerated by Faust. So, with an enthusiasm no disappointment can blemish, he recalls the "noble Argonauts": the young and ardent Dioscuri, the resolute, swift sons of Boreas, Jason, reflective, wary, beloved by women, the tender Orpheus who calmed the sea's waves with his lyre, Lynceus who scanned the distances with a look sharper than the sun, catching sight of remote shores and rocks that threatened their ship . . .[18] With a voice full of nostalgia, Chiron remembers Heracles, the most beautiful, divine man Mother Earth had ever generated, the hero statues and poets vainly tried to emulate. He recalls, too, the most beautiful woman, Helen, who when still a child had ridden on his back and stroked his mane.

But Chiron's grace does not hide the narrowness of his spirit. The Sphinxes and Sirens incarnate values he is unable to grasp; the Sibyls are possessed by divine inspiration to which he is completely alien. The heroic world, too, appears to him in an impoverished light. As he pictures her, Helen does not resemble that goddess on earth, that tragic incarnation of Beauty, who in Homer's verses conquers the souls of all those who look at her. The daughter of Zeus and Leda is merely a pretty woman, with a zest for life and joy, flattering and astute (7402–7404; 7423–7424); a figure whom we have met a thousand times in Fragonard's and Boucher's paintings and in the fashionable, worldly poems and novels of the eighteenth century.

No sooner does Chiron meet Faust than he feels great sympathy for him, and he is ready to reveal to him his own mythological knowledge. But Chiron does not understand Faust. A spirit such as his, so limited and so typical of the eighteenth century, cannot share the classical culture of this student of Winckelmann and Goethe. Faust's emotions, his religious veneration of ancient beauty, his hope of conquering fate and time and of wresting Helen's soul from the prison of Hades, seem to him the ravings of a diseased mind; and he takes him to Manto, Aesculapius's daughter, so that she might cure him with herbs and salutary waters.

If Chiron runs tirelessly in time, Manto, lost in her ecstatic dreams, lives outside history, with her eyes closed, confined within her own eternal time. If Chiron has renounced the gift of prophecy, Manto looks forward to the events her spirit has presaged (7481). Among men—all, perhaps, "rash" (7489)—she prefers the rashest ones, those who "long for the impossible" (7488), who dream of exploits superior to their powers, and who yearn, like Faust, to clasp Helen in desirous arms. So, instead of curing Faust's mind with the virtues of water and herbs, Manto helps him to realize his dreams. Many centuries before, she had led Orpheus before the throne of Persephone, among tenuous shadows and phantasms without light, numerous as the birds who hide among the leaves of the trees when the storm drives them from the mountains. Now Manto repeats the same route. She leads Faust, like a "second Orpheus," to a dark tunnel that opens at the foot of Mount Olympus and descends with him, into the abode of the queen of the nether region.

Mephistopheles's "Journey to Greece"

While the hours of the magical night give no sign of coming to an end, Mephistopheles listlessly carries out his *griechische Reise*. For the first time he becomes familiar with Greece; for the first time he sees Thessaly's mountains and plains, the Peneus's gentle banks, the fields and fires where the ghosts and witches of classical antiquity gathered. But the fresh air, the emotions and impressions of a journey which filled Faust with enthusiasm, as it would have enthused Winckelmann and Goethe, excite Mephistopheles not at all. We never hear from his mouth the words Goethe wrote from Rome to his friends in Weimar. No ancient spectacle immerses him in a bath of youthfulness, renders his spirit mobile and elastic once again, changes his skin, refreshes his eyes, smooths out the thousand wrinkles of his leathery heart. So he travels through the chaotic pit of the *Klassische Walpurgisnacht* like one of those curious, ironic, and impassive English tourists who, at the end of the eighteenth century, roamed the world to see a waterfall or a battlefield, to admire the ruins of the Baths of Caracalla, Paestum or the Parthenon, without ever relinquishing the manners of cold men of the world.

He was not pleased by Greece. Those blithe, serene sins committed without remorse; those naked figures; the immodest Sphinxes, the shameless Griffins, the shirtless Arimaspians—offend his *pruderie* as a Christian devil. The Sirens' famous trills and warblings do not move his spirit trained to listen to romantic German *Lieder*. In the end it seems to him that the whole *Klassische Walpurgisnacht* is an absurd masquerade, staged by a poet with abominable taste. As he stumbles among roots and rocks, grumbles and complains, he regrets the distant Northland, the smell of tar and sulphur of his native Harz, the old, beloved habits which he has abandoned for a few hours. That is his true homeland, and he remembers it with the nostalgia of a Philistine who feels unhappy as soon as he leaves the door of his house behind him, with the regret of an Adam driven from his earthly paradise.

As soon as he sees the Lamiae, lewd and brazen as prostitutes, he is unable to restrain himself; he hopes to experience with them the extraordinary erotic joy promised him by Homunculus; and he pursues them, dragging his stiff horse's hoofs. They flee from him and draw farther and farther away; they dance around him; they woo him, invite him, and maliciously excite him. When he succeeds in getting among them and stretches out his hands, the first beautiful Lamia is turned into a dried-out broom; the second shows him a repulsive face; the third slithers through his hands like a lizard; another, long and thin, becomes a thyrsus wand with a fir cone instead of a head. Still another, fat, round, plump, and full-bellied like a harem beauty, splits in two and disintegrates into dust. Finally, all together, they trace rapid, ghastly rings, skimming like black horrible bats around the "witch's son" who has penetrated into a world that is not his. On the soil of Greece, the lord

GOETHE

of appearances and metamorphoses is defeated by his own weapons; mocked at by demons who transform themselves in even more disconcerting ways than he.

Nothing contents and satisfies his embittered spirit. If he were seized by one of those grandiose moments of fury, sarcasm, and cynicism in which he demonstrates his genius, the spectacles of the *Klassische Walpurgisnacht* would have enchanted him. When that occurs, "wrathful Plutonic fire" erupts from the bowels of the earth; the ground swells under his feet; a mountain is born in an instant, meteors whistle across the sky as though all of nature were obeying the spirit of fire, violence, and destruction that Mephistopheles bears within him. But in Greece, as he stumbles over the rocky ground, not even the flames please him, and the ground's continual agitation and boiling annoys him. If he could listen to them, the speeches of his pupil Anaxagoras would provoke him to one of those irritated gestures of superiority caused by the speeches of presumptuous children.

In Greece, completely denying his own revolutionary past, Mephistopheles reveals to us only his nature as a conservative who loves immutable things such as the rocks of the Blocksberg and the slopes of the Pindus crowned by ancient oaks. Unfortunately, the exigencies of the play and Faust's demands force him to rush toward some unimaginable reincarnation. If he could stop, if destiny did not also oblige him to undertake so many futile journeys through the world, he would have found his ideal spot: the upper banks of the Peneus, where the Sphinxes stay—indeed, "my Sphinxes," as he calls them with an extremely warm and unusual upsurge of emotion (7689, 7806). He could remain there, where nothing changes in aspect, where nothing changes its place, where the world rests firmly on its foundation of granite, eternally solving riddles and charades with the Sphinxes and discussing God's strange pleasures.

The old pilgrim who ventured to the farthest eastern tip of the world, where the sun's flaming steps strike the soil, who crossed the ocean's tides and bore the furious noise of the crashing waves, ended up reaching the dark fields of Cistene. In those desolate places beyond the frontier of the night, never reached by even a glance of sun and moon, lived the three daughters of Phorcys and Ceto. Three old virgins whose hair was gray since birth and who draped beautiful crocus-colored veils around their elegant, sinuous, swanlike bodies. Medusa, their sister with whom they shared the same parents, could petrify with a look. And they, too, were flawed, their senile beauty marred. The three Phorkyads possessed but a single eye, which they lent each other to peer at the night's darkness; and a single tooth, which they passed from mouth to mouth.

Clambering up Pindus's slopes, Mephistopheles catches sight of the myth's three old sisters in a cave barely lit by the moon. But where are the "lovely cheeks," dear to Hesiod, the "swan's bodies" praised by Aeschylus, and the precious crocus-colored veils? That single eye and that single tooth in the probably monstrous faces, the shapes of bats and vampires, the chirping and hissing of nocturnal birds, the slithering, snakelike movements of the Phorkyads revolt even the lord of flies and mice. Just as the mystic tries to approach God's essence by multiplying metaphors and vocatives, so Mephistopheles seeks to accumulate examples of horror. He remembers mandrakes, the most abominable sins, the monsters who live on the threshold of the nether regions. Vying with him, Helen's maidservants evoke the calamities of war, the bronze voice of Discord, the stalking of irate gods among the flames that destroyed Troy (8704 ff.). All is in vain. The ugliness of the Phorkyads is so frightful it surpasses the delirium of the most corrupt human mind, the abject imagination of a devil; it even defeats the efforts of any language.

The real father of the three bat-vampires is not Phorcys, the god of the sea; nor is the mother Ceto of the lovely cheeks, as Hesiod had recounted. The genealogy, which Goethe works out for them, is infinitely more flattering. When the universe did not yet exist, Chaos, who was born before all else, generated them "in the portentous womb of ancient Night"; and Night gave birth to them together with a cortege · of terrors which, from then on, continued to traverse the earth like the fumes of fire (8010, 8028, 8649, 8665, 8812).[19] Later, light gleamed over the darkness: Elohim separated water and the earth, hung the sun and the moon in the firmament, created fishes, reptiles, domestic animals, and man; and the creatures assumed a form and were blessed by the light. But, at least in one place in the world, in Pindar's gloomy cave, in that sordid "temple" (7983), where the three Phorkyads twitter and hiss, Chaos and Night maintain their ancient rights. While gods and men have a distinct body, a persona, a name, and consciousness, the three sisters live sunk in the formless indistinctness of the origins. Their limbs are monstrously confused in a single serpentine tangle, their persons without name dissolve in an undifferentiated trinity, their consciousness is not yet awakened (8011). Someone has given them the gift of speech, perhaps only to appear in *Faust*. And yet, what use can they make of speech in the darkness that enfolds their existence on all sides, insinuates itself in their thoughts, obfuscates their emotions, and dazes them with its terrible fascination?

The kinship between Mephistopheles and the Phorkyads is much closer than he would like to think. Daughters of Chaos and the Night, the Phorkyads are not, as he says, his "distant relations," (7987), but

GOETHE

rather his maternal and paternal sisters, or, if we wish to accept another genealogy, both his sisters and his aunts (7990). As he looks into their cave, he is contemplating his own origins; he experiences the same freezing Chaos, the same desolate darkness that still lives within him; but purer, more profound and unconscious, as it was before his rationalism began to limit it. This spectacle of antiquity and horror fascinates him; this dark trinity leaves him speechless; and his emotions are like those Faust felt for the Mothers: a shudder of horror (7968), a profound astonishment (7969), wonder and ecstatic silence (7993).

Even this time Mephistopheles is true to himself. The journey to his origins, his descent into the Night from which he has sprung, takes place entirely under the sign of the grotesque and parody.[20] After halting at the entrance to the cave, Mephistopheles advances into the darkness, bows before the three sisters, indeed the three "very honorable," "very venerable" ladies (7984, 7997), and introduces himself as prescribed by the etiquette of the abyss. He has known many ancient divinities, he says—Ops, Rhea, and the Parcae—but he has never contemplated divinities such as they, capable of arousing such ecstatic admiration. And yet no poet has celebrated them in his songs; no chisel has ever tried to shape in marble the lineaments of their nocturnal trinity. Why do they live so far from the world, in that solitary "temple," hidden from the eyes of artists and admirers? More worthy places exist. Like the great goddesses, like Pallas, Venus, and Juno, they should live in one of those cities "where art and splendor reign on the selfsame throne" (8005). Where every day an artist sculpts a god or a hero in a block of marble. There some Praxiteles or Apelles could figure forth their immortal features.

Immured in their hovel, the three old sisters gladly listen to the voice that breaks the silence of centuries. Mephistopheles's virile compliments flatter them; and they hand around the single eye so as to see their unexpected guest. Perhaps, for a few instants, the Phorkyads' torpid imagination fondles the invitation of their infernal brother; and dreams of the unknown pleasures of the large cities and glory. But the sisters soon overcome this flattery. Daughters of the Night, they must remain eternally buried "in solitude and the most silent night"; joined to nocturnal things, unknown to everyone, and almost unknown to themselves.

Mephistopheles is not discouraged. Since the Phorkyads do not care to pose in the sculptors' studios, they could concentrate their mythological essence in only two figures and entrust the third figure to him, who thus would become their living image. Nothing prevents the three sisters from accepting Mephistopheles's new proposal. Faithful to their destiny, they will remain enclosed in the temple, while the new sister will conquer for them a small fame, perhaps even glory, in the distant world of men. Goethe does not explain to us what happens in the Pindus cave. How does one of the three Phorkyads succeed in canceling herself and being reborn in Mephistopheles's body? What happens at the moment when the two natures—Greek and Christian, male and female—merge in a single person? We only know that, as on so many other occasions, Mephistopheles has recourse to his talents as a mime and illusionist. Before the attentive eye of the Phorkyads, who help him with their advice, he recites his latest role. He shuts an eye, displays only one of his enormous incisors; he lets us see only his diabolic profile; and behold! his lineaments are confused with those of a Phorkyad.[21]

So, for the first time in the history of mythology, the daughters of Chaos and Night possess an image; they have found a living form, not less splendid than a masterpiece in marble. In a short while, through another person, they will make their appearance on the world's stage, and they will admire the radiant light of that sun which, so many centuries before, defeated Chaos and Night. Mephistopheles goes through an equally extraordinary metamorphosis. He leaves the North's ice and mist, his dear German cities, the ancient Gothic churches that protected him with their shadows; and he transforms himself into an ancient Greek goddess. While Faust and Manto descend toward the throne of Persephone, Mephistopheles hastens to reach the royal palace of Sparta. There, squatting like a servant near the hearth, he waits for Helen to return from the plains of Hades.

The Lunar Dew

As Pliny tells us, the ancient scholars and simple wayfarers, who enjoyed roaming about at night, beneath the pure brightness of a cloudless sky, contemplated the moon with a mixture of admiration and anguish. All the other stars—the sun which shines at the peak of space; white, cold, icy Saturn; mild and beneficent Jupiter; fiery Mars; Venus with its luminous rays; and Mercury—remain equal to themselves; yet who can calculate the incessant variety, the disquieting multiplicity of the moon's metamorphoses? Never immobile, forever growing or diminishing, now it traces a light, delicate sickle, now it exhibits the rotundity of a perfect circle, now half of itself; and now it disappears completely

GOETHE

from sight, as though it had never consoled the horror of our sleep. Sometimes it shows us a misty surface, covered with shadows and blotches, obfuscated by some unknown malady. Sometimes it illumines us with so clear and radiant a light that no shadow seems able to dim it. Now it watches over us throughout the night, like the most faithful of terrestrial sentinels. Perhaps it rises late, as if it were oppressed by a burden or a monstrous exertion, yet during the day it adds its light to that of the sun. At certain periods of the month it rises in space, at others it descends; but it isn't even regular in this because at times it goes to the very summit of the sky, then close to the mountains, elevated to the north or lowered to the south.

To what species of beings does this multiform and changing planet belong? Many believe that the queen of night is a true divinity, like the sun and the stars. But if Selene is a goddess, her worshippers should multiply the names they use to invoke her, to fit the multiplicity of appellations to the multiplicity of her forms. Like Lucius, at the end of Apuleius's *Golden Ass,* they called her sublime Ceres, celestial Venus, Artemis the protectress of women's birth pangs, and Proserpine. And they added still other names, almost exhausting the repertory of the Grecian-Oriental Olympus—Cybele, Minerva, the Paphos Venus, Diana Dictynna, Juno, Bellona, Hecate, Ramusia, and Isis . . . Many thought she was only a daimonic being, composed of equal and unequal things, of mortal passions and divine virtues. Then, as Macrobius writes in a passage well known to Goethe, we must see in her the mistress of ιυχη, "destiny," and expect from her all the innumerable pranks and caprices of chance. When we lift our eyes to Selene—as St. Basil and St. Ambrose commented—we see reflected the misery of passion and human affairs. They change, wax and wane, rise from nothing to perfection only to be consumed and destroyed, to assume ever new faces, aspects, and incarnations, subject—like the moon—to the single law of senseless inconstancy.

From the very inception of Greek scientific speculation, the astronomers—those Pliny symbolized in the figure of Endymion, who was attracted to and enamoured of the celestial queen—tried to discover the moon's substance. As happens in face of great mysteries or nearby and unfathomable things, their imaginations proposed hypotheses, refuted them, and advanced new ones, proposed again the old hypotheses, tried out the most ingenious and absurd combinations, which now intertwine before our eyes in the writings of the pre-Socratic thinkers and those of Posidonius, Pliny, Plutarch, Cicero, and Ptolemy, composing the most varicolored, fantastic tapestries. Some of them thought the moon's substance is the same as that of the stars: fire or pure ether, air and gentle fire, or a denser, colder fire than the sun's. Some considered it a star of the second magnitude, weary, feeble, and impure; the air that composes it is dirty and dark, like terrestrial air, afflicted by clouds and exhalations. Its murky flame, some said, burns in slow combustion, like the piles of carbonized and smoking firewood that mark the passage of shepherds and their flocks. Finally, others imagined it to be similar to our Earth—an "ethereal earth," no less venerable than a star, although it could not exhibit the mystical Oriental privilege of fire. Yet perhaps, the moon's body is not composed of fire or earth. Perhaps that arid globe watching us coldly from on high is made of congealed air, hailstones caught in a sphere of fire; or of pumice stone so porous it receives the light of the ether in itself. Perhaps that radiant body is made of glass, and it reflects the images and sights it receives from the entire universe with a fidelity much superior to that of our mirrors; or it is an immense, round, compact, and heavy cloud, each day extinguished and set afire again.

The ancient astronomers' imagination grew bolder. They began drawing the surface of the moon with the attentiveness with which the geographer draws on his globe the unexplored region he has just discovered. So those who thought that it was ethereal earth, discovered in it declivities and planes, inlets, cavities, and chasms; and described "regions of marvelous beauty, flaming mountains, and purple-colored areas, with gold and silver not scattered in the depths but which crop up abundantly like flowers in the plains or are visible on the smooth heights" (Plutarch, *De facie*, 935 A). Up there no cloud obscures the view; a tenuous air soughs, and tepid winds, loving breezes caused by the large body's regular movement, strew about dew and a light dampness sufficient to nourish roots and trees of every species. While the stars do not know all the terrestrial colors, every nuance of the spectrum gleams on the moon: a dreadfully somber black during the evening eclipse; a cerulean or bluish hue, like cyanose, during the eclipses of dawn; the same "wine-dark" color Homer attributes to the sea; a whiteness purer than milk; a brighter gold, a more delicate green . . . And yet the mystery continued to tempt audacious scientific conjectures. The dark blotches that shadowed Selene and at times appeared to imitate the eyes, nose, and lips of a bizarre human face, seemed to defy any plausible interpretation. What are these strange shapes? Do they perhaps like a mirror reflect the full tides and voids, the coasts, the abysses, gulfs, and isthmuses chiseled by the oceans on the earth's body? Or does the air of our globe, laden with filth and debris, rise up on high, besmearing the beautiful, unprotected face of the moon? Or is the lunar atmosphere agitated by sudden changes continually darkening it, like the sea when a ripple runs over its surface?

Despite this host of questions, certainties, and hypotheses, the chief

GOETHE

interest of astronomers and wayfarers who watched the heavens was something quite different. They were impassioned by the problem of the relationship between Helios and Selene, between Phoebus and Artemis, between brother and sister, as Sirens and Telchines will soon sing in the last hours of the Aegean festival. On one point all ancient writers agree. While the sun embodies the masculine principle, the moon represents the feminine one. "After chaos," Macrobius tells us, "when confused deformity begins for the first time to glisten in the different forms of things and the elements . . . the ethereal heat gradually augments its power; and from the fiery, burning seeds which descend onto the Earth are born—so it is believed—these two stars: the sun, which had received the greatest quantity of heat, was dragged into the upper regions, while the moon, detained by a more humid warmth and by its female sex, so to speak, occupied the lower regions; as though he especially preserved the substance of the father and she that of the mother" (*Saturnalia* I, XVII, 53). Thus the two stars share the characteristics of the two sexes: Helios assumes the generative and active functions and Selene the receptive and passive ones. When the sun's rays touch her surface, she receives them in her soft and yielding substance, as a mushroom absorbs water. She lets herself be penetrated by them and sends them, mixed perhaps with her own light, to the earth's anxious surface.

In this relationship the sun reveals his ambiguous character. Certainly, nobody could live without the "breath and brightness of the world," without the father of sea and soil. No life could subsist without his eye, open and flaming like the lion's, eternally embracing the earth with its unwearying stare. But those ardent and fiery beams which give life also take it away; those "points sharper and more pitiless" than the arrows of war kill everything they encounter in their passage. They burn, dry up, wither, wipe out the flourishing vegetation, render the soil arid and uninhabitable; they help "the dry, igneous, and parched" to triumph, where the sweet maternal power of humidity once reigned. If Typhon—the sun's negative aspect—does not encounter obstacles to his predominance, the breezes push the enfeebled Nile, contracted in a wretched, half-empty bed, toward the sea. The earth is stripped, the night grows longer, darkness increases, trees let their leaves fall and light's very force seems wan and annihilated. Lucan imagined the moment in which the parching tension of the sun, having completely drained the Syrtes, had consumed all the waters of our globe. To the potent and terrible face of her great brother, the moon counterposes her mild and benign figure—tepid or cold, like everything that is feminine. As soon as the solar light reaches it and spreads in that unsubstantial, translucid air, no obstacle augments or conserves its heat. The rays lose their fire, weaken, languish, and attenuate; just as voices attenuate when reflected in an echo, or as a fire striking a mirror from afar relays only its gleam, not its burning heat.

While the "dry" element comes from the sun, the "humid" element derives from the moon. The sun as well as the stars draw their alimentation and nutriment from terrestrial waters, and they have no other means to subsist and regenerate themselves. If the sun absorbs the saline waves of the sea, the moon feeds avidly on the sweet, soft exhalations that swamps, lakes, rivers, and springs send up to her as a tribute. When she wanes, when her globe thins down and grows pale in the sky, tending to consumption of herself, she is "dry" and "thirsty" *(sicca, sitiens)* like someone who has not drunk enough. But there is a substantial difference. Terrestrial humidity in the sun and stars is completely converted into the ardor of fire and ether; on the moon, it is not entirely consumed, or it is added to the copious springs that bathe it or actually form its substance. During the last centuries of the classical age, this idea of selenic humidity became a matter of common knowledge: Philolaus had already maintained that there is water in such abundance on the moon that one day it would bring about the end of the world; Plutarch insisted that Selene is a "gentle and watery" planet; and Methodius of Olympus asserted that "every form of humidity comes from Selene." The Manicheans and Martianus Capella took the final step: If the sun, the first said, is composed *"ex igneo bono,"* the queen of night is composed *"ex bona aqua."* It is a very tender body—the second adds —formed from the immaculate lightness of celestial dew.

During the splendid nights of full moon, when the sky is without clouds and not the slightest breath of wind breaks the interminable quiet, Selene particularly exerts her influence on earth. Then, extracting from it her very substance or mixing the heat of the sun with the exhalations of our rivers, she sends us an abundant "dew," which traverses the silence of the spaces together with her limpid, feminine light. Tepid as water barely set on the stove, this dew bathes and penetrates living things, and suckles them like a mother, warming them slowly. In this way, the moon renews her antithetic position to that of the sun. All the humidity the sun absorbs during the day, she restores at night, pouring out the treasure of her dew. While the sun contracts, she expands and relaxes; while the virile action of her celestial brother condenses and concentrates, the occult, insinuating activity of the sister releases, loosens, relaxes, frees, fuses, softens, and dissolves. So Pliny comments and Goethe could as well, since he conceived of reality according to the same fundamental principles, that is, that "Nature's

GOETHE

alternations"—the force of tension and the force of relaxation, the force of concentration and the force of resolution—follow and balance each other, assuring all that is necessary to the quotidian functioning of the world.

With the loving and scrupulous pleasure encyclopedic writers devote to the concrete as well as extravagant facts of our life, Plutarch and Macrobius, Aulus Gellius and St. Basil, St. Ambrose, and Anastasius Sinaita described the lunar influence on the terrestrial surface. Each detail was polished like the tessera of a mosaic, brought to the intangible perfection of the *topos,* knotted into a chain of other details, declined like the beads of a rosary. Then other writers, years or centuries later, again proposed the same *exempla* to an equally fascinated public. Without cruelty or violence, Selene's watery and expansive rays melt ice, soften the wood in trees, favor female menstruation, facilitate birth deliveries. They putrefy meats and foodstuffs; they have an influence on children's organisms, causing the flexibility of their bodies, the rapid growth and imperfect, disjointed condition of their souls. Also the movements of the tides—that swelling and falling, that disquieted, laborious panting of the waters, attracted by a force larger than themselves—come from the moon's liquefying action. But it would be wrong to abandon oneself incautiously to Selene's influence. In that complicated system of weights and counterweights, of forces and counterforces which is the classical cosmos, each principle contains its own danger. He who sleeps for long beneath her light, especially on the beneficent and maleficent nights of full moon, will awaken stunned, overcome by an intolerable torpor of the senses, capable of flinging him into the wildest insanity; for the rays open and dilate all the body's pores, through which the humidity penetrates deeply, to the point of altering the organism's equilibrium. As for suckling babies whom wet nurses leave for a few instants in the lunar atmosphere, their fate is sealed. Attacked by new humors, their slight limbs, already rich in so many natural liquids, are deformed and twisted, just as wood still green and moist bends in the heat of the fire.

On the other hand, these effects vary according to the moon's different phases. In the first quarter, the moon moistens things; in the second quarter when the moon puts on her luminous garb and begins to shine in her full roundness in the sky, she warms the terrestrial surface. Then, while she gradually strips off her clothes and seems obscured and as though widowed of light until she vanishes from space, she causes drought, aridity, and even cold inclement weather. So the moon reveals her influence on the genesis and unfolding of all things, above all in her first phases. Then she is truly *"mortalium corporum et auctor et conditrix,"* as Macrobius calls her, *"humanorum corporum mater,"* as Fir-

micus Maternus invokes her; *"rerum naturae parens, elementorum om-
nium domina, saeculorum progenies initialis,"* as she defines herself in
Apuleius's *Golden Ass.* When she waxes, all the bodies thronging the
land and sea swell and fill together with her. Her light satiates the clods
of earth, warms the seeds, makes the grass livelier, reinvigorates the
roots, rounds out fruits on trees and vines. Her luminescence makes the
blood in men's veins run more copiously, and favors the conception of
children and animals. During these fecund days of germination, who in
the vast terrestrial world escapes her influence? Even oysters, molluscs,
and sea urchins, clinging to the rocks and in the sea, acquire new flesh
and new juice. The pupil of that lunar animal the cat, so iridescent and
nocturnal, becomes wider and rounder; ants work actively even at
night. Flour kneaded by the baker's industrious hands ferments without
yeast; certain fishes of Gaul turn white; the stones in the Istaspe River
give off a harmonious sound . . .

When however the moon falls to her consumption, bodies diminish,
grow lighter, and are hollowed out. The soil becomes dry, the growth
of seeds and fruits slows, the body's blood thins, the flesh of oysters and
sea urchins grows lean and juiceless, the cat's pupil shrinks and darkens,
ants rest, fish turn black, the stones of the Istaspe become mute. And
if Selene vanishes from the sky, the Egyptian Ibis shuts its eyes and
takes no food, as if to share the grief of nature over the absence of the
mother of bodies and the mistress of the elements. This universal "sympathy" suffers a strange exception. Only the onion germinates and
flowers when the moon wanes, and diminishes when it waxes. As a
result, both Plutarch and Aulus Gellius report, Egyptian priests abstain
from mixing this impious and absurd vegetable in their food, since it
stubbornly opposes the natural rhythm of all things.

Having studied the moon in her relations with the sun, the ancient
astronomers tried to look more deeply into the whole treasure of "ardent luminaries," "eternally fragrant roses," and "vivid necklaces"
decorating the celestial spaces. The eye followed the relations among
the stars; it considered the links keeping the zodiacal system united,
and the bond tying stars to earth and bringing sun and earth together.
Each time they proposed the same symbol for meditation. If the universe is a great harmony, from the center to the extremities and from
the extremities to the center, if the sea and the land, the icy roughness
of the air and the surge of fire, the distant Milky Way and the sun,
Saturn and Jupiter merge their tones as one mixes Doric and Lydian
harmonies—then the moon is the key to this system of harmonies. The
principle of mediation, which upholds and administers the cosmos, finds
its very heart in her gentle feminine form.

The moon occupies an extreme position in the play of astral forces.

GOETHE

Above her begins the ether's brightness without shadow and without night, where all is immutable, uncorrupted, and divine. Below her begins the terrestrial realm of shadows, in which live mutable objects, deceitful, illusory, and rife with errors. So, last among the stars but close to the earth (or, as others insist, "ethereal earth"), she performs a double task. On the one hand, she oversees the sublunar world of birth and death, of generation and corruption. On the other, she mediates between the stellar universe and human life. She destroys everything in our world that tends to the savage and confused; she transmits to our minds, souls, and bodies the benefits and graces that descend from the highest supracelestial intelligence. But Posidonius attributes another mediating virtue to her. If the sun is the heart of the universe and distributes its heat and light almost as though they were blood and breath, the land and sea serve the cosmos in the way that the viscera and bladder serve animals. Halfway between these two poles, stands the moon performing the same functions as the liver in the human body. She transmits solar heat to us and terrestrial humidity to the stars; and meanwhile she elaborates, purifies, and refines, like the finest filter, everything that high and low continually send her.

Whoever mediates between the extremes of the world can only placate and mitigate the profound disquiet of things. What happens, in fact, at the end of each month? As soon as the moon leaves space empty —only a trace, a very labile sign indicates her remote presence—the temperature drops several degrees. Bad weather rages, clouds chase each other and clash. The waves of the sea, especially in straits and gulfs, begin an irresistible movement and agitation, until the nocturnal star reappears, assuring some regularity to the ebb and flow. Selene's true image is only manifested if the sky is completely serene; then she reveals her essence to human eyes. When the clouds rush like witches from some parts of the west, obscuring her, their triumph is brief. The winds, allies of the moon, chase them, shatter them, persecute them to the most distant horizon, and make her radiance shine out as before. In fact, the feast of Isis—the *Navigium Isidis*—was celebrated as soon as the winter storms were mitigated. On that day everything expressed happiness. "Drawn by the spring breezes, the songbirds intoned sweet chords, their insinuating speech caressing the mother of the stars and the mistress of the entire universe. The trees, not only those with fruitful buds but also sterile ones that gratify only with their shade, abandoning themselves to the south wind's breath and gleaming with the sheen of newly budding leaves, waved their branches with a soft, clement motion and gave off a pleasant rustling sound: the sea, having quieted the tempest's great roar and placated the waves' turbid swelling, resumed its quiet flow; while the sky, once all the cloudy mist was

dispersed, shone pure and serene in the splendor of its own light"
(Apuleius, *Golden Ass*, XI, 7).

The last questions confronted by the ancient astronomers touch our lives even more closely. What passion and desire, similar to human passions and desires, move the astral creatures? Do the sun's dry rays and the moon's tepid rays kiss? Does the earth reflect its mountains and oceans in Selene's enamoured face? Does the same alternation of encounters and separations, embraces and farewells which rules earthly loves, have its repercussions among the "eternally fragrant roses" and "vivid necklaces" of the stellar garden? Since our world is an imitation of the supralunary world, an incessant dance goes on among the flowers of the celestial meadow. Now the moon chases the sun, full of desire and attracted by everything divine shining in the figure of her older brother; now she runs away from him, like a wayward girl, and in the same way the sun flees and pursues her. Finally, on the day of the new moon, when the sky is empty and men tremble at the thought that perhaps that absence will be forever renewed and the dew will never again fall to moisten the world, behind the night's dark curtains takes place the encounter (ὀυνουϐια, the "coitus") between Helios and Selene, in which the brother pours the fecundating germ into his sister's womb. Meanwhile, another longer, slower pursuit traverses space. Demeter and Persephone, the mother and daughter of whom the myths tell stories, are images of earth and moon; and from the time they were separated when Persephone was carried off—was it an abduction as in the legend or a cosmic catastrophe?—they deeply miss each other, wander about and search for each other. Their encounter occurs every six months, and the mother welcomes and lovingly embraces the daughter with her shadow, eclipsing her face from human eyes. So nobody can be amazed that Selene is invoked in connection with all amorous matters, and that every sort of erotic spell is prepared beneath her protection.

Perhaps Selene also knows a sublimer form of love. When she is eclipsed, she slowly begins to lose her splendor. A bloody, then an ever darker, more blackish hue besmears her face; and finally that accomplished sphere of light, that tender globe of dew disappears for some time. Religious terror then grips men's hearts; nor does the furious sound of bronze instruments succeed in bringing them help and save her from the darkness enveloping her. During these hours of anguish, the queen of heaven suffers—according to Greek and Latin writers— her *labores:* labors, travails, sweats, and pains, which we must perhaps imagine as graver and more terrible than those suffered by any human creature.

But St. Ambrose interprets these *labores* in a much more significant manner when he alludes to the *"grande mysterium"* accomplished when the planet wanes or is eclipsed. Does the moon sacrifice and immolate herself for us? Does she diminish and disappear only to give new life to the exhausted elements? Are the pains of the moon only an announcement of Christ's ever renewed sacrifice? "The moon is diminished so that she may replenish the elements. This, therefore, is the great mystery. This was given her by him who gave grace to all. He lessened her so as to replenish he who also diminished himself to replenish all. Indeed, he diminished himself in order to descend to us, descended to us so as to ascend for all . . . Therefore the moon announced the mystery of Christ" (*Exameron*, IV, 8, 32). Neither Plutarch nor Macrobius, though open to every form of allegorical interpretation, would have understood these sentences. Here our circle is closed: The moon is no longer either a goddess or a demon, she is not a star of fire, earth, congealed air or glass. Completely abandoning her corporeal guise, she hovers in the sky like the symbol of a deed that cannot be exhausted by human words.[22]

The Miracle of the Sirens

The last part of the *Klassische Walpurgisnacht*—the most splendid in colors and melodies, the richest in profound meanings—takes place beneath the protection of the queen of night whom we have just celebrated. When Thales and Homunculus leave the realm of rocks, the violences of Plutonic fire, the battles of pygmies and cranes, and finally reach the shores of the Aegean Sea, the moon shines high in the sky's summit, as though she will never set again. They had seen her appear over the head of Erichtho, while the plain of Pharsalus seemed to burn with the fires of the Roman bivouacs; they had seen her hover and sway ironically over the prayers of Anaxagoras; her light had even penetrated into the cave of the Phorkyads; but now there is no place on earth that does not bear her mark. "From the arch of her night" (8037), the moon serenely contemplates the trembling waters swelling in fragile waves on the shore. She lights up the happy teeming, the free tumult of life, rising joyously from the depths of the ocean. With the etched clarity of her rays, she limns the coasts and winding inlets of the Aegean, the sea rocks on which the Sirens are stretched, the narrow tongue of sand where Homunculus has just stopped with Thales. Farther off, along the line of the horizon, she bathes the island of Samothrace where the Cabiri are honored, the blessed soil of Rhodes, and the island of Cyprus where Aphrodite is venerated.

The moon that appears at the end of *Klassische Walpurgisnacht* is still the ancient classical divinity of Plutarch and Macrobius: the same goddess who, in Apuleius's *Golden Ass*, emerged from the sea, illuminating "the silent mysteries of the shadowy night" with the extraordinary whiteness of her globe. Like Selene, Goethe's moon is a mild feminine figure *(Luna,* not *Mond)*, who tempers and mediates the power of the sun, that "boundless sea of fire" (4710) which blinds our eyes and kills our hopes. The same friendship ties her to the world of water. If Goethe says nothing of her own lakes and rivers, he reminds us twice that she is mirrored in the waves (7513, 8039), as if only in the "sweet humidity" (8458) from which life is perhaps born can she find the element that resembles herself. And, what matters most of all, on the lips of the Sirens we hear the final testimony, conserved for us in Western poetry, of a very ancient belief whose first expression can be found in Alcman's verses. Like Virgil and Philo, like Isidorus of Seville and Martianus Capella, the Sirens celebrate the moon's "sacred dew" (7514) which bathes and fecundates all things.

The friendship that ties moon and water together is perhaps deeper in Goethe's verses than in the classical sources. The "soft air" Homunculus breathes on the small beach, the "perfume," the ineffable vapor spread all around him by young, greening vegetation (8265–70); the impression, which Goethe can summon up in a few verses, of being enveloped by "sweet humidity," the "humidity of life" (8458, 8461), from which new creatures gush out and suddenly grow—this whole tangle of sensations derives from the fact that the lunar dew dissolves in the waves, which die out slowly on the shores. But there is something else. If this encounter between two different sources of life—between the tepid light and water swarming with light—had not taken place, at the end of the sea festival, when Homunculus dies and is resurrected on Galatea's seashell, we could not contemplate the mysteries of the origins of existence.

The correspondences between classical myth and the Goethean myth are not ended. Like Selene, the star of the Aegean festival blesses every form of Eros. The obscure, hindered, eternally nostalgic love of the first three Cabiri; the paternal and filial love of Nereus and Galatea who, like Demeter and Persephone, meet only after long separations; the love of the Dorides and the young sailors; the love of the white doves of Paphos consecrated to Aphrodite; the love that Homunculus feels for the illimitable richness of the All—are all intertwined, transforming the Aegean festival into a single celebration of lunar, aquatic Eros. Meanwhile, as this correspondence of hearts and beings makes the surface of the world vibrate, the moon soothes the tempests of land and sea, as happened during the *Navigium Isidis*. During the last hours of the mythical night, all demonic forces seem to have been exorcised. The moon forgets her Hecate face, and Seismos ceases to agitate the ground. The fury of the waves subsides, no longer wrecking ships and forcing the Nereids to take refuge at the bottom of the sea (8407, 8183, 8277–8282); nor are sailors lost because of the Sirens' seductions. All is placated, benign, friendly (8181, 8264), awaiting only the supreme pacification among the elements, which will be announced with the sacrifice of Homunculus.

But, at least at one point, Goethe seeks to vie with and surpass the classical myth. As we have seen, the Thessalian witches, mentioned several times in the *Klassische Walpurgisnacht* (7920–7924, 8034–8036), divert Selene from her path. With the help of the "rhomb" and magic formulas, they forced her to come down to earth where she grew pale and foamed on the grass. Now, during the Aegean festival, a new miracle takes place. Implored by the enthusiastic song of the Sirens, the bay's "demons" and priestesses, the moon consents to halt in the sky, motionless at the zenith, interrupting its course, on the basis of which men measure the days and months. So the night is prolonged for a few hours, and the "legions of Hellenic saga" are not driven off by the light of day. The two miracles are opposed to each other, like good and evil, light and darkness. The perverse magic of the Thessalian witches insulted and raped nature, casting horror and terror on the earth and breaking the rhythm of time to create disasters and disorders. The miracle of the Sirens—obtained without the help of magic, by the pure virtue of prayer—has only beneficent effects. The tranquil and radiant light descending on all things from the moon still at the zenith, for a few hours rescues our world from the prison of history and takes us into that infinitely prolonged moment which is the time of myth and solemn rites.

The great mythical spectacle to which we are all invited as "miraculous guests," is about to begin. Descending to the small strip of sand along with Thales and Homunculus, we too watch the splendid processions and choreographies of the divinities over waves bathed by the moon. We listen to the sounds of the flute, the elegant recitatives, duets, quartets, and full-voiced choruses of the mythical figures assembled from every part of the world. Before us lies the open sea, furrowed by thousands of Greek ships, trading and pirating; the sea that was thronged with Persian ships, Roman triremes, Genoan, Venetian, and Turkish galleys; the sea Hermes skimmed at great speed, carrying

Zeus's messages. And yet who can escape the impression of being in an enclosed spot and of seeing with a single glance all the processions and divinities, even the islands of Samothrace, Rhodes, and Cyprus filling the back of the scene like the magical views of mirages produced in a play on the stage?

A similar spectacle had occurred in the theater which two Florentine architects constructed in the park of the *Buen Retiro*. One evening in August 1635 the guests of Spain's Philip IV admired for the first time Calderon's *El mayor encanto Amor*. When the show was coming to an end, the imperial director removed the back of the stage, as if it were a flat: the stage grew larger, lost its fictitious character and the trees of the great park and an artificial lake appeared before the spectators' eyes. On the lake, the court's pyrotechnician created an ingenious spectacle of fire, which seemed to be burning the dark blue plains of the ocean and Ulysses's ship, ready to set out for his native land. But at this point Galatea appeared on a triumphal car, pulled by two dolphins and accompanied by a retinue of Tritons and Sirens with musical instruments, who swiftly cleaved the water's "silver" and "glass." The flames died and went out; the ship hoisted its sail; and Circe's enchanted palace vanished in a cloud of dust. A volcano rose in its place, vomiting fire against the moon and sun.[23]

At the beginning of *Faust*'s spectacle, the Sirens are lying on the rocks in the bay, looking down from on high at the approaching processions. The festival that is about to take place in the Aegean is their festival; they supervise it as priestesses of moon and water, and perhaps as very powerful witches, capable of arresting the stars. This bay is their temple, the theater of their solemn rites. Stretched on the rocks, the Sirens pray to, invoke, and praise "the beautiful Moon," "the sweet Moon"; and the words that flower on their lips are so ardent and deeply felt that they will be heard again from Doctor Marianus when he glorifies the Virgin (8034 ff.; 8078 ff.; 8206 ff.; 8285 ff.; 8339 ff.).[24] But the Sirens do not gaze at the summit of the world. Like heralds in a carnival masquerade, they announce and describe the groups as they move by; like soloists in a concert, they accompany the choreographies with the flute's melting sounds. Now their voices weave together with the deeper voices of the Tritons and Nereids, or are lost in the unanimous chorus of all the creatures. Now their sound stands out sharply like the voice of a famous soprano. They are like a skilled choirmaster who begins and leads a hymn to the mystery of the elements.

When the scene begins, the Sirens' music reaches the marine abyss where the dwellers of the deep have sought refuge from storms. Succumbing to their appeal, the Nereids and Tritons, decorated with chains of gold, diadems, precious buckles and belts, rise to the surface. But they remain for only an instant near the Sirens' rocks. Soon, Nereids and Tritons are again in the bay, returning from the island of Samothrace; they glide over the waves like very white sails pushed by the wind, bearing in their hands a gigantic sea turtle shell on which stand the three Cabiri, small as dwarfs. They sing in ever higher, more ringing voices, exulting in the fact that they have carried out an exploit even greater than the Argonauts' winning of the golden fleece.

When the Cabiri have disappeared, the waters of the Aegean are visited by the ambassadors of two primitive peoples. The first among them, the Telchines, were famous in antiquity as very industrious artificers, ingenious and demonic wizards, the first to shape iron and bronze and to forge Neptune's trident (Strabo, XIV, c. 654; Callimachus, *Hymn to Delos*, 31). At the Aegean festival, too—which they join mounted on sea horses and sea dragons—the Telchines bear Neptune's trident, which they use to calm the storms. As the Sirens sing, the Telchines are "consecrated" to Apollo (8285). For an instant, as the moon continues to shine on the water, the Telchines' words call up the solar world of Artemis's great brother who, like they, lives at Rhodes, the island that belongs "to the god who generates sharp rays, the master of horses that breathe fire" (Pindar, *Olimpica*, VII, 70 ff.), and enjoys the sun's continuous protection. From the summit of the heavens, Apollo looks lovingly down on the mountains, cities, shores, and waves; and if a veil of mist manages to creep in, a ray of sunlight or a gust of wind once again makes the air free and pure. In this immaculate light, which sculpts the profile of all things, the Telchines erect statues of the gods, to whom for the first time in history they have given noble human lineaments (8301–8302). They shape in bronze magnificent statues of Apollo, now graver, now more amiable, now young, now mature; and they hope, with the perfection of form, to overcome the encroachments and ambushes of time.[25]

The other primitive peoples of the *Klassische Walpurgisnacht*, the Psylli and Marsi, were both surrounded by the ambiguous fame of being witches. The Marsi of central Italy, descended from Circe's son, put snakes and vipers to sleep with the spell cast by their voices and gestures *(Aeneid,* VII, 752 ff.; Pliny, VII, 13–14, XXVIII, 19, 30). The Psylli inhabit the deserts of Libya, abode of the most poisonous scourges in the world—asps with hugely swollen heads, the gigantic haemorrhois, the chersydros, the chelidris which glide along, leaving behind a trail of smoke, the undulating horned viper, the chenchris with its checkered, spotted belly, the heavy two-headed amphisbena, and the basilisk which kills with only its hiss. The Psylli's entire existence is spent among these animals. At birth they are exposed to snakes—that dare not bite them. As children they play with them; then they begin to cure the most poisoned wounds with saliva, the touch of their hands, exorcisms and magical songs. They learn to know and use herbs—elder leaves, galbanum plants, the sad tamarisk, Thessalian centuary, hog's fennel, mullein of Erice—to put the desert's terrible inhabitants to flight. With the advent of historic times their art degenerated. Overwhelmed like all men by the greed for money, the few surviving Psylli had begun trading in poisons, invading Italy and the countries of the North with their deadly scourges (Lucan, IX, 700 ff.; Pliny, VII, 13–14, VIII, 93, XI, 89, XXVIII, 80).

Nobody could connect the witches of Virgil, Pliny, and Lucan with the mild, dreamlike figures of divine servitors who reach the Aegean festival riding on bulls, calves, and sea rams. Who knows what strange migration has torn them from the hot deserts of Libya, where Medusa dropped her poison, and from the arid hills of the Marsica. Attracted by the same appeal, the Psylli and Marsi have taken refuge in Cyprus, at first in Aphrodite's service and later in Galatea's. On Venus's island civilizations decline and die one after the other; the Greek temples have fallen into ruins, the dominion of the Roman eagle has ended, as well as that of the crusading knights, Venice's wingéd lion, and Ottoman's sickle moon. But the Psylli and Marsi have hidden in caves on the island, invisible to human beings, living as the mythical divinities lived when they reigned over the earth. The world around them has remained incredibly tranquil; neither Poseidon nor Seismos dare fill the caves with sand or disturb them. The breath of the eternal winds, the murmur of the nights, the loving interwining of the waves accompany, like a continuous echo, their tenuous, ghostly life. They do not act, they are not agitated, they do not become enraged: the sole aim of their existence is to guard Aphrodite's chariot of seashells, a reminder to them and us of how myth maintains itself untouched and immutable through the disasters of history.

Meanwhile a curious apparition attracts the eyes of the Sirens, of Nereus and Thales. A nocturnal wayfarer, who was lost in these places, might think that a group of cirrus clouds had enveloped the moon. But Nereus and Thales, who love to preserve something of the sacred in the "tranquil, warm nest" of their spirits (8358), recognize the figures of myth behind the outward appearances of natural phenomena. In reality, those cirrus clouds are passionate doves burning with love, their wings white as light, who form a precious halo around the moon. They live in the temple of Paphos; and they fly over the heads of the Sirens to announce that Galatea's seashell chariot, bequeathed from Aphrodite, is about to appear on the waters.

The procession approaches with a light movement. Nereus's daughters, the Nereids and Dorides, now weave ring on ring, now they move like snakes, tracing spirals around Galatea's chariot. The Nereids appear lusty and wild, as if the proximity to monsters had left a mark on their figures. The Dorides, "graces of the sea" (8137), are mounted on a cortege of dolphins and are so beautiful and delicate that they still seem part of the sea's foam. Just before, as the storm raged, they had saved some young sailors from the "furious teeth of the undertow" (8396). They had laid them on the reeds and moss, warming them and bringing them back to the light; and they implore the moon to grant the gift of immortal youth to their loved ones.

Other dolphins pull the chariot in which Galatea, the most beautiful of the Dorides, is seated. Like the white-winged doves, she comes from Paphos, where she is venerated in the temples of Venus. A thousand voices herald her, Nereus anxiously awaits her, the sea's creatures accompany her. With her the great Aegean festival reaches its climax.

Some spectators might expect that Goethe would portray, vying with Philostratus or Calderon, "Galatea's purple dress, which swells like a sail over her head, casting a shadow on it," and that he would make a reddish gleam shine on her forehead: the sharp, illimitable glances, the humid hair, the tender fingers that touch an ankle; "the elbow that dazzles with its pinkish white, the muscles of the arm that swell gently like small waves in the sea"; the sole of the foot which, swaying, grazes the water.[26]

But the Sirens only remind us that Galatea is "grave" like the immortal goddesses, and "attractive" like earthly women (8387–8390). We learn nothing else about her. She appears only for an instant in the moonlit bay; and for an instant she shines in the court theater packed with spectators. She exchanges a glance with her father, held fast by his look; she calls to him with a joyous cry and tries in vain to arrest her chariot's forward movement. The dolphins immediately drag her away, "in the élan of their circular movement," (8427) and they disappear in ever larger circles, while the seashell chariot continues to scintillate, clear and luminous, in the Aegean's distances.

Thales, Cabiri, Proteus, and Nereus

Seated in a corner of the Goethean theater, we have finished admiring the marvels of the "old fabulist," who plays and freely amuses himself, moves Nereids and Tritons, Cabiri and Telchines, Psylli and Marsi over the Aegean's waves, and seems concerned only with the grace of his gestures, songs, and light effects. Like the guests of Philip IV at the *Buen Retiro*, we cannot ask for anything more. Art is this, too: enamels, jewels, treasures dredged up from the sea, precious colors, perfect choreographies; the fantasy of a court poet put on a stipend by his sovereign to amuse the world's capricious guests. Yet on a part of the stage we have overlooked until now, the court poet tries to represent, with ever more meaningful "hints" and "allusions," ever more serious "jokes," the ultimate mysteries of Goethe's natural theology.

Upon exploration, all the elements of nature reveal complex and contradictory meanings. Anaxagoras's Jacobin philosophy, Mephistopheles's infernal theology, Homunculus's spiritual flame, the torment of Pater Profundus, the marvels of the night of carnival of the first act barely suffice to represent the contradictory aspects of fire. Jarno's silence, Mephistopheles's aridity, the immobility of Sphinxes and Dryads do not reveal to us all the meanings of the rocks. But what element is more ambiguous and elusive than water? So, with the idea of expressing all the sea's aspects, Goethe staged a small scientific comedy with a numerous cast of characters, a religious mystery sung by several voices, a chamber concert for many instruments, interweaving the speeches of Thales, Proteus, Nereus and the silence of the Cabiri. Only if we listen to all of them together, if we accustom ourselves to understand and hear their frivolous and grave senile chatter all at once, can we understand some of the secrets of the aquatic world.

The prime representative of the sea's realm is Thales, whom we have already met when he argued with Anaxagoras on the Peneus's banks. Amid rocks, oaks, volcanic creations, and the sanguinary revolts of the pygmies and ants, Thales moved uneasily. On the tongue of sand where he and Homunculus have now landed, he can contemplate the waves, enjoy the soft breath of the wind and inhale the sweet smells of cool marine vegetation. His happiness grows; his joy bursts open like a flower; his language, at first so precise, tinged at times by a faint high society irony, is traversed by an ecstatic élan, an enthusiastic impulse:

> Hail! Once more hail!
> How I bloom and regale
> On beauties' and truths' penetration!
> Everything live is water's creation!
> Water keeps all things young and vernal!
> Ocean, grant us thy rule eternal.
> Clouds—were it not for thee sending them,

GOETHE

> Nor fertile brooks—expending them,
> Rivers—hither and thither bending them,
> And Streams—not fully tending them,
> Then what would be mountains; what plains and earth?
> 'Tis thou giv'st livingest life its worth.*
>
> *(MacNeice translation)*

The sea's waves are the source from which the forms of life are born (7856, 8435) and the beneficent force that conserves it. If the ocean did not grant us its dominion; if it did not send us clouds and dispense brooks, if it did not everywhere guide the rivers' courses, what would become of mountains, plains, and the world? But, according to Thales, the waters possess an even more extraordinary quality. The beneficent force generates plankton and algae, crabs and small fishes, but is not satisfied to fashion such primordial animals. Slowly and gradually, through thousands of successive metamorphoses, obeying nature's "eternal laws," it produces the most differentiated organisms and the noblest forms, such as the dolphins escorting Galatea and the Dorides. It knows neither cessations nor interruptions; it is stopped by no difficulty—even its creation of man, the lord of nature who, as the providential *telos* of the universe, stands above all other creatures (8324–8326, 8331–8332).

There are gods who invite us to halt on the lowest steps of creation and to remain eternally in the ocean, where we can experience painless life. But Thales does not agree with this. The sea's waters, incessantly trying to surpass themselves, are the model in which we must mirror ourselves. Like Homunculus, each of us must "begin from the beginning" (8322) and so mount, one after the other, all the steps of the stairway of creation, tending toward the "higher orders" (8330), becoming, finally, capable of philosophizing and molding in bronze the statues of the celestial divinities (8324–8326, 8333–8334).

> *Heil! Heil! aufs neue!
> Wie ich mich blühend freue,
> Vom Schönen, Wahren durchdrungen . . .
> Alles ist aus dem Wasser entsprungen!
> Alles wird durch das Wasser erhalten!
> Ozean, gönn uns dein ewiges Walten.
> Wenn du nicht Wolken sendetest,
> Hin und her nicht Flüsse wendetest,
> Die Ströme nicht vollendetest,
> Was wären Gebirge, was Ebnen und Welt?
> Du bist's der das frischeste Leben erhält.
>
> *(8432–8443)*

Everyone knows who Thales is. But who are the Cabiri whom the Nereids and Tritons transport on the immense shell of a turtle, singing hymns in their praise? A curtain of obscurity seems to beshroud them ever since the beginnings of classical antiquity. Full of reticence, Herodotus alludes to the mysteries of the Cabiri, whom the Pelasgians worshipped on the island of Samothrace (II, 51). Strabo speaks at length of the Cabiri and of a whole picturesque horde of daemons, priests, and servants who accompanied the Great Mother; he describes how, inspired by Dionysian frenzy, they dance their war dances; they shout and raise an uproar, play flutes, tambourines, and drums, explode firecrackers, brandish weapons, filling whoever watches them with religious terror. But, in the end, Strabo, full of uncertainty and doubt, admits that he is unable to unveil all of the enigmas associated with the Cabiri—their nature, their identity, their sanctuaries (*Geography*, VII, 50; X, c. 466, 470, 472, 473, 474). As for Creuzer and Schelling, who can possibly venture without dismay into the forest of their symbolical and numerical speculations—the tangle of Egyptian, Phoenician, and Hebraic, Neoplatonic, Gnostic, and Masonic elements in which they end up concealing the figure of the gods of Samothrace?

Like Proteus, Goethe loves mysteries; and he thinks that if something is truly enigmatic and extravagant, it is (or can be) all the more respectable and venerable. So he makes no attempt to cast light on this very obscure material; he does not solve the enigmas of the Cabiri, but amuses himself by complicating them, vying in obscurantism with Demetrius of Scepsis, Strabo, and Creuzer.

When the Sirens, Nereids, and Tritons sing their agile, rhythmic strophes at the top of their voices, we believe that a procession of priests and initiates are intoning in the marine temple theological hymns, deeply emotional hymns of joy in homage to the very ancient and venerable divinity.

Sirens:	What do they think they are going to gain
	In the realm of the august Cabiri?
	They are Gods! . . .
Nereids and *Tritons:*	. . . They are gods, which we bring;
	You'll have to sing paeans.
Sirens:	Small in stature,
	Great in strength,
	Rescuers of the shipwrecked,
	Anciently venerated gods. . . .
Nereids and Tritons:	. . . These incomparables
	Want to go ever higher,

GOETHE

> Starvelings riddled with desire
> For the unattainable . . .*

A few instants go by, and the Sirens and Nereids amuse themselves by singing a scurrilous, riddling rondelay:

> Nereids and Tritons: We have brought with us three,
> The fourth would not come. . . .
> There are actually seven.
> Sirens: Where are the other three?
> Nereids and Tritons: We cannot say,
> You should inquire at Olympus;
> That's where the eighth resides,
> Of whom nobody has yet thought!†

Everything descends to the grotesque: the Cabiri become small, ludicrous monsters, ugly pots of terra-cotta, against which the scholars, Demetrius of Scepsis and Strabo, Creuzer and Schelling, vainly broke their stubborn heads (8219–8222).

Which songs should we believe? The sacred hymns or the farcical rondelays? Are the Cabiri venerable deities or ugly terra-cotta pots? If we wish to comprehend their nature we should listen to both the sacred

> *Sirenen: Was denken sie zu vollführen
> Im Reiche der hohen Kabiren?
> Sind Götter! . . .
> Nereiden und Tritonen: . . . Sind Götter, die wir bringen:
> Müsst hohe Lieder singen.
> Sirenen: Klein von Gestalt,
> Gross von Gewalt,
> Der Scheiternden Retter,
> Uralt verehrte Götter. . . .
> Nereiden und Tritonen: . . . Diese Unvergleichlichen
> Wollen immer weiter,
> Sehnsuchtsvolle Hungerleider
> Nach dem Unerreichlichen . . .
> (8073–8075, 8173–8177, 8202–8205)
> †Nereiden und Tritonen: Drei haben wir mitgenommen,
> Der vierte wollte nicht kommen. . . .
> Sind eigentlich ihrer sieben.
> Sirenen: Wo sind die dreigeblieben?
> Nereiden und Tritonen: Wir wüssten's nicht zu sagen,
> Sind am Olymp zu erfragen;
> Dort west auch wohl der achte,
> An den noch niemand dachte!
> (8186–8187, 8194–8199)

hymn and the riddle; fuse the gravity and buffoonery. We must venerate them as very potent deities and then immediately mock them, scoff
at the commentators and ourselves, who read *Faust II* without understanding it. Like Eros, the greatest of the Platonic demons, the mysterious Cabiri are double deities who in their own figure join the most
contradictory qualities the human mind can think of.[27]

Born in Zeus's garden, from the casual lovemaking of Πενία and
Πόφος, Eros inherited opposed qualities from father and mother. Since
he was born from Πενια, that is, Poverty, which begs and stretches out
its hand at doors, he was not a beautiful, delicate god, rich and happy,
as so many imagined; he was merely a coarse, poor, dirty demon who
went barefoot, had no roof and slept under the open sky, before the
doors of houses, and on the roads. He lacked everything, as is true of
someone eternally sharing the fate of indigence; life for him was only
a list of lacks—qualities he did not have, things he did not possess or
could not see, immediately present, before his yearning eyes.

But Eros also resembled his father, Πόφος ("Expedient Invention"),
who was the son in his turn of the goddess Μῆτις ("Technical and
Practical Knowledge"). So he was virile and audacious, like the most
terrible hunter—full of fantasies, fertile in ingenious expedients, like a
sophist, a magus, or the god Hermes. What did he care if he walked
barefoot, like the most miserable of beggars? His insatiable desire, his
daemonic hunter's instinct, the cunning of his sophist's and wizard's
mind incited him to conquer everything that he lacked. So he spent his
life philosophizing; chasing the truth he did not know, but which the
gods possess naturally. When close to anything beautiful he felt an inner
tumult and an equally enchanting calm, and his fecund spirit generated
a perfect interlacing of thoughts, a poem or ode to the gods, an invention useful to men, or the just laws of a city (Plato, *Symposium*, 199 c.
ff.).

The Cabiri of the *Klassische Walpurgisnacht* possess the same double lineaments as Eros. Like him, they are the children of Πενία, who
stretches out his hand before doors. They remain seated on the turtle's
shell, while the Sirens and Nereids sing at full voice; and they are as
silent as the water and the rock, for they have not been given the grace
of speech. If at least they meditated upon inexpressible thoughts concerning the world's essence! But the Cabiri cannot think; they do not
even know themselves, sunk as they are in the unconsciousness of
marine vegetation (8077). Whereas all organisms mount the stairway of
creation, assuming the elegant form of dolphins or the godlike form of
man, their ludicrous dwarfs' bodies continue to live in the formless,
incomplete and inconclusive.

GOETHE

In that part of their being which resembles instinct Πόφος, the Cabiri are seized by a noble hunger, by a very ardent desire, an illimitable nostalgia (8204–8205). So they constantly generate new Cabiris to multiply and spread through the world, swift as Thessaly's pygmies and Dactyls (8076). But this self-generation brings them back over their own tracks and is not satisfying enough for the small gods of Samothrace. Nostalgia and love force them to run farther, to where things exist that are unfamiliar to them, which are not and will not be, which they possess not and never will possess (8205). Some of them have succeeded in wholly imitating the great Sophist of the *Symposium* and spend their lives philosophizing. The fourth Cabiri is the one who "thinks for everyone" (8188–8189); the fifth, sixth, seventh, and eighth, who enjoy the pleasures of Olympian gods, surely know the art of writing philosophical dialogues, hymns to the gods, or the just laws of Athens and Sparta. Yet these Cabiri, disdaining the Aegean festival, have remained in Samothrace's temples or on the slopes and the summit of Mount Olympus, and from there mockingly deride their first three siblings (8191).

The three Cabiri, who protect the sea festival with their presence, are ignorant of these intellectual virtues. How many things about the universe they are ignorant of! And what do they know about nature's luminous formative activity, the progressive metamorphoses of organisms, the intellectual and plastic powers of human beings? For them the aquatic world so dear to Thales is a dead letter. While everything proceeds toward the heights, they remain prisoners of poverty and darkness, of incompleteness and imperfection—speechless, without thoughts, small, grotesque dwarfs, hampered even in the ardent amorous enthusiasm which at every moment inspires them.

Some mediocre student of Thales could situate the Cabiri on one of the lowest steps of the universe's staircase—down at the bottom, amid the seaweeds, shells, and crabs; and among the lowest demons, much darker than the ecstatic dancers and musicians who, according to Strabo, accompanied the Great Mother. Yet, in the *Klassische Walpurgisnacht,* the Cabiri are real and proper "gods," as the chorus repeats three times (8075, 8173, 8177), venerated since the most ancient times on the island of Samothrace.[28] Like the Great Mother, a retinue of demons, priests and servants—the Sirens, Nereids, and Tritons—exalts and worships them, extolling their graces. In the water no other god is more powerful than they, not even Poseidon, the shaker of the universe, or Galatea. The other ocean gods have an ambiguous aspect; now they make the sea calm and tranquil, now they overturn it from the depths, answering the fury of the lightning bolts with gigantic waves; now they help, now they destroy human beings. Only the Cabiri never deny their benign appearance. When their irresistible amorous force protects the waters, storms and winds are placated; and if Poseidon's fury flings a ship against the rocks along the shore, they save the seamen from death and destruction (8179–8185).

So, in the Aegean too, as in the *Lehrjahre,* we encounter one of Goethe's great paradoxes. The marine world is a staircase with a thousand steps rising slowly toward perfection and the light. But the gods whom we, singing with the Nereids and the Sirens, must venerate, the most sacred divinities who reign over the waters—from what do they draw their strength if not from the fatally imperfect love that animates them, from the hunger that tortures them, the silence that hides them, the darkness that envelops them?

While Homunculus and Thales watch the procession of the Cabiri, Proteus approaches, attracted by the flame that shines prettily in the small phial. Proteus has a long past: Menelaus met him on the island of Pharos, opposite Egypt, and Aristeus in the Carpathian sea, between Crete and Rhodes. In those days, when the sun kindled its midday fires, he emerged from the water and withdrew into an immense den, where the waves pushed by the wind broke in circular eddies. He watched and counted his school of seals, which gave off the sharp and dreadful odor of the abyss; and he slept among them like a shepherd in the middle of his flock of sheep. He knew all of the ocean's depths, caves, currents, and monsters. He was as truthful as Nereus, the other "old man of the sea," of whom Hesiod speaks (*Theogony,* 233–236); and he revealed present, past, and future, and the journeys, traps, and dangers the passage of time would bring. But those who knew him were particularly struck by the incredible variety of his deceptions. He was able to speak deviously, pretending ignorance, going around and about, as cunning and ingenious as Ulysses; and he assumed all the forms we meet on land and sea. If someone tried to seize or hold him, he turned into a lion, then a snake, a panther, a huge boar, a bull with great horns, or a scaly dragon; he would become a stone or a tree with towering foliage; he slithered away like a thin, limpid trickle of water or crepitated with the acrid sound of sudden flames (*Odyssey,* IV, 349 ff.; *Georgics,* IV, 387 ff.; Ovid, *Metamorphoses,* VIII, 732 ff.).

How many times Goethe thought he had caught a glimpse, in the realm of nature, of Proteus's restless lineaments! In Palermo's Villa Guilia, as rich in flowers and trees as Alcinous's garden, where he had discovered the *Urpflanze,* at Weimar when he studied the bones of monkeys, giraffes, and man, searching for the unique anatomical "type" —each time he had felt that he could see the ancient sea god of whom Homer, Virgil, and Ovid had sung. The *Urpflanze,* the *Urbild,* all the

GOETHE

universal forms Goethe had found in nature, Proteus-like, kept changing into ever new shapes (XI, 375: 28–32; XIII, 177: 13–17). They changed aspect and function, contracted and expanded, concealed themselves behind the most extravagant metamorphoses; they glided away before one's eyes, swift as God, who passes in front of Job and flees before Job can observe him (Job 9: 11).

In the years of maturity when he began his studies of morphology, these free games with which nature flaunts its wealth filled Goethe's soul with profound joy. But in the last period of his life, his feelings underwent a change. While his old friends walked in the garden, tranquilly comtemplating the trees or flowers, the idea of metamorphosis kept returning to his mind and tormented him (M. February 26, 1832). It seemed to him that it was one of the most "honorable and, at the same time, dangerous" gifts the gods or demons had bestowed on men. If it met no obstacles in its path, the force of metamorphosis transformed the species of plants into a quantity of individual varieties that eluded any determination, any specification of the taxonomic scientist. While his friends continued to converse in the garden, the almost terrified Goethe saw the splendid edifice of nature collapse into a formless rubble and its laws dissolve and become lost in the arbitrary (XIII, 35: 23–25; 36: 20–29; 37: 10).

To participate in the Aegean festival, Proteus has left his acrid-smelling school of seals. Curious and gay as a child, blithe and irreverent as Homunculus, he loves all fantastic things: the thousand marvels of the gods and the marine world, the fires that burn and scintillate on the ocean's surface. Since his old jokes never cease to amuse him, he changes shape; and in a few moments transforms himself into a giant turtle, a man with noble features, an elegant dolphin. Sometimes he is as spiteful as a gnome in a fairy tale; sometimes he diverts himself by imitating the scurrilous pranks of ventriloquists who put on exhibitions in the theater. He makes his voice come simultaneously from opposite places; and he says "farewell" as if he were calling from the most remote horizon, while, hidden in some mysterious form on the beach, he is very close to Homunculus and Thales.

Proteus is also a philosopher who has worked out his own conception of nature, a science "of being born and transforming oneself" (8153). At the start, he seems to share Thales's ideas. "One must begin," he tells advice-seeking Homunculus, "in the broad sea! There at the first one begins small . . . then one grows little by little and forms oneself for higher tasks" *(zu höherem Vollbringen)* (8260–8264). Thus we believe that Proteus also conceives of nature as a series of successive forms leading from plankton and tiny fish all the way to the earth's animals and man, the lord of creation. Certainly, to find Proteus too among the philosophers of *harmonia mundi;* to discover in him, who seems to play aimlessly with all forms, so much faith in the providential *telos* of creation, never ceases to astound us.

When Proteus reveals his thought more clearly, he makes us understand that these "higher tasks" mean nothing at all to him. Perhaps he has remembered them only to pay homage to Thales. Man, this distant, bizarre, unpredictable goal, this creature glorified by the humanists, by sculptors of nudes, and by a few mediocre theologians, does not please him. To live and to function on the Earth, among houses, temples, and earthquakes, seems to him an unbearable annoyance. When Thales proposes to Homunculus that he complete his transformation by becoming a man (8325–8326), Proteus invites him to plunge into the watery expanse and to live and move freely in the ocean. "But not to tend," he adds, "toward the higher orders *(nach höherem Orden):* for as soon as you become a man, then it's all up with you" (8327–8332). If he becomes a man, Homunculus must also stop his metamorphoses; he will be forced to live in the prison of the persona and descend, like Achilles and Helen, into the twilight of Hades. There can be no doubts about this. Proteus's philosophy of nature tries to halt the continual impulse toward metamorphosis at the most elementary levels, among the ocean's eternal, protective waves.

All man's works and activities, even his most noble ones, which seem to leap upward to the world of Olympian gods, arouse Proteus's pitiless mockery. As he converses with Thales and Homunculus, the Telchines pass by in the rocky bay, singing the praises of Apollo's immense bronze statue, adolescent and huge, amiable and grave, which they had shaped beneath the sun of Rhodes. Proteus remarks: "Let them sing, let them brag! To the sun's life-giving, sacred rays, dead works are just a joke."[29] What is left of those splendid statues, which tried to counterpose the closed perfection of form to the indefinite mobility of the waters, and which were supposed to conquer time? The soil of Rhodes was rent by earthquakes—the statues were destroyed; and someone has fused those forms again into different shapes—which are also mortal, as is everything that man creates upon the earth.

So, through Proteus's mouth, the sea mocks the land on which reign the Olympian gods, the light of the sun, and the dead works of art; there men try to escape the evasive and uninterrupted movement of the universe, tracing definite forms in flesh, stone, and bronze, which are supposed to defeat the snares of time. The maternal waves, the festive shoals of fish, the gods and demons of the depths try to avoid any sort of fixity. Just as Proteus constantly transforms himself, they continually

GOETHE

cancel all the forms they have sketched and replace them with new ones. They renounce themselves, dissolving in the flux of biological life; now frothy waves, now vegetation, now embryos, now fishes, now turtles, and now dolphins . . .

This uninterrupted movement, these metamorphoses without purpose and without goal are not embedded in the unconscious amorous darkness that prevented the Cabiri from thinking and expressing themselves. Proteus knows ingenious and artificial life, the cunning, deceits, and expedients of the intelligence. He can argue with a dialectical ability not inferior to that of Thales; he can joke with the light grace of Homunculus; and, sometimes, his sarcastic voice reminds us of the voice of another great humorist and illusionist who, at this moment, among the rocks of Thessaly, is being transformed into a Phorkyas. Thus, in the waters of the sea, in the dark, fragrant abyss from which life is born, we discover an irony infinitely more ambiguous and destructive than human irony; and with a kind of horror we encounter an indefinable force, as natural as it is intellectual, that dissolves forms, mocks any goal and any law, and continually astonishes and confuses us.

As in a drawing room full of mirrors the same figure is reflected full face and in profile, more faithful or more deformed, so in every part of the Aegean festival we discover a new self-portrait of Goethe. All the "old men of the sea"—both wise and puerile, melancholy and blithe, ironic and tender-hearted—resemble him profoundly. Imitating Thales, Goethe sang the praises of water and universal harmony; and his friends always thought he had Proteus's chameleonlike mobility. Also the third old man, Nereus, reminds us of Goethe during his last years, as we know him from his conversations with Eckermann, Chancellor von Müller, and other witnesses.

Truthful, just, and benign as in the *Theogony* (223 ff.), Nereus possesses two qualities that distinguished Goethe's old age: the tendency to play the part of the unheeded and disappointed prophet, the bizarre, splenetic grouse; and a kind of epicurean elegance (8414–8415). The passage of time, the long sequence of trials and experiences, has taught him that gods and men, the creatures who inhabit sea and land must "resign themselves once and for all" (X, 78: 6); they must renounce the most dearly desired things and above all the consolation of love. This experience has not made his spirit cold or withered. A melancholy sweetness surrounds his words, love still burns sorrowfully within him; and the inexorable harshness that upholds the order of the world does not prevent him from venerating sacred things, ancient religious traditions, and the white-winged doves that reach the temples of Paphos (8346–8354).

Like Goethe, Nereus does not love human beings. Holed up in a cave facing the seacoast, he declares he has never seen more capricious, irresponsible creatures. Men never listen to the advice of the wise; they obey only their own desires, though each time their foolish passions fill the world with misfortunes and death. Despite Nereus's warnings, Paris insisted on carrying off Helen; and so the walls of Troy collapsed in flames, a dense night filled the sky, and Pindus's eagles feasted on his brothers' corpses. Ulysses knew the future awaiting him; and yet he wandered for ten years along the shores of the Mediterranean, losing all his companions, victim of the cruelty of the Cyclops, the deceptions of Circe, the strange delays of his own spirit. That is how men are: incapable of improving themselves, "doomed to resemble themselves forever" (8097), they believe, hope, and strive to "reach the gods" (8096), children who want to repeat the great deeds of the Titans.

During the Aegean festival, the three old men of the sea and the Cabiri represent the different aspects of the marine world. Thales extolls the providential harmony of the waters; the Cabiri incarnate their dark, unfulfilled amorous strength; and Proteus their ironic ambiguity. To Nereus, the wisest, most experienced among them, falls the task of illustrating with two examples the ethic that rules in the ocean's waters; the moral principles obeyed by the gods and demons, dolphins and fishes assembled in the *Klassische Walpurgisnacht*. As he explains them, Nereus's bad temper is soothed, his rancor toward men is forgotten; his words are modest, cautious, and indirect, like those of a true teacher. Perhaps he speaks to the entire human race, respresented symbolically by Homunculus, and hopes to be able to persuade him by the simple grace of his fables.

The first of these fables is the simplest. When Nereus's dearly beloved daughters, the Dorides, arrive at the festival, they beg their father to grant immortality to the young sailors they have saved "from the undertow's enraged teeth." But Nereus replies: "Be happy with your fine catch, and mold the young man into a man. But I cannot give that which only Zeus can grant. The wave which cradles and rocks you does not grant stability even to love, and when caprice will have finished its pranks, place them tenderly on the shore."[30] Nereus repeats the words Goethe had hidden in the *Divan*'s strophes and in the *Wanderjahre*'s novellas. On the surface of the earth as in the mobile world of the waters, no passion can last; every encounter contains the sign and anticipation of the inevitable separation—love is a caprice, blithe, sweet, and sad.

When in the second fable, Galatea, in the seashell chariot approaches her father, a glance "chains" them together (8425), cries of joy burst from their throats. But, unconcerned with these "intimate motions of the heart" (8428), the dolphins flee rapidly in larger and larger circles, where glance cannot meet glance, and drag Galatea away, distant and unseizable as a star (8452). Of the expectation of an entire year, of so many hopes and desires that nourished the hearts of father and daughter, what is left? A single instant of happiness—akin to the moment that unites and separates Wilhelm and Natalia forever—and then Nereus and Galatea must renounce their proximity, the intimate warmth of everyday happiness.

For a moment Nereus allows himself to be overcome by discouragement and nostalgia, and dreams of being carried away with his daughter in that swift nocturnal flight. Then he bows his head to fate and resigns himself. But his renunciation is less bitter than that which saddens Wilhelm Meister's silent pilgrimages. The very rapid encounter has not been fruitless. In that intense and fleeting glance, that cry of joy which united them for an instant, are gathered all the emotions of an entire year (8430). When Galatea is far away, confused among the shoals of fishes or venerated in the temples of Paphos, she continues to shine and shimmer, "luminous and clear, always near and true," in the enamoured eyes of memory, as a great star shines in the sky to the eyes of our body (8452, 8454, 8456–8457). So, while he accepts the separation from Galatea, Nereus obtains something the Dorides will never know: the "stability" (8413) of love—close in the distance, luminous in the darkness of night and separation, eternally repeated like the return of the mythical figures, each year, to the Classical Feast of Walpurgis.

These continual renunciations—Nereus's renunciation and the Dorides', Wilhelm's, and Natalia's silence, the Sun's futile attempt to embrace Iris, the flights, tears, unbearable distances—do not diminish the love that travels through water and earth, air and fire. All the love we renounce as individuals increases and exalts the triumph of Eros, he who "has begun everything" (8479), as the unanimous voices of the great marine choir will shortly acclaim in triumph.

Mysterium Incarnationis

Enclosed in the fragile, transparent walls of glass, behind which his resonant flame moves, Homunculus possesses the loftiest qualities of the pure spirit. He knows things without being obscured by the burden of matter and the slowness of experience; and the secrets hidden from men and Mephistopheles let themselves be penetrated by his demon's intuition. This spiritual felicity does not last for long. A moment after being born, Homunculus contemplates in Faust's mind the embrace of the prince of swans and Leda's body, "the loveliest of all scenes," and the world of love and generation is revealed to him in its most fascinating colors.

While Homunculus describes Helen's conception to Wagner and Mephistopheles, his clear and ironic voice does not seem changed. But something has happened to his fiery temperament. Starting from this moment, the "enclosed space" (6884) in which he lives stifles him; his artificial existence as a spirit seems to him a stain—a kind of original sin —he must wipe out as soon as possible. He is no longer so certain, so childishly proud, so sure of understanding everything, and he pushes his humility to the point of asking advice of two human beings he has met by chance (7849). If so many men, immured in the prison of matter, dream at the end of their lives of donning the fiery robe of the demons, Homunculus, at the beginning of his life, experiences the opposite desire. Like all creatures who populate the air, who live on land and in the sea, he wants "to be born" with a body, shattering his walls of glass (7831–7832, 8252). Full of curiosity and impatience, he hopes to know the subtle sensations of incarnate creatures: the darkness, anxieties, pains, and exaltations of living matter, to lose himself finally in the illimitable space of nature (6883, 8328).

Having reached Thessaly, his curiosity aroused by all "the new, marvelous things" (7069) awaiting him on earth, he flits from place to place, illuminating with his now timid, now powerful light Greece's gods, demons, and landscapes. He contemplates the azure fires around which the spirits are seated; he skims over the Peneus's banks covered with bushes, rocks, and venerable oaks, observes the battles between the pygmies and cranes, and the meteor as it falls from the moon, whistling and rumbling. These "new, marvelous things," do not make him forget that he has come to Greece to be incarnated. But, if he does not know the procedures of generation, how can he be born? So when he hears Thales and Anaxagoras arguing about nature, he approaches them with the idea of asking for advice from one of them, in order "to be born in the best way" (7831).

Homunculus finds himself faced by the fundamental choice of his life. Which element should he prefer? In which element does he want to grow—among the flames of the earth and subterranean cavities, or in the waters of the Aegean Sea? Since he has a body of fire, we imagine that he is attracted by the "enraged Plutonic fires" (7865) as the element to which he has the greatest affinity. Anaxagoras also thinks so, and offers him the crown of the king of the pygmies, ants, and Dactyls. If he had succumbed to this flattery, Homunculus would have become one of the thousand earthly vassals of the king of the inferno, his father. With Thales's assistance, Homunculus escapes the temptation offered by Anaxagoras; he rejects the king's crown and follows the wise old man to the sea festival, as an obedient pupil follows his teacher. There he finds himself in his element, and breathes the enchanting aroma of young vegetation; he meets Nereus and vainly asks him for advice; he watches the procession of the Cabiri and Tritons, listens to the songs of the Telchines, Psylli, and Marsi. Finally he meets the only divinity who can teach him the art of being born and transforming himself: Proteus, the master of metamorphoses. He mounts Proteus's dolphinlike back and sets out with him over the waves of the sea, illuminating "life's sweet humidity" with his glitter.

As Galatea reaches the moonlit bay, a "glorious sound" (8463) echoes inside the phial. Leaving the back of Proteus-dolphin, Homunculus flies through the air; his flame spurting around the seashell chariot, he lands at the feet of the beautiful Galatea. Now he flares out more violently, now more gently and amiably, "as if he were moved by the pulse-beat of love" (8468). While he is swaying uncertainly between a moribund and a still unknown existence, how many emotions race through his soul! In a few moments, Homunculus experiences the anguish and fear and trembling of one about to renounce his own person forever; the desire for the beauty of all things; the nameless happiness of one about to break through his own limits and dissolve in the amorous embrace of universal life.

When the glass phial shatters against Galatea's throne, Homunculus's flame spurts out of its artificial envelope, expanding and flaring over the waters. A "miracle of fire" (8474) suddenly casts its radiance over the lunar night. An immense fire, more enchanting than that which rose above the stage of the *Buen Retiro*, sways over the small waves which, scintillating, clash against each other. It absorbs the timid light of the moon; tinges the Aegean horizon, the rocks on which lie the Sirens, the strip of sand where Thales still lingers. In a single conflagration it seems to burn in all the bodies of the sea's creatures—the bodies of the Nereids and Tritons, the "tender" bodies of the Dorides, Galatea's "grave" body, Proteus's dolphinlike body and Nereus's melancholy face.

Homunculus's destiny has been accomplished. The pure spirit has been reconciled with nature; the son of Wagner's artifices and combinations has experienced the generative power of life. If we could use this word, Homunculus is dead, and another creature has taken his place in the world. What this creature is, what name he bears, what he looks like, what his habits and functions are, we cannot know. But one thing is certain. While the Sirens and the Nereids, the Telchines and Tritons sing over the grave of Homunculus, he undergoes a fatal degradation. His spiritual flame is overcast; his light darkens; his mind loses that marvelous acumen that made him flit, like a young, soothsaying gnome, above the strange dreams of our nights and the obscure events of our past.

Perhaps Homunculus has become a heap of very damp algae, part of that vegetation that had just given off so sweet a perfume on the Aegean beach. With the passage of time he will perhaps become a crab, a blithe fish in the depths, a festive dolphin, a sea horse, a fantastic sea dragon. After having lived far and wide in the water, he will finally be elevated to the level of man. Like the Telchines, he will sculpt bronze statues; shut up in a dusty Gothic room he will experience Mephistopheles's temptation; he will be derided by Proteus and admonished by Nereus's vision. But then, after thousands of years, who will be able to remember his long past as a piece of seaweed and a fish?

Mysterium Crucis

The first Christian apologists saw the four arms of the cross stamped as an indelible sign in the "breadth and length, the depth and height" of the universe (Ephesians 3: 18). They saw it illuminate the highest summits of the heavens, shine in the middle of the atmosphere and delve down into the ground, connecting the sky with what lives on and under the earth. They observed it travel the world's immense expanse from east to west, from north to south. No visible or invisible place, no book, thought, or event existed that did not mirror this august figure. Wherever he might turn, the eyes of the believer could gaze at this sign of salvation: in the form of the praying human body and in the flight of birds, in the shape of the plough and in the banners of war, in the mainmast of ships and the tree of life that rose in the earthly paradise, and in the figures of the Old Testament.[31]

There is almost no one in Goethe's books who pronounces the name of Christ; or speaks of the cross on which he was immolated, remembering his martyrdom and his last sufferings, "the profound mystery in which is hidden the divine profundity of pain" (VIII, 164: 29–30). But

GOETHE

though Christ is not named, though Christ is hidden behind a veil of fear and horror, the symbol of the mediator and cosmic redeemer is the most sublime that Goethe knows. The deed he admires is of one who brings extremes together, mediates between light and darkness, makes peace between stars and stones, between the forces of "concentration" and "expansion." The action in which he sees the world's only salvation is that of one who buries himself in obscurity and sacrifices himself, so as to prepare the world's "future resurrection."

Just as Justin and Irenaeus discover the sign of the cross in the flight of birds and the masts of ships, so Goethe found the sign of mediation and redemption in the morning mists, the prism of colors, the clouds in the sky, the melodious arch of sounds and the colored reflections of the rainbow—now more evident and luminous, now hidden, now barely visible behind distant analogies. His theory of poetry and of colors, his doctrine of knowledge, his ethic, and his political hopes are all born under the sign of mediation; and even two chilly rationalists like Jarno and the astronomer try to mediate between the worlds of the stars and earth (VIII, 444–445). Eugenie, hidden at the end of *Natürliche Tochter;* Philerus, who throws himself in "the night's veiled waves" (*Pandora*, 983); Wilhelm Meister who, at the end of the *Wanderjahre,* saves his son by descending symbolically into the kindgom of death (VIII, 459: 30–32)—all of them imitate Christ's deed.[32]

Among these Goethean figures of mediators and redeemers, among these conscious and unconscious rivals of Christ, the greatest of all is the agile demon of fire whom we have just followed to the foot of Galatea's throne. Some might not want to believe this. What relationship could exist between the Son of God and the son of Mephistopheles; between the sorrowful figure of the Redeemer and the ironic and proud imp, so gay because of his prodigious knowledge; between the Christian God and this demon born in the margins of hermetic and Neoplatonic texts? But Goethe's allusions and hints about Homunculus's birth and death are too meaningful to be overlooked.

As he is born in Wagner's fantastic laboratory, Homunculus repeats the metamorphoses of the philosopher's stone and lights up the darkness like a "live coal," like a splendid red "carbuncle" (6825–6826). Now, in the books of the Christian alchemists, of Basil Valentine, Robert Fludd, Heinrich Khunrath, Georg von Welling, and Gottfried Arnold, Christ— our "cornerstone"—is clearly identified with the *lapis philosophorum.* Gottfried Arnold, whom Goethe read and admired in his youth, praised the "heavenly amiability" of that "ruby" or "carbuncle" stone which is Jesus Christ.[33]

Christ's earthly fate is condensed in two enigmas: the *Mysterium*

Incarnationis and the *Mysterium Crucis.* The immaterial light of the
Word encamps among men; and his body of earth mounts on the cross,
is buried, and is resurrected. When Homunculus descends at Galatea's
feet, he unites these two mysteries in a single act. Breaking the prison
of glass and dissolving himself in the waters, he is incarnated among the
marine creatures; and he sacrifices himself to reestablish nature's lost
unity. Galatea's chariot against which Homunculus suffers the shudders
and groans of death, the Aegean Sea in which he is lost and reborn, are
therefore his Bethlehem and Golgotha—his earthly cradle, his cross, his
sepulcher, the place of his eternal resurrection.

At this moment who can remember the days in which the flames and
waters displayed their demonic aspects, were unleashed against each
other, and Thales and Anaxagoras confronted each other with their
opposing principles? Who can remember the hatred, the darkness, the
heaviness, violence, and arbitrariness of nature? All the water of the
ocean and all the fire of the world, symbolically represented by Homunculus, show us only their "sacred" aspect (8481), fecund and loving.
Water and fire are reconciled; they rush toward each other and, obeying the laws of Eros, embrace ardently. The other elements accompany
their embrace. No lightning bolt, no storm, no cloud disturbs the sweet
air of the sky; and the earth, on which Seismos's capricious power and
Mephistopheles's rigidity reigned, reveals to us the profound, rich mysteries, the unlimited symbolic treasures hidden in its grottoes. So the
expectations, hopes, and desires of the creatures gathered together in
the *Klassische Walpurgisnacht* are fulfilled. For a moment outside of
time, while the moon is halted at the zenith, Homunculus has miraculously reestablished the unity and harmony of the universe; and the
world is returned to its origins, when it rested happily in God's eternal
bosom.

So the curtain can fall on the Aegean festival and, from the eyes of
the spectators seated in the court theater, hide the moon still arrested
in the sky, all the groups and processions that flocked to the shore of the
sea or on its rocks, or began traveling into the distance around Galatea's
throne. But before the festive sounds are hushed, before Helen's noble
and weary voice resounds on the banks of Peloponnesus, the Sirens
chant the triumphant praises of water and fire. Guided by their voices
and responding to their rhymes, the worshippers of Aphrodite and
Galatea, of the moon and the sun, the old gods of the sea, the great
magicians and wizards of Libya and Marsi, the marvelous sculptors, the
philosopher still lost on the banks of the Aegean, and creatures with the
bodies of fish—all extol in chorus the four sacred elements of the universe.

GOETHE

Sirens:	Hail to the sea! Hail the waves!
	Which this sacred fire enslaves!
	Hail to water! Hail to fire!
	Hail the daring of desire!
All Together:	Hail the breezes' gentle blisses!
	Hail, mysterious abysses!
	All things here let all adore—
	And the elements all four!*

(MacNeice translation)

Sirenen:	Heil dem Meere! Heil den Wogen,
	Von dem heiligen Feuer umzogen!
	Heil dem Wasser! Heil dem Feuer!
	Heil dem seltnen Abenteuer!
Alle-Alle:	Heil den mildgewogenen Lüften!
	Heil geheimnisreichen Grüften!
	Hochgefeiert seid allhier,
	Element'ihr alle vier!

(8480–8487)

Helen

VII

Before Persephone's Throne

When the curtain rises on the third act of *Faust II*, we are in the heart of the Peloponnesus. The sun's morning light sharply limns the severe mountains, among which stands out Mount Taygetus, encircling Sparta's green and fertile plain. The "sacred Eurotas" (8544, 9092) descends from the mountains as gaily as a brook, grows broader in the valley, and runs among the swampy reeds and sedge, nourishing the swans that glide over its water.[1] On the slopes of a hill, before the cyclopean walls, towers, and bronze portals of Tyndareus's palace, Helen is speaking to the maidservants who have just returned with her from Troy's ruins.

What has happened in the few hours which separate the end of the second act and the beginning of the third? Who has resurrected Leda's swans in the heart of the sixteenth (or nineteenth) century; who has rebuilt Menelaus's palace as it was in the past? And how in the world is Helen, who was dead, imprisoned in Persephone's kingdom, here once again, miraculously alive, as if she had just returned from her long wanderings? Goethe's first idea to answer a part of these questions was to describe Faust's descent into Hades as a "second Orpheus," and his speech to Persephone, "moving to the point of tears." Then he replaced the scenes in Hades with the simple, unfillable white space that divides the second and third acts. Just as Flaubert had left between two chapters of his *Sentimental Education* an "enormous white blank"—the most beautiful thing in the book, said Proust—Goethe also understood that nothing better than this blank space could suggest the impossible events that had taken place in Persephone's kingdom.

GOETHE

If we recall the episode of the Mothers, we can lift at least the edge of the veil Goethe has let fall. At that time Faust descended into the abyss, where the "forms," the "absolute images" of all creatures hovered around the Mothers' heads; and he evoked the figures of Helen and Paris before the uncomprehending eyes of the imperial courtiers. But when Faust tried to embrace Helen and to construct the "double, great realm" (6555) where absolute images and human creatures could live together, a violent explosion throws him in a faint to the ground, reminding him that the realms of Being and Reality are divided by boundless frontiers that never touch.

On the night of August 8, Faust followed Manto down into another abyss: "ungrateful, twilit Hades" (9119), the illustrious and sad Museum of the Past. There he saw rows of poplars, infertile willow trees, and meadows of asphodels where elusive hordes of nameless ghosts screech lugubriously like bats. Finally he reached the throne of Persephone, the queen of the dead and of history. He contemplated the shades of great historic personages—heroes and poets, kings and queens—all those who in life had performed noble deeds, winning a glorious name (9981) and so gaining the right to preserve a reflection of their terrestrial persona after death (9984).

Faust addresses "veiled" Persephone on her high throne, and begs her to bring Helen back to life, as so many centuries before she had permitted Orpheus to see Eurydice again and Admetus to embrace Alcestes a second time. A lover less wildly in love than Faust would have agreed to embrace Helen anywhere; even if she lived in Germany, wore modern clothes, and spoke the same language as himself. But Faust demands much more of the queen of Hades. With the same nostalgia that animates the great historians and archaeologists; with the same desperate desire that compels them to re-create a fragment of the past exactly as it was, he asks that Persephone resurrect not only Helen but also ancient Sparta with its palaces, its landscape, its language and customs.

When the past rises from the shadows and rubble; when Gibbon tearfully contemplates the fall of Constantinople, Burckhardt sees the courtiers of Urbino slip along the streets of Basil, and Huizinga lives at the court of Burgundy with Commynes; each of them knows that the fragment of the past, reconstructed with science and imagination, remains enclosed in its own sphere, as untouchable and unreachable as the images of Helen and Paris at the Emperor's court. But Faust cannot bear this radical separation once again; and he asks a favor of Persephone that no historian has ever obtained. Not even Goethe dared make the request as he wandered about his house looking at portraits of the dead, poring over time-yellowed letters and autographs, dreaming and fearing that those shades resurrected from the void might creep their way into his life. Faust asked her to create, beside the Eurotas River and among the hills of Laconia, the "double, great realm" of Present and Past where the shades inhabiting Hades and the fleeting creatures of life would lead—in time and outside time, in a single time and in all times—the same full existence.

The Mothers were averse to Faust's desperate prayer, but Persephone listened benignly to the request of the great lover, the great historian who knelt at her feet; she made a sign and the landscape of the Peloponnesus changed completely. Everything Chateaubriand had seen a few years before Goethe wrote *Faust II* vanished. Gone were the melancholy ruins of temples and palaces. No longer was the Eurotas a mere trickle, almost dry, the grass languishing, almost withered with not a bird, not an insect, not a plant, not a human being in sight—only a few wild horses and millions of lizards slithering up and down among the rocks beneath the silent light of noon. All this miserable rubble vanished, and thirty centuries of history were erased.

The Sparta of the Mycenaean age rose again from Hades, precisely as it had been. The plain of Laconia became rich and fertile, full of grain and barley, clover and oats, just as when it was crossed by Telemachus and Pisistratus; brimming Eurotas began flowing again among the canes and rushes of which Euripides had sung; and Leda's proud, delicate swans with resplendent feathers swam in the river. Tyndareus's palace displays its heavy, rough, cyclopean walls; the high stairs, on which Helen and Clytemnestra played; and the great bronze portals, which had opened to Menelaus's blithe, youthful step. After traversing three thousand years of history, the "true, authentic Helen" lived once again at Sparta, on her "ancient, tragic buskin"[2]; just as Homer had described her in the *Iliad* and *Odyssey* and Aeschylus and Euripides had represented her in the theaters of Athens.[3]

Helen in Classical Antiquity

In the *Iliad,* Helen lived in the beautiful house that Alexander, with the help of the most skillful craftsmen of Phrygia, built on the rock of Troy. She sat on the *megaron,* amid her slave girls, and wove a large purple cloth. But she did not embroider the earth and sea, the tireless sun and

GOETHE

the full moon, or the signs of the sky. Her design was not weddings, banquets, the work in the fields, vineyards loaded with grapes, the dances and races of the young, or the glory of the gods and heroes of the past. On her purple cloth Helen embroidered the struggles and sorrows that Achaeans and Trojans had suffered because of her; something of which she was the center, like the *Iliad* we are reading. When she left Alexander's house, Helen wrapped herself in one of those long veils, white, perfumed, and shimmering, which also accompany her in Goethe's *Faust.* Soon, she reached the Skaian gates where Priam's old companions, "like cicadas who, in the middle of the forest, rest on a tree to send forth a beflowered voice," sang the praises of the goddess's terrible beauty. The Trojan women, old and young, thronged around her; while on the plain Agamemnon and Odysseus, Ajax and Menelaus, Hector and Alexander prepared to fight for her. So on the walls of Troy, too, Helen was the obvious center of all the events on earth.

If Helen appeared as the focus of the cloth, if she was the heart of the Trojan war, it hadn't come about by chance. The gods had chosen her in advance. Aphrodite, who loved her immensely, had given her a beauty that could perturb and overwhelm men's minds. All the episodes of her existence—abandoning Menelaus, the flight with Alexander, the sojourn behind the walls; all the passions, ardors, furies, slaughters, conflagrations, and shipwrecks her ruinous beauty caused and would cause—had been prepared by those who live in the sky. Like all predestined creatures, Helen had to obey the signs of the gods and follow the roads they pointed out to her, wherever they might lead her.

Only the naïve believe that a predestined life is a privilege. When Helen considered her existence, what remained in her memory if not a long series of disasters? Her city, her parents, her first husband, and very young daughter abandoned; the dead beneath the walls of Troy; in her heroine's bed an unwarlike, cowardly man, unresponsive to the need for revenge; the shame and insults that would pursue her even into the most distant future. So, from the very first books of the *Iliad,* Helen cursed her fate, and regretted having followed Alexander; and precisely she, to whom the heavens had given all possible graces, hated herself. She wanted to die and would have preferred that a whirlwind had seized her on the day of her birth and had swept her into the tides of the sea.

One day Helen tried to break her predestined fate. When Menelaus and Alexander were about to confront each other in a duel, Aphrodite tore Alexander from Menelaus's hands. Then she grasped Helen by her veil to force her to return to the palace where her second husband was waiting for her, stretched out on the bed adorned with filigrees. He burned with desire, just like the first time he had slept with her, and was radiant with good looks and splendid clothes, like a man setting out for a ball. As soon as she recognized Aphrodite, Helen felt her heart leap in her breast and flung herself like a fury at the goddess, who had so shamefully insulted her heroine's dignity. She insulted the goddess as one might insult an old procuress; she proclaimed that she would never again climb into Alexander's odious bed, and urged the deity to share it and leave Olympus forever. But Homer's gods have over their favorites, their slaves, their victims, so complete a domination, made up of favors and threats, of flatteries and almost physical bullyings, that it is difficult for anyone to persevere in his rebellion. When Aphrodite became angry, threatening to change her immense love into an immense hatred, Helen bowed her head. She wrapped the bright white veil around her, recomposed her features distorted by anger and fear, and silently returned to her house. Thenceforth she no longer tried to rebel against her fate, but continued to share Alexander's bed, although shame and unhappiness darkened her life more and more.

Subterranean like all profound truths, but already formulated with precision, a question continually presented itself to the mind of Homer and his characters. Helen, the fated woman, she who lives a life imposed on her by the heavens, was she innocent or guilty? The misfortunes she had caused by her flight from Sparta, did they weigh only on her head, or on the heads of beings whom man cannot charge with the blame? Like all those who believe in the gods and in destiny, Homer replied in two ways to this question. In the first place, he absolved the fated creature. When Helen appeared at the Skaian gates, beside the men and women who soon would be dead because of her, Priam said to her in a loud voice: "Come over here, my dear girl, and sit down beside me. You will see your first husband, your relations, and friends; you have no guilt toward me; the gods have the guilt, who threw me into the doleful war with the Achaeans" (*Iliad,* III: 162–165).

But Helen was too noble a creature to accept Priam's words, which would cleanse her of all guilt. She made no excuses; she sought no justification for what she had done, although she knew how little she was the mistress of her own life. She spoke of herself as a "bitch," "hateful," "disgusting," the "intriguing creator of evil" (*Iliad,* III, 180, 404; VI, 344, 356); she accepted the guilt for the disasters inflicted on Troy and Greece (*Iliad,* III 173 ff.; VI, 355–356). Meanwhile, in ample Troad, everyone held her in horror: Her mother-in-law and her brothers and sisters-in-law had contempt for her and only spoke nastily to her. Waiting in a cluster on the shores of the sea, the Greeks hurled insults and slanders at her; and even Achilles deplored the fact that he had had to fight for a woman who "made him shudder with disgust" (*Iliad*, XIX: 325). Soon, all the shores of the Mediterranean would know Helen's name: even the swineherds would call down death on her lineage; and a single chorus of curses and imprecations would rise from every corner of the earth against the creature who occupies the center of the purple cloth.

In the *Odyssey* the palace in which Helen had lived was richer and more sumptuous than the palace in Troy. It glittered with bronze, gold, yellow, amber, silver, and ivory; it shone like the sun and moon, like Zeus's royal dwelling. The day on which Telemachus arrived in "concave Lacedaemon" in search of his father, Menelaus and his friends were banqueting joyously in the *megaron*. The bard was singing and playing the lyre; two tumblers were whirling about, and the servant girl was pouring water on the guests' hands, when Helen came out of her rooms looking like "an Artemis with a golden distaff." One handmaiden brought her a throne and footstool; another, a woolen rug; and a third, a basket with silver wheels rimmed in gold, and a gold distaff loaded with violet wool, the gift of a lord of Egypt. Seated in the *megaron*, like a very rich Oriental sovereign, Helen amiably performed her duties as the mistress of the house. She conversed with the guests; tried to cheer them with her stories; told her handmaidens to put beds in the porch and cover them with blankets and woolen rugs. And in the morning, before Telemachus left for Sparta, she gave him a present of the most luminous *peplos* embroidered with her own hands.

If she looked back, Helen saw greater misfortunes than those she had provoked in the *Iliad*. Because of her, Troy, which had taken her in as a guest for ten years, had been destroyed and burned down; Paris and Deiphobus were killed for love of her; Hector's son had been flung from the walls; the Trojan women, who had held her in horror, were dragged off to slavery in Greece; thousands of Greeks had died on their journey home; and Odysseus still suffered on the seas . . . But, on returning home, Helen found in the palace of gold and electrum a perfect reconciliation with her own nature: she had no remorse or sense of guilt; and she did not curse herself, or rebel against the will of the gods.[4] Seated on the throne, wrapped in the *peplos*, with the strange silver basket at her feet, she was calm, tranquil, and serene, as if nothing could trouble her. When she spoke about the past, it seemed that all those misfortunes were fictional episodes, picturesque adventures with which to distract her guests' preoccupied minds.

When Telemachus comes seeking his father, Helen tells him that in the last years of the war Odysseus had stolen into the fortress, covered with rags like a beggar. Nobody had recognized him; only she had discovered him, but she hid his plans and cunning tricks, for by now she desired only the fall of Troy, dreamed only of returning to Sparta to Menelaus's arms. Why doubt her words? But we also cannot doubt Menelaus's words describing how the day before the fall of Troy Helen had come, together with Deiphobus, to the Greeks' wooden horse. That day she circled three times around the "insidious hollow" packed with warriors; she palped it and then called by name the strongest among the Greeks, imitating the voices of their distant wives and trying to destroy not only the husband she claimed to love, but also Odysseus who admired her so much, Diomedes, Antichlos—and all of their hopes. The noble heroine of the *Iliad* would never have behaved so treacherously and deceitfully, without truth or loyalty, ready to betray both her new and old friends.

Yet whatever she did, even if she acted in the most equivocal fashion, the majestic queen of the *Odyssey* preserved a kind of miraculous innocence, a strange candor unknown to human creatures, who are torn between good and evil, innocence and guilt. So Menelaus's words show not even a shadow of rancor and hatred for the woman who had betrayed him and tried to destroy him. Perhaps he had forgiven her, during the years of wandering in Egypt, Phoenicia, and Libya; perhaps he had never assigned any guilt to her, as if her actions were above and beyond all human judgment, inexplicable and as free from culpability as the actions of the Olympian gods.

If in the *Iliad* Helen had been a great heroine, in the *Odyssey* she had by now left the ranks of mortals, becoming a divinity, similar to other ambiguous, insidious witch-goddesses who lived on the Mediterranean shores. Like Calypso, she conferred immortality on the man she married; like Circe, she knew the science of drugs, poisonous and deadly drugs as well as those that mitigate pain and suffering; and, just as Proteus transformed his body, so she knew how to transform her voice. The prestige of her beauty was no longer that of a simple female creature. Her terrible Siren-like voice gathered into itself the voice, memory, enchantment, and erotic fascination of all women. As soon as they heard it, heroes lost their wits, gave up all caution, and rushed with desire toward death.

In Aeschylus's *Agamemnon*, Helen never appears onstage but only in the background, seen obliquely and in a swift parenthesis, evoked by the dramatic, lightninglike voice of the chorus. Thus we learn about her flight—when she left the "soft veils" among which she had lived, when she passed through the walls of Sparta, bearing with her Menelaus's treasures, and sailed before Zephyr's violent breath. Meanwhile her phantom, her unforgettable and sinister presence reigned over the abandoned palace. During the hours of the day, she filled the mind of Menelaus, who sat in a corner, silent and humiliated, staring at beautiful statues of her which looked at him with only empty, hateful eyes. During the night, she filled his dreams, bringing him painful joys, and, in the morning, slipped out of his arms, going with swift wings down the path of sleep.

When seen with Menelaus's eyes, Helen, transformed into a nocturnal nightmare or a hateful, sightless statue, seems even more enchanting than in the *Iliad* and *Odyssey*. Nobody could withstand the "soft darts" thrown by her eyes, the "flower of desire" of her person, the "quiet splendor" that bathed her "treasures" (*Agamemnon*, 740–743). But this flower of desire was a miserable sinner, a "woman of many men" (*Agamemnon*, 63) who had forgotten the tragic nobility and divine innocence of the *Iliad* and *Odyssey*. This quiet splendor of treasures was a "mad woman," "who had violated all divine and human laws, bringing back to earth the ancient, atrocious 'excess' " (*Agamemnon*, 1454, 764). Not Aphrodite or the lords of Olympus, but a procession of demons had guided Helen's steps from the shores of the Peloponnesus all the way to the banks of the Simoeis—"bloody Discord" (*Agamemnon*, 698, 1461); and "infallible Wrath" (*Agamemnon*, 701); wicked, brazen, invincible. Ate, ruinous to the houses she strikes like a scourge (*Agamemnon*, 736, 770), and Ἀλάστωρ ("Alastor"), the terrible genie that weighs on the house of Tantalus (*Agamemnon*, 1468, 1501). Helen, too, was not a woman, but a destructive, maleficent goddess, an Eryinne, one of the daughters of the Night execrated by men and by Olympians, whom Zeus, the protector of guests, had sent against Troy (*Agamemnon*, 748).

All the troubles of the Trojans and Greeks had been provoked by this monstrous creature, born "to wreck ships, men, and cities" (ἑλένας, ἕλανδρος, ἑλέπτολις, *Agamemnon*, 689–690). If Troy's inhabitants clasped to their breasts the corpses of their fathers, brothers, and sons; if the great city perished in smoke and ashes; if the Argive warriors suffered the hardship of sleeping in the open in the bitter cold of winter and the burning torpor of summer when the sea sleeps in its meridian beds; if the battles had enfeebled the knees and broken the lances of its heroes; if Ares had sent home not living men but fragile vases full of ashes, and had buried their bones, in the hundreds and thousands, in enemy soil; if on the way back, the winds of Thrace, the crashing tumult of rainstorms, the vortex of typhoons had destroyed their ships, causing the Aegean to blossom with corpses and wreckage; if, finally, Agamemnon's indelible blood stained the walls of the palace of Argos—who must bear the blame for all this if not desire's flower, the eyes' soft dart, the Eryinne, daughter of Tyndareus and Leda?

In Euripides's theater, Helen's figure continually appears as a nightmare installed everywhere in the known world. We meet her on the plains of Troy. When the sanctuaries of the gods were flooded with blood, Priam lay mortally wounded on the steps of Zeus's altar, and the Trojan prisoners wept, as great birds shriek when they fly over their destroyed nests. We find her in the palace of Argos, where Menelaus had sent her out into the heart of the night to save her from acts of vengeance. And we see her again in Egypt, beside the waters of the Nile, where her handmaidens stretched out precious cloths beneath the rays of the sun. But where was she not spoken of, where was her infinitely repeated name not heard? It was heard in Aulis, where Agamemnon was about to immolate Iphigenia; on the soil of Tauris, where Iphigenia and her handmaidens dreamed of being freed; in Phthia, where Andromache, a prisoner, sought in vain for refuge in the sanctuary of the goddess Thetis . . .

In *The Trojan Women, Orestes, Hecuba,* the two *Iphigenias,* and *Andromache,* Euripides freely adopted the sinister image of the great sinner Aeschylus had hidden among the verses of *Agamemnon.* Helen was still "the loveliest woman that the sun with its golden light had ever shone on" (*Hecuba,* 635–636)[5]; but the splendor of her beauty was cruel and impassive. As if no other concern could touch her, as if no preoccupation could graze her—even the end of Troy, the blood shed in the palace of Atreus, or her own fate—she spent hours before the mirror, intent on saving her face's beauty from the assaults of time. When she heard that Clytemnestra had killed Agamemnon and later had been killed by Orestes, she refused to shave off her hair in sign of mourning; she cut off only a small lock, a few curls of her marvelous hair, so as to preserve her beauty unchanged.

Helen's image suffered a social degradation similar to the debasement that struck the great monarchs of the Mycenaean age after the Dorian invasions. Sparta's wealthy queen became a petty, grasping, provincial lady, living in a miserable corner of Greece and tortured by an insolent desire for luxury. As soon as she saw Alexander in his Oriental robes, glittering with gold, her heart began to rage; and with him she left Sparta for "the Phrygian city, where gold ran like a river" (*The Trojan Women,* 994–995). On her return from Troy, corrupted forever by Asiatic luxury, she brought with her a court of Phrygian slaves, soft, cowardly, and elegant, who lived in her gynaeceum, tending to the perfumes and mirrors and stirring the air with their exotic fans. But this mean, avid, cold woman still kept her fascination, which had lit up palaces of gold, ivory, and electrum. If she looked about her with her "very lovely eyes" (*The Trojan Women,* 772; *Hecuba,* 442, *Orestes,* 1386; *Iphigenia in Aulis,* 584), Helen conquered and imprisoned men's

GOETHE

eyes, arousing in them the fury of love and desire.[6] No warrior, perhaps not even a god, could defend himself from the terrifying enchantment of those eyes. So he who was accustomed to take was taken; he who was accustomed to possess was possessed; he who made people into prey became the prey of a furious, uncontrollable passion, never tempered by wisdom and moderation.

What, then, was the force that inspired this woman? Was it only the power of Aphrodite and Eros? Or was something more atrocious and ancient hidden behind her face? Euripides, this time too, picked up a suggestion of Aeschylus, constructing a new mythical genealogy for Helen. Inspired by the acumen of hatred, Andromache had proclaimed that Helen was not the daughter of Tyndareus or Zeus; she was not an earthly creature or a demigoddess, descended from the greatest god of Olympus. She had many fathers: Ἀλάστωρ, the genie of Revenge, the maleficent demon who brings down on the earth Envy (φθόνος), Murder (φόνος), and Death (θάνατος) (*The Trojan Women*, 768–769). By generating Helen, these demons had generated the spirit of Discord (*Iphigenia in Aulis*, 587); an Eryinne (*Orestes*, 1389); a Μιάστωρ ("Miastor"), a contaminating genie (id. 1584); and a Keres, the black demon of death (*The Trojan Women*, 771).

Listening to this procession of divinities and personifications, a modern reader might think that Andromache had flung at Helen the most terrible insults in the Greek vocabulary. But Euripides's Athenian audience understood his intentions perfectly. The demons he had listed, Death, Murder, Discord, the Eryinnes, and Keres, all belonged to the very ancient rule of "black," "fertile" Night, which Hesiod had represented in the *Theogony* (211, 212, 225, 228) and Aeschylus in the *Eumenides* (416, 1033). Thus the splendid solar light that shone on Helen in the *Iliad* and the *Odyssey* had deserted her head; and Zeus's daughter was lost among the monsters, nightmares, and horrors that live in the depths of darkness.

Stretched out on the ground, her face bathed in tears, Hecuba cursed "the hateful wife of Menelaus, the shame of Castor, the infamy of Eurotas, the murderer of Priam" (*The Trojan Women*, 131–136); Andromache blamed her for Hector's death and Astyanax's murder, with his skull shattered and besmeared with blood, and his poor inert hands at the foot of Troy's walls. Achilles's father thought her the most malevolent of all women, a "traitor," "a slut": even Clytemnestra called her dissolute and wicked; everyone saw in her something odious and abominable. When the Trojan women knew the victors' ships would soon carry them off as slaves to some Greek town where they would be forced to stand guard before the doors and to sleep, clothed in rags, on the naked earth—then their hatred for Helen became furious. They hoped soon to see her covered with rags, her head shaved like a Scythian, trembling with terror and humiliation; and they imagined her with her throat cut and a dew of blood on her headdress. Finally the hatred, so long nourished and fondled, had its consummation. When Orestes and Pylades attacked her with swords and Electra cried: "Murder! destroy! kill! slash with both edges, thrust with both points of your swords, strike her down" *(Orestes,* 1302–1304), it seemed that a very loud shriek of joy and thanksgiving rose to the sky from all the victims in Greece and Phrygia.

Helen tried to justify herself in a scene in *The Trojan Women.* The blame for everything that had happened, Helen maintained, was not hers but Hecuba's, who had generated Alexander; and the old servant, who had not killed him as soon as he was born; and Aphrodite, who had accompanied her all the way to Sparta; and Menelaus, who had left her alone, a prey to that demon, that true ᾽Αλάστωρ. As for herself, she dared to add, she deserved a crown because she had saved Greece from the barbarians; and, besides, as soon as Alexander was dead she had tried several times to escape from Troy, lowering herself on a rope over the walls, but each time the Trojan guards had surprised her. How painful and miserable these justifications sound; what a lack of style, of dignity and grandeur these studied words reveal! The heroine of the *Iliad* who led a fateful life, smitten by the divine will, the ambiguous witch-goddess of the *Odyssey,* the sinister phantom who reigned over the deserted palace of Sparta have all vanished. In their place is a paltry daughter of the Night, unworthy of her origins, a petty profligate, a worldly creature who has picked up her cunning tricks from the most mediocre of sophists.

The Athenian spectators, who admired *Helen* in March or April of the year 412, understood that Euripides had given himself the task of representing the luminous side of a great mythical creature of whom until then (and again in *Orestes* and *Iphigenia)* he had evoked only the darkest aspect. Probably, confronted by this extraordinary reversal, they were not astounded, since they were much more accustomed than we to accept the disquieting shifts in perspective with which gods, poets, and philosophers pursued the world's multiple and contradictory forms. The new Helen deeply loved and venerated the god or gods who lived among the stars of the sky, and stretched toward them, while praying, her enchanting hands. Her simple, mild soul hated—as the god hates—Envy, Discord, Violence, and Injustice *(Helen,* 903), and hoped that love and tenderness might rule over a world bloodied by hatred.

Among her handmaidens she seemed the same woman who had

conquered Paris's eyes and had appeared in a dream to the deserted Menelaus. But her eyes had lost that avid, predatory force; amorous deceits, perfidious tricks, and Aphrodite's philters revolted her; unchecked passions no longer lived in her heart. Her extremely beautiful face had for her become a curse, which she would have liked to cancel as one wipes out an ugly painting. Helen's new heart knew only emotions placated by the gentle breath of moderation, the profound and tender conjugal love that had accompanied her since the day she had left the happy home of her adolescence, seated beside Menelaus on a chariot drawn by four horses.

By tracing Helen's destiny, the gods sought to demonstrate the fickleness and inscrutability of their power. While Helen gathered roses to offer in the temple of Athena, Hermes abducted her and, wrapping her in a cloud, he carried her through the sky to the barbarous, desolate land of Egypt. Now Helen lived there, a prisoner in the king's palace, on the deep blue banks of the Nile. She had never been to Troy. The woman who had abandoned herself in Paris's arms and for whom so many Greeks and Trojans had lost their lives was simply a phantom of clouds and air, a vivid image, resembling Helen as she might look reflected in a mirror or the water of a lake.

So, in Euripides's new play, Helen also became an innocent victim, sacrificed by the world's mysterious destiny. How many hardships had offended her! Castor and Pollux had shortened their days and Leda had hanged herself because of shame over her; Menelaus had disappeared forever on the seas; her daughter, her joy, had grown old at Sparta, alone and without a husband. Everyone was unaware of her innocence: deceived by the phantom, the mothers who had lost sons, the virgins who, in memory of their brothers killed in battle, left locks of hair on the banks of the Scamander, the brides with their heads cropped in bereavement cursed her as the most pestilential woman in the world. Alone, abandoned on the banks of the Nile, threatened by the violence of a barbarian king, Helen lamented "the moist Eurotas, green with reeds" (Helen, 349–350) and the temples of Sparta. She remembered her lost husband, her distant youth, the days of her nuptials, when in the light of the torches the Dioscuri had proclaimed her happiness. When anguish attacked her with too sharp a bite, she burst into tears, sobs, pitying cries, sighing laments—sad elegies sung unaccompanied by the lyre, but perhaps the wingéd Sirens, shut up in Persephone's kingdom, accompanied her with the lugubrious echo of their flutes. She cursed her beauty and wanted to kill herself, to sink a sword into her breast and nobly end a very sad life.

Finally, Menelaus arrived in Egypt, at Proteus's palace, and the other

Helen, the image of clouds and air shaped by Hera, disappeared in the sky. And with what tender, loving ardor did Helen clasp her husband in her arms! She cried with joy and happiness; she embraced him, caressed him, removed his shipwrecked man's tatters, washed him in the Nile's cool current, warbled like an intoxicated singer. Then Helen and Menelaus boarded a Phoenician ship to leave the land where she had suffered so much. The mariners lifted the mast, loosed the sails, and dipped their swift oars in the water. Rivals of the clouds, the cranes took flight for Sparta, announcing Menelaus's return with their cries; and the beautiful dolphins began their dance. Riding on the backs of winged horses, the Dioscuri left the fires of the stars; they skimmed the foaming waves, riding over the sea's plain, alongside the ship bringing home— amid swans, roses, and rushes—the "most beautiful woman that the sun with its golden light had ever shone on."

The Realm of Light and Form

When Helen appears onstage in *Faust,* the demons of the night, who in the verses of Aeschylus and Euripides had been insinuated deep within her, abandon her. Neither Death, nor Murder, nor Discord, the Keres, or Eryinnes, enfold her in their frightful shadow. The sun, by now high in Sparta's sky, dedicates all the light of its rays to her "unique figure": "to the eternal being, equal to the gods, great and tender, sublime and loving."

Setting her foot on Laconia's shores Helen takes us into a mythical world we barely glimpsed in the song of the Telchines of Rhodes at the end of the *Klassische Walpurgisnacht.* Beneath the azure sky of Laconia and Arcadia, as beneath the sky of Rhodes, we live in the kingdom of Apollo, "the god generator of sharp beams, father of horses who breathe fire": the king and master who knows no darkness (8694, 8742– 8743) and cancels the veils of mist and cloud that darken the atmosphere. Apollo is the brother of Artemis who from the arch of night illuminated the Aegean Sea's quivering waters and happy creatures. But, if the moon blessed the uninterrupted and insidious metamorphoses of nature, the sun's fiery and extremely clear light protects the absolute splendors of form. Everything that moves and changes in the universe, everything that flees, showing us a thousand different faces, everything that dissolves, derides all law, and loses itself in the arbitrary, everything that succumbs to the violence of time—becomes fixed in a perfect organism. Here the spirit of choice and order, the forces of harmony and proportion are marvelously joined. The world's becoming is arrested; and everyone bows his head before a creation born of time —that has succeeded in conquering time.

The god of the sun celebrates his victory in great works of art, the statues of bronze and stone in which the gods assume a human face in order to lift men up to themselves, the miracle of painted surfaces, of lines and colors, "where only the form ennobles the content" (VII, 541–542; *Pandora,* 676); and the strophes stamped in the weak wax of words. But the sun is not satisfied with these triumphs and insists that nature vie with the sculptors and painters. Then nature seems to surpass herself. She develops and refines to the extreme her shaping qualities, generating men who reveal by their faces, the lines of their bodies, and the interlacing of spiritual qualities, the harmony, order, and proportion, the same "sacred measures" as works of art. Thus Greece's heroes (7363) are born; and Natalia (VII, 445: 35), Eugenie *(Natürliche Tochter,* 1495), Pandora and Epimeleia *(Pandora,* 461, 599, 791), and the daughter of Zeus and Leda—all the privileged creatures whom Goethe, to emphasize the perfection of their formal nature, called *Gestalten.*[7]

What is the fate of these marvelous creatures? If time destroys those *Gestalten* which are the bronze statues of Apollo, so much the more— we imagine—will the fragile, delicate, corruptible figures of flesh and blood wither and bend under the onslaught of time. But, in Apollo's world, it seems that Proteus's words have lost their weight.[8] Although Helen, Eugenie, and Ottilie die like other human beings, "the atoms collected in their precious figures" do not dissolve. Nor do the elements, deserted by the spirit of order that ruled them, easily destroy these divine images *(Natürliche Tochter,* 1494–1496, 1534–1535). So, in Hades, the great *Gestalten* of nature keep, though only as shadows, their noble form. They do not change; they are immobile, intact, eternally faithful to themselves, conserved in the empty, jealous museum of history, while other creatures are endlessly transformed.

Just as Galatea was the culmination of the lunar and aquatic world, so Helen is the supreme figure of the world of Apollo. No earthly creature is woven of light like Helen: no one lives in the sun's rays as in its proper element, and emanates so triumphant and continuous a splendor. The day on which she is born in the Peloponnesus, Helen leaps luminously out of her shell, dazzling the eyes of her mother and two brothers (9514–9521). As soon as she sets foot on the banks of the Laconia, the morning's mist and clouds vanish, and an unusual light, equal to the sun's brightness, blinds the eyes of the tower's sentinel

(9224 ff.). No light of our world is equal to hers: gold, pearls, emeralds, rubies, diamonds, the rarest treasures hidden in the earth and sea or visible at the surface, must give way before Helen's refulgence (8566–8567, 9297 ff.). Even the sun seems pallid, worn, and cold in comparison to her countenance (9353).[9]

By creating Helen, nature made a formal effort, which it never again wished or was able to repeat. Before knowing her on the soil of Greece, Faust calls her the "unique figure," indeed *die einzigste Gestalt* (7439). After seeing her beauty, Lynceus bows, together with reason, wealth, and power, before her "peerless figure"; and the chorus of handmaidens praise her as "the figure of all figures" *(die Gestalt aller Gestalten)*, that "the sun has ever shone on" (8907–8908). The spirit of distinction and order, the force of harmony and proportion were never before brought together in so perfect and spontaneous a fashion.[10]

When someone tries to see the face hidden behind this apotheosis of light and superlatives, he is frustrated. Like all symbols in which the world concentrates its meanings, Helen is indescribable—absolute form is not reflected in a real form; harmony, order, and proportion are not manifested in any evident figure. Although many readers might like to imagine her as a gigantic Hellenistic statue, Helen has no face, her hair and eyes have no definite color. Even those slight, marvelous details in the *Iliad*, the *Odyssey*, and *Orestes*—the very white, perfumed veils, the carpets, the peplums, the Orient's mirrors and perfumes—are lost among the iambic verses Goethe has given her to speak.

But if we do not know her face, we can yet recognize her presence in ourselves, in the terrible and radiant effects, the unthinkable perturbations provoked by the sight of her in reality or dream. He who sees Helen is unable to look at anything else, neither the towers on which he stands guard, nor the distant peaks and ravines, nor the immense spaces of earth and sky. He forgets his duties, renounces his reason and sense of responsibility, the power of his weapons, with which he had conquered an empire, and even his own ego, for which he had lived in the past. Everything he possesses seems to him "mown and withered grass" (9330); and the world becomes a sad "void," an enormous, insensible "nullity" (9355). Left alone in this canceled reality, lacking even the certainty of existing, he does nothing but look at the "unique figure." He stares at her as at the center of his own life; he directs at her the power of his eyes, the ardor of his heart, and blissfully sucks in "her sweet splendor" (9239).

Just as the daimonic light of Pandora's eyes subjugated Epimetheus's soul, just as the sea of fire attacked Faust from the eternal abyss of the sun, so Helen's beauty terrifies and ruins him who contemplates it. Her

GOETHE

face makes one fall in a "grim, dark dream" (9233); it dazzles defenseless and unprotected eyes; it masters spirits and, finally, it eludes all looks, which pursue it in vain (9280). But Helen can also heal our wounds. If her glance is serene, everything takes on meaning again, the eyes regain their sharpness, the soul rediscovers itself, the desire to act is once again vigorous, and the world's treasures resume their value (9331). Thus he will declare as did Faust at the Emperor's court:

> Have I still eyes? Now in my deepest mind
> Does beauty's source reveal its rich outpourings? . . .
> How the world seemed to me null, sealed, and inaccessible!
> And what is it now, since my priesthood?
> Now only desirable, firmly based, durable!
>
> *(6487–6492)*

Few men are satisfied, like Lynceus, to admire Helen's eyes and consecrate themselves to the contemplative life. Almost all, gods or demons, men or heroes, as soon as they are touched by desire for her, no longer respect anything sacred. They fight, kill, savagely torture, destroy cities, accumulating in their path ruins heaped on ruins, in order to pursue their dream. If Helen had dazzled them, turning them into her prey, they try in turn to transform her into prey: they abduct her and drag her with them, like a thing, in their long wanderings on land and sea. He who does not possess her, tears her away from the walls of her house or the portals of the temples; he who possesses her would rather kill than give her up to someone else; he who has lost her feels the claws of jealousy sunk deep in his breast, agonizing and as piercing as the shrill sound of battle trumpets.

All looks, thoughts, and human desires are therefore turned to Helen: all actions, real or dreamed, occur because of love for her who is the luminous heart of everything that happens, just as in the *Iliad* she was the center of the large purple cloth. But Helen does not act, she does not try in any way to shape her fate. She does not choose her men, but is chosen by them; she lets others conquer her and carry her over the seas. She remains immobile and passive, in the heart of Apollo's kingdom, illuminated and hidden by her apotheosis of light.

Living at the center of the world, Helen can see behind the appearances of things. Those gods, demons, and heroes who steal her away and drag her over the seas: Theseus, Menelaus, Alexander, Deiphobus, Achilles, and the new conqueror of the North who has settled on the mountains of Sparta, seem to her shadows, behind which a destiny even more inexorable than that of the *Iliad* appears. There, it had assumed

Aphrodite's lineaments, imperious but loving. In *Faust,* Helen's destiny is a force as dark and incomprehensible as storms at sea, pitiless and atrocious as the fate of Tantalus's grandchildren (8509, 8532–8534, 9247 ff.). And now this force brings her once again to the shores of the Peloponnesus to face a questionable future.

So, also, on the banks of this Eurotas and in this magically resuscitated palace, there reechoes the question that resounded through the *Iliad* and Euripides's plays. Is Helen innocent or guilty? Mephistopheles repeats Hecuba's accusations in *The Trojan Women:* Helen is a hardened, reckless sinner who outraged her sacred duties as a wife (8978 ff.; 8869). Mephistopheles is wrong, as were Hecuba, the Trojan women prisoners, and all those who, in Euripides's plays, curse the daughter of Zeus. Helen is neither innocent nor guilty; or she is both innocent and guilty, as Homer thought. What sin could we find her guilty of, if she obeyed the will of the gods? But, on the other hand, how could she be innocent, if the gods forced her to sin and to leave so many misfortunes on her path?

Helen can see no single moment in her past when she experienced the exultant sensation of being free. And yet she does not protest against the commands of Aphrodite, who pushes her into Alexander's bed, or of Persephone who sends her back into the world of men, perhaps against her wishes. In Hades, Helen learned a virtue she did not know in the *Iliad,* of accepting and venerating, in all events, the providential order of the universe. With the devotion of a stoical heroine, she bows her head before destiny; and she consents to the fact that "everything must be entrusted to the lofty gods, who do that which comes to their minds, whether this may be considered good or bad by men: we, mortals, must bear it" (8583–8586). How many terrible things occur in her life! The swift hand of fear grazes her, the terrors of ancient Night assail her like fiery clouds, Mephistopheles reveals his multiple past to her; and on the altar of sacrifice, the axe awaits her neck. Whatever threatens her, Helen "bears it"—without anxiety, without fear, without hope, maintaining on every occasion nobility of emotion, decorum of gesture, tragic loftiness of language, measure in expression, and regal dignity of comportment. This is the sole freedom Helen knows in the fateful and implacable realm of form: to change that which is imposed on her into the absolute style of her existence.

Is this privilege enough to make her happy? Is the perfection of regal form for her, too, the joy that all of us, mortal beings, desire? Those who accompany her on the stage of *Faust* are convinced of this. Her frivolous handmaidens think that Helen's beauty is "the highest good," "the greatest happiness on earth" (8518–8519), since the proudest heroes and gems bow before its splendor. Mephistopheles also seems to think this when he says that Helen, "favored immeasurably by the gods" (8845), has known long years of multiple happiness in which she has given herself up to "the inexhaustible joys of love" (8869). Helen does not share this estheticism. To her, beauty seems the most tragic and ambiguous of the gifts the gods can grant a human being (8531–8534). The "inexhaustible joys of love," which Mephistopheles perfidiously recalls, remind her only of the mass of sorrows that crashed down upon her head, the anguishing labyrinth of her existence, the infinite weariness of her journeys on land and sea. As she will say an instant before descending again into Hades, "Happiness and beauty never lastingly unite" (9940).

The world of form emits a light like the sun's; it possesses the perfection of lines and proportions, "shines and resounds in accordance with sacred measures"; it conquers time with its impeccable design. But it knows neither joy nor felicity. Dark, grim, mournful, it fears the brutal ardor of desire, the proud thrust of possession, the terror of force, the inexorable law of destiny, the blinding glitter of midday. Felicity prefers to live elsewhere: in the waters of the sea bathed by the moon, where the joyous throng of fishes swim about, where Thales lifts his hymns to the ocean, and where water and air, earth and fire embrace, celebrating the feast of Eros.

Helen As a Shade

Reading *Phaedra* and *Iphigenie auf Tauris*, we realize that Racine and Goethe have named their characters for two mythical figures, and have found many suggestions in two Greek tragedies. But when *"la fille de Minos et de Pasiphaé"* leaves her bed of anguish and drags herself out to see the sun after three days and three nights of sleeplessness, when Iphigenia ventures with a shudder into the shadows of "Diana's sacred, dense wood" and searches with her soul for the distant land of the Greeks, neither Racine nor Goethe claims their characters at one time were the bride of Theseus and the daughter of Agamemnon and Clytemnestra. The language of their heroines is not Greek, but rather the classical French of the time of Louis XIV and the elegant, purified, marvelously conventional German Goethe had fashioned in Weimar and Italy. As we listen to Phaedra and Iphigenia speak, we know that they are only Racine's and Goethe's creations.

Faust II

When Helen appears before Menelaus's palace, "still inebriated by the waves' mobile agitation," so uncertain, doubtful, disquieted, overwhelmed by the weight of her past—everything changes. Goethe does not want to present a creature freely imagined by his modern poet's imagination, but *die wahre Helena, die eigentliche Helena*—actually she, the real, historical Helen (if it is possible to use this word), the daughter of Zeus and Leda, the wife of Menelaus, who fled from Sparta together with Alexander, stayed for ten years behind the walls of Troy, brought about its ruin, returned home with her husband, died, and now is resurrected from the shadows of Hades. If we forget this intention, we will not understand Goethe's grandiose and mad attempt to sink into the pit of the past, to save a fragment from it and reproduce it in the monumental structure of his iambic trimeters.

Helen does not speak in any known language:

Greatly admired and greatly blamed, I, Helen,
Come from the beach where we landed a short while ago,
Still inebriated by the mobile agitation
Of the waves, which from the Phrygian plain,
On its high, crested back, by the favor of Poseidon
And the strength of Euros, has brought us here to our homeland's bays.

To the daughter of Zeus vulgar fear is not fitting,
And fright's fugitive, light hand does not touch her:
But the terror which, from the womb of ancient Night
In primeval times was born, still in a thousand forms
Like burning clouds out of the abyss of the mountain's fire
Burst forth on high, shaking even the hero's breast.*

The style of the girls in the chorus is even more extraordinary:

*Bewundert viel und viel gescholten, Helena,
Vom Strande komm'ich, wo wir erst gelandet sind,
Noch immer trunken von des Gewoges regsamem
Geschaukel, das vom phrygischen Blachgefild uns her
Auf sträubig-hohem Rücken, durch Poseidons Gunst
Und Euros' Kraft, in vaterländische Buchten trug . . .
                    (8488–8493)

. . . Der Tochter Zeus' geziemet nicht gemeine Furcht,
Und flüchtig-leise Schreckenshand berührt sie nicht;
Doch das Entsetzen, das, dem Schoss der alten Nacht
Vom Urbeginn entsteigend, vielgestaltet noch
Wie glühende Wolken aus des Berges Feuerschlund
Herauf sich wälzt, erschüttert auch Helden Brust.
                    (8647–8652)

GOETHE

Now, instead of a friendly word, richly endowed with comfort,
Which bestows the gift of oblivion, sweet and infinitely benign,
Lifts from you the burden of the entire past
Things more bad than good,
And darkens together
With the splendor of the present
Also the sweet,
Barely gleaming, light of hope in the future.

The lovely bank already gone,
The bank crowned by rushes, lost from our sight;
And the free, delicate, and proud swans which were gliding gently
In the companionable joy of swimming,
Alas! I see them no longer!
And yet, and yet
I hear them sing a distant, hoarse song!
Herald of death, they say!
Alas! may it not be that, for us,
Instead of the salvation of promised liberation,
It finally announces ruin:
For us, like the swans, with their long, beautiful, white necks; but also
For her who was born from a swan!
Woe is us, woe, woe!*

*Nun denn, statt freundlich mit Trost reich begabten
Letheschenkenden, holdmildesten Worts
Regest du auf aller Vergangenheit
Bösestes mehr denn Gutes
Und verdüsterst allzugleich
Mit dem Glanz der Gegenwart
Auch der Zukunft
Mild aufschimmerndes Hoffnungslicht . . .

(8895–8902)

. . . Schon entschwand das liebliche
Schilfumkränzte Gestade dem Blick;
Auch die frei, zierlich-stolz
Sanfthingleitenden Schwäne
In gesell'ger Schwimmlust
Seh ich, ach, nicht mehr!

Doch, aber doch
Tönen Hör' ich sie,
Tönen fern heiseren Ton!
Tod verkündenden, sagen sie.
Ach dass uns er nun nicht auch,
Statt verheissender Rettung Heil,
Untergang verkünde zuletzt;
Uns, den Schwangleichen, Lang-

Perhaps, for a moment, Goethe was tempted to let Helen and her handmaidens speak in Greek. And he thought he might insert in *Faust*'s bizarre structure an unknown play by Euripides, composed among the willows and asphodels of Hades; just as Venetian artists slipped into San Marco's façade the horses of porphyry stolen from Constantinople's St. Sophia, and the architects of Syracuse imprisoned the Doric columns of a classical temple in the walls of the Christian cathedral. But then he preferred to take the path of the pastiche. Helped by the natural flexibility of his language, he fashioned a new German tongue, and it followed Greek like a shadow, resembled it as the cast of a statue resembles a statue, as an image in a mirror the figure before it, as an inspired fake resembles a work of art. He hid many Greek modes and locutions among the German forms, and wrote it in such a way that they still transpired and stirred behind their light modern covering.

What Greek style is summoned up by the words of Helen and her handmaidens? Since she reflects the entire "saga" (8515) that had grown up around her and at once recalls Homer's, Aeschylus's, and Euripides's creations, Helen's words combine and blend the styles of the *Iliad*, *Odyssey*, Aeschylus's *Agamemnon*, and Euripides's plays. Thus the pleasure in verbal formulas, several metaphors, and the broad cadence of the iambic trimeters remind us of Homer. The daring verbal formations, the even more daring syntactical curves and torsions, the clusters of words, the tangles of adjectives, encountered especially in the choruses, remind us of some of the passages in *Agamemnon* and *Eumenides;* while the theatrical use of stichomythia comes from Euripides. In the end, the Greek and German seem to come together and embrace, merged in an unimaginable language; the expressions of Homer, Aeschylus, and Goethe speak to us *ex ore uno*, from a single mouth, just as a thousand years before, when Hebrew and Greek, as St. Augustine said, met on the lips of the seventy translators of the Old Testament.

Returning to earth, Helen faithfully maintains the *Gestalt* she had preserved intact for so many centuries in the museum of Hades. She cannot renounce, even for an instant, her noble forms, she cannot relinquish any element of her person, or transform herself into a living fragment of infinite, mutable nature—into a fish, a bunch of grapes, or a mountain's echo, as do her handmaidens and the figures in the *Klassische Walpurgisnacht*. How can one fail to bow before the perfection

---

Schön-Weisshalsigen, und ach!
Unsrer Schwanerzeugten.
Weh uns, weh, weh!

(9093–9109)

GOETHE

a bronze or marble statue? But only Helen knows how much the privilege of preserving the form costs, and how much she must give up in order to appear perfect and unchanged to Faust's desirous eyes.

Everything leads one to suppose that Persephone had given her the full gift of existence, for she has a body like all other human beings, speaks, breathes, couples with Faust in a cave and procreates a son, Euphorion. Yet at the end of the third act, a singular event takes place. Crushed by Euphorion's death, Helen dies and returns to Hades. Her body suddenly dissolves in the sky, as if it were made of air, and only her dress and veil are left in Faust's arms. The conclusion is clear. Just as Hera, in Euripides's *Helen*, had shaped an eidolon of air and cloud, identical to the daughter of Zeus and Leda, so Persephone, in Goethe's *Faust*, has entrusted Helen with the simulacrum of a body, similar to the real body of flesh and blood she possessed in her first existence.

As she appears to us among the hills of Laconia, Helen is only the cast, the *Nachgesicht* (7011), as Erichtho liked to say, of the resplendent Helen who had dazzled Menelaus and Alexander. The life she feigns for a few hours on the boards of the Goethean stage, imitates the breathing, joys, loves, fears, sufferings, even maternity of other human beings. But she never knows the full joy of existence as it smiles on the creatures of the *Klassische Walpurgisnacht;* for they have agreed to die and be transformed and so receive from nature the uninterrupted gift of life. If Helen were really alive, like Homunculus and Proteus, she would speak the language of all times. While the words she pronounces—the same iambic trimeters we have heard on Erichtho's lips—are a plaster copy of the words of Homer, Aeschylus, and Euripides, a pastiche that immures her in the prison of her own time and shrouds her in a funereal, antiquarian shadow.

Like every great *Gestalt*, like the great works of art and the heroes of humanity, Helen defeats the ambushes of time. The light of the sun, the spirit of harmony, order, and proportion, which are embodied in her figure, victoriously traverse the continual dissolution of things. But he who defeats time is a prisoner of his own time; he who is called up from death is not alive and inhabits the earth like a plaster cast still immersed in the spectral atmosphere of Hades. The Goethean creatures of form all resemble Helen. The immortality they know is conquered in the very bosom of death, beneath its mournful and august shadow, and their habitations are the museums of this and the other world, among Sphinxes, sarcophagi, and the decorations of that sumptuous cemetery, the Hall of the Past, through which Natalia led Wilhelm Meister by the hand.

The Light and the Night

At the beginning of the third act, Helen appears before the still closed portals of Sparta's ancient palace. Those stones, exactly like the stones of the past, awaken many memories. In that house built by Tyndareus, she had grown up happily together with Castor, Pollux, and Clytemnestra; on those high stairs she had played during her childhood; those great bronze portals, which are now about to open before her, were in the past flung wide apart to Menelaus's youthful step. The day she left the threshold of her house behind her, destiny began battering her with a whirlwind of misfortunes, on which her memory unwillingly dwells. That day Alexander, the "Phrygian bandit," surprised her in the temple of Aphrodite at Cythera, where she was performing a religious duty: he abducted her and brought her to the fortress town of Troy. There she went through ten years of battles, and the last, terrible night, when the flames burnt down the walls and houses; when Menelaus killed and ferociously mutilated Deiphobus; and when amid the tumult of warriors covered with dust, she heard the shriek of wrathful gods and the bronze voice of Discord.

Then she began the long, anguishing return. Menelaus made her come aboard his ship, not as a wife, not as the queen of Sparta, but as a reconquered prey. Throughout the voyage he sat before her, without looking at her, without saying a single word to her, as if he were meditating something atrocious. When they finally reached the bay of the Eurotas, he remained behind to pass his warriors in review on the shores of the sea; and he ordered her to go, guiding the horses, over the plain of Laconia and to reach Sparta. There she would have to oversee the handmaidens and the old guardian; to make sure that everything in the house was in order; and to prepare tripods, a basin, goblets, a sharply honed knife, an axe, amphoras full of pure water and dried-out wood for the fire, so as to perform a sacrifice to the gods. But he had not told her on whose neck the knife and axe would fall; perhaps on the neck of an animal; perhaps, as she feared, that knife would sacrifice precisely her, Helen, to the demons of jealousy and revenge.

Helen's story does not coincide with any of the many versions which the "saga" (8515) has woven around her return from Troy. In none of these versions does Menelaus so long continue his revenge against Helen. Certainly, in *The Trojan Women*, he ordered her servants to drag her by the hair and promised to kill her; in *Helen*, he seized her by her "wicked locks" and, in *Andromache*, he raised a sword to strike her. But, as soon as Helen looked at him with her beautiful eyes or showed him her naked breasts, all the hatred and rancor, accumulated

GOETHE

for so many years, left Menelaus's heart. He let the sword drop to the ground, and conquered once again by the charms of Aphrodite, embraced his unfaithful wife.

In *Faust*, Helen does not remember having returned from Troy once before and reaching the banks of the Eurotas, or of having spent the last part of her life in the palace of Sparta beside Menelaus, as the very loving mistress of the house. Above all, she does not remember having lived for thousands of years as a splendid ghost on the plains of Hades, together with the other heroes of Greece. If she feels so confused, uncertain, almost "drunk," it does not come, as she believes, from the sea's restless agitation during the voyage, but from the dizzying leap with which in an instant she traversed the space between the realms of the dead and the living. So, as Helen's ghost departed from Hades, someone magically expunged a part of her memory to make her forget her death and resurrection. Perhaps he has done something more. Who can assure us that what Helen tells her handmaidens really took place during her first life? That at that time Menelaus had continued to brood on revenge, instead of letting himself be conquered by his wife's charms? Nothing forbids us from imagining that the last part of Helen's memories—the voyage to Sparta, Menelaus's speech on the shores of the sea, the strange sacrifice she had to prepare in the palace—are only a manipulation of the queen of the past, who has insinuated a fictitious past in her fatigued memory.

Soon Helen gains control of herself, drives the fear of Menelaus from her mind, wipes out every painful memory, and mounts the high stairs of the paternal palace. The great bronze portals open, and her eyes gaze at the same stones, the same rooms, the same objects she had abandoned so many years before. Now the atrium is deserted. No watchman runs to meet his queen; no servant girl cleans the atrium or works at the loom; no rapid, hurried step resounds in the corridors. The house, which should have welcomed her joyously, seems deserted. Beside the womb of the hearth, where the tepid remains of the fire's ashes are guttering, sits a tall, thin, veiled woman, motionless like someone meditating. Helen calls to her imperiously; and the woman remains squatting on the floor without responding. When Helen hastens toward the bridal chamber, the mysterious creature moves her right arm to drive her away; then she springs up from the floor, threateningly bars her path and shows her horrible face from which stares an empty, bloody eye.

Looking at her, Helen feels that the "prodigious womb of ancient Night" (8649, 8664) has been flung open, and from it, as a cloud of smoke spews from the depths of a volcano, has surged one of the monstrous creatures of Chaos, one of those frightful creatures who at the beginning of time roamed our universe. Both the queen and her hand-maidens, all daughters of the solar light, feel threatened by this "mon-ster of cunning waiting in deep ambush" (8893–8894), more dreadful and atrocious than the monsters Hesiod remembered in the *Theogony*. Thus, on the threshold of the ancient palace of Sparta, there is reen-acted the clash between the world of light and the world of darkness, which Aeschylus had represented in the *Eumenides*. Here, too, the Eryinnes, the sad, unfertile, black-veiled daughters of the night, are seated before the temple of Apollo at Delphi. When the Pythia saw their eyes weeping drops of blood and the innumerable serpents twined around their heads, she stopped in horror. Even Apollo felt a shudder of revulsion when confronted by the evil and darkness that rose from the universe's ancient past. But, at the end of the *Eumenides,* the young gods of Olympus defeated their rivals and placated the powerful, avid gods of night, giving them a benign role in Zeus's luminous order.

In *Faust,* the daughters of light should not fear the phantoms of the night whom the gods of Olympus have defeated forever, driving them into odd corners of the created world. And yet Helen still feels over-whelmed. That figure fills her soul with terror; her mind fears it may see the harmonious order of things overturned; and her eye, accus-tomed to contemplate her own beauty and the world's, is offended by "unspeakable pain" (8746). With an agitated step she suddenly leaves the palace and returns to the sunlight, where Apollo, the friend of beauty, he who "never beheld the shadows," has his dominion (8693–8696, 8743). So, our encounter with the world of light and form reveals to us its fragility when faced by night's nightmares. Indeed, it requires only a veiled woman seated beside a hearth, a threatening gesture, an empty, bleeding eye to arouse the terrors vainly repressed by the mem-ory.

Confronted by this prodigious creature, in whom they have immedi-ately recognized Mephistopheles, *Faust*'s spectators and readers are undoubtedly much less moved than Helen and her handmaidens. But their wonder is boundless: Mephistopheles has really surpassed himself. If the spectators thought they might once again admire his abilities as a mime and clown, as in the second act when he flaunted his diabolical profile and let us see one of his enormous incisors, now he seems com-pletely transformed. Just as Christ encamps in a man's body, just as Homunculus is incarnated in the sea's waters, so Mephistopheles is embodied in a Phorkyad's revolting body. He has really become one of them, with gray hair, a single tooth, and an empty, grim, and bloodied eye standing out sinisterly in his face that is invested once again with

GOETHE

the dark grandeur he possessed at the world's origins.[11]

But, as soon as Mephistopheles appears between the lintels of the door, theatrical exigencies oblige him to conceal his double nature as the prince of hell and as a Phorkyad. Although Helen and her handmaidens may continue to suspect his demonic power (9072), Mephistopheles claims to be the stewardess chosen in advance by Menelaus. He is, he says, an old, faithful, Homeric slave who for years has watched over her master's house, guarded its treasures, and protected its roof from the rain's offenses, just as Eurycleia had protected Odysseus's palace and property from the greed of the suitors. With his marvelous actor's imagination he imitates the acid virtue, the moralism, the unshaken fidelity of old women servants; he feigns feminine emotions and habits, as though he had always dressed in nothing but women's clothes.

Thus disguised, Mephistopheles completely changes his language. His verses do not surprise us like those of the swift, elegant, and grotesque versifier; and the rhymes do not carry the cold acumen of the *pointe* to an extreme. The night spent on the soil of Thessaly and the first hours spent at the foot of Mount Taygetus, have refreshed his classical culture. Like Helen, he constructs slow iambic trimeters, he fashions epic formulas and maxims inspired by classicism's *topoi* (8754–8756); and the self-satisfied comparisons adorning his speech—"like a flock of raucous, sharp-voiced cranes who, flying over our heads in a long, screeching cloud, send down their continuous noise, making the tranquil wayfarer look up on high" (8765–8769)—try to improve on the comparisons in the *Iliad*. But Mephistopheles has read the classical epigrammatists with the same attention (8774–8782), and also Euripides's plays, from which he has learned the art of placing his pungent stichomythias.

In the course of an argument between Mephistopheles and the handmaidens certain grievous names crop up: Hades, from which Helen does not remember having come; Orion and Tiresias, who continue to hunt and prophesy on those melancholy wastes; souls from beyond the grave, as thirsty for blood as vampires . . . As soon as she hears these words, Helen is assailed by a throng of memories which until then she had expunged; and her first life on earth and her sojourn among the dead confusedly find their way into her memory. She wonders whether these images are memories or illusions (8838); whether she is alive or a phantom, a real person or a dream image (8839–8840); and an imperious force once again drags her toward Hades.

Troubled and threatened at the very foundations of her existence, Helen turns to the false stewardess. Although she does not know who she is, she imagines that the mysterious creature possesses certain extraordinary qualities, and begs for her help as from a "Sibyl" (8957), a "pythoness" (9135) endowed with divinatory powers. Since she cannot remember her own past, she asks the stewardess to reconstruct and interpret it; and she ardently hopes that her words might prove her to be a human creature like the others. So the world's two extremes draw close to each other and touch: the daughter of the sun and the monstrous creature of the Night collaborate in the same activity, as at the end of the *Eumenides*. But in the play the Eryinnes accepted a role in the kingdom of the gods of light and renounced their functions; here light's most splendid creature looks for assistance and guidance not from Apollo, her king and master, but from darkness, whom she asks to become her memory, the consciousness of her multiple past.

Like an old wet nurse who knows her master's secrets, like a Sibyl who foretells what her eyes have not seen, Mephistopheles tells the story of Helen's life. While she was a slender child of ten, Theseus carried her off and shut her up in Aphidnus's castle, from which Castor and Pollux freed her. Immediately after that, the greatest heroes of Greece asked for her hand in marriage, and although she preferred Patroclus, her father's will forced her to marry Menelaus, the daring navigator, with whom she generated Hermione. While her husband was beseiging and looting the coasts of Crete, Alexander appeared at Sparta (or at Cythera), abducted her and brought her with him to the "turreted city of Troy" (8868). Until then, as one can see, Mephistopheles has summoned up what Helen remembers quite well; perhaps more tragic and tumultuous, but akin to the life of all earthly creatures.

Then Mephistopheles remembers two traditions. The first is the tradition of the two Helens: the real person who stayed in Egypt, and the image of air, shaped by Hera, whom Alexander imprisoned in the walls of Troy. And yet, while Stesichorus and Euripides had distinguished between Zeus's authentic daughter and her fictitious image, Mephistopheles puts them on the same plane, as if they both possessed the same subtantiality, so as to confuse the queen's mind and lead it astray. The second tradition, recorded by Pausaniaus and Philostratus, recounted how Achilles, having gone down into the "hollow realm of shades" (8876), had been given the chance to return to earth and spend some time with Helen on a Black Sea island Poseidon had caused to be thrust up from the depths of the water. On this marvelous island, the ghosts of Achilles and Helen saw each other for the first time, fell ardently in love, and Poseidon, Amphitrite, the Nereids, the rivers and demons of Pontus and Maeotis celebrated their nuptials. As time passed without touching them, Achilles and Helen remained among the poplars and elms, banqueting, reciting Homer's verses and singing of their reciprocal love. Some of the Greek and barbarian sailors who crossed the Black Sea heard Achilles's quite terrifying voice resound over the waves, and the pounding of horses' hoofs, the cries of warriors, and the clash of weapons.

When Mephistopheles reminds her that she has already lived in Hades, Helen rebels with all her strength against the legend recorded by Philostratus. She tries to affirm another legend: the one told by Lycophron, according to which her lovemaking with Achilles did not take place in the remote Black Sea island, between two ghosts summoned up from Hades, but beneath the walls of Troy, in a dream, between two phantoms (*ich als Idol, ihm dem Idol,* 8879) as fragile as those of our own nights. If everything had been only a dream, she has never lived in Persephone's kingdom.

In the end, the truth appears in Helen's deeply troubled mind. The mysterious Sibyl, which issued out of Night's womb, had not lied to her. Like "a double image" (8872), she has lived in both Egypt and Troy. While she lived in the realm of the shades, she had joined with Achilles's loving shade on the island of Leucas. Even now, as her phantom resides in Hades, a body bearing her name is again in Sparta, awaiting Menelaus's revenge.[12] So who was, who is, the creature who bears the name of Helen? A living person or a phantom; a great heroine or only "the dream image of that destroyer of cities" (8840)? Crushed by those questions, Helen falls into an even more atrocious vertigo than that which, so many centuries ago, had seized her on the plains of Hades, and she faints into the arms of her handmaidens.

The Warriors of the North

When Helen, staggering, her bones mortally tired, left the desert of vertigo that enveloped her, Mephistopheles added a new revelation. Who will soon be sacrificed? Who must kneel humbly on a precious carpet and place her neck on the altar with its horns of gold; who will suffer the axe's violent blow and see her black blood run over the floor? It will be she herself, Helen, the victim of Menelaus's jealousy. The handmaidens who accompany her will have the same death that Ulysses, when he returned to Ithaca, meted out to his disloyal handmaidens; hanged from the highest rafter that supports the peak of the roof, they will kick their legs in a row, like thrushes caught in the hunter's snares. Pitilessly, in an increasingly ferocious voice, Mephistopheles tries in all ways to terrorize his victims. He makes a sign, claps his hands, and a group of masked dwarfs, round-bellied, hellish monsters, ferverishly run about, setting in place the axe, the altar, the amphoras of water, the carpet on which the beautiful head of the queen of Sparta will roll.

This evocation of dangers and infernal monsters is only a bit of playacting on Mephistopheles's part. For as soon as the old chorus leader turns to him for advice and the queen nobly asks for help, Mephistopheles promises his assistance. But, as Faust says, the devil is a pedant. Before putting his victims entirely at their ease, dissolving with a gesture the imaginary dangers he has evoked, he forces them to endure a minutely detailed lecture on the history of Sparta and the Peloponnesus. Menelaus—so he tells us—spent ten years before the walls of Troy; another ten years rowing from bay to bay, from island to island, looting ships and cities, accumulating the rich store of plunder now lying in the palace's rooms. During this time, a very bold band of warriors descended from the mists and darkness of the north, and nestled in the solitary mountain valleys in the northern part of Sparta. Among these rocks, they built a strong, inaccessible castle, such as Greek eyes had never seen. And they oppressed and imposed tributes on King Menelaus's subjects.

If we can accept Mephistopheles's chronology as true, the bold warriors of the north must be the Dorians who invaded and occupied the Peloponnesus about a decade after the fall of Troy. They set fire to and destroyed the fortress with its lions where Clytemnestra, "the two-footed lionness who slept with the wolf," murdered Agamemnon. They destroyed the lofty palace of Pylos where Nestor sat amid a crowd of his children and sons-in-law, the palace glittering with bronze, gold, and ivory, where Menelaus and Helen celebrated the nuptials of Hermione, and all the large and small fortresses of the Mycenaean age. But who could credit a chronology presented by the father of all lies and mystifications? Who can imagine that for the first time in his life, the devil has some respect for that complicated and boring affair that is the history of men?

As Mephistopheles begins his lecture the history of the world dissolves in prodigious clouds of smoke. His chronology goes berserk; thousands of years, from the Trojan war to the barbarian invasions, from feudal times to the battle of Missolonghi, overlap and straddle each other and are concentrated within the space of a few hours—as long as a theatrical performance lasts. Events lose their weight, objective consistency, and individual color; they become light, fatuous, and insub-

GOETHE

stantial as images of the night. If we examine them against the light, each event reveals in itself different, very distant events; and it is then set at different points of time—in the thirteenth century before Christ as well as the fourth and thirteenth centuries of our own era.

The Cimmerian warriors, whom Mephistopheles has installed on the mountains of Sparta, are theatrical phantoms living simultaneously in archaic, modern, and medieval Greece. One cannot exclude the possibility that they represent the Dorian warriors who, according to Thucydides, invaded the Peloponnesus. But they also represent the barbarian population, the Goths, Heruli, and Huns who submerged Greece and Europe in the fourth and fifth centuries.

> Out of the East we once descended,
> And then the West's dominion ended;
> A line of peoples long and vast
> The first one knew not of the last.
>
> One fell, a second made a stand,
> A third one's lance was close at hand,
> Strength hundredfold was each one's gain,
> Unnoticed went the thousands slain.
>
> We stormed our way with unstemmed pace
> We were masters from place to place,
> And where today my rule prevailed,
> Tomorrow others sacked and assailed.
>
> (9281–9292; Passage translation)

The warriors who came down from the mists and night above all represent the "flowering young manhood of the North, all clad in glittering steel" (9448), whom Guillaume de Champlitte and Geoffroy de Villehardouin, at the time of the Fourth Crusade, led through the classic landscapes of Greece. They disembarked at Methane, not far from Pylos, where Nestor's royal palace once stood (9454).[13] Then, in bands of a hundred, swift as lightning, they defeated the Byzantine armies and conquered and subjugated the Peloponnesus. "But behold the barbarians go swifter than my words," the Byzantine historian Nicetas Choniates wrote in tears. "They fly faster than the wing of history . . . : it has not even shown them yet and, Thebes sacked and Athens occupied, they penetrate into Euboea: yet they, not like pawns but airy birds, fly above history and race toward Isthmia, put the Roman army that stood guard at Isthmia to flight, enter the once rich city of Corinth, which stretches out near Isthmia. Then they go to Argos; roam about Laconia, and from there attack Achaea, reach Methane and fling themselves on Pylos, Nestor's homeland. . . ."[14]

Among the rugged mountains of the Peloponnesus, stuck between gloomy gorges and steep ravines, only a few hills covered with vineyards and the small plains of Elis and Laconia reminded the crusading knights of the broad plains of France. They knew nothing about the mythical and historical events that consecrated those mountains and hills. They did not know that, a short distance from them, Agamemnon had died naked under the blows of Clytemnestra's sword; that the Eryinnes had risen from the bowels of the night, weeping tears of blood; that Helen had lived at the foot of their castle, and Telemachus, searching for his father, had gone over the same roads they were traveling. They did not know who had erected the great Mycenaean tombs, of which they caught glimpses during their furious cavalry charges.

Not knowing this past, the "young flowers of Northern manhood" built their feudal castles near the ruins, similar to the fortresses that had already astounded Syria and Palestine. Thus Clemutsi, Nauplia, Acrocorinthus, the Alpheus valley, Kalamai, and Karitaina came to know the art of Frankish architects; and long lines of Greek masons hauled stone, plaster, and wood up the steep slopes of Mount Taygetus where Geoffroy de Villehardouin had them build the castle of Mistra. For more than two centuries, those castles, mountainous gorges, and plains witnessed the battles, tourneys, festivals, dances, songs, and hunts of France's knights, who led *"la meilleure vie que nul pût mener."* Then they, too, were defeated; and in those very places the Byzantines returned, then came the Turks, Albanians, and Venetians, killing each other in turn, "destroying cities and harvests," as on the soil of Cyprus (8376).

Six centuries later, while Goethe was writing *Faust II*, other "young flowers of the North" descended on the Peloponnesus, Byron among them. Villehardouin's Gothic castle was now but a grandiose, sad ruin. The ceilings had collapsed, great cracks had opened in the walls of once sumptuous halls, nobody stood behind the arrow-slit views; and in the vicinity who could distinguish the enormous Mycenaean sandstone blocks from the stones left behind by the Greeks, Romans, Franks, Byzantines, and Venetians, all equally corroded, polished, and assimilated by the hand of time? Yet, from the top of the tower, Chateaubriand's eyes could still gaze at the mountains of Laconia; the rich plain of wheat and clover that Telemachus had crossed on horseback; the hill where Tyndareus had built his palace, and the Eurotas River, luxuriant with rushes, where Helen's white swans had swum.[15]

GOETHE

The Meeting of Faust and Helen

Having ended his lecture, Mephistopheles hopes that Helen will want to follow him into the castle inhabited by the Cimmerians. But Helen hesitates and still puts her trust in Menelaus's forgiveness. So, to make her submit, Mephistopheles must employ other sorts of threats. At first, imitating the famous passage from the *Aeneid* (VI, 494 ff.), he reminds her how Menelaus's furious jealousy had offended and mutilated Deiphibos's corpse, her last Trojan husband. Then he falls back on his illusionistic arts: In the distance he makes the trumpets sound, sharp and lacerating as the claws of jealousy; he makes horns echo, weapons magically gleam; and he salutes his imaginary lord Menelaus, who is approaching the stage of *Faust*.[16] Helen bows her head. Although she distrusts the caliginous demon who succors and beseiges her, she follows him into the castle of the warriors from the North.

In this incomparable setting, at the foot of Mount Taygetus and before the Eurotas River, Mephistopheles stages the costumed spectacle he had for so long dreamed of showing to men. He presents an extravagant "historical phantasmagoria": a kind of fantastic, absurd musical opera, a dramatic vaudeville, which all Romantic librettists would have envied. Unnoticed, he slips behind the wings and abandons himself to his imagination as a manipulator of deceptions. As at the theater, when a scene must be changed stagehands drop a curtain between stage and orchestra, so a gesture of Mephistopheles brings down some bands of mist to cover both the backdrop and the upstage portion of *Faust*'s scene. The sunlight disappears. Mists that become grayer, heavier, thicker, and more impenetrable hide the Eurotas's banks and the superb, delicate swans gliding over the water.

Hemmed in by mist, Helen's handmaidens do not understand what is happening. They can no longer see each other; they do not know whether they are walking, standing still, or grazing the ground with tiny steps (9078, 9113–9115, 9144). Once again terror grips their mutable hearts. The distant, hoarse song of the swans, which rises from the Eurotas's banks, seems—to them, with their beautiful, swanlike white necks—the herald of approaching death. They think they can see Hermes, with his glistening wand of gold, come to make them return to odious Hades from which they have just escaped. But, suddenly, the strange journey comes to a halt and the mist dissolves. Everything is dark and gloomy. Tall, dark walls—of a ditch or courtyard in which, perhaps, they are prisoners—block their anxious sight. Has Mephistopheles actually brought Helen and her handmaidens into the turreted fortress inhabited by the Cimmerians—into the castle built by Geoffroy de Villehardouin on Mount Taygetus? Has he really in a few seconds dragged them through the rugged mountains and steep gorges, taking them with the help of the mist through the great, opened portals? Mephistopheles has once again deceived his ingenuous victims. He knows what they cannot have understood; that they are treading the boards of a stage. While the curtain of mist hid him, in a flash he built around them an edifice of cardboard and stone (9049), like the most adept scene designer.

Mephistopheles's castle resembles the "fantastic" (9126), ornate, be-flowered constructions, more "Gothic" than the true Gothic of Viollet-Le-Duc and his pupils. To the chorus leader it seems not just a castle but a "labyrinth" of rocks brought miraculously together (9145–9146). Regular, straight, well joined, the walls leap toward the sky, smooth as steel and resplendent as mirrors. Inside large courtyards enclosed by columns and pilasters there open up long colonnades, small arches, lunettes, terraces, and arcades. Strange coats-of-arms, emblazoned with lions, eagles, claws and beaks, buffalo horns, wings, peacock tails, bands of silver and gold, hang in halls as vast as worlds (9023 ff.). When Faust orders the servants to adorn the ceilings of the rooms with diamonds and colored stones, to imitate the splendor of the starry sky and the springtime meadows (9340–9341), the new Viollet-Le-Duc competes with the Arabian architects who decorated the palaces of the *Thousand and One Nights*.[17]

The scene becomes animated. A teeming crowd of servants moves quickly, and hurriedly, through the arcades, to give a worthy welcome to the queen of Sparta. A procession of young, handsome pages slowly and gracefully descends a stairway; and their blond, curly hair, their bright foreheads, red, downy cheeks arouse the maids' admiration. In the middle of the courtyard other pages set out the curtains, carpets, chairs, and steps of an extravagant medieval throne. On high, enveloped by a baldachin as by a crown of clouds, sits Helen.

When Faust, dressed like a medieval knight, appears at the top of the Gothic staircase and approaches the queen of Sparta, we think we can recognize him. We had left him in the middle of the second act, enthusiastic, overwhelmed, almost "mad" (7447) with the hope of embracing Helen. Now, in his serene face, in his tranquil figure, his slow, serious step, restrained by respect and reverence, his measured, solemn gestures, nothing recalls the passion that the night (of Act I) had set flaming in his heart. What experience has changed him so profoundly? What encounter along the paths leading to Hades or before the throne of Persephone has made of him, in a few hours, a completely different man? Faust has not changed and will never change, for he cannot

GOETHE

renounce the restless strength of his spirit. At this moment, like all those who pass before our eyes, he is an actor in a company that performs lyrical-dramatic operas. On the boards of a theater that appeared out of the void and in a few hours will dissolve again into nothingness, he is performing, as the young leading man, a "classico-romantic phantasmagoria" which, in the Goethean manner, could be entitled "The Love of Helen." The serenity and moderation we see on his face simply repeat the words of an imaginary libretto that he himself (together with Mephistopheles) has written and is still writing.

Like all the Cimmerian warriors, Faust plays a number of parts at the same time. So he wears the garb of a medieval knight and expresses himself like a *Minnesänger*, who lavishes his heart and kingdom on the lady of his dreams, and defends her, "covered in glittering steel," with the strength and ardor of his arms. His elegant demeanor is reminiscent of the manners of a seventeenth-century courtier; his ingratiating rhymes call up again the dainty charm of rococo poetry; while his gestures recall the proclivities of some Oriental tyrant who sacrifices the lives of his subjects to his own most idle whims.[18]

Faust descends the stairs, dragging along in chains the guardian of the tower, who forgot to announce Helen's arrival. The guardian's name is Lynceus, like the son of Aphareus (or Poseidon), who steered the Argonauts' ship all the way to Colchis (7377–7378). Even on the stage of *Faust*, amid Mephistopheles's theatrical prodigies, Lynceus still preserves the very sharp, pure, and immaculate eyes of his mythical predecessor. He lives at the top of the guard tower whence his eyes scan the vaults of the heavens, the ample space of the earth, where a wave of sheep and the threat of armies gather; and they delve to the very depths of land and sea.

In a passage of *Timaeus* (45 b–d), Plato described how the coarse, turbid fire stirring in human bodies reaches the walls of our eyes. The pupil filters it and allows a perfectly pure flame to pass through, a gentle flame, incapable of burning; a frail, dense, and continuous stream of light. When this flame encounters the rays emitted by objects outside us, then like falls on like—the inner fire meets the outer fire; and the two lights coalesce in space, forming a single, uniform, and homogeneous light.[19] The same phenomenon occurs when Lynceus contemplates things. As they fall like "rays" (9230), like "lightning flashes" (9199, 9279) to illuminate the world, his eyes are fascinated by light's countless miracles. They admire the beatitude of the dawn; the daily triumph of the sun at zenith; everything, in nature, welcomes the sun's radiance: gold, diamonds, emerald, the red ruby, the pearl's oval drop found in the chasms of the sea . . .

At the end of *Faust* Lynceus, old by now, serenely contemplates the beauty of the universe: things near and far, "the moon and the stars, the forest and the roe deer" (11294–11295).[20] But now, in the fullness of his strength, the joy of contemplating the miracles of light do not suffice for his soul. During very swift gallops on horseback, which took him through the world, his avid eyes had sought out and spied on the rarest things, including treasures hidden in other people's jewel cases. The hand grasps them, the sword conquers them; and diamonds, rubies, emeralds, gold, and pearls are accumulated, like prey, in strongboxes. So, misled by his youth, Lynceus fell victim to a naïve and fatal error. He believed he could possess the light; precisely he whom nature had entrusted with the infinitely more noble task of contemplating it with the radiant force of his eyes. So Plato's pupil, Apollo's mystical worshipper became an astute hermetic thief, a barbarous marauder, or a precious poet in love with the world's decorative magnificence.

During the early morning hours, Lynceus stood guard at the tower, waiting for the sun's solemn stride over the mountains to the east. When Helen set foot on the southern shore of the Peloponnesus, disembarking from her ship loaded with memories and ghosts, Lynceus saw the sun —Helen's sun—rise miraculously over the regions to the south (9225). From that moment on he could no longer look at the things of the world. The battlements of the tower, the mountains and distant ravines, the valleys through which the flocks moved, the immense spaces of the air seemed to him shrouded in "a dark, gloomy dream" (9233): even the sun seemed to him cold and pale. Lynceus could look only at Helen's beautiful shape, which dazzled his defenseless eyes; and turn to her the power of his eyes, the enthusiasm of his heart, the sharp blade of his thought.

Compared with Helen's face, what mattered the rolls of gold, the rubies and pearls of the sea, so jealously accumulated? Everything Lynceus possessed, everything that had seemed to him so lofty, true, and worthy of esteem, has become null and void—grass grown parched and withered under the too violent beams of the sun. So Lynceus, as soon as he is freed from his chains, leaves Helen's presence. When he returns with the servants he places before the throne, which is hidden in a baldachin of clouds, the strongbox filled with his treasures. Zeus's daughter has therefore cured him of his childish dream. Supreme beauty, incarnate light, the culmination of Apollonian form all teach him that the light slips through the hands of those who seek to possess it. We cannot imprison it in any earthly thing, even if it be something infinitely precious; but we must watch it with a deeply moved spirit each time the sun brings it over the earth, in whatever time and whatever aspect it chooses to reveal and hide itself.

Fantastic Gothic castles rise from nothingness; processions of servants

GOETHE

and pages prepare the most sumptuous welcome; Faust repeats the gestures of a medieval knight; Lynceus sings twice of his lover's anguish and felicity; battles flare on the horizon. And this feast of theatrical illusions, these choruses, these duets, these solo operatic singers, all occur only for the queen of Sparta, who as ever sits at the heart of the world, the center of the purple cloth, enfolded by the crown of the baldachin. But Helen does not react to or try to resist her fate. Now she, too, is a passive figure, an object of prey, who bows her head to others' words and will. Scarcely does she enter this fictitious medieval world than she gives up her tragic style; she steps down from her buskin, drops the Homeric formulas and iambic trimeters, heavy as the walls of Tyndareus's palace. Among papier-maché Gothic castles and the triumphs of Mephistopheles's magic, she, too, becomes an adept modern actress and even uses the couplets with which a *Minnesänger* like Faust loves to express himself.

She calls to her side the noble knight of the west, and he mounts the steps of the throne, kneels, kisses her hand and consecrates to her his love and his boundless kingdom. As in the theater, the love between Faust and Helen is born at the first glance—before an audience, before the complicitous chorus of the handmaidens. Seated on the throne's soft cushions, "shoulders touching, knee against knee, holding hands" (9403), they exchange precious couplets, like the soprano and tenor in a romantic opera.

> *Faust*:   And if the breast brims with desire,
>   We gaze around us asking——
> *Helen*:   who shares this joy.
> *Faust*:   Then the spirit does not look ahead or behind,
>   The present only——!
> *Helen*:   is our felicity.
> *Faust*:   It is a treasure, a lofty gain, a possession,
>   And a pledge; but who confirms it?
> *Helen*:   My hand.*

> **Faust*:   Und wenn die Brust von Sehnsucht überfliesst,
>   Man sieht sich um und fragt——
> *Helena*:   wer mitgeniesst.
> *Faust*:   Nun schaut der Geist nicht vorwärts, nicht zurück,
>   Die Gegenwart allein——
> *Helena*:   ist unser Glück.
> *Faust*:   Schatz ist sie, Hochgewinn, Besetz und Pfand;
>   Bestätigung, wer gibt sie?
> *Helena*:   Meine Hand.

> (9379–9384)

Meanwhile Mephistopheles rushes out to tell the audience that Menelaus is about to burst onto the stage, leading his band of Mycenaean-Byzantine pirates. Faust prepares to defend Helen and her realm of shades. Ponderous ranks of Frankish and Norman, Saxon and Goth knights dressed in armor, glittering with steel, file by on the stage. The leaders approach Faust, asking for instructions; meanwhile a rapid stage direction invites us to imagine "signals, explosions from the towers, trumpets and cornets, martial music" (stage directions, 9441). But the battle between Faust and Menelaus does not stain the boards with blood. All these ornate Gothic castles occupy no space, the crowds of servants and pages do not know the weight of human bodies, the proud feudal armies, light as ghosts, are but waiting to vanish into the mist from which Mephistopheles's magical hand has evoked them.

Helen As a Mythical Figure

So Helen and Faust meet and embrace in the scenes set by Mephistopheles. But what reader can fail to be disappointed? We have known Faust's anguish and horror on the road that led him to the Mothers, his uncontainable happiness at the first sight of Helen, to whom he consecrated passion, love, veneration, and delirium; and the dreams in which he evoked the encounter between Leda and the prince of swans. We have listened to the anxious questions he addressed to Chiron; and we have imagined the new horrors that must have assailed him on the road to Hades. In the end, this whole solemn prelude merely produces a costume vaudeville in which two actors intone some elegant duets. Are these embraces and kisses on the throne therefore the supreme love, conquered against the will of fate? Is this skillful actress, this astute coupler of rhymes really the great Helen of Troy?

As so often happens, Goethe has committed one of those "mistakes in addition" by which he tried to diminish the "sum total" of his text. He has let fall between the audience and his true intentions a curtain of theatrical fatuities, a parlor game purposely concocted to enchant that part of the audience who cannot help but applaud a demagogic device, such as the discovery of rhyme (9368–9384). But a few allusions and hints permit us to sense an idea of the mythical creature and an image of solar love, which Goethe has never before tried to express.

GOETHE

When Mephistopheles reminds her of her past, Helen faints, plunging into a desert of horror. As soon as she comes shakily to her senses, Mephistopheles with great élan salutes in her "the lofty sun of this day," which "breaks through the fleeting clouds": the sun which "even veiled filled us with enthusiasm, and now in dazzling splendor reigns" (8909–8910). Starting from this moment, Helen's sun will always remain high in the sky and no passing mist can darken it.[21]

Why does Mephistopheles salute with such enthusiasm the person he has offended and whom he will continue to defame? As she comes to her senses before Mephistopheles, though her behavior appears unchanged, Helen is transformed. Until then she thought she was an historical character, "the real Helen of Troy," who possessed a body like other human beings and led an absolutely linear existence, inhabiting a real and determined time and place. Now she has become a mythical creature; or, to put it more accurately, Mephistopheles, the secret artificer of this metamorphosis, has helped her to become aware of her mythical nature. She now understands that her life is "double," "triple," "quadruple"—infinitely multiple. She comprehends that all the antitheses and oppositions (past and present, death and life), all the dimensions which are in turn excluded, confused, and dissolve in men's normal consciousness, become in her existence a single dimension.

After Mephistopheles's revelations, Helen knows that she lives in Hades—where the entire past precipitates and accumulates, eternally petrified—as a dead woman among the dead, a ghost among ghosts. But she also lives on the earth, where she loves Faust, conceives a son, and is not unaware that this will be repeated each time a man's passion for her will be strong enough to conquer the laws of Hades. If before she belonged to Mycenaean Greece, now she is freed of all historical ties. She journeys through Greek civilization, the Middle Ages, and Goethe's times; the heroine of Homer and Euripides, a noblewoman whose praises have been sung by a *Minnesänger*, and a singer in a romantic opera. Finally, she remembers having lived contemporaneously in Troy and on the banks of the Nile, and perhaps, while she returns to Sparta's hills, another Helen occupies a different point in the world. Who, therefore, is more multiple than she who lives with both the living and the dead, in all times and in all possible places?

Although Helen tells us almost nothing about this new mythical existence, we can imagine the sort of sensations that pass through her mind. In each smallest portion of time, she encounters all the dimensions of time. For her, too, each instant is first of all a crumb of the present—something unrepeatable, which she lives through like all human beings, infinitely "near" (9411), abandoning herself to the new and unknown things that destiny prepares for her (9415–9416). But at the same time she feels infinitely "distant" (9411). The entire past—Theseus, Menelaus, Alexander, and Achilles—is present at each moment. The entire future, which she still must bear, but which she already knows and anticipates in her mind as a time when she will return to being "an image of dream and terror" (8839–8840), all the things other men know only as memory or expectation, interweave for her in every instant of the present. So, like Goethe's, Helen's existence acquires an extraordinary vastness, a profundity and plenitude, that no man, the prisoner of time, has ever been able to enjoy.[22]

But Helen experiences some less happy moments. Sometimes she understands that there is nothing real and truly alive in her existence: her body is a ghost's body. If she lives in all times and all places, she does not really live in any time and any place. And what are the acts of her life? Transparent ghosts, dream images that are repeated and recur, ever more unreal, down through history. When she looks around her, she must have the same sensation as Ottilie seated on a bench in the restored Gothic chapel. It must seem to her that "she exists and does not exist; feels and does not feel; as if everything is about to disappear before her and she before herself."[23] What profound vertigo, what anguish, perhaps what madness assail Helen's darkened mind at these moments.

So we can understand what seems at first sight the surprising relationship between Helen and Mephistopheles. If a mythical creature is a ghost rising over and over again, a phantom traversing death and life, all times and all places—the world to which Helen belongs borders on the vast realm of Mephistopheles, the lord of illusions. It is therefore not by chance that it is Mephistopheles himself who reveals her unreality to her; and that it is he again who constructs a theater around her, where she performs her mythical role alongside his weightless, insubstantial magical stunts, woven, like herself, out of air and clouds.

At the end of the *Klassische Walpurgisnacht*, in the realm of the moon and the waters, we become acquainted with the image of "possible" love, which the metamorphoses of nature, the laws of time, and the flight of emotions allow to the world's creatures. The very beautiful Dorides enjoy the embrace of young sailors, whom they have saved from "the teeth of the undertow," but they renounce keeping the sailors with them forever; whereas the eternal love of Nereus and Galatea must be satisfied with a look, a cry of joy, instantly lost in the ocean's immensity. The solar love of Helen and Faust is an "impossible" love (7488); it goes beyond the limits of nature and overcomes the sanctions

GOETHE

of destiny (7437). In fact, what does happen on the stage of Goethe's theater? The ardent power of love unites a living man and a dead woman, a body of earth and an idol composed of air; they embrace, creating around them "the double, great realm" of present and past. They do not bow their heads before the conditions and limits that weigh on earthly love. Instead, they insist on knowing that full and happy possession, that warm nearness, that Nereus and Galatea had renounced, and the "stability," the "lastingness," which the Dorides were obliged to sacrifice to nature's whims.

In order to assure the "lastingness" of their love, Faust and Helen abandon the barriers of time. As they embrace on the throne, around them "speech halts," "the day and place vanish" (9413–9414); time stops running and besieging them with its mortal beats. Faust and Helen go together into the luminous and immobile mythical present, which only the perfection of statuary forms and verses composed in accordance with "sacred measures" succeed in imitating on this earth; and which reigns uncontaminated on Olympus, where rain and snow do not fall and winds do not blow, but "the ether extends without clouds and rises white above the light" (*Odyssey*, VI, 44–45). The Gothic castle, the baldachins, the courtyards, the coats-of-arms, the battles and councils of war, the phantasmagoric inventions with which Mephistopheles imitated and parodied history, by now have become an irritating memory. At a sign from Faust, they dissolve into the air from which they came. A new scene, the mountains and hills of Arcadia, welcomes Helen and her court.

The Arcadian landscape to which Faust's grave and exalted words introduce us, recalls the fabulous golden age, which Hesiod had represented in *Works and Days,* Virgil in his fourth eclogue, and Ovid at the beginning of *Metamorphoses.* It was a time without miseries and without old age; a time without laws, without punishments, without judgments, without fears, without writings incised in bronze. In that time when there existed no ships and commerce, moats around cities, war's trumpets and horns, helmets, swords, and soldiers—an eternal springtime caressed with its tepid winds flowers born without seeds. The earth, which nobody dared offend with mattock and plough, was spontaneously covered with ears of wheat. Rivers of milk, rivers of nectar flowed through the world; the flocks did not fear the great lions; and without labor men harvested the tree's fruits, russet grapes dangling from wild briars, mountain strawberries, Cornelian cherries, blackberries, and honey distilled from the hard oak.

Over this marvelously conventional landscape, Faust, with a sure, majestic gesture, lets fall the images and colors he has seen in the paintings of Poussin and his imitators. Once again the sun wounds the tall, jagged mountains of Arcadia; springs gush from among rocks mottled with grass, and racing through gorges the brooks descend along slopes and over eternally green meadows. Goats avidly crop a meager forage, sheep graze on the undulating surfaces of a hundred hills, great-horned, yearling bulls advance cautiously to the edge of precipices. In the damp, fresh grottoes, in immense caverns, in unexplored pits that open behind clumps of bushes, Pan and his nymphs take refuge; while in the woods, full of silence and shadows, rigid oaks tenaciously intertwine their branches, mild maple trees, heavy with sweet syrups, play with their own weight, and honey drips from hollow trunks.[24]

Among these mountains and hills no Gothic castle was ever built, no fortress from which Agamemnon and Menelaus left for the conquest of Troy. The Heraclidae who disrupted Mycenaean Greece do not come here, nor the warriors of the Crusades, who overthrew the Byzantine empire. In Arcadia, the world's tumultuous past is forgotten: we are at the beginning or the end of all times, and nature reigns pure and without rivals, as in the golden age exalted by Hesiod and Virgil (9560, 9563–9565). The fates of gods, men, animals, and plants have not yet been distinguished from each other. The caves are inhabited by the nymphs of life; Pan protects the animals; and Apollo rules over the sheep, like the most beautiful of shepherds. Beneath the circle of darkness, the children live with the lambs, drinking the same milk; they grow up healthy and happy, with cheerful cheeks and mouths, guided by "an eternal youthful force" (9567). Men do not know hybris, passions and intemperate desires, restlessness and anxiety, which Nereus cursed. Who can distinguish them from the gods of Olympus who descend so gladly to earth and mix fraternally with them?

Although she has triumphed everywhere in the world, only among the hills of Arcadia can Helen have her supreme revelation. The "figure of all figures," she who never changes, forever faithful to herself, has found a world where nothing changes, nothing happens, and nothing can happen. Apollo's daughter, who radiates a light even more intense and dazzling than the sun's, has set foot in a land where the sun shines eternally at the zenith. What an apotheosis of light we can thus expect at the heart of the third act! But as always, at the very moment when he is about to reach the peak of the representation, Goethe chooses the most cautious expression. The life of Helen and Faust in Arcadia is only suggested by Faust's hymn in honor of the Peloponnesus. Then Helen and Faust leave the sun and take refuge in the darkness of the caves, where Euphorion's inspired and disquieting flame is about to scintillate.

GOETHE

Hermes

Shunning the society of the gods, Maia lived hidden in a solitary, very dark den whose entrance was located among the tree-covered mountains of Arcadia. It was an extraordinary abode. At times the poor, damp rocks shone like a vast subterranean palace, crowded with tripods and metal urns and populated by hundreds of servants; or like a very luxurious temple, where three *adytoi* contained the nectar and ambrosia, the gold and silver, and Maia's white vestments and purple gowns. There, as sleep possessed Hera, Zeus would furtively descend every night, unbeknown to gods and men—until, when the tenth moon rose in the sky, Hermes leaped forth from Maia's immortal loins (*Hymn to Hermes*, 19).

Then "a gaggle of garrulous nurses" put the new god in the cradle; wrapped and bound it tightly "in the purest bands of fleece," the purple "ornament of precious swaddling clothes" (*Faust*, 9647–9650). The sturdy, very precocious infant does not stay long in this prison; he frees his flexible limbs and climbs out of the cradle, stepping over the threshold of the dark and miserable cave, the sumptuous and luminous palace in which he was born. He has lived but a few hours and, like other children, he should have desired sleep, good swaddling clothes around his body, hot baths, and his mother's milk. But Hermes already possessed those gifts which both gods and men acquire only with the passage of time: he was candid and joyous as a child, skillful as a mature man, wise and ironic as someone who, after a thousand trials, has reached the end of his life.

He stood on the cave's threshold, looking around him as bandits do during the night hours. His newborn infant's eyes looked sharply (εὔσκοπος, *Hymn*, 73) at the things of the world; he moved rapidly and vivaciously, flashing and sparkling like a fire: so much so that, in order not to reveal his thoughts, he must hide them behind the screen of his lids. But how could he hide his talent, which gleamed in his every gesture, every act, every wandering glance? He had a multiple and versatile mind like Ulysses's (πολύμητις, *Hymn*, 319). It could assume all forms, travel all roads, and turn, always sinuous and flexuous, in all directions (πολύτροπος, *Hymn*, 13, 439; ἐπιστροφάδην, 210). He had a mind tinged by many different colors, like a painting, robe, carpet, embroidery, dance, or elegant speech. His mind was as entangled and insoluble as the knot Circe had taught to Ulysses; dark and equivocal as the oracles; complicated as Egyptian labyrinths, the constellations of heaven, and the work of bees. It was as bold and enigmatic as the art with which the gods or fortune, according to Euripides, govern the destinies of men (ποικιλομῆτις, *Hymn*, 155, 514).

To what could so restless a spirit apply itself? As soon as he issued from the cave, Hermes was tempted by one of the greatest pleasures of gods and men—inventing. Helped by the untiring patience of his hands, his mind continually devised new discoveries—new arts, new techniques, new expedients, new artifices. Within a few hours, the very young god had invented the seven-stringed lyre, Pan's pipes, and an extraordinary sandal. Prometheus, who resembled him in so many ways, had stolen from Zeus the "splendor of fire that one sees in the distance" *(Theogony,* 569), but Hermes was even more ingenious than he. Rubbing laurel and pomegranate branches together, he produced the "warm breath" *(Hymn,* 110), the ardent and beneficent spark of the flame.

But another τέχνη, "art," profoundly attracted his ambiguous soul: that of δόλος, "deception," carried out in the most surprising and acute manner: the very art practiced by Prometheus and Ulysses. The first evening of his life, as the sun was setting in the ocean, he ran off and reached the shadowy mountains of Pieria, where Apollo's cows grazed. During the night he stole fifty of the cows; drove them before him across sandy lands, mountains, hills, valleys, and magnificent meadows thickly covered with clover and sedge; and penned them in a cave near the Alpheus. Literary tradition later multiplied this theft *ad infinitum* and in Lucian's *Dialogues of the Gods* (VII) and in *Faust II* (9688–9678), we come across Hermes stealing Poseidon's trident, Ares's sword, Phoebus's bow and arrows, Hephaestus's tongs, and Aphrodite's girdle.

From his birth, Hermes was attracted by everything in the world that had a shady, equivocal aspect, that disgusts pure spirits; by all things furtive and brazen, and that offend moral, civil gentility. His interest was drawn even by scurrilous acts, reserved for characters in a farce, such as the sound of the belly's "reckless mercenaries," the "proud messengers" with which he liked to accompany his words *(Hymn,* 296). But when Hermes performed one of these indecent exploits, an unimaginable transformation occurred. The deceptions, lies, and obscenities acquired the same lightness and elegance as the noblest acts, as though he had to demonstrate that, when a god accepts and expresses it, any human quality can reveal an ineffable charm.

That night a vast part of the universe had finally found a divine protector. All those who practice the arts of deception: thieves who go at night into inhabited houses, stripping them noiselessly; bandits who steal herds of oxen and sheep; the ingenious horde of merchants would now turn to Hermes. The cunning adventurers, charlatans, tricksters, liars, and mystifiers; those who love to do things on the sly, lie secretly alongside women and possess them with violence; all who put their hopes in the assistance of fortune—from that moment on they would address their prayers to the god of Arcadia. Hermes could not refuse to satisfy them; and a shower of gifts began to fall from his hands, capricious as chance, onto the heads of his followers.

The next day the young god met the gods of Olympus: first Apollo, then the entire chorus of the immortals around Zeus. When Apollo came angrily into the den of Maia and Hermes, two contrasting worlds met. The radiant light of the sun shone beside a mocking little flame like that of Homunculus, which glittered in the darkness. A great, noble god of Olympus approached a "daimon" (*Hymn,* 551; *Faust,* 9665), a witty imp, a malicious and scurrilous spirit of air and night. The god of oracles, who revealed Zeus's real designs to men, encountered the friend of illusions and lies. The god of sacred gold saw the person who incited people to carry it off during insidious nocturnal hours. Between these two worlds, which seem irreconcilable to us, no clash occurs. When Hermes is led by Apollo to the summit of Olympus, he is greeted by an amused murmur. With the clownish grace and frivolity of his ways, the young god immediately won the sympathy of Zeus and of all the gods. He charmed them, as later he would charm the crowd of his admirers; and Apollo, his enemy and rival, became the first and dearest of his friends.

Perhaps the gods did not understand that Hermes's flamboyant and tortuous talent had, so as to conquer them, invented a new τέχνη, with which the world was unfamiliar. When Hermes spoke to Zeus, his words were not true and forthright as were those of Nereus and Apollo (*Theogony,* 233–235; *Hymn,* 315). They were insinuating and seductive, rich in strange artifices; now true, now false, full of reticences, mental reservations and irony, always complicated and sophistical. At that moment λόγος, "word," was born: the ambiguous, irresistible art of eloquence; this two-formed thing, as Plato called it, where the divine and human, the true and false, the smooth like perfect things and the harsh and rough like the billy goat, are confused in the most singular fashion (*Cratylus,* 408 a–d).

So Hermes is welcomed into the chorus of the Olympian gods, side by side with Zeus, Hera, Apollo, and Poseidon. He participates in their banquets, their loves, their joys, even their battles; and a vast growing realm, a hundred provinces at first sight distant and incompatible begin to follow his guidance and mirror themselves in his image. Black night, the thieves' friend, in which he had accomplished his first theft, remains his favorite time. As soon as the shadows had fallen on the earth; and when the streets were deserted, when sleep possessed gods and men, and even dogs no longer raised their voices, then Hermes slipped by as silent and invisible as the mist or an autumn breeze. With him he carried the immense populace of dreams, true and false. With his golden staff which strewed wealth and opulence, he touched men's foreheads; and he opened eyes, or with the force of sleep closed eyes still awake or drooping with weariness.

His eyes delved into the deepest darkness; they scanned, explored, and spied. But who could trust his intentions? According to the author of the *Hymn*, Hermes liked to deceive the wretched race of men. Homer preferred showing him in his beneficent aspect, as the companion of men surrounded by the thousand dangers of darkness, as the very shrewd friend and guide (πομπός), the silent succorer, of whom all the miserable, weak, and uncertain had need. He came down from the snowy peaks of Olympus like a young, extremely gracious prince, with his first down on his lips; he took people by the hand, consoled and calmed them with a kindly tenderness no modern reader would expect from so mocking a spirit. When salvation was near, he vanished and hid from men's eyes. "It would be blameworthy," he explained to Priam, "for an immortal god to love mortal men so openly" (*Iliad*, XXIV, 463–464).

Zeus appointed him his messenger, his herald; and the guide of the dead. As many centuries later he complained in a burlesque fashion, he was always in motion, balancing between heaven and earth, between life and death. Tying wingéd, golden sandals to his feet, he flung himself among the clouds; he flew over the snow-covered, wind-beaten mountains; he dove with his full weight from the azure of the sky into the azure expanse of the sea, like a seagull hunting for fish and wetting its wings in the salt water. Mild and inflexible, he accompanied souls, fluttering and gibbering around him, over the ocean's moist pathways —beyond the White Rock, the Gates of the Sun, and the people of dreams; all the way to the ocean's opposite shore, where stand the woods sacred to Persephone, the meadows of asphodels, poplars, and willow trees with fruits that do not ripen (*Odyssey*, XXIV, 1–14).

The still unexplored world of magic and witchcraft naturally invited his spirit, for he was enamored of all shadows, all the mysteries and artifices of existence. When Ulysses roamed among the oak groves and brushwood of Circe's island, Hermes appeared before him, like the young man who had guided Priam through the night's dangers. He seized the hand of the hero whose lineage he had protected for two generations (*Odyssey*, XIX, 397); he told him of the fate of his companions and the dangers that hung over him. And he offered him *moly*, the herb with black roots and a flower white as milk, with which he would be able to escape from Circe's power. So the prince of deceptions triumphed over her who meditated malign deceptions (*Odyssey*, X,

GOETHE

232). The great enchanter defeated the enchantress with the long wand (*Odyssey*, X, 291, 293); the wizard who knew the mysteries of the herbs, roots, and flowers, with his salutary drugs neutralized the amnesic drugs (*Odyssey*, X, 213, 236, 292). But some do not exclude the possiblity that he could even assume Circe's role, tearing from the soil insidious roots, poisonous and disquieting flowers capable of making one lose one's memory or of provoking terrible dreams.

Zeus's messenger, the protector of inspired inventions, the master of eloquence and dreams, the guide to the souls of Hades, the prince of roots and drugs—who can recognize in this very potent god, who possesses an unlimited kingdom, the small, rather shady gnome born in a dark den in Arcadia? Maia's cave had forever become a solemn and luxurious temple, where an innumerable throng of the faithful—thieves and merchants, liars, charlatans and critics side by side with Stoic and Neoplatonic philosophers, Fathers of the Church, Humanists, and alchemists—gathered to venerate the supreme wise man, the λόγος, the predecessor of Christ; the sublime mediator between heaven and earth, between white and black.

Hermes had renounced only one province of his kingdom. As the sun stood high in the sky, immediately after his birth he saw a mountain turtle feeding on grass in front of the entrance to his cave. Hermes laughed and made fun of the turtle, greeting it burlesquely with some of Hesiod's verses. Then a thought kindled the fire of his glance: He picked up the turtle, turned it over, and cruelly ripped out its vital core; he pierced its shell, fitted some cane sticks into the holes and stretched between them seven strings made from the guts of sheep. Thus the prince of bandits made his first lyre. His wise, light hands held it and strummed the strings with the plectrum, while his voice improvised some verses.

This was the first and only time in the history of poetry that Hermes would sing the songs his genius suggested to him. "Hermetic" poetry was born and died in these verses, welling up under the gay, violent, and sudden impulsion of his imagination. But, at that moment, nobody heard the great infant poet; neither Maia nor her many handmaids, neither Apollo nor the Muses who danced, sang, and played the flute on the summit of Olympus; and the author of the *Hymn* managed to furnish us with but a few, vague facts. Hermes's songs seem modest, even crude and elementary. Like young men who exchange banter and witticisms during banquets, he celebrated the furtive, amorous pleasures of Zeus and Maia and the tripods and metal urns his mother had hidden in her palace-den. What playfulness, what exquisite artifices Hermes could weave around these simple themes! Those songs, which no one could hear, must have been colored and embroidered like carpets and cloths; light as the dances of Phaeacian dancers; tortuous as the roads of the world; closely entangled as Circe's knots; complicated and entwining as the labyrinths of Egypt; candid as the daily work of bees among the flowers of the meadows of Arcadia.

The next day Hermes picked up his lyre for the second time. He was seated near the sandy banks of the Alpheus, where he had hidden the fifty stolen cows; and, since Apollo was listening to him, he decided to attempt the noblest subjects. He raised his voice, plucked harmoniously at the strings of his lyre, celebrating the Earth, Mnemosyne, the mother of the Muses, and each of the immortal gods—their birth, their exploits and their *moirai* (*Hymn*, 428). This time, Hermes had a model: the most famous epic *Theogony* with which the Muses of Helicon and Apollo had inspired Hesiod.

Seated silently to his right, Apollo listened, enthralled and wonderstruck, to the beautiful songs which τέχνη, the "industry," and σοφία, "ingenious wisdom," of Hermes accompanied with the lyre. What enchanted the protector of the Muses to such a degree? Certainly not the content of these poems; for he must have known much better than Hermes the *moira* of the gods. Hermes's new poems awakened in his soul certain effects and resonances, which till then he had never experienced listening to the voices and flutes of his Muses (*Hymn*, 452). When Hermes finished singing, Apollo tried to define the effect that the new poetry had on him; and Hermes completed his explanations, agreeing this once to interpret himself. The poems born on the seven-stringed lyre calmed and cured irremediable anxieties (*Hymn*, 447). They provoked laughter (*Hymn*, 420), gave rise to "the joy of day and night" (*Hymn*, 482, 449) in audiences at banquets and festivals; they excited the "sweet desire" of love (*Hymn*, 422, 434, 449); and they spread the soft enchantment of sleep (*Hymn*, 449).

These effects were not unknown to listeners of the Muses and the ancient poets. An adept cultivator of "the old poetry" like Apollo certainly remembered that the song of the Muses contained the virtue of calm and forgetfulness (*Theogony*, 55, 102–103); that Zeus laughed when their suave voices carried through Olympus (*Theogony*, 40); and that the voice of the bards in the *Iliad* and *Odyssey* awakened the desire for love and an even profounder "delight" than that produced by food and wine, athletic exercises, baths, the weeping which releases pain from one's breast and the contemplation of beauty. So what, therefore, was new in Hermes's poetry? Perhaps only one thing. Since the great wizard closed men's lids with his staff, his poems magically produced sleep in anxious, unhappy, or distracted souls.[25]

With this second exhibition, Hermes passed over the borders of his colorful and ambiguous world. To sing professionally as a bard inspired by the Muses of birth, of the exploits and *moirai* of the immortals; to compose *theogonias;* to divine the things "that were, are, and will be" —all this was not the task of the prince of thieves, liars, and wizards. So he left the seven-stringed lyre in Apollo's hands. In exchange, he was satisfied with the fifty cows he had stolen; with a flashing whip; the glowing, golden staff of prosperity and wealth; with prophecies, now true, now deceptive, so similar to his own words; with the *moirai*, the virgin bees; and a kind of protectorate over the livestock that roams the earth. From that day on he never again picked up the lyre; and it is probable that men have suffered from the stubborn silence of this mysterious and ingenious voice.

The seven-stringed lyre remained in the hands of Apollo who, sparks spurting from his feet and tunic, played it on the summit of Olympus. The Muses accompanied him, singing of the immortal gifts of the gods and of the misery of men unable to conquer old age; while the Graces, the hours, harmony, Hebe, and Aphrodite danced with their hands linked. But, according to Pindar, Hermes had taught something to his older brother. As soon as the first chords sounded from the golden lyre, the souls of the gods were charmed. Violent Ares, abandoning the sharp point of his lance, let drowsiness soften and soothe his soul; the fire of eternal lightning went out. And Zeus's eagle, overcome and possessed by the sounds' impetus, folded its wings, while the dark cloud of sleep —an Apollonian sleep, certainly purer, deeper, and more cathartic than that produced by the spells cast by the wizard of Arcadia—descended on his beaked head and softly closed his lids (*Pythian Ode*, I: 1 ff.).[26]

Euphorion, the Modern Hermes

Thousands of years later we are in the same places in Arcadia that witnessed Hermes's miraculous infancy. On the stage of *Faust* someone has swiftly reconstructed a classic landscape: caves, arbors, and a shadowy wood. Faust and Helen have disappeared behind the wings. On the stage's boards remain only Helen's frivolous handmaidens. Accustomed to Troy's luxuries and dances, to the almost incredible wonders of an adventurous life, they are bored in this extremely uniform landscape, in this world outside of time; and so they fall asleep beneath the shadow of the wood and arbors. Thus some time passes. We do not know how much, but it is probable that less than half an hour has gone by, just enough to make the change of scene, since the "bearded" spectators (9578) wait quietly for the drama or opera of Faust and Helen to come to an end before them.

Wearing his Phorkyad's costume, Mephistopheles returns to the stage, awakens the handmaidens from their sleep and stirs them up. He addresses the bearded spectators and all of us, promising us the "solution" of these "marvels worthy of belief" (9579). If he did not wear the mask and veils of the Phorkyad, we would have difficulty recognizing him. There is nothing that recalls the monstrous creature, born from the "womb of ancient Night," whom Helen had met beside the deserted hearth of Sparta's royal palace; nor the cruel Homeric servant, who threatened the Trojan servants; nor the wise Sibyl, who reconstructed Helen's forgotten past. Relinquishing the aura of mystery and darkness surrounding him, Mephistopheles seems merely a benign old woman telling tales, trying to alleviate the boredom of the young maids with marvelous, almost incredible *Märchen* (9582, 9583, 9595); similar to those other storytellers who, in the past in Ionia (9633), told stories about the prodigious feats of gods and heroes, or Scheherazade, who entertained the sultan every night with her tales.[27]

Those ancient storytellers, Mephistopheles says, were simply palming off tales based on falsehoods, and which vanished into the void together with the world of the ancient gods (9680, 9642). He, however, intends telling the maids true stories, everything that had actually taken place before his faithful witness's eyes. While the maids had slept, Faust and Helen left Apollo's luminous and immutable realm, taking refuge like "an idyllic pair of lovers" (9587) in a shadowy cavern in the rocks of Arcadia. This cavern had something in common with the poor Arcadian den, the magnificent palace, where Hermes and Maia used to live; and with the subterranean palaces, full of salons, rooms, courtyards, and gardens, which Prince Ahmed visited in the *Thousand and One Nights*. It was akin to the palace of the nymph Cyrene, the lakes enclosed by caves and resonant woods, under the waters of the Peneus River (Virgil, *Georgics*, IV, 335, 364).[28] Also, the cavern where Faust and Helen had taken refuge grew larger like Maia's den; and the two lovers discovered "unfathomed depths" (9596); spaces as immense as worlds; gigantic, fantastic subterranean palaces, larger than those magic had built on the hill of Sparta—room after room, courtyard after courtyard; woods and meadows, lakes and brooks (9595, 9598).

Only Mephistopheles followed them into those strange spaces. With them, he abandoned the light of the sun, so hateful to him; and he immersed himself in his element, going down into the dark bowels of the earth, its crevices and labyrinths (5015, 5030 ff.). There he offered them his services as a faithful servant. But suddenly, he left them alone, and began venturing among those rooms and courtyards, those lakes and woods. As if to imitate the arts of the herborist Hermes, he was searching for moss, roots, and barks that his hermetic knowledge would then transform into malign drugs similar to Circe's, or, perhaps, salutary medicines (9592).

When he heard an infant's laughter echo under the vaults, he returned to Faust and Helen. He saw a baby boy leap from his mother's lap to his father's; like a wingless genie or small faun. The infant shrieked and cried joyously, jumped to the ground, and the ground bounced him up again like a ball toward the cavern's high ceiling. Then he suddenly disappeared in the cleft of a ravine, to the distress of Faust and Helen. When he reappeared he was marvelously crowned. He was wearing clothes bedecked with flowers. Bows swayed at his arms, ribbons fluttered around his breast; he carried in his hands a golden lyre; and an ornament of gold or "a flame of very powerful spiritual force" (9624) shone around his head.

Who is the hero of Mephistopheles's truthful fable? Who is the portentous creature born suddenly from the love of Faust and Helen? Mephistopheles does not pronounce his name; we will learn later that he is called Euphorion, like the son that legends attributed to Achilles and Helen. But only the chorus of the maids, whom Goethe endows with the gift of his own mythological knowledge, reveals to us who the son of Faust and Helen actually is. Just as the furtive love of Zeus and Maia had generated the god Hermes, so the equally furtive love of Faust and Helen created the impetuous and fragile Hermes of modern times: the "marvel worthy of faith" whom Mephistopheles, the infernal Mercury, announces with an unusually excited voice to the silent, wonderstruck spectators of *Faust II*.[29]

Like Hermes, Euphorion is a daimon and an incredibly precocious genie (9603). Whereas the god had leaped from Maia's loins after nine months of gestation, Euphorion, as swift and artificial as Homunculus, was born immediately after having been conceived in Helen's spectral womb. His life confirms this prodigious birth. He is born and immediately he speaks, laughs, plays, leaps like an acrobat from one precipice to another; his fingers play marvelous melodies on the lyre, his feet and arms dance on the plain of Arcadia; his heart burns with amorous desire and warlike ardor. After an hour of theatrical life, he has already lived for a long time, more intensely and profoundly than many who travel the slow paths of this earth.

Cave-born Euphorion owes his gifts not to the light of the sun, which blesses Helen's existence, but rather to the earth and darkness. Without the assistance of the earth, without the talents given him by the caves, his genius would be quickly lost. When he wants to jump high, he must touch the earth with his foot; and immediately, like Antaeus, he is filled with the soil's marvelous nutritive and elastic strength, and flies up among mountains and gorges, vying with the wind's buoyancy. Also, poetic inspiration was not bestowed on him, as on the *Knabe Lenker* (5693), by the sky's "sweet radiance." Nor has he found the symbolic signs—the beflowered clothes, the golden lyre, the ornament of gold, or the inspirational flame—"in the cleft of a rugged ravine" (9614), in one of those chasms where, as Mephistopheles says, we must search for the treasures of knowledge. Euphorion possesses the same sort of mind as Hermes, multiple, versatile, and many-hued, full of resources and cunning devices; the same capacity of invention and metamorphoses; the same gnome's airy grace; the same infantile, daringly virile spirit, naïve and malicious, loving and cruel. Just as Zeus and Apollo gazed spellbound at the new god, so Faust and Helen, the chorus, even Mephistopheles, stare with enchantment at the new daimon who has descended to deceive the earth or to make it happy.

But "everything that happens in our day," as the maids of the chorus sing, is only the "sad echo of our ancestors' marvelous days" (9637–9640). Greece is covered with ruins; the gods of Olympus are dead; the myths, which modern men recount with the help of Mephistopheles, are much poorer than the "amiable lies" of ancient times. So the new Hermes is inferior to his model. He is not a god but only a theatrical ghost who is born, plays an instrument, and dances in stage settings built by the devil. He does not know how to fly freely; he cannot fling himself among the clouds like Hermes; and his impetuous leaps fall far short of his yearnings. Like men whom despite everything he resembles, Euphorion does not know himself; he does not possess that stupendous intuition of his own *moirai*—the role, limits, thoughts and actions belonging to each of us—which permitted the gods to live in the most harmonious and natural fashion.

Incapable of living within the confines of fate, Euphorion feels confined in an atrocious prison. An even more anxious restlessness than Faust's, a frenzy, a reckless hybris compels him to be lavish, to pour himself out, to rush into new activities, as if the center of his life were outside himself, at an unreachable point. His behavior becomes more violent; he challenges any danger; breaks through obstacles, real or imaginary; passes beyond the limits with which destiny has surrounded him. The only thing he desires is the beatitude of death; the definitive

GOETHE

consummation of those great and small forces nature has bestowed on him. So, toward the end of his life, Euphorion loses the gaiety and grace of his infancy. While in a fury he traverses the mountains and plains of Arcadia, he does not remind us of the prince of bandits, the restless spirit of the night, the seducer of all souls; but rather of one of those ancient and modern Titans who are fulfilled by shattering themselves against the barriers of their destiny. He reminds us of Icarus, who stretched out his wings to the sun and fell into the waters of the Aegean (9901); a wretched and talented *Stürmer;* a Byron who travels, as irresistibly as he, the dizzying steps of "a space full of pain" (9880).

His kingdom embraces a small part of the territories over which Hermes extended his rule. Thieves and traders, alchemists and herborists, liars, orators, sophists, actors and sleight-of-hand artists, inventors, magicians, and wizards no longer receive their powers from him but from Mephistopheles, the infernal Hermes. Euphorion possesses only the territory of music and poetry, still confused as at the time of Hermes and Apollo.[30] He has no rivals in this sphere. From birth, he displays the symbolic marks of the sovereign poet: the beflowered clothes and the golden lyre. The very genius of poetry—a potent spiritual flame, a precious gold ornament—splendidly encircles his young brow. So Mephistopheles can present him to the wonder-struck audience as "the future master of all beautiful things, through whose limbs course the eternal melodies" (9626–9627).

What does Euphorion sing on his lyre? What poetry inspires the flame encircling his head? Goethe does not make us listen to any of his songs or even indicate their subjects. Yet the new Hermes certainly does not try to evoke the world of deceptions and wealth which the old Hermes had summoned up, or the genealogies, the exploits, the *moirai* of the gods. For Euphorion, as for Mephistopheles, these subjects are merely very old "fables" (9680). In modern times, when all things are miserably humiliated and degraded, the objective splendor of Apollo's light does not graze the poets' brows (9691). A modern poet draws only from a source he bears within himself: the immense darkness of the human heart (9685, 9692–9694). But this "heart" contains many more things than a romantic reader might suppose. It includes the most subtle and ambiguous mysteries of consciousness concealed in hermetic labyrinths, in gorges full of roots, poisons, and drugs, in dangerous and unfathomable caves, where Euphorion has gathered the insignia of poetry.

When he touched the lyre with his plectrum, Hermes calmed and cured pains and anguish; he awakened joy, aroused amorous desire, and spread the spell of sleep. When Euphorion touches the lyre, his songs and words are insinuating and flattering (*Schmeichelton,* 9688) like those of the prince of liars; but they do not placate, do not cure, do not put sick souls to sleep. All who listen to Euphorion's songs seem the victims of a contagion. Their souls become soft and yielding (9690); a strange atmosphere of convalescence beguiles them (9698), the "plea-sure of tears" (9690) assails every heart, an intoxication confuses the most limpid minds (9964). So, in Euphorion's Dionysian and darkling poetry there is something of the impure: perhaps of the orgiastic (9964–9965). And yet, except for Panthalis, faithful student of Apollo's laws, the characters in the play, Helen, Faust, the chorus, even the mockingly cynical Mephistopheles,[31] applaud the new prince of poets, for they sense in Euphorion's words and sounds an even deeper seduction, an even more mysterious and irresistible charm than that which accom-panied Hermes's songs.

As we have seen, Hermes ceded the lyre and his new songs to Apollo and the Muses, enclosing the cycle of poetic activity in a perfect circle. If so many different intellectual and imaginative faculties flowed to-gether in the songs of the *aedi;* if ingenious technique and the genius of visionaries, the intricate, multiple mind and the simple, unified mind, the lie and the truth, the darkness of night and the light of the sun were equally useful to poetry, all these qualities gathered in the end under Apollo's imperious law. The conclusion of the Euphorion episode is different. The impetuous modern Hermes does not hand over the lyre to Apollo, or to some figure representing him, because he cannot re-nounce the unique, extremely rare virtue that is left him. He guards it jealously until the day of his death. He also keeps that faculty that had always possessed a profoundly Apollonian quality—*mania,* as Plato called it; creative genius, flaming, irresistible inspiration. In *Faust II,* this faculty always has an hermetic imprint; in fact, that other incarna-tion of poetry, the *Knabe Lenker,* is also a brother of Euphorion or Euphorion himself; a prodigious Narcissus who spreads his gifts with the same anxious and happy prodigality.[32]

So in *Faust II* Apollo is no longer the absolute sovereign, the cautious and violent dominator of poetry, as among the Greeks. Many of the poetic and intellectual qualities, which in the past were gathered about his figure, have escaped his control; and they are born, move about, erupt on the stage of literature, ignoring him completely. In Goethe's world, Apollo exercises his powers on a single aspect of poetic intelli-gence: absolute form, the harmonious, measured, and well-propor-tioned *Gestalt,* blessed by the splendor of the sun, which courses un-changed through the vicissitudes of time.

GOETHE

The Fate of Poetry

The life of Faust's and Helen's child in the woods and rocks of Arcadia lasts as long as a whirling, dizzying ballet. In the first scene, Euphorion leaps from one rock to another inside the cavern; and climbs light and agile as a chamois goat through the mountain groves of bushes, woods, and rocky gorges. He would like to climb ever higher, leave the ground (9724) and in the spaces of the air dissolve all that still remains in him of the terrestrial and dark. Like a butterfly leaving the constriction of the chrysalis, he would like to open the angelic and demonic wings he does not possess, flit capriciously through the layers of the ether, and finally touch the summit of the sky.

The ballet's second scene is milder. Euphorion accepts his parents' advice to practice moderation, and he goes down to the plain, where he drags Helen's maids into the dance. He lovingly waves his arms, shakes his blond curls, skims over the ground, while rapid strophes accompany his dance. This calm does not last for long. Just as Hermes pursued the nymphs, Euphorion runs after the girls among the wood's rocks and underbrush. He abhors "what he can reach easily"; only "what he must conquer by force" amuses him (9781–9784). So he pursues the wildest of the maids, a tart, shy girl, and clasps her to his breast; his race and her cries resound through Arcadia, savage and shrill as the clangor of trumpets.

With the last picture, the third act of *Faust II* takes a final leap in time, and the war of Greek liberation steps onstage like a phantasmagoria. From behind the wings, one hears thunders and roars from the sea; imaginary armies, reflecting the actions of too real armies, fight in the dust and on the waves. Meanwhile, Euphorion's exalted speech remembers Greece's men, women, and children who shed their blood, armed only with "unlimited courage" (9845). Euphorion participates in the war, flings himself into the dangers of the battles and seems encased in armor, refulgent with bronze and steel. "No sooner was he called to life, no sooner was he given to the serene day" (9877–9878) than he dreams of death. As if he wanted to repeat Icarus's attempt, he projects himself into the air, invoking the grace of flight: his clothes sustain him, his head shines, a stream of light follows him; then, to everyone's enormous grief, he falls to the ground at the feet of Faust and Helen.

Euphorion's death is as prodigious as his birth and life. The handsome earthly body, donned for so brief a time, resembles Byron's "well-known figure"; finally it disappears and dissolves in the air like Helen's, which was also woven out of air and illusions. The flame, the aureole of gold that encircled his head, rises toward the heavens like a comet: and the clothes, mantle, and lyre remain on earth, in Mephistopheles's hands.

When Euphorion descends into Hades, the chorus of Trojan girls intones a funeral lament:

> Lofty in lineage and power,
> Born for every earthly joy,
> Snatched away in youthful flower,
> Wrested from yourself too soon.
> Sharp eyes to contemplate the world,
> Sympathy for all the heart's deep woes,
> A flame of love to the noblest women,
> And your unique song.
> . . .
> Sublime the goals you set yourself,
> And yet you did not gain them.
>
> Who gains them? The dark question
> Before which fate dons its mask,
> While on this day of grief a nation
> Bleeds, and falls silent.[33]

Wem gelingt es? "Who gains from it?" This dark question assailed Goethe when confronted by the fate of any man, and it made him halt, deeply troubled or bitterly skeptical, before the inevitably imperfect results of his poetry. "It does not bring a gain" to anyone; here on this earth, imprisoned in the chrysalis of our bodies, none of us can attain "something of the sublime."

Then Mephistopheles strides onto the stage, picks up Euphorion's flowered garment, his mantle and lyre—all that is left of him in the world, his "mortal remains" (stage direction, 9954); his "works," as we might translate with a slight violence to the words. He holds them aloft and says ironically:

> There's always something gained!
> Of course the flame is out and doused,
> But this world doesn't make me weep.
> Enough is left for poet's consecration,
> To stir up envy in their guilds devout;
> And if I can't provide the inspiration,
> At least I'll lend his wardrobe out.[34]
> (*MacNeice translation, slightly revised*)

So, from Mephistopheles's lips, we listen again to Proteus's mockery of the fate of human works. Artists shape bronze statues in honor of the

GOETHE

gods; they paint surfaces and lines, masses and colors on the walls of temples and of funeral monuments; they intone their mysterious and pathetic songs on the lyre, hoping to win the eternity of fame. But what remains of those statues? Scattered fragments, destroyed by an earthquake's tremor, and soon melted down by other artists, perhaps with no memory of the original artists. And what remains of that poetry? The inspired flame disappears in the sky; while the clothes, mantle, and lyre, Euphorion's "works," fall into the hands of the mediocre, envious guilds of poets, and these fight over them, copy them more and more basely, thus giving them the grotesque immortality of history.

It seems therefore that an unappealable sentence weighs on all works of art: All inevitably are failures, and are offended by the counterfeits of time. Nothing "is gained" by anyone; and even we must fall silent, as do the Trojan girls, when faced by "the dark question before which fate dons its mask." But, just when they have touched the nadir of distress, the chorus invites us, with a Pindaric reversal, to forget our desolation. They ask us to remain no longer so deeply prostrated, and to "sing fresh songs" (9935–9936). A hope we had already renounced, an unexpected salvation appears on the horizon of the world and of poetry. Something will never die. If the bodies of poets go to Hades and their works are mocked by time, Mother Earth does not lose its inexhaustible generative power that with the same naturalness produces trees, luxuriant harvests, green grasses, and new artists (9937–9938). Other Telchines will model statues in honor of the celestial gods; newer Euphorions will be born in the caverns, finding inspiration in the enigmas of knowledge and the elastic impulsion of the soil; other Wielands, other Byrons, other Goethes, sprouting from the earth like mushrooms, will arouse the admiration of their deeply moved nations.

A part of that force that bore the name of Euphorion is also eternally preserved. While Mephistopheles mocks at the fate of his works, the indefinable quality that Goethe calls genius knows neither death nor the degradation of time. The "aureole" encircling his head, the "flame of a powerful spiritual force" that wreathed it as splendid as gold, ascends with the velocity of a comet toward the ultimate spaces of the sky, where nothing impedes the triumphs of lightness. It sails above the clouds, "high, always higher and unattainable," like the crown Tasso wanted to follow all his life; it shines "distant, ever more distant" like "a beautiful star" (*Faust*, 9863–9866), losing itself in infinite space.

When Helen appeared at Sparta's royal palace we believed that, despite Proteus's sarcasms, the measured and luminous forms of Apollo's kingdom have come perfect and immutable through the vortexes of history. But at the end of the act, what a reversal! Apollo's sad and sublime world is defeated by its own fundamental exigencies; human works, the creations of sculptors and poets, have never completely succeeded; they are never perfect; and they lie on the earth degraded by time. However, poetry's essential quality exists at two opposite poles —both hermetic—between which it moves. The first is the earth which inexhaustibly generates it. The second is the infinite force of flight, the indefinable impetus, the ever renewed desire that flings it toward the heavens. This second is like the impulse of true love, like the aspiration of Hope, which overcomes the walls of necessity with a beat of its wings and guides us into the illimitable realm of the eternal future; like Makarie's calm and uninterrupted movement through the heavens. Thus the essence of poetry does not rest in Apollo's firm and luminous hands, but in Hermes's dark and aerial ones. What does it matter if the life of Hermes-Euphorion lasts but an instant? At the moment he reaches Hades in tears he reveals to us that his flame, so active, mobile, and restless, is much less mortal than the static forms shaped by Apollo.

Yet this allegorical triumph of Hermes over Apollo does not express Goethe's last word on the nature of poetry. Like all of Goethe's ideas, his conception of poetry resembles a solar system, in which many planets move undisturbed along their orbits, bound together by a secret tie. In this planet which is the episode of Euphorion, Hermes's law defeats Apollo's, and kills the Apollonian life that had been realized among Arcadia's valleys and woods. But, in the other planet which is the first act of *Faust II*, Plutus and the *Knabe Lenker*—the rotund, peaceful Oriental Califf, and the anxious ephebe who lavishes the jewels and beetles of his rhymes, that is, Apollo and Hermes—collaborate harmoniously under Apollo's spiritual guidance.

If we wish to represent the Goethean idea of poetry, we must gather together many other characters, images, and symbols. He who shapes words is like the god of Leibniz, governing the edifice of the universe with the faint smile of the wise; but also like Faust, who rushes toward a goal he will never reach; and like Mephistopheles, who knows only the dry inspiration of irony, the elegant play of the epigram, the illusionistic spectacles of the theater. The poet is a sleepless nocturnal wayfarer, the victim of his own insatiable memory; an unahppy courtier whose blood is kindled by wine and drugs; a deformed young boy, who speaks the lost maternal language of the human race; a harpist, pursued by the Furies for a crime of which he is both innocent and guilty. The poet is a patient gardener who cultivates roses and prunes trees that grow wild; a cold, adept weaver who weaves on his loom magnificent and extravagant carpets like those of Samarkand; an old carpenter with gnarled, rough hands; a mathematician, who arrives by guesswork at all his sums by always making mistakes.

Poetry shines brightly like the gold that covered the island of Delos when Apollo was born, and like the bronze statues the Telchines constructed at Rhodes. It flows away, as mobile as the waters of the Euphrates. It sways in the air like a delicate veil woven from sunbeams and clouds, like a rainbow reflected in the spume of a waterfall, or a spectral echo of sounds. Poetry erupts from nocturnal dreams with the violence of a lightning bolt, sprouts like a colony of mushrooms under a sudden downpour; and it grows slowly, like the oak tree and the juniper. He who bears it within himself feels the fire consume his temples and his thoughts; and the cool wing of the evening wind calms his fatigued brow. He who listens to it during banquets and festivals, he who reads it in the silence of his room, experiences the dolorous, morbid intoxication of tears; and he is healed by sleep, which unties the knots of hard thoughts just as it closed the lids of Zeus's great eagle.

All these images and these characters, here collected almost at random on paper, present barely a shadow of the Goethean idea of poetry. He who will reconstitute it in its almost inexhaustible completeness, by describing the antitheses, contradictions, nuances, and ever renewed equilibriums, will probably realize that he has drawn the map of Goethe's entire world.

The Reign of Dionysius

When Euphorion disappears weeping, Helen embraces Faust for the last time; then her body of air dissolves and once again descends into the eternally full, eternally empty plains of Hades. Thus, after a brief resurrection, Helen is returned to the Museum of the Past, where she belongs. Like all the great figures of the solar world, she conserves in Hades her own persona, untouched by the metamorphoses of things, just as the hand of the Creator had formed her. She does not change, she is not transformed; she remains immobile, waiting for a new Faust to resurrect her for another very brief instant. But she does not leave our world entirely. While her historic "figure" lives in Hades, the Mothers' omnipotent hands continue to distribute her "absolute image" over the course of life, and renewed incarnations of Helen, changed and unrecognizable, illuminate the melancholy paths of the earth.[35]

Faust's existence in the woods and valleys of Arcadia has ended forever. He had hoped to reach the eternal present of myth, he had dreamed of conquering "impossible" love by living beside a light even purer than that of the sun. Nothing of all these dreams and hopes is left him. As hurried as Euphorion, he falls back into the tumult of time; his love for Helen has not been more lasting than the love between the Dorides and the young sailors; and the light of the sun is again hidden by the clouds whose role it is to conceal the splendor of the absolute.

But Faust's experience does not fall prey to the voracious demons beyond the grave, who try to snatch from us all the worthy things of our past. Of those enchanting "fugitive days" (10054), of those blessed instants outside of time, something remains in Faust's hands. Returning to Hades, Helen left him her dress and veil. They dissolve and are transformed into a cloud which lifts him on high and carries him across Europe's mountains and seas into the heart of Germany. There the cloud leaves him on the solitary brink of a mountain. Then as it drifts away it does not dissolve, but it condenses before Faust's marveling eyes. It divides as it travels through the sky, changes, sways, searching for a form; and it seems a gigantic figure of a woman—Juno, Leda, or Helen—majestically stretched out on cushions made radiant by the sun. Finally its aspect changes again. Broad, formless, towering like a "distant mountain of ice" (10053), it returns to the regions of the Orient, to the Greece where it was born.

Everything leads us to believe that Goethe was inspired by a famous tale from the *Thousand and One Nights* in which the daughter of the king of spirits escaped to heaven, wearing her magical gown of air.[36] But this episode in *Faust* is not simply an Oriental carpet woven with sumptuous and patient love. The very white gown and veil that remained in Faust's hands, the cloud lit by the sun, are the theatrical representation of the Helen that Faust preserves in his memory, like an undulating figure of mist expresses the memory that Epimethus possesses of Pandora. This "inestimable gift" (9951) reflects "the great meaning of the fugitive days" (10054) Faust lived with Helen. It will never dissolve into nothingness; like an infinitely precious treasure it will always preserve the reflected light of that dazzling past; and it will continue to guide him toward the highest ether (9952–9953).[37]

Among Helen's maids only Panthalis follows her queen to Persephone's throne without delay. All the others had never tried to win the glory of a name; they had not been true and proper "persons," coherent and enclosed figures like Helen. They had lived a capricious, sensual existence, enjoying the passing pleasures of the moment, loving only the privilege of beauty, the splendor of jewels, of pearls and gold, and of dancing wildly with the young stablemen of Troy and Mistra. In Hades, none of them could listen to the conversations around Persephone's throne. Lowly supernumeraries, they will remain in the back-

GOETHE

ground among the willows and rows of poplars, without experiencing even a pale echo of the joys that make life happy; and, right to the end of the centuries, they will continue to chitter lugubriously like bats, to whisper and hiss like sinister ghosts. So the girls of the chorus do not follow Helen and Panthalis into Hades. They remain on earth, among the elements, renouncing their weak individual figures. But, in exchange, they obtain from nature the gift Helen has never known: immortality of life; memoryless happiness and joy, the fire and moisture, the air and the weight of existence lost in the womb of nature.

Penetrating into the bark of trees, the first group stimulates the sources of life. Gently, almost playfully, they draw them up from the roots all the way to the trembling murmur, the swaying rustle of the highest branches; and they profusely adorn their tresses with a free vegetation of leaves, flowers, and fruits. Others bend caressingly, moving in soft waves along the bright mirror of the rock walls. They strain their ears, listen to all of nature's sounds—the songs of birds, the trills of flutes, whispers, thunders, Pan's terrible voice—and immediately respond with their echo, to double, triple, endlessly multiply those whispers, those thunders, those roars, and flute trills.

Other maids, more vagrant in spirit, become water and, attracted by the hills' profiles, run down to the valley. They undulate in sinuous meanderings, irrigate meadows, pastures, and gardens around the houses, where the tops of the cypresses mark off the line of the riverbanks. A last group remains higher up; and with its murmur surrounds the places where the vines grow green on the trellis poles, and the passion of the vineyard worker hoes, digs ditches, piles up the soil, prunes, and ties the tendrils of the vine. When the gods have filled the cornucopia of the grape clusters with air, humidity, and heat, something suddenly comes alive where the vineyard worker has labored in silence; something murmurs through every leaf and rustles from plant to plant. Soon the abundance of grape clusters make baskets creak, buckets clatter, and laden hods groan; and the grape treaders make the grapes spurt under the soles of their feet, dancing impetuously in the wine vats.

The earth gives nourishment to the trees; the air slides along the walls of rock; the water flows down to the valley; the fire burns in the cornucopia of grapes—Goethe has once again orchestrated his hymn to the four elements. But the nature triumphant at the end of the third act has nothing in common with the nature seen in the Aegean and the mythical nature of Arcadia. This world of trees, mountains, brooks, and vineyards conceals no theology; it is not inhabited by Cabiri, or by Thales, Proteus, or Homunculus; it does not reveal the harmony governing it, the eternally unfulfilled love that tortures it, the power of metamorphosis that makes it incomprehensible, or the élan that re-establishes its lost unity. Here we live in the heart of elementary nature among whispers and feminine allurements, prodigal lymphs, multiple, lucid echoes, warm rustles, and orgiastic vitality which now creeps underground, now erupts on the world's surface. This nature cannot grow and surpass itself; and it finds a kind of divinization only in the ecstasy—not superhuman but subhuman, not erotic but sensual—of Dionysian intoxication.

The god of this world is not Artemis, who guides the moon and the aquatic generations; nor Apollo, the god of form; nor Hermes, the poetic genius of the shadows; but Dionysius, who rules over the intoxi-cation of the senses and spirit. We see him under an arbor, or shut up in a grotto where the new, cool wines fill heaps of leathern flasks, jugs, and casks. Not at all concerned about the vineyard worker who toils for him, he lies there languidly, limply, the victim of a dreaming inebria-tion, and plays and frolics with the youngest of his fauns. When the wine treaders crush the grapes, Dionysius leaves his mysteries; the crash of brass cymbals shrieks and deafens; beside him advance the fauns and nymphs with goat's feet, and Silenus's shrilly braying ass. Their cloven hoofs do not respect anything sacred. Seized by vertigo, the senses totter, hands grope for more and more goblets and empty the old leathern flasks; heads and bellies are filled to bursting; the tumult in-creases, a deafening noise fills the ears.

At the end of this Dionysian orchestration, the curtain falls on the stage of *Faust II*. Mephistopheles steps out to the proscenium, gets down from his high buskin, removes his Phorkyas mask and veil. He declares that he is ready, if the spectators wish, to "comment" upon the drama of Helen and Euphorion. We do not know whether, among the young and bearded spectators who have seen the third act of *Faust II*, there is one who would dare to ask the prince of hell for explanations; and we cannot imagine all the interpretations that he might furnish. But one thing is certain. Vain as he is, Mephistopheles would have tried to demonstrate that it was he who pulled the strings of the play and guided Goethe's characters like puppets, when he was hidden behind the stage's wings. Without him, Helen would not have returned to illumine Greece; no Frankish castle would have adorned the mountains on Sparta's slopes; and who, if not he, could possibly understand Eupho-rion? "Everything," Mephistopheles would have said, "was only a game: an absurd spectacle in the theater, put on to amuse the bored Lord of the heavens and earth, to cheer myself and the spectators who, since the beginning of this world, have followed my exploits."

GOETHE

To contradict Mephistopheles; to confute, at least in part, the most scrupulous and impudent commentator that *Faust II* has ever had, may prove difficult, almost painful. But Mephistopheles is mistaken. As in the first act, so also in the third, so many things that he could not and did not want to foresee have crept onto a stage that was prepared with such knowing cleverness. For a few hours, the "double, great realm" of past and present, Helen's dazzling sun, the perfection of form, the mythical life in the absolute present, impossible love, the hermetic miracles of poetry have truly illuminated the stage of our world.

The Last Two Acts
of Faust II

VIII

Mephistopheles, Philospher of Nature and Politics

In the fourth act, Faust descends from the large cloud which, like a
magic vehicle, has transported him into Germany's mountainous heart.
The jagged peaks of the German Alps occupy the farthest horizon; and
the mountain solitude is populated only by horrible, gaping boulders,
crazy crags, and sharp, fragmented stones which thousands of years ago
an unknown hand had flung on the earth's surface. The sky is clear and
serene. As the cloud drifts slowly off, changeable and swaying as creatures of the air, a small ribbon of mist—Gretchen's image—rises hesi-
tantly from among the desolate rocks; it condenses, takes the form of
a cirrus cloud, and floats up into the limpid heights of the ether.[1]

Some minutes later, Mephistopheles sets his forked hoofs among the
stones of Germany. In Greece he has left his cloak swollen with combustible air, with which, emulating the *Thousand and One Nights* and the
brothers Mongolfier, he had brought Faust and Homunculus across the
world. This time he prefers a more homely and traditional vehicle: the
seven-league boots of German fairy tales, the same ones *Daumesdick*
or Thumbling had used to escape the ogre's ferocity. When he reaches
the mountains, Mephistopheles abandons the boots; indeed, he dismounts from them as if they were a pair of gigantic stilts. But the boots
do not stop. Animated by a mysterious force, they continue without him
their extremely rapid, ghostly race across the earth's surface, all the way
to the unbearable cold of the North Pole, the stifling heat of southern
China, the highlands of Tibet, the caves of the Thebaid, the snowy
mountain ranges and flaming volcanoes of the Cordilleras, and the

GOETHE

farthest tip of Cape Horn, like the boots of Peter Schlemihl.

Mephistopheles is happy to be home again, not far from Blocksberg, in the places dear to his crude pleasures. In Greece, beside the clear waters of the rivers and among the bushes inhabited by nymphs, in that world of monsters and incomparably beautiful women, he had suffered unheard-of humiliations. The Sphinxes had mocked him; the Lamiae and Empusa had defeated him in the arts of metamorphosis; Helen's maids had cursed his horrible forms; and in the end he had been reduced to being the servant of the sun's daughter. In that world so distant from his, he had actually passed beyond the limits of his own nature, and had almost come to grief. His style had imitated the rich, elaborate images of the *Iliad* and *Odyssey;* his heart had let itself be touched by Euphorion's poetry and music; his lips had commemorated Helen's death with a pathos and nobility of expression which, until that moment, no one would have dared attribute to him.

As soon as he touches his beloved German soil, these memories leave his mind; and we recognize the old Gothic devil—so arid and limited, so cynical, "bitter," and "pungent" (10194), so grandiosely abject— whom we met in *Faust I.* In these mountains, Mephistopheles reads only one book, the most ancient of books, written for his infamy and glory: the book that remembered the sin into which he had led Adam, Job's temptation, Christ's temptation, the futile battle with the archangels in the sky of the *Apocalypse.* The verses of the Old and New Testaments flower on his lips at every opportunity, and he recalls an exemplary episode in the Book of Kings (11287), images from Job (11809) and Isaiah (11639); or he impiously parodies the sayings in the Gospel of St. Matthew (11352, 10131), a famous passage in the Gospel of St. John (11594), or an entire section of the Letter to the Ephesians (10092–10094).

Mephistopheles realizes that for too long he has neglected his devil's duties, his tasks as tempter and corrupter. During the first three acts, he treated Faust as would an older, wiser companion; he helped him in all of his undertakings, arranging with him the carnival masquerade, the descent to the Mothers, the summoning of Helen from Hades; and had shared his experiences. Now Mephistopheles frees himself from this sort of dependence. At this moment, Faust is standing on the high mountain, among the rocks and huge boulders "stiff and crude" as the heart of the prince of hell—just as Christ, before he began preaching in Galilee, was dragged by the devil to the top of "an exceeding high mountain" (Matthew, 4: 8). The ancient situation is reproduced. As Satan had tempted Jesus Christ, showing him "all the kingdoms of the world, and the glory of them," Mephistopheles repeats the same words: "You will see from on high, in the immeasurable distance, the kingdoms of this world and their glory" (10130–10131).² But his temptation is subtler and more insidious than the extremely theatrical and spectacular one of his sublime colleague. Mephistopheles does not ask Faust to "fall down" and "worship him," he does not simply offer him worldly wealth. He expounds for Faust an unfamiliar aspect of his philosophy: the geological and political doctrines of the inferno; and so he tries to draw Faust into the orbit of his world.³

In a passage of the Letter to the Ephesians, St. Paul recalls that from the beginning of time the unfathomable mystery of Christ was hidden in the mind of God. Nobody could know it—neither the sons of men, nor the prince of darkness, nor the maleficent angelic powers that populated the regions of the air. Finally, the plan of this mystery was revealed to the Apostles, the prophets, and to him, Paul, the last and lowliest of the saints, so that he might preach and evangelize among the people.⁴ In his discussion with Faust, Mephistopheles recalls this passage from the Letter to the Ephesians; and he gives him to understand that, just as St. Paul had received the mystery of Christ through a revelation, he also knows by direct experience an unfathomable, very ancient cosmic enigma, which no one as yet has preached to the peoples of the universe (10093).

Many centuries before, at the time of the fall of Lucifer, Mephistopheles with his own eyes had seen the Lord God Almighty drive the demons down into the world's deepest regions. There they stayed for some time. Then the abyss began to swell, full of torrents of flame and clouds of gas that caused the still smooth crust of the earth, as Anaxagoras taught, to burst open with a roar. Then what was at the bottom of the abyss leaped to the surface. As the devils became masters of the regions of the air, mountain peaks suddenly rose out of the earth; and Moloch's enormous hammer flung everywhere very heavy rocks which still testify by their names—the "devil's rock," the "devil's bridge"—to the power of the spirits of the abyss.

This new cosmic secret, announced by Mephistopheles to Faust, confutes at every point the mystery preached by St. Paul. The Apostle had taught that Christ had descended from the heavenly regions, where he lived at the Father's right hand, to the lowest regions of this world; and he had reconciled and pacified heaven and earth, slaves and free men, Hebrews and Greeks, males and females, the length and breadth, height and depth of the universe. Mephistopheles teaches that it is not the supreme things (*das Oberste,* 10090) that come down on earth, but the lowest things (*das Unterste*)—the demons of the abyss, the gases and rocks—that rise to the sky, thus constituting the keystone and culmination of the universe; he proclaims that not peace but "tumult, violence, and senselessness" (10127), dominate the history of men as they do the everyday life of nature.

If St. Paul had claimed to see in Christ's person the central secret of the universe, he was deceived. That mystery, that "open mystery,"[6] was not Christ, but he himself, Mephistopheles, the ancient son of darkness and nullity; the power which, rising up from the pit, threatens earth and heaven; the eternal "tumult" and "violence" which cause the universe to go mad. He still cannot step forth openly; he must reveal himself only through enigmas and allusions to a few disciples; he must appear the apostle of a new revelation, whereas in reality he is the very content of the revelation: the Christ of the pit. But when the moment will have come, when for everyone there will arrive the final end of all time, he will appear to the inhabitants of the earth as the splendid, triumphant *Mysterium Iniquitatis.*[7]

Mephistopheles is too old and experienced, too bitter and subtle to believe in a single religion and a single system, or to preach to the people with the fervor of an apostle. Driven by his talent as an artist of the grotesque, he amuses himself by describing devils uncomfortably crushed one on top of the other in the bowels of the earth, huddled around a scorchingly hot fire and a much too bright light. Without batting an eyelash, as if he were expounding a fundamental scientific doctrine, he explains that the "Aeolian vapors" (7866), which according to Anaxagoras made the crust of our globe explode, were in fact the devils' coughs, their vapors, their sulphurous flatulence, the obscene gas of infernal bodies. So the great cosmic revelation promised us by the new St. Paul, the new "mystery," loftier and truer than Christ's, the very keystone of the universe plunges, to the joy of the readers of *Faust II*, into the stench of a disgusting satanic farce.

To illustrate his political program, Mephistopheles begins to draw, like the ancient theoreticians, the ideal capital of his earthly state.[8] He does not like the great cities of the classical world, Rome or Byzantium, from which Augustus, Constantine, and Justinian ruled like divinities over the peoples and multiple populations. Nor does he like London, with its immense suburbs of factories and workers' tenements; nor Paris, where the mob stormed the Bastille and unleashed the Revolution. The lord of flies and mice dreams of ruling over a German city: Frankfurt, Dresden, Leipzig, and even Karl August's small Weimar. Everything pleases him in these old, tranquil cities: the narrow, winding alleyways, the pointed roofs of the medieval quarter; the stench-ridden markets, full of cabbages, kale, onions, and greasy roasts over which saunter filthy swarms of flies; and outside the city's gates the large squares and broad avenues designed by seventeenth-century urbanists.

In these lazy, easygoing cities, among these stingy, modest burghers, Mephistopheles renounces without regret the dreams of "glory" (10185) desperately pursued by Alexander the Great and Napoleon. To drive with armies all the way to India or Moscow, to unleash revolutions, to be responsible for the construction of pyramids, or to put court poets on a stipend—all this seems to him a "madness" (10191) worthy of a crazed cicada like Faust. As every honest conservative, he is content to wield the good-natured, absolute power of an eighteenth-century German prince. Without worrying his head over the welfare of his subjects, he will live a few miles from the capital, in his small Versailles, among green trellises and velvety meadows, waterfalls and decorative fountains, geometric paths and the artificial shadows of an Italian-style garden. He will spend most of his time in his castle, surrounded by a bevy of loose, beautiful women. But sometimes, putting aside his pleasures for a few hours, he will come out on horseback or in a carriage and drive through the capital's new streets; admired and honored by hundreds of thousands of scattered ants—his modest, extremely devoted subjects.

With this political program, Mephistopheles concludes, at least for the time being, his role as tempter. As always he enjoys speaking at length about himself; nothing pleases him so much, nothing makes him so eloquent, witty, and amiable, especially if he has the good fortune to encounter an intelligent listener like Faust. But he does not delude himself that he has convinced his restless companion. By now he knows him in every corner of his soul; and he knows that the stench of infernal sulphur and filthy German markets cannot charm his exquisite, proud nostrils. If he has in any event tempted Faust, drawing for him a geological hypothesis and a political program, he has done so because he must repeat and parody on the stage the ancient deeds, replete with theological reality, which at one time he performed when he bore the name of Satan.

Faust and the Waters

Meanwhile Faust is still standing there, facing that sublime mountain scene, like a gloomy, melodramatic actor on a Romantic stage. With his haughty *grand seigneur* ways, he looks down his nose at Mephistopheles, scorns and insults him, as though he were the lowest of his lackeys, more contemptible than Leporello, more vulgar than Figaro. He does

GOETHE

not allow himself to be tempted by Mephistopheles; he does not even argue with him, or try to refute his statements. Standing on that stage, wrapped in noble pathos as in a ceremonial mantle, Faust in his turn expresses his idea of nature and politics.

Faust refuses to explain how the mountains were formed: "For me the mountain masses remain nobly mute, nor do I ask where they came from, nor even why" (10095–10096), he declares, echoing Jarno, who had affirmed: "the mountains are silent professors, and produce silent students" (VIII, 260: 25–26). To Mephistopheles's theories he counterposes his own symbolic image of nature, which dislikes the disorder and demented tumults so beloved by the spirits of the inferno. Nature has formed herself slowly and gradually, in accordance with eternal rules. After shaping the globe's sphere and setting the mountains and rocks in a row, she has let the grass-covered hills slope down gently. Then she contemplated her creation with joy. So this image of the universe is the same one that Thales had exalted in the *Klassische Walpurgisnacht*. It is the one Faust admired in Genesis—God, harmoniously and in an orderly fashion, created day and night, heaven and earth, sun and moon, green, seed-bearing plants, fruit trees, birds in the sky, fish, crawling animals, and man.

In any event, the Book of Job and Psalms 74 and 104 propose another story of the creation. When God fashioned the world, he encountered the resistance of the dark and savage forces of the sea, which had burst from the depths of the abyss. Then God sent it all away with a threatening, rumbling cry like thunder, and subjected it to his law and his order. He shut up the sea behind two gates, which he fastened with a lock; he constructed the dike of the banks; and he set beside it a watchman, so that it would not go beyond its new borders. Finally he proclaimed: "Up to here you can go and no farther: here your proud waves must halt!"[9]

Since that day, God hasn't yet completely defeated the powers of the abyss, which try to break down the gates and dikes and shatter the locks. As he flies across Europe's lands and seas, Faust views a desolate sight. The open sea rises, towering above itself; then, with unchecked arrogance, it flings itself in an assault on the land. The waves approach the shore and slither forward from a thousand sides; eternally unfertile and enthusiastic about their strength, they grow, swell, cover the squalid, deserted beach; and then they roll back, without having accomplished anything, atrociously monotonous . . . Mephistopheles was not mistaken when he proclaimed that the devil was everywhere (10125); for he had left his mark even on the water, the benign element that generates, maintains, and protects the fresh life of the world.

When Faust sees again in memory the unleashed waves besieging the land, anguish, desperation, and rage enflame his blood, as though confronted by a human act of arrogance. His spirit dreams of conquering the fury of the elements, as already in the past he had imagined coming to blows with tempests (466). If God, at the origins of the world, had sent the waters away with the thunder of his voice and had locked them behind two impenetrable gates, today he would like to complete the great, interrupted task. Immediately, without delay, he would like to "drive the imperious sea from the shore, narrowing the borders of the watery plain and pushing it far away, into itself" (10229–10231), canceling the violence, arbitrariness, sterility, and absurdity that still besiege the universe.

The goal Faust sets for himself is the loftiest symbolic goal that Goethe has ever proposed to men: to redeem and save nature; to force the rebellious elements to obey the gentle laws of the macrocosm, just as Homunculus has pacified water and fire.[10] Does this mean that Faust, in a few hours, has traveled the same distance on the road to perfection as Homunculus? Just as the young demon of fire had tempered his voice and mitigated his childish pride, has Faust too, under the influence of Helen's cloud and Gretchen's cirrus, freed himself of the anguish that tortured him? It would be naïve to believe this. The symbols of cosmic harmony console Faust's intelligence; the image of a nature that lets the hills gently slope down the valleys regales and brightens the eyes of his spirit; but it does not inspire his actions. Always enraptured, tense, and overly heroic, Faust is incapable of considering his life as the blithe and perishable reflection of a distant, mysterious network of laws. As he dreams of nullifying the pride of the oceans, the same pride, the same violence, and the same *Übermut* swell his breast (10202, 10224). So we wonder whether he really wants to pacify nature; or whether he is merely trying to prove the superhuman power of his Titanic spirit to himself, to Mephistopheles, and the God of the Bible.

Face to face with the shores of the ocean, bereft as they are of cities, houses, and human settlements, we imagine that Faust rejects all the political constrictions of human history. If he must struggle against the fury of the elements, as the first human societies struggled against the waters, the threat of lightning, and the land covered with forests, what necessity compels him to accept political institutions?[11] Is it not the moment to start all over again from the beginning, like those groups of *Wanderers* who founded a new civilization without capitals or royal seats in the towns of America? But Faust cannot free himself from the fatal entrapment of force; and he limits himself to counterposing a different political ideal to the one traced by the prince of stones.

Mephistopheles's political program seems to him intolerably "modern" (10176). That half-Gothic, half-rococo capital, miserable and inanely sumptuous; that life of a mediocre provincial prince spent in an insipid Versailles, surrounded by a retinue of beautiful women; that continuous, petty gratification of the pleasures of vanity—everything that attracts Mephistopheles seems irksome and odious to Faust. His political ideal comes down from those pages in the Bible, Tacitus, Plutarch, Machiavelli, and Shakespeare which portray in dark, grandiose hues tyrants devoured by the passion for power. If he had mounted the throne, he would have experienced only one joy: that of "commanding" (10252–10253). Like Alexander the Great, Caesar, Tamburlane, and Mohammed II, he would have attempted ever more enormous and audacious exploits; conquering empires, endlessly augmenting his activities and possessions (10187–10188). He would not be concerned about the welfare of his subjects, like the enlightened sovereigns of the eighteenth century who fed and educated them, and as a consequence brought up a generation of "rebels" (10155–10159). Imitating the great tyrants of history, Faust wants to put a distance between himself and the anonymous throng of his servants, hiding behind a screen of mystery and darkness, surrounding himself with a few trusted persons, whispering his intentions only to them, and astounding the world with his unimaginable deeds (10254–10259).

Enthralled by his gloomy ideal of domination, Faust wants "to drive the imperious sea from the shore," giving orders where nobody has ever done so; and he insists that Mephistopheles must "support" his aims (10233). What a paradox! While he imagines he can eliminate the arbitrariness of the elements, Faust turns for help precisely to the demon of the elements, the savage lord of fire. The noble intentions touching his spirit for a moment have no great importance. By now we are certain that Faust will only add other cruel wounds to the innumerable wounds which, during the course of the centuries, the elements and the princes of this earth have inflicted on nature's mild countenance.

Mephistopheles's Decisive Battle

At the moment, new misfortunes are about to strike the Holy Roman Empire, whose last, empty splendors we have seen. The empire has collapsed into anarchy: the small and great are fighting each other ferociously, cities have gone into battle against cities, castles against castles, guilds against noblemen, bishops against communes. Proclaiming that they intend to repress this license, the majority of the lay and ecclesiastical princes have rebelled against the authority of the cheerful, feckless Emperor and have elected a new sovereign. Sedition spreads rapidly. Gold-filled chests, magnificent furnishings, ancient treasures are gathered around the throne of the rebel Emperor; the people march behind his unfurled banners, as a flock of sheep follows the shepherd, as a river is propelled by its current.

With his princes and loyal troops, the Emperor takes shelter in the valleys at the base of the mountains and prepares to engage in the final battle. He is possessed by youthful and confused dreams of glory; his heart burns with martial passion; he dons his armor, breastplate, and helmet, picks up his sword, and challenges his rival to a duel. But the commanding general has already disposed his troops in accordance with the prescriptions in the manuals. Like a grim, heavy square, the infantry occupies the center of the plain; thousands of pikes lit by the sun glitter in the air through the misty vapors of early morning; higher up, a group of courageous men defends a narrow mountain pass. From the top of the mountain peaks, Faust and Mephistopheles listen to the trumpet blasts and rolling of drums of the two armies, and they watch the imperial cohorts take up their positions at the bottom of the valley. Ingenious as ever, Mephistopheles thinks of a way to support Faust's aim; once again he will run to the assistance of the weak Emperor. He will save his throne and country; and, in recompense, Faust will be able to obtain the beach lashed by the sea's wild waves. So Mephistopheles leaves the mountains with his proud, bored companion; and goes all the way down to the first redoubts, where the Emperor's tent is pitched.

As drums roll and trumpets reverberate fearfully, the armies confront each other beneath the sun's first rays. On high, alongside the Emperor, the commander-in-chief gives his battle orders; he has his troops perform the maneuvers he has studied in the manuals. He has the right wing advance impetuously; slowly moves forward, at the center, the powerful phalanx glittering with pikes; and makes sure that his valiant men-at-arms defend the narrow mountain pass from enemy violence. But of what use are these conscientious orders? The commander-in-chief is completely unaware that the guidance of the battle is taken away from him by Mephistopheles, who secretly assumes his insignia and transforms the war into a new spectacle of witchcraft, a lighthearted theatrical pastime.

The horizon darkens; a stifling, misty heat oppresses the combatants, a veil falls before their eyes, voices resound, whistle, and hiss in their

GOETHE

ears. A strange reddish gleam, the color of blood, makes their weapons gleam. A thousand agile little flames dance on the phalanx's lances and pikes; and an arm, then dozens of ghostly arms rise and wave furiously in the air, as often happens in Sicily, when imaginary cities and gardens waver, rise, and fall in the sky's misty vapors. The entire world has become weird and marvelous. Two ravens, the inferno's ancient and faithful messengers, alight on Mephistopheles's shoulders, whisper in his ear the battle's most recent tidings and receive his orders; an eagle and a fabulous griffin confront and tear open each other's breasts in the high regions of the sky. Meanwhile, Mephistopheles's three henchmen, Raufebold, Habebald, and Haltefest, three grotesque medieval allegories of violence, tear into the enemy's ranks—shattering necks, heads, and jaws, loosing rivers of blood, and running about wrathfully in search of loot, even to the rebel Emperor's tents.

To break the final resistance, Mephistopheles sends off the ravens to carry his orders to the elements of the universe, which obey him like a crew of docile supernumeraries. A swift, abundant spring seems to well up from the mountain's naked rocks; imaginary streams descend with a roar, issue doubled from the gullies, form the splendid arc of a waterfall, spread out gurgling over the rocks and rush down into the valley; and the rival Emperor's troops think they will drown, be swept away by these deceptive torrents of water. Denser shadows suddenly descend on the battlefield. Will-o'-the-wisps gleam everywhere, flashes fall on a tangle of bushes, stars hiss on the damp ground; a very bright flare explodes, shines, sparkles, suddenly blinding the enemy warriors.

And finally Mephistopheles's imagination loots the arsenals of feudal castles. He gathers among the clefts of the rocks the helmets, breastplates, swords, shields, and greaves that medieval emperors, kings, and knights had proudly worn. At first these weapons and pieces of armor are simply there, like the empty shells of snails. But the diabolical ghosts who then inhabit them share the political passions of their former owners. So, behind the combatants, the old weapons rehearse again the eternal hatreds and brawls of the Guelphs and Ghibellines. Their fury mounts, they strike each other with the roar of empty iron plates, they collide with a crash; and a strident sound echoes satanically over the entire valley.

The battle has ended. Disconcerted by so many marvels, confused by the miracles of water and fire, the rebel Emperor's troops flee precipitously. Cheerful military music played by *Faust*'s entire orchestra announces the Emperor's triumph, while, in the churches, the faithful are intoning a *Te Deum* of thanks to the Almighty. The Emperor has won; and what does it matter that Mephistopheles's magic helped him?

Standing in the tent of his defeated rival, surrounded by treasures and tapestries, he awaits the people's emissaries. The great figures of the empire surround him: the High Marshal, the High Chamberlain, the High Steward, the High Cupbearer and the omnipotent Archbishop-Lord High Chancellor. Richly adorned in new decorations and new ornaments, they dream together with him of further martial exploits, prepare solemn ceremonies, usurp ancient domains, impose taxes and tithes, draw up constitutions, sign scrolls . . .

For them, the world's history is a pompous baroque tragedy, just like those they admire on the stage. They believe they have composed it themselves, forming the rhymed Alexandrines dear to Corneille and Racine; and now they declaim them for the world's pleasure. How short their memories are! They have already forgotten that they owe everything—both life and power—to the prodigies of an infamous wizard. What would have become of them if Mephistopheles had not staged his tricks? As he was performing his miracles of illusionism, Mephistopheles demonstrated once again that he was the sole, authentic ruler of history. He is the puppet master who pulls the strings of the human comedy; the playwright with an extremely fertile imagination fabricating the events destined to be inscribed in epigraphs and books. While he is hidden in a corner of the scene, perhaps alone, perhaps with his ravens, the Emperor and his retinue think they are pronouncing Alexandrines as perfect as those Horace, Pompey, and Britannicus declaim on the stages of Paris. They do not realize that, an instant before they stepped onstage, Mephistopheles replaced these lines with amiable but clumsy Alexandrines, crammed with mistakes and lacking caesuras, like those the student Goethe composed in Leipzig for a joke.[12]

Baucis and Philemon

Many years later, traveling again the scenes of his restless pilgrimage, the wayfarer does not recognize the sterile, desolate dunes where in the past the waves had flung him half alive. As the last rays of the sun descend, he contemplates with amazement and terror "a paradisial image" (11086). Where the sea's wrath had raged, there now rises an immense garden: green meadows, pasture lands, woods, fertile orchards, populous villages pleasant to look at; and also dams and dikes that have tamed the water's impetus and kept it at a distance. One can barely catch sight of the sea, which is like the blue border of a painting. Over its peaceful waters pass sails, like birds searching for their nests; ships sail joyously into port, their colored flags flapping in the wind; and a small barge piled high with chests and strongboxes glides up the canal that leads to the heart of the colonized land, near Faust's palace.

Like the silent, melancholy wayfarer, anyone contemplating the "paradisial image" stretching along the empire's coast, will think Faust's dream has been realized. Like God at the world's origins, he has "narrowed the borders of the watery plain" (10230); he has pushed the sea farther and farther away, containing it inside the rigid confines of dams and dikes. At the foot of his palace, one sees no reminders of the world's past—neither Mycenaean fortresses, nor medieval castles, nor Gothic chambers. Old parchments, infinitely subdivided holdings, hereditary rights do not impede the free exploitation of the land. On this soil wrested from the chasms of the sea, in this happy America, everything is fresh and very new: The colors are brighter, the images purer, the eyes happier from gazing at the world's beauty.

But the verdant meadows and gaily colored flags are a deceptive mask. Faust's and Mephistopheles's broad realm is not the blissful place of Utopia, where men and the elements have been reconciled and live in the joy of a perennial present. All of history's sins and horrors are repeated and renewed, augmented gigantically on this long strip of land. Brute force rules without rivals; impiety is the unchallenged sovereign; and the presence of extraordinary technical and magical means —dams and dikes that rise overnight—make the dominion of violence even more unchallengeable.

Like a Dutch or English seventeenth-century sea captain, Mephistopheles commands Faust's fleet. His ships sail to the most distant seas; perhaps to the Americas and India, to buy spices, cloths, and the precious products of the East. But, since "war, commerce, and piracy" are an inseparable trinity (11187–11188), the captains transform their mercantile galleons into pirate ships and attack the ships met on the oceans, murder the crews, and fill Faust's palace with treasures. On land, too, Mephistopheles's maxim—"he who has might also has right"—will be confirmed (11184). The powerful lord's envoys and servants commit every sort of violence; they sow terror, kill mercilessly. At night, along the modern canals, they perform blood sacrifices resembling those that paid homage to Baal (11127). The reconciliation of the elements Faust had dreamed of is only apparent. Although Mephistopheles's magical inventions have driven "the imperious sea from the shore," other storms are being prepared behind the peaceful blue rim of the horizon, and the dark forces of the abyss are about to assail the land's feeble defenses and sweep away Faust's ambitious dream (11545 ff.). Meanwhile, on earth, infernal fire triumphs: wandering flames, torrents of fire accompany the nocturnal construction of the dikes; and even crueler flames will soon devour the hut of Baucis and Philemon.

In the midst of Faust's and Mephistopheles's impious world, a single fragment of the ancient world, fragile and infinitely precious, has remained. An old married couple, who bear the Ovidian names of Baucis and Philemon, live near the dunes not far from Faust's palace, in a wooden hut covered with moss. A wood of dark, century-old, sweet-scented lime trees stretches its branches over their garden. The wood casts a dense shadow around a small church, where every evening its bells' silvery peal commemorates the end of another day, the customary hour of prayer, the death that draws nearer for each of us, and the presence in heaven of the "old God" of the Bible (11142). Just like two characters from the *Metamorphoses*, priests and guardians of Jove's gold and marble temple, Baucis and Philemon are the priests, guardians, and sole worshippers in the simple house of God.

In this small space, hemmed in by the rapid prodigies of Mephistopheles's world, time flows by slowly, patiently, unnoticed. Each thing is imbued and saturated with time. The silent labor of the centuries has made the trees' trunks and branches grow; a God as old as the world has dictated the laws of men, the words of the prayers, the rites and gestures of the ceremonies, Baucis's and Philemon's sentiments and thoughts. And yet, beneath the lime trees' fragrant shade, who feels the weight of the past? Time has veiled its labors and hidden the smell of dust, tombs, and ghosts which it drags along with it. Of all the centuries that have passed over the earth, only the volatile essence, delicate as the sound of the bells pealing out at sunset, has remained here.

If someone from the distant country of the future questioned Baucis and Philemon, seeking to discover the persona, the individual "character" of each of them, the old married couple would not understand, or would offer the strangest replies. In fact, they are not individuals; and even their names are borrowed from a classical myth. Baucis and Philemon are exemplary figures who, without changing, traverse all of the world's epochs. They are like the lime and oak trees which, by dying, are transformed in the *Metamorphoses*; the trees are born, die, and rise up again forever the same, renouncing in every time and place the pride of being a "person." Like the life of trees, the lives of Philemon and Baucis are subject to a continuous interweaving of laws, conditions, and limitations. God has caused them to be born in that corner of the earth; he has made them live in that house, on that field inherited from their ancestors. He has subjected them to poverty and hard work, to the dangers of the sea, the customs of the past and the rituals of religion. With the joyous faith of pious souls, Baucis and Philemon accept these conditions and limitations; they love God with a pure spirit, they kneel every evening before him; they gaze happily at the meadows, gardens, the sea lit up by the sun, the miracles of nature and artifice. They work to the end of their lives, without desires or hopes, ignoring the rest of the world; they obey the Emperor's laws and speeches; they help their fellow men, who have been overwhelmed by the sea's tempests and the even more oppressive tempests of the heart.

So humble and confined, what can their lives mean to the lords of the earth, to those who declare wars and overthrow empires, who trade in distant countries and possess both might and right? The lives of Baucis and Philemon are, for such people, like a reed, a leaf of grass, a crumb one can sweep away with a swift movement of the hand. But innumerable other Baucises and Philemons, other wooden huts, other crumbling chapels, still populate the earth's surface. The "old God," before whom they trustingly kneel and pray, sees them with his all-seeing eye, and embraces all these huts, these reeds, these leaves of grass in a single cosmos, bound together and harmonious.

We cannot identify the other old man "born to see, ordered to look" (11288–11289), the man who watches from the tower of Faust's palace. Perhaps it is Lynceus, whom we have already seen in the fantastic medieval town above Sparta. At that time, he was living at the zenith of his existence. With the faith of youth, he dared contemplate the sudden flare of dawn and the splendor of noon, accumulating treasures of subterranean light in his strongboxes, and his eyes turned away in fright only before Helen's supreme beauty. Since those days, innumerable other spectacles have passed before the eyes of Lynceus, who is as old as Faust, Baucis, and Philemon. The light now enveloping him, and which he prefers, is the mild light of sunset; the veiled, adumbrated light that each night descends from the stars and moon to bathe the surface of the earth.

Old age has not covered his heart with wrinkles. No mist veils his soul; no passion darkens his mind. He is not disquieted by nostalgia for the past nor hope in the future, for he lives in the pure present of contemplation; he is not disturbed by the desire for possessions, because for him the empires and treasures of the earth are "dried-out grass"; he is not tortured by thoughts about himself, because he has renounced himself, like pilgrims who go about the world with their staffs. Lynceus's spirit is consumed and lightened, like the heart of eighty-year-old Goethe who, seated in his garden, contemplated the narcissi with their red-rimmed hearts. Sloughing off his entire outer crust, he has been reduced to the naked essence; that intangible core hidden within us, which only a few of us succeed in knowing during our lifetime.

Like Baucis and Philemon, Lynceus, with the passing of the years, has regained a naïve and childish candor; an innocence that is reflected in his simple, elementary language. His emotions in the past raised him to the peak of joy or sank him into the pit of despair. Now they have left him and his heart knows only an immutable and monotonous felicity. Perhaps his eyes are not as sharp as at one time they were, when they had the same power as the sun and, like "lightning bolts," plunged down to light up the world. But it is probable that they are purer, capable of receiving, without the slightest distortion, the design and profile of all things. When he looks around him, what atrocious sights he sees! Like every man, he lives in Mephistopheles's realm, knows the nocturnal exploits of magic and violence, sees the blood on the ships; and soon will witness the fire that burns down Baucis's and Philemon's hut. His eyes are not averted in horror, like the eyes of the midnight children at the end of *Faust*. Whatever it may be, the world "pleases" him (11291, 11298, 11301–11302), as it pleased the bitter and happy old man who bore the name of Goethe. Despite the terrible sights he witnesses, everything he sees seems to him infinitely beautiful: illuminated by the light of grace, worthy of being contemplated by his old man's candid and experienced eyes.

When he was young he thought that beauty concentrated its light in a few privileged symbols and objects: gold and emeralds, rubies and the sea's pearls, Helen's sovereign form. Now, from the height of the watch-tower, he looks at near and far things without choosing or preferring any of them, since eternal beauty is diffused in all the aspects of the world, even the most humble and quotidian (11297). He no longer glorifies things with the rich images he favored in the past; like children and wise men, who know only essences, he cheerfully takes in the setting sun and the fresh breeze of evening, the last ships which enter the harbor, the small boat with its tinted sails, Mephisto's strongboxes and bags; the moon and stars, the woods and the roe buck.

In the meantime, another old man, whose shoulders bear the burden of too many experiences, steps onstage. Faust paces restlessly back and forth in the large garden beside the canal; he argues angrily with Mephistopheles; and when night falls, tormented by insomnia, he comes out on the palace's balcony and looks toward the dunes . . . By now he has everything that he desired: "power" and "possessions" (10187). Endless treasures are piled up in his strongboxes; he owns huge cultivated tracts of land; he has under his command numerous subjects, ships that cross the oceans; his arm extends and embraces the entire created world (11226).

But of what use to him is the terrible gift of power? Like the grasping tyrants in the Bible and Shakespeare, he has dreamed of the bliss of commanding (10253); and he has discovered that the thirst for domination can never be quenched. In that immense territory, he feels that he lives in a narrow prison cell. There are many other things he would like to have—but if he did, a new desire would be born immediately in his soul, pushing him on and on. He had dreamed of remaining proudly alone; of hiding himself from men and confiding his wishes to the ears of a few loyal followers; yet, surrounded by Mephistopheles and his henchmen, he knows how grim the solitude of the powerful can be. He has neither peace nor happiness; he experiences none of the simple joys that console Philemon and Baucis; he lacks Lynceus's almost irrational visual bliss. Not a single instant of forgetfulness soothes his brow (11219).

During his long existence, he has gazed at the evening's misty veils, the great celestial lights and the small sparkles mirrored in the lakes at night; the vivid colors of morning, the haunting thrill of the rainbow. He has seen Greece's gods and monsters; the figures of dreams projected on the banks of the Peneus and the shades from Persephone's kingdom; he has even dared to stare at Helen's dazzling sun. Even now he dreams of building a lovely arboreal lookout, from which with a single glance he could take possession of the new earth torn from the sea, following the broad avenues of the sky until he was lost in the infinite (11245 ff., 11344–11346). But his eyes are sick; the sharp "thorn" (11161) of possession has irremediably wounded them; they are *düster* (11219), "dark and grim," like the eyes of Care's unhappy victims (11455, 11402, 11408). What could he see in the farthest distances of the sky's ultimate depths, if he cannot manage to see the beauty that surrounds him? If he cannot recognize the *ewige Zier*, the "eternal grace," in a few fragrant trees, verdant fields, and the sunset's joyous colors?[13]

In the world that spreads out before him, Faust's looks and thoughts discern only a single point. They alight not far away in the short tract of land beside the dunes where, among the lime trees, stands the crumbling church and Baucis's and Philemon's hut. With the insistence of a nightmare, those trees remind him that his magical realm knows neither the laws of nature nor time's slow wealth. Unexpected as a sudden, treacherous blow, nagging and tedious as a reproach, every evening the sound of the bell reminds him of everything he has lost, desires, and cannot bring himself to forget: the soul's simple joy, devotion to the "old God," the thought of the limits enclosing him on all sides; the consciousness of death, which makes all our undertakings futile and empty.

Thousands of years before, an exemplary event, destined to be repeated throughout the course of history, took place among the mountains and hills of Samaria. Ahab, the king of Israel, wanted to own

Naboth's vineyard which stretched at the foot of his palace, so that he could transform it into a herb garden; and he offered its owner a better vineyard or silver coins. But Naboth replied: "The Lord forbid it me, that I should give the inheritance of my fathers unto thee." When Ahab heard these words, he was seized by sadness, melancholy, and wrath. He returned home, "laid himself down upon his bed, and turned away his face, and would eat no bread." Jezebel, the queen, paid false witnesses, who said that Naboth had blasphemed the name of God and that of the king. So the devout Israelite, who had obeyed the law by protecting the inheritance of his fathers, was stoned and killed; and the bloodied vineyard, where a few years later dogs would eat Jezebel's flesh and bones, was added to the possessions of the sad king of Israel (I Kings 21).

The same episode is reenacted on the stage of *Faust*. Distressed, anxious, his eyes diseased, the gloomy sovereign of the realm of magic wishes to incorporate into his domain the vegetable garden, few trees, and hut owned by Baucis and Philemon, and also the small, crumbling church—that modest fragment, that pious relic of the ancient world. He sends his envoys to offer the two old people another, larger, more beautiful homestead on the newly reclaimed lands. Perhaps Philemon, more uncertain and more adventurous in spirit, might have let himself be tempted by Faust's enticing offer (11135–11136). But his wife does not want to live on Mephistopheles's untrustworthy, modern, unnatural land, which may sink again into the waters from which it rose (11137). As Naboth tried to preserve his vineyard, so she defends a priceless treasure, where her lares and penates exist, where the time in which she lives is gathered, where the daily presence of the "old God" can be felt.

Like Ahab with his face turned to the wall, Faust cannot bear this refusal. Each time the wind brings him the perfume of the lime trees and the sound of the evening bell he is pierced by an intolerable pang of rage and anguish (11236, 11258). His dominion over the world seems to him wretchedly marred by those few trees he does not own (11242); it seems to him that his will has been mocked and that his life has become a futile, vanished dream (11255, 11268). Like all great sinners, he lies abjectly to himself, searches for painful justifications, insists that only up there, on those trees, could he build his lookout from which to contemplate the infinite; he paraphrases the words of the most villainous character in *King Lear*, declaring that the old people's "resistance" and "obstinacy" make him "tired of being just" (11272). Swept away by this demonic thought, Faust orders Mephistopheles and his henchmen to forcibly remove Baucis and Philemon from their hut and take them to the new homestead.

GOETHE

Who can guide brute force once he has unleashed it; who can ask it to respect moderation, delicacy, and the lives of others? Impatient and furious as the inferno, Mephistopheles and his henchmen carry out their mission. In the middle of the night, they break down the door of the old hut; they kill Baucis and Philemon, who die at the same moment, as in the *Metamorphoses;* and with their swords they cut down the wayfarer who tries to defend them. Revived by Mephistopheles's deed, the infernal violence of fire is aroused and set loose again. And so, beneath "the lime trees' double night" (11309), a sudden shower of sparks is seen. The flames, fanned by the wind, envelop the black, moss-covered hut; and bright flashes, insidious tongues of fire leap up to the trees' leaves and dry branches, which go up in flames and crash to the ground. The chapel soon collapses beneath the weight of the branches; more jagged and crimson flames reach the tops of the lime trees and burn the hollow trunks right to their roots.

Thus, the mild, patient work of centuries has disappeared forever. That delicate interlacing of nature and history, love of God and family piety, is a burning coal soon to become ashes. On the watchtower, Lynceus's song changes tone, breaks off and dies. The pure and immaculate eye, the eye that sees far, the eye that loves all things has been forced to recognize the world's horror. In the heavens, the stars conceal their gaze and light; the fire of the conflagration dies down, almost gutters out; and all the way to Faust's balcony, a gust of wind carries the "smoke and vapor" (11382) of the atrocious crime of which he is guilty.

Care

How laden with crimes is the soul of the old tyrant! In the first part of the play Gretchen, because of her love for Faust, had known shame, madness, and death; and now, also because of Faust, three persons, Baucis, Philemon, and the wayfarer who resembles them like a brother, leave the pathways of the world streaming with blood. What does it matter that he did not order their murder? Or that the law of men cannot accuse him of it? The sickness of his eyes, the fury of domination polluting his existence, the insatiability of his desires, the painful justifications he offers to himself, the haste to give orders—all these are blameworthy sins that can never be canceled. Faust has never fallen so low, not even when he cursed Faith, Hope, and Charity, or rushed avidly toward the abyss, seized by a mania for destruction.

Having reached the ultimate brink, while the stars, shuddering, avert their eyes from him, Faust is startled awake and is fully himself again. Though he does not realize it, death—"his" death—is approaching from behind the clouds, and soon he too will lie motionless in a small, narrow pit. During these final hours of life, he begins to take his first uncertain —though, as he goes on, increasingly assured and triumphant—steps on the road to redemption. In a few hours the tyrant with bloodstained hands is freed of all his guilt, casts off the constriction of the chrysalis and flies boldly into the sky. When Elijah threatened Ahab with the Lord's revenge, the sad king of Israel rent his splendid vestments and put sackcloth on his flesh; and then he fasted, walking slowly, and slept wrapped in the sack of humiliation. So we imagine that this time, too, Faust will follow the Biblical example; we imagine that bitter darts of remorse will pierce his heart, that the crime will make him curse himself, and that, as in a medieval mystery play, the great sinner's life will end in an equally extraordinary conversion.

But the mantle of the sinner and the slow step of the humbled man are not suited to Faust's proud figure. Even during the final minutes of his life Faust does not repent: The word "sin" never reaches his lips; his ego is never a subject of discussion. So how can he redeem himself? In the course of four grandiose monologues, heard only by the night's phantoms, he rids himself of the experiences that have stifled his soul, tears off the scales that have darkened his sight. Quick and impetuous even at the point of death, one after the other he breaks the bonds that tied him to Magic, Care, and the spirit of Possession and Violence. At the end of this process of purification, Faust rediscovers the "primal source" (324) God had entrusted to him as the most certain guarantee of salvation.

As Faust stands on the balcony looking out over the dunes, the shades of four old, grim, gray women glide forward with swaying steps; farther away, another specter—death—is about to come from behind the clouds. On the palace's threshold, the four women halt and each pronounces her name: *der Mangel, die Schuld, die Sorge, die Not;* perhaps a last echo of the monsters—the revengeful *Curae,* pallid *Morbi, Luctus, Metus, Fames,* and the obscene *Egestas, Letum,* and *Labos*— Aeneas had seen in the house of Dis. They exchange some words and the empty, dull, gloomy, "spectrally muffled" (11402) sound of their voices reaches Faust's ears, and once again he senses the repugnant presence of ghosts.

Overwhelmed by this sudden sensation, still troubled by the murder of Baucis and Philemon, Faust now considers the years spent with

GOETHE

Mephistopheles. He has never attempted such a balance sheet; and he sees that, starting from the day he tied himself to the devil, his existence has been entrapped by the bonds of magic. Alien to anything free and natural, he has always lived in the darkest of nights (*im Düstern*, 11408). During all those years phantoms and demons have teemed in the air of the sky; magical formulas have allowed him to undertake almost any exploit; and if the day seemed clear and reasonable, a confused web of dreams crept into his sleep. So, little by little, he had become the victim of superstition. The world seemed to him a compact tangle of threatening allusions and mysterious revelations; if a bird croaked over spring fields, he felt the wing of misfortune graze his head.

This foreshortened view of Faust's existence debases some of the most important experiences he has had in Germany and Greece. Was Helen only a miserable ghost? And was Euphorion merely a shadow of the night? And didn't even the carnival spectacle reveal certain symbols to him? Didn't destiny, with its revelations, really protect Faust's existence? But Faust's soul is sad unto death; as murky and grim as the four gray women who, covered by darkness, glide about in front of the palace. At this moment we cannot expect from him greater justice toward his own past.[14] On the other hand, there is some truth in what Faust says. He has never fought simply with his own forces, as free men do; he has never stood up alone before maternal or hostile nature. All the actions, conquests, and extraordinary experiences of his life he owes to Mephistopheles's imagination, which has showered him with carnival pranks and metaphysical spectacles, victories in battle, and new countries. Now this wild round-dance of magical conquests deeply revolts Faust; he wants to drive magic from his path and forget forever the formulas and exorcisms. A few moments later he renounces uttering those "magical words" which, with no merit of his own, would have saved him once again (11423). He fights alone, supported only by his will and intelligence, fulfilling completely the first stage of the process of liberation and inner purification.

Three of the four gray women quickly leave Faust's palace: neither Want, nor Default, nor Necessity can live in the place where a rich man lives. But the fourth woman, Care, fears no obstacles. She frequents both the palaces of the rich and the hovels of the poor, the souls of ancient and modern men. So she slithers through the keyhole like an invisible shape of air; she makes Faust's door creak and menacingly approaches the old tyrant.

No one can look Care in the face, for she has neither a face nor a visible body; her long shadow is merged with and lost in the night. Perhaps Faust cannot even listen to Care's voice, since most likely the boring "litany" (11469) she declaims—those anxious, precipitous, almost whispered verses with which she presents herself—only echoes at the bottom of his sick heart. This terrible, bodiless, voiceless shadow, which perhaps does not even exist, is the sister of Death, of Want, of Default, and of Necessity. She is kin to all things that no longer are, that are lacking and render our lives empty and inert. Her gray figure, her monotonous words, her humiliating thoughts are born out of that interminable wasteland Goethe called *das Düstere* (11455): that is, all that is obscure, grim, gloomy, and tenebrous; the element in which Mephistopheles prepares his deceptions of men (6927), the Museum of the Past (7006) watched over by Erichtho, and phantoms, magic formulas, mysterious presentiments, and nocturnal dreams administered by magic (11408).

Just as she glides into Faust's palace, so Care nestles in our souls; she emanates around her the most complete darkness (11458); and her dolorous refrain falls with always the same dull reverberation within the narrow walls of our hearts. She pursues us over the pathways of land and sea, embarks on ships fitted out with bronze, runs after squadrons of horsemen, mounts on our horses' backs, swifter than the swiftest deer, faster than the wind that drives away the mist (11428; Horace, *Carmina*, II, 16, 21, ff.; III, 1, 38–40). She appears before us in a thousand guises: as the spirit of possession, as the feeling of affection for house and family, as the fear of death, as the morbid passion of love, as the obsessive memory of the past (644 ff., 11426; IV, 438–439; *Pandora*, 314). If we try to flee from her, flinging ourselves with open arms at the world, Care lets fall on things an uninterrupted twilight, like the twilight that colors our soul (11455). Then we no longer see the sun rise or set; we do not perceive the changing cycle of the seasons, the annual flowering of plants, the ripening of fruits (11456; IX, 578: 15 ff.). The treasures of life, the beauty and horror of the world, happiness and unhappiness, bliss and torments, all the variety of the universe is erased by the monotonous, anguished mania that inhabits us (11461, 11463). When we are her prey we live in the world as if we did not live there; we die of hunger amid the abundance that surrounds us (11462).

Possessed by Care, we forget every man's first obligation: to live in the present (11464–11465). The things surrounding us, the commitments we must meet each day, the joys and sorrows that must be borne vanish from our sight. Our indefatigable and tortuous imagination only considers that which is the future, that which will or may be, and it gets lost in the "murky realm of possibility which confuses the figures." We no longer know how to act. Whatever decision impends, we put it off till the next day, which will be followed by other, innumerable, equally

GOETHE

ineffective days. If someone or something compels us, we act against our will; and we go forward groping, taking short uncertain steps on the open road we have just begun to travel (11473–11474). As our imagination moves excitedly through time, we remain stockstill: motionless as statues, prisoners of the infernal chair to which we are bound.

If we reach the pinnacle of desperation, if tears rise impetuously from our breasts and we fall to the ground, overcome by sleep or the ponderous hand of the gods—then, like Orestes, we may hope to free ourselves from Care's entrapments. But he who lives in the country of Care is never so desperate as to be able to shatter the disease's nightmare (11480); he does not know the refreshment of sleep, which would allow him to forget the anxieties of the past (11484). Like the inhabitants of Limbo, he only half lives, torn and divided by every extremity. At almost any instant, he caresses and curses his own tortuous illness, now he breathes and now he suffocates; now he thinks he is free, now he is oppressed; he does not sleep and he is not awake; he is neither desperate nor resigned (11431, 11478, 11483, 11484, 11480). Half alive, like a shadow, he travels down the uncertain roads of an eternal twilight, brother to all those who lie beneath the earth (11479).

Listening to the portrait Care draws of the men she rules over, we ask ourselves how it is that she is here, in Faust's great palace. What has she in common with him? What are the relations between these two figures who confront each other in the night? If we remember the eternally dissatisfied élan, the temptestuous violence with which Faust rushed about the world during the first four acts, we must admit that he has never known Care and that she has chosen her victim badly. Yet, at the beginning of the fifth act, Faust is changed. Shadows reign in his spirit, as in the spirit of Care's victims; and his gloomy eyes *(düster)* do not like to contemplate the world's spectacles, dawn and the setting of the sun, the woods and roe bucks that attract Lynceus's pure eyes. "Starving amid plenty" (11462), he forgets to live in the present, to enjoy the world's thousand treasures; and he flings himself into the realm of the possible but denies himself the joy of sleep at the hour of midnight —"breathing deeply as he suffocates, not really dead, yet without life, neither desperate nor resigned" (11478–11480). If Care is lodged in the hearts of all mediocre men, binding them to the thought of their homes and possessions (648 ff.), does it not undermine Faust in the same way? What, if not Care, is the fury that drives him to make things "his" (11153, 11156, 11158, 11241), to incorporate a few trees and a crumbling house in "his" domains? For the first time in his life, the "fugitive," "the man without a house," has let himself be imprisoned by fatal human limitations, tying him to the things that we try to possess and never succeed in making ours.[15]

So Care has chosen her victim quite wisely. She knows that she has ruled for a long time in Faust's palace; she knows that her gloomy and insinuating refrain has resounded for years within the walls of that darkened heart; and now she tries to master him completely. When she asks him: "Have you ever known Care?", Faust, if he were sincere, would have to admit that he knew the nocturnal visitor better than himself. But at this moment he does not want to analyze his soul and describe his sins, like someone who finds himself before the open pages of a diary. With the rapidity that distinguishes him, he wants to free himself of the constrictions that bind him and rediscover his youthful spirit. As Care whispers her insidious temptations in his ear, he does not answer her; and with broad strokes, with the impetuousness of a painter of frescoes, he draws an image of himself.

The imaginary Faust is well aware that the view toward the summit of the heavens is blocked (11442). There, above the clouds, stretches nothing similar to our earth, but rather a terrible sea of fire that threatens to destroy and blind us (4710); perhaps insidious demons, perhaps a God we do not know, watch our lives from on high. So he renounces knowing the supreme things. His eyes do not look up toward the heights (11443); his imagination does not try to roam along the paths of eternity; his curiosity does not venture so far as to call upon the assistance of the spirits of the night (11447, 11450). Without disquietude or anguish, strong and tranquil, he "remains stockstill" on the surface of his earth, among the joys, sorrows, and thoughts born in the closed circle of life (11445, 1663 ff.).

As at the beginning of the second part of the play, when he awakens on the sunny meadow, Faust gazes lovingly at the world; he travels it from one end to another, and the world, as if to reward him, reveals its secret language to him (11441, 11446). The moment of action having come, he sets out without delay, without scruples, without doubts. He ardently desires something and possesses what he desires; he seizes every pleasure by the hair, drops what doesn't please him, forgets everything that escapes him; once again he desires, once again he possesses, and once again he desires, like an impetuous and violent wind coursing over the earth. What conquest, what pleasure, what joy could hold him? The only happiness he knows, the only torment that besieges him is his incessant journey through the world.

During his earthly existence, Faust has never realized this heroic and compendious image of himself. Perhaps only for a few hours, right after the pact with Mephistopheles was concluded and when he awoke on the mountain's meadows, had he renounced directing his eyes toward the summits of the sky. But the descent to the Mothers and the summoning of Helen, the desperate search for the forms of Being and the

GOETHE

figures of the past: weren't these two great undertakings of his life a way of scrutinizing, "above the clouds," that which men cannot and must not contemplate? And, during these last years—restless, his eyes diseased, trapped by the mania for possessions—had he ever looked freely at things? Had he ever been able to act with the naturalness and decisiveness of spontaneous, happy spirits?

The heroic self-portrait Faust paints for Care has a cathartic function. As he declares that he looks at the world with limpid eyes and acts with joy and decisiveness, with a single sweep of his hand Faust tears off all the bonds with which Care has furtively enveloped him. He maintains that he does not know what exists "above the clouds" and knows only his own human strength, and he emphasizes again that he does not need the spirits of the night. As he reaffirms his dissatisfaction, he sets in motion the spiritual energy that, during recent years, has been put to sleep. Thus he completes another stage in the process of inner liberation; he mounts another step on the stairway that must lead him back to the arms of God; and magic and Care, defeated, are driven from his path.[16]

The Great Vision and the Lemures

Having freed himself of these two distressing companions, Faust reacquires the ability to see. All the scales fall from his eyes; no "thorn" wounds him; he can look about him freely and soon, like a prophetic seer, perceive the distances of the eternal future (11504, 11579). Yet, at this very moment, Care takes revenge on the man who has resisted her so vigorously. She curses him, blows her spectral breath on his lids and blinds him forever. Another very deep dark night—a night no tender dawn could ever disperse—descends on the starless, fireless night covering the sleeping universe. By a tragic paradox, just when Faust's eyes become clear again, they can no longer see the sun's rays; they can only contemplate the "bright light" that is again filling the inner regions of his spirit (11500).

The light illuminates a bold project Faust has been brooding over for a long time. The work of land reclamation has not been completed. Despite years of activity and Mephistopheles's assistance, a large swamp stretches at the foot of the mountains and the miasmas from it taint the lands wrested from the fury of the elements. Blind, haunted by the presentiment of death, Faust cannot bear the thought that a shadow might obscure his terrestrial masterpiece, the paradisial country that Baucis and Philemon had admired beneath the light of the setting sun. He cannot tolerate further delays; and he decides immediately to dig a ditch that will collect and carry off the swamp's unhealthy waters. Supporting himself against the lintels of the door, staggering, the terrible old man comes out of the palace where he had experienced his deepest shame. In the middle of the night he orders his servants to come out of their hovels, and set to work with mattock and spade; he calls out the overseer and tells him to hire crowds of new laborers. For him these thousands of men are only "the hands" of his spirit, slaves, like those who built the pyramids; pure instruments, like the mattocks and spades they wield so laboriously. He also orders his overseer to entice them with pleasures, to buy them with money, to subject them to the strictest, most strenuous discipline, so that the ditch just begun will be quickly lengthened to the shores of the sea (11503, 11510, 11552–11554).

But, suddenly, Faust's profound eyes—the luminous eyes of his mind, not the blind ones of his body—abandon the procession of slaves surrounding him; he no longer sees them or cares about them. Even the thought of the barely initiated ditch no longer preoccupies him, as if the present, with its limits, conditions, and harsh necessities, had ceased to exist. The eyes of Faust's mind gaze only at the image of the future, which will be realized on his verdant land wrested from the water, even more marvelous than that which appeared beneath the sunset's light to the weary and fascinated pilgrim. Like prophetic blind men and dying men inspired by celestial revelations, he contemplates the ultimate incarnation of the world's eternal Hope, which, with a light flap of its wings, passes invisibly over the bronze doors and walls of Necessity, and flies above mists, rains, and heavy blankets of clouds, and all of the dimensions of time (*Urworte*, 33–40).

High above his territory, freed from the swamp's gloomy miasmas, Faust can see in the villages, fertile fields, among the gardens, vegetable plots, and woods, millions of active and happy inhabitants, children, men in the flower of their manhood, candid and wise old people like Baucis and Philemon, together with their sheep and cattle. This teeming, joyous mass will be able to carry out everything he has never achieved. Whereas he had relied on Mephistopheles's illusory assistance, the future inhabitants of the "paradisial land" (11569) will stand with their feet solidly planted on the ground, without looking beyond, at those dark places where the insidious traps of the phantoms gather. Alone before nature, surrounded by the everyday dangers of existence, active, laborious, and courageous, they will trust only in their own forces, conquering each day the right to liberty and life. Despite his desire to defeat the violence of the elements, Faust has never tamed the waters of the abyss or the infernal fires. Those children, those mature and old men will know how to impose on the savage, unchecked elements—our "colossal adversaries" (XIII, 309: 14)—the mild law that nature hides in our breasts; they will pacify water and earth, constructing new dikes, large and powerful as hills, and proclaiming to the sea, as God did in the Bible: "Hitherto shalt thou come, but no further: and here shall thy proud waves be stayed" (Job 38: 11).[17]

Intent on collaborating with and struggling against nature, the inhabitants of "the new land" (11566) will, without realizing it, break the dismal chain of violences, arbitrary events, stupidities, and mechanical necessities which, until that moment, had imprisoned universal history. Like the community of pilgrims in the *Wanderjahre*, they will no longer sleep in the hovels of slaves, they will not worship grim tyrants like Faust, surrounded by mystery and devoured by an insatiable passion to possess and dominate. These new men will live "free" on their "free land," subject only to the conditions that destiny and nature impose on each of us. The history of the world will undergo a complete transformation, an unprecedented reversal; and its course will ultimately resemble the tranquil course nature travels in its metamorphoses.

The vision, which comforts Faust at the supreme moment of his life, is a hope that flies above time and earthly conditions; the future that envelops and conceals it lies beyond all human limits and will never become the present. Yet, his spirit's eye already sees a joyous swarm of men cultivating the fields of the "paradisial land," building dikes, struggling with the waves. So that future, which will never be realized, is already present before his eyes; that hope, which flies eternally above time, has already descended on the land covered with the shadows of night. Thus a felicity he has never known descends on Faust's soul; a felicity as distant as his vision (*Im Vorgefühl von solchem hohen Glück*, 11585), yet warm and full as the real joys of existence (*Geniess' ich jetzt*, 11586).

Only now can Faust complete his inner purification. Since he defers to an eternal future all programs of action and avoids any confrontation with reality, no terrestrial condition arouses his disquietude and anxiety. The blissful, illimitable future, this place without conditions and necessities is the only one suited to the illimitable force of his spirit. Here, Faust has no need of dominating with violence; he no longer desires slaves as he did just a few moments before. Now he is calm and peaceful; he who has lived proudly alone can now see himself as a humble member of a community of equals.

The words of the wager with Mephistopheles come back to his mind:

> If ever I say to the passing moment
> "Halt here a while! Thou art so fair!"
> Then you may cast me into fetters,
> I will gladly perish then and there!
> Then you may set the death bell tolling,
> Then from my service you are free,
> The clock may stop, its hand may fall,
> And that be the end of time for me!
> *(MacNeice translation, slightly revised)*[18]

He had pronounced these words so many years before, when he was sure that he would never have told any "moment" to halt. But what has the moment of the pact in common with the moment he is now experiencing? That moment belonged to everyday life, made up of vulgar pleasures, insipid joys, of food that never satiates. This "moment" contains the vision of ultimate things, the full felicity of the present and the presentiment of that future, the guarantee of eternity; and Faust tries to detain it between his avid fingers, halting the course of time.

So, after so many foods that did not satiate, after so much gold that has slipped through his hands, after so many games impossible to win —Faust pronounces the words of the wager:

> Then could I bid the passing moment:
> "Halt here a while, thou art so fair!
> The traces of my earthly days can never
> Sink in aeons unaware."
> And I, who feel ahead such heights of bliss,
> At last enjoy my highest moment—this.
> *(MacNeice translation, slightly revised)*[19]

When he has finished saying these words, Faust drops to the ground. Death, which after the murder of Baucis and Philemon, was approaching from behind the clouds, death, which already lived within him, completely masters his body. The clock of his life stops, as mute as at midnight; the hands silently fall, abandoned by the force that guided them (11593–11594).[20]

A few minutes later a voice repeats the words that echoed over the hill of Golgotha when Christ, knowing that all things were fulfilled, wet his lips on the vinegar-drenched sponge and said: τετέλεϐται, *consum-*

matum est, then bowed his head and gave up the ghost (John 19: 30). Now, too, a voice—what does it matter if it is the voice of Mephistopheles?—proclaims to men: *consummatum est,* or *es ist vollbracht,* as Luther had translated it (11594). Another potent human energy has terminated the journey that God prescribed for it: marvelously fulfilled, like all celestial and earthly things that obey the providential design.[21]

What could be more majestic than Faust's end? In a few hours he rediscovers himself: he rends the nets of magic and defeats the gray women besieging him. But every event in *Faust II* must be contemplated from several points of view like a statue which achieves its definitive form only when we consider it from every side. If we tried to tell the story of Faust's death through the realistic, cynical, and illusionless eyes of Mephistopheles, our impression would be quite different. This noble death would seem a ridiculous end; this solemn tragedy, so similar to the tragedy of Golgotha, would seem to us a disreputable farce, performed on a coarse Elizabethan stage.

According to Mephistopheles's version, the clairvoyant blind man to whom the gods have granted the gift of prophecy, the great Utopian who dreams of "a free people on free land" is a poor old man who maunders on and raves deliriously without understanding what is happening around him. While Faust speaks the last monologue, no human being listens to his cries, his exhortations, his hopes. The gang digging with spades is not composed of hardworking laborers obedient to his orders. Mephistopheles has taken over the post of overseer, and in the realm of death he has hired a spectral group of Lemures who now, by the light of the torches, dance a grotesque *danse macabre.*

Gangling inertly, their bones, muscles, and tendons badly stitched together, the Lemures painfully imitate men's figures and gestures. What daring work of reclamation could be accomplished by these staggering skeletons? Their movements resemble those of Punch; their memories are as weak as idiots'; their lips repeat the ditties sung by the clown in the graveyard at Elsinore, for the Lemures perform the sad work of gravediggers. The spades which should have dug the great ditch that Faust had dreamed of, actually dig the miserable house, the small pit, where his own corpse will soon be placed.

When Faust sinks to the ground, Mephistopheles steps forward and, standing before the body, composes an atrocious epitaph. The proud man who had been his companion had gone through life like a whirlwind, embracing ever changing forms; and no pleasure had satisfied his senses, no happiness had contented his spirit. Having reached the end of existence, he, too, had bowed his head, proclaiming that he had experienced an instant of joy—indeed, the "highest moment," the supreme felicity. But what a base joy his had been! Precisely he, the eternally discontented, had embraced the last, empty, squalid moment he had been granted to live: the moment when the breath stops, the heart ceases to beat, and the pallid colors of existence vanish forever before one's blinded eyes (11589).

All of Faust's great dreams are doomed, Mephistopheles insists, to painful failure. The vision that had made him so happy, the image of the "free land," would never be realized. Nobody will ever succeed in shattering the circle of violences and stupidities traveled by universal history since the beginning of the world, or reconcile nature to itself. When the curtain falls on the stage of *Faust* the fragile realm constructed on the shores of the sea will collapse in ruins; the devil of the waters will awaken from his slumbers; the fury of the elements will again be aroused in the depths of the sea; and the waves will break and destroy the dams and dikes erected by magic's vain arts (11544–11545).

Now Faust lies there, like everyone, stretched out in a small pit—who knows where his soul is; and soon his body will be the prey of worms. The mistaken deed, the hopes of eternity, the much too grandiose dreams, all those light, imperceptible signs that distinguish one human existence from another—everything that was at one time called by the name of Faust—has been assailed by the terrible force of time, which "consumes" it, wears it out, and then flings it into the enormous pit of the past. But what is the past? What does this continual creation and formation of men and things, which are then abandoned to death, mean? "Past," Mephistopheles angrily declares, "and pure nullity absolutely the same." The past is a frightful desert, and only an appearance distinguishes it from the absolute emptiness that reigned over the universe before the creation. In this void, this nullity, even the memory of the person who was Faust, the "doctor," "my servant," is lost.

The Defeat of Mephistopheles

The stage of the Goethean theater is almost deserted. The proud master, the capricious companion of Mephistopheles's journey, lies in the gardens where he once anxiously paced. The spectral and bizarre voice of the Lemures is also silent. Now alone in the night, Mephistopheles advances to the proscenium; and, before leaving us, as if he needed to confide in us one last time, he reveals to the audience the pains, sorrows,

GOETHE

defeats, and disappointments afflicting his devil's soul. Mephistopheles has never been so sincere: never with such insinuating rhetoric has he displayed the wounds that bleed in his leathery heart; never has he so effectively depicted his own decadence—an obvious sign that we must not believe him at all.

With his conservative's well-bred nostalgia, Mephistopheles regrets the golden times when he bore the name of Satan, when he could flaunt all the infernal attributes, the horns, tail, claws, and the smell of pitch and sulphur. At that time God did not contest his sovereignty over his kingdom: Evil was the opposite of good, death negated life; and men venerated and respected the prince of hell. The ancient laws and customs regulating the infernal world were as stable as those in God's kingdom; none dared to doubt them or attempted to dispute the prime source of his power—the souls of sinners. When a sinner died, without delay the small winged soul left the constriction of the body, unable any longer to bear that nauseating abode. Mephistopheles lay in wait, all alone, beside the corpse; and as soon as the tiny soul began to fly off, he grabbed and clutched it tightly between his claws, as a cat clutches the quickest mouse. He would then strip it of its feathers, as a housewife plucks a chicken, until he had turned it into a revolting worm; then he branded it with his mark and threw it into the whirling tempests of hell.

How splendid the infernal city was in those days! It had innumerable, fearfully gaping gorges full of sharp teeth, like those of a colossal hyena. An eternal heat, furious torrents, savage seas of fire, of vapors and very thick smoke surged from the depths of the abyss. Sometimes a few of the damned would try to swim to safety; but as soon as they were in the jaws of the "hyena" those colossal teeth would rend them mercilessly. At the bottom of hell reigned the same admirable hierarchy God had imposed on earth. The souls of emperors and popes were burned by nobler flames; princes, bishops, great abbots, and simple knights were divided according to the rank they had held during their lifetime; and deeper down, in the last gloomy pits, a viler fire burned merchants, artisans, actors, and peasants.

In the irreligious modern age which Mephistopheles—perhaps out of calculation, perhaps out of light-mindedness—has helped to create, everything goes badly for him. Breaking his word, God occupies many of the territories that belonged to the devil, and establishes himself as the master among the germs of air, water, and land, and blesses the daimonic becoming of the universe. With a thousand cunning tricks and deceptions, the envoys of heaven wrest sinful souls from the devil, souls that rightfully belong to him. Laws and customs, gathered on parchments in the infernal archive, lose all value; the distinctions between good and evil no longer carry any weight, and men mock at Satan who must travel about the world in disguise.

Even death—"old death," Mephistopheles's surest ally—has lost its "swift strength" (11632). How many times has Mephistopheles stared in vain at stiffened limbs, seemingly abandoned by the slightest breath of life! When he was certain he could seize a small winged soul, those limbs have moved and were stirred again, forcing him sadly to renounce his prey. One couldn't even put one's trust in true, authentic deaths. Although the "genius" inhabiting it wants to leave the nauseating cadaver, the soul lingers lazily and remains fastened in all possible ways to its old abode. If the elements which hate and do battle with each other did not chase it ignominiously away, perhaps it would remain there for centuries, disappointing Mephistopheles's long wait (11626–11629, 11674–11675).

Cultivated and conscientious as he is, Mephistopheles has of course consulted the recent scientific literature dealing with the problems of life and death; for example, the studies of Sömmering, Goethe's old friend, on the "true abode of the soul."[22] But with what profit? Now he has forgotten his old anatomical convictions and does not know if the soul lives in the "nether regions" (11664), or whether it prefers to make its phosphorescent light shine in the navel (11668) or some other part of the body. So he cannot imagine from what aperture the soul, with the agile wings of a butterfly, escapes; and he cannot carry out by himself the noble functions of psychopomp or conductor of souls. If he wants to catch a soul, Mephistopheles must mobilize a regiment of demons. Just as a strategist positions his heavy troops, motionless and iron covered, in the vast plain, and the light troops, spread out, attack the enemy from the rear, so he deploys a group of devils—squat, fat devils with short horns, massive necks, blood-red cheeks, and bellies swollen like leather wine flasks—around Faust's body. In the meantime, he orders the devils with long, twisted horns—taller, thin and light—to flutter through the air with their arms and claws outstretched, so as to seize any soul that might try to reach heaven.

The ancient, venerable city of Dis has become a shadow of itself. Some unknown infernal artist has ably imitated Isaiah's *Sheol* (5: 14), Dante's Inferno, and Pisa's Campo Santo, painting on backdrops of canvas, cardboard, or wood the gaping jaws and hyena's teeth, the ocean of flames, the mysteries hidden in corners, the damned who try vainly to flee by swimming through the fiery waves. A squadron of devils drags onstage this masterpiece of theatrical decoration, just as in the seventeenth century the stagehands of the royal and popular theaters dragged their solemn and grotesque stage sets; and Mephistopheles

GOETHE

illustrates the marvels of his cardboard and canvas palace. But who could possibly fear these ridiculous colored flames, these canvas fangs? And who would flee from these fat devils stupefied by sulphur, or as vain as dancers? Despite Mephistopheles's protests, everything in the infernal world, too, is only "deception and illusion" (11655). In a few years, culture, progress, the immortal ideas of the French Revolution will triumph in the depths of the abyss. God (or a plenary assembly of demons) will insist that emperors and their servants, popes and sacristans, aristocrats and peasants must be devoured by the same jaws and burned by the same democratic fire (11642–11643).

Beneath the nocturnal sky, close to the pit in which Faust lies, Mephistopheles is waiting for the phosphorescent soul of his companion to abandon its old, now putrefying house with a light flap of its wings. He ought not to be worried. After a sinful, tumultuous life, Faust will plunge into the chasms of hell side by side with other great souls, who, like him, were devoured by the mania, frenzy, and passion of ruling. Mephistopheles's ears could not have deceived him. A moment before dying, as he began to rave, dreaming of a "free people," Faust pronounced the words of their wager before thousands of spectators. Magnanimous, grandiose, rhetorical as ever, he proclaimed to the "moment": *Verweile doch, du bist so schön.* "Halt here a while, thou art so fair!"

With his notarylike meticulousness, Mephistopheles has brought along the parchment that Faust had signed with his own blood so many years before; prepared to exhibit it if the soul of his companion and master intends to escape him. But he is not calm. A thousand anxieties harass him. He knows the fugitive, shifting world in which he is doomed to live: a world where parchments, property deeds, sworn agreements, the institutions sanctified by time all lie neglected in the archives of earth and hell, objects of indifference and mockery.

So what is the outcome of the wager between Mephistopheles and Faust? Can the lord of flies and mice conquer that "noble soul," that "great, unique prize" (11829) on which he has wasted so many years of his life, so much imagination and, if it were possible to use the word, so much love? Or will Faust's soul succeed in escaping him, protected by a good fortune that blesses even his mistakes? Everything depends on the composition of the tribunal which, in a place very far from the stage, perhaps in heaven, perhaps in some locality on earth, at this moment judges the wager on which the future of the modern world depends.

If this tribunal were composed of simple men and women; if it were made up of the spectators who anxiously await the end of the play, their decision would be immediate. Simple men detest legal quibbles, scorn what they call the "letter" of things; and they prefer to judge, as the saying goes, "according to the spirit." Now Faust, according to the spirit, has won his wager with the devil. He has not betrayed the "primal source" of his being (324); he has never let himself be deceived by the "moments" and pleasures of existence, he has never stretched out on a "bed of ease" (1692, 1696); and, even during the final instant of his life, he has remained faithful to the illimitable force of his soul. And what about God? If we were given the responsibility of judging, he too would reply without the slightest hesitation that Faust has won the wager with Mephistopheles. No mental bias and, above all, no antipathy for the "mocker" would influence his judgment. But God cannot bear words written on paper, printed in books, or incised in marble. He does not like the letter of the law; and much less juridical documents, notaries' offices, and lawyers' harangues. What counts for him is the eternal, loving, tireless activity of the universe, which has continued to pulsate in Faust's soul.

If he had heard the judgment of God and of men of good sense, Mephistopheles would not have been able to hide his anger. With a gesture more eloquent than any demonstration, once again flaunting the yellowed parchment, he would reply that this perverse worship of the "spirit" of things, worthy at best of the young Baccalaureus, leads the universe to its ruin. The judges of the great wager between him and Faust cannot be incompetents—not even God, who is one of the parties in the case and, as a result, runs the earth with such blameworthy light-mindedness. To judge a wager on which the world's future depends, we must call upon those very rare, learned, scrupulous legal minds, who know all the codes of heaven, earth, and hell; those exceptional men of letters who understand the supreme value of the "Word," and who, at the beginning, stood around God.

Mephistopheles will be in for an atrocious surprise. Having examined all the documents concerning Faust's case, and then having decided in a pure spirit, according to the letter of the law, without antipathy or prejudice for the prince of hell, the tribunal of jurists and literary men have judged the case as God and simple men do. The most important documents of the great trial—the wager between Faust and Mephistopheles, the first and second versions of Faust's last monologue—arouse not the slightest doubts or uncertainties.

In the first version of the *Mitternacht* scene, which goes back to the years around 1800, Faust pronounced the words of the wager:

> I can say to the moment:
> "So halt a while, thou art so fair!"

GOETHE

> The traces of my terrestrial days
> Cannot disappear into the Aeons.*

In the last version (which Mephistopheles, distracted, or too preoccupied, must not have listened to attentively), Goethe has canceled the indicative present, *darf*. Instead, he has put a conditional, *dürfte,* on Faust's lips, who no longer claims to halt a present instant (according to the conditions of the wager) but only a hypothetical, unreal future instant:

> Oh, that I might see such teeming and living,
> And tread a free earth with a free people,
> Then could I bid the passing moment:
> "Halt here a while, thou art so fair!"†

When the magistrates sit on the bench draped in their purple velvet robes; when the men of letters in their studies consult ancient parchments, venerable dictionaries, and writers of every period—none of them considers the fleeting thoughts that cross the mind, the doubts, or the first versions of books. They judge only on the basis of our actually accomplished deeds, our publicly spoken words, the definitive versions of our books as they are printed.

So God is amused at defeating Mephistopheles on his very own grounds: that of the word and the law. He has saved Faust with with the aid of a conditional—three miserable, invisible letters of our alphabet which, at the ultimate moment, he persuaded Goethe to modify on his manuscript. Grace loves to act in the most extravagant ways. This is not the first time that—for so little, for a breath, a "tiny tear," or a mistake in transcription—a "noble soul," a "great, unique treasure," who could have become the last of the damned, is welcomed by the angels and saints in the bizarre and loving kingdom of the heavens.

---

*Ich darf *zum Augenblicke sagen:*
"Verweile doch, du bist so schön!"
Es kann die Spur von meinen Erdentagen
Nicht in Äonen untergehn.
†Solch ein Gewimmel möcht' ich sehen,
Auf freiem Grund mit freiem Volke stehen,
Zum Augenblicke dürft'ich sagen:
"Verweile doch, du bist so schön!"

(11579–11582)

The Redemption of Mephistopheles

The night is about to end. On the palace and Faust's little realm, on the pit in which his mortal body lies, the first light of day begins to descend: "the undesired" (11686) gleam of dawn, when devils have had their worst defeats. The scene comes alive. On high, to the right, a band of very young people descends in a slow, lingering flight, singing at the top of their voices, accompanied by the paradisial music of the heavens:

> Follow, blest envoys,
> Heavenly convoys,
> In halcyon flight
> Sinners forgiving,
> Make the dust living,
> And in your soaring,
> Be you outpouring,
> On all the living
> Breath of delight!*
> *(Wayne translation)*

When he sees them, Mephistopheles feels all the violence of his ancient hatred. The celestial music seems to him a "strident strumming" (11685), that honeyed voice a confused, unharmonious blend of infantile and feminine voices: the warblings of eunuchs, dear for some mysterious reason to the deplorable tastes of the bigots of heaven and earth. As for the angels' virtues, Mephistopheles, who at one time belonged to their race, knows them all too well: diabolical arts, hidden behind a veil of disgusting hypocrisy (11693).

The young celestial hosts and the awkward infernal cutthroats around Faust's body renew once again the battle fought thousands of times, flinging themselves at each other, armed with crosses and pitchforks, as on the walls of Pisa's Campo Santo; or in the valley at the foot of the

---

*Folget, Gesandte,
Himmelsverwandte,
Gemächlichen Flugs:
Sündern vergeben,
Staub zu beleben;
Allen Naturen
Freundliche Spuren
Wirket im Schweben
Des weilenden Zugs!
(11676–11684)

Casentino, around Bonconte da Montefeltro's bloodied body. Like an old captain, Mephistopheles feverishly prepares his defenses, and deploys the two groups of devils—the fat and the thin, the devils with crooked horns and those with long ones—around the borders of Faust's grave. Then he gives them a rousing speech; calls on them to resist, reminds them of hell's illustrious traditions. To lose another battle, to yield a soul conquered with so much difficulty, would be a shame that they could never live down.

As Mephistopheles is exhorting his devils, the angels strew the sky with a fragrant rain of roses; barely opened buds, winged boughs, like a crimson and green spring, swaying above the earth. Mephistopheles, who has never fought against this new celestial weapon, imagines that the shower of petals intends to bury his troops beneath a blanket as fresh as snow, and orders his devils to puff out their fetid satanic breath from full lungs. As soon as the hot infernal breath touches them the crimson roses wither and are blighted. Then they grow pale, turn black, dry up, and burn; and some "bright, venomous flames" (11722), some agile and malicious will-o'-the-wisps flutter in the air and stick like burning hot pitch to the devils' necks. All of Mephistopheles's entreaties and commands are useless. Overcome by the unusual heat, burned by a fire more violent than hell's, Mephistopheles's clumsy soldiers pull back in disorder and, as they back up, throw themselves into the theatrical jaws that hell has gapingly opened onstage. The battle has lasted but a few seconds; the army of the abyss has never been defeated so ignominiously.

Mephistopheles remains alone at his battle post. He does not retreat a single step. But his head burns; his heart and liver are violently aflame; and a "superdiabolical element" (11754) has crept into his entire body. Although he again declares his satanic faith, he begins to give way to the insinuating heat, the witchlike spell the young angels have spread over the earth. He turns his head toward them; and his eye caresses their charms at greater length, like an unhappy lover gazing sadly at the loved one who disdains him.

Perhaps for the first time in the history of the world, despite his arid heart of stone and his bones filled with wintry ice, Mephistopheles has fallen in love. The flame of divine love has delved deep into his fibers. Passion burns in his heart, desire races through his old limbs; and he feels like a lascivious cat on a spring night. Almost beside himself, he implores the angels to come down to earth, to come close to him, to grant him a single, tender glance. He would like them to move their soft, supple limbs in a slightly more terrestrial manner; he would like them to smile at him with the ecstatic, yearning eyes of lovers; and he wants them to kiss him. Among others, he is particularly attracted by a gangly boy with the hypocritical face of a pastor, who wears a long, pleated robe, "excessively moral" (11798), which hides his angelic backside.

Insinuating and insidious as is his custom, divine love tries to seduce the ancient adversary with the innocent charms of very young angels. With not the slightest scruple, absolutely unprejudiced in the choice of the means, he tries to awaken homosexual passion in Mephistopheles's soul: even if the Epistle to the Romans had condemned all those who *"relicto naturali usu feminae, exarserunt in desideriis suis in invicem, masculi in masculos turpitudinem operantes. . . ."** Mephistopheles is just about to yield. Conquered by those shy glances, those treble voices, those young, overdressed bodies, he seems on the point of dissolving in the infinitely sweet, all-encompassing embrace of celestial love.

So, after a small battle between devils and angels, the history of the universe has reached a radical turn. The ancient separation and division of the world into two rival factions is about to end. The heavy force of concentration, tenebrous matter, the spirit that denies and contradicts will be joined, after centuries of hostility, with the free force of expansion, of light and love that moves the universe. Soon we will no longer hear Mephistopheles's sarcasms: his cynical moralist's *bons mots*, his destroyer's fury. He, too, will rise up to the heavens, again taking the place he had lost among the angelic hosts, alongside Raphael, Gabriel, and Michael; and dripping with pathos he will, together with them, glorify God's "lofty, incomprehensible works," "as splendid as on the first day" (249–250).

Many religious spirits will enthusiastically salute this most extraordinary conversion; and hymns of praise will echo from the summits of heaven down to the very depths of the earth. None of them will dare to cast doubt on the road chosen by grace and the means employed to seduce Mephistopheles. But other, perhaps less religious, spirits, though more concerned with the orderly administration of the universe, will not be able to share this joy. Won't the conversion of the devil deprive men, angels, and even God of a necessary stimulus and a profitable form of competition? Won't the world, once the infernal part is amputated, run the risk of being caressed by love's boring uniformity! What will become of the light without the darkness that accompanies it—light-

---

*"leaving the natural use of the women, burned in their lust one toward another; men with men working that which is unseemly. . . ."

GOETHE

ness without weight, the whole without the part, the spirit without the letter; the illimitable élan of the heart without the limited acumen of the intelligence, the dreams of the soul without the corrosive blade of irony?

Yet both the hymns of joy of religious spirits and the worries of the world's administrators are premature. While the angels continue melodiously to intone their strophes, Mephistopheles's diabolical nature again takes the upper hand over the celestial temptation. The infernal body expels the "ghost of [divine] love" (11814) which has wormed its way into him, insidious as a thief, violent as a disease. All extraneous elements, all celestial sensations, which the roses had helped to insinuate into his organism, break out on his skin in the form of disgusting boils, like those with which he himself had covered Job's body, from the tips of his feet to the top of his head. The devil is saved; the noble infernal race triumphs and regains faith in itself.

Mephistopheles can announce the great tidings to the spectators of *Faust,* and to all those who have anxiously followed his adventures: "The devil's noble parts are saved."* Almost identical words will soon resound in the loftiest regions of the atmosphere, when the angels will announce that Faust "the noble member of the world of spirits," has "been saved from evil" (*Gerettet* ist *das edle Glied* Der Geisterwelt vom Bösen, 11934–11935). So, with one of those light, glancing allusions so habitual to him, Goethe warns us that both of the play's great characters are, each in his own way, redeemed. Just as Faust had defended his "daimon," overcoming at the point of death the entrapments of Magic, Care, and Violence, Mephistopheles defends his infernal nature, conquering the temptation to throw himself into the bewitching waves of the "One-All."

At least this time, the scrupulous defenders of universal order have been reassured. Mephistopheles will remain excluded from the sweet bonds of divine love; his strident voice will not sing in chorus with the harmonious voices of the three archangels. Restricted to his world, he will continue to deny, to contradict, and to mock; to oppose with the rigid force of concentration the bouyant force of expansion that propels us to the stars. When the light will try to illuminate the entire universe, he will fight it with the enveloping, disquieting ambushes of darkness; when hope will lift us above the clouds, his sarcasm will bring us back to earth; when God will try to construct philosophical systems, he will demonstrate their lack of foundation. Strolling among us, his face hid-

*Gerettet *sind die* edlen *Teufel*steile
(11813).

den behind new, changing masks, with a nasty smile he will continue to show us all the imperfections of the creation; he will remind us that men suffer miserably; he will unleash tumults and violences. With the fury of fire and ice, he will try to cast into the frightful beatitude of the void everything that exists, the miserable remains of everything that has existed.

While Mephistopheles rediscovers himself, the host of angels rises in flight bearing Faust's immortal part to heaven:

> Holy fires!
> Whom you enfold
> Feels himself in life,
> And blessed by the good.
> All united,
> Rise up praising!
> The air is purified,
> The spirit breathes.*

Like a wretched, fifth-rate devil, Mephistopheles complains of his defeat; and, for a moment, he even thinks of demanding his just rights before God's tribunal. Then he gives up the idea, accusing only himself and his vulgar sodomitical lust, the "absurd" passion that tempted him (11838–11839). Without tragic gestures or heroic poses, with a bitter, elegant phrase, as befits an admirer of the eighteenth-century moralists, he departs forever from the stage of *Faust II;* and he abandons his vast readership, to whom he has given such exquisite, boundless joy.

Mephistopheles's defeat must not lead us to think that his power has diminished. If he travels about incognito; if his hell is made of canvas and wood, if his army of demons proves to be so mediocre, if infernal laws and customs have lost all value; if the angels seduce him and shamefully mock him—what does it matter? At the end of *Faust II* the kingdom of Mephistopheles has once again enlarged its immense frontiers.

In *Faust II* Mephistopheles is the first of the alchemists who search

---

*Heilige Gluten!
Wen sie umschweben,
Fühlt sich im Leben
Selig mit Guten.
Alle vereinigt
Hebt euch und preist!
Luft ist gereinigt.
Atme der Geist!
(11817–11824)

for the stone of the wise in the darkness underground. He is the father of the pure ironic spirit; the hidden kin of the nervous, prodigal modern poet; the lord of the appearances and pranks that triumph on the earth's stages. He knows the abysses, Hermes's magical herbs, and the analytical procedures of modern science; he navigates on the most distant oceans, decides the great battles and events of Europe's history; wrests the land from the sea, builds dikes and canals and undertakes reclamation projects, like the most audacious engineers; prints banknotes which spread an illusory wealth through the world, as do the banks of modern states.

When we wish to know the road which leads to the realm of Being, we must have recourse to his knowing guidance. When we try to transform the dead figures of the past into myths, we cannot do without his spectral assistance. Where does the power of the lord of flies and mice not reach? If we look with an attentive eye at the modern world, we rediscover the mark of Mephistopheles in the land and the sea's green distances, in the abysses, and perhaps even in the sky; we hear everywhere the echo of his laughter; we discover in every corner the shadow of his ambiguous and highly colored witch's gestures.

The Holy Anchorites

As the morning light spreads over the earth, our eyes can no longer see the dikes, canals, and fields torn from the ocean, or Faust's palace and garden, that artificial world where Mephistopheles accomplished his prodigies. The landscape now occupying the stage imitates the landscapes used as a background for the solitary life, temptations, tears, beatitudes, miracles, and prayers of the first Christian anchorites. As in the solitude of the Thebaid, so many times depicted by the brushes of medieval painters, inaccessible cliffs rest heavily on "profound chasms." A thousand brooks flow brightly down among the rocks and plunge with a savage, splashing roar into a dreadful gorge. Sturdy tree trunks sink their roots into the mountain's sides, and bend beneath the wing of the winds. An uncontainable force, a whirling, ecstatic tempest agitates the entire scene: Roots, trees, waters, and chasms undulate before our eyes, move, throw themselves on high, propelled by a single impulse of love.

Among these steep solitudes, some holy anchorites have found a "sacred refuge of love" (11853). As in the frescoes in Pisa's Campo Santo, they live in mountain caves, and lions stalk about near them, tranquil and friendly. Some of the anchorites live in a lower region; some halfway up the rocks; or even higher, "near the azure, outspread tent of heaven" (11999). Some live shut up in a tiny cell, occupied with their thoughts, or, freed from the body's weight, rise and fall in flight amid the caves and forests.

How many different voices, guided by an invisible orchestrater, resound in the mountain theater! A potent, unanimous chorus, repeated by the echo's multiple reverberations, opens the scene:

> Woods clamber tremblingly,
> Crags bear down weightily,
> Roots cling tenaciously,
> Trunks make a density;
> Spurting of wave on wave
> Deep lies our hermits' cave.*
> *(MacNeice translation)*

The enthusiastic voice of Pater Ecstaticus yields to the more meditative and dramatic voice of Pater Profundus; the light and serene voice of Pater Seraphicus intertwines with the treble, shrill voices of the children of midnight, whose voices remind us of the timbre of the three children in *The Magic Flute;* the naïve song of the novice angels sets up an echo to the more labored song of the full-fledged angels. The soft, tender, and ardent voice of Doctor Marianus sings praises to the Queen of Heaven; the chorus of penitents recalls verses that resounded earlier in *Faust I.* The Magna Peccatrix, Mulier Samaritana, and Maria Aegyptiaca weave a single, immense period, full of opulent Biblical figures; Gretchen repeats the prayer she had offered to the Virgin; Mater Gloriosa reveals the secret of her voice. Finally, the Mystic Chorus with its extremely clear-cut and obscurely symbolic accents concludes the scene and the book.

Pater Profundus lives in the lowest part of the mountain where nature shows its dark and savage countenance. Around his cave he sees grim chasms, waters plunge with a roar toward torrents and falls, light-

---

*Waldung, sie schwankt heran,
Felsen, sie lasten dran.
Wurzeln, sie klammern an,
Stamm dicht an Stamm hinan.
Woge nach Woge spritzt,
Höhle, die tiefste, schützt.
(11844–11849)

GOETHE

ning bolts flashing and spreading desolation—just as the archangels had seen the night's horrors and Thales had witnessed the eruptions of Seismos. But he is not content, like the archangels, to exalt the incomprehensible wisdom that God has hidden in his works; nor does he encase himself in Thales's dogmatic candor, ignoring the disasters of creation. With the acute and dramatic attention of his eyes and intelligence, he interrogates things, and clarifies the great problems of theodicy. The waters of the torrents, which seemingly useless and destructive, descend to lovingly irrigate the valley (11876–11878); the lightning, in which the archangels see only a "flaming ruin" (263), purifies "the atmosphere, which bore poison and vapors in its womb" (11880–11881).

So disorder and violence, offensive to the world's beautiful surfaces, are a vain appearance deluding our confused senses. Whoever lives in the deepest regions and looks deeply at things, perceives God's omnipotent, amorous, and laborious power triumph in all the places of the universe. He sees the revelatory signs in the sky and the chasms; among the rocks and waters, in the limpid or cloudy spaces of the air and in the fire. Ceaselessly, this force leaps up toward the sky as, obeying its own impulse, the trunk of the ancient tree flings its branches into the air; and just as, down below, rock rests on rock, torrents and streams plunge toward the falls (11866 ff.).

But Pater Profundus's soul is burdened by a strange curse. He who has the task of demonstrating to other men the harmony of the universe pays for this privilege with his own spiritual disharmony; he who sees everywhere "almighty Love, which forms all and sustains all" (11872–11873) is not himself inhabited by the ardent and continuous impulse of love (11884). Pater Profundus's spirit, which certifies the glory of God, is "cold and confused," possessed by images of the world, tortured by the barrier of the obtuse senses, wounded by the enclosed recurrence of terrestrial pains (11885–11887). His mind, which frees other minds, is heavy and disquieted (11888); his heart is dark and full of anguish (11889). So he begs God to warm his spirit with the everyday gift of love, soothe his worries, and cast light on his needy heart.

So the final intellectual justification of the universe, which Goethe attempts in *Faust*, is not less paradoxical than that of others. What was offered by the angels ended in absurdity; around the theodicy of God and Thales the light of parody danced glintingly; whereas Pater Profundus's justification, the only one carried victoriously to the very end, occupies a much lower step on the stairway to perfection. So any theodicy is merely a humble introduction to the road that leads to God. What saves the harmony of the world is the pure impulse that leads

Homunculus to sacrifice himself in the sea's waters, and the innocence and lightness of just-born infants, the prayers of Gretchen and of the three penitents to the Virgin, the mild and infinitely beneficent gaze of the Mater Gloriosa.

All of Pater Ecstaticus's thoughts and limbs are invaded by unbearable divine love. It possesses him like an eternal conflagration, awakening in his breast a joy and pain more piercing that any pleasure and pain of the senses; and fragmenting his style in a procession of vocatives, implorations, and interjections. But at the same time divine love frees him from the weight of the body. While Pater Profundus, Pater Seraphicus, and Doctor Marianus remain immured in their cells, he experiences the joys of ecstasy, and rises and falls among the forests and gorges, like St. Philip Neri, who lifted himself off the earth by praying (XI, 470. 12–5). Something ephemeral still oppresses his spirit—not the worries of Pater Profundus, but the shadow of the execrable ego, *das Nichtige*, which he curses four times in four lines all ending with word "myself" (*Mich ... mich ...mich ... mich.* 11858–11861). Assailed by an intense desire for annihilation, he invokes the signs of martyrdom; the arrows that transfixed the bodies of Christian martyrs, the spears that struck them down, the cudgels that crushed them, all preparations for eternal beatitude—even lightning bolts, which in the past would fall from the sky to incinerate rebels and wicked men. These arrows, these cudgels, these lightning bolts must destroy *das Nichtige* which casts a darkness on him, just as the fire burns away and evaporates the transient part of all things. At the end of the process of purification, his "crust," his individual "mask" will disappear completely. Incorruptible as the diamond, eternal as a star, there will shine in him only the core *(Kern)*, the deepest core of his soul (11865).[23]

Pater Seraphicus lives in a cave halfway up the mountain, where the fir trees grow more thickly. His voice does not share Pater Profundus's intellectual despair, or Pater Ecstaticus's mystic ardors. Love confers on his words a mild and charming calm. So he can look with clear eyes, without terror or attraction, at the spectacle of things, the "rugged pathways of the earth" (11904), the rocks, the waters descending with enormous leaps to the abyss. Without thinking of himself, but still not completely lost in contemplative bliss, he helps the souls who turn to him and guides them toward the ether's sphere.

The last anchorite, Doctor Marianus, lives in the highest cave, the "purest cell" (11988), where nothing hides the "azure, outspread tent of heaven." From that aerial observatory he contemplates the Mater Gloriosa in her crown of stars, together with the repentant sinners who cluster about her knees. His life subsists only in this contemplation. As

GOETHE

the most mighty pontiff of the world's feminine religion, he knows all the names of the Mater Gloriosa; he understands or glimpses the mysteries that form her essence; he follows the grave or tender story of earthly loves; he directs the chorus of praise and prayers which from every part of the earth rise to the feet of the Mother of God.

As the voices of the anchorites continue to weave together in the sky, a small cloud creeps among the swaying crests of the fir trees. In this cloud Pater Seraphicus sees a host of very young spirits: the "infants of midnight," who, with their spirits and senses barely budding, died right after birth, who know nothing about themselves (11895) or the world's spectacles, and have neither the eyes to see them nor the minds to meditate upon them. But does this matter if "the earth's pressure" (11973) does not weigh them down? In compensation for what they do not know, these cloudy buds possess that infantile virtue—lightness, candor, simple gaiety of soul, grace of speech—without which nobody can enter the kingdom of heaven. Before moving into the ether, the spirits of midnight must have some experience—even if indirect and mediated—of what happens on the "rugged pathways of the earth" (11904). Thus, on the stage of *Faust,* one sees again the spectacle which the visionary genius of Swedenborg had imagined in his *Arcana coelestia.* Pater Seraphicus takes the infants into himself, and lends them his eyes so that they may look with him at the rocks, the torrents, the trees clinging to the rocks. Enclosed in that trustworthy observatory, the blessed children are horrified by this grievous vision of the universe: terror possesses them; and they beg Pater Seraphicus to let them go off into the regions of the air.

The just-born spirits rise into the upper zones of the sky, reaching the summits of the mountains, like those tenuous slithers of cirrus cloud, those veils of mist our eyes see on clear summer mornings. They link hands and dance in a circle around the rocks: they sing cheerfully, full of faith in him whom they soon will contemplate; and they gaze gratefully at the "new spring and ornament" (11976) of the celestial world, just as Lynceus, in the depths of the night, gazed at "the eternal grace" of the terrestrial world (11297). But their journey has not ended. Soon, because of the counsel and the will of the angels, they will receive as a pledge and token Faust's immortal part and will rise with him toward the ultimate confines of the world.[24]

Grace

The scene becomes animated again. The angels who had acquainted the earth with heaven's melodies and songs, who had let fall, like a red and green spring, the perfumed shower of roses, rise in flight into the highest zones of the atmosphere, bearing with them Faust's immortal part. There are among them "more perfect" angels and the host of the younger angels who, wearing the long pleated robe, set fire to Mephistopheles's lust, and who remember with childish joy the victory they won over the prince of hell. All together they sing in chorus:

> Saved from evil is the noble part
> Of the world of spirits:
> 'He who always strains and strives
> We can ever redeem.'
> And if love also from on high
> Has helped him through his sorrow,
> The hallowed legions of the sky
> Will give him glad good morrow*
> *(MacNeice translation, revised)*

How should we interpret the words that Goethe has emphasized by direct quotation? Why has God saved Faust, his "servant," the man who desired the most beautiful stars in the sky and the greatest pleasures on earth? From the beginning, accustomed as we are to the idea of salvation obtained by works, all seems clear to us, God has rewarded and redeemed Faust for his works; since he "has striven," as the angels say; since his "activity becomes constantly higher and purer," as Goethe remarked when talking with Eckermann (E. June 6, 1831). But what are Faust's works? He has not performed a good deed: in fact he has not performed any deed and, in the last instant of his life, while the elements were about to destroy his realm, he was satisfied to contemplate with the eyes of the spirit an eternal future vision, a dream which never would have descended through our mists, rains, and blankets of clouds.

> *Gerettet ist das edle Glied
> Der Geisterwelt vom Bösen.
> *Wer immer strebend sich bemüht*
> *Den können wir erlösen.*
> Und hat an ihm die Liebe gar
> Von oben teilgenommen,
> Begegnet ihm die selige Schar
> Mit herzlichem Willkommen.
> (11934–11941)

GOETHE

God does not absolve or condemn the deeds we do not perform; he does not know them, or he knows that they are all mistaken, improper, and confused. He considers only our souls: the "primal source" he has placed in each of us; and he absolves or condemns us, takes us with him or leaves us the victim of the despair that he himself has bestowed on us. Just as he had chosen Saul and given him a kingdom though he had done nothing to deserve it; just as he had granted Natalia, the "fruit of gold," and the "gift long and sagaciously prepared" to Wilhelm Meister, who had erred in all of his actions, so, now, he exclusively rewards Faust's "nature," the inexhaustible *Streben* which he has given him as the rarest of all graces. Faust's sole "merit"—if in Goethe's world we can speak of merits—has been that of preserving this grace and of having defended it during the last moments of his life.

But no man can be certain of being saved by the hand of God, not even the "sons of Kish," the Wilhelm Meisters, the Fausts, all those chosen by nature. God rewards whomever he wishes and he cannot bear that his decisions must obey a rule that can be explained, contested, and impugned. So that Faust may rise up into heaven, divine love must choose him a second time, it must intercede and participate in his destiny (*und hat an ihm die Liebe gar von oben teilgenommen . . .*); it must go down to meet him with its softest graces, scattering sprigs of roses, singing with the childish voices of angels. If this had not taken place, Faust's soul would still be in its disgusting corpse; and, soon after Mephistopheles would stamp it with his seal, dragging it into the vortices of hell.

When the dark body of water and earth, of air and fire, which has contained us as in a prison, dies and dissolves into nothingness, our divine intellect is not yet completely pure—this is what Plotinus, Porphyry, Iamblichus, Proclus, Macrobius, and the hermetic and alchemical texts tell us. Over its naked spiritual qualities are worn immaterial bodies, the "clothes," the "tunic" the soul had received when coming down through the spheres of the stars on the day when, through fate, error, or some fault, it was incarnated on this earth. As it travels again over the same astral route, rising toward the place above the heavens, the intellect little by little gives up these incorporeal clothes, this very fine tunic; just as he who mounts toward the sanctuaries of the temples and the holy mysteries, purifies himself, abandoning his old garments (Plotinus, *Enneads*, I, 6, 7).

No sooner does it reach the sphere of the moon than it leaves there the most material and feminine of these garments: a lunar robe, formed of the atmosphere's vapors and mists, which had furnished it with vital and nutritive energy. To the sphere of Mercury it leaves avid cupidity and the faculty of interpreting, to Venus the amorous inclinations, to the Sun the imagination, to Mars combative ardor, to Jove ambition and the strength to act—until it has stripped itself of even the most immaterial, finest, and most rarified of robes, the "ethereal garment" which it had donned first of all. Then our intellect is wholly pure, with none of the faculties, energies, perceptions, passions, and emotions that accompanied it during its lifetime. Having attained its true homeland, in the place high above the heavens—as Plato says, the place above Uranus—where it once lived, with amusement and joy mixed with fear it contemplates immutable, motionless Being, which takes nothing in itself and bestows beauty on all things; the Being toward which everything looks and on which everything depends.[25]

After thousands of years this eschatological vision, which the youthful Goethe had seen in the Neoplatonic and alchemical texts, reappears in the last scene of *Faust*—like a tenuous shadow, like a pale but visible echo, which alone can explain certain curious expressions. When Faust's "immortal part" attains the atmosphere, we must imagine that we see, above the mountain peaks and the forests of fir trees, a robust spiritual body—"powerful limbs" (12077)—the pneumatic double of Faust's earthly limbs. His is now "a transfigured body," similar to that which Mignon, at the end of the *Lehrjahre*, dreamed of possessing among the "celestial figures" (VII, 516: 1–4).[26] But his pneumatic body is not yet completely pure. Not the subjection to sin, as Christian doctrine teaches; but rather a "residue of earth" (11954), the shadow of matter, the obscure weight of the elements, as in the Neoplatonic cosmology, enfolds his already resplendent spiritual substance.

So also Faust's "immortal part," like the νοῦς and the λόγος of the Neoplatonic and hermetic texts, begins silently to rise through "the spheres" (12094), from whence it had at one time descended. As it ascends, it grows lighter, becomes purified, divests itself of the garments concealing it, as the butterfly leaves "the rigid constriction of the chrysalis" and journeys through "the ether traversed by the sun's rays" (9658–9660, 11982–11986). The process of purification is gradual; and we glimpse only the first two phases. When it meets the host of midnight spirits, Faust's immortal part leaves the "cocoon" (or "tufts of wool" *Flocken*) that enveloped it (11982–11985); frees itself violently from all the "earthly bonds of the old integument" (12088–12089). Then, as Gretchen prays to the Mater Gloriosa for him, Faust is also about to leave the "ethereal raiment" (12090), which, according to Porphyry, was the first, most immaterial, and finest of the garments we wear on earth.[27]

GOETHE

This progressive abandonment of outer garments takes place quite easily with simple, weak, and pure souls who barely know the ways of the world. But Faust's "robust spiritual strength" had clung to the world with solid organs and the "harsh pleasure of love" (1114): he had desired, possessed, abandoned, and desired once again; he had attracted the elements to him, merging with them (11960). So Faust cannot by his own efforts free himself from his terrestrial shadow, and not even the most perfect angels can divide his "double, reunited nature" (11962). God is the only one who can separate this otherwise indivisible combination (11964), and He sends His faithful envoys to greet Faust.[28]

The first of these envoys are the children of midnight, who looked upon things with the eyes of Pater Seraphicus. Between these spirits and Faust, due to the advice and incitement of the angels, there takes place a reciprocal exchange of gifts. The children reveal to Faust qualities he has never known: innocence of heart, the soul's limpid joy, the capacity to contemplate the world's springtime, and Faust teaches the children, whom death had so quickly removed from the "choirs of life," at least a part of what he learned during his long experience. A little while later an even more efficacious female mediator awaits his transfigured body. At the beginning of the fourth act, among Germany's mountain peaks, a "tender, light ribbon of mist, fresh and caressing" had grazed the breast and forehead of Faust, who recognized Gretchen's image—"Aurora's love," the "first, swiftly felt and scarcely comprehended glance" which more than any other treasure could have illuminated his life (10061–10062). This band of mist has come all the way up here, to the highest part of the atmosphere, like one of those small clouds clustered about the knees of the Mater Gloriosa.

Gretchen has not yet been accepted into the presence of the queen of the world. Although she has known tears at the feet of the Mater Dolorosa: shame, humiliation, sin, the terrible song of the *Dies irae*, and an ignominious death, although even at the end of her days she invoked the name of the Father, she has never been forgiven by the Mater Gloriosa. Yet Faust has not uttered a single word of repentance, as though he could neither sin nor repent; and yet, since "much has been given to him," God saves him, the angels descend to meet him and lead him to the choir of the blessed. So even in the realm of the heavens there is repeated the theological injustice which on earth offended the harpist, Mignon, and all those to whom God, as the Gospel of St. Matthew says, had not "given" any of his gifts.

When, through the intercession of the great female sinners, Gretchen is admitted into the choir of blessed spirits, she repeats the prayer that in the past with the sword of anguish in her heart and pain gnawing at her bones, she pronounced at the feet of the Mater Dolorosa:

> Oh, bow,
> Thou rich in sorrows
> Benignly your face to my pain.*

What a different background her words now have! The sorrowful mother of Christ has become the glorious, radiant mistress of the world; no longer anguish, but an unexpected felicity fills her soul, while Faust returns to our true homeland. No longer terrestrial ignorance, but a mysterious knowledge of the enigmas of heaven illuminate her ingenuous spirit (12092–12093).

> Bow, bow
> Thou incomparable being,
> Rich in radiance.
> Benignly bow thy face to my felicity.
> My love of old,
> Now free from stain,
> Comes back to me!†

Gretchen's prayer is heard and accepted by the Mater Gloriosa. Like Mignon and the harpist, like all souls crushed without reason by the burden of guilt, Gretchen possesses a strength which happy spirits, favored by God and nature, rarely know. The love kindling her soul is not enough to redeem her, but it can redeem the universe, and dissolve the last earthly vestiges that cast their shadow on Faust's immortal part.

Divesting itself first of its earthly integument, and then of its very delicate, ethereal garment, Faust's pneumatic body is completely invaded by "the primal strength of youth" (12091). Without a morsel left of his human doctrine, with eyes still weak and unable to bear the light of the new day (12093), he returns to what he had been before coming down through the sphere of the stars. He rediscovers the source of his life, of which he had had a profound presentiment during his early

---

*Ach neige,
  Du Schmerzenreiche,
  Dein Antlitz gnädig meiner Not!
      (3587–3589)
†Neige, neige
  Du Ohnegleiche,
  Du strahlenreiche.
  Dein Antlitz gnädig meinem Glück!
  Der früh Geliebte,
  Nicht mehr Getrübte,
  Er kommt zurück.
      (12069–12075)

GOETHE

childhood years, "when the kiss of divine love" was sent to him in the "solemn peace of Holy Sabbath"; when "an inexpressibly sweet yearning" drove him to roam the fields and woods, and he felt a world being born within him (771 ff.). As always in Goethe, Faust's leap forward, his eschatological flight toward the eternal future is at the same time a return—an immersion in the symbolic youthfulness of his life and the universe.[29]

The astral ascent and the successive metamorphoses of the Neoplatonic νοῦς ended in the high place, far above the heavens, before the immutable splendor of Being. Faust's immortal part, having regained the strength of youth, does not halt before God's blinding light, nor around a point or a circle, in which the essence of the universe seems to be concentrated. Not the mountains' wild peaks and chasms, nor the tepid bays of the sea, nor the sun's eternal splendor, nor the night's eternal darkness—no terrestrial limit, no astral sphere can stand in the way of his illimitable forward leap. In the free zones of the ether, he has the powerful wings of birds, of which he had at one time vainly dreamed. He experiences the lightness of the lark, the wings of the eagle stretched high above the mountains covered with fir trees, the crane's yearning flight over lakes and plains. Gay, tranquil, silent, in eternal movement and eternal repose, he continues his incessant activity: He moves and is transformed, subject to the law of universal metamorphosis.

We know that the "world's spirit" will find ever new occupations for him (March 19, 1827); but we do not know what they will be. We can imagine that, at some time in the future, Faust will once again come down to the earth in the form of a friend of knowledge and beauty, of a king who obeys the laws; or in the form of a swan, a lion, an eagle, as did happen, according to the Platonic tale of Er, to the souls of Orpheus, Ajax, and Agamemnon. Or perhaps the regions of the ether may detain him indefinitely, like the monads of Wieland and Makarie. There he will know the blessed games of the gods; he will transform the comet's nebulous essence into clarity; he will revolve like a star of the first magnitude; and he will penetrate deeper into the spaces beyond Jupiter, beyond Saturn, beyond the confines of our small solar system . . .

Mysterium Lunae

The traveler who has come so high among these tall mountain peaks, and sees the five acts of *Faust II* stretched out at his feet—as the calm world, radiant heights, and tranquil valleys, the rivers of gold and silver stretched at Faust's feet—what is his impression now? Perhaps at this distance he cannot see the orderly procession of events, forgets Faust, Mephistopheles, Helen, and Euphorion—all the characters of flesh or cardboard who have performed in Goethe's play. In the valleys he left but a short time ago, only the large masses, the intense colors and contrasts catch his attention. Perhaps, out of the entire plot of *Faust*, he sees only the tragic drama, the festive, brilliant dance of the elements; the spectacles of fire and water, of earth and air, which Goethe dedicated to the most faithful and subtle of his spectators.

If he looks more intently at these apparitions, it seems to him that, in each act, the drama of the elements exalts a fundamental element. In the first act, the marvelous aquatic palaces, with their lucent green walls and purple borders, the pygmies' troglodytic caves, the mists, the clouds, and flares of heat provoked by Pluto's wand cluster around the very high cupola blazing with flames, where the Emperor walks like the prince of salamanders. In the second act, the fires that warm the monsters of antiquity, the rocks in movement or unshakable as granite, the hiss and windlike breath of celestial meteors, the nocturnal clouds that announce Galatea's arrival—all the events of the "infamous night" lead to the waves of the Aegean Sea, bathed by the moon's dew. And finally, in the third act, the last fire of Troy and the agitation of the Aegean are the background against which one sees, as in relief, the supple forms that gods, nature, and men shape on the surface of the earth lit by the sun.

Having reached the topmost peak of *Faust II*, our traveler sees the most spiritual of elements: air; indeed its purest part, which the ancients and Goethe called the "ether" (11732, 11923, 12018). "Blankets of clouds, mists, rainy whirlwinds" never come up there, nor does the rumble and flare of the tempest ever trouble Pater Profundus. Indeed, around him everything is serene, tranquil, warm, and infinitely luminous. Charmed by this spectacle, the traveler of the elements—like another traveler who during the Aegean festival gazed at the moon enveloped by a circle of clouds (8347 ff.)—sees only the "azure, outspread tent of heaven." He looks at the moon's sickle or disk as it appears in the limpid morning sky; the fragile streak of mist wreathed about the summit of the mountains, the cirrus clouds rising higher and higher until they dissolve in the Father's "lap and hand."[30]

GOETHE

But Pater Profundus, Pater Ecstaticus, and Doctor Marianus would have accused this traveler of being myopic; for what to his earthly eyes seemed only an aerial spectacle, was also a divine revelation. Just as, at the close of the Aegean festival, Nereus and Thales had affirmed that each of us must preserve something of the sacred in his breast, as within "a tranquil, warm nest," so, at the end of *Faust*, Doctor Marianus proclaims that the keen eyes of his body and the pure eyes of his spirit contemplate the Mater Gloriosa, the "lofty mistress of the world," accompanied by a choir of repentant sinners.

Hidden in the highest of the mountain cells, Doctor Marianus glorifies the Mother of God with the images of Christian tradition. He sees her surrounded by a "crown of stars" (11994); just as in the Apocalypse or Book of Revelations, after lightning flashes, clamors, thunders, and earthquakes, Mary had appeared "clothed with the sun, and the moon under her feet, and upon her head a crown of twelve stars" (12, 1). He calls her the "queen of heaven, high mistress of the world"; "Virgin, pure in the most beautiful sense, Mother worthy of honors," "untouchable," "incomparable" "rich in grace," "rich in radiant beams" (11995, 11997, 12009–12010, 12020, 12035–12036, 12071, 12102); and as for centuries in the darkness and magnificence of baroque churches, the throng of the faithful have extolled Mary: *"Mater Christi, Mater divinae gratiae, Mater purissima, Mater castissima, Mater inviolata, Virgo prudentissima, Virgo venerabilis, Virgo predicanda, Vas spirituale, Vas honorabile, Rosa mystica, Domus aurea, Janua coeli, Stella matutina, Regina angelorum . . ."*

Other expressions surprise us on the lips of a mystical Christian like Doctor Marianus. After having called her mother and queen, he invokes Mary as *Göttern ebenbürtig* and *Göttin* (12012, 12103), that is, as "equal to the gods," indeed a "goddess"; the same words with which Faust and Mephistopheles had extolled Helen (7440, 9949), and Nereus and the Sirens had praised Galatea (8147, 8387, *den Göttern gleich zu schauen*). Who are the other gods to whom Doctor Marianus compares Mary? Without a doubt, Jesus Christ, the Holy Ghost, all the saints of "Catholic mythology"; but also Apollo, Artemis, Aphrodite, Zeus, the great gods of pagan mythology, whom Christ should have defeated. On Doctor Marianus's lips the confines of Christian religion are enlarged, merging into a single indeterminate mythology, which tends to include in itself all of the religions on earth.[31]

So Mary is not only the Virgin extolled by the angel Gabriel, the Mater Dolorosa invoked by Gretchen's desperate devotion, the benign, succoring Madonna who protects the crowds that lift up their prayers to her. All the thoughts, desires, and emotions that the men of any

civilization have devoted to woman; all the personifications and religious or profane symbols that glorify "the eternal feminine," are gathered around the radiant head of this "great goddess," this "mistress of
the world" who hovers at the very summit of space. Although she may
seem so far from their sphere, Mary includes in herself the memory of
Galatea, who had inherited Aphrodite's beauty and temples; and of
Helen, who confused, overwrought, and bedazzled men in each of her
epiphanies.

When Doctor Marianus asks the best souls "to consecrate themselves
to the service" of the Mater Gloriosa (*Dir zum Dienst erbötig,* 12101) and
implores the Virgin, Mother, and Queen, surrounded by light clouds of
penitents, "to remain compassionate" (*bleibe gnädig,* 12103), he only
repeats the words of the Sirens—priestesses of the lunar festival, just as
Doctor Marianus is the priest of the feast of Mary—who had evoked the
moon stationary in the sky (*Dir zu jedem Dienst erbötig,* 8042; *sie uns
gnädig, bleibe . . . gnädig,* 8043, 8078–8079), surrounded by a rich circle
of "cloudlets" (8339). As the aerial traveler has seen, a subtle relationship ties the Virgin's sweet look to the tranquil light of the celestial
moon. None of the anchorites could accuse Doctor Marianus of offending Christian tradition by these parallels: for the Apocalypse or Revelation (or its very first interpreters) had shown the moon at Mary's feet.
The Church Fathers, the sculptures in medieval churches, the precious
miniatures of the codexes, the piety of the crowds saw in the Virgin the
true moon, from which "the sun of Justice, Christ, our God" is born; St.
Ambrose had identified the *Mysterium Lunae* with the *Mysterium
Mariae,* that *Geheimnis* which is not yet completely revealed to Doctor
Marianus's contemplative eye (12000).[32]

How many other times had Goethe contemplated the light of the
moon around female images! Frau von Stein's face had shone sweetly
and calmly on him, just as the misty beams of the moon shone on the
valley and river; Eleonora d'Este's passions had illuminated the world,
like the moon's calm, cold, parsimonious light; Iphigenia had looked at
the rediscovered Orestes, just as Artemis turned her silent, virginal face
to Apollo; and Galatea had glistened beneath the beams of the August
moon . . .[33] This light seems pallid, weak, only capable of illuminating
the dark paths of the night: so much less intense than Pandora's and
Helen's dazzling, possessive solar light. And yet, in the last verses of
Faust II, while Helen's ardor is hidden in Hades or is lost in the regions
of the East, "the eternal feminine" chooses Artemis's mild, reflected
rays as the highest, most delicate form by which to reveal herself to
men.

Around the knees of the Mater Gloriosa are gathered, like a ring of very light clouds, a "gentle populace" of repentant sinners (12016). When they lived on earth, will-less and without strength, a look, a greeting, a caressing sigh would be enough to perturb them: their feet slid gladly on the smooth, inclined terrain; and who among them was able to break the chain of amorous pleasures? Now they are here, repentant, and they pray, singing in chorus, invoke the forgiveness of the Mater Gloriosa, sip ether, just as the gods on Olympus feed only on ambrosia and nectar.

Some had sinned more gravely or were able by themselves to break the chain of pleasures. These sinners remember their distant pasts, which the Gospels and the *Acta Sanctorum* have already rendered symbolic. So we listen to the Magna Peccatrix, who bathed the feet of Jesus Christ, anointed them with drops of ointment made of nard, washed them with the balsam of her tears, and dried them with the softness of the hairs of her head (Luke 7: 37–38); the Mulier Samaritana, who met Christ beside the well, where they watered Abraham's camels and offered him a bucket to cool his parched lips (John 4: 5 ff.; Genesis 24: 10 ff.); Mary Aegyptiaca, who sinned, was driven out of the church of the Holy Sepulcher, retreated into the desert, where she died tracing the last of her prayers on the sand.

To the topmost summit of the heavens, where the Mater Gloriosa lives, there rises from every place on earth the love that, each day, is born, burns, and dies in men's breasts. Here is gathered Pater Profundus's anxious love; Pater Ecstaticus's boiling and painful love, Pater Seraphicus's pure brotherly love, Doctor Marianus's contemplative thoughts, the infantile emotions of the spirits of midnight, and the tears of shame of the repentant women sinners. But here is also gathered the love lost pursuing profane, confused, wayward, perhaps unworthy objects, trampled underfoot by him who should have enjoyed them. Here is found "the harsh pleasure of love" with which Faust seized the world's joys, and the anxieties, sighs, looks, greetings, flatteries, emotions as sweet smelling as drops of spikenard, soft as the tresses of the Magna Peccatrix, which the penitent women sinners gave as gifts to too many creatures on earth.

Purified by the Virgin's blessing, this manifold earthly love can remain beneath the world's vault in the hands of the penitents who magically transform it into roses; and rise toward the ultimate summits of space until it dissolves "in the lap and hand" of God. Meanwhile, ceaselessly, incessantly, it descends to earth like the water of the "pure, rich source," gushing from Abraham's well and, "superabundant, eternally clear, runs through all the worlds" (12051–12052); like the perfumed shower of roses the angels scatter over Faust's body.[34]

When the waters of celestial love descend again to the earth, they heal our wounds, like a miraculous balsam (11170; *Zueignung*, 35–36). They soothe our ardor, tame our furies, mitigate the passions that dig deep into our limbs, refresh our hot and weary brows like the wings of Truth and the winds of poetry (12007–12008; *Zueignung*, 43 ff.; 97 ff.).[35] This water is also a fire; this very fresh spring is a crimson springtime of roses, hotter than the infernal flames. If its petals fall on us our heads burn, our hearts begin to flame; something irresistible, more sinful in appearance than earthly Eros, finds its way into our souls, possesses us, encloses us in its infinitely sweet embrace (11699, 11725, 11753–11754, 11802, 11817).

As she traverses the world with her waters and flaming roses, feminine celestial love purifies everything she touches and grazes; she destroys the things that live in us and are not part of us, defeats the external influences that miserably stifle our souls; she overcomes the limits of the opaque senses and makes the intangible purity of our inner beings shine out (11753–11756 ff., 11864–11865). She forgives miserable sinners, redeems and reawakens those who have died beneath the burden of guilt and the shadow of the body, spreading joy in this life and preparing the beatitude of Paradise (11679–11680, 11727, 11729, 11818–11820). Finally, as Faust's last words announce, she leads us up to the heights where the luminous words of truth live their happy life (11731 ff., 12110–12111).

The Chorus Mysticus

So, after so many thousands of verses, after so many symbols hidden inside each other like the butterfly in its cocoon, *Faust* has found its proper conclusion. While the word *finis* is about to descend on the boards of a stage that expands and extends as far as the eye can see, who can say that Goethe has not kept the promises which, more than thirty years before in his *Prelude in the Theater*, the Director, Poet, and Clown made in his name?

As the Poet wished, we have listened to songs welling from the deepest part of the breast, and in which were released at one and the same time the impulse to truth and the pleasure of deception, the indomitable upsurges of the soul, dolorous felicity, the force of hate and the impetus of love. We heard songs that distinguished the eternally equal flow of things in accordance with the precise measure of a rhythm, lifting the individual to sacred universality where he pulsates with a magnificent harmony bringing together a thousand scattered notes in the architecture of the Whole. Meanwhile, as the Clown had recommended, fantasy, assisted by a pinch of madness, told a story. It was akin to one of those adventures of love which are born by chance and grow little by little. Such stories end by generating incredible romances—drawing highly colored images, where little clarity, many errors and an imperceptible spark of truth stand side by side—not certainly a Whole but a ragoût without beginning or end, which any spectator can distractedly enjoy. As the Director of the company had desired, onstage were enacted adventures from the *Thousand and One Nights,* prodigies, fires, earthquakes, battles, murders, lootings, and edifying spectacles; while, hidden behind the wings, some imaginative stagehands lifted into the sky the moon and the sun, lavishly pouring out stars, water, fire, rocky precipices, beasts and birds, as though all of creation wished to be concentrated in this narrow house made of boards and stage flats.

And the motley crowd that had pushed and shoved before the box office as if in front of a bakery on a day of famine, with what emotion has it followed the spectacle of *Faust II?* Many of the spectators had gone to the theater to outwit the torments of boredom; some after having read the newspaper; the ladies to make a display of themselves and their clothes; others had thought they might pick up partners for a game of cards, or dreamed of a night of wild pleasures on some young girl's breast. Off in a corner, only a group of young people—still ready to cry and laugh profoundly, to honor enthusiasms, to love fleeting appearances—seemed disposed to absorb from the verses a delicate and melancholy nourishment. And yet the miracle dreamed of by the Poet, Director, and Clown has taken place. During the five interminable acts, almost none of these ladies and gentlemen, these old and young people, these cultivated and coarse persons have regretted the money paid at the box office to acquire the ticket.

Before the curtain falls forever on the stage, a few more minutes are left for Goethe to try to sum up the meaning of *Faust* in a mathematical formula, as simple on the surface as it is rich in subtle meanings and implications. For the last time, the voices of the penitent women sinners, the saintly anchorites, the spirits of midnight, Faust and Gretchen, the voices of all the saints who inhabit the supreme regions of the universe and speak in the name of the citizens of the earth, intone a solemn *Chorus Mysticus:*

Faust II

All that passes
Is only a comparison;
The inaccessible,
Happens here;
The indescribable
Fulfills itself here;
The eternal feminine
Draws us on high*

As the first scene of *Faust II* has reminded us, fugitive things, the phenomena, events, and persons of the earth are comparisons, examples, symbols, parables, shimmering rainbows to help us to know, though mediated and reflected, the light of the sun, the splendor of truth, the grace and power of God.[36] Up there on high, around the Mater Gloriosa, we glimpse the first term of the comparison which till now someone has concealed from us, the other face of the symbol, the mysterious meaning behind the example and the parable. Divine love, the mystery of salvation, the ascent and purification of spirits, the Mater Gloriosa as the sign of the eternal feminine, all the things that were inaccessible to us on earth now are clear before our eyes, "the events" (*Ereignis*), "fulfilled" (*getan*), fulfilled and palpable as those of our world.

But *das Ewig-Weibliche*—is it truly the culmination of *Faust II?* Does everything happen here, does everything complete and realize itself, as the mystic chorus sings? Do there not exist other inaccessible things which escape our sight and our tongues? Do we really know the first, obscure term of comparison, the mysterious meaning of the parable, the hidden face of the symbol? Do we no longer see, as Prometheus said, "illuminated things," but the same dazzling, inconceivable light (*Pandora*, 958)? Has the restless movement—which has agitated this book as it has its terrible hero—finally come to a halt while the uninterrupted line curves in a circle of perfection?

Perhaps the Mater Gloriosa, the penitent women sinners, the children of midnight, Gretchen and Faust will know the definitive splendor

*Alles Vergängliche
Ist nur ein Gleichnis;
Das Unzulängliche,
Hier wird's Ereignis;
Das Unbeschreibliche
Hier ist's getan;
Das Ewig-Weibliche
Zieht uns hinan.
(12104–12111)

GOETHE

of the "new day" (11933, 12093). Without pain or mediation, they will blissfully contemplate the rays of the sun which had seemed to Faust a boundless conflagration, a hostile sea of fire, full of love and hate. As for us, as Emil Staiger writes, we have barely lifted "the hem of the curtain of eternity." We do not contemplate the light of the sun, but merely the mild, pallid lunar light surrounding the Virgin. We have not reached the final goal; all that is possible has not been accomplished before our yearning eyes. Just as the "fleeting things" were the symbol of that which gathered around the Mater Gloriosa, so in its turn the *Ewig-Weibliche* is the symbol of the ultimate Reality, still distant and veiled. But this Reality will never reveal itself, this definitive event can never take place, this absolute light will continue to hide behind a cloud of love and hate, the ultimate significance of the comparison will never slough off the cocoon that encases it. Behind the examples and the words vainly trying to express it, there will continue to move that unnamable, unattainable, indescribable upward trajectory to which, in the words of human language, we give the name of God.

So, after the last verses have dropped from Goethe's hand, the culmination of *Faust II*, like the culmination of the *Lehrjahre*, does not remain within the confines of the book but outside of it. As the curtain falls on the final words of the *Chorus Mysticus*; as the spectators return to their houses—some to a quiet game of cards, some to the wild pleasures of love, some to their favorite newspaper, some to savor again the triumphant and melancholy revelations—the great book, which has occupied us for so long a time, continues to pursue its goal just as Euphorion's inspired aureole restlessly rises toward the sky of poetry, just as Makarie's star is lost beyond Jupiter, beyond Saturn, beyond the confines of our solar system.

Notes

All Roman and Arabic numerals in parentheses in the text refer to the volume, page, and line of the complete edition of Goethe's works edited by Erich Trunz (Wegner edition). Those preceded by *W.* refer to the Weimar edition; those preceded by *A.* to the Artemis-Verlag edition. The dates preceded by *E.*, *M.*, or *B.* refer, respectively, to the conversations with Eckermann and Muller, and to the collection edited by Wilhelm Bode, *Goethe in vertraulichen Briefen seiner Zeitgenossen*, Berlin, 1918–1923. All simple dates, with no other indication, refer to the collection of Goethe's letters.

In the chapters on the Lehrjahre, parenthetical numerals refer to the page and line of the Wegner edition (volume VII) of the *Lehrjahre*. In the chapters on *Faust II*, the parenthetical numerals refer to the lines of the Wegner edition (volume III) of *Faust*.

I am not certain I can remember the whole long list of my debts to the many scholars of Goethe, and so I want to express my gratitude here by recording all of the books and essays that have been most useful to me: Charles Du Bos, *Goethe*, Paris: Editions Corrêa, 1949; Ernst Robert Curtius, *Kritische Essays zur europäischen Literatur*, Bern: Francke, 1954; Gottfried Diener, *Fausts Weg zu Helena*, Stuttgart: Klett, 1961; Wilhelm Emrich, *Die Symbolik von Faust II*, Bonn: Athenäum, 1957; R. D. Gray, *Goethe the Alchemist*, New York: Cambridge, 1953; Hermann Hess, "Goethe und Bettina" and "Wilhelm Meisters Lehrjahre" in *Dank an Goethe*, Zurich: W. Classen, 1946; Max Kommerell, "Faust II; Zum Verständnis der Form" in *Geist und Buchstabe der Dichtung*,

GOETHE

Frankfurt-on-Main: Klostermann, 1944; Thomas Mann, "Über Goethes Faust" in *Neue Studien*, Stockholm: Bermann-Fischer, 1948; Ladislao Mittner, "Paessagi italiani di Goethe" in *Letteratura tedesca del novecento*, Turin: Einaudi, 1960, and the chapters on Goethe in the *Storia della letteratura tedesca. Dal pietismo al romanticismo*, Turin: Einaudi, 1954; Katharina Mommsen, *Goethe und 1001 Nacht*, Berlin: Akademie-Verlag, 1960; Karl Reinhardt, *Die klassische Walpurgisnacht*, in *Antike und Abendland*, I, 1945; Emil Staiger, *Goethe*, Zurich: Atlantis, 1952–1959, 3 vols.; and the commentary of Erich Trunz, especially to volumes III and VIII of the edition over which he presided.

PART ONE

CHAPTER I

1) Found among several descriptions of Rome under the moonlight, all in *Italienische Reise (Italian Journey*, English version translated by W.H. Auden and Elizabeth Mayer, 1968), see XI, pages 168, 371, 373, 408, 554–555.

2) See the oldest conclusion of *Italienische Reise* in XI, page 677 ff.

3) "So lebe ich den glucklich, *weil ich in dem bin, was meines Vaters ist*" (XI, 400: 37). And *Luke* 2: 49 in Luther's translation: "Wisset ihr nicht, dass ich sein muss in dem, das meines Vaters ist?"

CHAPTER II

1) On Goethe's garden, see Wilhelm Bode, *Goethes Leben im Garten am Stern*, Berlin, 1909, and Georg Balzer, *Goethe als Gartenfreud*, Bruckmann, 1966.

2) Concerning the dangers of metamorphosis in *Faust II*, see Part II, Chapter VI, pages 297–298. On the games of nature in classical writers, one can read Karl Deichgraber's excellent essay, *Natura varie ludens*, Akademie der Wissenschaften und der Literatur in Mainz, Abh der Seistes-und Sozialwissen-schaftlichen Klasse, 1954, Number 3 and *Die Musen, Nereiden und Okeaninen in Hesiods Theogonie*, ibid., 1965, Number 4.

3) On repetition in history and in nature, the figure of Erichtho, Part II, Chapter VI, pages 245–247.

4) See farther on, Part I, Chapter VI, pages 95–96; Part II, Chapter III, page 169; Chapter VI, pages 264–265 and pages 301–302; Chapter VII, page 364 ff.; Chapter VIII, page 395 ff.

CHAPTER III

1) For the theme of incest in the *Lehrjahre*, see also Chapter VI on page 94 ff. One would never come to an end if one were to try to track down in Goethe's books the most complicated variations on incest. See, in any case, *Die Geschwister* written in 1776, where Wilhelm loves Mariane like a brother, a putative father, a lover, and a husband; and a

novella in the *Wanderjahre*, "The Man of Fifty," in which the baroness attempts to satisfy her unconscious incestuous passion for her brother by marrying him to her daughter.

2) Marie Delcourt, *Hermaphrodite*, P.U.F., 1958, pages 35–81.

3) R. D. Gray, *Goethe the Alchemist*, New York: Cambridge, 1953, page 222 ff., fundamental for these problems.

4) The definition that Aurelie gives of Wilhelm (obviously shared by Goethe) coincides with the definition that Goethe gives of the poet and of himself. "Without having ever observed the objects in Nature, you recognize the truth in the image; it seems that there lies in you a presentiment of the entire world, awakened and developed by means of the harmonious contact with poetry" (VII, 257, 16–21). "As one says of the poet, that the elements of the visible world are hidden in his deepest nature, and must only develop gradually from within him, in such a manner that he does not contemplate anything in the world which he has not already lived through in his presentiments . . ." (VIII, 126, 7–11). "Thus some time before he had said to me that the true poet possesses, from birth, knowledge of the world and that he has no need, in order to depict it, of a great deal of practice and experience. 'I wrote my *Götz von Berlichingen*,' he said, 'when I was twenty-two; and ten years later I was amazed at the truth of what I had depicted. . . . If I had not already borne inside myself the entire world, I would have remained a blind man with open eyes, and all my studies and experiences would have been only a dead, useless labor. The light is there, and the colors enswathe us; but if we do not have the light and the colors in our eyes, we can never perceive them outside of ourselves' " (E. February 26, 1824).

CHAPTER IV

1) Diderot, *Oeuvres*, Paris: Bibliothèque de Pleiade, 1954, page 1066. The *Paradox* was written in 1773 but was published as late as 1830. In 1805 Goethe translated *Rameau's Nephew*, in which a number of analogous motifs appear.

2) On Jarno as a messenger of the "tower," see the next chapter.

3) See Schiller's letter to Goethe on July 3, 1796: "No single action, none of his speeches represent him: one must see him, must feel him, must live with him."

CHAPTER V

1) We cannot know, for example, if the unknown person with whom Wilhelm discusses destiny in the ninth chapter of the second book is the Abbé (as it would seem from 420: 27–28) or the Abbé's brother (as is suggested on 494: 34–36).

2) Cagliostro's speech in *Der Gross Kophta:* ". . . a secret society of men spread over the entire earth, men who are more or less alike, who rarely appear personally but manifest themselves by their actions" (A. VI, 633), is a perfect definition of the Society of the Tower. Also the chorus sung in Cagliostro's Egyptian loggia (*"Bringet Ernst zur ernsten Sache,"* A. VI, 630) reminds one a little of the chorus sung in the *Lehrjahre* at Mignon's burial: *". . . nehmet den heiligen Ernst mit hinaus, denn der Ernst, der heilige, macht allein das Lieben zur Ewigkeit"* (578: 14–16).

3) See Chapter IV, pages 49–50.

CHAPTER VI

1) In *Iphigenie auf Tauris* Goethe does not credit the classical tradition, according to which Tantalus offered his own son to the gods as a sacrifice. Just as in Euripides Iphigenia

GOETHE

considered this tradition unworthy of belief (*Iphigenia in Tauris*, 387), so also in Goethe Iphigenia declares that Tantalus *"unedel war er nicht und kein Verräter, Allein zum Knecht zu gross, und zum Gesellen Des grossen Donnrers nur ein Mensch"* (319–321).

2) See Gray, *op. cit.*, page 168.

3) See Chapter III, pages 38 ff.

4) See Chapter II, pages 29–32.

5) See Chapter VI, pages 94–96.

6) See Part II, Chapter VII, page 358 ff.

7) In the Greek world, Marie Delcourt (*op. cit.*, page 68) writes, "androgyny occupies the two poles of the sacred. Pure concept, pure vision of the spirit, it appears rich in the loftiest values. Once actualized in a being of flesh and blood, it is a monstrosity, and nothing else: it attests to the wrath of the gods against the group which has had the misfortune to reveal it; and they free themselves as soon as possible from the unfortunates who represent it."

8) The "carbuncle stone" (sign of the *lapis*) was an image Goethe had drawn from alchemy's great metaphoric repertory.

CHAPTER VII

1) This cosmological mosaic was composed by using the following texts: Plato: *Phaedrus, Phaedo*, and *Timaeus;* Aristotle: *On the Heavens;* Lucretius: *De Natura Rerum;* Cicero: *De Natura Deorum, Somnium Scipionis;* Philo: *De Opifico Mundi, Legum Allegoriae, De Somniis;* Ovid: *Metamorphoses;* Seneca: *Naturales Quaestiones, Ad Helviam, Ad Marciam, Epistolae ad Lucilium;* Lucan: *Pharsalia;* Pliny: *Natural History, Corpus Hermeticum;* Iamblichus: *De Mysteriis.* The major part of these books, ideas, and images were known to Goethe, and appear in his writings.

2) This last detail appears only in the 1821 edition of the *Wanderjahre*, Max Hecker, ed., Berlin: Dom-Verlag, 1921, page 201.

3) On the symbol of the Amazon in Goethe, see Gray's fine analysis, *op. cit.*, pages 228 ff., to which there is nothing to add.

4) Jarno seems to attribute to Natalia the three theological virtues, Faith, Hope, and Charity, which Theresa does not know (523: 3–7).

5) See the fine description of Natalia's character in Schiller's letter of July 3, 1796.

6) Goethe writes: *"sie streckte ihre Hand . . . aus";* and Matthew 8:3, in Luther's translation: *"streckte seine Hand aus."*

7) See Part II, Chapter III, pages 164–165.

8) See Chapter VI, pages 101–102.

9) *". . . Ich fand mich ganz in der Nähe des angebeteten Wesens. Dies ist ihre reine, holde Gestalt, ihre schlanken Arme, die mir einst so hülfreuch erschienen und mich, nach unseligen Leiden und Verworrenheiten, endlich doch, wenn auch nur für Augenblicke, teilnehmend umfassten . . ."* (*Wanderjahre*, in the 1821 version, *ed. cit.*).

10) Goethe began to think of the *Wanderjahre* soon after the publication of the *Lehrjahre;* he wrote the first chapters in May 1807. It is impossible to establish when he decided to separate the paths of Wilhelm and Natalia forever. Certainly the motif of distant and impossible love above all returns in his later writings: *Hochbild* was written in 1815, while the *Klassische Walpurgisnacht*, with the episode of Nereus and Galatea, dates from 1830

(see Part II, Chapter III, pages 169–170, and Chapter VI, pages 301–302).

11) The passage of the figure of Natalia to that of Makarie is evident in the section of the 1821 version published by Trunz on pages 643–644 of his edition.

<h2 style="text-align:center">CHAPTER VIII</h2>

1) From the "first preface" to *Lucien Leuwen*, Stendhal, published in English in two volumes as *The Green Huntsman* and *Telegraph*, New York: New Directions, 1950.

2) In the first chapter of *Theatralische Sendung*, mention is made of "M., a free city of a medium size."

3) See Chapter II, pages 31–32.

4) Discussing with Wilhelm immediately after Mignon's death, Friedrich informs him that Philine is going to have a child, conceived at about the time of the first production of *Hamlet* (559: 16). Therefore, from the production of the play to Mignon's death, about nine months have gone by. In the second chapter of the fifth book, just before the play is produced, Werner announces his coming marriage to Wilhelm's sister. At the beginning of the eighth book, just before Mignon's death, he says that his "sons" give promise of becoming "level-headed youngsters" (501: 1). In this case, at least three to four years must have passed. In the first version, as Schiller observed, the incongruence was much more evident, since Werner's sons were already able "to write and calculate, trade and do business as merchants" (Schiller's letter of July 5, 1796 and Goethe's reply of July 9).

5) See *Wanderjahre* in the 1821 version, *ed. cit.*, page 178.

6) There are a few small exceptions. Although the "beautiful soul" does not possess a personal style, we can find in her lexicon some influences of pietistic language: Wilhelm's letter in Chapter XVI of the first book carries to an extreme the lyrical-rhetorical richness of the narrative sections here. A small "stylistic portrait" is that of Norberg, Mariane's first lover. His two love notes (74–75: 487) reveal a certain coherence and autonomy in the tone and images. But the person who has written these notes is not a coarse German merchant; he is somewhat of a rhetorician, nourished on classical culture, who finds it amusing to copy the vulgarity and truculence of his bourgeois correspondent.

7) In *Theatralische Sendung*, intellectual psychology played a much more important part than in the *Lehrjahre*. As he was reworking his old book, Goethe cut out some very fine pages which analyzed Wilhelm's disease and his idea of language (see Book II of *Theatralische Sendung*, Chapters I and II). Some of the analytical elements manage to find their way into the autobiography, "Confessions of a Beautiful Soul"; while the entire sixth book is composed according to principles different from those operating in the rest of the *Lehrjahre*.

8) Sometimes Goethe went so far as to practice a kind of illusionistic psychology: the unconscious reconciliation achieved between Wilhelm and his father takes place through the words of the Abbé's brother, who appears before him disguised as a ghost during the initiation ceremony (see Chapter IV, pages 70–71). Later on, especially in *Wahlverwandschaften*, Goethe is concerned with the enumeration of objects and events, in which the heart's boundless wealth is expressed. "He felt a profound sadness, which he had rarely experienced. The swaying movement of the boat, the splash of the oars, the sowing of the wind which seemed to shiver on the mirror of the water, the rustle of the reeds, the last flights of the birds, the intermittent glistening of the first stars: everything had a touch of the ghostly about it . . ." (VI, 324: 39–325: 5). We are close to Flaubert's most proverbial

GOETHE

effects: *"Il voyagea. Il connut la mélancholie des paquebots, les froids réveils sous la tente, l'étourdissement des paysages et des ruines, l'amertume des sympathies interrompues."*

9) The motif of "destiny" is born in the *Lehrjahre*. Natalia's motif is almost entirely new: the painting of the "father's bride," the connection that links the apparition of the Amazon, Clorinda, and the painting, Natalia's handwriting and the countess's—of all this there was not a trace in *Theatralische Sendung* (which is interrupted at the beginning of the fifth book of the *Lehrjahre*).

10) On poetry as a "veil," see Part II, Chapter III, pages 165–166. Proust wrote in 1904 to Countess de Noailles: *". . . si on cherche ce qui fait la beauté absolue de certaines choses, des fables de La Fontaine, des comédies de Moliere, on voit que ce n'est pas la profondeur, ou telle ou telle autre vertu qui semble éminente. Non, c'est une espèce de fondu, d'unité transparente, où toutes les choses, perdant leur premier aspect de choses, sont venues se ranger les unes à côté des autres dans une espèce d'ordre, pénétrées de la même lumière, vues les unes dans les autres, sans un seul mot qui reste en dehors, qui soit resté réfractaire à cette assimilation. . . . Je suppose que c'est ce qu'on appelle le Vernis des Maîtres . . ."* (*Correspondance générale*, Plon 1931, volume II, pages 86–87.) I am not familiar with really satisfactory critical evaluations of the style of the *Lehrjahre*. Having grown over the course of twenty years, the book bears the signs of many different formal studies, as does *Faust*. In the same chapter, the soft lyrical waves, drenched with Biblical and rhetorical allusions from Goethe' youth, are combined with the more prudent and intellectual prose of his maturity. But we never have the impression, as in the case of *Faust*, of holding in our hands a prodigious and monstrous accumulation, the encyclopedia of all possible styles; nor do we admire, as in *Faust*, off-key notes and sudden, leaping changes in tone. In the course of his revision, Goethe has moderated, shaded, softened, making sure that the extreme poles of his style would appear as variations of a fundamental tonality.

11) On granite see XIII, 255: 11–12 and 256: 6–7 (and the essay *Der Dinamismus in der Geologie*, A. XVI, 585 ff.). On purplish red see Chapter II, page 23.

PART TWO

CHAPTER I

1) Ernst Robert Curtius has devoted an excellent essay to Goethe the "administrator" in *Kritische Essays zur europäischen Literatur*, Bern: Francke, 1954.

2) See especially the letter to Zelter of March 16, 1827, and the conversation with Falk of January 25, 1813.

3) In the fifth chapter of the eighth book of the *Lehrjahre*, Wilhelm visits the Hall of the Past, constructed by Natalia's uncle. "What a life," he exclaimed, "in this Hall of the Past! One might with equal justice call it the Hall of the Present and the Future. So all things were, and so they will always be. Nothing is transitory, save for the person who looks at it and enjoys it. Here, this image of the mother clasping her baby to her breast, will survive many generations of happy mothers. Centuries from now, perhaps, some father will take pleasure in contemplating this bearded man, who puts aside his gravity and plays with his son . . ." (VII, 541: 1 ff.)

4) It suffices to recall Mignon's embalming in the *Lehrjahre*, the duke's dream of rescuing Eugenie's body from putrefaction (*Natürliche Tochter*, 1481–1496); and the fate of Ottilie, who also escapes putrefaction. Why do the Abbé and the Society of the Tower decide to

embalm Mignon? Certainly so as to give "some lastingness" to her body. But it is possible that Goethe wanted to suggest another idea. Mignon dead lies stretched out beneath a veil, wearing her clothes, the angel's white wings, and the band around her head (VII, 575: 9–11; 577: 6–8). Now these clothes are, as we know, "the appearance" (VII, 515: 31) symbolic of her angelic soul. By preserving her so carefully, the members of the tower's society are attempting perhaps to preserve the terrestrial image of her privileged nature.

In the *Wahlverwandschaften*, Ottilie's profoundest aspirations are to live the silent life of portraits; and to know the "second life," which begins for some after death. She writes in her diary: "Sometimes one has relations with a living man as with a portrait. It is not necessary that he speak to us, that he look at us, that he concern himself with us: we see him, we feel our relation with him, indeed our relations with him can develop without any action on his part, without his even realizing that he behaves toward us as to a portrait" (VI, 569: 14–20). Later, after entering the restored Gothic chapel, Ottilie remembers an ancient belief which held that the dead live in huge caves, "sitting in silent conversations." "Yesterday, when I sat in the chapel and, before my carved pew, I saw many others arranged in a circle, that thought seemed to me friendly and benign. 'Why can't you remain seated?' I thought to myself. 'Sit quietly and all wrapped up in yourself, for a long, long time, until the day that your friends come: then you may rise to your feet and show them their places, with a friendly wave of greeting.' The colored panes of glass convert the day into a solemn twilight, and someone should procure an eternal lamp, so that the night, too, does not remain completely dark" (VI, 575: 25–34).

Involuntarily, Ottilie satisfies both of these aspirations. She realizes the first during the last days of her existence, during that atrocious interregnum between life and death, when she is in "silent conversation," alongside Eduard, silent as a portrait, repeating like an automaton the gestures of the year before. Then she dies: she is buried in the Gothic chapel, beneath a light slab of crystal, and her body remains uncorrupted. The coffin of Eduard's child rests at her feet, Eduard's beside her; while a perennial lamp illumines the church. As she had dreamed, during that limbo which is our "second life" after death, she continues her silent conversation with those who had loved her on earth.

5)   ... gebietend uns wieder zurück
               Zu dem unerfreulichen, grautagenden,
               Ungreifbarer Gebilde vollen,
               Überfüllten, ewig leeren Hades?
                       (*Faust,* 9118–9121)

Concerning the Goethean sense of history and myth, see particularly Emrich, *op. cit.*, page 110 ff.; and the pages on mythical figures and Erichtho in Chapter VI, and those on Helen in Chapter VII in Part II.

CHAPTER III

1)   Ich bringe süsses Rauchwerk in die Flamme
               O lass den reinen Hauch der Liebe dir
               Die Glut des Busens leise wehend kühlen
                 (*Iphigenie auf Tauris,* 1156–1158)

And *Zueignung,* 46: *"am heissen Tag die Stirne sanft gekühlt."* This relationship of mediation between the light of the sun and that of truth was already announced in a letter of February 13, 1769, at the time of his readings in alchemy: "The light is the truth, but the sun is not the truth, although the light pours from the sun."

2) In a strict sense, the "crown" should be the symbol of poetic glory, which exults and terrorizes Tasso's soul. But the value of the image is richer. In verse 496, Leonore declares that the crown "refreshes the brows" of those who walk in the torrid regions of glory; in

GOETHE

the same way, as we have seen, in the verses of *Zueignung* (46, 99) the wings of truth and the veil of poetry refresh the brows of their devotees. In *Tasso* verses 2026 ff., Leonore compares the poet's crown of laurel and the martyr's aureole; and Goethe, commenting on the scene with Euphorion, sees in the aureole the symbol of poetic inspiration (see Chapter VII, pages 358, 362; *Faust*, 9624, stage direction after 9902, and Goethe's letter to Iken on September 27, 1827). So it does not seem to me excessive to see in the "crown" the same force as poetry. On the theme of the inachievability, ineffability, and unreachability of poetry, see farther ahead, in relation to Euphorion (Chapter VII, pages 363–365). Tasso's sensation is similar to Ottilie's (VI, 374: 1–8).

3)   Hoffnung breitet leichte Schleier
        Nebelhaft vor unsern Blick
        (*Chinesisch-Deutsche Jahresund Tageszeiten*, III, 5–6).

4)   . . . Steht Wolke hoch, zum *Herrlichsten geballt*,
        Verkündet, *festgebildet*, Machtgewalt . . .
            (*Trilogie zu Howards Wolkenlehre*, 35–36).
                And *Faust*, 10044–54.

5) As Gray comments (*op. cit.*, pages 133–134), at Karlsbad, on the Day of Ascension in 1820, Goethe had observed some cirrus clouds which rose and dissolved in the sky; and he had associated this phenomenon with the ascension of Christ. The last verse devoted to the *cirrus*, in the poem in honor of Howard—"*So fliesst zuletzt . . . Dem Vater oben still in Schoss und Hand*"—alludes to a phrase in John: "*unigenitus Filius qui est in sinu Patris* (1: 18; in Luther's translation: "*der in des Vaters Schoss ist*").

6) When writing the chorus of the elves in the same scene in *Faust II, Anmutige Gegend*, it is probable that Goethe remembered the Platonic myth of the cave. In the passage of the *Republic* (515c–516b), the prisoner, coming out of the cave, is blinded by the sun's light: he tries to accustom himself slowly to it; and, at first, he sees the *shadows*, then the images of men and of objects reflected in the *water*, the light of the *stars* and the *moon*, and finally, he can look directly at the sun. Thus the chorus of elves, which wants to give Faust back to the "sacred light," first remembers the "sweet vapors" of twilight (4636), then the light of the stars reflected in the lake and the magnificence of the moon (4642–4649), until Faust is urged to look at the day's splendor (4659).

7) See Chapter VII, pages 366–367.

8) On the images of the veil and the cloud, see Emrich's excellent analysis, *op. cit.*, pages 44 ff. From Gray's research, *op. cit.*, pages 146–159, it becomes clear in this case too, that alchemy had furnished the suggestion for Goethe's metaphoric constructions. Indeed, alchemical texts associated clouds, garments, doves, and infants as a group (8340 ff.).

9) On the task which Goethe imposed on his readers, see the statements contained in the letters of November 19, 1796; November 15, 1809; March 11, 1816; November 14, 1827; and September 8, 1831.

CHAPTER IV

1) See Chapter VI, pages 262–264; Chapter VIII, pages 373–374, 376.

2) On the relationship between Mephistopheles and Hermes, see Chapter VII, page 359 ff.

3) Emrich's interpretation, according to which Faust, in the second part of the play, is completely changed, does not seem to me acceptable. If Faust had really decided to know the light of the sun in its "colored reflections," all his attempts would have no meaning. Both that of founding the "double realm" of Being and Reality, and those of summoning

up a dead person, possessing Helen's love and conquering the unleashed forces of the elements are obviously infractions of the limits of human nature (see Chapter VIII, page 393).

4) See Chapter V, page 000; Chapter VII, pages 000–000; Chapter VIII, pages 000–000.

5) Thomas Mann, "Über Goethes Faust," in *Neu Studien*, Stockholm: Bermann-Fischer, 1948, pages 670 ff.

6) At the start, Goethe really thought of having Satan appear on the Brocken (see A., III, 552–554).

7) On Mephistopheles's decadence, see Chapter VIII, pages 399 ff.

8) Mephistopheles slightly corrects Hesiod, for whom "at the beginning" there was Chaos, from which Erebus and "black Night" were born (*Theogony*, 116 ff.).

9) The source is again the *Theogony* (124), where the Night generates the ether and the light. It is necessary to remember that, in Goethe, it is always God, not the darkness, that creates light.

10) See the profession of vulcanist faith on the part of Mephistopheles, Chapter VIII, pages 000–000; and Anaxagoras's statement, Chapter VI, pages 000–000.

11) For Jarno's figure, Part I, Chapter IV, pages 63–64. On matter as *"schwer," "fest," "finster," "starr,"* VIII, 444: 26–29; IX, 351–352; *Faust*, 1353–1358.

12) Concerning Mephistopheles the conservative, see farther on in Chapter VI, page 000, and Chapter VIII, 000–000.

13) It is enough to recall the relationship between Mephistopheles and the Mothers (Chapter V, pages 000–000) and the Phorkyads (Chapter VI, pages 000–000). As for Mephistopheles the "specialist," see also Jarno in the *Wanderjahre*.

14) What Mephistopheles says to the student (1908 ff.) has a double meaning, at least in the final version of *Faust*. Mephistopheles makes fun of the science of his time and recognizes in it one of his ideals.

15) On the relationship between Mephistopheles and Wagner, see Chapter VI, pages 000–000.

16)   Du bist am Ende—was du bist.
                    Setz dir Perücken auf von Millionen Locken,
                    Setz deinen Fuss auf ellenhohe Socken,
                    Du bleibst doch immer, was du bist
                                (1806–1809)

CHAPTER V

1) Goethe has presented Cagliostro's figures and deeds in *Gross-Koptha* (1791).

2) This enumeration is inspired by one of tales from the *Thousand and One Nights*, the "Story of Prince Seyen-Alasman and the King of the Spirits." See Katharina Mommsen, *Goethe und 1001 Nacht*, Berlin: Akademie-Verlag, 1960, page 191.

In all probability, one of the sources for the entire act and the figure of the Emperor are Chapters 1–3 of Book XVI of Tacitus's *Annals* in which Nero (hungry for gold, just like the Emperor in *Faust)* is deceived by Cessellius Bassius, who promises him the gold buried under the ground near Carthage.

3) See Gottfried Diener, *Fausts Weg zu Helena*, Stuttgart: Klett, 1961, page 34.

4) See verses 10089–10090, wherein Mephistopheles expounds his vulcanist philosophy:

. . . Sie gründen auch hierauf die rechten Lehren,
Das *Unterste* ins *Oberste* zu kehren.

And verses 5467–5469, on the lips of Mephistopheles disguised as Zoilo-Thersites:

Das Tiefe hoch, das Hohe tief,
Das Schiefe grad, das Grade schief,
Das ganz allein macht mich gesund. . . .

5) Verse 6115, *"Die Phantasie, in ihrem höchsten Flug,"* alludes to verse 640: *"Wenn Phantasie sich sonst mit kühnem Flug."*

6) See Gray, *op. cit.*, pages 31 and 202; Diener, *op. cit.*, page 77. There is no doubt that Goethe wanted to represent the descent to the Mothers as an equivalent of the alchemical opus. Mephistopheles says:

Ist mein Kumpan doch deshalb weggegangen;
Er weiss schon, wie es anzufangen,
Und *laboriert verschlossen still,*
Muss ganz besonders sich befleissen;
Denn wer den Schatz, das Schöne, heben will,
Bedarf der *höchsten Kunst, Magie der Weisen*
(6311–6316)

But I believe that this is chiefly a verbal equivalence; there does not seem to me to be anything truly alchemical in the representation of the realm of the Mothers. Yet, in any event, consult Gray, *op. cit.*, pages 201–204.

7) *Hoffnung* here incarnates only the negative face of Hope (see Chapter III, pages 168–169).

8) In appearance, it is Faust with his magic wand who causes most of the prodigies. But the true magician is undoubtedly Mephistopheles, who has conferred a part of his powers on Faust. In fact, the passage from a simple masquerade to the illusionist spectacle is provoked by the metamorphosis of Zoili-Thersites (Mephistopheles); while in verses 6031 ff., the emperor recognizes in Mephistopheles, whom he compares with Scheherazade, the true author of the prodigies. See the analogous scenes in the third act (Chapter VII, page 340 ff.) and the fourth act (Chapter VIII, page 379 ff.; and also Mommsen, *op. cit.*, page 229).

9) On the Mephistophelean element in Proteus and nature, see Chapter VI, pages 299–300.

10) As Goethe said to Eckermann, the *Knabe Lenker* is a first incarnation of Euphorion: "Euphorion is not a human being but allegorical. In him is personified poetry, which is not tied to any time, place or person. The same spirit, who would later like to be Euphorion, now appears as the boy charioteer, and in this is similar to the ghosts who are present everywhere and can appear at any time" (December 20, 1829). On Euphorion, the *Knabe Lenker* and poetry's young demons, see Chapter VII, pages 360–361.

11) The theme of gold as the symbol of inspiration returns in the figure of Euphorion, see Chapter VII, pages 358, 364, and Wilhelm Emrich, *Die Symbolik von Faust II,* Bonn: Athenäum, 1957, pages 149 ff., 171 ff. On the relationship between Plutus and the boy charioteer, see the pages on the relationship between the worlds of Apollo and Hermes, Chapter VII, pages 365–366.

12) As to the Oriental sources, see Mommsen, *op. cit.*, page 222 ff.

13) On the theory of money in the sixteenth century, see Michel Foucault, *The Order of Things,* New York: Pantheon, 1970, pages 168 ff.

Notes

14) Talking with Eckermann, Goethe observed that he had found the name of the Mothers in Plutarch (see Chapter V, page 220). "This is what I owe to tradition; the rest is my invention" (January 10, 1830). But I believe that the correspondences with *Phaedrus*, indicated farther on, express an allusive intention.

15) To emphasize that the Mothers live outside of time, Goethe writes:

Versinke denn! Ich könnt'auch sagen: *steige!*
(6275)

But, in fact, in Goethe's metaphoric representation, the Mothers live in the depths.

16) In the first version, verses 6431–6432 declare: *"Was war, was ist, was kommt in Glanz und Schein, /Es wogt einher, als wollt'es ewig sein."* In this version, the "images of life," which exist before phenomena, were therefore similar to Platonic ideas.

17) See Chapter VII, page 310 ff.

18) On the cultural sources for this passage, see Gottfried Diener's excellent book, *op. cit.*, pages 62 ff. On the eventual relationship between the Mothers and the moirai *("diese sind, wie ihr Name besagt, die Verteilerinnen* [6433] *die jedem Seienden seine Portion* [*"Meros"*] *zuteilen"),* Wolfgang Schadewaldt, *Goethe-Studien,* Munich: Artemis, 1963, page 185.

19) One can never be cautious enough in interpreting this episode, which has no other examples anywhere in Goethe, and where the summary and allusive art of *Faust II* attains an extremity of concentration. But I believe that it is possible to suppose that, according to Goethe, three Helens, three Parises, and three Achilles coexist contemporaneously in the universe. Their absolute images hover like a light mist around the heads of the Mothers; their "historic" figures are conserved in Hades; while, on earth, ever different bodies and spirits are born without knowing their immortal traces.

20) On the significance of *"schaudern"* (6218, 6265, 6272), see Diener, *op. cit.*, pages 100 ff. In *"schaudern,"* at verse 6272, one can hear the echo of another verb that is not pronounced: *"erstaunen,"* in which Goethe like Plato ($\theta\alpha\nu\mu\acute{\alpha}\xi\epsilon\iota\nu$) saw a supreme value; see Eckermann, February 18, 1829; XIV, 36, 38 and a passage in the *Wanderjahre* in which the very same words of our passage return: *"Ergriffen und erstaunt hielt er sich beide Augen zu. Das* Ungeheure . . . *droht, uns zu vernichten"* (VIII, 119: 6–8). Here: *"Ergriffen, fühlt er tief das* Ungeheure" (6274).

21)   Du bist's, der ich die Regung aller Kraft,
          Den Inbegriff der Leidenschaft,
          Dir Neigung, Lieb', Anbetung, Wahnsinn zolle"
          (6498–6500)

22) The allusion to the famous passage in *Phaedrus* seems obvious to me. There is a perfect correspondence between the effects of the "divine countenance" on the lover in *Phaedrus* and those of the Mothers and image of Helen on Faust. Fear: "$\delta\epsilon\iota\mu\acute{\alpha}\tau\omega\nu$"(*Phaedrus*, 251 a), "$\check{\epsilon}\delta\epsilon\iota\sigma\epsilon$"(*Phaedrus*, 254 b), *"aufgeschreckt"* (62126). *Shudders, shivers of horror:* "$\check{\epsilon}\varphi\rho\iota\xi\epsilon$" (254 a) and *"schaudert's dich"* (6216), *"schaudernd"* (6265). *Beside oneself:* "$\check{\epsilon}\kappa\pi\lambda\eta\tau\tau o\nu\tau\alpha\iota$ $\kappa\alpha\grave{\iota}$ $o\grave{\nu}\kappa\epsilon\theta$'$\alpha\nu\tau\tilde{\omega}\nu$ $\gamma\acute{\iota}\gamma\nu o\nu\tau\alpha\iota$"(*Phaedrus*, 250 a) and *"aus sich selbst entrückt* (6485). *Veneration:* "$\sigma\acute{\epsilon}\beta\epsilon\tau\alpha\iota$" (*Phaedrus*, 251 a) and "$\sigma\epsilon\varphi\theta\epsilon\tilde{\iota}\sigma\alpha$" (*Phaedrus*, 254 b) and *"Anbetung"* (6550)/*Delirium;* "$\mu\alpha\nu\acute{\iota}\alpha$" (*Phaedrus*, 244 ff.) and *"Wahnsinn"* (6500). One might also add that the *"Erstarren,"* which Faust rejects (6271), corresponds to the rigidity ("$\sigma\kappa\lambda\eta\rho\acute{o}\tau\eta\tau o\varsigma$" *Phaedrus*, 251 b), which prevents the wings from growing.

23) While this book was already in galleys, I received Harold Jantz's *The Mothers in Faust, The myth of time and creativity,* Baltimore: Johns Hopkins Press, 1969. Jantz has found a print, contained in *Iconologia Deorum, Oder Abbildung der Götter* by Joachim Sandart,

GOETHE

published in Nuremburg in 1680 and reprinted in 1768–1775, which most likely constitutes a source for the episode of the Mothers.

CHAPTER VI

1) In verses 6850 ff., the infinitives which rhyme, *komponieren, verlutieren, kohobieren, probieren, organisieren,* and *kristallisieren* are the homage that Goethe and Wagner pay to alchemy. In the *Aurea catena Homeri,* which Goethe knew very well, we encounter in a few lines an analogous group of infinitives in *ieren* and *iren: "Nun wollen wir . . . das Wasser in seine Theile . . .* separieren, *solche* examinieren *und ihre Wirckung* anatomieren, solviren, *erlösen,* separieren, *solche . . . dann wieder . . .* conjungiren, coaguliren *und* figiren . . ." (Gray, *op. cit.,* page 254).

2) See Goethe's texts in Diener, *op. cit.,* pages 253–255.

3) There are two dates (according to the ancient Roman and the Julian calendars) of the night that precedes the battle of Pharsalus, on the anniversary of which the *Klassische Walpurgisnacht* takes place. But Goethe mocked and made fun of this chronology; and in the outlines for act two he had Homunculus and Mephistopheles fight (which was based on the Benedictines' chronology) around about this date.

4) On the relationship between the myth of Homunculus and the *lapis,* see the chapter devoted to Homunculus in Gray, *op. cit.;* and also see Chapter VI, page 306.

5) This representation is almost a commonplace in hermetic and Neoplatonic texts: see treatise X, 16–18 in Pliny's *Corpus Hermeticum;* and the passages in Plotinus, Porphyry, Iamblichus, and Proclus quoted in the A. J. Festugière's commentary on the *Corpus* (volume I, page 131, Belles Lettres, 1960). I do not know what Goethe's direct source could be; but a study of the alchemical texts of his youth should certainly track them down.

6) See page 302 ff.

7) See Staiger, *op. cit.,* volume III, page 352, and Karl Reinhardt, *Die Klassische Walpurgisnacht* in *Antike und Abendland,* Marion von Schröder, 1945, volume I, pages 153 ff.

8) The sources I have used are the most obvious ones. For the peoples of the North, Herodotus, III, 116; IV, 7–9, 13–14, 23–28; Lucan, III, 280. For the Griffins, Aeschylus, *Prometheus Unchained,* 803; Herodotus, III, 116, IV, 13; Pausanias, I, XXIV, 6; Aelian, IV, 27; Philostratus, *Apollonius of Tyana,* III, 48. For the ants, Herodotus, III, 101–105. For the race of Echidna, Hesiod, *Theogony,* 295–332. For the Sphinxes, Aeschylus, *Seven Against Thebes,* 538, 541, 558; Sophocles, *Oedipus the King,* 36, 130, 371; Euripides, *The Phoenician Women,* 806 ff.; 1018 ff., *Electra,* 471; Apollodorus, *Library,* III, V, 8. For the Sirens, Hesiod, *Theogony,* 340; Homer, *Odyssey,* XII, 39 ff.; Plato, *The Republic,* X, 617 b; *Cratylus,* 403 d–e; Apollonius Rhodius, IV, 891 ff.; Ovid, *Metamorphoses,* V, 385 ff., 553 ff.; Euripides, *Helen,* 168; Apollodorus, *Epitome,* VII. 18–19. For the birds of Stymphalus, Pausanias, VIII, 22, 3–9; Apollodorus, *Library,* II, V, 6; Apollonius Rhodius, II, 1037 ff. For the Hydra of Lernae, Pausanias, II, 36, 6–8, 37, 1–6; Apollodorus, II, V, 2; Euripides, *Hercules,* 419–420; Ovid, *Metamorphoses,* IX, 69 ff. For the Empusa and Lamiae, Philostratus, *Apollonius,* IV, 25; Aristophanes, *The Frogs,* 288 ff., and the texts cited by Rhode in *Psyche,* Paris: Payot, pages 332 and 607 ff. On the effects aroused by poetry according to Homer and the ancients and on the value of θέλγειν ("delight," "giving pleasure"), Carlo Diano, "La catarsi tragica" in *Saggezza e poetica degli antichi,* Venezia: Neri Pozza, 1968, page 249.

9) The combination in a single group of the monsters of the North and India can be traced back to Arrian, *Anabasis* V, 43, and is a topic in Clement of Alexandria's *Paidgógos,* 11, 12, 120.

10) See Emrich, *op. cit.*, pages 263 ff.

11) On relations between Mephistopheles and the Sphinxes, Chapter IV, page 190.

12) The allusion to Poseidon is in the verses 7530–7532. On earthquakes and upheavals in antiquity, Herodotus, VII, 129; Seneca, *Natural Questions,* II, 26; Callimachus, *Hymn to Delos,* 28 ff.; Pliny, *Natural History,* II, 202 ff.

13) On the figure and philosophy of Thales, see farther on at pages 291–293.

14) See the page on the wild elements in *Versuch einer Witterungslehre,* XIII, 309; and Part II, Chapter IV, page 178; Chapter VIII, page 376.

15) See pages 306–307 and Chapter VIII, pages 376–377.

16) Reinhardt, *op. cit.*, pages 142–143. See also, Chapter VII, pages 310–311.

17) Pindar, *Pythian III,* verses 1 ff., 45 ff.; *Pythian IX,* verses 30 ff.; Aeschylus, *Prometheus,* verses 1028 ff.

18) On the Argonauts, *Philostratus Gemälde,* in Artemis-Ausgabe, XIII, 814–815.

19) On the Phorkyads in classical antiquity: Hesiod, *Theogony,* 270–273; Aeschylus, *Prometheus,* 794–797; Ovid, *Metamorphoses,* IV, 774–777. Sometimes Faust's genealogies are more tangled than those of the *Theogony* and the *Gotha.* At verse 7990, the Phorkyads seem to be sisters, not daughters of Chaos: but daughters of whom, if Chaos is the first god? Verse 8812 assigns Erebus as their father (who, according to Hesiod, is the son of Chaos and the brother of Night). Verses 8728–8729 claim that Phorcys is their father (as in the *Theogony).* Thus the Phorkyads have three fathers: Chaos, Erebus, and Phorcys; but they might also have an unknown father, who in his turn is the father of Chaos. The mother, however, is certain: Night. Everything leads one to think that this genealogical confusion is not casual: Goethe must have amused himself drawing up a parodistic *Theogony.*

20) The Phorkyads were already grotesque figures in the *Metamorphoses,* IV, 775 ff.

21) In the course of the third act, it will no longer be a matter of a theatrical representation but of a true incarnation. However, at the end of the act, the scenic aspect will reemerge (see Chapter VII, pages 333 and 369).

22) Here are the principal sources for this paragraph. The testimony of the Pre-Socratics —particularly Xenophanes, Heraclitus, Parmenides, Empedocles, Ion of Chios, Philolaus and Diogenes of Apollonia—are of course taken from the edition edited by Diels: Thucydides, VII, 30; Aristotle, *Problemata,* XXIV, 14; *De generatione animantium,* II, 4; IV, 2; IV, 10; *De historia animalium,* VII, 2, 1; Philo. *De providentia,* II, 77; *De somniis,* I, 145; Varro, *De re rustica,* I, 37; Lucretius, V, 575–585, 705–737; Cicero, *De natura deorum,* II, 19, 50; II, 21, 56; II, 40, 103; II, 46, 118–119; III, 14, 37; *De divinatione,* II, 14, 33–34; Virgil, *Georgics,* III, 337; Horace, *Satires,* II, IV, 30; Pliny, *Natural History,* II, 41–58, 109, 212–233; IX, 18; XI, 109, 212–233; XVI, 190, 193–194; Seneca, *De beneficiis,* IV, 23, 1; *Naturales quaestiones,* V, 6; *Medea,* 790; Lucan, IX, 313–338; Curtius, IV, 10, 6; Plutarch, *De Iside et Osiride; De facie quae in orbe lunae apparet; De Pythiae oraculis;* 400 A, 404 D, 416 EF; *Quaestiones conviviales,* III, 10; *Aemilius Paulus,* 17; Ptolemy, *Tetrabiblos,* 2, 4, 6, 7, 8; III, 12; IV, 4, 10; Apuleius *The Golden Ass,* XI; *De magia,* 30; *De mundo,* 16, 16; Lucian, *Icaromenippus,* 13; Aulus Gellius, XX, VIII; Porphyry, *De antro nympharum,* 11; Julian, *Discourse on Helios-the-King*(?), 149 D; *Discourse on the Mother of the Gods,* 167 D; Macrobius, *Saturnalia,* I, XVII; I, XVIII, 23; I, XIX, 17; I, XXI, 4–5; I, XXIII, 22; VII, XVI, 15–34; *Somnium Scipionis,* I, II, 6–8; I, 19, 12–13; I, 19, 23; I, 21, 33; Phirmicus Maternus, *Mathesis,* I, IV, 9; I, 10, 14; preface to V; St. Basil Methodius of Olympus, *Hexaemeron,* VI, 3–4, 10–11; St. Ambrose, *Exameron,* IV, 2, 5; IV, 2, 7; IV, 7, 29–30; IV,

GOETHE

8, 31; IV, 8, 32; Metodio d'Olimpo, *Symposium*, VIII, 4, 6; Anastasius Sinaita, *Hexaemeron*, IV, 975 ABC; Martianus Capella, *De nuptiis Philologiae*, II, 169; VI, 583. As for a bibliography, I limit myself to recording the essential texts: the pertinent essays in Pauly-Wissowa (especially *Mond* by W. Gundel); W.H. Roscher, *Selene und Verwandtes*, Leipzig 1890; Karl Reinhardt, *Kosmos und Sympathie*, Leipzig 1926; Hugo Rahner, *Symbole der Kirche*, pages 91–173, Salzburg 1964; and the commentary of Harold Cherniss to the Loeb edition (1957) of Plutarch's *De facie*.

23) I take this information from the commentary on *Faust* by Ernst Beutler, Artemis, V, 597–599.

24) See Chapter VIII, pages 422–423.

25) See Chapter VII, pages 327 ff. and page 299.

26) I translate from Goethe's reworking of Philostratus's *Eikones* (A. XIII, 821).

27) Karl Reinhardt has devoted some fine pages to the Cabiri, *op. cit.*, pages 146–150, which show how Goethe took the idea of the combination of the Cabiri and the Platonic Eros from Schelling's book, *Ueber die Gottheiten von Samothrake*.

28) I believe that the insistence upon the divine qualities of the Cabiri (*"Sind Götter!*, 8075; *"Sind Götter, die wir bringen,"* 8172; *"Uralt verehrte Götter*, 8177, aims at confuting Strabo's theory, which presents them as demons and servants of the gods (X, c. 466).

29)
> Lass du sie singen, lass sie prahlen!
> Der Sonne heiligen Lebenstrahlen
> Sind tote Werke nur ein Spass.
> Das bildet, schmelzend, unverdrossen:
> Und haben sie's in Erz gegossen,
> Dann denken sie, es wäre was.
> Was ist's zuletzt mit diesen Stolzen?
> Die Götterbilder standen gross—
> Zerstörte sie ein Erdestoss;
> Längst sind sie wieder eingeschmolzen
> (8303–8312)

30)
> Mögt euch des schönen Fanges freuen,
> Den Jüngling bildet euch als Mann;
> Allein ich könnte nicht verleihen,
> Was Zeus allein gewähren kann.
> Die Welle, die euch wogt und schaukelt,
> Lässt auch der Liebe nicht Bestand,
> Und hat die Neigung ausgegaukelt,
> So setzt gemächlich sie ans Land
> (8408–8415)

31) The texts of Justin, Hippolytus, Irenaeus, St. Gregory of Nyssa, Massimo di Torino in Hugo Rahner, *op. cit.*, pages 58 ff., and Jean N. Daniélou, *Théologie du Judéo-Christianisme*, Paris: Desclée, 1958, pages 305–315.

32) The necessity of an eternal, incessant redemption is affirmed at the end of Chapter VIII of the second part of *Dichtung und Wahrheit* (IX, 353: 4 ff.).

33) On Gottfried Arnold, *Dichtung und Wahrheit* (IX, 350), at the beginning of the famous theological-cosmological summary. See the quotation in Gray, *op cit.*, pages 20 and 266 (other examples in the first chapter of the same book). The alchemical image of the carbuncle stone (or ruby) returns in *Natürliche Tochter* (65), apropos Eugenie, who belongs to the same group of mediator-saviors.

34) At the end of the Aegean festival is the harmony of the universe truly complete? Have all the destructive forces really been driven off? Since Homunculus is Mephistopheles's son, someone might suppose that even the lord of the inferno, of rocks and fire might be reconciled, for an instant, through his son, with the divine force of nature. Yet nothing permits us to affirm this. Nothing allows us to believe that, even with but a "hint" or a "slight allusion," Goethe might try to suggest that Mephistopheles also melts, for an instant, into the harmony of the universe.

CHAPTER VII

1) On Goethe's historical and geographical sources, the excellent study by Johanna Schmidt, *Sparta-Mistra, Forschungen über Goethes Faustburg,* "Goethe," n. 18, 156, pages 132 ff. It seems almost impossible to me that Goethe did not read Chateaubriand's *Itinéraire de Paris à Jerusalem,* Paris, 1811. At one point there could be a textual correspondence: "*Vue du chateau de Mistra [Faust,* 9001], *la vallée de la Laconie est admirable: elle s'étend à peu près du nord au midi: elle est bordée à l'ouest par le Taygète* [8996], *et à l'est par les monts Tornax, Barosthènes, Olympe et Ménélaïon; des petites collines obstruent la partie septentrionale de la vallée, descendent au midi en diminuant de hauteur [das Talgebirg, das hinter Sparta nordwärts in die Hohe steigt* 8994-8995] *et viennent former de leurs dernières croupes les collines où Sparte étoit assise. Depuis Sparta jusqu'à la mer se deroule une plaine unie et fertile arrosée par l'Eurotas* [the final phrases could recall the verses 8498, 8544-8547, written however in 1800]. *L'Eurotas mérite certainement l'epithète de* καλλιδόναξ, *aux beaux roseaux, que lui a donnée Euripide; mais je ne sais s'il doit garder celle d' olorifer, car je n'ai point aperçu de cygnes dans ses eaux*" (on pages 144-145 and 154 of the Garnier edition, 1904). Here Chateaubriand in his turn borrowed from *Voyage du jeune Anacharsis* by Abbé Barthelemy, also known to Goethe: "*En certains temps il est couvert de cygnes d'une blancheur éblouissante, presque partout de roseaux très recherchés parcre qu'ils sont droits, élevés, et variés dans leurs couleurs*" (volume IV of the 1789 edition, pages 93-94).

2) "*Die wahre Helena auf antik-tragischem Kothurn vor ihrer Urwohnung zu Sparta auftreten könne*" (*Faust,* Artemis edition, page 574).

3) The majority of scholars who have written about *Faust II* see in the *Klassische Walpurgisnacht* "the rebirth of Helen on a biological-natural base" (Emrich); they find in Galatea a heralding of Helen; and the incarnation of Homunculus would seem to prefigure the birth of Helen, as a Venus risen from the waves, the foam of the sea. These reconstructions clash with the very letter of Goethe's text. Helen does not come from the world of life but rather from that of death; and the sphere in which she lives is exactly the opposite from that of the Aegean festival (see pages 322-323, 325-326, 329-330).

4) At verse 145 of the fourth book of *The Odyssey* Helen calls herself once again a "bitch," But it is, I believe, above all an echo of much more intense passages in *The Iliad.* On the figure of Helen in Greek literature and art, see Lilly B. Ghali-Kahil, *Les enlèvements et le retour d'Hélène dans les textes et les documents figurés,* Paris: De Boccard, 1955.

5) Goethe, from this, has copies verses 8907-8908 in *Faust: "Die Gestalt aller Gestalten Welche die Sonne jemals beschien."*

6)
$$\text{Ὀοῶν δὲ τήνδε φεῦγε, μή σ'ἕλη πόθω.}$$
$$\text{Ατθεῖ γὰο ἀνδοων ὄμματ', ἐξαιοει πόλεις,}$$
$$\text{πίμποησι δ'οἴκους: ὠδ'ἔχει κηλήματα}$$

$$(891-893)$$

7) On physical beauty and its relation with works of art, the famous page of the essay on Winckelmann: "the final product of Nature, which ascends into eternity, is the *beautiful*

GOETHE

man. Truly, Nature can bring it birth only rarely, since too many conditions contradict her ideas, and not even her omnipotence can remain for long in perfection and confer lastingness on the beauty which she has created. In reality, one might say that there exists only a single instant when the beautiful man is truly beautiful.

"But, in exchange, art steps forward. When man is set on the summit of Nature, then he regards himself as a complete Nature, who must in his turn create a summit. So he develops and improves himself, suffusing himself with all the perfections and virtues, calling upon Choice, Order, Harmony, Significance, and finally succeeds in producing the work of art, which occupies a splendid place beside his other actions and works. Once created, the work of art stands before the world in its ideal reality, and exerts a lasting effect, indeed the most sublime among the effects; while it develops spiritually from conjoined forces, it gathers in itself all that there is of the magnificent, venerable and lovable; animating the human figure, it lifts man above himself, concludes the circle of his life and deeds, and deifies him for a past, in which past and future are included" (A. XIII, 421–422).

8) Ibid., pages 441–442.

9) Other verses on the relationship between Helen and the sunlight: 8601, 8657, 8695, 8900, 8907, 8909, 10054.

10) At other times the word *Gestalt* is used to define Helen: 6495, 6561, 8532, 9352. See also *Polygnots Gemälde* (Artemis-Ausgabe, XIII, 382): *"Des höchsten irdischen Gutes, des Anblicks einer vollkommenen Gestalt."* On the value of "forms" in the Greek world, see Carlo Diano, *Forma ed evento*, Neri Pozza, 1967.

11) During all of the third act, Mephistopheles identifies himself completely with a Phorkyad; but at the end of the act, Goethe repeats that it has been only a theatrical game: "The Phorkyad dismounts from the tragic buskin, lays aside mask and veil, and appears as Mephistopheles. . . ."

12) That Helen accepts Mephistopheles's version and knows that she is dead, is never said explicitly; but it is evident from 9254 ff. See also at pages 340 ff.

13) Goethe could read in Chateaubriand's *Itinéraire* that Methane in Messenia was two hours by ship from "ancient Pylos, hidden by the island of Sfacteria": now it was precisely at Methane, as Chateaubriand and almost any history book recounts, that Geoffroy de Villehardouin, returning from the Holy Land, had disembarked. So it is not by chance that Faust says: *"An Pylos traten wir zu Lande, / Der alte Nestor ist nicht mehr"* (9454–9455).

14) Nicetas Choniates, *Historia ex recensione Immanueli Bekkeri*, Bonnae, 1835, page 806.

15) There is no doubt that Goethe knew of the existence of both Geoffroy de Villehardouin and the Gothic castle above Mistra. See the essay by Johanna Schmidt, *op. cit.*

16) Above all, Menelaus is a theatrical invention of Mephistopheles. But perhaps Goethe also wanted to represent in him an historically double phantasm, similar to the Cimmerian warriors. We know that piracy is his profession: *"Raubschiffend ruderte Menelas von Bucht zu Bucht, / Gestad' und Inseln, alles streift' er fiendlich an, / Mit Beute wiederkehrend . . ."* (8985–8987); *"Drängt ungesäumt von diesen Mauern / Jetzt Menelas dem Meer zurück; / Dort irren mag er, rauben, lauern, / Ihm war es Neigung und Geschick"* (9458–9461); and several times in his outlines. Goethe probably wanted to define the nature of Mycenaean civilization, gathering together the information from the *Odyssey* (III, 301–302; IV, 89–91) and from Thucydides (1, 5 ff.) But I would not exclude the possibility that he also wished to allude at the same time to the Byzantines, Villehar-

douin's enemies. In Paolo Ramnusio's book, *Della guerra di Constantinopoli per la restituzione degli imperatori*, Venice: *Comneni*, 1604, it is said that the Greeks of the Morea, defeated by the Crusaders, devoted themselves to a war of piracy. (Ramnusio was well known to the historians of Goethe's time; yet we do not know whether Goethe actually read him. See Schmidt's essay, *op. cit.*)

17) See Mommsen, *op. cit.*, page 270 ff.

18) See Mommsen, *op. cit.*, page 266.

19) Goethe agreed with the theory set forth in *Timaeus*. Here is the introduction to the *Farbenlehre:* "The eye owes its existence to the light. From subsidary indifferent animal organs, the light gives birth to an organ which becomes similar to herself: thus the eye is formed in the light by the light, so that the inner light runs to meet the outer light.

"Here we want to recall the ancient Ionian school, which continued to repeat always with great understanding that like is known by like; and the words of an ancient mystic, which I will translate in German verses in this manner:

> If the eye were not solar,
> How could we contemplate the light?
> If the true force of God did not live in us,
> How could divine matters put us in ecstasy?

"No one can deny this immediate kinship between the light and the eye; but it is more difficult to think of them as a single, identical thing. We would understand each other better if we said that the eye is inhabited by a light in a state of quiet, which at the slightest stimulus is excited from within and from without" (XIII, 323–324).

20) See Chapter VIII, pages 384 ff.

21) In Mephistopheles's words, the sun is obviously both that which shines in the sky (8911) and that of Helen (which in fact has been covered by "passing clouds").

22) See Part II, Chapter I, page 151 ff.

23) See *Die Wahlverwandschaften*, Chapter III (VI, 374: 4–9); and Emrich's acute pages on the relationship between Ottilie and Helen, *op. cit.*, page 319 and in the index of names.

24) See Ernst Robert Curtius, *European Literature and the Latin Middle Ages*, Bollingen, 1953, Chapter X, entitled "The Ideal Landscape."

25) On "delight" in Homeric poetry, Wolfgang Schadewaldt, *Von Homers Welt und Werk*, 1965, *Hoehler, pages 83 ff.; on the magical effects of poetry in antiquity*, Carlo Diano, *Saggezza e poetiche, op. cit.*, pages 249 ff. As for the figure of Hermes, see *Forma ed evento, op. cit.*, pages 56–59; out of an immense bibliography, I mention only Karl Kereny, *Hermes als Seelenführer*, Rhein Verlag, 1944.

26) What classical sources concerning Hermes did Goethe keep in mind in *Faust II?* In the hymn which the chorus sings in honor of Hermes (9630 ff.), the protective demon of thieves and of *Schälke*, all the details derive from Lucian's *Dialogues of the Gods*, VII; perhaps through the mediation of Hederich. As is quite natural, Goethe knew the passages dealing with Hermes in the *Iliad* and the *Odyssey;* and he remembers his function as the guide of the dead (9115 ff.) and messenger (4956). In the chorus, no obvious sign seems to link it with the Homeric *Hymns*, which has served as the basis for my story. But it seems to me, as will become clear, that the correspondences between the *Hymn* and the entire myth of Euphorion are much too numerous to be simply due to chance.

27) On Mephistopheles-Scheherazade, see Mommsen, *op. cit.*, page 281 ff.

GOETHE

28) As a source, Mommsen mentions the fable of Pari-Banu in the *Thousand and One Nights (op. cit.*, pages 258 ff.); Diener indicates the myth of Aristaeus *(op. cit.*, page 547); and an equally and perhaps most possible source the *Hymn to Hermes*, in which the Arcadian cave is at the same time a palace and a temple.

29) We must remember that Goethe defines Hermes twice with the same term *("der Schalk")*, which belongs by right to Mephistopheles; see 339, 6885 and 9652 and 9663. See Chapter IV, page 181.

30) One might say that, from the beginning, Euphorion is only a musician, not a poet (stage directions on 9678, 9679); but verses 9695, 9863, 9922, 9935, 9958 convince us that he was, like Hermes and Apollo, both musician and poet.

31) What is the reason for the very evident sympathy of Mephistopheles for Euphorion? Let us recall, first of all, the relationship between Mephistopheles and Hermes; and, secondly, that Euphorion, born in the subterranean darkness, is protected by the earth's power; now darkness and the earth are among Mephistopheles's favorite elements. As for the glorification of the "heart" (9685–9686), expressed by Mephistopheles, we should remember that he is the prince of mystifiers and that once already, arousing the contempt and mockery of the Sphinxes, Mephistopheles had laid claim to a very sensitive heart (7176–7177).

32) On the relations among Mignon, the *Knabe Lenker*, and Euphorion, I refer once again to Emrich's excellent demonstration, *op. cit.*, pages 171 ff. and 350 ff.

33)
> Ach! zum Erdenglück geboren,
> Hoher Ahnen, grosser Kraft,
> Leider früh dir selbst verloren,
> Jugendblüte weggerafft!
> Scharfer Blick, die Welt zu schauen,
> Mitsinn jedem Herzensdrang,
> Liebesglut der besten Frauen
> Und ein eigenster Gesang.
>
> . . .
>
> Wolltest Herrliches gewinnen,
> Aber es gelang dir nicht.
> Wem gelingt es?—Trübe Frage,
> Der das Schicksal sich vermummt,
> Wenn am unglückseligsten Tage
> Blutend alles Volk verstummt.
> (9915–9922; 9929–9934)

34)
> Noch immer glücklich aufgefunden!
> Die Flamme freilich ist verschwunden,
> Doch ist mir um die Welt nicht leid.
> Hier bleibt genug, Poeten einzuweihen,
> Zu stiften Gild—und Handwerksneid;
> Und kann ich die Talente nicht verleihen
> Verborg'ich wenigstens das Kleid
> (9955–9961)

35) See Chapter V., page 222.

36) See Mommsen, *op. cit.* page 236. On the relation between this scene and the images of the veil and the clouds, see Chapter III, pages 171–172.

37) Many scholars are astonished that solemn verses such as 9945 ff. have been put on Mephistopheles's lips:

> Halte fest, was dir von allem übrigblieb.
> Das Kleid, lass es nicht los. Da zupfen schon
> Dämonen an den Zipfeln, möchten gern
> Zur Unterwelt es reissen. Halte fest!
> Die Göttin ist's nicht mehr, die du verlorst.
> Doch göttlich ist's. Bediene dich der hohen,
> Unschätzbaren Gunst und hebe dich empor:
> Es trägt dich über alles Gemeine rasch
> Am Äther hin, so lange du dauern kannst.
> Wir sehn uns wieder, weit, gar weit von hier.
>
> Hold fast to what is left to you.
> Do not let this garment go. Already
> The demons tug at its hems, and want
> To drag it down to Hades. So hold fast!
> It is not the goddess whom you have lost,
> Yet it is godlike too. Make use of this high,
> Inestimable favor and soar aloft!
> It will bear you quickly over all common things,
> Toward the ether—so long as you persevere.
> We shall meet again, far, very far from here.

The tone of these verses certainly is not suited to the cynical lord of the flies and mice; and perhaps here Mephistopheles has gone completely out of true role, as before the girls in the chorus did (E. July 5, 1827). But it is well to remember one fact. In *Natürliche Tochter*, when the duke laments the death of his daughter *("Getrenntes Leben, wer vereinigt's wieder? / Vernichtetes, wer stellt es her?"*, 1698–1699: "a life that's been divided, who will unite it? That which is annihilated, who will recreate it?"), a Mephistophelean-like character, the Abbott, replies to him: *"Der Geist! / Des Menschen Geist, dem nichts verlorengeht . . . So lebt Eugenie vor dir, sie lebt / In deinem Sinne, den sie sonst erhub . . .; / So wirkt sie noch / Als hohes Vorbild, schützet vor Gemeinem, Vor schlechtem dich, wie's jede Stunde bringt, Und ihrer Würde wahrer Glanz verscheuchet Den eitlen Schein, der dich bestechen will* (1699 ff.): "The spirit! man's spirit, of which nothing is lost. . . . Thus Eugenie lives before you, lives in your mind, which at one time rose up. . . . Thus she still acts as a sublime image, protects you from common things, from bad things, which are brought to us by each hour, and the true splendor of her dignity frightens the vain appearance, which wants to corrupt you." Both Mephistopheles and the Abbott therefore urge Faust and the duke to relive in memory "the separated, annihilated life," and help them to free themselves from the anguish of death. It should be remembered that Mephistopheles is as much a conserver as a destroyer of the past (see Part II, Chapter II, pages 190–192). If here he helps Faust to conserve it, soon after this (9955 ff.) he mocks the past, poking fun at Euphorion's miserable poetic inheritance.

CHAPTER VIII

1) On Faust's initial monologue, Part II, Chapter III, pages 171–172.

2) Of course, Mephistopheles knows Luther's translation: *"zeigte ihm alle Reiche der Welt und ihre Herrlichkeit."* (This verse, which Goethe loved greatly, continually crops up in his books and letters.)

3) After the first three acts, so distant from *Faust I*, the entire beginning of act four (after verse 10067) seems to hark back intentionally to the two *Studierzimmer* scenes. Mephistopheles's geological doctrine enlarges the cosmology of verses 1747 ff.; his political

GOETHE

doctrines apply the ideal of life sketched in verses 1688 ff.; while the definition that Faust offers of Mephistopheles in verses 10193–10195 echoes again the sarcasm of verses 1675 ff.

4) In the margin beside verse 10094, Goethe refers to the Epistle to the Ephesians 6: 12. But the citation (I do not know whether it is intentional) happens to be mistaken; it is verse 10092 which recalls the Ephesians 6: 12, while verses 10093–10094 allude quite obviously to Chapter 3: 1–12 of the same epistle.

5) Mephistopheles's theory about the formation of mountains is identical with Anaxagoras's, who had maintained that the mountains owe their origin to the conjoined force of fire and subterranean winds. Mephistopheles refurbishes this theory, about which, in the *Klassische Walpurgisnacht*, he seemed to harbor a certain diffidence: he pays homage, by the clever play of rhymes and assonances, to one of his most talented pupils (the verses which contain Anaxagoras's doctrine have the following words in rhyme: *Feuer, ungeheuer, Kruste, musste* (7865–7868); those which contain Mephistopheles's doctrine: *säure, Ungeheure, Kruste, musste* (10083–10086); and he asserts that without the gases (10084) and the flames which torrentially agitate (10078, 10108) in the earth, the Alpine mountain ranges, rocks, and scattered boulders would never have come to light.

6) The Goethean formula *Ein offenbar Geheimnis*, which we encounter again in Mephistopheles's discourse (10093), also recalls an expression in the Epistle to the Ephesians, *"dass mir ist kund geworden dieses Geheimnis durch Offenbarung,"* 3: 3, referring to Christ.

7) The "open mystery" will be revealed to the peoples "only later," Mephistopheles says (10094). What does "later" signify? Does it refer to the end of time, when the anti-Christ will appear? Or does Mephistopheles allude to Goethe's times, when geological vulcanism flourished, almost three centuries after the time (very unreal) during which *Faust*'s action takes place?

8) On Mephistopheles the conservative, see Part II, Chapter IV, pages 191–192.

9) It seems to me quite likely that Goethe, when he wrote the part dealing with Faust and the waters, had in mind the very famous Psalm 104 and Job 38. There are some correspondences (though vague) between these Biblical passages (in Luther's translation) and the verses of *Faust*. *"Die Berge gingen hoch hervor, und die Täler setzten sich herunter zum Ort, den du ihnen gegründet hast* (Psalm 104: 8); and *"Als die Natur sich in sich selbst gegründet . . . Und Fels an Fels und Berg an Berg gereiht, Die Hügel dann bequem hinabgebildet, Mit sanftem Zug sie in das Tal gemildet (Faust, 10097, 10100–10102); "Du hast eine Grenze gesetzt, darüber kommen sie nicht und dürfen nicht wiederum das Erdreich bedecken* (Psalm 104: 9), *"hier sollen sich legen deine stolzen Wellen!* (Job 38: 11), *"da ihm der Lauf brach mit meinem Damm* (Job 38: 10); and *"Das herrische Meer vom Ufer auszuschliessen, Der feuchten Breite Grenzen zu verengen Und, weit hinein, sie in sich selbst zu drängen"* (10229–10231), *"Den Wellen ihre Grenze setzt, Das Meer mit strengem Band umzieht"* (11542–11543), and the dikes which Faust will have Mephistopheles construct in act five (11126). On the sea in the Old Testament, see Edmond Jacob, *Théologie de l'ancien Testament*, Paris: Delachaux and Niestlé, 1955, pages 112–114.

10) See Part II, Chapter VI, pages 306–308.

11) This motif, which barely filters through the definitive text, was much more obvious in previous drafts: "Mephistopheles describes a Sardanapalian life. Faust retorts with a description of revolt. For him the inhabitants of the shore of the sea, which they want to rescue from the waves, are enviable. He wants to associate himself with them. First form and then go to work. *The superiority of human society to its own beginnings"* (A. V, 588).

12) The fine page written by Staiger, *op. cit.*, III, 419, about the end of the fourth act.

13) The terms of the vision continually return in the last act of *Faust II*, which is first of all a tragedy of the eye. The wayfarer would like to *schauen* at the boundless sea (11076): Philemon invites him to *sehen*, to *schauen*, to *erblicken* (11085, 11086, 11095, 11103) the image of the new paradisial land: therefore, together with him, he goes to *schauen* the sunset (11140). Lynceus, born for *sehen*, predisposed to *schauen* (11288–11289), is all eye: *"ich* blick' *in die Ferne, ich* seh' *in der Näh' " (11292–11293): and again sehen* 11296, 11301, 11308; *Blick*, 11336; *Augen*, 11328–11329). In Faust's speeches (or in those of Mephistopheles reported to Faust) *Augen* recurs in verses 11153, 11161, *schauen* in 11243, 11247, 11345, *sehen* 11246, 11346, *Blick* in 11219, 11245. Farther on, as one will see in the text, the theme becomes even more significant. In the *Mitternacht* scene, Faust speaks of himself as of someone who does not lift his *blinzelnd* eyes on high (11443), who looks *("sehe . . . um")* around himself, at this world (11445). He who is persecuted by Care *siehet* all *schiefer* things (11476). Care blinds Faust (11497), who, however, feels gleaming in himself "a bright light" (11500), wants to *schauen* the work of his mind (11504), and *sehen* the spectacle of a free people on free soil (11579).

14) It seems undeniable that the image of magic, given in verses 11404 ff., should be so less rich in content than the image which magic assumed in *Faust II*. Perhaps the explanation should be sought in the fact that a sketch or a large part of this scene dates back to the years around 1800, when for Goethe magic had a more limited significance. See Alexander R. Hohfeld, "Die Enstehung des Faust-Manuskripts von 1825–26," *Euphorion*, volume 49, 1955, page 283 ff.

15) The relationship between the tyrant Faust and Care is very clear in a fragment:

> *Faust:* Muss befehlen.
> *Sorge:* Das hilft dir nichts, du wirst uns doch nicht los:
> Grad *im Befehlen wird die Sorge gross*
> (A. III, 615).

In any case, Faust knows Care so profoundly that, before she describes the symptoms which afflict her victims, he anticipates them—turned upside down—in the monologue where he describes himself. The verses 11433–11434 are the opposite of the verses 11459–11460 and 11463–11464; verse 11452 the opposite of verses 11480 and 11482.

16) Emil Staiger, *op. cit.*, III, 440 ff., calls attention to some incongruencies in Faust's second monologue in respect to the first part of act five and explains them by the fact that they were written many years before. In my opinion, the only true incongruence is verse 11440 *("Mein Leben durchgestürmt; erst gross und mächtig, Nun aber geht es weise, geht bedächtig"),* where Goethe (as he represents himself in a famous poem in the *Divan, Mich nach—und umzubilden)* appears from behind Faust's words. In any event, everything can be explained if one interprets Faust's monologue not as a confession but as an attempt at catharsis.

17) On the failure of the pacification of nature imagined by Faust, see page 399. In Faust's last monologue, verses 11567–11568 leave the impression that the dikes are no longer those built by Mephistopheles (11126); but others, completely new, built only by the men; as if Faust wanted to cancel every trace of magic from the "extremely new land." I do not believe that this can be explained only by the long reworking of this episode (on which, however, see the essay by Hohfield already cited).

18)   Werd'ich zum Augenblicke sagen:
                  Verweile doch! du bist so schön!
                  Dann magst du mich in Fesseln schlagen.

GOETHE

> Dann will ich gern zugrunde gehn!
> Dann mag die Totenglocke schallen,
> Dann bist du deines Dienstes frei,
> Die Uhr mag stehn, der Zeiger fallen,
> Es sei die Zeit für mich vorbei!
> (1699–1706)

19)
> Zum Augenblicke dürft ich sagen:
> Verweile doch, du bist so schön!
> Es kann die Spur von meinen Erdetagen
> Nicht in Äonen untergehn.—
> Im Vorgefühl von solchem hohen Glück
> Geniess'ich jetzt den höchsten Augenblick
> (11581–11586)

20) Why does Faust die? He dies because he is old: because the time set for his death has arrived (11397, 11592). Owing to his relations with all the demons, Mephistopheles knows that he is going to die and prepares his grave. Yet this death, which is being prepared in Faust's organism, happens, "is precipitated," only when he pronounces the words that, according to the agreement, would be his funeral knell. Faust's death, in a word, is half a physical event; as for the other half, he is like a notary, who punctiliously carries out the conditions established by the pact.

21) On the different value of *"es ist vollbracht,"* see farther on at page 398.

22) Recalled in *Tag- und Jahreshefte.* A. XI, 67 (the title of the essay by Sömmering was *Über das Organ der Seele*).

23) As a parallel passage, besides the verses of *Gott, Gemüt und Welt*, noted by Lohmeyer *(Denn was das Feuer lebendig erfasst, Bleibt nicht mehr Unform und Erdenlast, Verflüchtigt wird es und unsichtbar")*, one might recall a passage in the *Wanderjahre*, in which Makarie (the star) contemplates, through *"die ihn umgebende individuelle Maske,"* through *"die Schale," "die innere Natur," "den gesunden Kern"* of each individual (VIII, 116: 9–14).

24) On these verses, see Gray, *op. cit.*, page 154 ff.

25) On the Neoplatonic and hermetic doctrine of astral clothes (and the parallel one of vehicles), see the texts recorded or quoted by Paul Moraux in the article "quinta essentia" in Pauly-Wissowa, vol. XXIV, 1, col. 1251 ff.; and by Franz Cumont, in *Lux perpetua*, Paris: Genthner, 1949, pages 181 ff., 358 ff.; and by A. J. Festugiere, in *La Révélation d'Hermès Trismégiste*, Paris: Gabalda, 1949–54, vol. III, pages 131 and 237, and the comment to *Corpus hermeticum*, volume I, pages 128, 129. As for Goethe's direct source: whether he went right back to the Neoplatonic texts or (as I believe more probable) to the late alchemical texts which had inherited their ideas and images, I cannot say. Certainly *"ätherischem Gewande"* (12090) is a technical Neoplatonic expression.

26) The stage directions accompanying verses 11824, 11933 bear, instead of *"Faustens Unsterbliches,"* *"Faustens Entelechie."* Perhaps the substitution has been motivated by the fact that the expression *Entelechie* does not go in accord with the image of a "spiritual body."

27) This reconstruction is slightly conjectural; and it emphasizes elements which, in Goethe, are barely touched on. Thus the Mater Gloriosa speaks of "spheres" only in verse 12094 and then in a generic manner: but it seems to me impossible that, given the context, he did not want to allude to successive spheres of the stars. Whereas Porphyry defines precisely the sucessive ethereal, solar, and lunar clothes (or vehicles, or bodies)—although other Neoplatonic thinkers are much less precise—Goethe's eschatology is not equally

well defined. What may be, exactly, the superficial garment, *"der alten Hülle,"* with its "earthly ties" (12089) (which is compared to *"die Flocken"* of the chrysalis, 11985), is not easy to imagine. It certainly is not a matter of a lunar or solar garment; but rather of an integument formed of earthly elements (it is well to remember, however, that *"Hülle* has the value of garment in a parallel passage, VII, 515: 37, which refers to Mignon). As for "ethereal garment," this is, instead, as I have said, a technical Neoplatonic expression.

28) The "stronger" spirits are also those more tied to earth: one cannot possibly imagine an idea less Neoplatonic (and more Faustian).

29) W. Emrich, *op. cit.,* page 415.

30) See Part II, Chapter III, page 171.

31) In the *Italienische Reise,* Goethe already described Mary as a *"Göttin"* (XI, 46: 6); and spoke *"der katholischen Mythologie"* (XI, 102: 23). In *Kunst und Altertum am Rhein und Main,* the same syncreticism leads him to remember that "schon *im* heidnischen Altertum *war Jungfräulichkeit und Mutterschaft verbunden denkbar"* (XII, 145: 26 ff.).

32) On the relationship between the Madonna and the moon in Goethe, see Gray, *op. cit.,* page 517. On Mary and the moon in the Christian tradition, Hugo Rahner, *Griechische Mythen in Christlicher Deutung,* pages 99–100, 142–143, 149 ff. To the numerous verbal and imaginative correspondences between the last scene of *Faust* and the *festa egea,* one might add what occurs between verse 8049 *("Holder Sang zieht uns heran")* and the last verse of *Faust, "zieht uns hinan."* In the first case, she who attracts is the song of the Sirens, the Moon's priestess; in the other, *"das Ewig-Weibliche."*

33) *Jägers Nachtlied,* verses 1–4, 13 ff.; *An Lida,* verses 7 ff; *An dem Mond,* first draft, verses 1 ff.; *Torquato Tasso,* verses 1956 ff.; *Iphigenie auf Tauris,* verses 1317 ff.

34) Thus the Mater Gloriosa, according to a gesture dear to Goethe, looks toward the earth: *"die angehende Göttin nicht Himmelwärts, sondern* herab *nach ihren Freunden blickt"* (XI, 46: 7–9); *"Dort bewegt sich in höchster Glorie eine* herabwärts *teilnehmende Mutter"* (XI, 128: 37–38).

35) See Chapter III, page 165.

36) See Chapter III, page 171; and the famous passage with which the *Versuch einer Witterungslehre* begins: "The truth, identical with the divine, never lets us recognize it directly, and we contemplate it only in the reflection, the example, the symbol, in single and conjoined apparitions: we consider it an incomprehensible life, and yet we cannot renounce the desire to comprehend it" (XIII, 305: 26–31).

Index

INDEX

INDEX

INDEX

INDEX

INDEX

INDEX